FROM THE KITCHEN OF:

THE MARTHA STEWART LIVING

# Christmas Cookbook

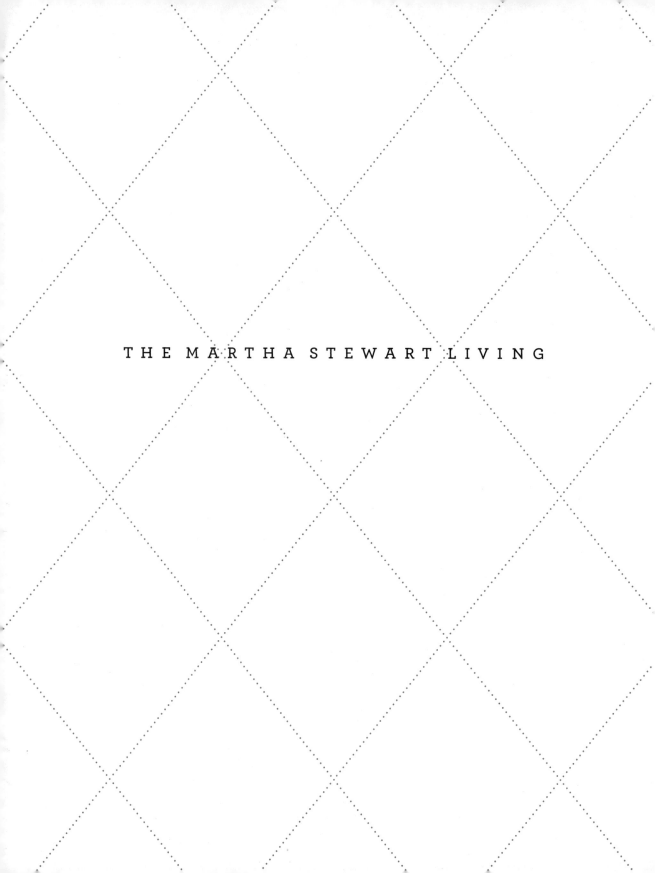

THE MARTHA STEWART LIVING

# Christmas Cookbook

### A COLLECTION OF FAVORITE
### HOLIDAY RECIPES

*from the editors of* MARTHA STEWART LIVING

*To all of the employees of* Martha Stewart Living Omnimedia *who have worked diligently and enthusiastically to produce more than twelve years' worth of wonderful, original recipes that celebrate the best that the Christmas season has to offer.*

ORIGINALLY PUBLISHED IN BOOK FORM BY MARTHA STEWART LIVING OMNIMEDIA, INC., IN 2003.
PUBLISHED SIMULTANEOUSLY BY CLARKSON POTTER / PUBLISHERS AND OXMOOR HOUSE, INC.

ALL OF THE RECIPES IN THIS BOOK HAVE BEEN PREVIOUSLY PUBLISHED IN SLIGHTLY DIFFERENT FORM BY MARTHA STEWART LIVING OMNIMEDIA, 1990–2003.

PRINTED IN THE UNITED STATES OF AMERICA.

LIBRARY OF CONGRESS CATALOGING-IN-PUBLICATION DATA

THE MARTHA STEWART LIVING CHRISTMAS COOKBOOK / BY THE EDITORS OF MARTHA STEWART LIVING.

1. CHRISTMAS COOKERY. 1. MARTHA STEWART LIVING OMNIMEDIA.

TX739.2.C45 M39 2003

641.5'68—DC21                    2003006588

ISBN 0-8487-2739-8

10 9 8 7 6 5 4 3 2 1

FIRST EDITION

# *acknowledgments*

✳

THE RECIPES IN THIS cookbook represent more than a decade's worth of developing, testing, retesting, writing, and editing. We extend our gratitude toward every editor and member of the food department, past and present, who had a hand in the creation of this book.

A very special thank you to Susan Spungen, Susan Sugarman, Lori Powell, Jennifer Aaronson, Tara Bench, Frances Boswell, Heidi Johannsen, Anna Kovel, Judith Lockhart, Melissa Perry, Elizabeth Pilar, Gerry Porter, and Laura Trace. Thank you to the editors in our books department, Ellen Morrissey and Christine Moller, for overseeing the creation of this book from its inception almost a year ago, and to senior recipe editor Evelyn Battaglia, whose gift for rigorous recipe editing is reflected on every page. Thanks to Mary Jane Callister, who, with the help of Alanna Jacobs and direction from Eric A. Pike, created a wonderful design with the cook in mind. Thank you to editors Debra Puchalla and Natalie Ermann, as well as Chris Borris, for their attention to accuracy and clarity, and to the production team of Brian Baytosh, Duane Stapp, and Matthew Landfield.

Thank you, too, to everyone else who contributed their time and energy to putting this book together, among them Annie Armstrong, Roger Astudillo, Dora Braschi Cardinale, Peter Colen, Richard P. Fontaine, Stephanie Garcia, Amanda Genge, Eric Hutton, Jennifer J. Jarett, Johanna Kletter, Jim McKeever, Melissa Morgan, Elizabeth Parson, Meg Peterson, George D. Planding, Romy Pokorny, Lesley Porcelli, Meera Rao, Margaret Roach, Colleen Shire, Lauren Podlach Stanich, Gael Towey, Miranda Van Gelder, Alison Vanek, and Alicia White, and to everyone at Oxmoor House, Clarkson Potter, R.R. Donnelley and Sons, AGT. seven, and Satellite Graphics. Finally, thank you to Martha, for inspiring us to take a fresh look at those tried-and-true recipes and to create innovative dishes to serve friends and family.

# contents

✸

# introduction

✳

SOME OF MY MOST CHERISHED MEMORIES *have to do with the celebration of the holiday season. Christmas taught me about family, traditions, and holiday entertaining—and a lot about fun and food. In the weeks leading up to Christmas each year, we enjoyed baking and decorating cookies, and making rich fruit-cakes (quickly eating up the one we always got from our beloved neighbors). When Christmas Eve finally arrived, we feasted into the night. We began Christmas morning with stacks of fluffy pancakes topped with real maple syrup. Later there was the traditional ham—and so much more—for dinner. The holidays meant eggnog and roast goose,* delicious stuffing and apple pie. For more than a decade, the food editors at MARTHA STEWART LIVING have been celebrating the holiday season with classic dishes such as these, plus many, many others. Each one is as delicious as the next! We've collected more than six hundred recipes in this indispensable cookbook. We hope you'll like flipping through these pages as much as we do—and more important, trying different recipes, whether new or familiar, to the delight of those closest to you. Think of each one as a Christmas present from us to you and your family. Enjoy! *Martha Stewart*

# the tastes of Christmas

✳

CHRISTMAS TRADITIONS VARY THROUGHOUT THE WORLD, BUT SOME THINGS, PARTICU-LARLY CULINARY SPECIALTIES, ARE UNIVERSAL FAVORITES. WHAT FOLLOWS IS A LIST OF SOME OF THE TREATS THAT SEEM TO GRACE OUR TABLES EACH HOLIDAY SEASON.

**BABA AU RHUM** Babas are yeast-leavened cakes that are steeped in rum- or kirsch-flavored syrup after baking. Legend has it that they were invented by Polish King Stanislas Leszczynsky in the 1600s. Upon finding kugelhopf—a cake studded with raisins, candied fruits, and nuts—too dry, he soaked it in rum to improve its texture. Delighted with the result, he named it in honor of his favorite literary character, Ali Baba. These days, babas are most often baked in tall, cylindrical molds, but the cakes are also made in different sizes and shapes. We bake our ginger-flavored version (page 374) in miniature brioche molds.

**BEEF WELLINGTON** Beef Wellington was the high point of any formal meal in America in the 1960s, largely because it was a state-dinner favorite of President and Mrs. Kennedy. Indeed, the beef tenderloin, covered with a savory mousse and wrapped in puff pastry, still makes a fittingly fancy Christmas dinner. Although Beef Wellington is clearly a relative of boeuf en croute (French for "beef in a crust"), no one knows exactly when the dish was invented, nor whether it was named for the Duke of Wellington, the British military hero who defeated the French at the Battle of Waterloo in 1815. Some culinary historians believe that the beef dish takes its name from the appearance of the Duke's glossy brown leather footwear, known as Wellington boots. Regardless, adorned with decorative pieces of pastry in the shape of holly leaves and berries, our Beef Wellington (page 194) is simply a festive, delicious dish.

**BRITTLES AND TOFFEES** Handmade brittles and toffees have long been a Yuletide staple for making, eating, and gift giving. In Wales, it was once customary for families to stay up all night on Christmas Eve, hanging garlands, telling stories, and making toffee. Perhaps the allure of these sweets is that their complex flavors, colors, and textures come from one humble ingredient, sugar, which is cooked until it caramelizes. Nuts provide additional flavor and extra crunch to the trademark texture of brittle (pages 436 and 444). Butter or cream is added to make toffee (pages 439 and 444), with its chewier consistency.

**BUCHE DE NOEL** A traditional Christmas cake served first in France and subsequently around the world, bûche de Noël translates as "yule log." The cake is baked in a jelly-roll pan, topped with mousse or buttercream, and then rolled into a log. Sometimes, the ends are sliced on the diagonal, with one or both of the cuttings placed atop the cake to resemble branches growing out of the log. The bûche is usually covered with buttercream frosting. Our chocolate rendition (page 356) is decorated with traditional meringue "mushrooms," topped with chocolate shards, and given a snowy dusting of confectioners' sugar. We've also included a white icing–covered version, our birch de Noël (page 358).

**CHESTNUTS** The opening lyrics of Mel Torme's "The Christmas Song"—"Chestnuts roasting on an open fire"—forever linked the nuts to the holiday season. Even though chestnuts are harvested in the fall, they've always been associated with the winter months. Chestnuts make regular appearances in stuffing. But they are a much more versatile ingredient than that; we've used them in a wide range of recipes, from Chestnut Mushroom Soup (page 178) to Chestnut-Espresso Caramel-Swirl Ice Cream (page 339). And for many people, chestnuts need little more than roasting (page 211) to be a delicious holiday treat.

**CHOCOLATE TRUFFLES** Chocolate truffles, named for their likeness to the savory delicacies dug from woodland soil, are a traditional Christmas gift in France. Typically, they are made by pouring hot cream over chopped chocolate; then they are sometimes enhanced with such flavorings as vanilla, spices, coffee, nuts, chopped candies, and spirits. Our truffles (pages 440–443) include hazelnuts, candy canes, coconut, and sambuca. Because they are made with cream, chocolate truffles only keep for about a week. But their popularity makes worries over storage time unnecessary.

**COOKIES** Throughout the world, festive occasions have long been celebrated with cookies. Such traditions date to a time when sugar, nuts, and spices were rare ingredients reserved for the most exalted circumstances. For many Americans, sugar and gingerbread cookies, shaped like Christmas trees and angels and sprinkled with sanding sugar, are a sure sign that Christmas has arrived. We've gathered here more than 40 holiday cookie recipes (pages 404–436).

**CRANBERRIES** More than any other fruit, the cranberry belongs to Christmas. Its deep scarlet color is made to order for holiday decorating, and its flavor—at once tart and sweet—is worth celebrating in itself. In North America, cranberries are native and abundant in the fall and winter. Centuries ago, they were a wintertime staple in Native American diets and were included in the earliest settlers' holiday feasts. We've used them in an array of dishes, from Cranberry-Glazed Turkey with Cranberry-Cornbread Stuffing (page 213) to Pistachio-Cranberry Biscotti (page 433). However you choose to incorporate cranberries into your holidays, you'll be taking part in a tradition that is centuries old.

**CROQUEMBOUCHE** Literally translated from the French as "crisp in mouth," this classic dessert is made with puffs of choux pastry filled with pastry cream, dipped in caramel syrup, stacked in a tall cone, and surrounded by a ring of spun sugar. We make our pecan version (page 332) as a wreath instead. The caramel holds the individual pastries in place and crisps as it cools; each bite is both crunchy and melt-in-your-mouth. Croquembouche is a popular wedding dessert in France, but it has become a favorite Christmas treat as well.

**EGGNOG** A Christmas party hardly feels complete without a cup of eggnog. This creamy punch made from milk or cream, eggs, sugar, nutmeg, and usually rum, brandy, whiskey, or a combination of all three, is so rich and nourishing it used to be recommended for children and the sick to drink regularly (without the alcohol). There are many recipes for eggnog; some are made by separating the eggs and stiffly beating the whites before adding them to the yolk mixture; others recommend lightly cooking the yolk mixture to thicken it, similar to a custard. We've included a traditional version (page 123), Cooked Custard Eggnog (page 124), and White-Russian Eggnog (page 124).

**EPIPHANY CAKE** Epiphany Cake, also known as Kings' Cake, is traditionally served on the twelfth night of Christmas—or the eve of the epiphany—in honor of the three kings who came bearing gifts twelve nights after the birth of Christ. Our version (page 335) is made from puff pastry filled with ground almonds, egg, rum, and raspberry jam. Baked inside the cake is a coin, a bean, or a small figurine symbolizing the Christ child; whoever finds the prize is crowned king or queen for the day.

**FRUITCAKE** Recipes for fruitcakes date back to the seventh century. The Persians knew how to preserve fruit in sugar and grind almonds and sugar into the paste we know as marzipan. Over time, Europeans embraced the custom of adding candied fruit and ground nuts to their breads and cakes. By the nineteenth century, the English had perfected the art of the fruitcake. Making one requires a large quantity of ingredients—candied citrus peel, glacéed cherries, currants, nuts, butter, eggs, flour, and, of course, brandy—which yields a small number of cakes. Consequently, fruitcakes have always been reserved for special occasions, Christmas in particular. Once baked, fruitcakes are wrapped in cheesecloth or muslin, kept in a cool, dry place, and occasionally doused with liquor; traditional fruitcakes should be stored for at least one month before serving. We included one exception: Our Chocolate Panforte (page 378) can be eaten as soon as it cools.

**GINGERBREAD** "Of all the Christmas pastries, the gingerbread cookie was the one most loved by early American children," writes food historian William Woys Weaver in *The Christmas Cook*. Gingerbread became popular because it was inexpensive to make; gingerbread aficionados, however, will tell you that gingerbread came to be loved for its taste—a combination of molasses, ginger, cinnamon, and nutmeg. Gingerbread has been baked since early Christian times, but by the Middle Ages, Bavarian bakers had virtually cornered the market on gingerbread; they maintain an international reputation in the field today. The confection was so popular during the reign of Elizabeth I that the royal family employed its

own gingerbread baker. Gingerbread became synonymous with extravagant decoration; cut into shapes, it was iced with sugar and gilded. According to Weaver, the practice of building gingerbread houses dates back at least to the 1500s, but it surged in popularity with the opera *Hansel and Gretel*, which was first performed in 1893—and featured a life-size gingerbread house. Our Gingerbread Cookies (page 428) and sweetly shaped Gingerbread Angels (page 432) can be served plain or decorated with Royal Icing (page 428).

**GOOSE** Most of us know the old ditty that starts, "Christmas is coming, the goose is getting fat." Or, for many of us, it's the goose dinner relished by the Cratchit family in Dickens' "A Christmas Carol" that makes us associate the game bird with the holiday. In fact, the succulent roast goose was the old world's celebratory dish. Today, it is still the centerpiece of the holiday table in Scandinavian and Central European households. A few initial preparations are necessary: The goose must be trimmed of as much fat as possible (there will be plenty remaining). Since the wings have so little meat, the first and second joints should be removed before cooking. With a sharp knife, the outer skin of the goose should be pricked all over to help release the fat while cooking. Goose requires no basting, as its fat melts and bastes the meat as it roasts. Our favorite recipe for Roast Goose can be found on page 225.

**GRAVLAX** This Scandinavian specialty is a staple on any Christmas Eve smorgasbord. From the Danish *gravad*, meaning "buried," gravlax refers to salmon that has been cured in a mixture of salt, sugar, fresh herbs, spices, and liquor. Our Classic Gravlax is on page 160. Once seasoned, the salmon is weighted with cans or heavy pans and chilled; the fillets slowly "cook," absorbing the preserving brine. Crushed coriander seed, white pepper, and juniper berries add subtle, exotic, piney notes to gravlax; a layer of coarsely chopped dill sandwiched between two fillets infuses the fish with bold flavor. Vodka and aquavit are the most common liquors used to cure gravlax, though gin and Cognac are appropriate as well. Once cured, gravlax is sliced paper-thin. It can be served with eggs for breakfast, or with simple starches such as boiled potatoes, but it is most often presented as an hors d'oeuvre, such as our Star-Anise Gravlax (page 162), where it is served atop star-shape crackers.

**OYSTERS** In parts of France, oysters are traditionally eaten on Christmas Eve, as part of the meal—known as Le Reveillon—eaten before or after Midnight Mass. The old adage of eating oysters only in the months with an "R" in their name is no longer a strict rule; today's superior refrigeration reduces any risk. But oysters really are at their best—particularly for serving raw on the half shell—during fall and winter because their summer-month spawning softens them unpleasantly. Oysters are often served with a mignonette (we offer two versions of the sauce on page 156), but they are also delicious with a squeeze of lemon or a dash of hot sauce.

**PRIME RIB ROAST WITH YORKSHIRE PUDDING** No meal better embodies the right combination of special-occasion comfort food than Prime Rib Roast with Yorkshire Pudding (page 196). A thick slice of this roast beef, cooked medium-rare, is supremely satisfying, while the pudding, really a savory pastry baked in the beef drippings, is tender and delicious. Prime rib needs to rest right after cooking so that its juices can redistribute before carving; this is when the Yorkshire pudding is made. Named for England's northern county of Yorkshire, the pudding may be prepared in the roasting pan in which the roast beef was cooked, or the drippings may be transferred to muffin tins. The drippings must be piping hot and the batter very cold to get a puffed, golden exterior. By the time the pudding is done, the meat, too, is ready to be carved and served.

**TRIFLE** An array of colors and flavors, trifle (also known as tipsy cake) is as festive to the eye as it is to the palate. Trifle gets its tastes and textures from sponge cake or ladyfingers spread with preserves and custard, and topped with whipped cream, fruit, nuts, and sometimes chopped chocolate. Since it's a layered dessert, it's best arranged in a large glass serving bowl, so that its colorful striations are visible. Trifle is refrigerated for a few hours, cooling the dessert into a smooth, pudding-like treat. Our recipes highlight seasonal ingredients—there's Gingerbread Trifle with Cognac Custard and Pears (page 328) and Poached Pear and Almond Holiday Trifle (page 329). But the trifle is not just for Christmas; in Britain, it is a popular year-round party dish, particularly with children who love all the layers of cake, fruit, custard, and cream.

# menus

FOLLOWING IS A SELECTION OF OUR FAVORITE HOLIDAY MENUS,
FROM RELAXED BREAKFASTS TO FORMAL DINNERS.

## CHRISTMAS MORNING BREAKFAST
### SERVES 6

*apple ginger sparklers* · 128

*white hot chocolate* · 130

*rolled omelet with spinach
and goat cheese* · 84

*multigrain hot cereal with
cranberries and oranges* · 92

*almond brioche toasts* · 90

## SOUTHERN OPEN-HOUSE BRUNCH
### SERVES 10 TO 12

*spiked fruit punch* · 126

*black-eyed pea dip* · 134

*cheese coins with jalapeño jelly* · 146

*shrimp cocktail* · 158

*mushroom quiche* · 84

*glazed ham* · 206

*beaten biscuits* · 112

*sour cream–corn muffins* · 93

*cranberry chutney* · 303

*oyster pie* · 241

*marinated green-bean and
lima-bean salad* · 270

*pickled-beet salad* · 235

*pecan pie* · 390

*brown-sugar pound cake* · 119

*bourbon pralines* · 437

## HOLIDAY TEA
### SERVES 10

*apricot-onion tartlets* · 144

*crunchy chicken salad on brioche* · 142

*twice-baked cheese strudel* · 151

*cornmeal-pear loaf with
pear-raspberry butter* · 120

*whole-wheat apple cake* · 96

*poppy-seed layer cake* · 363

*currant scones* · 94

*classic shortbread wedges* · 433

*pomegranate punch* · 129

*iced spice tea punch* · 128

## COCKTAILS AND HORS D'OEUVRES
### SERVES 8 TO 10

*cherry bombs* · 128

*holiday bloody mary* · 122

*brie en croute* · 145

*warm olive buffet* · 132

*rock-shrimp snowballs* · 158

*leek dip with crudité* · 135

*pomegranate dipping sauce with
walnut chicken strips* · 136

*blini with caviar and
cucumber-dill dressing* · 153

*porcini-stuffed mushrooms
with camembert* · 150

## CHRISTMAS EVE FAMILY DINNER
### SERVES 6

*finnan-haddie canapés · 141*
*shrimp-salad rolls · 142*
*endive petals with smoked scallops · 158*
*crown roast with gravy · 203*
*wild-rice stuffing · 295*
*twice-baked potatoes stuffed with
spinach and parsnip soufflés · 263*
*citrus salad · 167*
*gingerbread-pear upside-down cake · 369*
*tiny tartes tatin · 401*

## ITALIAN CHRISTMAS EVE
### SERVES 10 TO 12

*rosemary breadsticks · 106*
*shrimp bruschetta · 143*
*citrus and rosemary olives · 132*
*prosciutto bread · 106*
*tortellini soup · 187*
*red snapper livornese style · 231*
*roasted fennel · 276*
*polenta wedges · 297*
*arugula with shaved pecorino · 164*
*eggnog panna cotta · 316*
*pistachio-cranberry biscotti · 433*

## VEGETARIAN HOLIDAY DINNER
### SERVES 8 TO 10

*parmesan-herb twists · 111*
*vegetarian pâté · 140*
*french lentil soup · 182*
*chestnut salad with hazelnuts,
frisée, and pear · 166*
*wild mushroom and spinach lasagna · 252*
*chocolate-applesauce cake · 345*
*coconut almond cookies · 423*

## TURKEY DINNER
### SERVES 8 TO 10

*cheese straws and poppy-seed straws · 146*
*three-peppercorn spread · 139*
*red-pepper vegetable soup · 185*
*cranberry-glazed turkey with
cranberry-cornbread stuffing · 213*
*cranberry-fig relish · 309*
*braised onions · 281*
*balsamic-roasted sweet potatoes
and butternut squash · 265*
*wilted brussels sprouts salad with
warm vinaigrette · 176*
*caramel-coated seckel pears · 312*
*autumn harvest pie · 389*
*spice ice cream · 340*

## ELEGANT BUFFET
### SERVES 12

*pear-champagne punch · 125*
*crab salad in daikon-radish boxes · 156*
*wild mushroom pâté · 140*
*sole florentine · 237*
*stuffed rib-pork-chop paillard · 207*
*frisée salad · 169*
*braised leeks, parsnips, and fennel · 277*
*root vegetables anna · 286*
*birch de noël · 358*
*sabayon with roasted chestnuts · 324*
*sambuca truffles · 443*

## TRADITIONAL CHRISTMAS DINNER
### SERVES 6

cooked custard eggnog · 124

ramos gin fizz · 123

spicy pecans · 133

garlic-thyme popovers · 118

chestnut mushroom soup · 178

roast goose · 225

gratin dauphinoise · 261

waldorf salad · 168

fig holiday roll · 352

cranberry noëls · 421

## FIRST NOEL DINNER
### SERVES 6

lentil stars · 144

chestnut mushroom soup · 178

jerusalem artichokes and mixed
greens with roasted tomatoes · 171

shepherds' crooks · 171

shepherd's pie with sweet-potato crust · 198

green-beans vinaigrette · 271

epiphany cake · 335

mini angel-food cakes · 375

clementine mousse · 375

## HOLIDAY LAMB DINNER
### SERVES 4

pear caponata · 138

olive-filled rolls · 114

ricotta salata with roasted red peppers
and marinated baby artichokes · 174

braised lamb shanks with
tomato and fennel · 197

soft polenta · 298

toasted-almond milk with honey · 123

three-nut torte · 367

## SWEDISH HOLIDAY DINNER
### SERVES 8 TO 10

homemade aquavit · 127

glögg · 125

potato pancakes with gravlax and dill · 155

whole roasted salmon with
christmas glaze · 236

sweet-and-sour red cabbage · 274

potato gratin with onions and herring · 262

pomegranate, fennel, and
green bean salad · 173

linzertorte with lingonberry jam · 365

## CORNISH GAME HEN DINNER
### SERVES 4

triple-crème cheese with
armagnac-soaked raisins · 139

puréed spinach-potato soup · 187

winter greens and bacon · 288

roasted cornish game hens with
pomegranate-molasses glaze · 223

pomegranate pilaf · 296

lemon tart with candied lemons
and kumquats · 398

# *the photographs*

CHRISTMAS MEANS AFTERNOONS IN A
WARM KITCHEN AND TREATS FRESH FROM
THE OVEN. IT'S ALWAYS TIME WELL SPENT,
ESPECIALLY WHEN YOU SEE EVERYONE'S
EYES WIDEN IN DELIGHT. HERE ARE
SOME OF OUR MOST BEAUTIFUL DISHES
FROM THE SEASON. ENJOY!

# breakfast

(clockwise from top left)

classic french toast PAGE 88

yeasted coffee cake
with poppy-seed filling PAGE 98

puffy maine pancakes PAGE 86

*(clockwise from right)*

*blueberry sticky buns* PAGE 100

*buckwheat sour-cream waffles* PAGE 87

*old-fashioned oatmeal* PAGE 90

# breads

*miniature panettone* PAGE 104 · *(opposite) sour rye pretzels* PAGE 108

*parker house rolls* PAGE 116        *buttery crescents* PAGE 115

*(opposite) olive-filled rolls* PAGE 114

*rosemary breadsticks* PAGE 106

*(opposite) ear of wheat* PAGE 105

# drinks

*flavored vodkas* PAGE 126

*chocolate-bar hot chocolate* PAGE 130

**26**  (opposite) *planter's punch* PAGE 126 · *iced spice tea punch* PAGE 128 · *chilled rosé wine*

*holiday bloody mary* PAGE 122 · *pear-champagne punch* PAGE 125

**28**   (opposite) *ramos gin fizz* PAGE 123 · *cooked custard eggnog* PAGE 124 · *spicy pecans* PAGE 133

*shrimp cocktail* PAGE 158

*(opposite) pomegranate dipping sauce with walnut chicken strips* PAGE 136

*(clockwise from top left)*
*cheese straws and poppy-seed straws* PAGE 146

*apricot-onion tartlets* PAGE 144

*curry waffles with gravlax* PAGE 154

*(clockwise from right)*

*sun-dried tomato palmiers* PAGE 150

*chicken-liver pâté with white truffles* PAGE 139

*twice-baked cheese strudel* PAGE 151

*brie en croûte* PAGE 145

*(opposite, clockwise from top right) finnan-haddie canapés* PAGE 141
*shrimp-salad rolls* PAGE 142 · *endive petals with smoked scallops* PAGE 158

# salads

*(clockwise from top left)*

*frisée and fennel with dried apricots
and crumbled roquefort* PAGE 169

*warm goat-cheese salad* PAGE 175

*honey tangerines and kumquats with
walnuts and shaved celery* PAGE 172

*(opposite) pomegranate, fennel, and
green bean salad* PAGE 173

*chestnut salad with hazelnuts, frisée, and pear* PAGE 166

*(opposite) jerusalem artichokes and mixed greens with roasted*
*tomatoes* PAGE 171 · *shepherds' crooks* PAGE 171

*soups*

*(from top) wild mushroom stock* PAGE 182
*tortellini soup* PAGE 187 · *french lentil soup* PAGE 182

*(opposite) chestnut mushroom soup* PAGE 178

*cream of belgian-endive soup* PAGE 180

*spicy sweet-potato soup* PAGE 189
*whole-grain crackers* PAGE 111

*(opposite) classic mushroom soup* PAGE 180

*main courses*

*stuffed rib-pork-chop paillard* PAGE 207

*(opposite) roast goose* PAGE 225

*choucroute garni* PAGE 202

*cranberry-glazed turkey with
cranberry-cornbread stuffing* PAGE 213

*(opposite) roasted cornish game hens with
pomegranate-molasses glaze* PAGE 223 · *pomegranate pilaf* PAGE 296

(opposite) whole roasted salmon
with pickled-beet salad PAGE 235

(this page, clockwise from top left)

striped sea bass with
blood oranges and olives PAGE 236

sole rolls with spinach and lemon slices PAGE 238

scallops in white wine PAGE 241

*perciatelli with roasted chestnuts, butternut squash, and goat cheese* PAGE 246

*(opposite) crab-stuffed shells with peas and leeks* PAGE 247

*baked rigatoni with sausage meatballs
and broccoli rabe* PAGE 250

*wild mushroom and spinach lasagna* PAGE 252

*(opposite) butternut squash cannelloni with sage-walnut cream sauce* PAGE 249

*risotto with three mushrooms* PAGE 300

(opposite) *baked sweet potatoes and pecans* PAGE 264
*roasted-garlic mashed potatoes* PAGE 256 · *chunky apple-cranberry sauce* PAGE 310      **57**

*(opposite) savory twice-baked
sweet potatoes* PAGE 264

*(this page, clockwise from right)*

*oyster brioche stuffing* PAGE 293

*gratin dauphinoise* PAGE 261

*wild-rice and fruit salad* PAGE 302

polenta wedges PAGE 297

mushroom-potato pie PAGE 278

(opposite) cranberry-bean salad with butternut squash and broccoli rabe PAGE 270

*desserts*

*peppermint semifreddo* PAGE 341

*vacherin* PAGE 313

*(opposite) coconut snowmen* PAGE 338

**63**

*gingerbread semifreddo roll* PAGE 354 · *(opposite) date-nut puddings* PAGE 320

*epiphany cake* PAGE 335
*mini angel-food cakes with clementine mousse* PAGE 375

*mr. and mrs. maus's fruitcakes* PAGE 382

*(opposite) pistachio charlotte* PAGE 326

*three-nut torte* PAGE 367

*(opposite, clockwise from top left) pecan croquembouche ring* PAGE 332
*chocolate cake with golden leaves* PAGE 344 · *lemon tart with candied lemons and
kumquats* PAGE 398 · *pear and raisin upside-down cake* PAGE 370

*gingerbread-pear upside-down cake* PAGE 369
*tiny tartes tatin* PAGE 401

*black-bottom tart* PAGE 394

*(opposite) chocolate-applesauce cake* PAGE 345

# cookies and confections

(clockwise from top) hazelnut truffles PAGE 441
coconut truffles PAGE 442 · classic truffles PAGE 440
candy cane truffles PAGE 441
pistachio truffles PAGE 442 · orange truffles PAGE 442

peppermint bark PAGE 443

(opposite, clockwise from top) bourbon pralines PAGE 437 · chocolate-covered turtles PAGE 438
chocolate-covered almonds PAGE 440 · chocolate-nut patties PAGE 437

# *breakfast*

EGG DISHES

PANCAKES, WAFFLES, AND FRENCH TOAST

CEREAL AND GRANOLA

MUFFINS AND SCONES

CAKES AND PASTRIES

✷

EGG DISHES

## holiday frittata
### SERVES 6

*This versatile Italian omelet can be made with many different fillings.*

 1  red bell pepper
12  large eggs, lightly beaten
 1  cup milk
 ¾  cup sliced scallions, white and light-green parts only (about 1 small bunch)
 1  tablespoon fresh tarragon, coarsely chopped, plus a few sprigs for garnish
 1  teaspoon coarse salt
 ½  teaspoon freshly ground black pepper
 5  ounces goat cheese, crumbled
 ½  tablespoon unsalted butter
 ½  tablespoon olive oil
 2  small red potatoes, sliced ⅛ inch thick

**1.** Roast pepper over a gas flame or under a broiler until blackened. Place in a bowl; cover with plastic wrap, and let steam 5 minutes. Peel and seed, then cut into ¼-inch-wide strips.

**2.** In a bowl, place pepper strips, eggs, milk, most of the scallions, the tarragon, salt, pepper, and half the goat cheese; whisk to combine. Set aside.

**3.** Preheat oven to 350°F. Heat butter and oil in a 10-inch ovenproof skillet (preferably nonstick) over medium heat. Add potatoes; cook until tender on both sides, about 8 minutes.

**4.** Reduce heat to medium-low, and pour egg mixture over potatoes. Using a rubber spatula, pull edges into the center, tilting skillet so egg mixture fills the gaps, until frittata is partially set, about 8 minutes. Sprinkle remaining cheese over frittata.

**5.** Transfer skillet to oven. Bake until top is set and edges are golden brown, about 25 minutes. Garnish with tarragon sprigs and remaining scallions. Serve hot, warm, or at room temperature.

## frittata with sausage and pecorino
### SERVES 4

 1  teaspoon olive oil
 6  ounces sweet fennel sausage, casings removed
1½  tablespoons unsalted butter
 8  large eggs, lightly beaten
    Coarse salt
 4  cups mizuna or watercress leaves (4 ounces)
 3  ounces pecorino or Gruyère cheese, grated
 ½  cup ricotta cheese
    Freshly ground pepper

**1.** Preheat oven to 425°F. Heat oil in a 10-inch ovenproof skillet (preferably nonstick) over medium-high heat. Add sausage; cook, breaking up meat, until well browned, 2 to 3 minutes. Using a slotted spoon, transfer sausage to a bowl; set aside. Discard fat and wipe out skillet.

**2.** Return skillet to medium heat; add butter. When melted, add eggs, season with salt, and cook until eggs begin to set on the bottom, about 10 seconds. Using a rubber spatula, pull edges into the center, tilting skillet so eggs fill the gaps. Sprinkle with 1 cup mizuna, the sausage, and both cheeses. Continue pulling edges toward center until frittata is nearly set, about 4 minutes.

**3.** Transfer skillet to oven; bake until top is set and edges are golden brown, 6 to 8 minutes. Season with pepper, and serve hot, warm, or at room temperature, garnished with remaining mizuna.

## poached eggs on rounds of polenta

### SERVES 10

*Milk helps give this polenta a creamy texture and wonderfully rich flavor. The eggs can be poached ahead of time and refrigerated in a bowl of cold water. To reheat, transfer eggs to a pan of hot water for a few minutes, drain, and serve.*

- 2 tablespoons unsalted butter, plus more for dish
- 3 cups milk
- 1 teaspoon coarse salt, plus more for water
- 1½ cups yellow cornmeal
- ⅓ cup freshly grated Parmesan cheese
  Freshly ground pepper
- 10 large eggs
  Herb Beurre Blanc (recipe follows)
  Chopped fresh chives, for garnish

**1.** Lightly butter a 9-by-13-inch baking dish; set aside. In a large saucepan, combine milk, 4 cups water, and the salt. Bring to a boil; slowly sprinkle in cornmeal, whisking constantly to break up lumps. Reduce heat to low, and cook, stirring constantly with a wooden spoon, about 15 minutes.

**2.** Stir in 1½ tablespoons butter and the cheese; season with pepper. Pour into prepared dish; cover with plastic wrap, and refrigerate until firm, at least 1 hour and up to 2 days.

**3.** Preheat oven to 200°F. Use a 3-inch cookie cutter or inverted glass to cut out 10 rounds of polenta. In a large nonstick skillet over medium heat, melt remaining ½ tablespoon butter. Cook rounds in skillet until brown, about 3 minutes per side. Transfer to a baking sheet; keep warm in oven.

**4.** In a large saucepan, bring about 3 inches of water to a boil; add salt, then reduce heat to a bare simmer. One at a time, carefully crack eggs into a small shallow bowl, and gently slide into water.

Poach two or three at a time until just set, 3 to 5 minutes. Remove with a slotted spoon; drain well. Continue until all eggs are poached.

**5.** On serving plates, top each polenta round with a poached egg; spoon a little butter sauce on top, sprinkle with chives, and serve.

## herb beurre blanc

### MAKES ABOUT 1 CUP

*This butter sauce should be made as close to serving as possible; if reheated, it will separate. To keep it warm, set pan in a larger pan of warm—not hot—water; stir in herbs just before serving.*

- 3 shallots, minced
- 2 cups dry white wine
- ½ pound (2 sticks) cold unsalted butter
  Coarse salt and freshly ground pepper
- 2 tablespoons mixed chopped fresh basil, chives, flat-leaf parsley, and tarragon

**1.** In a small saucepan, bring shallots and wine to a boil. Reduce the heat to medium, and simmer the liquid until it is reduced to approximately 2 tablespoons, about 20 minutes.

**2.** Reduce heat to lowest possible flame. Whisk butter into wine mixture 1 tablespoon at a time, adding a new piece as each previous one just melts. Don't allow sauce to become too hot.

**3.** Remove from heat. Season with salt and pepper, and stir in the herbs.

## rolled omelet with spinach and goat cheese

SERVES 6 TO 8

*Mustard greens, Swiss chard, or arugula can be used instead of or in combination with the spinach.*

- 4 tablespoons unsalted butter
- 1 small onion, diced
- 6 cups fresh spinach (about 10 ounces), rinsed well and stems discarded
  Coarse salt and freshly ground pepper
- ¼ teaspoon ground nutmeg
- 12 large eggs
- 3 ounces goat cheese

**1.** Melt 2 tablespoons butter in a large sauté pan. Add onion; cook until soft and translucent, about 8 minutes. Add spinach, one handful at a time, letting each batch wilt before adding more. Season generously with salt and pepper; add nutmeg. Remove from heat. Let stand until mixture is cool enough to handle. Squeeze moisture from spinach, and coarsely chop leaves. Set aside.

**2.** Preheat oven to 200°F. Whisk together 6 eggs and 1 tablespoon water in a medium bowl. Season with salt and pepper. Melt 1 tablespoon butter in a 12-inch nonstick sauté pan over medium heat. Add egg mixture; as eggs begin to set, pull edges into the center of the pan with a rubber spatula, tilting the pan so eggs fill the gaps.

**3.** When eggs are cooked but not yet completely dry, slide omelet onto a baking sheet. Crumble 1½ ounces goat cheese in a line, across bottom half of omelet; cover with half the spinach filling. With your hands, carefully roll omelet into a neat log. Transfer sheet to oven to keep warm.

**4.** Repeat process with remaining ingredients. Using a large metal spatula, transfer omelets to a serving platter with the seam side down. Cut logs on the diagonal into individual pieces; serve.

## mushroom quiche

SERVES 6

*This recipe, a brunch favorite, was developed by John Barricelli, kitchen manager of the Martha Stewart Living television studio. You will need three-quarters of the pâte brisée dough; instead of dividing the dough in half, as instructed, pinch off one-quarter, and save for another use (dough can be stored in the freezer for up to one month). Pat the rest of the dough into a disk, and cover with plastic wrap until ready to use.*

- All-purpose flour, for work surface
  Pâte Brisée (page 389)
- 2 tablespoons olive oil
- 2 medium shallots, thinly sliced
- 1 pound white button mushrooms, quartered
  Coarse salt and freshly ground pepper
- 6 ounces Gruyère cheese, grated (1½ cups)
- ½ cup milk
- ½ cup heavy cream
- 2 large whole eggs
- 1 large egg yolk
  Pinch of ground nutmeg

**1.** On a lightly floured work surface, roll out dough into a 12-inch round, about ⅛ inch thick. Fit into a 10-inch fluted round tart pan with a removable bottom, pressing dough into edges and up sides. Trim dough flush with edge. Prick bottom all over with a fork. Refrigerate at least 30 minutes.

**2.** Preheat oven to 375°F. Line tart shell with parchment paper and then aluminum foil; press into edges. Fill with dried beans, rice, or aluminum pie weights. Bake until pastry is golden brown and dry, 40 to 50 minutes. Transfer tart pan to a wire rack to cool while making filling. Carefully remove weights, foil, and parchment paper.

**3.** Heat oil in a large nonstick skillet over high heat. Add shallots; cook, stirring, until translucent but not brown, about 1 minute. Add mushrooms, and season with salt and pepper. Continue cooking, stirring frequently, until mushrooms are dark golden brown and their released juices have evaporated, 8 to 10 minutes.

**4.** Transfer tart pan to a baking sheet. Sprinkle half the cheese evenly over the bottom of the crust. Sprinkle with mushrooms, and top with remaining cheese. In a medium bowl, whisk together milk, cream, eggs, and egg yolk. Add nutmeg; season with salt and pepper. Pour over cheese. Bake until quiche is just set in the center, 30 to 35 minutes. Let cool on a wire rack about 10 minutes; slice into wedges, and serve.

...........................................................

PANCAKES, WAFFLES,
AND FRENCH TOAST

...........................................................

## apple pancake

SERVES 4

- 4 tablespoons unsalted butter
- ¼ cup packed dark-brown sugar
- 1 large McIntosh apple (about 8 ounces), cored and sliced ⅛ inch thick
- 5 large eggs
- 1 cup all-purpose flour
- 1 cup milk
- ½ teaspoon ground cinnamon
   Pinch of coarse salt
   Confectioners' sugar, for dusting

**1.** Preheat oven to 400°F. In a 10-inch cast-iron skillet, melt the butter and 3 tablespoons brown sugar over medium heat. Add apple slices; cook, stirring occasionally, until starting to brown, about 5 minutes. Remove from heat.

**2.** In a medium bowl, whisk together eggs, flour, milk, cinnamon, salt, and remaining tablespoon brown sugar. Pour batter slowly over cooked apple

mixture. Transfer skillet to oven, and bake until pancake is dark golden brown, set in the center, and puffed around the edges, about 15 minutes. Dust with confectioners' sugar, and serve.

## best quick pancakes

MAKES 9 FOUR-INCH PANCAKES

- 1 cup all-purpose flour
- 2 teaspoons baking powder
- ½ teaspoon salt
- 2 tablespoons sugar
- 1 large egg, lightly beaten
- 1 cup milk
- 2 tablespoons unsalted butter, melted, plus ½ teaspoon for griddle

**1.** In a medium bowl, whisk together flour, baking powder, salt, and sugar. Add egg, milk, and 2 tablespoons butter; whisk to combine. Batter should still be slightly lumpy.

**2.** Preheat oven to 200°F. Heat a griddle or heavy skillet over medium heat until it is hot enough to make a few drops of water bounce. Using a pastry brush or paper towel, lightly coat griddle with the remaining ½ teaspoon butter.

**3.** Working in batches, ladle about ¼ cup batter onto griddle in pools, 2 inches apart. Cook until bubbles on surface break and edges begin to look dry, about 2 minutes. Flip pancakes, and cook until bottoms are brown, about 1 minute more.

**4.** Transfer pancakes to a heatproof plate or baking sheet, and keep warm in oven while cooking remaining batter. You may need to lightly re-oil the griddle between batches.

## cornmeal pancakes with cranberry-maple compote

MAKES 9 FIVE-INCH PANCAKES

¾  cup all-purpose flour
2  tablespoons sugar
½  cup yellow cornmeal
4  teaspoons baking powder
¾  teaspoon salt
1  cup milk
5  tablespoons unsalted butter, plus more for serving
2  large eggs, lightly beaten
   Vegetable oil
   Cranberry-Maple Compote (recipe follows)

1. In a large bowl, whisk together flour, sugar, cornmeal, baking powder, and salt.

2. Combine milk and butter in a small saucepan, and place over low heat until butter melts. Remove from heat; let cool slightly. Whisk in eggs.

3. Pour egg mixture over dry ingredients; using a wooden spoon, combine with a few swift strokes. Batter may still be slightly lumpy.

4. Preheat oven to 200°F. Heat a griddle or skillet over medium heat until hot enough to make a few drops of water bounce. Lightly oil griddle using a brush or paper towel.

5. Working in batches, spoon batter onto griddle to make 5-inch rounds, 2 inches apart. Cook until bubbles on surface break and edges begin to look dry, about 2 minutes. Flip pancakes, and cook until bottoms are brown, about 1 minute more.

6. Transfer to a baking sheet, and keep warm in oven while cooking remaining batter. (You may need to lightly re-oil the griddle between batches of pancakes.) Serve with butter and compote.

## cranberry-maple compote

MAKES ABOUT 2 CUPS

*Store compote in an airtight container in the refrigerator for up to one week.*

1  cup fresh cranberries
1  cup pure maple syrup

Combine cranberries and syrup in a small saucepan. Heat over medium-low heat until mixture comes to a simmer. Cook until cranberries soften and burst and syrup turns red, about 10 minutes. Serve warm over pancakes.

## puffy maine pancakes
*photograph on page 18*
MAKES 3 FOUR-INCH PANCAKES

*These pancakes are best if you make the batter a day ahead and chill it overnight; whisk to combine again just before cooking. You can easily double this recipe.*

2  large eggs, lightly beaten
½  cup all-purpose flour
½  cup milk
   Pinch of salt
   Pinch of freshly grated nutmeg
3  tablespoons unsalted butter
   Confectioners' sugar, for dusting

1. Preheat oven to 425°F. In a medium bowl, whisk together eggs, flour, milk, salt, and nutmeg until well combined. Batter may still be slightly lumpy.

2. For each pancake, working with one at a time, melt 1 tablespoon butter in a 4-inch crêpe pan or ovenproof skillet over medium-high heat. Ladle one-third of the batter into hot pan; transfer immediately to oven. Bake until pancake is golden brown and very puffy, about 10 minutes. Transfer to a plate. Dust with confectioners' sugar; serve immediately. Repeat with remaining butter and batter.

## banana-nut buttermilk waffles

SERVES 4 TO 6

2 cups all-purpose flour

½ cup packed light-brown sugar

2 tablespoons granulated sugar

1 tablespoon baking powder

½ teaspoon salt

½ teaspoon ground cinnamon

¼ teaspoon ground nutmeg

3 large eggs, separated

2 cups nonfat buttermilk

½ cup (1 stick) unsalted butter, melted

1 teaspoon pure vanilla extract

3 very ripe bananas

1 tablespoon freshly squeezed lemon juice

⅔ cup walnuts, coarsely chopped

**1.** Preheat oven to 200°F. Heat a waffle iron. Into a large bowl, sift together flour, sugars, baking powder, salt, cinnamon, and nutmeg. In a medium bowl, whisk together egg yolks, buttermilk, butter, and vanilla. Pour mixture into dry ingredients; stir until just combined.

**2.** In a nonreactive bowl, coarsely mash bananas and lemon juice; stir into batter along with the walnuts. In a medium bowl, beat egg whites until stiff but not dry. Fold into batter.

**3.** Ladle about ⅓ cup batter onto each section of the waffle grid, filling grid almost to the edges. Close lid; cook 5 to 6 minutes, or until no steam emerges from waffle iron.

**4.** Transfer cooked waffles to a baking sheet, and keep warm in oven while cooking remaining batter. Serve warm.

## buckwheat-sour cream waffles

*photograph on page 19*

SERVES 4 TO 6

*Adding buckwheat flour to the batter gives these waffles an earthy flavor. If desired, sauté fresh blueberries in about one tablespoon melted butter over medium heat, until just starting to burst, three to five minutes.*

1 cup buckwheat flour

1 cup all-purpose flour

2 tablespoons light-brown sugar

1 tablespoon baking powder

1 teaspoon salt

¼ teaspoon ground cinnamon

3 large eggs, separated

1 cup sour cream

1½ cups milk

½ cup (1 stick) unsalted butter, melted
   Fresh blueberries, for serving (optional)
   Whipped crème fraîche, for serving (optional)

**1.** Preheat oven to 200°F. Heat a waffle iron. Into a large bowl, sift together flours, sugar, baking powder, salt, and cinnamon. In a medium bowl, whisk together egg yolks, sour cream, milk, and butter. Pour egg mixture into dry ingredients; stir until just combined.

**2.** In a medium bowl, beat egg whites until stiff but not dry. Fold into batter.

**3.** Ladle about ⅓ cup batter onto each section of the waffle grid; filling grid almost to the edges. Close lid; cook 5 to 6 minutes, or until no steam emerges from waffle iron.

**4.** Transfer cooked waffles to a baking sheet, and keep warm in oven while cooking remaining batter. If desired, serve warm with blueberries and a dollop of whipped crème fraîche.

## savory potato waffles

SERVES 4 TO 6

*Closely related to potato pancakes, the potato waffle has one advantage—it reheats exceptionally well and therefore can be made in advance. Serve with your favorite brunch foods, such as soft-boiled eggs and poached asparagus.*

2  medium (about 13 ounces) Yukon gold potatoes

1½  teaspoons salt, plus more for saucepan

2  cups all-purpose flour

1  teaspoon sugar

1  teaspoon baking soda

1½  teaspoons baking powder

3  large eggs, separated

2  cups nonfat buttermilk

½  cup (1 stick) unsalted butter, melted

**1.** Peel potatoes; cut each into eighths. Place in a medium saucepan of cold water. Bring to a boil; add salt, and simmer until potatoes are fork-tender, about 8 minutes. Drain; set aside in a bowl to cool. Mash coarsely with a fork.

**2.** Preheat oven to 200°F. Heat a waffle iron. Into a large bowl, sift together flour, sugar, baking soda, baking powder, and salt. In a medium bowl, whisk together egg yolks, buttermilk, and butter. Pour egg mixture into dry ingredients; stir until just combined. Stir in potatoes.

**3.** In another medium bowl, beat egg whites until stiff but not dry. Fold into batter.

**4.** Ladle about ⅓ cup batter onto each section of the waffle grid, filling grid almost to the edges. Close lid; cook 5 to 6 minutes, or until no steam emerges from waffle iron.

**5.** Transfer waffles to a baking sheet; keep warm in oven while cooking remaining batter. Serve.

## classic french toast

*photograph on page 18*
SERVES 6

*We used challah, but any dense bread, such as brioche or sourdough, will work just as well. We served crisp slices of bacon on the side.*

6  large eggs

1½  cups heavy cream, half-and-half, or whole milk

2  tablespoons pure vanilla extract

½  teaspoon ground cinnamon

Pinch of ground nutmeg

Pinch of salt

6  slices bread (1 inch thick), preferably day-old

4  tablespoons unsalted butter, plus more for serving

4  tablespoons vegetable oil

Pure maple syrup, for serving (optional)

**1.** Whisk together eggs, cream, vanilla, cinnamon, nutmeg, and salt in a large bowl; set aside.

**2.** Place bread in a shallow baking dish large enough to hold slices in a single layer. Pour egg mixture over bread; let soak 10 minutes. Turn slices; let soak 10 minutes more or until soaked through.

**3.** Preheat oven to 200°F. Place a wire rack on a baking sheet; set aside. Heat 2 tablespoons each butter and oil in a large skillet over medium heat. Cook half the bread slices until golden brown, 2 to 3 minutes per side, turning once. Transfer to prepared baking sheet; keep warm in oven.

**4.** Wipe skillet with a paper towel, and repeat with remaining butter, oil, and bread. Serve warm with butter and maple syrup, if desired.

## *orange croissant french toast*

### SERVES 6

- 6 *large eggs*
- 1½ *cups heavy cream, half-and-half, or whole milk*
- 2 *tablespoons Grand Marnier, or other orange-flavored liqueur*
- 1 *teaspoon pure vanilla extract*
- ½ *teaspoon ground cinnamon*
  - *Pinch of ground nutmeg*
  - *Pinch of salt*
  - *Grated zest of 1 orange*
- 4 *ounces cream cheese, softened*
- 2 *tablespoons confectioners' sugar*
- 6 *croissants, preferably day-old*
- ½ *cup orange marmalade, plus more for serving, if desired*
- 2 *tablespoons unsalted butter, plus more for serving, if desired*
- 2 *tablespoons vegetable oil*
  - *Orange Syrup, for serving (recipe follows)*
- 2 *oranges, segmented, for serving (optional)*

**1.** Whisk together eggs, cream, Grand Marnier, vanilla, cinnamon, nutmeg, salt, and orange zest in a large bowl; set aside. Stir together cream cheese and sugar in a small bowl.

**2.** Halve croissants horizontally. Spread bottom half of each with some cream-cheese mixture, then with some marmalade. Replace tops. Place stuffed croissants in a shallow baking dish large enough to hold them in a single layer. Pour egg mixture over croissants; let soak 5 minutes. Turn croissants; let soak 5 minutes more or until soaked through.

**3.** Preheat oven to 250°F. Place a wire rack on a baking sheet; set aside. Heat 1 tablespoon butter and 1 tablespoon oil in a large skillet over medium heat. Cook half the croissants until golden brown, about 3 minutes per side. Transfer to prepared baking sheet, and keep warm in oven.

**4.** Wipe skillet with a paper towel, and repeat with remaining butter, oil, and croissants. Serve warm with orange syrup, marmalade, butter, and orange segments, if desired.

### *orange syrup*

#### MAKES 1¼ CUPS

*This syrup can be poured over French toast or pancakes as an alternative to maple syrup.*

- 1 *tablespoon cornstarch*
- ¾ *cup freshly squeezed orange juice*
- 1 *cup sugar*
- 2 *tablespoons unsalted butter*

**1.** In a small bowl, whisk cornstarch into orange juice until dissolved; set aside.

**2.** Combine sugar and ½ cup water in a small saucepan. Bring to a boil over medium-high heat, stirring until sugar has dissolved. Reduce heat to low; pour orange juice mixture into sugar syrup, stirring to combine. Simmer gently until thick, 6 to 8 minutes; stir in butter until melted. Remove from heat; serve warm.

### THE BEST FRENCH TOAST

*As its original name (***pain perdu***, or "lost bread") suggests, French toast really is better when it is made with day-old bread. The extra firmness helps the bread hold together as it soaks in the batter and fries in the pan.*

## almond brioche toasts

MAKES 10 SLICES

10  tablespoons (1¼ sticks) unsalted butter, room temperature

⅔  cup granulated sugar

5  ounces finely ground almonds (1½ cups)

1  large egg

1  teaspoon pure almond extract

1  loaf (12 ounces) brioche, preferably day-old, sliced into 10 pieces

⅓  cup sliced almonds
   Confectioners' sugar, for dusting

1. Preheat oven to 350°F. In the bowl of an electric mixer, cream butter and granulated sugar. Scrape down sides of bowl. Add ground almonds, egg, and almond extract; beat until well combined.

2. Spread 3 tablespoons mixture on top of each brioche slice. Sprinkle with sliced almonds, and place on a large baking sheet in a single layer.

3. Bake until brioche are golden brown on top, about 20 minutes. Transfer toasts to a wire rack to cool. Dust with confectioners' sugar. Serve warm or at room temperature.

### THE BEST OATMEAL

*Many of us think of oatmeal as a ready-to-eat wonder that comes in a carton or envelope. But quick and instant oats are relatively modern inventions, made by processing the steamed, flattened grains into small pieces so they cook faster. This processing can diminish texture and flavor—and oats have so much of both. Instead, try either rolled oats or steel-cut oats. How you prepare them will alter the flavor and consistency of the resulting porridge.*

CEREAL AND GRANOLA

## old-fashioned oatmeal

photograph on page 19

MAKES 3¼ CUPS

*Serve this oatmeal with your choice of toppings. We use a soaking method, which produces creamy oatmeal. If you prefer, you can simply cook the oats immediately after adding them to the boiling salted water; reduce heat to a simmer, and cook until tender but still chewy, about thirty minutes.*

   Pinch of coarse salt

1  cup Irish, Scottish, or other steel-cut oats
   Sautéed Pears (recipe follows; optional)
   Stewed Fruit (recipe follows; optional)
   Vanilla Cream (recipe follows; optional)
   Infused Honey (recipe follows; optional)

1. Bring 4 cups water to a boil in a medium saucepan; add salt. Turn off heat, and stir in oats; cover, and let stand overnight.

2. Place pan of soaked oatmeal over medium-low heat; cook, stirring occasionally, until creamy and heated through, 8 to 10 minutes. Serve hot with desired toppings.

### sautéed pears

SERVES 4 TO 6

1  tablespoon unsalted butter

3  ripe Bosc pears, peeled, cored, and thinly sliced

1  tablespoon sugar

In a large skillet, melt butter over medium-high heat. Add pears and sugar; sauté pears until tender and caramelized, about 10 minutes. Transfer to a plate, and keep warm until ready to serve.

## stewed fruit
MAKES 1 CUP

*If you like, the stewed fruit may be rewarmed as needed in a small saucepan over low heat.*

¼ cup brandy or apple cider
1 vanilla bean, split lengthwise and scraped
8 pitted prunes
12 dried apricot halves
¼ cup golden raisins

Combine brandy, vanilla bean and scrapings, prunes, apricots, and raisins in a medium saucepan with 2 cups water. Bring to a boil, then reduce to a simmer. Cook until liquid is reduced by about three-quarters. Discard vanilla pod. Serve warm.

## vanilla cream
MAKES 2 CUPS

2 cups heavy cream
1 vanilla bean, split lengthwise and scraped

Heat cream with vanilla bean and scrapings, in a small saucepan over very low heat until cream is just bubbling. Remove from heat; let steep about 20 minutes. Discard vanilla pod, and serve warm.

## infused honey
MAKES 1 CUP

*This flavorful honey may be made ahead and kept up to ten days in an airtight container at room temperature.*

1 cup honey
4 whole star anise
4 cinnamon sticks

Warm ingredients in a small saucepan over medium-low heat, 5 to 10 minutes. Turn off heat; let honey mixture steep 30 minutes or overnight. Serve over hot cereal.

## brûléed irish oatmeal with dried fruits
SERVES 6

*We adapted this recipe from one that was developed by Katy Sparks, the former chef of Quilty's in New York City.*

¼ cup packed light-brown sugar
3 cups milk
1½ cups McCann's Irish Oatmeal (not instant)
¼ teaspoon salt
  Apple and Pear Chips (recipe follows)
1 cup stewed prunes, for serving (optional)
  Pure maple syrup, for serving (optional)
  Heavy cream, for serving (optional)

**1.** Crumble the brown sugar into a baking pan or shallow dish in an even layer; let dry, uncovered, overnight at room temperature. Press through a fine sieve or grind in a spice grinder.

**2.** In a large saucepan, bring milk and 3½ cups water to a boil over medium-high heat; stir in oatmeal and salt. Cook over medium heat, stirring often, about 15 minutes. Reduce heat; simmer, stirring often, until oats have absorbed almost all liquid and are al dente, about 25 minutes.

**3.** Heat broiler. Transfer oatmeal to a 6-cup oven-proof dish at least 2 inches deep; sprinkle with dried brown sugar. Place oatmeal under broiler; cook until sugar melts and forms a crust, about 2 minutes. Serve with fruit chips, prunes, maple syrup, or heavy cream, if desired.

## apple and pear chips
MAKES ABOUT 1½ DOZEN

*Use unblemished, slightly underripe fruit.*

- 1 apple
- 1 pear
- ¾ cup sugar

**1.** Preheat oven to 200°F. Place a Silpat baking mat on a baking sheet. Using a Japanese mandoline or very sharp knife, slice apple and pear into very thin translucent rounds (slice pears lengthwise). Do not worry about removing seeds or cores. Spread sugar on a plate; dip apple and pear slices in sugar, turning to coat both sides.

**2.** Transfer slices to prepared baking sheet. Bake until edges begin to ruffle, about 1 hour. Turn slices; continue baking until golden brown, about 1 hour more. Transfer chips to a wire rack in a single layer to cool and harden. Once cool, chips can be stored in an airtight container between layers of parchment paper, up to 3 days.

## multigrain hot cereal with cranberries and oranges
SERVES 4

*Soy and other whole-grain flakes can be found at most natural-food markets.*

- 1 cup fresh or frozen cranberries
- 2 oranges, peeled and segmented
- 2 cups unsweetened apple juice
- 1 cup cracked wheat
- ½ cup soy or other whole-grain flakes
- ½ cup kasha
- ¼ cup toasted hazelnuts

**1.** Heat a medium skillet over medium-high heat. Add cranberries and 2 tablespoons water. Cook until cranberries soften and release their juices,

about 2 minutes. Stir in orange segments. Remove from heat, and set aside.

**2.** Bring apple juice and 3 cups water to a boil in a large saucepan. Add cracked wheat; reduce to a simmer, cover, and cook 15 minutes. Add soy flakes; cook, covered, 5 minutes. Add kasha; cook, covered, 10 minutes more.

**3.** Continue cooking, uncovered, about 5 minutes more to let excess liquid evaporate. Spoon mixture into individual bowls. Sprinkle with hazelnuts, and spoon reserved fruit on top. Serve.

## homemade toasted granola
MAKES 1 POUND

- 1 cup rolled oats
- 1 cup soy flakes
- 1 cup wheat flakes
- ½ cup packed light-brown sugar
- 1 cup roughly chopped pecans
  Grated zest of 1 orange
- ½ teaspoon freshly grated nutmeg
- ¼ teaspoon ground cinnamon
- ½ cup (1 stick) unsalted butter
- ¼ cup honey

**1.** Preheat oven to 350°F. Combine oats, flakes, sugar, pecans, zest, nutmeg, and cinnamon in a bowl. Melt butter and honey in a saucepan over low heat; pour over oat mixture.

**2.** Spread mixture evenly in a 7-by-11-inch baking pan; bake until just golden, about 10 minutes, stirring occasionally. Let cool completely in pan. (Mixture will harden.) Break into pieces before serving. Granola can be stored in an airtight container at room temperature up to 10 days.

MUFFINS AND SCONES

## sour cream-corn muffins
MAKES 1 DOZEN

*You may add up to one-and-one-quarter cups of the following to the prepared batter: corn kernels, crumbled cooked bacon, chopped fresh chives, grated cheddar cheese, or diced jalapeño.*

- 10 tablespoons (1¼ sticks) unsalted butter, room temperature, plus more for tin
- 1 cup yellow cornmeal
- 1 cup all-purpose flour
- ¾ teaspoon baking powder
- ¾ teaspoon baking soda
- ¾ teaspoon salt
- ¾ cup sugar
- 1 large egg
- ¾ teaspoon pure vanilla extract
- ¾ cup sour cream

**1.** Preheat oven to 375°F. Butter a standard muffin tin. In a large bowl, whisk together the cornmeal, flour, baking powder, baking soda, and salt.

**2.** In the bowl of an electric mixer, cream butter and sugar until light and fluffy. Add egg; beat until fully incorporated. Beat in vanilla. Add flour mixture and sour cream in four alternating batches, starting with the flour; beat until just combined.

**3.** Spoon ¼ cup batter into each prepared muffin cup. Bake until tops are golden, 15 to 17 minutes. Remove from oven; let cool in pan 15 to 20 minutes before transferring to a wire rack. Serve warm or at room temperature.

## breakfast muffins
MAKES 1 DOZEN

*If using strawberries, cut them into small pieces. You can also use other fruit, such as peaches; peel and chop them before adding to batter.*

- 10 tablespoons (1¼ sticks) unsalted butter, melted, plus more for tin
- 1¾ cups all-purpose flour
- 1 tablespoon baking powder
- 1¼ teaspoons ground cinnamon
- ¼ teaspoon salt
- ½ vanilla bean, split lengthwise and scraped
- ⅔ cup sugar
- ⅔ cup milk, room temperature
- 1 large egg, room temperature
- 1¼ cups mixed fresh berries
  Streusel Topping (recipe follows)

**1.** Preheat oven to 400°F. Butter a standard muffin tin. In a large bowl, whisk together the flour, baking powder, cinnamon, and salt.

**2.** In a bowl, whisk together butter, vanilla-bean scrapings, sugar, milk, and egg. Fold butter mixture and the fruit into flour mixture, using no more than 10 strokes.

**3.** Spoon ¼ cup batter into each prepared muffin cup; gently press 2 tablespoons streusel on top of each. Bake until tops are golden, 15 to 17 minutes. Remove from oven; let cool in pan 15 to 20 minutes before transferring to a wire rack. Serve warm or at room temperature.

### streusel topping

MAKES ENOUGH FOR 12 STANDARD MUFFINS

⅔ cup all-purpose flour

⅔ cup confectioners' sugar

¼ teaspoon ground cinnamon

  Pinch of salt

5 tablespoons unsalted butter, melted

In a medium bowl, whisk together flour, sugar, cinnamon, and salt. Add melted butter; combine, using your fingers, until mixture is crumbly.

# carrot and fig muffins

MAKES 1 DOZEN

*You can also bake these muffins in a standard muffin tin; use a quarter-cup batter for each cup.*

  Unsalted butter, for tin

1 cup whole-wheat flour

1 cup wheat bran

3 tablespoons flax seed, ground, plus more, whole, for garnish

1¼ teaspoons baking powder

1¼ teaspoons baking soda

¾ teaspoon ground nutmeg

½ teaspoon salt

5 carrots, finely grated

10 ounces (about 15) dried figs, each sliced into eighths

⅔ cup unsweetened applesauce

⅔ cup honey

5 large eggs, lightly beaten

1 teaspoon pure vanilla extract

**1.** Preheat oven to 375°F. Butter a ⅔-cup muffin tin. In a large bowl, whisk together flour, bran, flax seed, baking powder, baking soda, nutmeg, and salt. Add carrots, figs, applesauce, honey, eggs, and vanilla. Using a large rubber spatula, stir until mixture is just combined.

**2.** Spoon ½ cup batter into each prepared muffin cup. Bake until tops are golden, 15 to 17 minutes. Remove from oven; let cool in pan 12 to 15 minutes before transferring to a wire rack. Serve warm or at room temperature.

# currant scones

MAKES 10 TO 12

*If not eaten warm from the oven, scones are best split, toasted, and spread with butter or clotted cream and jam.*

6 tablespoons unsalted butter, chilled, plus more for baking sheet

2 cups all-purpose flour, plus more for work surface

1 tablespoon baking powder

3 tablespoons granulated sugar, plus more for tops

½ teaspoon salt

½ cup dried currants

2 large eggs, plus 1 egg, lightly beaten, for tops

⅓ cup heavy cream

**1.** Preheat oven to 400°F. Lightly butter a baking sheet, and set aside. Into a medium bowl, sift together the flour, baking powder, sugar, and salt two times. Using a pastry cutter or two knives, cut butter into flour mixture until mixture resembles coarse meal. Add currants; stir to combine.

**2.** In a separate bowl, beat together eggs and cream. Make a well in the center of the flour mixture, and pour in egg mixture. Stir lightly with a fork until dough just comes together.

**3.** Turn out onto a lightly floured surface, and knead a few times. Pat dough into a rectangle or round about ¾ inch thick. Cut into 2½-inch triangles with a floured knife or into shapes with floured cookie cutters.

4. Transfer shapes to prepared baking sheet. Lightly brush top of each with beaten egg; sprinkle with sugar. Bake until golden, 12 to 15 minutes. Transfer to a wire rack to cool.

✳

## lemon poppy-seed scones
### MAKES 6

*For convenience, mix the dry ingredients and the liquid ingredients separately the night before baking; refrigerate the liquid. When ready to bake, just combine the two.*

- 3 cups all-purpose flour, plus more for work surface
- 2 tablespoons baking powder
- 1 teaspoon salt
- 1 tablespoon sugar, plus more for tops
- 2 tablespoons poppy seeds
  Grated zest of 1 lemon
- 1 large egg
- 2 tablespoons unsalted butter, melted, plus more for baking sheet (if needed)
- 1¼ cups buttermilk

1. Preheat oven to 425°F. Sift together flour, baking powder, salt, and sugar into a large bowl. Stir in poppy seeds and lemon zest.

2. In a separate bowl, whisk together egg, butter, and buttermilk. Pour liquid into dry ingredients, and combine with a few swift strokes.

3. Turn out dough onto a lightly floured surface, and knead once or twice. Pat dough into a rectangle or round about ¾ inch thick; cut into rounds using a floured 3-inch cookie cutter. Re-roll scraps and cut again until all dough has been used.

4. Place rounds a few inches apart on a buttered or parchment-lined baking sheet. Sprinkle tops with sugar, and bake until golden brown, 10 to 15 minutes. Serve warm.

## classic crumb cake
### MAKES 1 NINE-INCH CAKE

- 2½ cups all-purpose flour
- 1 teaspoon baking soda
- 1 teaspoon baking powder
- ¼ teaspoon salt
- 10 tablespoons (1¼ sticks) unsalted butter, room temperature, plus more for pan
- 1 cup granulated sugar
- 3 large eggs
- 1 teaspoon pure vanilla extract
- 1¼ cups sour cream
- 3 cups blueberries (optional)
  Crumb Topping (recipe follows)
  Confectioners' sugar, for dusting (optional)

1. Preheat oven to 350°F. Sift together flour, baking soda, baking powder, and salt into a bowl; set aside. Butter a 9-inch square baking pan; set aside.

2. In the bowl of an electric mixer, cream butter and granulated sugar until light and fluffy, about 4 minutes. Add eggs, one at a time, beating until combined before adding the next. Add vanilla, and stir until combined. Add reserved flour mixture and sour cream, and stir just until well combined. Fold in 2 cups blueberries, if desired.

3. Spoon batter into prepared pan. Toss remaining cup blueberries, if desired, with the crumb topping. Sprinkle topping over cake. Bake until golden brown and a cake tester comes out clean, 50 to 60 minutes. Dust with confectioners' sugar before serving, if desired.

## crumb topping

MAKES ENOUGH FOR 1 NINE-INCH CAKE

*The easiest method of combining the ingredients is to use your fingers. But if you want to blend them quickly without getting your hands messy, you can mix them in the bowl of an electric mixer fitted with the paddle attachment.*

- 1½ teaspoons ground cinnamon
- ½ teaspoon salt
- ½ cup packed light-brown sugar (or ¾ cup confectioners' sugar)
- 1½ cups all-purpose flour
- 12 tablespoons (1½ sticks) unsalted butter, room temperature

In a medium bowl, combine cinnamon, salt, sugar, and flour. Using your hands, two knives, a pastry cutter, a blender, or an electric mixer's paddle attachment, cut in butter until well combined and mixture is crumbly. Topping can be stored in an airtight container in the refrigerator up to 1 week or frozen up to 2 months.

### MAKE-AHEAD COFFEE CAKE

*Typically served at breakfast or brunch, coffee cake is best eaten warm the day that it's made, but it can also be wrapped airtight and frozen for up to three weeks. This makes it ideal for an easy breakfast or snack when guests pop in unexpectedly over the holidays.*

## whole-wheat apple cake

MAKES 1 NINE-INCH CAKE

*For a hearty twist on traditional coffee cake, we have substituted whole-wheat flour for some of the all-purpose flour and replaced the milk with yogurt. Chopped green apples add a moist tartness to the dense, rich cake sprinkled with brown sugar, which caramelizes into a crisp topping. For an elegant snack, pair this cake with sharp English cheddar and a glass of white wine.*

- 3 Granny Smith apples, peeled, cored, and cut into ½-inch pieces
- ¾ cup packed light-brown sugar
- 2 teaspoons ground cinnamon
  Pinch of ground cloves
- 1¼ cups all-purpose flour
- 1¼ cups whole-wheat flour
- 1 teaspoon baking soda
- 1 teaspoon baking powder
- ¼ teaspoon salt
- 10 tablespoons (1¼ sticks) unsalted butter, room temperature, plus more for pan
- 1 cup granulated sugar
- 3 large eggs
- 1 teaspoon pure vanilla extract
- 1¼ cups plain whole-milk yogurt

1. Preheat oven to 350°F. In a medium bowl, combine apples, ½ cup light-brown sugar, cinnamon, and cloves; set aside. Sift together the flours, baking soda, baking powder, and salt into a medium bowl; set aside. Butter a 9-inch springform pan.

2. In the bowl of an electric mixer, cream butter and granulated sugar until light and fluffy, about 4 minutes. Add eggs, one at a time, until well combined. Add vanilla extract, and combine. Add reserved flour mixture and yogurt; stir until well combined. Fold in two-thirds of the reserved apple mixture.

3. Spoon half the batter into prepared pan. Sprinkle remaining apple mixture evenly over batter. Top

with remaining batter; smooth with a spatula. Sprinkle top with remaining ¼ cup brown sugar.

**4.** Bake cake until golden brown and a cake tester inserted in center comes out clean, 1 hour 10 minutes to 1 hour 20 minutes. Cover with foil after 45 minutes of baking. Let cool 20 minutes before releasing cake from the pan.

## ultimate streusel cake
### MAKES 1 TEN-INCH BUNDT CAKE

*Literally meaning "strew" or "sprinkle" in German, streusel is usually reserved for topping. We concealed some of ours inside the cake. As the cake bakes, the streusel becomes firm and candylike. Drizzle the cake with icing, and slice it thickly for the perfect complement to a steaming cup of café au lait.*

2½  cups all-purpose flour
 1  teaspoon baking soda
 1  teaspoon baking powder
 ¼  teaspoon coarse salt
 10  tablespoons (1¼ sticks) unsalted butter, room temperature, plus more for pan
 1  cup granulated sugar
 3  large eggs
 1  teaspoon pure vanilla extract
1¼  cups sour cream or 1 cup buttermilk
    Pecan-Streusel Filling (recipe follows)
2½  cups sifted confectioners' sugar
 ¼  cup milk

**1.** Preheat oven to 350°F. Sift together flour, baking soda, baking powder, and salt into a bowl; set aside. Butter a 10-inch Bundt pan (or other tube pan with a 3-quart capacity); set aside.

**2.** In the bowl of an electric mixer, cream butter and granulated sugar until light and fluffy, about 4 minutes. Add eggs, one at a time, beating until well combined. Beat in vanilla. Add reserved flour

mixture and sour cream in alternating batches, starting and ending with the flour; beat just until combined. Spoon half the batter into prepared pan. Make a well in the center, and crumble two-thirds of the streusel mixture into well. Spoon in remaining batter, smoothing top; sprinkle with remaining streusel. Bake until golden brown and a cake tester comes out clean, about 1 hour.

**3.** In a medium bowl, whisk together confectioners' sugar and milk until combined; set icing aside, covered with plastic wrap, until ready to use. Let cool slightly before drizzling over cake.

## pecan-streusel filling
### MAKES ENOUGH FOR 1 TEN-INCH CAKE

1½  cups packed light-brown sugar
 ½  cup granulated sugar
1½  cups chopped pecans
 ½  cup all-purpose flour
 1  tablespoon ground cinnamon
    Pinch of ground cloves
 ½  cup (1 stick) unsalted butter, softened

Combine both sugars, the pecans, flour, cinnamon, and cloves in a medium bowl. Using your hands or a pastry cutter, cut in butter until combined and mixture is crumbly; transfer to the refrigerator until ready to use.

## yeasted coffee cake with poppy-seed filling

*photograph on page 18*

MAKES 2 NINE-INCH CAKES

*Our yeast coffee cake is sweetened mainly by a filling of brown sugar, butter, walnuts, and poppy seeds—there's not much sugar added to the dough itself. The result falls somewhere between a sweet cake and a bread. After cooling completely, the cakes can be frozen and wrapped in two layers of plastic wrap, up to one month.*

1½ cups warm milk

½ cup (1 stick) unsalted butter, melted, plus more for bowl, plastic, and pans

1 tablespoon salt

½ cup granulated sugar

1 teaspoon ground cardamom

2 large eggs

2 envelopes active dry yeast (2 scant tablespoons)

10 cups all-purpose flour, plus more for work surface

½ cup packed dark-brown sugar Poppy-Seed Filling (recipe follows)

**1.** Combine 1½ cups warm water, milk, 4 tablespoons butter, salt, sugar, cardamom, and eggs in the bowl of an electric mixer. Sprinkle yeast over top; let stand until foamy, 10 to 15 minutes.

**2.** With the mixer running, gradually add flour. Mix until well combined; dough will be sticky. Turn dough out onto a floured surface, and gently knead until it forms a ball. Place in a large buttered bowl to rise, covered with plastic wrap, until doubled in bulk, about 1½ hours.

**3.** Butter two 9-inch tube pans; sprinkle bottom of each with ¼ cup brown sugar. Punch down dough; turn out onto lightly floured surface. With a rolling pin, roll into a rectangle that is about 14 by 17 inches and about ½ inch thick. Brush a third of the remaining butter over the middle third of

the dough, and sprinkle with 1 cup filling. Fold bottom third of dough over filling and overlap top third, forming an envelope. Rotate dough 90 degrees. Roll dough again into a rectangle of roughly the same size, and repeat with half of the remaining butter and filling. Repeat one more time (three times total) using remaining butter and filling. Rotate dough 90 degrees, and let rest, covered with a damp cloth or plastic wrap, 15 minutes.

**4.** With a sharp knife, cut a 1-inch slice from one short end of dough. Pick up slice, twisting it gently into a spiral. Place the twist in bottom of pan, forming a circle. Repeat process, using remaining dough, filling each tube pan with two layers of twisted dough. Cover each cake with plastic wrap; let rise until doubled in bulk, about 45 minutes.

**5.** Preheat oven to 375°F. Bake cakes until golden brown, 40 to 50 minutes. Let rest in pans 15 minutes before inverting. Flip cakes over so attractive side is up. Serve warm or at room temperature.

### poppy-seed filling

MAKES ENOUGH FOR 2 NINE-INCH CAKES

1 cup packed dark-brown sugar

½ cup all-purpose flour

½ cup finely chopped walnuts

¼ teaspoon ground cinnamon

¼ teaspoon ground nutmeg

⅓ cup poppy seeds

½ cup (1 stick) unsalted butter, room temperature

Combine sugar, flour, walnuts, cinnamon, nutmeg, and poppy seeds in a medium bowl. Using your hands or a pastry cutter, cut in butter until well combined and crumbly; chill until ready to use.

## YEASTED COFFEE-CAKE TECHNIQUE

*This coffee cake may take longer to make than others, but the result is definitely worth it. Similar to rolling out puff pastry, the process incorporates the filling into the dough, forming many layers.*

**1.** *After the dough has risen, punch it down, then roll it out on a lightly floured surface into a large rectangle about ½ inch thick.*

**2.** *Brush a layer of melted butter across the middle of the rectangle, and sprinkle one-third of the filling over the butter. Then fold the dough over at the center to make an envelope, and rotate 90 degrees.*

**3.** *Repeat the process in step 2, rolling the dough into another rectangle of approximately the same size. Brush the top with butter, and sprinkle half the remaining filling over the center.*

**4.** *Repeat the rolling and filling process a third and final time, to form a multilayered dough.*

**5.** *Using a large sharp knife, cut the dough crosswise into 1-inch-wide strips, and gently pull and twist each strip so that the filling spirals through the dough.*

**6.** *Place half of the twists in each of two buttered pans, forming circles around pans and creating two layers in each. Set the dough aside to rise until it has doubled, then bake.*

# blueberry sticky buns

*photograph on page 19*

MAKES 1 DOZEN

*You can bake these buns up to one day ahead; keep them in the pan, and cover with plastic wrap. To make it easier to remove them from the pan, place it over low heat, rotating constantly until the buns are loosened.*

      4  tablespoons unsalted butter, melted,
         plus more for bowl, plastic wrap, and pan
      1  envelope active dry yeast
         (1 scant tablespoon)
   1½  tablespoons sugar, plus a pinch for yeast
      1  cup warm milk (about 110°F)
      ½  teaspoon salt
      1  large egg, lightly beaten
      3  cups all-purpose flour, plus more
         for work surface
      3  cups fresh blueberries (about ¾ pound),
         picked over and rinsed
      1  cup packed dark-brown sugar
   1½  tablespoons ground cinnamon
      ½  cup light corn syrup

**1.** Butter an 8-inch square baking pan; set aside. In the bowl of an electric mixer, sprinkle the yeast and a pinch of sugar over ¼ cup warm water (about 110°F). Let stand until foamy, about 5 minutes. Whisk in milk, remaining 1½ tablespoons sugar, 2 tablespoons butter, the salt, and egg.

**2.** Attach bowl to mixer fitted with the paddle attachment. With mixer on low speed, gradually add 2 cups flour; continue beating until fully incorporated. Switch to the dough-hook attachment. With mixer on low, gradually add remaining cup flour to create a sticky dough. Continue kneading until dough is smooth, about 5 minutes. Scrape onto a well-floured work surface; dust dough with flour. With floured hands, knead until dough is no longer sticky, about 1 minute.

**3.** Transfer dough, smooth side up, to a large buttered bowl. Cover with a lightly buttered sheet of plastic wrap; let rise in a warm place until doubled in bulk, about 1 hour.

**4.** Heat 1 tablespoon butter in a medium sauté pan over medium heat. Add berries; cook, stirring constantly, until juicy, about 5 minutes. Remove from heat; let cool completely.

**5.** In a small bowl, combine brown sugar and cinnamon. Sprinkle ¼ cup brown-sugar mixture into prepared pan, reserving the rest, and drizzle with corn syrup. Set aside.

**6.** Preheat oven to 350°F. Divide dough into two equal pieces. On a lightly floured work surface, roll out one piece into a 9-by-12-inch rectangle. Brush with ½ tablespoon melted butter. Sprinkle half the reserved brown-sugar mixture over butter; top with half the berries. Starting with one short side, roll dough into a 9-inch log, pinching to seal the seam. Repeat with remaining dough, melted butter, brown-sugar mixture, and berries.

**7.** Cut each log into six rounds; place, cut side up, in prepared pan. If any fruit mixture spills out of the rolls, spoon into pan. Cover with plastic wrap, and let rise 15 minutes.

**8.** Transfer pan to oven, and bake until centers spring back and tops are deep golden brown, 40 to 45 minutes. Remove from oven, and let cool in pan 10 minutes. Run a knife around the edge of the pan to loosen; invert buns onto a serving plate. Serve warm or at room temperature.

# *breads*

YEAST BREADS

BREADSTICKS AND CRACKERS

BISCUITS AND ROLLS

QUICK BREADS

✳

## country wheat bread

MAKES 2 LOAVES

*We let these loaves rise in* Brotformen, *German baskets that shape and mark the dough as it rises. If you're not using a* Brotformen, *shape dough following directions, and then place on parchment paper dusted with coarse cornmeal; coat bottom and one inch up sides with cornmeal. Cover loosely with oiled plastic wrap and then with a clean towel.*

2¼ cups warm water (about 110°F)

1½ teaspoons active dry yeast (½ envelope)

2 tablespoons honey

½ cup Sponge (recipe follows), pulled into small pieces

4 cups bread flour, plus more for work surface and pans

¼ cup plus 2 tablespoons white, light, or medium rye flour

¾ cup whole-wheat bread flour

1 cup rye meal

¼ cup plus 2 tablespoons cracked wheat

4 teaspoons salt

Vegetable oil, for bowl and plastic wrap

Coarse cornmeal, for dusting

**1.** In the bowl of an electric mixer, combine ¼ cup warm water, yeast, and honey. Let stand until foamy, about 10 minutes. Add sponge; mix on low speed, using paddle attachment, until combined, about 1 minute. Add remaining 2 cups warm water, flours, rye meal, cracked wheat, and salt; mix on low speed 2 minutes. Switch to dough-hook attachment; mix on medium-low speed until dough is smooth and tacky, about 8 minutes. Alternatively, knead dough by hand, 15 to 20 minutes.

**2.** Transfer dough, smooth side up, to a lightly oiled bowl; cover with oiled plastic wrap, and let rise in a warm place until 1½ times its size, about 2 hours.

**3.** Punch down dough, and knead in bowl 4 or 5 times. Turn folded side down; replace plastic, and let rise again until doubled in bulk, about 1 hour.

**4.** If using, sprinkle two braided Brotformen liberally with flour. Turn out dough onto a lightly floured surface; divide in half. Cover one piece of dough loosely with oiled plastic wrap. On an unfloured surface, knead the other piece of dough into a ball. Cup your hands around it and move it on the work surface in small, circular motions, until top is rounded and bottom is smooth.

**5.** Place shaped loaf, bottom side up, in prepared pan. Cover loosely with lightly oiled plastic wrap and then with a kitchen towel. Repeat shaping process with second piece of dough. Let loaves rise in a warm place until doubled in bulk, about 1 hour.

**6.** Meanwhile, 30 minutes before final rise is complete, preheat oven to 450°F. Place a baking stone, if using, in lower third of oven and an empty baking pan on lowest shelf.

**7.** Transfer one loaf to a baker's peel or baking sheet dusted with cornmeal. Using a razor blade or serrated knife, slash an X on top ¼ to ½ inch deep. Slide loaf onto baking stone. Repeat with second loaf. Quickly and carefully pour 2 cups very hot water into heated baking pan to create steam; close oven door.

**8.** Bake loaves until dark golden brown and hollow sounding when tapped on the bottom, 25 to 30 minutes. If bread begins to darken too quickly, lower oven temperature to 425°F after 15 minutes of baking. Transfer loaves to a wire rack; let cool at least 30 minutes before slicing.

### *sponge*
MAKES ABOUT 3½ CUPS

*Sponge can be refrigerated for up to one week or frozen for up to three months. Bring to room temperature before using.*

1½ cups warm water (about 110°F)
½ teaspoon active dry yeast
3½ cups bread flour
    Vegetable oil, for bowl

**1.** In the bowl of an electric mixer, combine ¼ cup warm water and yeast. Let stand until foamy, about 10 minutes. Add remaining 1¼ cups warm water and flour; mix on low speed 2 minutes. Sponge will be the consistency of a wet dough.

**2.** Place sponge in an oiled bowl. Cover with plastic wrap; let stand at room temperature 24 hours.

### *la pompe à l'huile*
MAKES 2 TWELVE-INCH ROUND LOAVES

*This Provençal brioche, made with olive oil, is part of a traditional Christmas Eve display of pastries and other sweets. It is called* pompe, *which translates to pump, because when it is dipped in wine, the bread is supposed to "pump" up. La Pompe is also delicious with morning coffee or afternoon tea.*

7 cups bread flour
1 tablespoon salt
¼ cup sugar
¼ cup finely chopped candied orange peel
1 tablespoon anise seeds
1 envelope active dry yeast
   (1 scant tablespoon)
   Grated zest and juice of 1 orange
2 large eggs, lightly beaten
½ cup extra-virgin olive oil, plus more
   for bowl, pans, and plastic wrap
1 tablespoon orange-flower water
   All-purpose flour, for work surface

**1.** In the bowl of an electric mixer, place bread flour, salt, sugar, candied orange peel, anise seeds, yeast, and zest. Using the dough-hook attachment, mix ingredients on low speed until combined.

**2.** Place orange juice, eggs, oil, and orange-flower water in a 4-cup liquid measuring cup. Fill cup with enough warm water to measure 2½ cups. Pour mixture over the flour mixture; mix on low speed until shiny and elastic, 4 to 5 minutes.

**3.** Lightly oil a large bowl; set aside. Turn out dough onto a lightly floured work surface. Gather into a smooth ball, and place in oiled bowl. Cover bowl with oiled plastic wrap; let rise in a warm place until doubled in bulk, about 2 hours.

**4.** Lightly oil two large baking sheets. Turn out dough onto a lightly floured work surface; divide into two equal pieces. Roll one piece into a 12-inch disk, about ⅓ inch thick. Cut three short decorative slits in dough, starting near the center, and cutting out toward the edge; stretch each slit to widen. Transfer disk to one of the prepared baking pans; cover loosely with plastic wrap, and let rise in a warm place until about 1 inch high, about 50 minutes. Repeat with remaining piece of dough.

**5.** Preheat oven to 400°F. Bake loaves until golden brown, 20 to 25 minutes. Transfer to a wire rack to cool completely. Wrap bread in plastic, and store at room temperature up to 2 days.

## miniature panettone

*photograph on page 20*

MAKES 1 DOZEN

*We baked these panettone in half-pound brown paper bags (3 by 1¾ by 4¾ inches). After baking, we wrapped each bag with a piece of colored ribbon, for gift giving.*

### for sponge:

⅓  cup warm water (about 110°F)

1  envelope active dry yeast
(1 scant tablespoon)

½  cup all-purpose flour

### for bread dough:

½  cup warm milk (about 110°F)

1  envelope active dry yeast
(1 scant tablespoon)

⅔  cup sugar

4  large whole eggs

3  large egg yolks

1  teaspoon pure vanilla extract

¾  cup (1½ sticks) chilled unsalted butter,
plus more, melted, for bowl, plastic
wrap, and bags

3½ cups all-purpose flour, plus more
for work surface

2  cups mixed dried and candied fruit,
such as currants, orange peel, apricots,
and cherries, finely chopped

Grated zest of 1 lemon

Grated zest of 1 orange

1  tablespoon heavy cream

Confectioners' sugar, for dusting

**1.** Make sponge: Pour the warm water into a small bowl, and sprinkle with yeast. Stir with a fork until yeast has dissolved. Let stand until foamy, 5 to 10 minutes. Stir in flour, and cover bowl with plastic wrap. Let rise in a warm place until doubled in bulk, about 30 minutes.

**2.** Make the dough: Pour warm milk into a small bowl, and sprinkle with yeast. Stir to dissolve, and let stand until foamy, 5 to 10 minutes. In a medium bowl, whisk together sugar, eggs, 2 egg yolks, and vanilla. Whisk milk mixture into egg mixture.

**3.** In the bowl of an electric mixer, beat butter and flour on medium speed until mixture is crumbly. With mixer on low speed, slowly add egg mixture; continue beating on medium speed until smooth.

**4.** Add sponge mixture; beat on high speed until dough is elastic and long strands form when dough is stretched, about 5 minutes. Beat in dried fruit and grated zests. Transfer dough to a buttered bowl, and cover with a piece of buttered plastic wrap. Let rise in a warm place until doubled in bulk, about 2 hours.

**5.** Fold twelve paper bags down to make cuffs about 3 inches deep. Generously butter the bags inside and out; set aside. Turn out dough onto a lightly floured surface; knead a few times, turning each time, until smooth. Divide dough into 12 equal parts, and knead into balls. Drop balls into prepared bags. Place bags on a large rimmed baking sheet; cover loosely with buttered plastic. Let rise in a warm place until dough reaches just below the tops of the bags, 45 to 60 minutes.

**6.** Preheat oven to 400°F, with rack in lower third. In a small bowl, whisk together remaining egg yolk and the cream. Brush tops of dough with egg mixture. Using kitchen scissors, cut an X, centered, in the top of each loaf. Bake 10 minutes. Reduce oven temperature to 375°F; continue baking until loaves are deep golden brown, about 20 minutes, rotating baking sheet halfway through. If they start to get too brown, drape a piece of aluminum foil over tops. Transfer baking sheet to a wire rack; let panettone cool completely; dust with confectioners' sugar.

# ear of wheat

*photograph on page 25*

MAKES 2 RING-SHAPED LOAVES

1½ cups warm water (about 110°F)

1 teaspoon active dry yeast

3½ cups plus 3 tablespoons bread flour, plus more for work surface, parchment paper, and dusting

½ cup white, light, or medium rye flour

1½ teaspoons salt

Oil, for bowl and plastic wrap

**1.** In the bowl of an electric mixer, combine ¼ cup warm water and yeast. Let stand until foamy, about 10 minutes. Add remaining 1¼ cups warm water, both flours, and salt; using paddle attachment, mix on low speed 2 minutes. Switch to the dough-hook attachment, and mix on medium-low speed until firm, about 8 minutes. Alternatively, knead the dough by hand 15 to 20 minutes.

**2.** Turn out dough onto a lightly floured surface, and knead into a ball. Place smooth side up in an oiled bowl; cover with oiled plastic wrap, and let rise in a warm place until doubled in bulk, about 2 hours.

**3.** Punch down dough, and knead in bowl 4 or 5 times. Turn folded side down. Replace plastic; let rise again in a warm place until doubled in bulk, about 1 hour.

**4.** Line two baking sheets with parchment paper; lightly dust paper with flour. Turn out dough onto a floured surface, and divide in half. Pat one piece into an 8-by-11-inch rectangle. Fold in half width-wise; press down to seal edge. Repeat, folding two more times; place dough, seam side down, on unfloured surface. Roll dough back and forth, gently stretching it out to 28 inches long. Pinch ends together, forming a circle. Transfer loaf to a prepared baking sheet; correct shape, if necessary, and cover loosely with oiled plastic wrap. Let rise in a warm place until doubled in bulk,

about 45 minutes. Meanwhile, repeat with other piece of dough.

**5.** Meanwhile, 30 minutes before final rise is complete, preheat oven to 450°F. Place a baking stone, if using, in lower third of oven and an empty baking pan on lowest shelf.

**6.** Dust loaves with flour. Holding kitchen scissors at a 45-degree angle to top of one loaf, make a cut across the width three-quarters of the way through. Fold the V-shaped flap of dough to the right. Keep making cuts every 1½ inches, alternating folds to the left and right. Repeat with other loaf.

**7.** Place sheets directly on stone, if using. Pour 2 cups hot water into baking pan. Bake until loaves are medium golden brown and hollow sounding when tapped on bottom, 20 to 25 minutes. Let cool on a wire rack at least 30 minutes before slicing.

### FORMING THE EAR OF WHEAT

*For a wreath, make deep cuts across the width of the ring of dough, holding scissors at a forty-five-degree angle. Alternate turning the resulting V-shaped flaps of dough to the left and right.*

## prosciutto bread

MAKES 1 LOAF

*This is a savory version of traditional sweet yeast breads from Verona. Sweet breads are usually baked in pandoro molds in Italy, but any heavy metal nine-cup mold may be used. Cooking times may vary.*

- 1 envelope active dry yeast (1 scant tablespoon)
- 2 teaspoons sugar
- 1¾ cups warm water (110°F)
- 4 cups all-purpose flour, plus more for work surface
- 2 teaspoons salt
- 2 teaspoons very coarsely ground pepper
- ¾ cup prosciutto, cut into ¼-inch dice (about 4 ounces)
- ¾ cup Italian fontina cheese, cut into ¼-inch dice (about 4 ounces)
  Olive oil, for bowl, plastic wrap, and mold
- 1 large egg, lightly beaten

**1.** In the bowl of an electric mixer, combine yeast and sugar with the warm water. Let stand until foamy, about 10 minutes.

**2.** Add flour, salt, and pepper to yeast mixture. Using the dough-hook attachment, mix on low speed until a smooth ball forms (dough will be slightly sticky), about 5 minutes. Turn out dough onto a lightly floured surface; pat into a 10-inch square. Scatter prosciutto and cheese over the top; press into dough. Fold corners of dough toward center, and shape into a round; transfer folded side down to a large, lightly oiled bowl. Cover with oiled plastic wrap. Let rise in a warm place until doubled in bulk, about 1 hour.

**3.** Punch down dough; knead again into a round, and turn folded side down. Replace plastic wrap; let rise again until doubled in bulk, about 1 hour.

**4.** Preheat oven to 425°F, with rack in lower third. Punch down dough. Fold corners toward center, and shape into a round; place in an oiled mold, seam side up. Cover with plastic; let rise until even with top of mold and slightly mounded, 30 minutes.

**5.** Brush top of dough with beaten egg. Bake until top is dark golden brown, about 35 minutes. Cover bread with tented aluminum foil; reduce oven heat to 350°F. Continue baking until base of bread sounds hollow when tapped and sides are golden brown, 30 to 40 minutes more.

**6.** Unmold bread onto a cooling rack, top side down; let cool completely, about 1 hour. (If sides of bread are not brown, return bread to oven, placing it directly on the rack, top side down, for about 5 minutes.) Bread will keep wrapped in plastic wrap 1 to 2 days at room temperature.

BREADSTICKS AND CRACKERS

## rosemary breadsticks
*photograph on page 24*
MAKES 35 TO 40

*These crisp breadsticks keep for up to ten days in an airtight container at room temperature.*

- 1¼ cups plus 2 tablespoons warm water (about 110°F)
- 3½ teaspoons active dry yeast
- 1 teaspoon barley malt
- 3 tablespoons olive oil, plus more for plastic wrap, parchment paper, and brushing dough
- 3¾ cups bread flour, plus more for work surface
- 1½ teaspoons salt
- 1 tablespoon plus 1 teaspoon vegetable shortening
- 3 tablespoons chopped fresh rosemary
- ½ cup freshly grated Parmesan

**1.** In the bowl of an electric mixer, combine ¼ cup warm water, yeast, and barley malt. Let stand until foamy, about 10 minutes. Add oil, flour, salt, shortening, and remaining 1 cup plus 2 tablespoons warm water; mix on low speed 1 minute using the paddle attachment. Switch to dough-hook attachment; mix on medium-low speed until dough is soft but not tacky, about 2 minutes. Add rosemary and cheese; mix 1 minute more. Alternatively, knead dough by hand 5 to 10 minutes.

**2.** Turn out dough onto a floured surface; knead 4 or 5 times, forming dough into a ball. Cover with lightly oiled plastic wrap; let rest 10 minutes.

**3.** Place a piece of parchment paper on a clean work surface; brush with oil. Transfer dough to parchment; pat into a 22-by-4-inch rectangle. Brush surface with oil. Cover with oiled plastic, and let rise until almost doubled in bulk, about 1 hour.

**4.** Preheat oven to 400°F. Line four baking sheets with parchment; oil parchment generously. Slice a ½-inch-wide piece of dough off short side of rectangle. Holding strip by the ends, stretch it to the length of the baking sheet. While stretching dough, keep shape as uniform as possible to prevent uneven baking. Form ends into hooks, loops, S curves, or knots. Place on a prepared baking sheet. Repeat with remaining dough, placing shapes about 1 inch apart. Let rise in a warm place, uncovered, 10 minutes.

**5.** Bake two sheets at a time on separate shelves, until breadsticks are crisp and golden, 20 to 25 minutes, rotating sheets halfway through. Let cool completely on wire racks before serving or storing.

## sesame star crackers
### MAKES ABOUT 4 DOZEN

*Use a one-and-a-half-inch star-shaped cookie cutter to make bite-size crackers. Toast sesame seeds in a saucepan over medium heat, shaking frequently, until fragrant, two to three minutes.*

- 2 cups all-purpose flour, plus more for work surface
- ¾ teaspoon salt
- ¼ cup plus 2 tablespoons black sesame seeds, toasted
- ¼ cup plus 1 tablespoon dark sesame oil

**1.** Preheat oven to 325°F. In a medium bowl, combine flour, salt, and sesame seeds. Stir in sesame oil with a fork until fine crumbs form. Add ½ cup water, and stir until dough comes together.

**2.** Turn out dough onto a lightly floured work surface, and knead a few times until smooth. Wrap in plastic, and let rest 10 minutes.

**3.** Divide dough into four equal pieces, and roll out each to ⅛ inch thick. Cut into stars using a cookie cutter. Prick top of each star with a fork in several spots, and place, at least 1 inch apart, on an ungreased baking sheet.

**4.** Bake until crackers are just golden, 20 to 25 minutes. Transfer crackers to wire racks, and let cool. Store crackers in an airtight container, at room temperature, up to 1 week.

## sour rye pretzels

*photograph on page 21*
MAKES 3 DOZEN

*It is important to allow the sautéed onions to cool completely before adding to yeast mixture so they do not hinder the rising.*

¼ cup extra-virgin olive oil, plus
   more for bowl and plastic wrap

1 onion, finely chopped

1½ envelopes active dry yeast
   (1½ scant tablespoons)

¼ cup warm water (about 110°F)
   Pinch of sugar

2¼ cups plain whole-milk yogurt

2½ tablespoons caraway seeds

2 tablespoons table salt

½ tablespoon freshly ground pepper

2 large whole eggs

3 cups rye flour

4½ to 5 cups all-purpose flour, plus
   more for work surface
   Yellow cornmeal, for baking sheets

1 large egg yolk, lightly beaten
   with 1 tablespoon water, for egg wash

5 tablespoons coarse salt

**1.** Heat oil in a large sauté pan over medium heat. Add chopped onion; cook, stirring occasionally, until translucent, about 6 minutes. Remove pan from heat; set aside to cool.

**2.** In the bowl of an electric mixer, whisk together yeast, the warm water, and sugar. Let stand until foamy, about 6 minutes.

**3.** With mixer on low speed, using the dough-hook attachment, add yogurt, cooled onion, caraway seeds, table salt, pepper, whole eggs, and rye flour. Slowly add 4½ cups all-purpose flour to make a soft dough; if dough is still sticky, add just enough of remaining ½ cup flour to achieve desired consistency. Knead on medium-low speed until dough springs back when pressed with a finger, about 6 minutes. Transfer dough to a lightly oiled bowl; cover with oiled plastic wrap. Let rise in a warm place until doubled in bulk, about 2 hours.

**4.** Sprinkle cornmeal over three large baking sheets. Punch down dough to remove air pockets. Turn out onto a lightly floured work surface. Knead once or twice, and divide into 36 equal pieces (about 2 ounces each). Roll out dough, one piece at a time, into 12- to 14-inch-long strips. Twist into pretzel shapes, and transfer to prepared baking sheets, placing them 1 to 1½ inches apart. Cover with oiled plastic wrap; let rise in a warm place until almost doubled in bulk, about 25 minutes.

**5.** Preheat oven to 350°F. Brush tops of pretzels with egg wash; sprinkle with coarse salt. Bake until golden, 20 to 25 minutes. Let cool on a wire rack at least 5 minutes before serving.

## soft pretzels

MAKES 16

*These pretzels make great gifts, especially when packaged with any of our Homemade Mustards (page 110).*

2 cups warm water (about 110°F)

1 tablespoon sugar

1 envelope active dry yeast
   (1 scant tablespoon)

5½ to 6 cups all-purpose flour, plus
   more for work surface

1 tablespoon table salt
   Canola oil, for bowl

2 tablespoons baking soda

1 large egg, lightly beaten
   with 1 tablespoon water, for egg wash
   Coarse or pretzel salt
   Vegetable-oil cooking spray

1. Pour the warm water into a mixing bowl. Add sugar; stir to dissolve. Sprinkle with yeast; let stand until foamy, about 5 minutes.

2. Using the dough-hook attachment, beat 1 cup flour into yeast mixture on low speed until combined. Beat in table salt and 4 cups flour until combined, about 30 seconds. Raise speed to medium-low; continue beating until dough pulls away from sides of bowl, about 1½ minutes. Add ½ cup flour; knead on low speed 1 minute more. If dough is still wet and sticky, add ½ cup more flour; knead until combined, about 30 seconds.

3. Turn out dough onto a lightly floured work surface, and knead until smooth, about 10 times. Transfer dough to a lightly oiled bowl. Cover with a kitchen towel, and let rise in a warm place until dough has doubled in bulk, about 1 hour.

4. Preheat oven to 450°F. Lightly coat two baking sheets with cooking spray; set aside. Punch down dough to remove air pockets. Turn out onto a lightly floured work surface. Knead once or twice, and divide into 16 equal pieces (about 2½ ounces each); wrap each piece in plastic.

5. Roll out dough, one piece at a time, into 18-inch-long strips. Twist into pretzel shapes; transfer to prepared baking sheets. Cover with a kitchen towel. Let dough rise slightly, about 15 minutes.

6. Meanwhile, fill a large, shallow pan with 2 inches of water; bring to a boil. Add baking soda. Reduce to a simmer; carefully drop three to four pretzels into the water. Poach 1 minute. Use a slotted spoon to return pretzels to baking sheet. Continue until all pretzels have been poached.

7. Brush pretzels with egg wash, and sprinkle with coarse salt. Bake pretzels until golden brown, 12 to 15 minutes. Remove from oven, and let cool on a wire rack. Pretzels will keep at room temperature up to 2 days. Do not store them in a covered container. Serve warm or at room temperature with homemade mustards, if desired.

### SHAPING PRETZELS

*For Soft Pretzels, begin with an 18-inch-long strip of dough in an upside-down U shape.*

*1. Cross the right end over the left, forming a large loop with the top part of the dough.*

*2. Cross the ends of the dough strip over each other one more time in the same direction to twist the strip further.*

*3. Complete the pretzel shape by folding the bottom (twisted) part of the strip up to meet the top of the loop. Pinch ends onto top of dough to seal.*

## homemade mustards

MAKES ABOUT 3 CUPS EACH

*All of these mustards are created the same way; just use the ingredients you like best. They can be served with homemade pretzels or crackers and cheese as an hors d'oeuvre. We also love them with country ham and biscuits. And, of course, they make wonderful holiday gifts when presented in small, hand-labeled jars.*

### english mustard:

- 1 cup brown mustard seed
- ¼ cup yellow mustard seed
- 1¼ cups white-wine vinegar
- 1 cup dark beer
- 1 cup mustard powder combined with 1 cup water (let sit 20 minutes)
- 1 teaspoon sugar
- 1 teaspoon coarse salt
- 1 teaspoon ground allspice
- ¼ teaspoon ground turmeric
- ¼ teaspoon ground mace

### red-wine mustard:

- ⅔ cup yellow mustard seed
- ½ cup brown mustard seed
- 1 cup red-wine vinegar
- ½ cup dry red wine
- 1 teaspoon freshly ground pepper
- 2 tablespoons sugar
- 2 teaspoons coarse salt
- 1 tablespoon dried marjoram

### green-peppercorn mustard:

- ½ cup yellow mustard seed
- ¼ cup black mustard seed
- ¾ cup balsamic vinegar
- ½ cup dry sherry
- 2 tablespoons whole green peppercorns
- ⅓ cup olive oil
- 2 teaspoons coarse salt

### pink-peppercorn mustard:

*Same ingredients as Green Peppercorn, but substitute whole pink peppercorns for the green, and white-wine vinegar for balsamic; add 3 tablespoons chopped fresh tarragon.*

**1.** In a nonreactive container, combine mustard seeds with vinegar and alcohol. Let stand, covered, 48 hours at room temperature. Check periodically to make sure seeds are covered by liquid; add more vinegar if necessary.

**2.** Transfer seeds and liquid to a food processor. Add remaining ingredients. Process until mixture is creamy, 4 to 6 minutes. Store in jars or containers with tight-fitting lids.

## whole-grain crackers

photograph on page 42

MAKES ABOUT 3 DOZEN

*The dough can be frozen for up to two months, making it perfect to have on hand for holiday entertaining. Slice off just what you need, returning any unused portions to the freezer.*

- 1½  cups all-purpose flour, plus more for work surface
- ¼  cup rolled oats
- ¼  cup packed light-brown sugar
- 2  tablespoons toasted wheat germ
- 2  tablespoons flax seed
- ½  teaspoon salt
- 6  tablespoons chilled unsalted butter, cut into pieces
- ½  cup smooth peanut butter
- ¼  cup milk

**1.** In a food processor, combine flour, oats, sugar, wheat germ, flax seed, and salt. Pulse a few times to combine. Add butter; pulse just until mixture is crumbly. Add peanut butter; pulse a few more times. Add milk; pulse until combined and mixture holds together.

**2.** Turn out dough onto a lightly floured surface; divide in half. Roll out each piece into a 6-inch log about 1½ inches in diameter. Wrap logs tightly in plastic; freeze until firm, at least 45 minutes. Remove logs from freezer; wrap parchment or wax paper over plastic. Freeze until ready to bake.

**3.** Preheat oven to 350°F. Remove the logs from freezer; let stand until slightly softened, about 5 minutes, depending on how long they have been frozen. Using a serrated knife, slice log into ¼-inch rounds. Place rounds on a baking sheet.

**4.** Bake until crackers just start to brown, about 12 minutes per side, turning once and rotating pan halfway through. Transfer to wire racks to cool. Store crackers in an airtight container at room temperature up to 1 week.

## parmesan-herb twists

MAKES 28

*Serve these breadsticks before an Italian-inspired meal, or bundle them together and pair them with a bottle of wine for a nice gift.*

- 1½  cups all-purpose flour, plus more for work surface
- ½  teaspoon salt
   Pinch of freshly ground pepper
- 2  tablespoons mixed fresh herbs, such as sage, thyme, or rosemary, finely chopped
- 2  tablespoons vegetable oil
- 1  large egg white
- 1  teaspoon milk
- ¼  cup grated Parmesan cheese (about 1 ounce)

**1.** Preheat oven to 325°F. In a food processor, pulse together flour, salt, pepper, and herbs. Add oil, and pulse until mixture resembles coarse meal. With machine running, add ¼ cup cold water; process until dough just comes together.

**2.** Turn out dough onto a lightly floured surface; divide in half. Roll out one piece of dough into a 7-by-9-inch sheet, ⅛ inch thick. In a small bowl, whisk together egg white and milk. Brush dough with egg mixture; sprinkle generously with cheese.

**3.** Cut dough along long edge into ½-inch strips. Twist each strip, and pull until 16 to 18 inches long. Transfer to an ungreased baking sheet. Repeat with other piece of dough.

**4.** Bake until dough just begins to brown and is firm to the touch, 20 to 25 minutes. Transfer strips to a wire rack to cool. Store in an airtight plastic container at room temperature up to 5 days.

## *wheat squares*

MAKES 14 DOZEN

1   cup all-purpose flour, plus more
    for work surface

1   cup whole-wheat flour

2   tablespoons toasted wheat germ

2   teaspoons table salt

2   tablespoons chilled unsalted butter,
    cut into small pieces

1   tablespoon honey

¾   cup milk

1   large egg white, lightly beaten
    Coarse salt, for sprinkling

**1.** Preheat oven to 325°F. In a food processor, pulse the flours, wheat germ, and table salt. Add butter; pulse until mixture resembles coarse meal. With machine running, gradually add honey and milk; process until dough just comes together.

**2.** Transfer dough to a lightly floured work surface, and divide into four equal pieces. Roll each piece into a 9-by-10½-inch sheet, ⅛ inch thick. Transfer to four baking sheets. Use a paring knife to score dough into 1½-inch squares. Using a fork, pierce each square three times.

**3.** Brush beaten egg white over dough; sprinkle with coarse salt. Bake until dough is stiff, about 20 minutes. Turn with a spatula; bake until light brown and firm to the touch, 6 to 8 minutes. Transfer to a wire rack to cool. Break sheet into crackers. Store in an airtight container at room temperature up to 1 week.

BISCUITS AND ROLLS

## *beaten biscuits*

MAKES 3 DOZEN

*These breads, which are small and firm, are really more like soda crackers than flaky, doughy biscuits. We like to serve them cut in half with very thin slices of baked country ham, at a holiday open house.*

1¾  cups all-purpose flour, plus more
    for work surface

2   teaspoons salt

3   tablespoons chilled unsalted butter,
    cut into small pieces

¼   cup solid vegetable shortening

¼   cup milk

¼   cup ice water

**1.** Line two baking sheets with aluminum foil, with the dull side facing up; set aside. In a food processor, pulse to combine flour and salt. Add butter and shortening, and pulse until mixture resembles fine meal. With the machine running, pour in milk and the ice water. Mix until most of the dough has come together to form a ball, then continue to process 2 minutes more.

**2.** Preheat oven to 300°F, with rack in center. Transfer dough to a lightly floured work surface. The dough will appear wet and slick. Sprinkle top of dough lightly with flour. Use a rolling pin to tamp across top of dough, beating in flour, until dough is about 10 inches long and ½ inch thick.

**3.** Fold dough loosely into thirds, then sprinkle again with flour, and beat in flour with a rolling pin. Stretch out dough until it is about ¼ inch thick. Sprinkle again with flour, and repeat process for about 10 minutes. The dough will become very smooth, with little bubbles inside.

**4.** When dough is smooth and satiny, roll out until about ⅜ inch thick. Cut out rounds with a 1½-inch biscuit cutter. Transfer rounds to prepared baking sheets, placing them about 1 inch apart. Prick each round twice with a small fork, poking fork all the way through the dough. Gather scraps, and continue process until all dough has been used.

**5.** Bake biscuits, one sheet at a time, 15 minutes; reduce oven heat to 200°F. Continue baking until biscuits are golden brown on bottom but still white on top; watch carefully, as this can take anywhere from 15 to 30 minutes more. Biscuits will turn a very slight white-pink when done; they should not be golden or brown on top at all. Biscuits freeze well in an airtight container, up to 1 month.

## angel biscuits

### MAKES 2 DOZEN

*Yeast is used as part of the leavening to give these biscuits the light, airy texture that inspired their name.*

- 6 cups all-purpose flour, plus more for work surface
- 2 teaspoons sugar
- 1 tablespoon baking powder
- 1½ teaspoons salt
- 1 teaspoon baking soda
- 1 envelope active dry yeast (1 scant tablespoon)
- ¼ cup warm water (about 110°F)
- 1 cup (2 sticks) unsalted butter, melted and cooled to 115°F
- 2 cups buttermilk, room temperature

**1.** In a medium bowl, sift or whisk together flour, sugar, baking powder, salt, and baking soda; set aside. In another bowl, sprinkle yeast over the warm water; let stand until foamy, about 5 minutes.

**2.** In a medium bowl, combine 1 cup flour mixture with the yeast mixture, melted butter, and 1 cup buttermilk. Stir to combine. Add remaining flour mixture and buttermilk alternately, stirring between additions. When a sticky dough forms, cover it with plastic wrap, and refrigerate 2 hours.

**3.** Preheat oven to 450°F. Remove dough from refrigerator; turn out onto a lightly floured work surface. Knead a few times; roll out ½ inch thick. Cut out rounds with a 2¼-inch biscuit or cookie cutter; place rounds 1 inch apart on a baking sheet. Bake until golden on top and dry in middle, 12 to 15 minutes. Let cool on a wire rack. Serve warm.

### HOW TO BAKE THE BEST BISCUITS

• *Start with a clean work surface. As you work, scrape up loose bits of dough with a bench scraper or spatula, and incorporate them into the rest of the dough.*

• *Don't overwork the dough. To avoid getting tough results, mix dough with your hand or a fork until it just comes together.*

• *Cold dough is easier to roll. Chill the dough thoroughly before rolling. Wrap dough well with plastic, and place in the refrigerator for at least 1 hour or overnight.*

• *When making yeast biscuits, prewarm the bowl and ingredients. Keeping all items at about the same temperature will give the dough a good environment for rising.*

• *Don't butter the baking sheet. There's no need—the butter in the batter should prevent the biscuits from sticking to the sheet.*

## buttermilk biscuits

MAKES 15

*The buttermilk in this recipe makes these biscuits very light in texture, with a tangy flavor.*

- 4 cups all-purpose flour, plus more for work surface
- 4 teaspoons baking powder
- 1½ teaspoons salt
- 1 teaspoon baking soda
- 1 teaspoon sugar
- 1 cup (2 sticks) chilled unsalted butter, cut into small pieces
- 2 cups buttermilk

**1.** Preheat oven to 375°F. In a medium bowl, whisk together flour, baking powder, salt, baking soda, and sugar. Add butter; using a pastry blender or two knives, cut in butter until the mixture resembles coarse crumbs.

**2.** Add buttermilk to flour mixture; stir just until mixture comes together; batter will be sticky. Transfer to a lightly floured work surface; use floured fingers to pat dough to a 1-inch thickness. Use a 2½-inch biscuit or cookie cutter to cut rounds as close together as possible to minimize scraps.

**3.** Transfer rounds to a baking sheet. Bake until lightly browned, 18 to 20 minutes. Let cool on a wire rack. Serve warm.

## olive-filled rolls

*photograph on page 23*

MAKES 18 TO 20

- 1¼ cups plus 1 tablespoon warm water (110°F)
- ¾ teaspoon active dry yeast
- ½ cup Sponge (page 103), pulled into small pieces
- 5 tablespoons olive oil, plus more for bowl, plastic wrap, and pans
- 3¾ cups bread flour, plus more for work surface
- 2½ teaspoons salt
- ¾ cup olive paste

**1.** In the bowl of an electric mixer, combine ¼ cup warm water and yeast. Let stand until foamy, about 10 minutes. Add the sponge and 2 tablespoons oil; using the paddle attachment, mix on low speed until combined, about 2 minutes.

**2.** Add flour, salt, and remaining 1 cup plus 1 tablespoon warm water; mix 1 minute. Switch to the dough-hook attachment, and mix on medium-low speed until dough is soft and smooth, about 6 minutes. Alternatively, you can knead the dough by hand 15 to 20 minutes.

**3.** Transfer dough to a lightly floured surface, and knead by hand 4 or 5 times, shaping dough into a ball. Place dough, smooth side up, in a large, lightly oiled bowl, and cover with oiled plastic wrap. Let rise in a warm place until doubled in bulk, about 2½ hours.

**4.** Brush two 9-by-5-inch loaf pans liberally with olive oil, and pour 1 tablespoon oil into each. Turn out dough onto a lightly floured work surface, and cut into 18 to 20 equal pieces (about 2 ounces each). Working with one piece at a time, flatten dough with fingertips into a 4-by-5-inch rectangle. Spread with about 1 teaspoon olive paste, roll up tightly, and pinch long edge to seal. Place roll, seam side down, in prepared pan. Repeat this process until you have filled the bottom of the pan with rolls fitting snugly; the pan should accommodate about nine. Repeat process with remaining dough and pan. Cover with lightly oiled plastic wrap, and let rise 1 hour.

**5.** Thirty minutes before final rise is complete, preheat oven to 450°F. Place a baking stone, if using, in lower third of oven and an empty baking pan on the lowest shelf.

**6.** Use a razor blade or sharp knife to make a lengthwise slash on each roll until olive paste is visible. Transfer loaf pans to oven. Pour 2 cups very hot water into heated baking pan to create steam; close oven door. Bake until dark golden brown, 30 to 40 minutes. Remove pans from oven; turn out rolls onto wire rack to cool. If bottom and sides of loaves are not dark enough, return to oven, placing loaves directly on shelf; bake until golden. When finished baking, brush tops with remaining tablespoon oil; let cool on wire racks at least 30 minutes before serving.

## buttery crescents
*photograph on page 22*
MAKES 35 TO 40

*1 cup (2 sticks) salted butter, cool but not cold, plus more for plastic wrap*
*Classic Light Rolls dough (recipe follows), made through step 2*
*All-purpose flour, for work surface*

**1.** Place butter in the bowl of an electric mixer. Beat on low speed until spreadable. Turn dough out onto a floured work surface. With a floured rolling pin, roll into a 10-by-25-inch rectangle. Spread with butter. Fold both 10-inch edges of dough toward the middle, then fold in half to form a rectangle, about 10 by 6 inches. Wrap dough in buttered plastic; place on a baking sheet. Chill 40 minutes.

**2.** Remove dough from refrigerator. On a floured work surface, roll dough again into a 10-by-25-inch rectangle. Fold into a 10-by-6-inch rectangle as in step 1. Wrap in plastic; return to baking sheet. Chill 40 minutes more.

**3.** Line two large baking sheets with parchment paper. Roll dough into a 15-by-25-inch rectangle. Using a pizza wheel or sharp knife, trim edges of dough so they are straight. Cut rectangle lengthwise into four equal strips. Cut each strip into elongated triangles, about 3 inches wide at the base. Starting at base, roll and shape into crescents. Transfer to baking sheets, 1 inch apart. Cover with buttered plastic wrap. Let rise in a cool place 1 hour.

**4.** Preheat oven to 350°F. Bake until crescents are golden and cooked through, about 20 minutes. Let cool on a wire rack 5 minutes before serving.

### SHAPING CRESCENT ROLLS

*To ensure even baking, keep rolls uniform in size and shape. Cut strips of dough into triangles three inches wide at the base; roll from base, then curve ends slightly to form crescent shapes.*

## classic light rolls

MAKES 2 DOZEN

¼ cup warm water (about 110°F)

½ cup plus a pinch of sugar

1 envelope active dry yeast
   (1 scant tablespoon)

1¼ cups milk

¾ cup (1½ sticks) unsalted butter, melted and
   cooled, plus more for bowl and plastic wrap

2½ teaspoons salt

2 large eggs

4½ to 5 cups all-purpose flour, plus more
   for work surface and rolling pin

1 large egg, lightly beaten with 1 tablespoon
   water, for egg wash

1 tablespoon poppy seeds

**1.** In the bowl of an electric mixer, whisk the warm water with a pinch of sugar and the yeast. Let stand until foamy, about 6 minutes.

**2.** With mixer on low speed, using the dough-hook attachment, add milk, butter, remaining sugar, salt, and 2 eggs. Gradually add 4½ cups flour; if dough is still sticky, add up to ½ cup more. Brush inside of a large bowl with butter. Transfer dough to bowl; cover with buttered plastic wrap. Let rise in a warm place until doubled in bulk, about 2½ hours.

**3.** Line a large baking sheet with parchment paper. Turn out dough onto a floured work surface. With a floured rolling pin, roll dough out ¾ inch thick. With a 2¼-inch cookie cutter, cut out 24 rounds as close together as possible. Place rounds ¼ inch apart on baking sheet. Cover with buttered plastic wrap; let rise until they do not spring back when pressed with a finger, about 30 minutes.

**4.** Preheat oven to 350°F. Brush egg wash on tops of rounds; sprinkle tops with poppy seeds. Transfer baking sheet to oven. Bake until rolls are golden brown, 20 to 23 minutes. Transfer to a wire rack to cool at least 5 minutes before serving.

## parker house rolls

photograph on page 22

MAKES 2 DOZEN

1 envelope active dry yeast
   (1 scant tablespoon)

¼ cup warm water (about 110°F)

3 tablespoons plus a pinch of sugar

¾ cup (1½ sticks) plus 1 tablespoon unsalted
   butter, melted and cooled, plus more for
   bowl, plastic wrap, and pan

1 cup milk, room temperature

1 tablespoon salt

3 large eggs

4½ to 5 cups all-purpose flour, plus
   more for work surface

**1.** In the bowl of an electric mixer, whisk together yeast, the warm water, and a pinch of sugar. Let stand until foamy, about 6 minutes.

**2.** With mixer on low, using dough-hook attachment, add 7 tablespoons butter, milk, salt, remaining 3 tablespoons sugar, and eggs. Add 4½ cups flour. If dough is still sticky, add up to ½ cup more. Place dough in a lightly buttered bowl; cover with buttered plastic wrap. Let rise in a warm place until doubled in bulk, about 2½ hours.

**3.** Butter a 9-by-13-inch baking pan. On a floured work surface, roll dough into a 12-by-16-inch rectangle; brush with 3 tablespoons butter. Using a pizza wheel or knife, cut dough lengthwise into 6 equal strips; cut crosswise into 4 equal parts. You will have 24 strips. Fold strips in half; place in prepared baking pan, four across and six down. Brush with remaining 3 tablespoons butter. Cover pan with buttered plastic wrap. Let rise until dough does not spring back when pressed with a finger, 25 to 30 minutes.

**4.** Preheat oven to 350°F. Bake until golden, 35 to 40 minutes. Let cool at least 5 minutes on a wire rack before inverting onto rack. Reinvert; serve.

## cornmeal rolls

MAKES 20

1¼  cups milk

 4  teaspoons salt

 ½  cup yellow cornmeal, plus more for sprinkling

 1  envelope active dry yeast
    (1 scant tablespoon)

 ¼  cup warm water (about 110°F)

 2  tablespoons dark-brown sugar

 2  large eggs, plus 1 lightly beaten, for glaze

3½  to 4 cups all-purpose flour, plus
    more for work surface
    Olive oil, for bowl and plastic wrap

**1.** Place the milk and salt in a large saucepan over medium heat, and bring to a simmer. Gradually whisk in the cornmeal. Cook, stirring, until mixture is thickened, about 2 minutes. Remove from heat; set aside to cool.

**2.** In the bowl of an electric mixer, whisk together yeast, the warm water, and brown sugar. Set aside until foamy, about 6 minutes. In a small bowl, whisk together 2 eggs; set aside.

**3.** With mixer on low speed, using the dough-hook attachment, add cooled cornmeal mixture and reserved 2 eggs. Slowly add 3½ cups flour, beating until a soft dough forms. If dough is still sticky, add up to ½ cup more flour, a little at a time. Knead on medium-low speed until dough springs back when pressed with your finger, about 5 minutes. Place dough in an oiled bowl; cover bowl with oiled plastic wrap. Let rise in a warm place until doubled in bulk, about 3 hours.

**4.** Sprinkle two 13-by-18-inch baking sheets with cornmeal. Turn dough out onto a floured work surface; divide into 20 pieces. Roll each piece into a ball. Place balls 1½ inches apart on prepared baking sheets. Cover with oiled plastic wrap. Let rise until dough does not spring back when pressed with your finger, about 30 minutes.

**5.** Preheat oven to 375°F. Brush remaining egg over tops of dough; sprinkle with cornmeal. Using a sharp knife, cut two parallel slits in the top of each ball. Bake until rolls are golden, about 20 minutes. Transfer to a wire rack to cool at least 5 minutes before serving.

## classic popovers

MAKES 6

*Popover tins are special pans that allow the hot air to circulate fully around each popover, creating a dramatic top; regular muffin tins may be used instead.*

2½  tablespoons vegetable oil,
    plus more for pan

1½  cups milk

1½  cups all-purpose flour

 ½  teaspoon salt

 4  large eggs

**1.** Preheat oven to 425°F, with rack on lowest level. Brush a 6-cup popover tin or 6 cups of a standard muffin tin with oil; set aside. In a medium bowl, combine 1½ tablespoons oil with the milk, flour, and salt; stir until just moistened. Whisk in eggs one at a time until fully incorporated.

**2.** Heat popover tin in oven 5 minutes; remove from oven. Working quickly, pour ½ teaspoon oil into each cup. Divide batter evenly among cups.

**3.** Return pan to oven; bake 20 minutes. Reduce oven temperature to 350°F without opening oven. Continue baking until sides of popovers are crisp and firm, about 20 minutes more. Remove from oven, and poke centers with a sharp knife to release steam. Serve immediately.

## garlic-thyme popovers

MAKES 1 DOZEN

*If serving popovers with Roast Goose (page 225), goose fat can be used in place of the vegetable shortening in this recipe. Popover batter may be made up to one day ahead and stored, covered, in the refrigerator.*

2½ tablespoons pure vegetable
  shortening, plus more for pans
 3  small garlic cloves, minced
2½ tablespoons chopped fresh thyme
 2  tablespoons unsalted butter, melted
 2  cups milk
 2  cups all-purpose flour
 2  teaspoons salt
 5  large eggs, lightly beaten

**1.** Preheat oven to 450°F, with rack on lowest level. Lightly coat two 6-cup popover tins or one 12-cup standard muffin tin with shortening; set aside.

**2.** Heat 1½ teaspoons shortening in a small sauté pan over low heat. Add garlic; cook until soft, about 3 minutes. Add thyme; set aside.

**3.** In an 8-cup glass measuring cup or bowl, whisk together melted butter, milk, flour, and salt. Gradually whisk eggs into milk mixture. Whisk in reserved garlic mixture.

**4.** Heat popover tins in oven 5 minutes; remove from oven. Divide remaining 2 tablespoons shortening among tins; transfer to oven, and heat until it sizzles, about 10 minutes. Remove from oven; quickly divide batter evenly among cups, filling each about halfway.

**5.** Bake 15 minutes; reduce heat to 350°F without opening oven. Continue baking until popovers puff up and are golden brown, about 15 minutes more. When done, sides should be crisp and firm. Remove from oven; poke each with a sharp knife to release steam. Serve immediately.

QUICK BREADS

## banana-nut bread

MAKES THREE 3¼-BY-5¾-INCH LOAVES

*When baked in small French Panibois molds and wrapped in cellophane and decorative papers, these individual loaf cakes, as well as the pound cakes and carrot cakes that follow, are delicious holiday gifts.*

 5  tablespoons unsalted butter, room
  temperature, plus more for pans
1½ cups all-purpose flour
 1  teaspoon baking soda
 1  teaspoon salt
 1  cup sugar
 2  large eggs
 1  cup mashed very ripe bananas
  (3 small bananas)
 ½  cup sour cream
 1  teaspoon pure vanilla extract
 ½  cup coarsely chopped pecans
  (about 2 ounces)

**1.** Preheat oven to 350°F. Butter three 3¼-by-5¾-inch mini loaf pans; set aside. Into a medium bowl, sift together flour, baking soda, and salt; set aside.

**2.** In the bowl of an electric mixer, cream butter and sugar on medium-high speed until light and fluffy, 2 to 3 minutes. Add eggs, and beat until incorporated, scraping sides of bowl as needed.

**3.** Add reserved flour mixture to butter mixture; beat on low speed until combined. Add bananas, sour cream, and vanilla; beat until well combined. Stir in pecans. Divide mixture evenly among the prepared loaf pans.

**4.** Place pans on a baking sheet, and transfer to the oven. Bake until loaves are golden brown and a cake tester inserted in the center comes out clean, 30 to 35 minutes. Transfer pans to a wire rack to cool completely before removing loaves. Store, wrapped well in plastic wrap, at room temperature, up to 5 days, or freeze up to 1 month.

## brown-sugar pound cake

MAKES FIVE 3¼-BY-5¾-INCH LOAVES

1  cup (2 sticks) unsalted butter,
    room temperature, plus more for pans

3  cups sifted all-purpose flour

2  teaspoons baking powder

½  teaspoon salt

2¼  cups packed light-brown sugar

5  large eggs

¾  cup buttermilk

**1.** Preheat oven to 325°F. Butter five 3¼-by-5¾-inch mini loaf pans; set aside. Into a medium bowl, sift flour, baking powder, and salt; set aside.

**2.** In the bowl of an electric mixer, cream butter and sugar on medium speed until light and fluffy, 2 to 3 minutes. Add eggs, one at a time, beating until incorporated after each and scraping down sides of bowl as necessary.

**3.** Add one-third of reserved flour mixture, beating on low speed just until combined. Add half the buttermilk, and another one-third of the flour mixture; beat just until incorporated. Repeat, adding remaining buttermilk and flour mixture. Pour about 1½ cups batter into each prepared pan. Spread batter evenly with an offset spatula.

**4.** Place pans on a large baking sheet; transfer to oven. Bake until tops of loaves are golden brown and a cake tester inserted into the centers comes out clean, 40 to 45 minutes. Transfer pans to a wire rack to cool completely before removing loaves.

## mini carrot cakes

MAKES THREE 3¼-BY-5¾-INCH LOAVES

1  cup (2 sticks) unsalted butter,
    room temperature, plus more for pans

2  cups all-purpose flour, plus more for pans

½  cup granulated sugar

½  cup packed light-brown sugar

3  large eggs

1  teaspoon baking powder

1  teaspoon baking soda

2  teaspoons ground cinnamon

1  teaspoon salt

3  cups finely grated carrots (14 ounces)

1  cup coarsely chopped walnuts
    (about 4 ounces)

**1.** Preheat oven to 350°F. Butter three 3¼-by-5¾-inch mini loaf pans; dust with flour, and tap out excess. In the bowl of an electric mixer, cream butter and sugars on medium-high speed until light and fluffy, 2 to 3 minutes. Add eggs one at a time, beating after each until smooth and scraping down sides of bowl as necessary.

**2.** Into a medium bowl, sift together flour, baking powder, baking soda, cinnamon, and salt. Add flour mixture to the butter mixture all at once, and beat on low speed until combined. Add carrots and walnuts, and beat until combined. Divide batter evenly among prepared pans.

**3.** Place pans on a baking sheet, and transfer to the oven. Bake until loaves are golden brown and a cake tester inserted into the centers comes out clean, 35 to 40 minutes. Transfer pans to a wire rack to cool completely before removing loaves.

## cornmeal-pear loaf
MAKES ONE 9-BY-4½-INCH LOAF

1⅓  cups all-purpose flour
⅔  cup yellow cornmeal
½  cup packed light-brown sugar
1  tablespoon baking powder
1  teaspoon baking soda
½  teaspoon ground cinnamon
¼  teaspoon salt
¾  cup nonfat buttermilk
2  large whole eggs
1  large egg white
3  tablespoons unsalted butter, melted, plus more for pan
2  ripe Bosc pears, peeled and cut into ¼-inch dice (about 1½ cups)
⅓  cup golden raisins
   Pear-Raspberry Butter (recipe follows)

1. Preheat oven to 375°F. Butter a 9-by-4½-by-2¾-inch loaf pan; set aside. In a medium bowl, whisk together flour, cornmeal, sugar, baking powder, baking soda, cinnamon, and salt. In another bowl, whisk together buttermilk, eggs, egg white, and melted butter. Stir buttermilk mixture into flour mixture. Stir in pears and raisins until combined.

2. Fill prepared pan with batter. Place in the oven, and bake until a cake tester inserted into the center comes out clean, 45 to 50 minutes. Transfer pan to a wire rack to cool before removing loaf. Serve with pear-raspberry butter.

## pear-raspberry butter
MAKES 2 CUPS

*The cooking time for this fruit butter will vary with the juiciness of the pears; to avoid scorching, watch closely as the purée becomes thick.*

3  pounds ripe Comice pears (about 6 large), peeled and cored
1½  cups fresh or thawed frozen raspberries (6 ounces)
2  tablespoons sugar

1. Cut pears into chunks, and place in a food processor. Process until finely chopped, 20 to 30 seconds. Transfer to a medium saucepan.

2. Purée raspberries in a food processor. Pass purée through a fine sieve into saucepan; discard seeds. Add sugar; stir to thoroughly combine.

3. Place saucepan over medium heat, and bring just to a boil. Reduce heat to medium-low, and cook, stirring frequently, adjusting heat to low as the liquid cooks out and purée becomes very thick, 3 to 4½ hours. Remove from heat; serve warm or at room temperature with cornmeal-pear loaf.

# *drinks*

COCKTAILS AND PUNCHES

NONALCOHOLIC "COCKTAILS"
AND PUNCHES

HOT CHOCOLATES

COCKTAILS AND PUNCHES

## holiday bloody mary

*photograph on page 28*

SERVES 8

- 1 can (46 ounces) low-sodium tomato juice
- 2 tablespoons hot sauce, such as Tabasco
- 1 tablespoon freshly grated horseradish, or 2 tablespoons prepared
- ½ cup freshly squeezed lemon juice (4 lemons)
- 2 cups vodka

In a large pitcher, combine tomato juice, hot sauce, horseradish, lemon juice, and vodka; stir well. Serve immediately over ice, or refrigerate until very cold, up to 3 hours.

## hot buttered rum with ginger and cinnamon

SERVES 4

- 4 tablespoons Ginger Simple Syrup (recipe follows)
- 1 cup dark rum
- 4 whole cinnamon sticks
- 4 cups boiling water
- ½ recipe Ginger Butter (recipe follows)

**1.** Divide simple syrup among four heatproof glasses or mugs; add ¼ cup rum, 1 cinnamon stick, and 1 cup boiling water to each. Stir well.

**2.** Top each serving with a round of ginger butter. Serve immediately.

## ginger simple syrup

MAKES ¾ CUP

- 4 ounces fresh ginger, thinly sliced
- ½ cup granulated sugar

In a small saucepan, bring ginger, sugar, and ½ cup water to a boil over medium heat. Cook 2 minutes. Strain mixture through a fine sieve; discard ginger. Store syrup in an airtight container in the refrigerator up to 1 week.

## ginger butter

SERVES 8

- 3 pieces crystallized ginger, finely chopped (about 2 tablespoons)
- ½ teaspoon ground cinnamon
  Pinch of ground cloves
  Pinch of freshly grated nutmeg
- ½ cup (1 stick) unsalted butter, room temperature

In a small bowl, combine all ingredients; stir with a fork until blended. Shape into a log by rolling in parchment paper or plastic wrap. Chill until firm, about 1 hour, before slicing into eight rounds.

## ramos gin fizz

*photograph on page 29*

SERVES 1

   1  *ounce gin*
   3  *dashes freshly squeezed lime juice*
   3  *dashes freshly squeezed lemon juice*
   3  *dashes orange-blossom water*
   2  *teaspoons superfine sugar*
   1  *large egg white*
   4  *tablespoons light cream*
   ¼  *cup seltzer water*
      *Ground cinnamon, for garnish (optional)*

**1.** Combine gin, lime juice, lemon juice, orange-blossom water, sugar, egg white, and cream in a cocktail shaker. Shake over ice; pour into glass.

**2.** Top off drink with seltzer, and garnish with cinnamon, if desired; serve immediately.

**Note:** Raw eggs should not be used in food prepared for pregnant women, babies, young children, the elderly, or anyone whose health is compromised.

## toasted-almond milk with honey

SERVES 4

   8  *ounces sliced or slivered almonds*
   4  *cups milk*
  4½  *tablespoons honey*
   4  *ounces amaretto (optional)*

**1.** Preheat oven to 350°F. Spread almonds in a single layer on a rimmed baking sheet, and toast until golden and fragrant, about 10 minutes. Remove from oven; let cool, and roughly chop.

**2.** Place almonds and milk in a medium saucepan; cook over medium heat just until milk begins to steam, 5 to 6 minutes. Remove from heat; let steep, covered, about 30 minutes.

**3.** Strain milk mixture into a warmed pitcher or another saucepan; discard almonds. Stir in honey. Divide among four coffee cups; add 1 ounce of amaretto, if desired, to each. Serve immediately.

## the original eggnog

SERVES 26

*For eggnog like Martha's, use Maker's Mark bourbon, Mount Gay rum, and Grand Cru Cognac.*

  12  *large eggs, separated*
  1½  *cups superfine sugar*
  1½  *quarts heavy cream*
   1  *quart whole milk*
   3  *cups bourbon*
   ½  *cup dark rum*
   2  *cups Cognac*
      *Freshly grated nutmeg*

**1.** In the bowl of an electric mixer fitted with the paddle attachment, beat egg yolks until thick and pale. Gradually add sugar, beating until combined. Switch to the whisk attachment; beat in 1 quart cream and milk. Stir in bourbon, rum, and Cognac.

**2.** Just before serving, beat egg whites until stiff. Fold egg whites into mixture. Whip remaining 2 cups heavy cream until stiff, and fold into mixture. Sprinkle with nutmeg.

**Note:** Raw eggs should not be used in food prepared for pregnant women, babies, young children, the elderly, or anyone whose health is compromised.

## white-russian eggnog

SERVES 6

*This recipe can easily be doubled.*

3½  cups milk
  5  large egg yolks
  ¾  cup sugar
  2  cups heavy cream, chilled
  ¾  cup vodka
  ½  cup Kahlúa

**1.** Prepare an ice bath; set aside. Place 2 cups milk in a small saucepan; bring to a boil over medium-high heat. Combine egg yolks and sugar in the bowl of an electric mixer; whisk on medium speed until mixture is pale and thick, 3 to 5 minutes.

**2.** Pour half the hot milk into egg-yolk mixture in a steady stream, whisking constantly. Return mixture to pan, and cook over low heat, stirring constantly with a wooden spoon, until mixture is thick enough to coat the back of the spoon.

**3.** Remove from heat; immediately stir in 1 cup cream and remaining 1½ cups milk, and transfer to the ice bath. Let stand until chilled, about 30 minutes, stirring frequently.

**4.** Stir vodka and Kahlúa into egg mixture. In a medium bowl, whip remaining cup cream until soft peaks form. Ladle eggnog into six serving glasses; top each with a dollop of whipped cream.

## cooked custard eggnog

*photograph on page 29*

SERVES 8 TO 10

3½  cups milk, chilled
  5  large egg yolks
  ¾  cup sugar
  2  cups heavy cream
  1  cup dark rum
     Freshly grated nutmeg

**1.** Prepare an ice bath; set aside. Bring 2 cups milk to a boil in a medium saucepan over medium-high heat. Combine egg yolks and sugar in the bowl of an electric mixer; whisk on medium-high speed until mixture is very pale and thick, 3 to 5 minutes.

**2.** Pour half the hot milk into egg-yolk mixture in a steady stream, whisking constantly. Return mixture to pan, and cook over low heat, stirring constantly with a wooden spoon, until mixture is thick enough to coat the back of the spoon.

**3.** Remove from heat; immediately stir in 1 cup cream. Pass mixture through a fine sieve into a medium bowl set in the ice bath; let stand until chilled, about 30 minutes, stirring frequently. Stir in remaining 1½ cups milk and the rum.

**4.** Transfer mixture to a large serving bowl, or ladle into glasses. In a medium bowl, whip remaining cup cream until soft peaks form. Top eggnog with whipped cream, and sprinkle with nutmeg.

### EGGNOG PREPARATION TIP

*Eggnog can be refrigerated in an airtight container for up to two days. Mix in spirits and top with whipped cream just before serving.*

## glögg
### SERVES 4

*This hot spiced wine, a version of mulled wine, is a traditional Swedish and Finnish drink.*

   1   *bottle dry red wine*
   1   *cup Madeira*
   1   *tablespoon ground cardamom*
   1   *whole cinnamon stick*
        *Peel from ½ lemon*
   ¼   *cup packed light-brown sugar*
   ¼   *cup whole blanched almonds*
   ½   *cup raisins*

**1.** Combine red wine and Madeira in a saucepan. Add cardamom and cinnamon, and bring to a simmer over low heat. Add lemon peel and sugar; stir to dissolve sugar. Remove from heat, and let steep at least 2 hours.

**2.** Strain liquid into a clean saucepan; discard solids. Reheat wine mixture over low heat. Divide almonds and raisins among four mugs, fill with glögg, and serve.

## pear-champagne punch
*photograph on page 28*
### SERVES 8

*Poire Williams is a pear-flavored brandy. Pear nectar can be found in gourmet shops and many supermarkets.*

   3   *tablespoons pear nectar*
   3   *tablespoons Poire Williams*
   2   *750-ml bottles chilled champagne*
        *Pear Chips (recipe follows)*

Combine nectar, Poire Williams, and champagne in a large pitcher. Gently stir; serve in individual glasses, each garnished with a pear chip.

## pear chips
### MAKES ABOUT 1½ DOZEN

*Use unblemished, slightly underripe fruit.*

   1   *pear*
   ¾   *cup confectioners' sugar*

**1.** Preheat oven to 200°F. Line a baking sheet with a Silpat baking mat. Using a mandoline or very sharp knife, slice pears lengthwise into very thin translucent rounds. Don't worry about removing seeds or cores. Sift sugar over both sides of each pear slice, coating completely.

**2.** Transfer slices to baking sheet. Bake until edges begin to ruffle, 1 to 1½ hours. Turn slices, and bake until golden brown, 1 to 1½ hours more.

**3.** Transfer chips to a wire rack in a single layer to cool and harden. Once completely cooled, chips may be stored in an airtight container between layers of parchment paper up to 3 days.

### CHAMPAGNE FOR A CROWD

*Most of us associate Champagne with celebrations and good cheer, but few know that it comes in many-size bottles. If you're hosting a holiday party, you can make a big impression with one of the larger sizes. Plan on one-half standard bottle (750 ml) per guest for a sit-down dinner. A Magnum, the size of two standard bottles, is handy for couples dining together. For larger crowds, choose from a Jeroboam, which equals four bottles, or a Rehoboam, made up of six. A Methuselah equals eight bottles of champagne, and a Salmanazar equals twelve. Next up is the Balthazar, holding the equivalent of sixteen bottles, and the very biggest, the Nebuchadnezzar, contains twenty.*

## planter's punch

*photograph on page 27*
SERVES ABOUT 24

*Serve this punch icy cold. In lieu of ice, which may dilute the punch as it sits, you can freeze whole citrus fruits, and add them to the punch just before serving.*

1⅓ cups freshly squeezed orange juice
(4 to 5 oranges)
¾ cup freshly squeezed lime juice
(about 5 limes)
⅔ cup freshly squeezed lemon juice
(about 4 lemons)
1½ cups dark rum
1 can (46 ounces) pineapple juice
½ cup sugar
¼ teaspoon bitters
1 liter sparkling water or club soda, chilled

Combine orange, lime, and lemon juices in a large container. Add rum, pineapple juice, sugar, and bitters, and stir to combine. Transfer mixture to the refrigerator, and chill. Just before serving, stir in cold sparkling water or club soda.

## spiked fruit punch

SERVES 12 TO 20

*This recipe is courtesy of Sheila Bridges.*

6 lemons
4 navel oranges
2 cans (6 ounces each) frozen lemonade
1 can (6 ounces) frozen orange juice
2 liters lemon-lime soda
1 liter Southern Comfort
Ice, for serving

**1.** Line two baking sheets with plastic wrap, and set aside. Slice lemons as thinly as possible into rounds. Arrange slices in layers on one of the prepared baking sheets. Repeat with oranges; layer

on second baking sheet. Transfer to the freezer until fruit slices are frozen, 2 to 2½ hours.

**2.** Just before serving, drop whole logs of frozen lemonade and orange juice into a large punch bowl. Add soda, Southern Comfort, and several handfuls of ice. Remove frozen fruit slices from freezer, and arrange over top of punch. Serve.

## flavored vodkas

*photograph on page 26*
MAKES THREE 750-ML BOTTLES

*Flavored vodkas make attractive holiday gifts. If you like, return the fruit to the cranberry and orange vodkas after decanting, and store in the refrigerator or freezer, up to four months. Unlike the other flavors, pineapple vodka must be refrigerated while curing.*

3 750-ml bottles vodka
1 cup fresh or thawed frozen cranberries
1 orange, such as navel or blood
1 large ripe pineapple, trimmed and peeled

**1.** Decant 2 bottles of vodka into two clean 2-liter glass containers. Soak vodka bottles to remove paper labels. Let dry; reserve for gifts.

**2.** Make cranberry vodka: Rinse cranberries, and place in one container of vodka. Allow to cure, covered, in the refrigerator or a cool, dark place at least 1 week and up to 3 weeks.

**3.** Make orange vodka: Cut orange in half through stem (do not peel). Place on a clean work surface, cut sides down, and halve again into quarters. Slice each quarter into ¼-inch-thick wedges. Add orange wedges to second container of vodka. Allow to cure, covered, in the refrigerator or a cool, dark place at least 1 week and up to 3 weeks.

**4.** Make pineapple vodka: Slice pineapple into ½-inch-thick rings. Arrange rings in a clean, wide-mouthed 3-liter glass container. Pour vodka from third bottle over slices and into container. Allow to cure, covered, in the refrigerator at least 1 week and up to 2 weeks.

**5.** If giving as gifts, use a funnel to pour cranberry and orange vodkas back into their original reserved bottles. Decant the pineapple vodka: Use tongs or

## vin d'orange

MAKES 5 QUARTS

*This wine drink needs to be made at least one week ahead to allow the flavors to develop. For best results, let stand one month. Sweetened with Orange Syrup and poured over ice, it makes a delicious apéritif.*

   10  oranges
    5  lemons
    6  750-ml bottles dry, fruity white wine
 1½  cups brandy
    1  vanilla bean, split lengthwise
       Orange Syrup (recipe follows)

**1.** Rinse oranges and lemons; cut into quarters, and place in a large jar with a tight-fitting lid. Add wine, brandy, and vanilla bean. Cover, and store in a cool, dry place up to 1 month.

**2.** Strain liquid; discard solids. Pour liquid into glass bottles; refrigerate. Serve over ice with orange syrup, as desired; garnish with candied zest.

### orange syrup

MAKES 1 QUART (INCLUDING ZEST)

*Keep the strips of orange zest in the finished syrup to use as a garnish for the Vin d'Orange.*

    4  oranges
    3  cups sugar

**1.** Using a vegetable peeler or sharp paring knife, remove the zest from the oranges in long strips. Reserve oranges for another use.

**2.** In a medium saucepan, combine zest, sugar, and 3 cups water; bring to a boil over medium heat. Wash down sides of pan with a wet pastry brush to prevent crystals from forming. Reduce heat to low, and simmer until very fragrant, 30 to 40 minutes. Let cool. Refrigerate in an airtight container up to 2 weeks.

NONALCOHOLIC
"COCKTAILS" AND PUNCHES

## iced spice tea punch

*photograph on page 27*

SERVES ABOUT 12

*The frozen clove-spiked lemons replace ice cubes in this nonalcoholic punch, which can be made up to one day ahead.*

    6  lemons
       Whole cloves, for lemons
    6  cranberry-flavored tea bags
    6  whole cinnamon sticks
    ¼  cup whole star anise
    2  tablespoons allspice

**1.** Pierce skin of a lemon with a wooden skewer, creating a decorative design; fill each hole with a single clove. Repeat with remaining lemons. Transfer studded lemons to the freezer, and freeze at least several hours, preferably overnight.

**2.** Combine tea bags, cinnamon sticks, star anise, allspice, and 1½ quarts water in a medium saucepan. Cover, and bring to a simmer over medium heat; continue simmering, uncovered, to allow flavors to blend, about 15 minutes. Let cool to room temperature. Transfer to an airtight container, and refrigerate until cold.

**3.** To serve, strain the cold tea into a punch bowl; discard solids. Add frozen lemons.

## apple ginger sparklers

SERVES 6

    Ginger Simple Syrup (page 122)
    4½  cups sparkling apple cider
    6  whole cinnamon sticks
    6  pieces crystallized ginger

Place 2 tablespoons syrup in each of six glasses. Fill glasses with ice cubes; pour in cider, dividing evenly. Garnish each with a cinnamon stick and a piece of ginger. Serve immediately.

## cherry bombs

SERVES 6

    1  cup grenadine
    1  liter lemon-lime soda or seltzer
    18  maraschino cherries

Place 2 cups water in a medium saucepan, and bring to a boil over medium-high heat. Add grenadine, and stir to combine. Pour mixture into two ice-cube trays. Freeze until solid, 2 hours or overnight. Fill six glasses with prepared ice cubes. Top with soda, and garnish with cherries.

## pink grapefruit "margaritas"

### SERVES 6

- 2 tablespoons colored sanding sugar
- 1 lime
- 6 teaspoons pomegranate syrup or grenadine
- 1½ cups pink-grapefruit juice

**1.** Spread sugar on a plate. Slice six thin rounds from middle of lime, and set aside. Rub cut side of one end of lime around rims of six glasses; dip each glass in sugar to coat rim. Pour 1 teaspoon pomegranate syrup into each glass.

**2.** In a blender, combine grapefruit juice and 2 cups ice. Process on high speed until ice is crushed coarsely. Pour frozen mixture over pomegranate syrup in glasses; garnish each with a reserved lime round. Serve immediately.

## pomegranate punch

### MAKES 2 QUARTS

*For a pretty presentation, serve punch with ice made by freezing pomegranate seeds and water in ice-cube trays.*

- 8 cups pomegranate seeds (about 5 pomegranates)
- ¾ cup sugar
- 1 bunch fresh mint, trimmed and rinsed
- ¼ cup freshly squeezed lemon juice (about 2 lemons)

**1.** Place pomegranate seeds in a food processor, and pulse until smooth. Strain liquid through a fine sieve into a bowl; discard solids. You should have about 3⅓ cups juice.

**2.** Place sugar and 2 cups water in a small saucepan, and bring to a boil. Reduce heat to a simmer, and stir until sugar has dissolved. Add pomegranate juice, mint, and lemon juice. Reduce heat,

and cover; let steep 30 minutes. Remove mint with a slotted spoon; discard. Let punch cool completely. Transfer to an airtight container; chill until ready to serve, up to 2 days.

## steamed milk

### SERVES 6

*This drink is a wonderful alternative to eggnog.*

- 6 tablespoons honey
- 1 quart milk
- 1 teaspoon ground cinnamon
- 3 whole cloves
  Freshly grated nutmeg

**1.** Place 1 tablespoon honey in each of six serving glasses; set aside. In a medium pan over medium-high heat, heat milk just until it begins to steam. Remove from heat; add cinnamon and cloves. Let steep, covered, 20 minutes. Return pan to heat, and bring mixture just to a boil. Remove from heat.

**2.** Remove and discard cloves. Working in batches so as not to fill more than halfway, transfer hot-milk mixture to a blender. Blend on high speed until frothy, about 30 seconds. Pour into glasses, topping each with some foam; repeat with remaining hot milk. Sprinkle nutmeg over tops, and serve.

## chocolate-bar hot chocolate

*photograph on page 26*

SERVES 4

*Hot chocolate made from candy bars is a child's idea of heaven. It also saves time since the sugar is already added. Candy-cane stirrers give the chocolate a hint of peppermint flavor.*

- 1 chocolate bar (8 ounces), finely chopped
- 1 quart milk
- 4 candy canes, for garnish

Combine chocolate and milk in a medium saucepan. Place over medium heat; whisk frequently until chocolate has melted, about 5 minutes. Whisk mixture to combine well, then divide among 4 mugs. Serve garnished with candy canes.

## malted hot chocolate

SERVES 4

- 1 quart milk
- 1 teaspoon pure vanilla extract
- 4 ounces semisweet chocolate, coarsely chopped
- ¾ cup malted-milk powder

**1.** In a medium saucepan, heat milk and vanilla over medium heat just until milk begins to steam, 5 to 6 minutes. Add chopped chocolate, and whisk until completely melted and combined.

**2.** Pour malt powder into a warmed pitcher or another saucepan. Add hot chocolate mixture, whisking thoroughly until powder dissolves. Divide among four mugs; serve immediately.

## spicy hot-chocolate with cinnamon

SERVES 4

*An ancho chile lends a touch of heat.*

- 1 quart milk
- 1 ancho chile, quartered, seeds removed
- 2 whole cinnamon sticks, plus 4 for garnish
- 4 ounces semisweet chocolate, coarsely chopped

**1.** In a medium saucepan over medium heat, combine milk, ancho chile, and cinnamon; heat just until milk begins to steam, 5 to 6 minutes. Remove from heat; let steep, covered, 10 minutes.

**2.** Place chocolate in a medium bowl; strain milk mixture into bowl, whisking to combine thoroughly. Discard solids. Return mixture to saucepan; continue whisking over medium heat until chocolate has completely melted. Divide among four mugs; serve immediately, garnished with remaining cinnamon sticks.

## white hot chocolate

SERVES 4

- 1 quart milk
- ½ teaspoon pure vanilla extract
- 4 ounces best-quality white chocolate, finely chopped

In a medium saucepan, heat milk and vanilla over medium heat just until milk begins to steam, 5 to 6 minutes. Add white chocolate, and whisk until completely melted and combined. Divide among four mugs; serve immediately.

# hors d'oeuvres

OLIVES AND NUTS

DIPS, RELISHES, AND SPREADS

CANAPES, BRUSCHETTA, AND CROSTINI

BAKED BITES

SAVORY PANCAKES

FISH AND SHELLFISH

✳

### citrus and rosemary olives
MAKES ABOUT 2 CUPS

Grated zest of 1 lemon

Grated zest of 1 orange

8 to 10 ounces (2 cups) assorted olives, such as Niçoise, Nyon, Picholine, Kalamata, or Cerignola

2 garlic cloves, minced

1 small shallot, minced

¼ cup extra-virgin olive oil

2 teaspoons minced fresh rosemary or 1 teaspoon crumbled dried rosemary

In a medium bowl, combine all ingredients. Marinate 2 to 4 hours at room temperature, stirring occasionally. Olive mixture may be kept in an airtight container, in the refrigerator, up to 1 week. Let sit at room temperature at least 30 minutes before serving.

✳

### marinated black olives
MAKES ABOUT 2 CUPS

Use Kalamata or Provençal olives. If you can't find hot paprika, substitute sweet Hungarian paprika plus a pinch of cayenne.

1 pound oil-cured black olives

5 garlic cloves, crushed

¾ cup extra-virgin olive oil

⅓ cup red-wine vinegar

2 tablespoons hot paprika

2 sprigs rosemary

2 sprigs thyme

2 sprigs oregano

In an airtight container, mix all ingredients. Cover, and marinate in the refrigerator overnight or up to 1 week. Serve at room temperature.

### warm olive buffet
SERVES 6 TO 8

Heating herbed olives before you serve them is an excellent way to bring out their flavor. Marinated olives will keep up to one week in an airtight container in the refrigerator; bake just before serving.

1½ pounds assorted olives, such as Picholine, Kalamata, or Niçoise, rinsed and drained

2 tablespoons extra-virgin olive oil

**for spicy olives:**

1 chile pepper, seeded and thinly sliced

2 garlic cloves, halved

**for fennel-seed olives:**

1 dried bay leaf

¼ teaspoon fennel seeds

**for lemon-thyme olives:**

Zest of ½ lemon, cut into strips

1 teaspoon coarsely chopped thyme leaves

Preheat oven to 350°F. Divide olives into thirds; place each third in a baking dish. Toss each with 2 teaspoons olive oil and the ingredients for one of the variations. Bake 15 to 25 minutes. If using garlic, remove before serving. Transfer olives to serving dishes; serve immediately.

#### THE FLAVOR OF OLIVES

There are dozens of types of olives varying in size and flavor. Underripe olives are always green, whereas ripe olives may be either green or black. Green olives, such as Picholine, Cerignola, and Kalamata, tend to be sharper and more pungent, whereas black ones, such as Niçoise, taste richer. The flavor of olives is enhanced by the use of herbs and spices, which are often added to the brine to form marinades.

## kalamata olives with fennel and orange

MAKES ABOUT 2 CUPS

- 1 orange
- 2 cups Kalamata olives
- ½ fennel bulb, trimmed and thinly sliced crosswise
- 1 teaspoon fennel seeds

Using a vegetable peeler, remove orange zest in long strips, avoiding pith. With a sharp paring knife, remove pith; cut between membranes to remove sections, and cut sections into thirds. In a medium bowl, toss orange zest and pieces with remaining ingredients, and serve immediately.

## spicy pecans

photograph on page 29

MAKES 5 CUPS

You can substitute almonds, walnuts, or cashews for the pecans, or any combination of mixed nuts. Store nuts in an airtight container at room temperature for up to one week.

- 1 tablespoon coarse salt
- 2 tablespoons cayenne pepper
- 1½ teaspoons paprika
- ½ cup sugar
- 2 large egg whites
- 5 cups pecan halves

**1.** Preheat oven to 300°F. Line two rimmed baking sheets with parchment paper. In a small bowl, combine salt, cayenne, paprika, and sugar.

**2.** In a medium bowl, whisk egg whites until foamy. Whisk in spice mixture. Stir in pecans. Spread coated pecans in a single layer on prepared baking sheets. Bake 15 minutes, then reduce oven temperature to 250°F. Rotate sheets in oven; cook until nuts are browned and fragrant, about 10 minutes more. Immediately transfer pecans in a single layer to another piece of parchment. Let cool.

## warm mixed nuts

MAKES 5 CUPS

The nuts may be refrigerated up to two days; reheat in a 300 degree oven for ten minutes.

- 5 cups mixed nuts, such as walnuts, cashews, almonds, pecans, and hazelnuts
- 3 tablespoons unsalted butter
- 2 small shallots, thinly sliced crosswise into rings (about ¼ cup)
- 3 garlic cloves, thinly sliced lengthwise
- ¼ cup coarsely chopped fresh rosemary
- ¼ teaspoon cayenne pepper
- 1 tablespoon dark-brown sugar
- 1 tablespoon coarse salt

**1.** Preheat oven to 350°F. Place nuts in a single layer on two rimmed baking sheets. Toast until nuts are golden and fragrant, 8 to 12 minutes, rotating sheets halfway through cooking. Transfer nuts to a large bowl, and set aside.

**2.** Heat 1 tablespoon butter in a small skillet over medium heat. Add shallots and garlic; sauté until golden, 3 to 5 minutes. Transfer shallots and garlic to a paper towel–lined plate. Set aside.

**3.** Melt remaining 2 tablespoons butter, and pour over nuts. Add rosemary, cayenne, brown sugar, and salt; stir well to combine. Toss in the garlic and shallots. Serve warm.

DIPS, RELISHES, AND SPREADS

## asian dipping sauce with winter rolls

MAKES 24

6 tablespoons seasoned rice vinegar

4 tablespoons mirin (Japanese cooking wine)

2 tablespoons sugar

½ teaspoon coarse salt

7 ounces rice noodles or cellophane noodles

1 cucumber, peeled, seeded, and cut into 3-inch-long matchsticks

½ small jícama, peeled and cut into 3-inch-long matchsticks

24 rice-paper wrappers

½ cup fresh mint leaves

1 small bunch fresh chives, cut into 3-inch-long pieces

¼ teaspoon Asian fish sauce

1 small red chile pepper

1 tablespoon finely grated carrot

**1.** Combine vinegar, mirin, sugar, and salt in a small bowl. Set aside.

**2.** Bring a pot of water to a boil; cook noodles until tender, according to package instructions, about 3 minutes. Drain in a colander; transfer to a bowl.

**3.** Pour 2 tablespoons vinegar mixture over noodles; set aside. Place cucumber and jícama in a bowl; combine with 2 tablespoons vinegar mixture.

**4.** Fill a medium bowl with warm water; dip rice-paper wrappers, a few at a time, in water until soft and pliable. Lay each wrapper on a clean kitchen towel; arrange a small bundle of noodles, 4 pieces of cucumber, 2 pieces of jícama, several mint leaves, and 1 chive piece across lower quarter of wrapper. Roll, folding in ends as you go, to form a tight roll. Place on a plate lined with damp paper towels, and repeat with remaining wrappers and

filling. Keep covered with damp paper towels until ready to serve.

**5.** Make dipping sauce: Stir fish sauce, chile pepper, and carrot into remaining vinegar mixture. Just before serving, cut rolls in half on the diagonal; arrange on serving plate with dipping sauce.

## black-eyed pea dip

MAKES 4 CUPS

*Black-eyed peas make a velvety dip that is good with corn chips. The peas are traditionally eaten on New Year's Day in the southern United States; they are thought to bring good luck in the new year to those who eat them.*

5 sprigs cilantro, plus 2 tablespoons chopped cilantro, for garnish

10 whole black peppercorns

2 cups dried black-eyed peas

1 ham hock (12 to 14 ounces)

4 stalks celery, 2 quartered, 2 finely chopped

2 onions, 1 quartered, 1 finely chopped

2 tablespoons olive oil

½ jalapeño chile, seeded and finely chopped

1 teaspoon crushed red-pepper flakes

1½ teaspoons coarse salt

1 teaspoon freshly ground black pepper

2 tablespoons freshly squeezed lime juice

**1.** Make bouquet garni: Place cilantro sprigs and peppercorns on a cheesecloth square; tie with kitchen twine to form a bundle.

**2.** Place peas, ham hock, quartered celery and onion, and the bouquet garni in a large saucepan. Add water to cover by 2 inches; bring to a boil over medium heat. Reduce heat; simmer gently, uncovered, until peas are tender, about 50 minutes. Remove from heat; drain, reserving cooking liquid. Discard ham hock, celery, onion, and bouquet garni.

**3.** Heat 1 tablespoon oil in a medium skillet over medium heat. Add chopped onion; cook until translucent, about 5 minutes. Add chopped celery, jalapeño, red-pepper flakes, and ½ teaspoon each salt and black pepper; cook until softened, about 5 minutes.

**4.** Set aside ½ cup cooked peas and ½ cup cooked celery and onions. Place remaining peas, celery, and onions in a food processor; add 1 tablespoon chopped cilantro. With motor running, slowly add 2 cups reserved cooking liquid and remaining tablespoon oil; process until a rough paste forms. Add remaining teaspoon salt and ½ teaspoon black pepper with the lime juice.

**5.** Transfer dip to a serving bowl, and garnish with reserved whole peas, vegetable mixture, and chopped cilantro.

## flame-grilled eggplant dip

MAKES ABOUT 1½ CUPS

- 1  large eggplant (about 1½ pounds)
- 1  tomato, coarsely chopped
- 2  tablespoons finely chopped red onion
- 1  tablespoon olive oil
- 1  teaspoon balsamic vinegar
- 2  tablespoons chopped fresh flat-leaf parsley
   Coarse salt and freshly ground pepper
   Crudités, bread, and crackers, for serving

**1.** Roast eggplant over a gas burner or under the broiler until blackened and soft, turning as needed, about 35 minutes. Set aside to cool. Remove skin; discard. Coarsely chop eggplant; drain in a colander 15 minutes.

**2.** In a serving bowl, combine eggplant, tomato, onion, oil, vinegar, and parsley; season with salt and pepper. Serve at room temperature with crudités, bread, and crackers.

## leek dip with crudité

MAKES 3½ CUPS

*We served dip with cucumber, cauliflower, fennel, daikon radishes, jícama, kohlrabi, and celery.*

- ¼  cup slivered almonds
- 2  tablespoons unsalted butter
- 2  medium leeks, white and pale-green parts only, thinly sliced, washed well and dried
- 2  cups sour cream
- 1  log (14 ounces) fresh goat cheese
- 1  tablespoon chopped fresh flat-leaf parsley
   Coarse salt and freshly ground pepper
   Crudités, for serving

**1.** Preheat oven to 350°F. Spread slivered almonds on a rimmed baking sheet; toast until lightly golden, about 10 minutes. Let cool. Coarsely chop.

**2.** Melt butter in a medium sauté pan over medium-low heat, and add leeks. Sauté until soft and translucent, about 5 minutes. Set aside to cool.

**3.** Place sour cream and goat cheese in a medium bowl, and stir until combined. Add reserved almonds and leeks with the parsley; season with salt and pepper. Keep covered with plastic wrap in the refrigerator, up to 1 day. Serve with crudités.

## pomegranate dipping sauce with walnut chicken strips

*photograph on page 30*

MAKES ABOUT 2 CUPS SAUCE
AND 4 DOZEN PIECES

*When juicing a pomegranate, you need not separate the seeds first; just halve it, and crush each section with a citrus reamer.*

### for chicken strips:

1½ cups coarsely chopped walnuts
(about 6 ounces)

¾ cup all-purpose flour

1½ teaspoons coarse salt

½ teaspoon ground cinnamon

¼ teaspoon freshly ground pepper

1 cup heavy cream

4 boneless and skinless chicken breasts (about 2 pounds)

½ to ¾ cup vegetable oil

### for sauce:

2 tablespoons unsalted butter

2 small shallots, finely chopped

½ cup finely chopped walnuts
(about 2 ounces)

½ cup dry white wine

1½ cups homemade or low-sodium canned chicken stock

½ cup freshly squeezed pomegranate juice
(about ½ pomegranate)

2 tablespoons pomegranate molasses

2 tablespoons all-purpose flour

1 cup pomegranate seeds
(1 large pomegranate)

Coarse salt and freshly ground pepper

**1.** Preheat oven to 350°F. Make chicken strips: Place walnuts, flour, salt, cinnamon, and pepper in a food processor. Process until finely chopped and well combined; transfer to a shallow bowl. Pour heavy cream into another shallow bowl.

**2.** On a clean work surface, place chicken between two pieces of plastic wrap or waxed paper. Using a meat pounder, flatten to an even thickness, about ½ inch. Cut chicken into ½-by-3-inch strips. Working with one at a time, dip strips in heavy cream with one hand, letting excess drip off; using your other hand, dredge in flour mixture, turning to coat both sides and tapping off excess. Place on a baking sheet.

**3.** Heat 2 tablespoons oil in a large skillet over medium-high heat. Working in batches, add chicken strips; cook, turning occasionally, until golden brown all over, about 3 minutes. Transfer to a wire rack set over a rimmed baking sheet. Wipe out skillet; repeat with remaining chicken, adding 2 tablespoons oil with each batch. Transfer baking sheet with chicken to oven, and bake until chicken is cooked through, about 10 minutes.

**4.** Meanwhile, make sauce: Melt butter in a clean skillet over medium heat. Add shallots and walnuts; cook until shallots are tender and nuts are golden, about 2 minutes. Add wine; cook until most of the liquid has evaporated. Add 1¼ cups stock, the pomegranate juice, and molasses. Raise heat to medium high, and cook until liquid is reduced by half, about 10 minutes.

**5.** Whisk together remaining ¼ cup stock with flour in a bowl until well combined. Stir into sauce; simmer until thickened, about 1 minute. Stir in pomegranate seeds; season with salt and pepper. Serve hot with chicken strips.

## roasted red-pepper and walnut dip

MAKES 2¼ CUPS; SERVES 10 TO 12

*For best results, make the dip a day ahead to let the flavors mellow and blend. Serve with toasted pita triangles.*

- 3   red bell peppers (about 1 pound)
- 1   six-inch pita bread (2 ounces)
- 1   small garlic clove
- ¾   cup toasted walnut pieces (4 ounces), plus more for garnish
- 1½  teaspoons paprika, plus more for garnish
- ¾   teaspoon ground cumin
- 1   tablespoon balsamic vinegar
- 1   tablespoon freshly squeezed lemon juice
- 2   teaspoons extra-virgin olive oil, plus more for drizzling
- ¾   teaspoon coarse salt
  Freshly ground black pepper

**1.** Roast peppers over a gas burner or under the broiler until blackened all over, turning with tongs as each side is blistered. Transfer to a bowl, and cover with plastic wrap; let stand about 15 minutes. Peel, and discard skins, stems, and seeds. Set peppers aside.

**2.** Toast pita bread until crisp and golden. Break into 2-inch pieces; place in a bowl, and cover with water. Soak until soft, about 10 minutes. Transfer to a sieve; drain well, pressing out excess water.

**3.** Combine garlic and walnuts in a food processor; process until fine crumbs form, about 10 seconds. Add paprika, cumin, and reserved peppers and pita bread; process until smooth, about 10 seconds. Add vinegar, lemon juice, oil, and salt; season with black pepper. Pulse to combine.

**4.** Transfer to a serving bowl; cover with plastic wrap. Refrigerate at least 1 hour or overnight. Before serving, bring to room temperature. Drizzle with oil; garnish with walnuts and paprika.

## eggplant-pomegranate relish

MAKES ABOUT 2⅓ CUPS

*Serve with toasted pita bread or lavash.*

- 1   large eggplant (about 1½ pounds)
- 2   tablespoons plain yogurt
- 1   tablespoon pomegranate molasses
- 1   tablespoon freshly squeezed lemon juice
  Coarse salt and freshly ground pepper
- ½   red onion, cut into ¼-inch pieces
- 1   garlic clove, minced
- ½   cup chopped toasted walnuts (about 2 ounces)
- ½   cup pomegranate seeds (about ½ pomegranate)
- 2   tablespoons finely chopped fresh flat-leaf parsley

**1.** Heat broiler. Place eggplant on a baking sheet, and pierce a few times with a fork. Cook, turning occasionally as skin blackens, until very tender, about 35 minutes. Remove from oven, and let cool.

**2.** Scrape flesh of eggplant into a food processor; discard skin. Add yogurt, molasses, and lemon juice; season with salt and pepper. Pulse a few times until almost smooth, but with some chunks remaining.

**3.** Transfer mixture to a serving bowl; stir in onion, garlic, walnuts, pomegranate seeds, and parsley. Cover with plastic wrap; chill until ready to serve.

## pear caponata
SERVES 8

*This relish is also delicious as a side dish with roasted pork or poultry.*

1   can (28 ounces) peeled Italian plum tomatoes
1   medium eggplant (about 1 pound)
    Coarse salt
¼   cup plus 2 tablespoons olive oil
2   teaspoons sugar, plus more for seasoning
1   large onion, coarsely chopped
2   garlic cloves, minced
2   tablespoons capers
2   Bosc, Anjou, or Bartlett pears
¼   cup currants
2   teaspoons balsamic vinegar
    Freshly ground pepper
1   baguette (10 inches), sliced diagonally and toasted

**1.** Drain tomatoes, reserving juice. Seed tomatoes, chop coarsely, and set aside.

**2.** Slice eggplant into ¾-inch rounds. Place on a wire rack. Sprinkle with salt; let drain 30 minutes. Rinse well and pat dry. Cut slices into ¾-inch cubes.

**3.** Preheat oven to 425°F. Heat a 12-by-14-inch baking pan in oven 5 minutes. In a bowl, toss eggplant with ¼ cup oil and 1 teaspoon sugar, then spread out in pan. Return to oven; roast until eggplant is tender and well browned, about 25 minutes, shaking pan after 15 minutes. Remove from oven.

**4.** In a large sauté pan, heat 1 tablespoon oil over medium heat. Add onion and garlic; cook, stirring, until golden, about 7 minutes. Add eggplant, reserved tomatoes and ⅔ cup tomato juice, and capers. Cook, stirring occasionally, over medium-low heat 10 minutes. Remove from heat; keep warm.

**5.** Return baking pan to oven 5 minutes. Peel pears, and cut into ¾-inch chunks. In a bowl, toss with remaining tablespoon oil and teaspoon sugar; spread out in warmed pan. Roast until pears are tender and golden brown, about 25 minutes, shaking pan after 15 minutes. Remove from oven.

**6.** Add pears and currants to eggplant mixture in skillet. Stir in vinegar; season with sugar, salt, and pepper. Cook over medium heat until heated through, 5 to 10 minutes. Add more tomato juice, as needed, to keep caponata from becoming dry. Serve warm on toasted bread.

## herbed goat-cheese spread
MAKES 2 CUPS; SERVES 8 TO 10

*Serve this tangy spread with crackers.*

1   package (8 ounces) cream cheese, room temperature
1   log (11 ounces) fresh goat cheese, room temperature
¾   teaspoon coarse salt
¼   teaspoon freshly ground pepper
4   teaspoons freshly squeezed lemon juice (about ½ lemon)
3   tablespoons chopped fresh flat-leaf parsley
1   tablespoon chopped fresh tarragon
1   tablespoon chopped fresh dill
1   tablespoon snipped fresh chives

In a food processor, combine cream cheese and goat cheese; process until smooth and creamy. Add salt, pepper, lemon juice, parsley, tarragon, dill, and chives; pulse until thoroughly combined, scraping down sides of bowl as needed. Transfer spread to an airtight container. Refrigerate until ready to serve, up to 2 days.

## three-peppercorn spread

SERVES 8

*This pretty and easy appetizer is delicious with toasted whole-grain bread or crackers.*

- 1 log (5½ ounces) fresh goat cheese, room temperature
- 1½ teaspoons coarsely ground black pepper, plus more for garnish
- 1½ teaspoons whole pink peppercorns, plus more for garnish
- 1½ teaspoons whole green peppercorns, plus more for garnish
- 2 teaspoons extra-virgin olive oil

**1.** Place goat cheese in a small bowl. Add black pepper and pink and green peppercorns. Stir until combined.

**2.** Line an 8-ounce ramekin or 1-cup bowl with plastic wrap. Transfer cheese mixture to ramekin or bowl, and press down with the back of a spoon. Unmold mixture onto a serving plate. Smooth surface with a heated knife, and drizzle with oil. Garnish with pepper and peppercorns.

## triple-crème cheese with armagnac-soaked raisins

SERVES 8 TO 10

*Raisins can be soaked for up to one month ahead, and kept refrigerated. Serve with crackers.*

- ½ cup golden raisins
- ¼ cup Armagnac
- 1 whole rindless triple-crème cheese, such as Brillat-Savarin (1⅓ pounds)

**1.** In a nonreactive container, combine raisins and Armagnac. Let stand at room temperature 24 hours; refrigerate if not using immediately.

**2.** When ready to serve, bring cheese to room temperature; place on a serving plate. Pour raisins and soaking liquid over cheese.

## chicken liver pâté with white truffles

*photograph on page 33*

MAKES 2 CUPS; SERVES 8 TO 10

*If making ahead, top pâté with a layer of melted butter to prevent discoloration.*

- ½ cup (1 stick) unsalted butter, room temperature, plus more for serving dish
- ⅓ cup olive oil
- ½ cup finely diced yellow onion
- 1 pound chicken livers, trimmed and halved
  Coarse salt and freshly ground pepper
- 6 tablespoons Cognac
- 1 small fresh white or black truffle (about 1 ounce)

**1.** Butter the inside of a small crock or terrine mold; set aside. Heat oil in a large skillet over medium-low heat. Add onion; cook, stirring frequently, until translucent, 8 to 10 minutes. Reduce heat to low; add livers, and season with salt and pepper. Cook, stirring frequently, until just cooked through, about 15 minutes. Transfer liver mixture to a bowl until completely cool.

**2.** Return skillet to medium heat; add Cognac to pan juices. Tilt pan to ignite Cognac; cook until most of the liquid has evaporated, about 4 minutes. Remove from heat; set aside until completely cool.

**3.** In a food processor, combine reserved liver mixture and the pan juices. Chop truffle; add truffle and butter to the food processor. Process until smooth. Season with salt and pepper. Transfer pâté to prepared crock, and smooth top. Cover, and refrigerate until ready to serve, up to 3 days.

## vegetarian pâté

MAKES 3 CUPS; SERVES 12 TO 14

5   *large eggs*

¼   *pound string beans, trimmed and cut into 1-inch pieces*

1   *tablespoon unsalted butter*

1   *red onion, cut into ¼-inch dice (1 cup)*

¾   *cup toasted walnuts (3 ounces)*

1   *tablespoon soy sauce*

2   *tablespoons mayonnaise*

1   *tablespoon olive oil*

2   *tablespoons finely chopped fresh chives*
    *Coarse salt and freshly ground pepper*
    *Bread or crackers, for serving*

**1.** Prepare an ice bath; set aside. Place eggs in a medium saucepan with enough water to cover by 2 inches. Place over high heat; bring to a boil. Turn off heat; cover. Let stand 12 minutes. Transfer eggs to ice bath to stop cooking. When eggs are cool, peel under cold running water; cut into quarters, and set aside.

**2.** Return cooking water to a boil; blanch string beans 2 to 3 minutes. Transfer to ice bath to stop cooking. Drain; dry on paper towels.

**3.** Melt butter in a medium sauté pan over medium heat. Add onion; cook, stirring occasionally, until lightly caramelized, 8 to 10 minutes. Remove from heat; let cool to room temperature.

**4.** In a food processor, combine eggs, string beans, walnuts, soy sauce, mayonnaise, and oil. Pulse until finely chopped but not puréed. Transfer to a bowl; stir in sautéed onion and the chives. Season with salt and pepper. Serve at room temperature with bread or crackers.

## wild mushroom pâté

SERVES 12

*The pâté, which should be chilled at least eight hours, may be made up to one day ahead. To make toast points for serving, remove crusts from thinly sliced white sandwich bread; cut into triangles, and toast just until golden.*

1   *cup finely chopped walnuts (4 ounces), plus more for garnish*

6   *tablespoons unsalted butter*

2½   *pounds assorted fresh mushrooms, such as cremini, shiitake, portobello, and white button, cleaned and coarsely chopped, plus 14 to 16 small mushrooms, halved, for garnish*

6   *scallions, white and pale-green parts only, finely chopped*

1½   *tablespoons fresh thyme leaves, finely chopped, plus more for garnish*
    *Coarse salt and freshly ground pepper*

⅓   *cup dry sherry*
    *Juice of 1 lemon*

1   *cup packed fresh flat-leaf parsley, finely chopped*
    *Dash of hot-pepper sauce, such as Tabasco*

1   *package (8 ounces) cream cheese, room temperature*
    *Toast points, for serving*

**1.** Preheat oven to 350°F. Spread walnuts in a rimmed baking sheet. Toast until fragrant, about 7 minutes, shaking pan occasionally. Transfer walnuts to a bowl; set aside to cool.

**2.** In a large heavy skillet over medium heat, melt 4 tablespoons butter; cook chopped mushrooms and scallions, stirring occasionally, until mushrooms have released their liquid and the skillet is almost dry, about 20 minutes.

**3.** Stir thyme, salt, and pepper into mushroom mixture; cook 2 minutes more. Add sherry, and cook, stirring, until skillet is almost dry, about 4 minutes. Stir in lemon juice. Remove from heat, and let cool.

**4.** In a large bowl, combine mushroom mixture with toasted walnuts, parsley, hot sauce, and cream cheese. Season with salt and pepper.

**5.** Line a 12¼-by-4-by-3-inch terrine mold (or 6-cup mold) with plastic wrap, leaving a 4-inch overhang on all sides. Spoon mushroom mixture into terrine. Firmly press down all over terrine with the back of a spoon, spreading mixture as evenly as possible. Cover mold with overhanging plastic wrap; refrigerate at least 8 hours or overnight.

**6.** Just before serving, melt remaining 2 tablespoons butter in a medium skillet; cook halved mushrooms just until tender, about 5 minutes. Remove from heat; season with salt and pepper.

**7.** Unwrap chilled terrine, and invert it onto a large serving platter. Drape a warm, wet kitchen towel over the mold, if necessary, to help loosen the pâté. Garnish platter with cooked mushroom halves, walnuts, and thyme. Serve pâté with toast points.

## finnan-haddie canapés
*photograph on page 35*
SERVES 6

*Smoked haddock, known as finnan haddie after the Scottish village Findon, is available in some fish markets. Salt cod makes a good substitute; soak it twelve hours, changing water several times, and begin with step two.*

- ¼ pound smoked haddock or salt cod
- 4 cups milk
- 1 garlic clove
- 6 sprigs thyme, plus more for garnish
- 1 small potato, peeled and quartered
- 2 tablespoons heavy cream
    Coarse salt and freshly ground pepper
- 3 tablespoons freshly grated horseradish, plus more as needed
- 1 baguette (12 inches), sliced ¼ inch thick on the diagonal
- 1 tablespoon olive oil

**1.** Place smoked haddock in a large bowl, and cover with cold water. Soak fish 4 hours, changing water every 30 minutes.

**2.** Remove fish from water; discard any bones. Transfer fish to a saucepan. Add milk, garlic, thyme, and potato. Set over medium-low heat; simmer until fish is very soft, about 1 hour. Pour mixture through a sieve set over a bowl; discard thyme and milk. Transfer solids to a large bowl.

**3.** Preheat oven to 400°F. Using a fork, gently mash fish, potato, and garlic, adding enough cream to make a thick paste. Season with salt and pepper, and stir in horseradish.

**4.** Place bread slices on a baking sheet, and toast until golden. Brush toast with oil; spread fish paste on top. Garnish with thyme. Serve immediately.

## crunchy chicken salad on brioche

MAKES ABOUT 4 DOZEN

1 loaf brioche or white bread, thinly sliced

3½ cups homemade or low-sodium canned chicken stock

1 boneless and skinless chicken breast (12 ounces)

1 Granny Smith apple

Juice of 1 lemon

½ cup diced celery

½ cup mayonnaise

1 tablespoon chopped fresh tarragon, plus more for garnish

1½ teaspoons coarse salt

¼ teaspoon freshly ground pepper

**1.** Preheat oven to 350°F. Using a 2-inch cookie cutter, cut out about 4 dozen rounds from the brioche slices. Place rounds on a baking sheet; transfer to oven until they are lightly toasted, about 3 minutes per side.

**2.** Place stock in a medium saucepan; bring to a boil. Add chicken breast; reduce heat to a simmer. Poach until chicken is cooked through, about 15 minutes. Drain, reserving stock for another use; set chicken aside to cool, then shred into bite-size pieces.

**3.** Peel and core apple; cut into ¼-inch dice. Place in a large bowl, and toss with lemon juice to coat. Add shredded chicken, celery, mayonnaise, tarragon, salt, and pepper.

**4.** When ready to serve, top each brioche toast with 1 heaping teaspoon chicken salad; garnish with a pinch of freshly chopped tarragon.

## shrimp-salad rolls

photograph on page 35

SERVES 6

Look for the smallest shrimp available. Serve the salad on Parker House Rolls (page 116) or other small dinner rolls.

1 pound small shrimp, peeled and deveined

1 tablespoon unsalted butter

Coarse salt and freshly ground pepper

3 tablespoons freshly squeezed lemon juice (about 1 lemon), plus more as needed

¾ cup mayonnaise

1 scallion, finely chopped

24 Parker House Rolls (page 116) or other small rolls

1 small head Bibb lettuce, washed and trimmed

**1.** Rinse shrimp under cold running water, and pat dry. Heat butter in a large skillet over medium heat. Add shrimp; season with salt and pepper. Cook shrimp until bright pink and opaque, about 2 minutes per side. Add lemon juice; remove from heat.

**2.** When shrimp are cool, cut into ½-inch pieces. In a large bowl, combine shrimp, mayonnaise, and scallion; toss to combine. Season shrimp salad with salt, pepper, and more lemon juice, if desired. Cover with plastic; refrigerate until chilled.

**3.** To serve, split open the rolls. Gently press a lettuce leaf into each roll, and fill with a heaping teaspoon of shrimp salad. Serve.

## shrimp bruschetta
MAKES 6 TO 8

*If using medium shrimp, halve them crosswise through the back, and devein.*

- 1 loaf rustic bread, sliced ¾ inch thick
- 1 tablespoon olive oil, plus more for brushing
- 1 tablespoon minced garlic (about 1 clove)
- 2 teaspoons sliced red chile pepper
- 1½ pounds rock or medium shrimp, peeled
- 1 cup dry white wine
- ¼ cup packed chopped fresh flat-leaf parsley
  Coarse salt and freshly ground black pepper

**1.** Heat grill or grill pan. Brush bread with oil; grill until golden brown on both sides, turning once.

**2.** Heat a cast-iron skillet over medium heat on grill or stove. Add 1 tablespoon oil. When hot, add garlic and chile; sauté until lightly browned, 2 to 3 minutes. Add shrimp; cook, stirring, until pink and opaque, about 3 minutes.

**3.** Add wine to skillet, and cook, stirring up any browned bits from bottom of pan, until liquid has reduced by half, about 5 minutes. Remove from heat. Stir in parsley, and season with salt and pepper. Top each bread slice with shrimp mixture, and serve warm.

## grilled porcini mushroom and goat cheese crostini
MAKES 4

*Look for crottins that have a thick rind.*

- 2 to 4 fresh porcini mushrooms
- ¼ cup olive oil, plus more for brushing and drizzling
  Coarse salt and freshly ground pepper
- 4 slices rustic bread
- 4 goat-cheese crottins (2 ounces each)
- 1 bunch watercress, trimmed

**1.** Heat grill or grill pan to medium hot. Clean mushrooms: Scrape dirt from stem ends with a mushroom brush or paper towel. Cut mushrooms lengthwise into ½-inch-thick slices, keeping cap and stem attached as much as possible.

**2.** Place mushrooms in a large bowl, and add ¼ cup olive oil; season with salt and pepper, and toss gently to combine. Immediately arrange mushrooms on grill. (If working in batches, add oil and seasonings just before grilling.) Grill until golden outside and soft inside, about 3 minutes per side. Set mushrooms aside.

**3.** Arrange bread and cheese on grill; cook until bread is well toasted and cheese is hot in the center, about 3 minutes per side. Brush bread with oil.

**4.** To serve, spread cheese on the bread, top with mushroom slices, and drizzle with oil. Serve watercress on the side.

## lentil stars

MAKES 2 DOZEN

2 dozen slices white sandwich bread

2 tablespoons unsalted butter, melted

⅓ cup French green lentils

1 cup homemade or low-sodium canned chicken stock

5 garlic cloves

10 sprigs thyme

2 tablespoons vegetable oil

1 slice slab bacon (about 1 ounce)

Freshly ground pepper

1. Preheat oven to 350°F. Using a 2½-inch star-shaped cookie cutter, cut a star from each slice of bread. Brush each star with melted butter, and place on a parchment-lined baking sheet. Toast in oven until golden brown, 8 to 10 minutes. Transfer stars to a wire rack.

2. In a medium saucepan, combine lentils, stock, 2 garlic cloves, and 7 thyme sprigs. Cover, and bring to a boil. Uncover, reduce heat to medium-low, and simmer until lentils are tender, about 25 minutes. Pick leaves from remaining 3 thyme sprigs, and set leaves aside.

3. Meanwhile, thinly slice the remaining 3 garlic cloves. Heat oil in a small skillet over medium heat. Add garlic; cook until lightly golden, about 2 minutes. Transfer to a paper towel–lined plate.

4. Pour oil from skillet; return to medium heat. Add bacon, and cook until browned, 4 to 6 minutes. Drain on paper towels, and dice finely. Add cooked lentils and bacon to hot skillet; toss well. Season with pepper.

5. To serve, spoon some lentil mixture on each toasted star. Garnish with a slice of sautéed garlic and a few reserved thyme leaves.

## apricot-onion tartlets

*photograph on page 32*

MAKES 2 DOZEN

*If the pan begins to get too dry while the onions are cooking, add a few tablespoons of water. Taleggio cheese, made from cow's milk, has an edible rind, a creamy interior, and a nutty flavor. You can substitute another soft aged cheese.*

2 tablespoons olive oil

4 white onions (about 2 pounds), thinly sliced

1 tablespoon sugar

¼ cup brandy

Pinch of crushed red-pepper flakes

½ cup dried apricots (about 4 ounces), finely chopped

Coarse salt and freshly ground black pepper

3 tablespoons fresh thyme leaves

Walnut Tartlet Shells (recipe follows)

½ pound Taleggio or other soft cheese

1. Heat oil in a large skillet over medium heat. Add onions and sugar; cook, stirring occasionally, until dark brown and caramelized, about 40 minutes. Add brandy; deglaze pan, stirring up any browned bits from bottom of skillet with a wooden spoon.

2. Stir red-pepper flakes and apricots into onion mixture; season with salt and pepper. Cook until all liquid has evaporated. Stir in 2 tablespoons thyme. Remove from heat.

3. Preheat oven to 350°F. Place tartlet shells on a baking sheet. Cut cheese into 24 equal pieces; place 1 slice in each tartlet shell. Spoon 1 to 2 tablespoons onion mixture on top of each shell.

4. Bake tartlets until cheese melts, 5 to 8 minutes. Sprinkle with remaining tablespoon thyme; serve.

## walnut tartlet shells
### MAKES 2 DOZEN

*If you don't have forty-eight tartlet pans (you'll need two for each shell), bake shells in batches.*

- 2 cups all-purpose flour, plus more for work surface
- ¼ teaspoon salt
- ½ cup (2 ounces) walnuts
- ¾ cup (1½ sticks) chilled unsalted butter, cut into small pieces
- ¼ cup ice water

**1.** Place flour, salt, and walnuts in a food processor. Pulse until small but not fine crumbs form. Add butter; pulse until pea-size clumps remain.

**2.** With the machine running, gradually add the ice water through the feed tube; pulse until dough just starts to come together when you pinch it with your fingers. If dough is crumbly, add 1 to 2 more tablespoons cold water; pulse to combine.

**3.** Form dough into a ball. Flatten into a disk, and wrap in plastic. Refrigerate at least 1 hour.

**4.** Preheat oven to 350°F. Place twenty-four 2-inch tartlet pans on a large rimmed baking sheet. On a lightly floured work surface, roll out dough to about ⅛ inch thick. Using a paring knife, cut dough into twenty-four squares slightly larger than pans. Press dough into pans; trim edges. Gently press a second tartlet pan into each lined pan to help hold shape. Refrigerate 30 minutes.

**5.** Transfer sheet to oven; bake tartlet shells until edges are lightly browned, about 10 minutes. Remove top pans; continue baking until crust is cooked through and golden all over, 12 to 15 minutes more. Remove from oven; invert shells onto wire racks to cool. Store shells in an airtight container up to 3 days, or freeze up to 1 month; thaw frozen shells at room temperature before using.

## brie en croute
*photograph on page 34*
### SERVES 12

*All-purpose flour, for work surface*

- 1 package (17.3 ounces) frozen puff pastry, thawed
- 1 round (8 inches) ripe brie
- 1 large egg, lightly beaten with a pinch of salt, for egg wash

**1.** On a lightly floured work surface, roll out 1 sheet of puff pastry into a 12-inch square. Using a large plate as a guide, cut out a 12-inch round with a paring knife. Transfer round to a parchment-lined baking sheet. Place cheese in the center; fold pastry just over edge of cheese, and crimp edge.

**2.** Roll out the second pastry sheet into a 12-inch square. Using a cake pan as a guide, cut out an 8-inch round.

**3.** Brush egg wash over crimped edge of dough. Place smaller round on top; gently press against crimped edge to seal.

**4.** Use a ⅝-inch pastry tip to cut out rounds from remaining dough for a decorative grape garnish, if desired. Using a paring knife, cut out stem and vine tendrils from dough. Brush top of cheese package with egg wash; gently press grapes on top to form a cluster. Press stem and tendrils in place. Carefully brush surface with egg wash. Refrigerate at least 30 minutes.

**5.** Preheat oven to 400°F. Transfer cheese package to a baking sheet. Bake 10 minutes, then reduce oven temperature to 350°F. Continue baking until pastry is golden brown, 35 to 40 minutes more. Transfer to a wire rack to cool about 30 minutes before serving.

## cheese straws and poppy-seed straws

*photograph on page 32*

MAKES ABOUT 40

*To keep the twist in the cheese straws, it is essential that they be very cold when they go into a very hot oven. The standard size for one sheet of store-bought frozen puff pastry is a ten-inch square. To toast sesame seeds, spread in a small skillet; cook over medium heat, shaking pan frequently, until golden, about three minutes.*

- 1 to 2 ounces Parmesan cheese, grated on the small holes of a box grater (about ⅓ cup)
- 1 teaspoon cayenne pepper
- 3 tablespoons sesame seeds, lightly toasted
- 3 tablespoons poppy seeds
- 1½ teaspoons coarse salt
- 1 sheet frozen puff pastry (from a 17.3-ounce package), thawed
- 1 large egg, lightly beaten

**1.** In a small bowl, combine cheese and cayenne pepper. In another small bowl, combine sesame and poppy seeds with the salt. Set both aside.

**2.** Place puff pastry on a work surface. Cut in half. Brush each half with beaten egg. Sprinkle one half with cheese mixture and the other with seed mixture. Using a pastry cutter or paring knife, cut each half crosswise into twenty ½-inch-wide strips.

**3.** Working one at a time, twist each strip into a spiral; transfer to parchment-lined baking sheets, placing them ½ inch apart. Using your thumb, press ends of strips down into the parchment to help twists hold their shape.

**4.** Preheat oven to 425°F, with racks in upper and lower thirds. Transfer baking sheets to freezer; chill until dough is very firm, at least 20 minutes. Check strips periodically to make sure they stay twisted.

**5.** Bake straws until golden, 10 to 15 minutes, rotating baking sheets halfway through. Transfer straws to wire racks to cool completely. Store straws in an airtight container at room temperature up to 1 day.

## cheese coins with jalapeño jelly

MAKES ABOUT 6 DOZEN

*Logs of dough can be frozen for up to one month before baking. Coins can be baked up to one week in advance and stored at room temperature.*

- 2 cups all-purpose flour, plus more for work surface
- 1 teaspoon salt
- 1 teaspoon paprika
- ½ teaspoon cayenne pepper
- 1 cup (2 sticks) chilled unsalted butter, cut into small pieces
- 1 cup grated sharp cheddar cheese
- ⅓ cup jalapeño jelly

**1.** Combine flour, salt, paprika, and cayenne in a food processor; pulse to blend. Add butter; pulse until mixture resembles coarse meal. Add cheese; process until dough starts to hold together.

**2.** Turn out dough onto a lightly floured surface. Knead a few times. Divide into four equal pieces, and roll each into a log about 1 inch in diameter. Wrap in plastic, and chill until firm, at least 1 hour and up to 3 days.

**3.** Preheat oven to 350°F. Cut dough into ⅓-inch-thick rounds, and place 2 inches apart on parchment-lined baking sheets. Bake until rounds are lightly browned, about 20 minutes, rotating sheets halfway through. Let cool on baking sheets 1 minute, then transfer to wire racks.

4. When ready to serve, warm the jalapeño jelly in a small saucepan over low heat until almost melted, 10 to 15 minutes. Remove from heat. Spoon jelly onto center of each coin, making sure to get some pepper flecks on each one.

## goat cheese and spinach triangles

### MAKES 2 DOZEN

*Once formed, triangles may be frozen for up to one week before baking; transfer them directly from the freezer to the oven.*

⅓ cup olive oil

6 large scallions, white and pale-green parts only, finely chopped

2 packages (10 ounces each) frozen chopped spinach, thawed, liquid reserved, or 3 pounds fresh spinach, trimmed and washed well, with water clinging to leaves

1 bunch fresh flat-leaf parsley, leaves roughly chopped (about 1 cup)

1 bunch fresh dill, roughly chopped (about 1 cup)

1 log (12 ounces) fresh goat cheese, crumbled, room temperature

2 large eggs, lightly beaten
 Coarse salt and freshly ground pepper

1 package (16 ounces) phyllo dough

2 cups (4 sticks) unsalted butter, melted and kept warm

1. Heat oil in a large skillet over medium heat. Add scallions, and cook, stirring frequently, until translucent, about 4 minutes. Add spinach and reserved liquid, and cook until heated through, about 1 minute. Transfer mixture to a clean kitchen towel or cheesecloth; wring out liquid into a bowl. Reserve 2 tablespoons liquid.

2. In a food processor, combine spinach and reserved liquid with parsley, dill, goat cheese, and eggs. Season with salt and pepper, and pulse until thoroughly combined.

3. Preheat oven to 375°F, with racks in upper and lower thirds. On a clean work surface, lay phyllo sheets flat between damp paper towels. Place one phyllo sheet flat on work surface; brush with butter. Place second phyllo sheet on top; brush with butter. Cut stacked phyllo lengthwise into four strips, each about 3 inches wide.

4. Working with one strip at a time, place 2 tablespoons spinach mixture at one end, in a corner. Fold corner over to form a small triangle; brush with melted butter. Fold triangle over again; brush with butter. Repeat until strip is rolled into a layered triangle; trim excess with a paring knife. Brush triangle with butter; place on a parchment-lined baking sheet. Repeat with remaining strips phyllo dough, filling, and butter.

5. Bake until golden, 15 to 20 minutes, rotating sheets halfway through. Transfer triangles to wire racks. Serve warm or at room temperature.

### HOW TO WORK WITH PHYLLO DOUGH

*If you can't find fresh phyllo dough, thaw frozen dough overnight in the refrigerator before using. In a pinch, you can defrost phyllo at room temperature in about an hour, but it may be harder to work with. Once thawed, unfold the dough and lay it flat on a work surface. Remove as many sheets as you will need for your recipe, plus one or two extra in case of tearing (chill the rest and reserve for another use, but do not refreeze). To prevent the dough from drying out, keep any unused portion covered with damp paper towels while you work (the sheets dry out very easily and cannot be saved). Mend any rips or tears in the dough by brushing them with melted butter or oil, and then patching with another piece of phyllo.*

**147**

## gougères

MAKES 12½ DOZEN

Pâte à Choux (recipe follows)

4  ounces Gruyère cheese, finely grated
   (1 cup), plus more for sprinkling

1  teaspoon salt

½  teaspoon freshly ground pepper

¼  teaspoon ground nutmeg

1  large egg, lightly beaten with 1 tablespoon
   water, for egg wash

   Vegetable oil, for plastic wrap

**1.** Preheat oven to 425°F, with rack in center. Line two baking sheets with parchment paper or Silpat baking mats; set aside. Add cheese, salt, pepper, and nutmeg to pâte à choux dough.

**2.** Fill a pastry bag fitted with a large round tip (we used an Ateco #804) with batter; pipe ¾-inch rounds about ½ inch high onto baking sheets, about 2 inches apart. Use your finger to gently coat tops with egg wash, being careful not to let wash drip onto surrounding baking sheet (it will inhibit rising). Sprinkle with grated cheese.

**3.** Cover one baking sheet with lightly oiled plastic wrap; place in refrigerator. Transfer other to oven. Bake 10 minutes; reduce oven temperature to 350°F. Continue baking until golden brown, about 15 minutes more. Turn off oven; prop open door slightly to let steam escape. Let gougères dry in oven until crisp, about 10 minutes. Transfer to a wire rack. Raise oven heat to 425°F. Repeat process with remaining baking sheet. Serve warm.

## pâte à choux

We used this dough to make Gougères. If not using immediately, the dough can be refrigerated in an airtight container up to two days (add the cheese and other ingredients in the Gougères recipe first). Remove dough from refrigerator, and stir to soften before filling piping bag.

½  cup (1 stick) unsalted butter

1  teaspoon sugar

½  teaspoon salt

1  cup all-purpose flour

4  large eggs, plus 1 lightly beaten

**1.** In a medium saucepan, combine 1 cup water with the butter, sugar, and salt. Bring to a boil over medium-high heat, and immediately remove from heat. Stir in the flour. Return to heat. (This mixture is called a panade.) Dry panade by stirring constantly for 4 minutes. It is ready when it pulls away from the sides and a film forms on bottom of pan.

**2.** Transfer panade to the bowl of an electric mixer; beat on low speed until slightly cooled, about 2 minutes. With mixer on medium speed, add eggs, one at a time, letting each one incorporate completely before adding the next. Add the beaten egg a little at a time, until batter is smooth and shiny. Test by touching it with your finger: If a string doesn't form, add more egg. If you have added all the egg and batter still doesn't form a string, add water 1 teaspoon at a time.

## guacamole
## and crab corn cups

### MAKES 4 DOZEN

- 2  ripe avocados, pitted and peeled
- 1  tablespoon freshly squeezed lime juice
- 6  cherry tomatoes, finely chopped
- ½  jalapeño chile, minced
- ¼  cup packed fresh cilantro, finely chopped, plus more sprigs for garnish
   Coarse salt and freshly ground pepper
   Toasted Corn Cups (recipe follows)
- 4  ounces fresh lump or king crabmeat

In a medium bowl, mash together avocado and lime juice until almost smooth. Add tomatoes, jalapeño, and cilantro; season with salt and pepper. Stir until combined. Place 2 teaspoons guacamole in each corn cup. Top each with a piece of crabmeat and a cilantro sprig.

### toasted corn cups

### MAKES 4 DOZEN

Corn cups may be made several days ahead and kept in an airtight container at room temperature or frozen up to three weeks. If using frozen cups, thaw at room temperature; spread them on a rimmed baking sheet, and warm in a 250-degree oven three to five minutes.

- 24  corn tortillas (6 inches each)
   Canola or corn oil, for brushing

**1.** Preheat oven to 350°F. Using a 2¾-inch cookie cutter, cut out 48 rounds from tortillas. Working in batches, place tortillas in a steamer basket set over a pan of simmering water until they are slightly softened and warm to the touch. Transfer to a baking sheet; brush both sides with oil.

**2.** Press half the rounds into a 24-cup mini-muffin tin. Bake until tortillas are crisp and just beginning to brown, about 20 minutes. Remove from oven; transfer cups to a wire rack to cool completely. Repeat with remaining tortillas.

## oven-baked
## sweet-potato chips

### MAKES ABOUT 3 DOZEN

These chips are made without any fat. For attractive, circular chips, look for sweet potatoes that are round rather than long. It is best to make very thin slices using a mandoline.

- 1  large sweet potato (about 9 ounces), rinsed and dried
   Coarse salt and freshly ground pepper

**1.** Preheat oven to 200°F, with racks in upper and lower thirds. Line two rimmed baking sheets with parchment paper, and set aside. Slice potato crosswise, as thinly as possible. Arrange slices on prepared sheets, leaving space in between. Sprinkle lightly with salt and pepper.

**2.** Place in oven; cook 50 minutes. Slices will be drying and shrinking; turn chips, and rotate baking sheets. Continue cooking until slices are crisp and fluted around edges and centers are still orange, not brown, 30 to 40 minutes more.

**3.** Transfer to wire racks; let cool on baking sheets. (Chips will be soft when removed from oven and will crisp as they cool.) Store in an airtight container, at room temperature, up to 3 days.

## porcini-stuffed mushrooms with camembert

MAKES 2 DOZEN

*If you can't find fresh porcini, substitute one ounce dried porcini and three ounces white button mushrooms; soak dried mushrooms in hot water ten minutes before using.*

- 1  *tablespoon unsalted butter*
- 1  *small shallot, minced*
- 4  *ounces fresh porcini mushrooms, roughly chopped*

    *Golden Mushroom Caps (recipe follows), stems reserved, cleaned, and roughly chopped*
- 2  *tablespoons dry white wine*

    *Coarse salt and freshly ground pepper*
- 3  *ounces Camembert cheese*

**1.** Melt butter in a medium skillet over medium heat. Add shallot; cook until soft, 1 to 2 minutes. Add porcini mushrooms and reserved golden mushroom stems; cook until mushrooms have released their juices and most of the liquid has evaporated, 4 to 5 minutes. Add wine; deglaze pan by stirring up any browned bits from the bottom with a wooden spoon. Continue cooking until wine has evaporated, 1 to 3 minutes. Season with salt and pepper; remove from heat.

**2.** Heat broiler. Slice Camembert into 24 small pieces, about ½ inch each; set aside. Using a small spoon, fill golden mushroom caps with porcini mushroom mixture.

**3.** Place caps on a baking sheet. Broil until heated through, 2 to 3 minutes. Remove from oven; place a cheese slice on each mushroom. Serve.

## golden mushroom caps

MAKES 2 DOZEN

- 24  *small white button mushrooms*

    *Extra-virgin olive oil, for brushing*

    *Coarse salt and freshly ground pepper*

**1.** Preheat oven to 400°F. Remove stems from mushrooms; reserve for the filling. Clean caps with a damp paper towel or mushroom brush. Brush each with oil; sprinkle with salt and pepper.

**2.** Place mushroom caps, cavity side down, on a baking sheet. Roast until mushrooms are golden and beginning to release liquid, 6 to 7 minutes. Transfer to paper towels, cavity side down; let drain. Once cooled, mushroom caps can be stored in an airtight container up to 4 hours.

## sun-dried tomato palmiers

*photograph on page 33*

MAKES ABOUT 1 DOZEN

*Sun-dried tomato halves can be used in place of tomato paste: Cover fifteen halves with boiling water, and let stand until softened, about five minutes. Drain, then purée in a food processor with three tablespoons olive oil. For sun-dried tomatoes packed in oil, simply remove fifteen halves from oil; process until puréed.*

- 1  *package (17.3 ounces) frozen puff pastry, thawed*
- 6  *tablespoons ricotta cheese*
- 6  *tablespoons sun-dried tomato paste*
- 1  *cup grated Parmesan cheese (4 ounces)*

**1.** On a clean work surface, roll out one sheet of pastry into a rectangle about ⅛ inch thick. Trim to approximately 8 by 11 inches. Spread half the ricotta over pastry. Spread half the sun-dried tomato paste on top. Sprinkle with half the Parmesan. Roll each long edge of the pastry into the center of the rectangle, making sure pastry is tight and even (see page 427). Repeat process with the remaining sheet of pastry, ricotta, tomato paste, and Parmesan.

**2.** Wrap rolls separately with plastic wrap, and transfer to refrigerator until firm, about 30 minutes. (Rolls can be frozen at this point up to 1 month. When ready to bake, remove rolls from freezer; let stand at room temperature until a sharp knife can slice through without compressing them, about 10 minutes.)

**3.** Preheat oven to 425°F. Remove rolls from refrigerator, and cut into ½-inch-thick slices. Place 2 inches apart on a parchment-lined baking sheet. Bake until puffed and lightly golden, 8 to 9 minutes. Turn palmiers, and bake until golden, 5 to 6 minutes more. Let cool completely on a wire rack.

## twice-baked cheese strudel
*photograph on page 33*
SERVES 10 TO 12

*To prevent the phyllo dough from drying out, keep the unused portion covered with damp paper towels while you work. Logs can be frozen, wrapped tightly in plastic, for up to one month before baking.*

 7  *sheets frozen phyllo dough, thawed*
 ½  *cup (1 stick) unsalted butter, melted*
 ¾  *cup (12 tablespoons) finely grated Parmesan cheese*
 ½  *cup plus 2 tablespoons finely grated Asiago cheese*
 ½  *cup plus 2 tablespoons finely grated Pecorino Romano cheese*
5½  *tablespoons poppy seeds*

**1.** Preheat oven to 350°F. On a clean work surface, lay phyllo sheets flat between damp paper towels. Place one sheet flat on work surface; brush with butter. Place second phyllo sheet on top; brush with butter. Repeat with one more sheet of phyllo. Sprinkle third layer of buttered phyllo evenly with 2 tablespoons of each cheese and 1 tablespoon poppy seeds. Add four more layers, brushing with butter and sprinkling each with cheese and seeds, for a total of seven.

**2.** Carefully roll pastry and filling lengthwise into a tight log, no more than 1½ to 2 inches in diameter. Brush outside with butter, and sprinkle with remaining 2 tablespoons Parmesan and ½ tablespoon poppy seeds. Slice in half crosswise, and place on a parchment-lined baking sheet.

**3.** Bake until pastry is deep golden, 20 to 25 minutes. Transfer to a wire rack to cool slightly.

**4.** Using a serrated knife, cut logs into ½-inch-thick slices; return to baking sheet. Bake until golden throughout, about 10 minutes. Transfer to wire racks to cool. Serve warm or at room temperature.

## twice-cooked potatoes with caviar

MAKES 2 DOZEN

28  small red potatoes (about ¾ pound)

½  cup plus 2 tablespoons milk

1  tablespoon unsalted butter, plus 2 tablespoons melted, for brushing

¼  cup crème fraîche

1  tablespoon finely chopped fresh chives,
   plus more for garnish
   Coarse salt and freshly ground pepper

3  ounces sevruga, osetra, or American
   sturgeon (paddlefish) caviar

**1.** Place potatoes in a large saucepan, and cover with cold water. Bring to a boil; reduce heat, and simmer until tender but still quite firm when pierced with the tip of a sharp knife, 15 to 20 minutes. Remove all but 4 potatoes, and set aside; continue cooking 4 in pan until soft, about 5 minutes.

**2.** When cool enough to handle, carefully cut off the very tops of reserved potatoes. Using a melon baller, scoop out as much flesh as possible while leaving at least ¼-inch-thick shell. Place flesh in a small heatproof bowl set over a pan of simmering water. Peel and add remaining 4 potatoes. Cut a small slice off the bottom of each potato shell so it will stand upright.

**3.** Preheat oven to 375°F. Heat milk and 1 tablespoon butter in a small saucepan until butter melts. Push potato flesh through a ricer, food mill, or wide-mesh sieve into a bowl. Stir in milk and butter a little at a time until creamy. Stir in crème fraîche and chives; season with salt and pepper.

**4.** Place potato mixture in a pastry bag fitted with a large plain tip. Arrange potato shells on a rimmed baking sheet. Pipe filling into shells, making sure to cover cut edges.

**5.** Bake 15 minutes, or until filling is golden brown and slightly puffed. Brush with melted butter, and bake 15 minutes more. Top each potato with about ¼ teaspoon caviar, and sprinkle with chives.

## walnut blue-cheese coins

MAKES 30

These crackers are very rich with the taste of blue cheese, yet still quite light and crisp.

1  cup toasted walnuts (3¼ ounces)

¾  cup all-purpose flour, plus more for
   work surface

½  teaspoon coarse salt

¼  teaspoon freshly ground pepper

¼  teaspoon baking soda

2  tablespoons chilled unsalted butter,
   cut into small pieces

4  ounces blue cheese, crumbled
   Coarse salt, for sprinkling

**1.** In a food processor, finely grind ½ cup toasted walnuts. Add flour, salt, pepper, and baking soda; pulse to combine. Add butter; pulse until mixture resembles coarse meal. Add cheese; pulse until dough just comes together, about 15 times.

**2.** Preheat oven to 350°F. Transfer dough to a floured work surface; divide in half. Using your hands, roll one half into a 1½-inch-diameter log. Repeat with other half. Coarsely chop remaining ½ cup walnuts; sprinkle over a clean work surface. Roll logs in walnuts. Wrap each log separately in plastic; chill until firm, at least 3 hours.

**3.** Remove logs from refrigerator. Slice into ¼-inch-thick coins. Transfer to a baking sheet; sprinkle lightly with salt. Bake until centers are firm to the touch, about 15 minutes. Transfer to a wire rack to cool. Store in an airtight container up to 3 days.

SAVORY PANCAKES

## blini with caviar and cucumber-dill dressing

MAKES ABOUT 54

*Sourdough starter gives blinis their tangy flavor. They are delicious served with sour cream, smoked salmon, capers, and diced red onion.*

- 4  cups milk
- 10  large eggs
- 2  teaspoons salt
- 2  cups Rye Sourdough Starter (recipe follows)
- 4  cups all-purpose flour
- 1  cup rye flour
- 3  tablespoons unsalted butter, room temperature
- 3½  cups salmon roe
    Cucumber-Dill Dressing (recipe follows)

**1.** In a large bowl, whisk together milk, eggs, and salt. Add sourdough starter and the flours; whisk until mixture is well combined. Cover with a clean kitchen towel, and let stand 1 hour.

**2.** Preheat oven to 200°F. Heat a griddle or large cast-iron skillet over medium heat. Brush bottom with ½ teaspoon butter. Working in batches, ladle about ¼ cup batter (enough to make 4-inch blinis) onto griddle, being careful not to crowd pan; cook until bubbles form on surface and underside is golden brown, about 1 minute. Turn blinis; cook until underside is golden brown, about 1 minute.

**3.** Transfer to a large ovenproof plate or baking sheet, and place in oven. Repeat with remaining batter, brushing pan with ½ teaspoon butter before each batch. Serve hot, with salmon roe and cucumber-dill dressing on the side.

## rye sourdough starter

MAKES 3¼ CUPS

*Once it is fermented, the dough can be stored in the refrigerator indefinitely as long as it is replenished every two weeks by adding equal parts flour and water. You can substitute two cups starter for one quarter-ounce package active yeast in most recipes.*

- 1  teaspoon active dry yeast
- 1  cup warm water (about 110°F)
- 2  cups buttermilk, room temperature
- 2  tablespoons sugar
- 1¾  cups rye flour

**1.** In a large bowl, combine yeast with the warm water; let stand until foamy, about 5 minutes.

**2.** Stir buttermilk, sugar, and 1½ cups flour into yeast mixture. Cover with a clean kitchen towel; let stand in a warm place 24 hours. Whisk in remaining ¼ cup flour until well combined. Set aside, covered, at room temperature, another 24 hours before using or storing in a jar or airtight container.

## cucumber-dill dressing

MAKES 6 CUPS

- 2  cucumbers, peeled, seeded, and cut into ¼-inch pieces
- 2  cups mayonnaise
- 2  cups sour cream
- 1  small onion, finely chopped
- 1  large garlic clove, finely chopped
- ¼  cup finely chopped fresh dill
- 1  teaspoon freshly ground pepper
- ½  cup white vinegar

Stir together all ingredients in a large bowl. Cover with plastic wrap, and place in refrigerator until dressing is well chilled, at least 1 hour.

## buckwheat blinis with avocado and caviar

MAKES 4 DOZEN

1½  cups milk

1  teaspoon sugar

1  envelope active dry yeast
  (1 scant tablespoon)

¾  cup buckwheat flour

¾  cup all-purpose flour

½  teaspoon salt

4  tablespoons unsalted butter, melted

3  large egg yolks

1  ripe but firm avocado

2  large egg whites
  Vegetable oil, for frying
  Crème fraîche or sour cream, for garnish

12  ounces sevruga, salmon, or American
  sturgeon (paddlefish) caviar

**1.** Heat milk in a small saucepan until lukewarm. Transfer to a large bowl; stir in sugar and yeast, and let stand until foamy, about 5 minutes.

**2.** Whisk in flours, salt, butter, and egg yolks until smooth. Let rise, covered, in a warm place until doubled in bulk, about 1 hour.

**3.** Peel avocado, and cut into ¼-inch pieces; stir into batter. In a separate bowl, beat egg whites until stiff, and fold into batter.

**4.** Preheat oven to 200°F. Heat 1 tablespoon oil in a large nonstick skillet over medium-low heat. Add batter by the tablespoon, 1 inch apart. Cook until edges are golden brown, about 1 minute. Turn blinis, and cook 30 seconds. Transfer to a baking sheet; keep warm, covered loosely with foil, in oven. Repeat with more oil and remaining batter.

**5.** Serve blinis warm, topped with a dollop of crème fraîche and a spoonful of caviar.

## curry waffles with gravlax

*photograph on page 32*
MAKES 30

Curry Waffles (recipe follows)

1  pound Classic Gravlax (page 160),
  thinly sliced

¼  cup crème fraîche

4  ounces salmon roe
  Fresh chives, finely chopped

Top each waffle with sliced gravlax. Garnish with crème fraîche, salmon roe, and chives.

## curry waffles

MAKES 30

1  cup all-purpose flour

1  teaspoon curry powder

½  teaspoon baking soda

½  teaspoon baking powder

½  teaspoon sugar

½  teaspoon coarse salt

2  large eggs, separated

1  cup nonfat buttermilk

4  tablespoons unsalted butter, melted

**1.** Preheat oven to 200°F, with rack in center. Line a rimmed baking sheet with parchment paper; transfer to oven. Heat a waffle iron.

**2.** Sift flour, curry powder, baking soda, baking powder, sugar, and salt into a large bowl. In a medium bowl, whisk egg yolks, buttermilk, and butter. Pour egg mixture into dry ingredients; stir until just combined.

**3.** In a medium bowl, beat egg whites until stiff but not dry. Fold into batter.

**4.** Pour about 1 tablespoon batter onto each section of waffle grid. Close lid; cook 3 minutes, or until no steam rises from iron. Transfer waffles to baking sheet while cooking remaining batter.

## mini corn cakes with goat cheese and pepper jelly

MAKES 42

*An old-fashioned cast-iron skillet with shallow round indentations is ideal for making uniform corn cakes. Since these pans can be hard to find, you can use a regular cast-iron skillet and achieve lovely, if less uniform, results. Pepper jelly adds subtle heat and a bit of sweetness.*

1½  cups all-purpose flour

½  cup yellow cornmeal

¼  cup sugar

1  tablespoon baking powder

½  teaspoon salt

1¼  cups milk

2  large eggs, room temperature

⅓  cup vegetable oil, plus more for skillet

3  tablespoons unsalted butter, melted and cooled

1  15¼-ounce can corn kernels, drained

1  log (8 ounces) fresh goat cheese, thinly sliced

1  cup pepper jelly, for serving

**1.** Whisk together flour, cornmeal, sugar, baking powder, and salt in a medium bowl. In a separate bowl, whisk together milk, eggs, oil, and butter until smooth and combined. Add milk mixture to flour mixture, and stir just until batter is combined; fold in corn kernels.

**2.** Heat a cast-iron skillet over medium heat, and rub with enough oil to coat surface. Working in batches, drop batter by the tablespoon into skillet to make 2-inch cakes. Cook until undersides are golden brown, 45 to 60 seconds; turn, and continue cooking until other side is browned and cakes are heated through, about 1 minute. Transfer to a platter. To serve, top each cake with a slice of goat cheese and some pepper jelly.

## potato pancakes with gravlax and dill

MAKES 3 DOZEN

1  small yellow onion, grated on the large holes of a box grater

3  Yukon gold potatoes (about 1 pound), peeled and grated on the large holes of a box grater

1  tablespoon chopped fresh dill, plus sprigs for garnish

½  teaspoon salt

Pinch of freshly ground pepper

1  large egg white, lightly beaten

4  ounces Classic Gravlax (page 160), or store-bought, thinly sliced gravlax

¼  cup sour cream

Olive-oil cooking spray

**1.** Preheat oven to 450°F. Place onion in a fine sieve; press out as much moisture as possible. Combine onion, potatoes, chopped dill, salt, pepper, and egg white in a medium bowl; stir to combine.

**2.** Coat two baking sheets with olive-oil cooking spray. Form pancakes by dropping batter by the tablespoon on baking sheets and flattening into disks. Bake until golden brown on bottom, about 10 minutes, rotating sheets once during cooking. Remove from oven, and flip pancakes. Return to oven, and continue baking until brown on both sides, about 7 minutes more.

**3.** Serve pancakes topped with gravlax and a dab of sour cream. Garnish with dill sprigs.

## crab salad in daikon-radish boxes

MAKES 2 DOZEN

- 3 to 4 large daikon radishes (about 3 pounds)
- ½ pound lump crabmeat (1 cup), picked over and rinsed
- ½ cucumber, peeled, seeded, and cut into ¼-inch dice
- 2 tablespoons mayonnaise
- 1 tablespoon freshly squeezed lemon juice
- 1 teaspoon Dijon mustard
- 1 teaspoon coarse salt
- 1 teaspoon fresh chervil leaves, plus more for garnish

**1.** Cut daikon radishes into 1¼-inch cubes (make sure bottoms are cut evenly so cubes will stand upright). Use a 1-inch melon baller to scoop out the center of each cube.

**2.** Bring a pot of water to a boil, and blanch daikon boxes 3 minutes. Drain, and set aside.

**3.** Place crabmeat and diced cucumber in a medium bowl, and add mayonnaise, lemon juice, mustard, salt, and chervil leaves. Stir to combine.

**4.** Place 1 heaping teaspoon crab salad into each daikon box, and garnish with remaining chervil leaves. Serve immediately.

## shucked oysters with mignonette

SERVES 8

*Each mignonette variation makes enough for two dozen oysters. Look for oysters with tightly sealed shells; discard any that are open.*

- 2 dozen fresh oysters

### for festive mignonette:

- 1 tablespoon whole pink peppercorns
- 1 tablespoon whole green peppercorns
- 1 tablespoon fennel seeds, lightly toasted
- ½ cup red-wine vinegar
- ½ cup champagne vinegar
- ½ teaspoon coarse salt

### for classic champagne mignonette:

- 2 shallots, finely minced
- 1 cup champagne vinegar
- 4 tablespoons dry Champagne or sparkling wine (optional)
- 1 teaspoon freshly ground pepper

**1.** Make mignonette: Stir together all ingredients. Cover with plastic wrap, and refrigerate until ready to serve.

**2.** Shuck oysters just before serving; arrange on a bed of crushed ice. Drizzle with mignonette, or serve on the side. Serve immediately.

### PRESENTING OYSTERS

*As an alternative to crushed ice, try serving raw oysters on a bed of salt and seaweed. The salt, unlike ice, will not melt, and the seaweed will keep the oysters upright.*

## baked oysters with spinach and champagne beurre blanc
### MAKES 2 DOZEN

- 2 to 3 cups rock or coarse salt, for baking sheet
- 2 dozen oysters, shucked, liquor and bottom shells reserved separately
- 1 cup heavy cream
- 1 cup dry Champagne or sparkling wine
- 3 large shallots, minced (about ½ cup)
- ¼ cup white-wine vinegar
- 1¼ cups (2½ sticks) chilled unsalted butter, cut into small pieces
  Coarse salt and freshly ground white pepper
- 1 pound fresh spinach, trimmed and rinsed well, or 2 ten-ounce packages frozen spinach, thawed
  Snipped fresh chives, for garnish

**1.** Pour salt onto a rimmed baking sheet. Nestle oyster shells in salt; set aside.

**2.** Bring cream to a simmer in a small saucepan; cook until reduced by half. Remove from heat.

**3.** Meanwhile, bring Champagne, shallots, and vinegar to a simmer in another small saucepan. Cook until liquid has almost evaporated. Add reduced cream, and cook 1 minute more.

**4.** Remove pan from heat, and whisk in butter, one piece at a time, adding each piece just before the previous one has melted completely. (The sauce should not get hot enough to liquefy; it should be the consistency of heavy cream.) Stir in ½ cup reserved oyster liquor, and season with salt and white pepper. Keep warm.

**5.** If using fresh spinach, rinse it thoroughly several times, and place in a large saucepan with just the water that clings to the leaves. Cover pan, and cook spinach until bright green and just tender, about 2 minutes. Drain well, and roughly chop. (Squeeze excess moisture from thawed frozen spinach; do not cook.)

**6.** Heat broiler, with rack 5 inches from heat. Divide spinach equally among reserved shells. Top each with a shucked oyster. Spoon enough sauce (about 1 tablespoon) over oysters to cover them. Broil until sauce bubbles and edges of oysters start to curl, about 1 minute. Remove from oven. Garnish with chives; serve immediately.

## scallop ceviche
### MAKES 2 DOZEN

*We served the ceviche in scallop shells, available at fish markets. You can also use spoons.*

- 3 limes plus ½ cup freshly squeezed lime juice
- 1 pound bay scallops, halved if large
- 1 tablespoon extra-virgin olive oil
- 4 hearts of palm, sliced into ½-inch-thick rounds
- 1 avocado, pitted, peeled, and cut into ½-inch pieces
- ½ cup fresh cilantro leaves
  Coarse salt and freshly ground pepper

**1.** Slice the ends off the limes, and stand on one end. Use a paring knife to remove peel and pith, following the curve of the fruit. Working over a bowl to catch the juices, cut between membranes to remove whole sections; cut into ½-inch pieces, and add to bowl.

**2.** Add lime juice, scallops, oil, and hearts of palm to bowl; toss to combine. Cover with plastic wrap; refrigerate at least 2 hours or overnight.

**3.** Just before serving, add avocado and cilantro to scallop mixture; season with salt and pepper. Fill scallop shells, if using, with 1 heaping tablespoon ceviche; serve on a tray lined with coarse salt.

## rock-shrimp snowballs

MAKES 2 DOZEN

*Dip your fingers in a bowl of water before shaping the rice; the water will prevent the rice from sticking to your hands.*

- 2 tablespoons sesame seeds
- 1½ cups sushi rice
- 3 tablespoons seasoned rice-wine vinegar
- 6 tablespoons mirin (Japanese cooking wine)
- 1 tablespoon sugar
- ¾ teaspoon coarse salt
- 1 tablespoon canola oil
- 2 shallots, minced (3 tablespoons)
- 1 teaspoon soy sauce
- ¾ pound rock shrimp or small shrimp
- 2 scallions, white and pale-green parts only, thinly sliced on the diagonal

**1.** Place sesame seeds in a skillet over medium heat, and cook, stirring, until lightly toasted and fragrant, about 4 minutes. Set aside.

**2.** Cook rice according to package directions. Combine vinegar, mirin, sugar, and salt in a small saucepan, and bring to a boil. Stir until sugar is dissolved, and remove from heat. Pour vinegar mixture over rice; stir to cool, and set aside.

**3.** Place a medium skillet over medium heat; add oil. When hot, add shallots; cook, stirring, until translucent, about 2 minutes. Add soy sauce and shrimp; cook until shrimp are opaque, about 2 minutes. Stir in scallions; cook until all liquid has evaporated, about 5 minutes. Set aside to cool.

**4.** Form rice into 1-inch balls. Using your thumb, make an indentation in the center, and fill with shrimp mixture. Cover shrimp with rice, and dip one side of ball into toasted sesame seeds. Place on a tray, seed side down. Keep covered with plastic in the refrigerator until ready to serve.

## endive petals with smoked scallops

*photograph on page 35*

SERVES 6

- 2 small red beets
- ½ pound smoked sea scallops, cut into ¼-inch dice
- ½ cup coarsely chopped fresh flat-leaf parsley
- 1 tablespoon freshly squeezed lemon juice
- 2 tablespoons olive oil
- ½ teaspoon coarse salt
- ¼ teaspoon freshly ground pepper
- 2 heads Belgian endive

**1.** Fill a small saucepan with water. Add beets, and bring to a boil. Reduce heat; simmer until fork-tender, about 45 minutes. Remove pan from heat. Drain; let cool. Peel and chop beets into ¼-inch dice.

**2.** Combine beets, scallops, and parsley in a bowl. Add lemon juice, oil, salt, and pepper. Toss to combine. Serve scallops on individual endive leaves.

## shrimp cocktail

*photograph on page 31*

SERVES 12

*Arranging the shrimp on a platter of ice keeps them chilled for a party. Serve with one or all three of the accompanying sauces (recipes follow).*

- 5 dozen large shrimp, shells and tails intact
- 2 dried bay leaves
- 1 tablespoon whole black peppercorns
  Coarse salt
  Lemon Aïoli (recipe follows)
  Cocktail Sauce (recipe follows)
  Ginger-Cilantro Cocktail Sauce (recipe follows)

**1.** Fill a large stockpot three-quarters full with water. Cover, and bring to a boil over high heat.

Prepare an ice bath; set aside. Rinse shrimp in a colander; place in the sink to drain.

**2.** When the water comes to a full boil, add bay leaves, peppercorns, and a generous amount of salt. Keep the heat on high, and carefully add all the shrimp. Cook, stirring often, until shrimp turn opaque and start to float to the surface, about 4 minutes. Drain shrimp; transfer to ice bath until cool.

**3.** Carefully peel shrimp, making sure to leave tails and last shell section intact. To devein shrimp, run a sharp paring knife down back of shrimp, cutting deeply enough to meet the thin black intestinal tract. Remove vein with the tip of the paring knife. Refrigerate deveined shrimp until ready to serve, up to several hours. Serve with dipping sauces.

### lemon aïoli
MAKES 1 CUP

1 large egg
1 teaspoon coarse salt, plus more for seasoning
½ cup canola oil
¼ cup extra-virgin olive oil
3 tablespoons freshly squeezed lemon juice
    Zest of 1 lemon

Place egg and salt in a food processor, and blend until foamy. With the machine running, add the canola oil and then the olive oil, starting with a few drops at a time and ending in a slow, steady stream. Add lemon juice and zest, and pulse to combine. Season with more salt. Refrigerate in an airtight container up to 2 days.

**Note:** Raw eggs should not be used in food prepared for pregnant women, babies, young children, the elderly, or anyone whose health is compromised.

### cocktail sauce
MAKES 1 CUP

¾ cup ketchup
2½ tablespoons prepared horseradish
2 tablespoons freshly squeezed lemon juice
½ teaspoon coarse salt
¼ teaspoon hot-pepper sauce

In a small bowl, whisk together all ingredients. Refrigerate in an airtight container up to 3 days.

### ginger-cilantro cocktail sauce
MAKES 1⅓ CUPS

*The fresh ginger and cilantro give this sauce an Asian flavor. The sauce may be made up to three hours ahead and refrigerated.*

2 cans plum tomatoes (28 ounces each)
1½ tablespoons cider vinegar
3 cups sugar
    Coarse salt and freshly ground black pepper
¼ teaspoon ground allspice
¼ teaspoon ground cloves
¼ teaspoon ground ginger
¼ teaspoon cayenne pepper
    Pinch of dry mustard
2 tablespoons grated fresh ginger
1 tablespoon chopped fresh cilantro
1 teaspoon finely chopped jalapeño chile
    Juice of 3 limes, plus more for seasoning

**1.** Push tomatoes and their juice through a fine sieve or food mill into a medium bowl. Transfer to a large saucepan; place over medium heat, and add vinegar, sugar, salt, black pepper, allspice, cloves, ground ginger, cayenne, and mustard. Simmer until consistency is a little thinner than that of ketchup, about 50 minutes. Remove from heat; let cool.

**2.** Add fresh ginger, cilantro, jalapeño, and lime juice; chill at least 1 hour. Season with additional salt, pepper, and lime juice, as desired.

**159**

## classic gravlax

SERVES 4 TO 6

½  cup sugar

¼  cup coarse salt

1  tablespoon whole white peppercorns, crushed

1  tablespoon coriander seeds, crushed

2  center-cut salmon fillets (1 pound each), skin on

1  bunch fresh dill, coarsely chopped

¼  cup aquavit or vodka

**1.** Combine sugar, salt, peppercorns, and coriander seeds in a small bowl. Set aside. Place salmon fillets on a parchment-lined work surface, and remove any remaining bones.

**2.** Cover flesh side of each fillet with spice mixture, gently rubbing it onto the flesh.

**3.** Spread dill over spices, then pour aquavit or vodka over the dill.

**4.** Stack one fillet on top of the other, and wrap tightly in plastic wrap.

**5.** Place wrapped fillets in a glass or enamel baking dish. Place heavy objects, such as canned goods, on a platter, and place platter on top of fish. Transfer to the refrigerator, and chill 12 hours. Remove dish from refrigerator. Remove wrapped fish; pour off liquid that has accumulated in dish. Turn fish, and replace weighted platter on top.

Return to the refrigerator; let cure 3 more days, turning fish every 12 hours.

**6.** Remove dish from refrigerator. Remove plastic wrap from fish. Scrape dill and spices from the surface of both fillets. To serve, slice each fillet on the diagonal, as thinly as possible. Wrap any remaining gravlax in plastic; refrigerate up to 3 days.

## coriander-cured gravlax
### SERVES 10 TO 12

*To toast coriander seeds, spread in a small skillet; cook over medium-high heat, shaking pan frequently, until fragrant, two to three minutes.*

- 1  salmon fillet (3 to 3½ pounds), skin on
- ½  cup coarse salt
- ½  cup sugar
- 2  tablespoons whole black peppercorns, crushed
- 2  tablespoons coriander seeds, toasted and crushed
- 2  bunches fresh cilantro, plus more for garnish
- 4  limes
- 3  to 4 jalapeño chiles, finely chopped (½ cup), for serving
- 1  red bell pepper, finely chopped (1 cup), for serving
- 1  large onion, finely chopped (1 cup), for serving
-    Mustard Sauce, for serving (recipe follows)

**1.** Rinse salmon, and pat dry. Make a few shallow slashes on skin side. In a small bowl, mix salt, sugar, peppercorns, and coriander. Rub ¼ cup spice mixture on skin side of salmon. Place salmon, skin side down, in a glass baking dish. Rub remaining spice mixture over flesh side. Coarsely chop cilantro; spread evenly over salmon. Cover with 2 thinly sliced limes.

**2.** Cover dish with plastic wrap. Place a smaller dish on top; weight with canned goods. Refrigerate at least 48 hours, turning salmon every 12 hours and basting with any released liquid.

**3.** Scrape off limes, cilantro, and spice mixture. Place salmon on a serving platter, and garnish with remaining 2 limes, thinly sliced, and cilantro sprigs. Serve with chopped jalapeño, red pepper, onion, and mustard sauce on the side.

### mustard sauce
#### MAKES 1½ CUPS

- ½  cup red-wine vinegar
- 2  shallots, finely diced
- 1  cup Dijon mustard
- 1½  tablespoons honey
- ½  teaspoon ground coriander
-    Freshly ground pepper
- ¼  cup fresh cilantro leaves, coarsely chopped

In a small saucepan over medium heat, combine vinegar and shallots. Cook until liquid is reduced to 1 tablespoon, about 8 minutes. In a small bowl, combine mustard, 2 tablespoons water, the honey, and coriander; season with pepper. Stir in shallot mixture and chopped cilantro.

## star-anise gravlax

MAKES 4 DOZEN

*It will take a few fennel bulbs to yield two cups fronds, the feathery leaves on top of the stalks.*

3   tablespoons coarse salt

2   tablespoons sugar

12   whole black peppercorns

4   whole star anise

1   salmon fillet (2 pounds), skin on, bones removed

2   cups fennel fronds, chopped, plus more whole for garnish

1   lemon, thinly sliced

2   tablespoons vodka
    Sesame Star Crackers (page 107)

½   small bulb fennel, sliced paper thin

1   small red onion, sliced paper thin

**1.** Combine salt, sugar, peppercorns, and star anise in a spice grinder or mortar and pestle, and grind until spices are crushed. Rub both sides of salmon well with spice mixture.

**2.** Arrange chopped fennel fronds, lemon slices, and any leftover spice mixture in a glass baking dish large enough to hold the fish flat. Sprinkle the flesh side of the fish with vodka, and place in dish, skin side up.

**3.** Cover dish with plastic wrap; place a smaller dish on top, and weight with canned goods. Let cure in the refrigerator 2 to 3 days, turning salmon every 12 hours, and basting with any released liquid. The salmon should look opaque when cured.

**4.** Remove fish from baking dish, and scrape off seasonings. Serve immediately, or rewrap and refrigerate 1 to 2 days.

**5.** To serve, slice fish very thinly on the diagonal down to the skin, using a very sharp slicing knife. To assemble hors d'oeuvres, layer each cracker with a slice of gravlax, fennel, and red onion; top with a fennel frond. Serve immediately.

### CHOOSING SALMON FOR GRAVLAX

*When making gravlax, any variety of salmon will work, as long as it is the freshest available. Ask the fishmonger to cut your fillet from the center of a side of salmon; make sure the skin is intact, because this helps ensure freshness and holds the fish together as you slice it.*

# salads

✳

## arugula with shaved pecorino
### SERVES 4

*It is easiest to work from a larger chunk of pecorino cheese, although you will not need more than four ounces. For best results, make sure the cheese is at room temperature; this will help keep it from cracking. Promptly wrap the remaining cheese with plastic wrap.*

- 4 ounces pecorino cheese
- 2 bunches arugula, trimmed, washed well, and drained
- 4 teaspoons extra-virgin olive oil
  Coarse salt and freshly ground pepper

**1.** Using a vegetable peeler, shave pecorino cheese into thin strips.

**2.** Arrange a large handful of arugula on four salad plates. Scatter pecorino shavings over arugula. Drizzle each salad with 1 teaspoon olive oil, and season with salt and pepper. Serve.

## avocado grapefruit salad with lime dressing
### SERVES 10 TO 12

*Deconstructing the salad and serving it in separate bowls, instead of tossing it together, allows guests to compose their own and keeps all the ingredients crisp and fresh.*

- ½ cup freshly squeezed lime juice (about 3 limes)
- 1 tablespoon honey
- ½ cup extra-virgin olive oil
- ½ teaspoon crushed red-pepper flakes
  Coarse salt and freshly ground black pepper
- 4 ruby-red grapefruit, peel and pith removed
  Seeds from 2 pomegranates
- 4 ripe avocados
- 3 heads Bibb lettuce (about 2 pounds), leaves separated

**1.** Make dressing: Combine ¼ cup lime juice and the honey in a small bowl. Whisk in oil and red-pepper flakes, and season with salt and black pepper. Transfer to a glass cruet or small glass pitcher for the table.

**2.** Slice grapefruit crosswise into ¼-inch-thick rounds; place in a serving bowl. Place pomegranate seeds in another bowl.

**3.** Halve avocados, and remove pits. Peel; cut avocados into 1-inch pieces, and toss in a bowl with remaining ¼ cup lime juice.

**4.** Place lettuce in a large salad bowl; season with salt and pepper. To serve, arrange all ingredients, in bowls, and serve.

## beets with blood oranges and watercress

SERVES 4

5 beets (about ¾ pound),
 trimmed and scrubbed

2 tablespoons extra-virgin olive oil
 Coarse salt

4 blood oranges

1 small shallot, minced (about 1 tablespoon)

1 teaspoon red-wine vinegar
 Freshly ground pepper

2 ounces (1 bunch) watercress,
 trimmed and rinsed

1. Preheat oven to 375°F. Place beets in a baking pan; drizzle with ½ tablespoon oil, and season with salt. Toss to combine. Pour ¼ cup water into pan; cover with foil. Cook until beets are easily pierced with the tip of a paring knife, about 45 minutes.

2. Remove pan from oven; remove foil, and let beets cool completely. Peel beets, and slice into thin rounds using a mandoline or sharp knife. Divide beets among four salad plates, arranging the slices in a circular pattern.

3. Peel blood oranges: Using a sharp paring knife, slice off both ends. Carefully slice downward, following the curve of the fruit, to remove peel and pith. Working over a bowl to catch the juices, cut between membranes to remove whole segments. Set segments aside.

4. Make dressing: Pour 2 tablespoons of the blood-orange juice into a small bowl. Add shallot and vinegar; season with salt and pepper. Whisk in remaining 1½ tablespoons oil in a slow, steady stream until emulsified.

5. Divide watercress and blood-orange segments among plates of beets, mounding them in the center. Drizzle all with dressing; serve immediately.

## brussels sprouts salad with roasted shallot vinaigrette

SERVES 10 TO 12

Separating the brussels-sprout leaves allows them to maintain their bright-green color and crisp texture; the salad will hold up for several hours on a buffet table.

6 shallots (unpeeled)

6 tablespoons olive oil, plus more
 for roasting shallots
 Coarse salt

2½ pounds brussels sprouts, trimmed
 and leaves separated

2 tablespoons balsamic vinegar
 Freshly ground pepper

1. Preheat oven to 400°F. Line a small roasting pan with aluminum foil. Place shallots in pan, and toss with a little oil. Roast until soft, about 15 minutes. Set aside to cool.

2. Prepare an ice bath; set aside. Bring a large pot of water to a boil; add salt, and blanch brussels-sprout leaves until bright green and tender, 1 to 2 minutes. Using a slotted spoon, transfer leaves to ice bath to stop cooking. Drain, and set aside.

3. Peel shallots, and place in a blender or food processor. Add vinegar, and season with salt and pepper; process until coarsely chopped, leaving some large pieces. Transfer to a small bowl, and whisk in oil. The vinaigrette will be quite thick. Just before serving, toss brussels sprouts with vinaigrette, and season with salt and pepper.

## chestnut salad with hazelnuts, frisée, and pear

*photograph on page 38*

SERVES 6 TO 8

2 ounces hazelnuts (½ cup)

8 ounces fresh chestnuts

1 tablespoon unsalted butter

1 pound Forelle or Seckel pears, peeled, cored, and cut into ½-inch-thick wedges

1 tablespoon sugar

4 ounces pancetta or bacon, cut into ½-inch dice

⅓ cup sherry vinegar

¾ cup extra-virgin olive oil

Coarse salt and freshly ground pepper

1 large head frisée lettuce

**1.** Preheat oven to 375°F. Spread hazelnuts on a rimmed baking sheet; toast in oven until fragrant and skins are beginning to split, about 10 minutes. Remove from oven; wrap nuts in a clean kitchen towel, and rub vigorously to release skins. Roughly chop nuts, and set aside.

**2.** Raise oven heat to 400°F. Score each chestnut using a sharp paring knife or a chestnut knife: Make an X on one side of each chestnut or make one long slit crosswise around circumference. Place chestnuts in a single layer on a rimmed baking sheet; roast until flesh is tender and golden, about 25 minutes. Remove from oven. Immediately rub in kitchen towel to remove shells.

**3.** Melt butter in a medium skillet over medium-high heat. Add pears and sugar; cook, stirring occasionally, until caramelized, 6 to 8 minutes. Transfer pears to a dish.

**4.** Place pancetta in skillet, and cook until crisp, about 5 minutes. Using a slotted spoon, transfer to paper towels to drain; set aside.

**5.** Carefully add vinegar to skillet with rendered fat. Raise heat to high, and cook, stirring, until liquid is reduced by one-quarter, about 2 minutes. Whisk in olive oil until combined. Add chestnuts; season with salt and pepper. Reduce heat to low, and simmer 5 minutes.

**6.** Tear frisée into large pieces, and place in a large salad bowl. Add reserved hazelnuts, pears, and pancetta. Pour hot dressing and chestnuts over salad; toss to combine, and serve immediately.

### SALAD-GREEN GLOSSARY

• **ARUGULA:** *This aromatic green, widely used in Italy, is increasingly popular in the United States. It has a peppery flavor that lends itself to cooking as well as salads.*

• **ROMAINE:** *Also called Cos lettuce, romaine has dark green, slightly bitter outer leaves and hearts that are crisp and very pale green.*

• **WATERCRESS:** *A member of the mustard family, watercress's dark-green leaves are tender, with a peppery flavor. When using the leaves raw as a salad green, reserve the thickest stems to add to stock.*

• **CHICORY:** *This relative of endive has brightly colored, bitter-tasting leaves; the white heart has a more delicate flavor.*

• **ESCAROLE:** *A milder member of the chicory family, escarole has broad, pale-green leaves.*

• **FRISEE:** *Another member of the chicory family, frisée has pale, curly leaves and a bitter taste.*

• **RADICCHIO:** *With tender leaves and a pronounced bitter flavor, this red-leaf chicory is usually paired with milder greens.*

## chicory salad with lemon-anchovy vinaigrette

### SERVES 4

Finely grated zest and juice of 1 lemon

½ teaspoon Dijon mustard

3 anchovy fillets, rinsed and finely chopped

Coarse salt and freshly ground pepper

6 tablespoons extra-virgin olive oil

1 small head radicchio

1 small head escarole

1. Make vinaigrette: Combine lemon zest and juice, mustard, and anchovies in a small bowl; season with salt and pepper. Whisk in oil in a slow, steady stream until emulsified.

2. Discard outer leaves of radicchio and escarole; tear remaining leaves into bite-size pieces. Place in a salad bowl. Season with salt and pepper, and drizzle with just enough vinaigrette to coat. Serve with remaining vinaigrette on the side.

## citrus salad

### SERVES 10 TO 12

Ruby-red grapefruit is at its peak in December.

4 ruby-red or pink grapefruit

5 navel or blood oranges

3 tablespoons sherry vinegar

1 tablespoon honey

Coarse salt and freshly ground pepper

5 tablespoons extra-virgin olive oil

¼ cup canola oil

2 large heads radicchio, leaves separated

2 heads Belgian endive, leaves separated

¼ small red onion, very thinly sliced

1. Using a sharp paring knife, slice off both ends of grapefruit, and remove peel and pith, following the curve of the fruit. Working over a bowl to catch the juices, use a paring knife to slice between sections of each grapefruit to remove whole segments. Place segments in bowl. Repeat process with oranges; add to bowl with grapefruit. Transfer to refrigerator until ready to serve, up to 1 hour.

2. Make vinaigrette: In a small bowl, combine vinegar and honey; season with salt and pepper. Slowly whisk in olive oil, then canola oil, until emulsified. Set aside.

3. Just before serving, arrange radicchio and endive leaves on a large serving platter. Arrange reserved grapefruit and orange segments in center of platter. Scatter red-onion slices over top and drizzle with vinaigrette.

## waldorf salad

SERVES 6 TO 8

4   ounces (1 cup) pecans
1   bulb fennel, trimmed (1 pound)
2   tablespoons plus 1 teaspoon freshly
    squeezed lemon juice (about 1 lemon)
1   Granny Smith apple
1   bunch seedless red grapes,
    halved (about 1½ cups)
4   stalks celery, thinly sliced crosswise
6   to 8 escarole leaves, stacked,
    cut crosswise into thin strips
¼   cup chopped fresh dill
¼   cup plain yogurt
2   tablespoons extra-virgin olive oil
    Coarse salt and freshly ground pepper

**1.** Preheat oven to 350°F. Spread pecans in a single layer on a rimmed baking sheet; toast in oven until golden and fragrant, 10 to 15 minutes. Let cool, then halve pecans, and set aside.

**2.** Very thinly slice fennel bulb using a mandoline or sharp knife. Transfer to a large bowl; add 1 teaspoon lemon juice, and toss to coat.

**3.** Slice apple into thin wedges; add to bowl with fennel, and toss to coat with the juice. Add grapes, celery, escarole, and half the dill to bowl. Toss to combine. Salad may be made up to this point 4 hours ahead, and refrigerated, covered.

**4.** In a small bowl, combine remaining 2 tablespoons lemon juice with the yogurt and oil; season with salt and pepper. Toss salad with just enough vinaigrette to lightly coat. Transfer to a serving bowl; garnish with remaining dill and reserved pecans halves. Serve salad with remaining vinaigrette on the side.

## escarole with persimmons, pomegranate seeds, and lemon-shallot vinaigrette

SERVES 12 TO 14

*For this salad, look for Fuyu persimmons, which can be enjoyed while they are still firm, unlike the larger Hachiya persimmons, which can only be eaten when very soft.*

¾   cup freshly squeezed lemon juice
    (3 to 4 lemons)
¼   cup minced shallots (about 4 shallots)
2   tablespoons grainy mustard
2   tablespoons chopped fresh marjoram
    Coarse salt and freshly ground pepper
1   cup extra-virgin olive oil
2   heads escarole, washed and torn
    into bite-size pieces
5   Fuyu persimmons, very thinly sliced
    Seeds of 1 pomegranate

**1.** Make vinaigrette: In a small bowl, combine lemon juice, shallots, mustard, and marjoram; season with salt and pepper. Whisk in oil in a slow, steady stream until emulsified.

**2.** Toss escarole with just enough vinaigrette to lightly coat. Arrange persimmon slices over greens, and sprinkle with pomegranate seeds. Serve remaining vinaigrette on the side.

## frisée and fennel with dried apricots and crumbled roquefort

*photograph on page 36*

SERVES 4 TO 6

*Roquefort is best kept cold until you are ready to crumble it into the salad.*

- 2 small heads frisée
- 2 small bulbs fennel
- ½ cup dried apricots, cut into ¼-inch-thick strips
- 4 to 5 ounces Roquefort cheese
- ¼ cup extra-virgin olive oil
- Coarse salt and freshly ground pepper

**1.** Discard outer leaves of frisée. Tear remaining frisée into bite-size pieces; place in a serving bowl. Using a mandoline or very sharp knife, shave fennel as thinly as possible. Transfer to bowl.

**2.** Scatter apricots over frisée and fennel. Crumble Roquefort directly into bowl. Just before serving, drizzle salad with oil, and season with salt and pepper; toss to combine.

## frisée salad

SERVES 12

- 2 ounces (⅓ cup) pine nuts
- 4 thick slices baguette, cut into ½-inch cubes
- 3 tablespoons plus ¼ cup extra-virgin olive oil
- Coarse salt and freshly ground pepper
- ¼ cup red-wine vinegar
- 1 garlic clove, minced
- 2 heads frisée (about 1 pound)
- 6 ounces Roquefort cheese, crumbled (about 1½ cups)

**1.** Preheat oven to 375°F. Spread pine nuts in a single layer on a rimmed baking sheet; toast in oven until golden, about 8 minutes. Set aside to cool.

**2.** Make croutons: In a medium bowl, toss bread cubes with 3 tablespoons oil, and season with salt and pepper. Spread cubes in a single layer on a rimmed baking sheet; toast in oven until golden brown, about 15 minutes. Set aside to cool.

**3.** Make vinaigrette: In a bowl, whisk together vinegar and garlic, and season with salt and pepper. Whisking constantly, add remaining ¼ cup oil in a steady stream until emulsified.

**4.** In a large serving bowl, toss together frisée and Roquefort with reserved croutons and pine nuts. Drizzle just enough vinaigrette to coat salad, and toss to combine. Serve immediately with remaining vinaigrette on the side.

## fruit and fennel salad

SERVES 8 TO 10

2  bulbs fennel (2¼ pounds), trimmed

2  stalks celery, trimmed

1  Fuji or other sweet, crisp apple

2  lemons

¾  cup dried apricots, cut into bite-size pieces

¼  cup unsalted pistachios or almonds, coarsely chopped, plus 1 tablespoon for garnish

1  tablespoon extra-virgin olive oil
   Coarse salt and freshly ground pepper

1  log (4 ounces) fresh goat cheese

1. Using a mandoline or sharp knife, slice fennel lengthwise as thinly as possible. Transfer to a large bowl. Cut celery diagonally into very thin slices, and add to bowl with fennel.

2. Quarter and core apple. Cut each quarter lengthwise into thin slices. Add to bowl; squeeze juice from 1 lemon over mixture, and toss to combine. Stir in apricots and ¼ cup chopped nuts.

3. Squeeze juice of remaining lemon over mixture. Drizzle with oil, and season with salt and pepper; toss to combine. Transfer salad to a serving bowl. Crumble goat cheese over the top; garnish with remaining tablespoon nuts. Serve immediately.

## mixed greens with orange vinaigrette and toasted sesame seeds

SERVES 12

*Toasting whole cumin seeds before grinding them is the best way to bring out their distinctive flavor. Add slices of avocado to this salad for a delicious variation.*

¼  cup sesame seeds

1  teaspoon cumin seeds

⅔  cup freshly squeezed orange juice (about 2 oranges)

3  tablespoons red-wine vinegar

1  teaspoon coarse salt

1  teaspoon sugar
   Freshly ground pepper

½  cup extra-virgin olive oil

1½  to 2 pounds mixed lettuces, such as romaine, radicchio, and frisée, finely sliced or torn into bite-size pieces (20 to 24 cups)

1. In a small skillet over medium heat, toast sesame seeds, shaking skillet until seeds are fragrant, 2 to 3 minutes; set aside to cool. Repeat to toast cumin seeds; grind cumin in a clean spice or coffee grinder or with a mortar and pestle until it becomes a fine powder.

2. Make vinaigrette: In a medium bowl, whisk together orange juice, vinegar, salt, sugar, and pepper. Whisk in oil in a slow, steady stream until emulsified. Whisk in ground cumin.

3. Arrange greens in a large serving bowl. Drizzle salad with just enough dressing to coat, and sprinkle with sesame seeds. Serve immediately with remaining dressing on the side.

## jerusalem artichokes and mixed greens with roasted tomatoes

*photograph on page 39*

SERVES 6

*Jerusalem artichokes are also called sunchokes.*

- 8 ounces cherry tomatoes, halved
- 1 small garlic clove, minced
- 1 tablespoon plus ¼ cup extra-virgin olive oil
  Coarse salt and freshly ground pepper
- 10 cups mixed field greens (4 ounces)
- 12 ounces Jerusalem artichokes, peeled and thinly sliced crosswise
- 2 tablespoons fresh tarragon leaves
- 2 teaspoons Dijon mustard
- 2 tablespoons tarragon vinegar
  Shepherds' Crooks (recipe follows)

**1.** Preheat oven to 300°F. In a medium bowl, combine tomatoes, garlic, and 1 tablespoon oil. Season with salt and pepper, and toss to combine. Arrange tomatoes, cut side up, on a rimmed baking sheet; roast until wrinkled and slightly dried, about 1 hour. Set aside to cool.

**2.** In a large serving bowl, combine field greens, artichokes, and tarragon. In a small bowl, whisk together mustard and vinegar; season with salt and pepper. Whisk in remaining ¼ cup oil in a slow, steady stream until emulsified. Drizzle salad with just enough vinaigrette to coat; toss to combine. Divide among six serving plates; garnish each with a shepherds' crook, and serve with remaining dressing on the side.

## shepherds' crooks

MAKES ABOUT 2 DOZEN

- 2 cups all-purpose flour, plus more for work surface
- 1½ teaspoons baking powder
- ½ teaspoon table salt
- 3 tablespoons solid vegetable shortening
- ½ cup plus 2 tablespoons ice water
- 2 cups very finely chopped hazelnuts (about 8 ounces)
- 1 teaspoon coarse salt
- 3 large egg yolks, lightly beaten with 3 tablespoons heavy cream, for egg wash

**1.** Preheat oven to 350°F. Line a baking sheet with parchment paper; set aside. Place flour, baking powder, and table salt in a food processor; pulse to combine. Add shortening; pulse until mixture resembles coarse meal. With machine running, gradually add ice water until dough just comes together, about 1 minute.

**2.** Turn out dough onto a lightly floured work surface. Pat dough into a smooth rectangle, about 6 by 4 inches. Roll out dough into a 12-by-9-inch rectangle about ¼ inch thick. Using a pizza wheel or sharp knife, cut dough on one long side into 24 strips, each ½ inch wide and 9 inches long.

**3.** Stir together hazelnuts and coarse salt, and spread out on a clean work surface. Dip one strip into egg wash, turning to coat; let excess drip off, and lay flat on nut mixture. Gently roll back and forth to form a ¼-inch-thick, 20-inch-long rope. Place on prepared baking sheet, curve one end down slightly to form crook shape. Repeat with remaining dough strips.

**4.** Bake until breadsticks are golden, about 20 minutes. Transfer to a wire rack to cool completely. Store breadsticks in airtight containers at room temperature up to 5 days.

## honey tangerines and kumquats with walnuts and shaved celery

*photograph on page 36*

SERVES 4

*The combination of walnuts, Pecorino Romano cheese, and palate-cleansing citrus makes this a fine after-dinner salad.*

- 3 honey tangerines
- 6 kumquats (about 2 ounces)
- 4 stalks celery
- 1½ ounces (about ½ cup) walnut halves
- 1 tablespoon plus 1 teaspoon freshly squeezed lemon juice (about 1 lemon)
- 2 teaspoons extra-virgin olive oil
  Freshly ground pepper
- 1 ounce Pecorino Romano cheese

**1.** Using your hands, peel tangerines; separate fruit into segments, and pop out seeds. Slice kumquats into very thin rounds; remove seeds. Combine tangerines and kumquats in a large bowl.

**2.** Using a mandoline or sharp knife, slice celery very thinly on the bias. Add to bowl with fruit. Add walnuts, and toss to combine.

**3.** In a small bowl, whisk together lemon juice and oil; season with pepper. Drizzle dressing over citrus mixture, and toss to combine. Divide among four salad plates. Shave cheese with a vegetable peeler over each salad, and serve immediately.

## jícama and orange salad with citrus-cumin vinaigrette

SERVES 4

- 2 oranges
- 1 jícama (about 1½ pounds), peeled and julienned
- 3 ounces baby spinach
  Citrus-Cumin Vinaigrette (recipe follows)

Using a sharp paring knife, cut off both ends of oranges, and remove peel and pith, following the curve of the fruit. Slice fruit crosswise into ¼-inch rounds, and remove any seeds. Transfer slices to a large bowl; combine with jícama and spinach. Toss with vinaigrette; serve immediately.

### citrus-cumin vinaigrette

MAKES ¾ CUP

- 1 teaspoon cumin seeds
- ½ cup freshly squeezed orange juice (about 2 oranges)
- 2 tablespoons freshly squeezed lemon juice (about 1 lemon)
- 1 tablespoon extra-virgin olive oil
- 1 tablespoon honey
- 2 teaspoons Dijon mustard
  Coarse salt and freshly ground pepper

In a small skillet over medium-high heat, toast cumin seeds until fragrant, about 2 minutes, shaking skillet to toast evenly. Let cool slightly, then finely grind in a clean spice or coffee grinder. Combine all ingredients in a blender; process until smooth. Store vinaigrette in an airtight container in the refrigerator up to 3 days.

## mixed lettuces with grapefruit, goat cheese, and black pepper

SERVES 4

1  pink or ruby-red grapefruit

2  teaspoons white-wine vinegar
   Pinch of coarse salt

1  tablespoon plus 1 teaspoon
   extra-virgin olive oil

1  head Belgian endive

6  ounces mixed baby lettuces, such as
   frisée, mizuna, arugula, and tatsoi

1  log (3 ounces) fresh goat cheese, cut in half
   Freshly ground pepper

**1.** Before peeling grapefruit, zest one quarter (about 1 teaspoon zest). Set aside in a small bowl. Peel grapefruit: Using a sharp knife, cut off both ends. Carefully slice downward, following the curve of the fruit, to remove large strips of rind. Be sure to remove all white pith, as it is quite bitter. Slice grapefruit in half vertically, and place cut side down on a cutting board. Slice each half into six semicircles, and set aside.

**2.** Make vinaigrette: Add vinegar and salt to the reserved grated zest. Whisk in oil in a slow, steady stream until emulsified, and set aside.

**3.** Slice endive in half lengthwise, and remove core with a small knife. Slice each half lengthwise into ¼-inch-wide strips. Place in a medium bowl along with the mixed greens; drizzle salad with just enough vinaigrette to coat, and crumble half the goat cheese over salad. Toss to combine.

**4.** Divide salad among four plates, and arrange three grapefruit slices on top of each serving. Slice remaining goat cheese into four rounds, and place one on each salad. Season with pepper, and serve immediately with remaining dressing on the side.

## pomegranate, fennel, and green bean salad

photograph on page 37

SERVES 4 TO 6

1  small bulb fennel, trimmed
   Juice of 1 lemon
   Coarse salt

6  ounces green beans, trimmed and
   cut into 2-inch lengths

2  tablespoons Dijon mustard

2  tablespoons pomegranate molasses

1  tablespoon honey
   Freshly ground pepper

½  cup extra-virgin olive oil

1  bunch watercress, trimmed and rinsed

2  ounces crumbled feta or goat cheese

½  cup pomegranate seeds (from about ½
   pomegranate)

**1.** Cut fennel lengthwise in half through root. Thinly slice each half crosswise; place slices in a small bowl. Toss with lemon juice, and set aside.

**2.** Prepare an ice bath; set aside. Bring a small saucepan of water to a boil; add salt and beans. Cook until bright green, about 1 minute. Using a slotted spoon, transfer beans to ice bath to stop cooking. Drain; pat dry with paper towels.

**3.** In a bowl, whisk together mustard, molasses, and honey; season with salt and pepper. Whisk in oil in a slow, steady stream until emulsified.

**4.** Arrange watercress on a serving platter, and place fennel and green beans on top. Sprinkle with cheese and pomegranate seeds. Drizzle with just enough dressing to coat lightly, and serve immediately with remaining dressing on the side.

## ricotta salata with roasted red peppers and marinated baby artichokes

SERVES 4

*Because ricotta salata is so easy to slice, it's nice in a selection of antipasti. For a more substantial dish, add olives and grilled vegetables.*

- 3 cups chicken stock, preferably homemade (page 179), or low-sodium canned chicken broth
- 2 tablespoons extra-virgin olive oil, plus more for drizzling
- 1 tablespoon whole black peppercorns
- 1 tablespoon coarse salt, plus more for seasoning
  Several sprigs of fresh thyme
- 3 garlic cloves, smashed
- 2 shallots, quartered
- 3 lemons
- 6 baby artichokes
- 1 red bell pepper
  Freshly ground black pepper
- 6 ounces ricotta salata
  Small handful of tender sprouts or greens

**1.** Combine chicken stock, 2 tablespoons oil, peppercorns, salt, thyme, garlic, and shallots in a medium saucepan. Cut 2 lemons in half, and squeeze juice through a small sieve directly into saucepan. Set lemon halves aside.

**2.** Using a paring knife, trim about ½ inch from top of each artichoke. Remove and discard outer leaves. Use a paring knife to trim stem end and to peel away tough outer skin. Slice artichokes in half. Carefully carve out purple choke, and discard. Rub each artichoke with reserved lemon halves; place artichokes in saucepan. Cover surface of cooking liquid with cheesecloth to help keep artichokes submerged during cooking.

**3.** Set pan over medium heat, and bring mixture to a boil. Reduce heat; simmer until artichokes are just fork-tender, 35 to 40 minutes. Remove pan from heat; let artichokes cool in cooking liquid.

**4.** Roast red pepper over a gas burner or under the broiler until charred, turning as each side becomes charred. Place in a bowl, and cover with plastic wrap; let stand until cool enough to handle, about 10 minutes. Remove skin by rubbing with a paper towel. Cut pepper in half; remove seeds and stem, and slice flesh into long, thin strips. Place strips in a small bowl; drizzle with oil.

**5.** Drain artichoke halves, discarding peppercorns and other solids. Place halves in a bowl. Squeeze juice of remaining lemon over artichokes, and drizzle with oil. Season with salt and black pepper.

**6.** Using a sharp knife, cut cheese into thin slices. Divide cheese, peppers, artichokes, and sprouts evenly among four serving plates. Serve.

## oranges with olives, parsley, and paprika

SERVES 4

- 4 navel oranges
- ¼ cup Niçoise olives, pitted and halved
- ½ teaspoon paprika
- 2 tablespoons freshly squeezed lemon juice (about 1 lemon)
- 1 tablespoon extra-virgin olive oil
- 1½ tablespoons finely chopped fresh flat-leaf parsley, plus more leaves for garnish

**1.** Peel oranges: Using a sharp knife, cut off both ends. Carefully slice downward, following the curve of the fruit to remove wide strips of rind. Be sure to remove all white pith, as it is quite bitter. Slice each orange crosswise into about six rounds, and arrange them in overlapping rows on a serving plate. Scatter olives over oranges.

**2.** In a small bowl, combine paprika and lemon juice; whisk in oil in a slow, steady stream until emulsified. Add parsley, and whisk to combine. Drizzle dressing over oranges and olives; garnish with parsley, and serve immediately.

## spinach salad with fennel and blood oranges

SERVES 4

3 blood oranges
  Juice of 1 lemon
2 tablespoons sherry vinegar
  Coarse salt and freshly ground pepper
1 bulb fennel, trimmed and very thinly sliced
16 cremini mushrooms, trimmed and very thinly sliced
1 red onion, very thinly sliced
6 ounces baby spinach
3 slices cooked bacon, finely crumbled

**1.** Using a sharp paring knife, slice off both ends of 2 oranges; carefully slice downward, following the curve of the fruit to remove peel and pith. Cut between membranes to remove whole segments. Place in a small bowl; set aside. Juice remaining orange into a separate bowl or glass measuring cup. Whisk lemon juice and vinegar into orange juice; season with salt and pepper.

**2.** In a large serving bowl, combine fennel, mushrooms, onion, and spinach. Add reserved orange segments and juice mixture; toss to combine. Divide among four serving plates, and sprinkle each with crumbled bacon. Serve immediately.

## warm goat-cheese salad
*photograph on page 36*
SERVES 4

⅓ cup extra-virgin olive oil,
  plus more as needed
½ cup fine breadcrumbs
  Coarse salt
1 log (12 ounces) fresh goat cheese,
  sliced into eight ¾-inch-thick disks
½ shallot, minced (about 1 teaspoon)
1½ tablespoons red-wine vinegar,
  plus more as needed
  Freshly ground pepper
1 teaspoon Dijon mustard
6 ounces mixed tender greens
  (enough for 1 large handful per salad)

**1.** Pour oil into a shallow dish. Place breadcrumbs in a separate shallow dish, and season with salt.

**2.** Carefully dip cheese disks one at a time in oil, turning to coat both sides. Transfer disks to breadcrumb mixture, and turn to coat evenly. Place disks on a plate, cover with plastic wrap, and chill until firm, at least 1 hour or overnight. Pour remaining oil into a glass measuring cup; set aside.

**3.** Make dressing: Combine shallot and vinegar in a small bowl, and let stand at least 20 minutes. Season with salt and pepper. Whisk in mustard, then whisk in the reserved oil in a slow, steady stream until emulsified.

**4.** Preheat oven to 400°F. Transfer cheese disks to a parchment-lined baking sheet. Cook until cheese is warm and soft to the touch, 8 to 10 minutes.

**5.** Place greens in a large bowl. Drizzle with dressing; season with salt and pepper, and toss to combine. Divide salad among four serving plates. Place two cheese disks on top of each, and serve.

## wilted brussels sprouts salad with warm vinaigrette

### SERVES 6

1 pound brussels sprouts, trimmed, leaves separated

4 ounces spinach (about 3 cups), trimmed and washed

1 small head radicchio, trimmed

1 garlic clove, finely chopped

⅓ cup cider vinegar

2 tablespoons honey mustard

1½ tablespoons sugar

Coarse salt and freshly ground pepper

½ cup extra-virgin olive oil

Crumbled goat cheese, for garnish

Toasted caraway seeds, for garnish

**1.** Thinly slice brussels-sprout leaves crosswise into strips. Repeat with spinach and radicchio. Combine all in a large bowl; set aside.

**2.** Make vinaigrette: In a small saucepan over medium heat, whisk together garlic, vinegar, mustard, and sugar; season with salt and pepper. Whisk in oil in a slow, steady stream until emulsified. Bring to a simmer; cook until mixture thickens slightly, about 3 minutes.

**3.** Pour vinaigrette over salad mixture; toss to combine. Serve immediately, garnished with goat cheese and caraway seeds.

## winter white salad

### SERVES 4

*Hazelnut oil has a subtle, nutty flavor that is perfect with winter vegetables. You can also use walnut oil or extra-virgin olive oil.*

1 bulb fennel, trimmed and quartered

1 stalk celery

3 ounces (½ cup) whole hazelnuts

2 tablespoons white-wine vinegar

½ teaspoon Dijon mustard

Coarse salt and freshly ground pepper

6 tablespoons hazelnut oil

1 small head frisée or escarole, leaves torn into bite-size pieces

2 large heads Belgian endive, leaves separated

1 small leek, halved lengthwise, then thinly sliced crosswise and washed well

**1.** Using a mandoline or sharp knife, slice fennel quarters as thinly as possible. Slice celery paper-thin on the bias. Refrigerate fennel and celery in separate covered bowls until ready to use.

**2.** Preheat oven to 350°F. Spread hazelnuts in a single layer on a rimmed baking sheet; toast in oven until fragrant and skins are starting to split, about 10 minutes. Remove from oven; rub warm nuts vigorously in a clean kitchen towel to remove skins. Set aside to cool.

**3.** In a bowl, whisk together vinegar and mustard, and season with salt and pepper. Whisk in oil in a slow, steady stream until emulsified.

**4.** Place frisée, endive, leeks, and reserved fennel and celery in a salad bowl. Drizzle with just enough vinaigrette to coat and arrange on chilled plates. Crush hazelnuts lightly with the side of a knife, and sprinkle over salad. Serve immediately with remaining vinaigrette on the side.

# soups
# and stews

*

## carrot soup

SERVES 6

1   tablespoon unsalted butter

1   onion, coarsely chopped

1   pound carrots, coarsely chopped

2   cups (16 ounces) freshly made or
    store-bought carrot juice

2   cups chicken stock, preferably
    homemade (page 179), or low-sodium
    canned chicken broth

1   tablespoon honey

2   teaspoons coarse salt

½   teaspoon ground cumin

¼   teaspoon freshly ground white pepper

2   tablespoons half-and-half (optional)
    Chopped fresh chives, for garnish
    Cayenne pepper, for garnish

**1.** Heat butter in a large saucepan over medium-low heat. Add onion, and cook, stirring, until translucent, about 5 minutes. Add carrots; cook, stirring occasionally, until very tender, about 15 minutes. Do not brown. Add carrot juice, stock, honey, salt, cumin, and white pepper. Bring to a simmer; cook until vegetables are very soft, about 30 minutes.

**2.** Remove from heat; let cool slightly. Working in batches so as not to fill more than halfway, purée soup in a blender or food processor until smooth. Return to pan, and warm over low heat, thinning with stock or water if needed. Stir in half-and-half, if using. Divide soup among bowls, and garnish with chives and a sprinkling of cayenne.

## chestnut mushroom soup

*photograph on page 40*

SERVES 4 TO 6

1   pound fresh chestnuts

6   ounces cremini mushrooms

2   ounces shiitake mushrooms, stems removed

1   tablespoon extra-virgin olive oil

2   tablespoons unsalted butter
    Coarse salt and freshly ground pepper

1   small onion, coarsely chopped

1   garlic clove, halved

8   sprigs thyme, plus leaves, for garnish

1½  quarts chicken stock, preferably
    homemade (recipe follows), or low-sodium
    canned chicken broth

½   cup heavy cream

**1.** Preheat oven to 400°F. Score each chestnut using a sharp paring knife or a chestnut knife: Make an X on one side of each chestnut or make one long slit crosswise around circumference. Place chestnuts in a single layer on a rimmed baking sheet, and roast until flesh is tender and golden, about 25 minutes. Remove from the oven. Using a clean kitchen towel, immediately rub to remove shells; set chestnuts aside.

**2.** Set aside 2 each cremini and shiitake mushrooms, and roughly chop the rest. Heat oil and 1 tablespoon butter in a stockpot over medium-high heat. Add chopped mushrooms, and season with salt and pepper; cook, stirring occasionally, until mushrooms start to brown, about 5 minutes. Add onion, garlic, and thyme sprigs. Reduce heat to medium-low, and cook, stirring frequently, until onions are translucent, about 8 minutes.

**3.** Set aside 4 chestnuts, and add the rest to the pot; cook until they are golden, about 5 minutes. Add chicken stock and 2 cups water; increase heat to high, and bring to a boil. Reduce heat, and simmer until chestnuts are tender and falling apart, about 1 hour. Remove from heat; discard thyme. Let cool about 10 minutes.

**4.** Pass soup through a fine sieve into a bowl, reserving liquid. Working in batches so as not to fill more than halfway, transfer solids to a blender or food processor. Purée until soup is very smooth. Add reserved liquid to last batch, and process 1 minute more. Season with salt and pepper. Return to pot; stir in cream, and place over low heat until soup is just heated through.

**5.** Slice reserved chestnuts and mushrooms ¼ inch thick. Melt remaining tablespoon butter in a small skillet over medium-high heat. Add chestnuts and mushrooms; cook, stirring, until they are crisp and golden brown, 3 to 4 minutes. Remove from heat. Divide soup among bowls, and garnish with sautéed chestnuts and mushrooms and a sprinkling of thyme leaves.

### basic chicken stock
MAKES ABOUT 5 QUARTS

*Refrigerate stock in airtight containers for up to three days or freeze for up to six months. We added canned broth to fortify the stock's flavor, but you can replace it with water, if you prefer.*

- 3 *carrots, cut into thirds*
- 2 *stalks celery, cut into thirds*
- 1 *bulb fennel, cut into large chunks*
- 3 *tablespoons fennel seeds, toasted*
- 1 *teaspoon whole black peppercorns*
- 1 *whole chicken (4 to 6 pounds)*
- 2 *pounds chicken wings, necks, and backs*
- 3 *quarts low-sodium canned chicken broth (two 48-ounce cans)*
- 2 *quarts cold water*

**1.** In a large stockpot, combine all ingredients. Cover, and bring to a boil over medium-high heat, then reduce heat to a very gentle simmer. Cook, uncovered, 1 hour, checking occasionally to make sure the liquid is barely bubbling, and skim surface with a large metal spoon as needed.

**2.** Transfer whole chicken to a cutting board. Let cool slightly, and pull meat from sides. (Reserve meat for another use; store in refrigerator up to 3 days, covered with plastic wrap.)

**3.** Return chicken bones to pot. Place a smaller pot lid on surface of stock to keep ingredients submerged. Simmer until bones fall apart when poked, 2½ to 4 hours. Skim surface as needed.

**4.** Prepare a large ice bath. Strain stock through a fine sieve into a large heatproof bowl, discarding solids. Set bowl in ice bath, and let stock cool to room temperature, stirring frequently.

**5.** Transfer stock to airtight containers. Refrigerate at least 8 hours or overnight. With a large metal spoon, skim off and discard fat layer that has collected on the top. If storing, leave fat layer intact; it helps to seal in the flavor.

## classic mushroom soup

*photograph on page 43*

SERVES 6 TO 8

*The wine adds sweetness to balance the earthy flavor of this rich soup.*

- 1 ounce each dried porcini and dried morel mushrooms
- 1½ quarts boiling water
- 4 tablespoons unsalted butter
- 1 onion, cut into ¼-inch dice
- 3 garlic cloves, minced
- 1½ pounds fresh wild mushrooms, cleaned and coarsely chopped
- ¼ cup Madeira or Cognac
- 2 tablespoons all-purpose flour
- 1 tablespoon chopped fresh flat-leaf parsley, for garnish
- ½ cup heavy cream
  Coarse salt and freshly ground pepper

**1.** Place dried mushrooms in a large heatproof bowl; pour the boiling water over mushrooms. Let stand until softened, about 20 minutes. Remove mushrooms with a slotted spoon; coarsely chop, and set aside. Pour mushroom liquid through a cheesecloth-lined sieve into a bowl, discarding any solids; reserve liquid.

**2.** Melt butter in a stockpot over medium heat. Add onion and garlic, and cook, stirring, until softened, about 5 minutes. Add fresh and reserved dried mushrooms, in two batches if necessary, and cook, stirring occasionally, until they have released all of their juices and most liquid has evaporated. Add Madeira, and cook, scraping up any browned bits from bottom of pot with a wooden spoon, until liquid has evaporated, about 2 minutes. Sprinkle mixture with flour, and stir to coat.

**3.** Stir reserved mushroom liquid into pot; bring to a boil. Reduce heat, and simmer, stirring occa-sionally, about 30 minutes. Using a slotted spoon, transfer 1 cup mushroom mixture to a bowl, and toss with parsley. Cover bowl to keep warm; let liq-uid in pot continue to reduce slightly.

**4.** Working in batches so as not to fill more than halfway, pour remaining soup into a blender or food processor; purée until smooth, and return to pot. Stir in cream, and season with salt and pep-per. Divide soup among bowls, and garnish with reserved mushroom mixture.

## cream of belgian-endive soup

*photograph on page 42*

SERVES 8 TO 10

- 8 heads Belgian endive, plus leaves for garnish
- 2 russet potatoes
- 3 tablespoons unsalted butter
- 2 leeks, white and pale-green parts only, cut in half lengthwise and thinly sliced crosswise, washed well
- ½ cup dry white wine
- 1¼ quarts chicken stock, preferably homemade (page 179), or low-sodium canned chicken broth
- 1 cup heavy cream
- 1½ teaspoons coarse salt
- ¼ teaspoon freshly ground white pepper
  Pinch of freshly grated nutmeg

**1.** Cut each head of endive in half lengthwise; cut out and discard cores. Thinly slice crosswise; set aside. Peel potatoes; cut into ½-inch pieces. Place in a bowl of cold water to prevent discoloration.

**2.** Heat butter in a stockpot over medium heat. Add leeks, and cook until they start to soften, about 3 minutes. Drain potatoes well, and add to pot along with sliced endive. Cook, stirring occa-sionally, until vegetables begin to soften, about 10 minutes; do not brown.

3. Pour wine and stock into pot, and bring to a gentle simmer. Cook until vegetables are very soft, about 1 hour. Remove from heat; let cool slightly.

4. Working in batches so as not to fill more than halfway, purée soup in a blender or food processor until smooth. Return to pot, and stir in cream. Bring to a simmer; remove from heat. Add salt, pepper, and nutmeg. Divide soup among serving bowls, and garnish with endive leaves.

## creamy tomato soup
### SERVES 6 TO 8

2  tablespoons unsalted butter
1   onion, finely chopped
3  garlic cloves, minced
10  cups crushed tomatoes
1¼  quarts chicken stock, preferably homemade (page 179), or low-sodium canned chicken broth
3  sprigs oregano, plus more for garnish
½  to 1 cup half-and-half
   Coarse salt and freshly ground pepper

1. Melt butter in a large saucepan over medium-low heat. Add onion and garlic; cook, stirring, until translucent, about 6 minutes.

2. Add tomatoes, stock, and oregano, and bring to a boil. Reduce heat; simmer gently until thickened, about 45 minutes. Remove oregano. Working in batches so as not to fill more than halfway, purée soup in a blender or food processor until smooth. Return soup to saucepan.

3. Slowly add half-and-half to soup, stirring constantly, until desired consistency is reached. Season with salt and pepper. Divide soup among bowls, and garnish with oregano.

## lentil and escarole soup
### SERVES 4

*You can substitute brown lentils for green.*

1  tablespoon unsalted butter
1  small onion, finely chopped
1  small garlic clove, finely chopped
1  small carrot, coarsely chopped
¾  cup French green lentils
1  dried bay leaf
2  whole canned plum tomatoes, drained, seeded, and coarsely chopped
   Coarse salt and freshly ground pepper
2  slices Italian bread, cut into ¾-inch cubes
½  head escarole, cut crosswise into 1-inch strips
   Extra-virgin olive oil, for drizzling

1. In a small stockpot, melt butter over medium heat. Add onion, garlic, and carrot; cook, stirring occasionally, until tender, about 5 minutes. Add lentils, bay leaf, tomatoes, and 1¼ quarts water; season with salt and pepper. Bring to a boil, then reduce heat, and simmer, covered, until lentils are just tender, about 40 minutes.

2. Meanwhile, preheat oven to 425°F. Toast bread cubes on a baking sheet, turning occasionally, until golden brown, about 7 minutes.

3. Add escarole to soup, and cook 5 minutes more. Season with salt and pepper. Divide soup among bowls; garnish with croutons, and drizzle with oil.

## french lentil soup

*photograph on page 41*

SERVES 8 TO 10

*You can easily double this recipe and refrigerate any leftovers in airtight containers for up to three days. The soup can also be frozen for up to three months. We used French lentils, but brown lentils may also be used.*

- 2 tablespoons olive oil
- 1 small onion, finely chopped
- 2 carrots, finely chopped
- 1 stalk celery, finely chopped
- 1 small red bell pepper, seeds and ribs removed, finely chopped
- 1 teaspoon dried oregano
- ½ cup French green lentils, picked over and rinsed
- 3 tablespoons bulghur wheat
- 1½ quarts Wild Mushroom Stock (recipe follows)
  Coarse salt and freshly ground black pepper

**1.** Heat oil in a large stockpot over medium heat. Add onion, and cook, stirring occasionally, until translucent, about 5 minutes. Stir in carrots, celery, bell pepper, and oregano until combined. Stir in lentils and bulghur wheat.

**2.** Pour stock into pot; cover, and simmer over low heat just until lentils are tender, about 45 minutes. Remove from heat; season with salt and pepper. Divide soup among bowls, and serve.

## wild mushroom stock

*photograph on page 41*

MAKES 3 QUARTS

- 4 ounces dried porcini mushrooms
- 1 quart boiling water
- 2 tablespoons unsalted butter
- 2 tablespoons olive oil
- 1 large onion, coarsely chopped
- 2 large carrots, coarsely chopped
- 2 parsnips, coarsely chopped
- 2 stalks celery, coarsely chopped
- 1 bunch (about 1½ pounds) red or green Swiss chard, cut into 1-inch pieces
- 1 dried bay leaf
  Several sprigs thyme
  Several sprigs flat-leaf parsley

**1.** Place dried mushrooms in a medium heatproof bowl; pour the boiling water over mushrooms. Let stand until softened, about 20 minutes. Strain through a fine sieve into another bowl, leaving behind any sediment. Reserve liquid and mushrooms separately. Set aside.

**2.** In a stockpot, cook butter and oil over medium heat. Add onion; cook until caramelized, stirring occasionally, about 20 minutes. Add reserved mushrooms along with the carrots, parsnips, and celery; cook, stirring often, until vegetables are softened, about 20 minutes.

**3.** Stir chard into vegetable mixture in pot. Add 3½ quarts water, reserved mushroom liquid, bay leaf, thyme, and parsley. Cover, and bring to a boil; reduce heat, and simmer, uncovered, 1 hour.

**4.** Remove pot from heat; strain mixture through a cheesecloth-lined sieve into a large heatproof bowl or saucepan, pressing down on vegetables with the back of a wooden spoon to extract as much liquid as possible. Discard solids. Store stock in airtight containers in the refrigerator up to 3 days or in the freezer up to 6 months.

## pea bisque with shrimp and tarragon

SERVES 6

½ pound green split peas, picked over and rinsed

2 bottles (8 ounces each) clam juice

1 onion, chopped

1 package (10 ounces) frozen baby green peas, thawed

1 pound medium shrimp, peeled, deveined, and halved lengthwise

3 garlic cloves, minced

4½ teaspoons finely grated lemon zest

1 teaspoon paprika

¼ teaspoon coarse salt

1 tablespoon unsalted butter

1 tablespoon freshly squeezed lemon juice

1 tablespoon finely chopped fresh tarragon

**1.** Place split peas in a large bowl with enough water to cover by 2 inches; let stand 6 hours or overnight at room temperature.

**2.** Drain peas; transfer to a stockpot. Add clam juice, 1½ quarts water, and onion. Bring to a boil; reduce heat, and simmer, stirring occasionally, until split peas are just tender, 35 to 40 minutes.

**3.** Stir baby peas into pot. Simmer 5 minutes; let cool slightly. Working in batches so as not to fill more than halfway, purée mixture in a blender or food processor until smooth. Press through a fine sieve into a large saucepan; discard solids, and keep mixture warm over low heat.

**4.** In a large bowl, stir together shrimp, garlic, lemon zest, paprika, and salt. Melt butter in a nonstick medium skillet over medium-high heat. Add shrimp mixture; cook, stirring, until shrimp begin to turn opaque. Add lemon juice, and stir 1 minute more. Remove from heat; stir in tarragon.

**5.** Divide bisque among bowls, and place a mound of shrimp mixture in the center of each.

## potato, shrimp, and white bean soup

SERVES 6

This soup can be made through step two up to one day ahead; store puréed mixture in an airtight container in the refrigerator.

1 teaspoon olive oil

1 teaspoon unsalted butter

1 garlic clove, minced

2 medium leeks, white and pale-green parts only, halved lengthwise, sliced crosswise into ¼-inch half moons, and washed well

Coarse salt and freshly ground black pepper

1 quart chicken stock, preferably homemade (page 179), or low-sodium canned chicken broth

2 large Yukon gold potatoes, peeled and sliced ¼ inch thick

½ cup skim milk

1½ cups cooked or canned cannellini beans, rinsed and drained

½ pound medium shrimp, peeled, deveined, and halved lengthwise, tail intact

¼ red bell pepper, cut into ⅛-inch dice

1½ tablespoons snipped fresh chives

**1.** In a stockpot, heat oil and butter over medium-low heat. Add garlic and leeks, and season with salt and pepper; cook, stirring frequently, until leeks are translucent, about 10 minutes.

**2.** Add chicken stock and potatoes to pot, and bring to a boil. Reduce heat to medium, and simmer until potatoes are tender when pierced with a fork, 12 to 15 minutes. Working in batches, if needed, so as not to fill more than halfway, purée soup in a blender or food processor until smooth.

**3.** Return mixture to stockpot, and place over medium heat. Add skim milk and cannellini, and bring to a simmer. Add shrimp, and cook until just opaque, about 2 minutes. Divide soup among bowls, and garnish with red pepper and chives.

## potato seafood chowder

SERVES 6

*The clams will not open at the same time. To prevent overcooking, check the pot frequently, and remove clams as soon as they open.*

2   pounds littleneck clams, scrubbed well

2   tablespoons unsalted butter

1   yellow onion, cut into ½-inch dice

2   stalks celery, cut into ⅛-inch-thick slices

1   tablespoon all-purpose flour

1½  pounds small Yukon gold potatoes, peeled and cut into ¾-inch dice

1   dried bay leaf

4   sprigs thyme

1   pound firm white fish, such as cod or red snapper, cut into bite-size pieces

½   pound medium shrimp, peeled, deveined, and cut in half crosswise

1½  cups half-and-half

Coarse salt and freshly ground pepper

**1.** Bring 2 cups water to a boil in a medium saucepan over medium-high heat. Add clams; cover, and cook, stirring occasionally, until clams have opened, 5 to 8 minutes. Remove clams; let cool slightly. Remove clam meat; discard shells. Set meat aside. Pass liquid through a cheesecloth-lined sieve into a bowl; set broth aside.

**2.** Melt butter in a stockpot over medium heat. Add onion and celery; cook, stirring frequently, until onion is translucent, 8 to 10 minutes. Add flour; cook, stirring, 1 minute. Add reserved clam broth, potatoes, bay leaf, and thyme. Cover, and simmer until potatoes are tender, 10 to 12 minutes.

**3.** Add fish and shrimp to pot. Simmer, uncovered, until seafood is cooked through and opaque, about 3 minutes. Add half-and-half and reserved clam meat; season with salt and pepper. Cook until just heated through, about 3 minutes; serve hot.

## ALL ABOUT CHOWDER

*The word chowder is derived from the Breton chaudrée, a fish stew cooked in a chaudière, or cauldron. This technique was probably brought to Canada and Colonial America by French settlers, and later spread throughout New England. Early American settlers made chowder from household staples: rendered salt pork, locally caught fish, and biscuit crackers. In the nineteenth century, potatoes replaced the crackers, and soon, creamy chowders, such as corn chowder and New England clam chowder, became popular fare. Still, some chowders, such as Manhattan clam chowder, which has a tomato base, more closely resemble the creamless chowders popular before the nineteenth century.*

## poached salmon, leek, and fennel soup

SERVES 6

- 1 tablespoon extra-virgin olive oil
- 3 leeks, white and pale-green parts only, sliced into ¼-inch-thick rounds and washed well
- 3 carrots, cut into ¼-inch-thick rounds
- 2 stalks celery, cut into ¼-inch-thick slices
- 1 small bulb fennel, trimmed and cut into wedges, fronds reserved for garnish
- 4 sprigs flat-leaf parsley
- 4 sprigs thyme
- 1 can (14½ ounces) low-sodium vegetable broth
  Coarse salt and freshly ground pepper
- 1 salmon fillet (1 pound), skin removed, cut into 1-inch cubes
- 1 bunch (about 3 ounces) spinach, washed and cut into 1½-inch-wide strips

**1.** Heat oil in a large saucepan over medium heat. Add leeks, carrots, celery, and fennel. Cook, stirring, until softened, about 5 minutes. Add parsley, thyme, broth, and 1¼ quarts water; season with salt and pepper. Bring to a boil; reduce to a simmer, and cook, covered, 30 minutes.

**2.** Turn off heat; add salmon and spinach to pan. Cover, and poach fish until just cooked through and opaque, about 3 minutes. Divide soup among bowls, garnish with fennel fronds, and serve.

## red-pepper vegetable soup

SERVES 8 TO 12

*The roasted red peppers lend a wonderful smoky taste and a rosy hue to this soup.*

- 6 red bell peppers
- ½ cup (1 stick) unsalted butter
- 2 large onions, coarsely chopped
- 2 garlic cloves, minced
- 4 large carrots, coarsely chopped
- 1 large baking potato, peeled and coarsely chopped
- 2 ripe but firm pears, peeled and coarsely chopped
- 1¼ quarts chicken stock, preferably homemade (page 179), or low-sodium canned chicken broth
- 1 tablespoon coarsely chopped fresh flat-leaf parsley
  Coarse salt and freshly ground pepper
  Crème fraîche or sour cream, for garnish
  Herb sprigs, for garnish

**1.** Roast peppers over a gas flame or under the broiler until skin is charred, turning as each side blackens. Place in a bowl. Cover with plastic wrap; let steam about 10 minutes. Using a paper towel, rub off skins. Discard seeds; coarsely chop flesh.

**2.** Melt butter in a stockpot over medium heat. Add onions and garlic, and cook, stirring frequently, until translucent, about 10 minutes. Add carrots, potato, and chopped red pepper; cook 10 minutes more. Add pears, chicken stock, and parsley. Bring to a boil; reduce heat, and simmer until vegetables are just tender, about 20 minutes. Season with salt and pepper.

**3.** Working in batches so as not to fill more than halfway, purée soup in a blender or food processor until smooth. Return to pot, and place over low heat until heated through. Divide among bowls, and garnish with crème fraîche and herbs.

## squash and parsnip soup

### SERVES 6

*Winter squash include acorn, butternut, turban, and kabocha, with flesh colors ranging from deep yellow to orange. Store them out of the refrigerator in a cool, dark place.*

2   *orange-fleshed winter squash (2¾ pounds)*

2   *tablespoons olive oil*

1   *leek, white and pale-green parts only, cut into ¼-inch rounds, washed well*

3   *garlic cloves, minced*

1   *teaspoon finely grated fresh ginger, or more, if desired*

1   *parsnip (4 ounces), peeled and cut into ¼-inch pieces*

1   *quart chicken stock, preferably homemade (page 179), or low-sodium canned chicken broth*
    *Coarse salt and freshly ground pepper*

2   *slices (about ¾ inch thick) whole-wheat bread, crusts removed, bread sliced into ½-inch pieces*

3   *tablespoons freshly grated Parmesan cheese*

**1.** Cut squash in half lengthwise. Remove seeds and fiber, and peel. Cut squash into ½-inch pieces, and set aside.

**2.** In a stockpot, heat oil over medium-low heat. Add leek and garlic; cook, covered, until softened, 3 to 5 minutes. Add reserved squash, the ginger, and parsnip. Stir to combine, and cook over medium heat 3 to 5 minutes. Add stock, and season with salt and pepper. Cover, and bring to a boil. Reduce to a simmer, and cook until squash and parsnip are tender, 12 to 15 minutes.

**3.** Working in batches, so as not to fill more than halfway, purée half the soup in a blender or food processor until smooth. Return mixture to stockpot, and cook over low heat until heated through. Season again with salt and pepper.

**4.** Meanwhile, preheat oven to 425°F. Toast bread on a baking sheet until golden brown, about 7 minutes. Sprinkle bread with Parmesan; return to oven until cheese begins to melt. Divide soup among bowls; garnish with cheese croutons.

## spicy sweet-potato soup

*photograph on page 42*

### SERVES 10

*This soup can be stored in airtight containers in the refrigerator for up to three days or in the freezer for up to three months.*

1¼  *teaspoons ground cardamom*

1   *teaspoon ground turmeric*

¾   *teaspoon ground cinnamon*

⅓   *teaspoon chili powder*

1   *tablespoon unsalted butter*

1   *tablespoon olive oil*

2   *leeks, white and pale-green parts only, coarsely chopped, washed well*

1   *large onion, cut into ¼-inch dice*

4   *sweet potatoes, peeled and cut into ½-inch dice*

1   *butternut squash (about 1½ pounds), peeled and cut into ½-inch dice*

2   *carrots, cut into ½-inch dice*

3   *quarts chicken stock, preferably homemade (page 179), or low-sodium canned chicken broth*
    *Coarse salt and freshly ground pepper*
    *Radish sprouts, for garnish (optional)*

**1.** Combine spices in a small bowl. In a medium saucepan, heat butter and oil over medium heat. Add leeks and onion; cook, stirring frequently, until translucent, about 8 minutes. Sprinkle with spices, and add sweet potatoes, squash, and carrots. Stir well to combine.

**2.** Add chicken stock to mixture in saucepan, and simmer over low heat, partially covered, until vegetables are tender, about 40 minutes. Season with salt and pepper. Remove from heat.

**3.** Working in batches, so as not to fill more than halfway, purée half the soup in a blender or food processor until smooth. Return to saucepan and place over low heat until heated through. Divide soup among bowls, and garnish each with a handful of radish sprouts, if using.

## puréed spinach-potato soup
SERVES 4

2  tablespoons unsalted butter

1  onion, cut into ½-inch pieces

3  garlic cloves, minced

1½  pounds (about 5 small) Yukon gold potatoes, peeled and cut into ½-inch pieces

¼  cup dry sherry or white wine

1  quart chicken stock, preferably homemade (page 179), or low-sodium canned chicken broth

2  bunches (about 1¼ pounds) spinach, trimmed and washed well

Coarse salt and freshly ground pepper

**1.** Melt butter in a large saucepan over medium heat. Add onion, garlic, and potatoes; stir to coat. Cook, stirring, 2 minutes.

**2.** Pour sherry, chicken stock, and 2 cups water into pan, and stir to combine. Bring to a boil. Reduce heat to a simmer; cover, and cook until potatoes are very tender, about 15 minutes.

**3.** Stir spinach into pan; cook until wilted and bright green, about 3 minutes. Season with salt and pepper. Working in batches so as not to fill more than halfway, purée soup in a blender or food processor until smooth. Return to pan; place over low heat until heated through. Serve.

## tortellini soup
*photograph on page 41*
SERVES 10

2  quarts Wild Mushroom Stock (page 182)
   Coarse salt and freshly ground pepper

1  pound fresh or frozen tortellini filled with sausage or cheese

In a large saucepan, bring mushroom stock to a boil over medium heat. Season with salt and pepper, and stir in pasta. Cook until pasta is al dente according to package instructions (tortellini should float to the top). Remove from heat. Serve hot.

## lamb and chestnut stew
SERVES 6

*Stews are best when cooked the day before they are served. Store in the refrigerator, covered, overnight. When ready to serve, place the covered stew over medium-low heat, until hot. Just before the stew is ready, prepare the polenta.*

14  ounces fresh chestnuts

2  pounds lamb stew meat, cut into 2-inch pieces
   Coarse salt and freshly ground pepper
   All-purpose flour, for dredging

3  tablespoons olive oil

6  ounces pearl onions, peeled

12  ounces small button mushrooms

1  cup dry red wine

3½  cups beef stock, preferably homemade (page 189), or low-sodium canned beef broth

4  canned Italian plum tomatoes, drained and seeded

2  teaspoons chopped fresh sage

2  teaspoons chopped fresh rosemary

½  cup dried cranberries
   Quick Polenta (recipe follows)

1. Preheat oven to 400°F. Score each chestnut using a sharp paring knife or a chestnut knife: Make an X on one side of each chestnut or make one long slit crosswise around circumference. Place chestnuts in a single layer on a rimmed baking sheet, and roast until flesh is tender and golden, about 25 minutes. Remove from oven. Using a clean kitchen towel, immediately rub to remove shells; set chestnuts aside.

2. Season lamb with salt and pepper. Dredge meat in flour, and shake off excess. Heat 2 tablespoons oil in a Dutch oven or stockpot over medium-high heat. Add half the lamb in a single layer without crowding pot; cook until browned all over, about 5 minutes. Transfer lamb to a dish. Repeat browning with remaining tablespoon oil and the meat.

3. Add onions to pot, and cook, stirring occasionally, until golden, about 4 minutes. Add mushrooms; season with salt and pepper, and cook until well browned, 5 to 6 minutes. Add red wine, and deglaze pot, scraping up any browned bits from bottom with a wooden spoon. Cook until liquid is reduced by half, about 5 minutes.

4. Add reserved chestnuts, lamb, beef stock, tomatoes, sage, and rosemary; bring to a boil. Reduce heat to medium-low, and simmer until meat is very tender, 1½ to 2 hours. Add cranberries, and cook 2 minutes. Serve the stew with hot polenta, or let cool and refrigerate overnight.

## quick polenta
### SERVES 6

*Coarse salt*
2 *cups quick-cooking polenta*
*Freshly ground pepper*

Pour 2 quarts water into a large saucepan; season generously with salt. Bring to a boil over high heat. Whisking constantly, pour in polenta in a slow, steady stream. Reduce heat to medium-low; cook, stirring constantly with a wooden spoon, until polenta thickens, 3 to 5 minutes. Season with salt and pepper. Remove from heat; serve.

## hearty beef stew
### SERVES 10

*This recipe uses the tomato and shredded meat that are left over from making the beef stock. Serve this stew over egg noodles or rice.*

*Basic Beef Stock (recipe follows)*
1 *pound pearl onions, peeled*
5 *carrots, cut into 2-inch-long matchsticks*
*Several sprigs dill, coarsely chopped*
*Coarse salt and freshly ground pepper*
1 *package (10 ounces) frozen green peas, thawed*

1. In a stockpot, combine stock and reserved beef and tomato pieces. Cover; bring to a simmer over medium-high heat. Add onions, carrots, and dill. Cook, uncovered, until vegetables are soft, about 30 minutes. Season with salt and pepper.

2. When ready to serve, add peas, and cook just until tender and heated through, about 3 minutes.

## basic beef stock

MAKES 3½ QUARTS

*Refrigerate stock in airtight containers up to three days, or freeze up to six months.*

- 6 pounds beef short ribs, trimmed of excess fat
  Coarse salt and freshly ground pepper
- 1 can (28 ounces) peeled whole tomatoes, coarsely chopped, juice reserved
- 2 dried bay leaves
- 10 whole black peppercorns
  Several sprigs dill, coarsely chopped

**1.** Preheat oven to 450°F. Arrange ribs in a large roasting pan; season generously with salt and pepper. Roast until browned and meat is tender, about 1½ hours, turning ribs halfway through.

**2.** Combine 3 quarts water and tomatoes and their juice in a large stockpot. Bundle bay leaves, peppercorns, and dill in a small piece of cheesecloth; tie with kitchen twine, and add to pot.

**3.** Transfer roasted ribs to pot. Pour off and discard fat from roasting pan. Pour 1 cup water into pan; place over medium-high heat. Bring to a boil, scraping up any browned bits from the bottom with a wooden spoon; boil until water is reduced by half. Transfer liquid and solids to stockpot.

**4.** Bring mixture in pot to a simmer over high heat; do not boil. Reduce heat to a gentle simmer; place a lid smaller than pot directly on surface of stock to keep ingredients submerged. Cook until meat is very tender and pulls away from bone, about 1½ hours. Skim surface with a spoon as needed.

**5.** Prepare a large ice bath. Remove herb bundle from pot; squeeze it over pot, and discard bundle. Strain stock through a sieve into a large heatproof bowl set in the ice bath; let stock cool to room temperature, stirring frequently.

**6.** Transfer ribs and tomato pieces to another bowl. When cool enough to handle, pull meat from bones, and shred with your fingers. Discard bones. Store meat and tomato pieces in an airtight container in refrigerator, up to 3 days.

**7.** Transfer cooled stock to airtight containers; refrigerate at least 6 hours or overnight. With a large metal spoon, skim off and discard fat layer that has collected on top. If storing, leave fat layer intact; it helps to seal in the flavor.

### MAKING STOCK AHEAD

*Homemade soup may require a bit more effort, but there is a way to cut down on last-minute work. Prepare a big pot of stock well in advance of the holiday season, and freeze it in airtight plastic containers. It will keep for up to six months and can be used to fix quick, fresh soups during the holidays, when you don't have a lot of time to spare. Making the stock requires an afternoon of tending, but the actual work takes less than an hour, most of which is spent chopping and sautéing the ingredients.*

## winter vegetable chicken stew

SERVES 6

12  ounces boneless and skinless chicken thighs (about 4 pieces)

 1  pound boneless and skinless chicken breast halves (about 3 pieces)

    Coarse salt and freshly ground pepper

 3  tablespoons unsalted butter

 4  carrots, cut into ¾-inch pieces

 3  large stalks celery, cut into ¾-inch pieces

 2  parsnips (6 ounces), peeled and cut into ¾-inch pieces

 4  small onions, quartered lengthwise, with roots intact

 2  cups chicken stock, preferably homemade (page 179), or low-sodium canned chicken broth

 1  tablespoon fresh rosemary leaves or 1 teaspoon dried

 ½  pound wide egg noodles

 ¼  cup finely chopped fresh flat-leaf parsley

 4  garlic cloves, thinly sliced

 1  bunch (1½ pounds) Swiss chard, stems and leaves coarsely chopped

 2  ounces freshly shaved Parmesan cheese, for garnish

**1.** Cut chicken thighs and breasts into 1-inch pieces, and season with salt and pepper. Melt 2 tablespoons butter in a 6-quart Dutch oven over medium heat. Add half the chicken; cook, stirring occasionally, until browned, about 7 minutes. Transfer to a large bowl. Repeat with remaining chicken.

**2.** Add carrots, celery, parsnips, onions, 3 cups water, stock, and rosemary to Dutch oven; deglaze pot, scraping up any browned bits from bottom with a wooden spoon. Cover; bring to a simmer over low heat. Cook, stirring occasionally, until vegetables are barely tender, about 10 minutes.

**3.** Meanwhile, bring a large pot of water to a boil; add salt. Cook noodles in boiling water until al dente according to package instructions; drain. Stir noodles, parsley, reserved chicken and any collected juices into mixture in pot. Cook on low heat until chicken is heated through, 1 to 2 minutes. Remove from heat; cover to keep warm.

**4.** Melt remaining tablespoon butter in a large nonstick skillet over medium-high heat. Add garlic; stir until golden, about 1 minute. Add chard; cook, stirring occasionally, until tender, about 5 minutes. Divide chard among bowls. Ladle soup into bowls, and garnish with shaved Parmesan.

# main courses

BEEF, LAMB, PORK

VENISON, TURKEY, CHICKEN

GAME BIRDS

FISH AND SHELLFISH

PASTA

✳

BEEF

## boeuf bourguignon
*photograph on page 45*
SERVES 8; MAKES 2½ QUARTS

1  large onion, coarsely chopped

2  carrots, coarsely chopped

1  head garlic, cloves separated and
   lightly crushed (unpeeled)

10  sprigs flat-leaf parsley, halved,
    plus 3 tablespoons chopped for garnish

6  sprigs thyme

4  sprigs rosemary

2  dried bay leaves

½  teaspoon whole black peppercorns

2  tablespoons olive oil

6  ounces salt pork, trimmed of rind
   and cut into ¼-by-1-inch pieces

3  pounds beef chuck, cut into 2-inch cubes
   Coarse salt and freshly ground pepper

3  tablespoons all-purpose flour

3  cups beef stock, preferably
   homemade (page 189), or low-sodium
   canned beef broth

1  750-ml bottle dry red wine,
   preferably Burgundy

1  teaspoon tomato paste

1  pound frozen pearl onions

1  tablespoon unsalted butter

1  tablespoon sugar

10  ounces large white mushrooms,
    trimmed and quartered

**1.** Cut two 12-by-22-inch pieces of cheesecloth; lay them on a clean work surface, overlapping each other perpendicularly in the center to form a cross. Pile the onion, carrots, garlic, parsley, thyme, rosemary, bay leaves, and peppercorns in the center.

**2.** Gather the ends together to enclose contents completely, and tie the top with kitchen twine. Place in an 8-quart Dutch oven, and set aside.

**3.** Preheat oven to 300°F. Heat oil in a large skillet over medium heat. Add salt pork, and sauté until brown and crisp, about 7 minutes. Using a slotted spoon, transfer pork to Dutch oven, leaving rendered fat in skillet.

**4.** Season beef cubes with salt and pepper. Working in two batches, place beef in skillet in a single layer; cook until browned on all sides, about 6 minutes total. Transfer beef to Dutch oven.

**5.** Whisk the flour into fat in the skillet. Slowly whisk in beef stock, and bring to a simmer over medium heat, stirring frequently until thickened.

**6.** Pour mixture into Dutch oven around cheesecloth bundle. Add wine and tomato paste, and season with salt and pepper; stir to combine. Bring to a boil over high heat. Cover; transfer to oven. Cook until beef is very tender, about 2½ hours.

**7.** Remove pot from oven, and transfer cheesecloth bundle to a large sieve set over a bowl. With a wooden spoon, press on bundle to release as much liquid as possible. Discard bundle, and pour accumulated juices into pot.

**8.** Remove beef and pork from pot; reserve. Return liquid to a boil; reduce to 4 cups, about 10 minutes. Skim surface as needed with a metal spoon. Reduce heat to low; return beef and pork to pot.

**9.** While sauce is reducing further, set the skillet over high heat. Add the pearl onions, ½ cup water, the butter, sugar, and a pinch of salt. Bring to a boil, then reduce heat to medium; simmer until almost all the liquid evaporates, 5 to 8 minutes. Raise heat to medium-high, and add the mushrooms. Cook, stirring occasionally, until vegetables are browned and glazed, about 5 minutes.

**10.** Remove skillet from heat. Transfer contents to Dutch oven; simmer over medium heat until just heated through. Season with salt and pepper, and serve garnished with chopped parsley.

## beef tenderloin
## with herb-salt crust
### SERVES 6 TO 8

*Salt dough is distantly related to huff paste, a concoction of salt, flour, and water used to protect meat from the heat of an open spit; herbs and garlic infuse this wrapped tenderloin with incredible flavor while it cooks. When finished, the salt crust will be discarded.*

- 2 cups plus 2 tablespoons coarse salt
- ¼ cup plus 3 tablespoons fresh thyme leaves
- ¼ cup plus 3 tablespoons fresh rosemary leaves
- 2 large eggs, separated
- 2 to 2½ cups all-purpose flour, plus more for work surface
- 2 to 3 pounds beef tenderloin, trimmed and tied
- 1 tablespoon unsalted butter
- 1 tablespoon extra-virgin olive oil
- 10 fresh sage leaves
- 2 fresh bay leaves
- 1 cup fresh flat-leaf parsley leaves
- 6 garlic cloves, peeled and thinly sliced
  Freshly ground pepper

**1.** In the bowl of an electric mixer, combine 2 cups salt with 3 tablespoons each thyme and rosemary. Add egg whites and ⅔ cup water; beat until thoroughly combined. Gradually add 2 cups flour, beating on medium speed, until mixture forms a smooth dough, 2 to 3 minutes. The dough should be firm but not too moist or sticky. If necessary, knead in an additional ½ cup flour, a little at a time. Pat dough into a square; wrap in plastic. Let rest at room temperature at least 2 hours or up to 24 hours.

**2.** Preheat oven to 375°F, with rack in center. Rinse tenderloin, and pat dry. Heat butter and oil in a large skillet over medium-high heat. Add beef;

sear on all sides until browned, about 1½ minutes per side. Transfer tenderloin to a wire rack set over a baking pan to cool, about 5 minutes.

**3.** On a lightly floured work surface, roll out dough to a rectangle ¼ inch thick and large enough to encase the beef. Sprinkle dough with the remaining ¼ cup each thyme and rosemary, along with the sage, bay leaves, parsley, and garlic. Remove and discard twine from tenderloin; place beef in the center of the dough. Wrap dough around beef, completely encasing it. Press edges together to seal. Carefully transfer the wrapped beef to a roasting pan. In a small bowl, whisk together egg yolks and 2 teaspoons water; brush entire surface of dough with egg wash. Sprinkle remaining 2 tablespoons salt over the top.

**4.** Place roasting pan in oven. Roast until crust is light golden and an instant-read thermometer inserted into center of tenderloin registers 125°F to 130°F for medium-rare (10 to 12 minutes per pound). Remove pan from oven, and let beef rest at room temperature 1 hour.

**5.** When ready to serve, slice off the crust at one end, and remove beef; discard crust. Season the beef with pepper, and cut into slices.

### PREPARING BEEF TENDERLOIN

*One end of a strip of tenderloin is generally thicker than the other. To cook the tenderloin evenly, trim excess meat from the thicker side, then tie to other end with string, so thickness is uniform. This technique will help ensure that the tenderloin stays moist while cooking.*

## beef wellington

*photograph on page 44*

SERVES 6 TO 8

*Beef Wellington's ingredients make it exceptionally rich fare. Serve it with simple boiled vegetables, such as new potatoes, and a traditional Madeira sauce or a Bordelaise sauce made with red wine.*

2½ to 3 pounds beef tenderloin, trimmed and tied

2 teaspoons coarse salt

½ teaspoon freshly ground pepper

1 tablespoon oil

2 tablespoons unsalted butter

1 small onion, finely chopped

1 pound white mushrooms, stems removed, caps finely chopped

¼ cup dry sherry

All-purpose flour, for work surface

1 pound frozen puff pastry, thawed, plus more for garnish, if desired

4 ounces duck, chicken-liver, or peppercorn mousse, room temperature

1 large egg, lightly beaten

Sea salt, for seasoning (optional)

**1.** Rub beef with 1 teaspoon salt and ¼ teaspoon pepper. Place a large cast-iron or heavy skillet over medium-high heat, and add oil. When oil is very hot, add beef; sear on all sides until browned, about 1½ minutes per side.

**2.** Transfer tenderloin to a platter; let rest until cool. Pour off any accumulated juices, and transfer to the refrigerator until ready to assemble and beef is cold, at least 1 hour or overnight.

### ASSEMBLING BEEF WELLINGTON

*1. On a floured surface, roll puff pastry into a rectangle big enough to enclose the beef. Spread the top of the tenderloin evenly with mousse, and then spread sautéed mushrooms evenly over the top.*

*2. Invert the coated tenderloin into the middle of the puff pastry, and spread the other side with mousse and sautéed mushrooms. Fold up the long sides of the dough to enclose the tenderloin, brushing edges with egg wash to seal. Trim the ends if necessary, then fold up, and seal.*

*3. Roll out extra dough, and cut into holly or other desired shapes. Chill dough and shapes. Attach shaped cutouts to pastry with egg wash; brush entire surface with egg wash, then bake.*

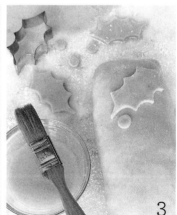

**3.** In clean skillet, melt butter over medium heat. Add onion; cook until soft, about 4 minutes. Add mushrooms; season with remaining teaspoon salt and ¼ teaspoon pepper. Cook, stirring occasionally, until tender and released liquid has evaporated, 8 to 10 minutes. Add sherry; cook until mixture is dry, about 4 minutes more. Remove from heat; let cool at room temperature. The mushroom mixture can be refrigerated up to 1 day.

**4.** On a floured work surface, roll out puff pastry into a rectangle ¼ inch thick and large enough to encase the beef. (It may be necessary to lay out two pieces, overlapping, and roll them out into one piece.) Spread top of tenderloin evenly with half the mousse, then with half the mushroom mixture.

**5.** Carefully invert tenderloin onto middle of puff pastry, coating side down. Spread the remaining mousse over rest of tenderloin, then spread remaining mushroom mixture over mousse. Fold up long sides of dough to enclose tenderloin, brushing edges with egg wash to seal. Trim short sides, if necessary, then fold up and seal.

**6.** Carefully transfer wrapped tenderloin, seam side down, to a baking sheet; cover with plastic wrap, and chill at least 2 hours or overnight. Roll out any extra dough; cut into holly or other shapes if desired, and chill on baking sheet with beef. Cover and chill egg wash.

**7.** Preheat oven to 425°F. Heat a baking sheet on middle rack of oven, about 15 minutes. Decorate top of pastry with shaped pastry cutouts, if desired; brush with beaten egg. Make 2 to 3 slits in pastry for venting steam. Sprinkle with sea salt, if desired.

**8.** Carefully transfer beef to preheated baking sheet. Bake until pastry is golden brown and beef registers 130°F to 135°F for medium-rare, 35 to 50 minutes. Cover pastry with foil if it starts to become too brown while cooking. Transfer beef to a cutting board; let rest 10 minutes before slicing.

## beef tenderloin with shallot mustard sauce
### SERVES 4

*We used a mixture of Dijon and grainy mustards, but you may use either on its own.*

1½   *pounds beef tenderloin, trimmed and tied*
2   *teaspoons coarse salt*
1   *teaspoon freshly ground pepper*
1   *tablespoon olive oil*
3   *large shallots, cut into ¼-inch-thick rounds*
2   *tablespoons balsamic vinegar*
1   *cup beef stock, preferably homemade (page 189), or low-sodium canned beef broth*
1   *tablespoon Dijon mustard*
2   *teaspoons grainy mustard*
2   *tablespoons unsalted butter*

**1.** Preheat oven to 425°F. Rub beef with salt and pepper. Place an ovenproof skillet over medium-high heat; add oil. When oil is very hot, add beef; sear until browned, about 1½ minutes per side.

**2.** Transfer to oven; roast 10 minutes. Add shallots; roast 15 to 20 minutes more, or until a meat thermometer registers 135°F for medium-rare. Transfer beef to a cutting board; let rest at least 10 minutes.

**3.** Place skillet with shallots over medium-high heat; add balsamic vinegar, and deglaze pan, stirring up any browned bits from the bottom with a wooden spoon. Add stock, and simmer until slightly reduced, 2 to 3 minutes. Reduce heat to low, and stir in mustards and butter. Keep sauce warm. When ready to serve, cut beef into ½-inch-thick slices, and spoon sauce over the top.

## prime rib roast

### SERVES 6 TO 8

*To ensure even cooking, let roast sit at room temperature about two hours before cooking. Reserve pan drippings in step three for Yorkshire Pudding (recipe follows).*

- 1  three-rib prime-rib roast, trimmed and tied
- 1  tablespoon freshly ground pepper
- 2  tablespoons coarse salt
- 3  short ribs, tied
- 1½  cups dry red wine
   Yorkshire Pudding, for serving
   (recipe follows)

**1.** Preheat oven to 450°F, with rack on lower level. Rub roast all over with the salt and pepper. Transfer to a heavy 13-by-16-inch roasting pan, fat side up. Place short ribs in pan next to roast.

**2.** Transfer to oven; cook 20 minutes. Reduce oven heat to 325°F, and continue cooking until a meat thermometer inserted in thick end of roast (avoiding bone) reaches 115°F, about 1 hour 25 minutes.

**3.** Transfer roast to a platter; let rest in a warm spot to allow juices to collect. (As roast rests, temperature will increase about 10°F.) Do not cover, or crust will get soggy. Raise oven heat to 425°F. Discard short ribs. Pour fat and all drippings from pan into a glass measuring cup; reserve for pudding.

**4.** Place roasting pan over medium-high heat. Pour red wine into pan, and deglaze, scraping up any browned bits from bottom of pan with a wooden spoon. Cook until reduced by half, 5 to 8 minutes. Place a fine sieve over a medium heatproof bowl. Pour mixture through sieve. Using a wooden spoon, press down on solids to extract juices. Discard solids. Cover bowl tightly; keep sauce warm by placing in a saucepan filled with 1 inch barely simmering water. Serve roast hot with pan sauce and pudding.

## yorkshire pudding

### SERVES 6 TO 8

*Yorkshire Pudding batter needs to be cold. For best results, make a day ahead, and refrigerate.*

- 2  cups all-purpose flour
- 1  teaspoon coarse salt
- 6  large eggs
- 2½  cups milk

**1.** Sift together flour and salt into a medium bowl; make a well in the center, and place eggs in well. Slowly whisk eggs into flour mixture until a paste forms. Gradually whisk in ½ cup milk until well combined; whisk in the remaining 2 cups milk. Cover with plastic wrap; chill at least 4 hours.

**2.** When roast is finished, raise oven temperature to 425°F. Once pan is deglazed, pour ¼ cup reserved pan drippings into pan. Heat pan and drippings in oven until very hot, about 5 minutes. Remove batter from refrigerator; shake or whisk well. Quickly pour into hot pan. Return to oven, and cook until pudding has risen and is golden brown in center and well browned around edge, 20 to 30 minutes. Serve warm with prime rib.

## *braised lamb shanks with tomato and fennel*

SERVES 4

*We served this dish with Soft Polenta (page 298).*

4  *lamb shanks (about 1½ pounds each), trimmed*

  *Coarse salt and freshly ground pepper*

½  *cup all-purpose flour*

¼  *cup extra-virgin olive oil*

2  *tablespoons unsalted butter*

2  *onions, sliced ¼ inch thick*

1  *large leek, white and pale-green parts only, halved lengthwise, sliced into ¼-inch half moons, washed well and drained*

4  *garlic cloves, thinly sliced*

1  *cup dry red wine*

2  *cups chicken stock, preferably homemade (page 179), or low-sodium canned chicken broth*

1  *can (28 ounces) peeled whole plum tomatoes, drained*

2  *tablespoons tomato paste*

1  *tablespoon fresh thyme leaves*

2  *dried bay leaves*

2  *fennel bulbs, trimmed and sliced ¼ inch thick*

**1.** Preheat oven to 375°F. Rub lamb all over with salt and pepper. Place flour in a shallow bowl. Dredge lamb shanks, one at a time, in flour, turning to coat evenly; shake off excess. Heat oil and butter in an 8-quart Dutch oven or ovenproof skillet over medium heat. Working in two batches, sear shanks until browned, about 5 minutes per side. Transfer to a large plate; drain off all but 2 tablespoons fat from pot.

**2.** Return pot to medium heat. Add onions and leek; sauté until lightly browned, about 6 minutes. Add garlic; cook 4 minutes more. Add red wine; deglaze pot, scraping up any browned bits from bottom with a wooden spoon. Return shanks to pot, and add chicken stock, tomatoes, tomato paste, thyme, and bay leaves. Bring to a boil; cover, and place in oven. Braise 2 hours; add fennel, and cook 30 minutes more.

**3.** Using a slotted spatula, transfer shanks and vegetables to a large bowl. Cover; set aside. Using a ladle, skim fat from surface of cooking liquid; cook over medium heat until liquid has thickened, 5 to 7 minutes. Return shanks and vegetables to pot; cook just until heated through. Remove from heat; season with salt and pepper. Serve immediately.

### CHOOSING LAMB CHOPS

*When buying lamb, look for meat that is firm and bright, pink to light red in color, with smooth, white fat rather than yellow. The cut surface of the bones should be red and moist. Avoid meat that is darker, slightly purplish, strong-smelling, or with bones that are white and dry—these are signs of an older animal. Most American lamb, which is largely grain-fed, has a milder flavor and is slightly more tender than grass-fed imported lamb.*

## leg of lamb with spicy mustard marinade

SERVES 8 TO 10

*For the most flavorful results, the lamb should marinate overnight. Have your butcher remove the hip bone, leaving leg bone intact.*

½ cup Dijon mustard

3 tablespoons chopped fresh rosemary

3 tablespoons soy sauce

2 garlic cloves, minced

¼ teaspoon ground ginger

2 tablespoons olive oil

1 leg of lamb (7 to 8 pounds), trimmed of excess fat

**1.** Whisk together mustard, rosemary, soy sauce, garlic, ginger, and oil in a nonreactive bowl. Place lamb on a rack in a roasting pan. Using a pastry brush, coat lamb with marinade. Cover with plastic wrap. Marinate in the refrigerator at least 6 hours or overnight.

**2.** Remove lamb from refrigerator; let stand at room temperature 1 hour.

**3.** Preheat oven to 450°F. Place lamb in oven; immediately reduce oven temperature to 350°F. Roast 15 to 20 minutes per pound, or until an instant-read thermometer inserted into thickest part of meat (avoiding bone) registers 135°F to 140°F for medium-rare (2 hours 15 minutes for a 7½-pound leg of lamb). Remove from oven; let rest at least 15 minutes before carving.

**4.** On a cutting board, place tip end of lamb closest to you. Slice on the bias, as thinly as desired. Flip the lamb as you carve to reach bottom of meat. Transfer to a platter, and serve.

## shepherd's pie with sweet-potato crust

SERVES 6

*You can use ground lamb instead of cooked stew meat: Brown the ground meat first, remove from skillet, and continue with step two.*

2 pounds sweet potatoes (about 6)

3 tablespoons olive oil

1 yellow onion, finely chopped

1 garlic clove, minced

1 stalk celery, finely chopped

2 carrots, cut into ¼-inch dice

½ pound white button mushrooms, trimmed and cut into ½-inch pieces

1¼ pounds cooked lamb stew meat, cut into chunks

1 can (6 ounces) tomato paste

1⅔ cups beef stock, preferably home-made (page 189), or low-sodium canned beef broth

1 teaspoon dried oregano
Coarse salt and freshly ground pepper

½ cup heavy cream, heated

2 tablespoons unsalted butter, melted

**1.** Preheat oven to 450°F. Pierce sweet potatoes with a fork; place on a baking sheet, and bake until tender, 30 to 45 minutes. Remove from oven; set aside to cool slightly. Reduce oven heat to 400°F.

**2.** Meanwhile, heat oil in a large skillet over medium heat. Add onion, garlic, celery, and carrots; cook, stirring frequently, until onion is translucent, 8 to 10 minutes. Add mushrooms; cook until softened, 5 to 7 minutes. Stir in lamb, tomato paste, stock, and oregano; season with salt and pepper. Cook until mixture bubbles and thickens, 10 to 12 minutes. Remove from heat; transfer to a 6-quart casserole or a deep-sided ceramic pie dish.

**3.** Peel potatoes; pass through a food mill or potato ricer into a medium bowl. Add hot cream and butter; season with salt and pepper. Stir until mixture is combined and smooth. Spread potatoes over lamb mixture, leaving a 1-inch border. Bake until potatoes are browned and meat is heated through, about 40 minutes. Remove from oven; let stand 5 minutes before serving.

## stuffed lamb chops
### SERVES 8

*This recipe calls for boning lamb chops; boned chops can also be ordered from a good butcher.*

8   *double-thick loin lamb chops*

4   *tablespoons unsalted butter*

3   *leeks, 2 whole, 1 julienned and washed well*

2   *red bell peppers, ribs and seeds removed, julienned*

3   *garlic cloves, minced*

½   *cup plain breadcrumbs, preferably homemade*

4   *sprigs rosemary, leaves picked and chopped*

12  *sprigs thyme, leaves picked from 4 and chopped*

    *Coarse salt and freshly ground pepper*

3   *tablespoons olive oil, plus more for baking dish*

**1.** Remove the bone and all fat from each lamb chop; set chops aside. Melt butter in a skillet, and sauté julienned leek, bell peppers, and garlic over medium heat until just tender, about 5 minutes. Add breadcrumbs and chopped rosemary and thyme. Season with salt and pepper. Reduce heat to low, and cook 5 minutes.

**2.** Spoon stuffing onto each lamb chop. Roll each chop tightly, and tie with kitchen twine. Heat oil in a skillet until it sizzles. Add stuffed chops and remaining 8 sprigs thyme; season with salt and pepper. Cook until chops are lightly browned all over, about 3 minutes per side. Remove chops from skillet; let cool slightly before removing twine from each chop.

**3.** Meanwhile, bring a large pot of water to a boil. Prepare an ice bath; set aside. Carefully separate leaves of whole leeks; wash off all dirt. Blanch 10 to 30 seconds, plunge into ice bath, and drain.

**4.** Preheat oven to 350°F. Wrap one leek leaf around each lamb roll, and tie with ends to form a bow.

**5.** Place chops in a baking dish with a small amount of oil, and bake until heated through and lamb is browned, 12 to 15 minutes; serve immediately.

## LAMB-CHOP CUTS

*A lamb chop's flavor, texture, and cost are largely determined by where the cut is made on the body. The most tender meat comes from the lamb's loins and ribs; the loin is leaner, the rib more flavorful. The sirloin chop, taken from the leg or hip, is less expensive, but the meat, like that of the shoulder cut, can be tough.*

PORK

## brown-sugar-glazed pork loin
SERVES 10 TO 12

*Use a combination of the pan drippings and marinade to brush on the pork while roasting to give it an appealing burnished color.*

¼ cup packed dark-brown sugar

2 tablespoons Dijon mustard

¼ cup balsamic vinegar

¾ cup freshly squeezed orange juice

4 garlic cloves, peeled and crushed
Freshly ground pepper

10 whole sage leaves, plus more for garnish

1 pork loin (3 to 5 pounds)
Coarse salt
Prune and Apple Chutney (page 305)

**1.** In a shallow dish, whisk together sugar, mustard, vinegar, orange juice, and garlic; season with pepper. Add sage leaves, and bruise them with the whisk. Place loin in marinade; turn to coat all sides. Refrigerate, covered, 1 hour or overnight.

**2.** Preheat oven to 375°F. Place a wire rack in a roasting pan. Remove loin from marinade, letting excess drip off; place loin, fat side up, on rack. Salt, then dot loin with sage leaves from marinade. Reserve marinade. Roast, basting often with pan drippings and marinade, until a meat thermometer inserted into center registers 150°F, 1 to 1½ hours.

**3.** Garnish with sage, and serve warm or at room temperature with chutney.

## cider-braised pork loin with mashed roasted butternut squash
SERVES 4

1 pork loin and 1 rack of 8 ribs (about 5 pounds total)

2 tablespoons coarse salt, plus more for seasoning

2 teaspoons freshly ground pepper, plus more for seasoning

2 tablespoons canola oil, plus more for frying

4 cups apple cider

6 cups no-salt chicken stock, preferably homemade

2 tablespoons cider vinegar

2 onions, cut in half

4 sprigs thyme

2 sprigs flat-leaf parsley

4 Granny Smith apples, 2 halved, 2 peeled, cored, and sliced into eighths

2 teaspoons sugar

8 fresh sage leaves (optional)
Mashed Roasted Butternut Squash (recipe follows)

**1.** Preheat oven to 250°F. Rub rack of ribs with 1 tablespoon salt and 1 teaspoon pepper. Place a 7-quart Dutch oven or flameproof casserole over medium heat. Add 1 tablespoon oil, and heat until hot but not smoking. Add ribs; sear until brown, 8 to 10 minutes per side, and remove. Pour off excess fat from pot.

**2.** Add 2 cups cider to pot; deglaze pot, stirring up browned bits from the bottom with a wooden spoon. Add stock, vinegar, onions, thyme, and parsley. Return ribs to pot; add halved apples. Bring to a simmer; transfer pot to oven, and cook 2 hours.

3. Heat remaining tablespoon oil in a large skillet. Season pork loin with 1 tablespoon salt and 1 teaspoon pepper. When oil is hot but not smoking, add pork loin; sear until golden brown on all sides, 10 to 15 minutes.

4. Remove pot from oven. Transfer 2 cups cooking liquid from pot to a shallow bowl; let stand until cool. Transfer loin to pot; return to oven, and continue cooking until a meat thermometer inserted into loin registers 150°F, about 40 minutes more.

5. Skim fat from reserved cooking liquid. Strain liquid into a medium saucepan; add remaining 2 cups cider. Simmer over medium heat until reduced by a little more than half; liquid should be amber with a slightly viscous consistency.

6. Place a large skillet over medium heat. Arrange sliced apples in a single layer in the hot skillet. Sprinkle with sugar, and season lightly with salt and pepper. Cook until sugar melts, 2 to 3 minutes, then reduce heat to low. Continue cooking until sugar starts to caramelize, 7 to 8 minutes. Apples should soften and puff, and bottom sides should start to brown.

7. When the apple slices loosen on their own from pan, turn and cook until other sides are browned, 5 to 7 minutes. Add reduced cider mixture to skillet; cook just until heated through.

8. If using sage leaves, heat about ½ inch oil in a heavy skillet over medium heat to just below smoking point. Add sage leaves; fry until crisp, about 1 minute. With a slotted spoon, transfer leaves to paper towels to drain.

9. Slice loin ¼ inch thick, and cut rack into individual ribs. Serve pork with apples and butternut squash. Garnish with fried sage leaves.

## mashed roasted butternut squash
### SERVES 4

*If making squash to serve with Cider-Braised Pork Loin, use some of the cooking liquid from braising the pork instead of chicken stock.*

- 2 small butternut squash (3 to 4 pounds total)
- 2 tablespoons unsalted butter
- 2 shallots, finely chopped
- ¼ teaspoon ground ginger
- ½ cup no-salt chicken stock, preferably homemade, plus more if needed
- Coarse salt and freshly ground pepper

1. Preheat oven to 400°F. Line a baking sheet with parchment paper. Cut each squash in half lengthwise. Place halves, cut sides down, on baking sheet; roast until very tender, about 45 minutes.

2. Remove squash from the oven. When just cool enough to handle, scoop out seeds. Spoon flesh into a bowl; discard seeds and skin.

3. Melt butter in a medium saucepan over medium heat. Add shallots; cook until translucent, about 5 minutes. Add ginger and squash; stir to combine. Pour in stock; using a fork, mash squash to a purée. Add more stock as needed. Season with salt and pepper, and serve warm.

## pork loin braised in milk
*photograph on page 45*
SERVES 4

*We served this dish with Butternut Squash with Brown Butter (page 276) and Sautéed Brussels Sprouts with Raisins (page 274).*

2  tablespoons olive oil
8  boneless pork loin chops (about 1¼ pounds)
   Coarse salt and freshly ground pepper
2  cups milk
5  to 6 sprigs thyme, plus 1 teaspoon
   fresh thyme leaves
1  tablespoon cornstarch

**1.** Heat oil in a large skillet over medium heat. Season pork chops on both sides with salt and pepper. Working in batches if necessary, sear the chops until brown, about 3 minutes per side. Transfer chops to a large plate.

**2.** Pour off fat from skillet, and place skillet over low heat. Return pork and any accumulated juices to skillet; add milk and thyme sprigs. Bring to a boil over high heat; cover, and reduce heat to low. Simmer until pork is cooked through and tender, turning once, about 45 minutes.

**3.** Transfer pork to a serving platter, and cover with foil to keep warm. Return skillet to medium-high heat, and bring remaining liquid to a boil. Whisk together cornstarch and 1 tablespoon water in a small bowl; whisk into liquid in skillet, and boil 1 minute. Transfer mixture to a blender or food processor. Add thyme leaves; purée until smooth. Pour sauce over pork, and serve immediately.

## choucroute garni
*photograph on page 49*
SERVES 10 TO 12

*You can substitute hard-to-find meats, such as dry-salted bacon, with more available ones, such as sausage. The overall quantity is more important than using any one particular variety.*

5  to 6 pounds sauerkraut
25  whole black peppercorns
1½  teaspoons coriander seeds
5  whole cloves
15  juniper berries
6  sprigs flat-leaf parsley
4  sprigs thyme
2  dried bay leaves
½  cup goose fat or unsalted butter
4  onions, sliced ⅛ inch thick
1½  cups Riesling or other dry white wine
2  cups chicken stock, preferably homemade
   (page 179), or low-sodium canned
   chicken broth
1  slab (1½ pounds) dry-salted bacon,
   rinsed and dried
1  slab (1½ pounds) smoked bacon
2  dry-salted pig's knuckles (about 1½ pounds)
1  pound smoked pork butt
3  carrots
¼  cup finely minced garlic
2  teaspoons coarse salt
8  small red potatoes, peeled
4  white veal sausages (weisswurst or
   bockwurst; about 4 ounces each)
4  smoked country sausages (bauerwurst;
   about 4 ounces each)
4  knackwurst sausages (about 4 ounces each)

**1.** Place sauerkraut in a colander; rinse with warm water, and drain well.

**2.** Make bouquet garni: Place peppercorns, coriander seeds, cloves, juniper berries, parsley, thyme, and bay leaves on a square of cheesecloth, and tie with kitchen twine.

**3.** Melt goose fat in a very large Dutch oven over medium heat. Add onions; cook, stirring frequently, until translucent but not brown, about 10 minutes.

**4.** Add wine, stock, and 2 cups water to Dutch oven; stir to combine. Add both bacons, the pig's knuckles, pork butt, carrots, garlic, salt, and bouquet garni. Spread drained sauerkraut on top of mixture. Add enough cold water to bring liquid to 1 inch below sauerkraut. Cover, raise heat to high, and bring liquid to a boil. Reduce heat to low; cook at a full simmer 1½ hours.

**5.** Add potatoes to pot; simmer, covered, until potatoes are just tender when pierced with a fork, about 30 minutes. Add sausages; simmer, covered, until heated through, about 10 minutes more.

**6.** Remove bouquet garni, and discard. Transfer meat, potatoes, and carrots to a cutting board. Drain sauerkraut, and place in the middle of a large serving platter. Slice bacon and pork butt. Arrange meat, potatoes, and carrots around sauerkraut on platter. Serve warm.

## crown roast with gravy

*photograph on page 45*

SERVES 12 TO 18

*Ask your butcher to remove the chine (backbone), feather bones, and any excess fat from the crown roast.*

 1  crown roast of pork (8 to 9 pounds)
    Coarse salt and freshly ground pepper
 ¼  cup plus 1½ tablespoons olive oil
    Grated zest of 1 orange
 4  large garlic cloves, minced
 2  tablespoons chopped fresh rosemary
    Wild-Rice and Sausage Dressing (page 294)
 ¾  cup dry white wine
 ½  cup apple cider
1½  cups chicken stock, preferably
    homemade (page 179), or low-sodium
    canned chicken broth
 1  tablespoon unsalted butter,
    room temperature
 2  tablespoons all-purpose flour

**1.** Preheat oven to 425°F, with rack in lower third. Season crown roast with salt and pepper, and brush with ¼ cup oil.

**2.** In a small bowl, combine orange zest, garlic, rosemary, and the remaining 1½ tablespoons olive oil. Spread mixture evenly over meat, inside and out. Place meat in a large, heavy roasting pan fitted with a rack.

**3.** Transfer pan to oven. Roast 15 minutes. Reduce oven heat to 375°F. Continue roasting, rotating pan after 45 minutes, until meat is well browned and a meat thermometer inserted into meaty center of crown (avoiding ribs) registers 150°F, about 1½ hours. (Take several readings in different spots to ensure that temperature is even all around.)

**4.** Remove roasting pan from oven; transfer roast to a cutting board with a drainage well, and let stand 20 minutes.

**5.** Raise oven temperature to 425°F. Place dressing in oven, and bake until heated through, about 20 minutes; remove from oven. Meanwhile, pour pan juices into a glass measuring cup, and let stand 5 to 10 minutes; skim fat from surface, and discard. Return juices to pan.

**6.** Place roasting pan over medium-high heat. Add wine, and bring to a boil; deglaze pan, stirring up any browned bits on bottom of pan with a wooden spoon. Boil until liquid has reduced by half, 5 to 7 minutes. Stir in apple cider and chicken stock. Season with salt and pepper; return liquid to a boil.

**7.** In a small bowl, combine butter with flour; mix until smooth. Add flour mixture to roasting pan, and whisk constantly until gravy has thickened slightly, 4 to 5 minutes. Remove from heat, and strain liquid into a gravy boat.

**8.** Transfer the roast to a serving platter. Spoon dressing into center of the roast, and carve. Serve roast and dressing with gravy on the side.

### ABOUT CROWN ROASTS

*Crown roasts are often made with lamb, but pork may be a better choice, partly because it is less expensive, and also because it is meaty enough to remain succulent after roasting. Pork today is lean and mild, perfect as a complement to a rich and flavorful dressing. You'll also need a group with an appetite, since a crown requires twelve to fourteen chops; fewer will not provide a large enough circumference when bent into a full circle.*

## roasted loin of pork with orange, fig, and prune dressing
### SERVES 6

*The pork marinates overnight in the refrigerator, so plan ahead. Use a heavy roasting pan if you don't have a skillet large enough to hold the loin.*

¼ cup plus 3 tablespoons extra-virgin olive oil

¼ cup honey

¼ cup cider vinegar

2 teaspoons crushed red-pepper flakes

8 shallots, 6 whole, 1 thinly sliced, 1 minced

1 cinnamon stick

1 boneless loin of pork (3 pounds)

8 ounces dried figs, tough stems removed

8 ounces pitted prunes

3 tablespoons Armagnac, Cognac, or water

4 garlic cloves, minced

2 tablespoons finely chopped fresh rosemary, plus sprigs for garnish

2 tablespoons fresh thyme, plus sprigs for garnish

2 tablespoons balsamic vinegar

Grated zest and juice of 1 orange, plus more zest for garnish

Coarse salt and freshly ground black pepper

2 cups dry red wine or water

**1.** In a medium bowl, combine ¼ cup oil, honey, vinegar, red-pepper flakes, sliced shallots, and cinnamon stick. Place pork loin in a shallow glass baking dish or a large resealable plastic bag. Pour marinade over pork, cover or seal, and marinate overnight in the refrigerator.

**2.** Make dressing: Place the figs, prunes, and Armagnac in a food processor. Pulse until combined, but still quite chunky. Transfer to a bowl, and add garlic, rosemary, thyme, balsamic vinegar, orange zest, and juice; season with salt and black pepper. Stir until well combined; set aside.

**3.** Remove pork from marinade, and blot dry. Butterfly the loin lengthwise: Use a large knife to cut halfway into the loin down its entire length. With the knife inside the cut loin, turn the knife perpendicular to the first cut, and slice into the loin on both sides of the original cut at a 90-degree angle so that the loin will open up like a book.

**4.** Press open loin; cover with plastic. Pound lightly with the flat side of a meat pounder or heavy pan to achieve an even thickness, ¾ to 1 inch. Season both sides with salt and pepper.

**5.** Spread about half the dressing over center of loin, leaving a 1-inch border. Reserve remaining dressing for serving. (Store in an airtight container in the refrigerator up to 24 hours.)

**6.** Roll up loin starting on a long side; tie at 1-inch intervals with kitchen twine. (The loin may be prepared up to this point up to 24 hours in advance, and refrigerated, wrapped in plastic wrap; bring to room temperature before proceeding.)

**7.** Preheat oven to 350°F. Heat remaining 3 tablespoons oil in a large ovenproof skillet over medium heat. Sear loin briefly until browned on all sides, about 5 minutes. Add 6 whole shallots to pan, and transfer to oven.

**8.** Roast until a meat thermometer inserted into loin registers 145°F, 50 minutes to 1 hour, basting occasionally with any pan drippings. Transfer loin and shallots to a cutting board or a serving platter; let rest at least 10 minutes before serving.

**9.** Transfer reserved dressing to a small saucepan; stir over medium heat until hot, about 5 minutes. Transfer to a platter; set aside.

**10.** Meanwhile, make the gravy: Return skillet to medium heat. Add minced shallot, and cook until translucent, about 3 minutes. Add wine over high heat; deglaze pan, stirring up browned bits from bottom of skillet with a wooden spoon. Continue cooking until liquid has reduced by half, about 5 minutes. Strain into a gravy boat.

**11.** To serve, garnish platter with rosemary, thyme, and the cooked whole shallots. Remove twine from loin, top with warm dressing, and garnish with orange zest. Serve gravy on the side.

## glazed ham

SERVES 16

*Cookware shops sell specialized ham knives with long, thin blades for carving, but any sharp knife with a long blade will do.*

1   whole smoked ham (14 to 18 pounds), bone in and rind on

1   cup apple cider

¼   cup yellow mustard seeds

2   tablespoons whole cardamom pods

1   tablespoon whole fennel seeds

2   teaspoons ground cinnamon

1   tablespoon ground ginger

¾   cup prepared mustard

1   cup plus 2 tablespoons packed light-brown sugar

¾   cup packed dark-brown sugar

3   tablespoons light corn syrup

2   tablespoons unsulfured molasses

2   to 3 tablespoons whole cloves

4   fresh bay leaves (optional)

**1.** Rinse ham with cool water; dry with paper towels. Let stand 2 hours at room temperature.

**2.** Preheat oven to 350°F, with rack on lowest level. Line a roasting pan with heavy-duty aluminum foil. Place a wire rack in pan. Transfer ham, with the thicker rind on top, to rack. Pour ½ cup apple cider over ham. Cook 2 hours, or until a meat thermometer registers 140°F.

**3.** Meanwhile, make glaze: Toast mustard seeds, cardamom, and fennel seeds in a heavy skillet over medium-low heat until aromatic, 3 to 4 minutes. Transfer to a spice grinder or mortar and pestle; grind to a powder. Combine spice powder with cinnamon, ginger, prepared mustard, 2 tablespoons each light-brown and dark-brown sugar, corn syrup, and molasses. Mix well; set aside.

**4.** Let ham cool about 30 minutes. Using a sharp knife, trim the hard rind from the ham. Carefully trim fat to a ¼-inch layer all over ham. The bottom side of ham will have less fat and more skin. Place ham bottom side down in pan.

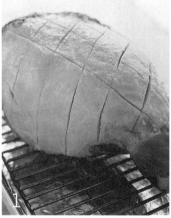

### GLAZED HAM

*1. Score the layer of fat on top of the ham into a pattern of 1- to 2-inch diamonds, making the cuts about ¼ to ½ inch deep, through the fat and partially into the meat.*

*2. Insert a whole clove into the intersection of each diamond. Using a pastry brush or your fingers, rub the glaze all over the ham and into each of the cut diamonds.*

**5.** Score remaining fat on top of the ham into a diamond pattern, making cuts about ¼ to ½ inch deep, through the fat and into the meat. Insert a whole clove into intersection of each diamond. Using a pastry brush or your fingers, rub glaze all over ham and into cut diamonds.

**6.** Combine remaining cup light-brown sugar and ½ cup plus 2 tablespoons dark-brown sugar. Use your hands to gently pack sugar mixture all over scored fat. If using bay leaves, secure them with toothpick halves around the shank bone, pushing toothpicks all the way into meat. Cover toothpicks by inserting cloves on top of them.

**7.** Return ham to oven, and cook 20 minutes. Sugar will begin to crystallize, but there will be some hard spots; gently baste these areas with the remaining ½ cup cider (never baste with pan juices as they will cloud the glaze). Continue cooking 40 minutes more, basting with remaining glaze after 20 minutes. The ham should be dark brown and crusty; cook 15 minutes more if necessary.

**8.** Remove ham from oven, and let cool slightly. Transfer to a serving platter or carving board, and let stand about 30 minutes before carving.

**9.** Before carving, cut a few thin slices from the end of the ham that is rounder and protrudes more. Stand the ham on this cut side; the meatiest part of the ham is now on top, ready to be sliced. (It will still be slightly unsteady, however, so make sure to carve carefully.) Slice straight down in ¼-inch intervals until you hit the bone. In one motion, run the knife horizontally along the top of the bone. Slices will lift out easily and can be placed, overlapping, on a serving platter.

## stuffed rib-pork-chop paillard

*photograph on page 47*
SERVES 12

*Ask your butcher to remove the chine (backbone), and to cut each chop three-quarters of an inch thick. The rib bone should also be trimmed to a three-inch length and then frenched.*

  *3  tablespoons unsalted butter*
  *2  tablespoons olive oil*
*1⅓  cups shallots, minced*
  *1  tablespoon minced garlic*
  *3  tablespoons finely chopped fresh sage, plus sprigs for garnish*
  *¾  cup plain breadcrumbs, preferably homemade*
  *8  ounces fontina cheese, grated (about 2 cups)*
  *8  ounces white seedless grapes, quartered (about 1½ cups), plus clusters for garnish*
    *Coarse salt and freshly ground pepper*
*12  rib pork chops, trimmed and pounded ¼ inch thick*
  *3  tablespoons vegetable oil*

**1.** Preheat oven to 400°F. Make filling: Heat butter and olive oil in a medium skillet over medium-low heat. Add shallots; cook until soft and translucent, about 8 minutes. Add garlic and sage; cook until mixture is fragrant, about 3 minutes. Remove from heat; transfer to a large bowl. Add breadcrumbs, cheese, and grapes; stir to combine. Season well with salt and pepper.

**2.** Place chops on a clean work surface, and season with salt and pepper. Place about ⅓ cup filling in center of each. Starting at the bone, roll meat tightly to completely encase filling. Tie with kitchen twine at 1-inch intervals.

**3.** Heat a large skillet over medium heat. Season chops again with salt and pepper. Working in three batches, add 1 tablespoon vegetable oil to pan; add chops, being careful not to overcrowd. Cook until chops are browned on all sides, about 8 minutes. Transfer to a rimmed baking sheet. Wipe skillet with a paper towel; repeat with remaining oil and chops.

**4.** Transfer sheet to oven; bake chops until a meat thermometer inserted into thickest part (avoiding bone) registers 160°F and meat is no longer pink, 18 to 20 minutes. Remove from oven; remove twine. Garnish with sage and grape clusters.

VENISON

### *loin of venison with red-currant bordelaise*
SERVES 8 TO 10

*Ask your butcher for a boneless saddle of venison, which will yield two loins, each weighing about two pounds.*

1 tablespoon juniper berries
1 tablespoon whole black peppercorns
1 tablespoon whole allspice
2 venison loins (2 pounds each)
4 shallots, minced
1 750-ml bottle dry red wine
2 cups veal or game stock
3 tablespoons red-currant jelly
  Coarse salt and freshly ground pepper
2 teaspoons vegetable oil

**1.** Combine juniper berries, peppercorns, and allspice in a spice or coffee grinder, and process to a powder. Rub spice mixture over meat; place in a dish, and refrigerate several hours.

**2.** Make sauce: Combine shallots and wine in a medium saucepan. Bring to a boil; reduce heat, and simmer until reduced by three-quarters, about 45 minutes. Add stock; return mixture to a boil. Simmer until reduced by half, about 30 minutes. Sauce should be thick enough to coat the back of a spoon. Stir in jelly; season with salt and pepper.

**3.** Meanwhile, preheat oven to 400°F. Heat oil in a large, heavy skillet over medium heat. Add venison loins; sear quickly on all sides until brown, about 3 minutes. Transfer to a roasting pan; roast in oven 12 to 16 minutes for rare to medium-rare (6 to 8 minutes per pound).

**4.** Remove venison from pan, and season lightly with salt. Let rest 10 minutes. Slice on an angle, and serve with sauce.

# roasted rack of venison with cranberry sauce

### SERVES 6 TO 8

*You can also use this recipe to make rack of lamb; choose racks that are about one-and-a-half pounds each, and cook twenty-five to twenty-eight minutes for medium-rare.*

- 4 tablespoons juniper berries
- 4 tablespoons whole black peppercorns
- 4 tablespoons dried rosemary
- 4 cups beef stock, preferably homemade (page 189), or low-sodium canned beef broth
- 2 fresh bay leaves
- 1 bunch fresh thyme
- ¾ cup ruby port
- 1 one-inch piece fresh ginger, peeled and chopped
- ½ cup red-currant jelly
- 1 tablespoon coarse salt
- 2 racks (1½ to 2 pounds each) venison, well trimmed
- 1 tablespoon olive oil
- 1 tablespoon plus 2 teaspoons unsalted butter
- 2 teaspoons all-purpose flour
- 1 cup fresh or frozen cranberries

**1.** Combine the juniper berries, peppercorns, and rosemary in a spice grinder. Process until coarsely ground; set aside.

**2.** Combine stock, bay leaves, thyme, port, ginger, and jelly in a large saucepan. Bring mixture to a boil. Reduce heat; simmer until stock has reduced to 1 cup, about 1 hour. Remove from heat, strain, and transfer to a clean small saucepan; set aside.

**3.** Preheat oven to 350°F. Place a large roasting pan in oven. Salt both sides of venison well, and rub spice mixture into meat.

**4.** Heat oil and 1 tablespoon butter in a large skillet over medium-high heat. Place venison in the skillet, and sear until brown, about 2 minutes per side, using tongs to maneuver racks in skillet. Transfer venison to preheated roasting pan.

**5.** Roast venison 30 to 35 minutes for medium-rare. Remove pan from oven, and transfer meat to a cutting board; let rest 15 minutes.

**6.** In a small bowl, combine remaining 2 teaspoons butter with the flour; mix to form a paste. Return sauce to a boil over medium-high heat. Reduce heat, and stir in cranberries; let simmer until berries are soft and sauce is shiny, about 5 minutes. Whisk in butter mixture. Serve sauce with venison.

## CHOOSING ROASTING PANS

*If you need a new roasting pan, select one that's small enough to fit your oven, large enough to fit a large bird or cut of meat, and two to three inches high. Don't choose nonstick pans— you'll never get the good browned bits that, deglazed, make such delicious gravies and sauces. Avoid the disposable aluminum kind. They're flimsy and dangerous, since it's far too easy to spill grease and burn yourself, or drop whatever you're roasting.*

## *classic roast turkey*

SERVES 12

*A turkey this size generously serves twelve for dinner, or it can serve twice as many guests as part of a buffet. Covering the turkey with the moistened cheesecloth while cooking enables it to cook evenly and protects the delicate breast meat. Stuff turkey just before it goes into the oven to prevent bacteria; also, don't pack it too tightly or the stuffing won't cook evenly. Cook any extra stuffing in a buttered baking dish for about forty-five minutes in a 375 degree oven.*

- 1½  cups (3 sticks) unsalted butter, melted, plus 4 tablespoons, room temperature
- 1  750-ml bottle dry white wine
- 1  fresh whole turkey (20 to 21 pounds), giblets and neck removed from cavity, turkey rinsed and patted dry
- 2  teaspoons coarse salt
- 2  teaspoons freshly ground pepper
  Classic Stuffing (page 290)

**1.** Preheat oven to 450°F, with rack on lowest level. Combine melted butter and wine in a large, shallow bowl. Fold a large piece of cheesecloth into quarters; cut it into a 17-inch, four-layer square. Immerse cheesecloth in wine mixture; let soak.

**2.** Fold wing tips under turkey. Sprinkle ½ teaspoon each salt and pepper inside cavity. Fill large cavity and neck cavity loosely with stuffing. Clean off any stuffing that falls onto outside of bird. Fold neck flap under; secure with toothpicks.

**3.** Place turkey, breast side up, on a wire rack in a heavy roasting pan. Tie legs together loosely with kitchen twine. Rub turkey with 4 tablespoons butter; sprinkle with remaining 1½ teaspoons each salt and pepper.

**4.** Remove the cheesecloth from the wine mixture; squeeze it lightly, leaving it very damp. Spread cheesecloth evenly over breast and about halfway down sides of turkey; it can cover some of the leg area. Place turkey, legs first, in oven. (If your roasting pan only fits sideways in the oven, turn the pan every hour so the turkey cooks and browns evenly.) Cook 30 minutes.

**5.** Use a pastry brush to baste the cheesecloth and any exposed parts of the turkey with the wine mixture. (Basting should always be done in the oven and as quickly as possible so the oven temperature doesn't drop.)

**6.** Reduce oven temperature to 350°F, and continue cooking turkey 2½ hours more, basting every 30 minutes with wine mixture. Watch cheesecloth carefully to make sure it does not dry out and burn; baste more often if necessary. (If using an electric oven, make sure cheesecloth does not come into contact with heating element.)

**7.** Carefully remove and discard cheesecloth; it will have turned quite brown. Turn roasting pan so that breast is facing back of oven. Baste turkey with pan juices. If there are not enough juices, continue to use wine mixture. The skin becomes fragile as it browns, so baste carefully.

**8.** Continue cooking until a meat thermometer inserted into thickest part of thigh (avoiding bone) registers 180°F (stuffing should be at least 165°F), about 1 hour more; baste after 30 minutes.

**9.** Transfer turkey to a serving platter, and let rest about 30 minutes before carving into thin slices.

## *roast free-range turkey with pear-and-chestnut stuffing*

SERVES 8 TO 10

*The stuffing may be baked in a buttered casserole dish at 375 degrees until heated through, about forty-five minutes.*

¾ cup (1½ sticks) unsalted butter

6 stalks celery, cut into ¼-inch dice

2 large onions, cut into ¼-inch dice

¼ cup finely chopped thyme leaves

1 teaspoon finely chopped sage leaves

1 tablespoon coarsely chopped fresh flat-leaf parsley

½ pound Roasted Chestnuts (recipe follows), chopped

27 slices day-old white bread (1½ pounds), crusts trimmed, cut into ¼-inch dice (about 8 cups), lightly toasted

1¼ cups turkey stock, preferably homemade (page 273), or low-sodium canned chicken broth

4 firm, slightly underripe Anjou pears, cored, peeled, and cut into ½-inch dice

1 tablespoon coarse salt

1 whole free-range turkey (12 to 14 pounds), rinsed and patted dry, giblets reserved for gravy
Giblet Gravy (recipe follows)

**1.** Preheat oven to 375°F. In a large skillet, melt 4 tablespoons butter over medium heat. Add celery and onions; cook, stirring, until translucent, about 10 minutes. Stir in 2 tablespoons thyme, along with the sage, parsley, chestnuts, and bread. Add stock, ¼ cup at a time, until bread becomes moist. Stir in pears; remove from heat.

**2.** Place remaining ½ cup butter and 2 tablespoons thyme, and 1 teaspoon salt in a food processor. Pulse until combined; set aside.

**3.** Place turkey, breast side up, on a wire rack set in a large roasting pan. Season cavity with remaining 2 teaspoons salt. Fill cavity loosely with stuffing. Clean off any stuffing that falls onto outside of bird. Tie legs together with kitchen twine. Fold neck flap over; secure with toothpicks. Rub thyme-butter mixture all over turkey.

**4.** Transfer pan to oven; roast 2½ hours, basting every 30 minutes. Continue cooking until a meat thermometer inserted in thickest part of thigh (avoiding bone) registers 180°F (stuffing should be at least 165°F), 30 to 45 minutes. If turkey starts to become too brown, tent with aluminum foil. Transfer to a serving platter; reserve roasting pan and juices for giblet gravy. Let turkey rest 20 to 30 minutes before carving. Serve with gravy.

## *roasted chestnuts*

MAKES 1 TO 2 POUNDS

*1 to 2 pounds fresh large chestnuts*

Preheat oven to 400°F. Score each chestnut using a sharp paring knife or a chestnut knife: Make an X on one side of each chestnut or make one long slit crosswise around circumference. Place chestnuts in a single layer on a rimmed baking sheet, and roast until flesh is tender and golden, about 25 minutes. Remove from oven. Using a clean kitchen towel, immediately rub to remove shells. Chestnuts can be refrigerated up to 1 week in an airtight container.

### HOW MUCH TURKEY?

*With a fifteen- to twenty-pound turkey, count on one to one-and-a-half pounds per person; with smaller birds (twelve pounds or less), two pounds per person. A turkey that's fifteen pounds or more, however, will cook up better, and it will be juicier, than a smaller one.*

## giblet gravy
### MAKES 2 CUPS

1 tablespoon olive oil

Turkey giblets (neck, heart, gizzard, and liver)

2 stalks celery, coarsely chopped

1 carrot, coarsely chopped

1 leek, white and pale-green parts only, coarsely chopped and washed well

1 cup dry white wine

1 cup Madeira or dry sherry

4 cups turkey stock, preferably homemade (page 273), or low-sodium canned chicken broth

6 whole black peppercorns

1 dried bay leaf

3 tablespoons all-purpose flour

Coarse salt and freshly ground pepper

**1.** Heat oil in a medium saucepan over medium-high heat. Add giblets; cook, stirring, until browned all over. Remove giblets; set aside. Reduce heat to medium; add celery, carrot, and leek. Cook until leek begins to brown, about 10 minutes. Add white wine and Madeira; cook until reduced by half, 15 to 20 minutes. Add stock, reserved giblets, peppercorns, and bay leaf. Simmer 40 minutes. Strain; discard solids. Set stock aside.

**2.** Pour reserved juices from roasting pan into a glass measuring cup. Let stand 10 minutes; skim fat from surface, and reserve. Place pan over medium heat; add juices, scraping up browned bits from bottom with a wooden spoon. Add 3 tablespoons reserved turkey fat and flour; cook, stirring, until brown, about 2 minutes. Whisk in strained stock, 1 cup at a time, until incorporated.

**3.** Remove pan from heat; strain mixture into saucepan. Over medium-high heat, cook until gravy has thickened, 10 to 15 minutes. Season with salt and pepper; serve hot.

## turkey with pomegranate glaze and vegetable gravy
### SERVES 8 TO 10

When juicing a pomegranate, you need not separate the seeds first; just halve it, and crush each section with a citrus reamer.

1 fresh whole turkey (12 to 14 pounds), rinsed and patted dry

Coarse salt and freshly ground pepper

2 onions, cut into wedges

3 carrots, halved lengthwise

3 stalks celery, halved lengthwise

3 parsnips, peeled and halved lengthwise

Cornbread Stuffing with Sage, Sun-dried Tomatoes, and Sausage (page 290)

2 tablespoons unsalted butter, room temperature

4 pomegranates (about 2 pounds)

4 cups turkey stock, preferably homemade, (page 273), or low-sodium canned chicken broth

3 tablespoons red-currant jelly

2 tablespoons all-purpose flour

¼ cup Cognac

**1.** Preheat oven to 425°F. Season turkey inside and out with salt and pepper. Arrange vegetables in a large, heavy roasting pan in a single layer.

**2.** Fill cavity of turkey loosely with cooled stuffing. Clean off any stuffing that falls onto outside of bird. Tie legs together with kitchen twine. Rub bird with butter, and place turkey in roasting pan on top of vegetables.

**3.** Transfer pan to oven; roast turkey 30 minutes. Reduce oven heat to 350°F, and continue roasting, basting every 30 minutes with pan juices, until a meat thermometer inserted into thickest part of thigh (avoiding bone) registers 170°F, about 3 hours 15 minutes. If turkey starts to become too brown, tent with aluminum foil.

**4.** Meanwhile, make pomegranate glaze: Juice pomegranates; strain liquid through a sieve lined with cheesecloth into a small saucepan. Add 1 cup stock; cook over high heat until thick enough to coat the back of a spoon, about 20 minutes. Stir in currant jelly; set aside.

**5.** Remove turkey from oven; brush evenly with pomegranate glaze. Reduce oven heat to 325°F, return bird to oven, and continue roasting 5 minutes. Brush again with pomegranate glaze; roast 5 to 10 minutes more (turkey should register 180°F). Watch carefully to keep glaze from burning.

**6.** Remove turkey from oven, and let cool slightly. Transfer turkey to a serving platter. Let rest 20 minutes before carving.

**7.** Meanwhile, make gravy: Using a slotted spoon, transfer vegetables from roasting pan to a food processor, and process until smooth.

**8.** Pour off all but 2 tablespoons drippings from pan into a large glass measuring cup; let stand 10 minutes, then skim fat from surface. Place pan over medium-low heat; add flour, stirring with a wooden spoon until mixture is smooth. Add 3 tablespoons puréed vegetables to pan, and stir until smooth. (Remaining purée can be served as an additional side dish or discarded.)

**9.** Add Cognac to pan; deglaze pan, stirring up any browned bits from bottom with a wooden spoon. Continue cooking slowly over medium-low heat, stirring constantly while adding degreased pan juices and remaining 3 cups stock. Raise heat to medium-high, and cook until gravy thickens, 10 to 15 minutes. Season with salt and pepper. Serve in a gravy boat alongside turkey and stuffing.

### cranberry-glazed turkey with cranberry-cornbread stuffing
*photograph on page 49*
SERVES 8 TO 10

*Cranberry glaze adds a beautiful, rich sheen and a slightly tart flavor to the turkey.*

- *2 cups (4 sticks) unsalted butter, plus 4 tablespoons, room temperature*
- *1 750-ml bottle dry white wine*
- *1 fresh whole turkey (16 to 18 pounds), rinsed and patted dry*
  *Coarse salt and freshly ground pepper*
  *Cranberry-Cornbread Stuffing (page 292)*
- *5 red onions (about 2 pounds), peeled and quartered*
  *Cranberry Glaze (page 216)*
- *1 cup dry red wine or water*
- *2 cups turkey stock, preferably homemade (page 273), or low-sodium canned chicken broth*

**1.** Preheat oven to 450°F, with rack on lowest level. In a large saucepan, melt 3 sticks butter; add white wine. Turn off heat, leaving mixture on top of stove to keep warm. Fold a large piece of cheesecloth into quarters; cut it into a 17-inch, four-layer square. Immerse cheesecloth in wine mixture, and set aside to soak.

**2.** Place turkey, breast side up, on a clean work surface. Fold wing tips under turkey. Season cavity with salt and pepper.

**3.** Fill large cavity loosely with 7 to 8 cups stuffing. Clean off any stuffing that falls onto outside of bird. Tie legs together loosely with kitchen twine. Fold neck flap under, and secure with toothpicks. Brush bird with 4 tablespoons butter, and season with salt and pepper.

**4.** Remove cheesecloth from liquid; squeeze it lightly, leaving it very damp. Spread it evenly over breast and about halfway down sides of turkey; it can cover some of the leg area.

**5.** Arrange onions in a large, heavy roasting pan. Place turkey on top of onions; transfer to oven, and cook 30 minutes. Reduce oven temperature to 350°F. Brush a quarter of the wine mixture over cheesecloth and exposed parts of turkey; continue cooking 2 hours more, basting every 30 minutes.

**6.** When all the wine mixture has been used, melt the remaining stick of butter. Baste turkey with half of that butter; continue cooking until a meat thermometer inserted into thickest part of thigh (avoiding bone) registers 170°F, about 30 minutes more. If necessary, baste turkey with remaining melted butter, and return to oven. Be careful to watch the pan juices; if pan gets too full, spoon out juices, reserving them for gravy.

**7.** Carefully remove and discard cheesecloth. Brush half the cranberry glaze on the turkey. Cook turkey 10 to 15 minutes more. Brush remaining glaze on turkey, and continue cooking 10 minutes more to set the glaze (the turkey should register 180°F, and the stuffing should register 165°F).

**8.** Transfer turkey and onions to a carving board; let rest about 30 minutes before carving.

**9.** Meanwhile, make the gravy: Pour the pan juices into a large glass measuring cup. Let stand 10 minutes, then skim off the fat that has risen to the surface; discard fat.

**10.** Meanwhile, place roasting pan over medium-high heat. Add the red wine or water, and bring to a boil; deglaze pan, stirring up browned bits from bottom with a wooden spoon. Add stock to pan. Stir well, and return to a boil. Cook until liquid has reduced by half, about 10 minutes. Add defatted pan juices; cook over medium-high heat 10 minutes more. You should have about 2½ cups gravy. Season with salt and pepper. Strain into a warm gravy boat; serve with turkey and onions.

### CARVING TIPS

*To prepare for carving, have handy a warm platter, a pair of kitchen scissors, and a sturdy and sharp slicing knife, about 10 inches long. After being removed from the oven, the bird should stand at room temperature for about 30 minutes to allow the juices to saturate the meat. Transfer the turkey from the roasting pan or platter to a carving board. The best way to hold the turkey steady is to use your hand instead of the carving fork. A carving fork, while useful for arranging the meat once it is carved, will pierce and tear the flesh; it also won't provide as good a grip. Do not use a serrated blade to cut as it, too, will tear the flesh.*

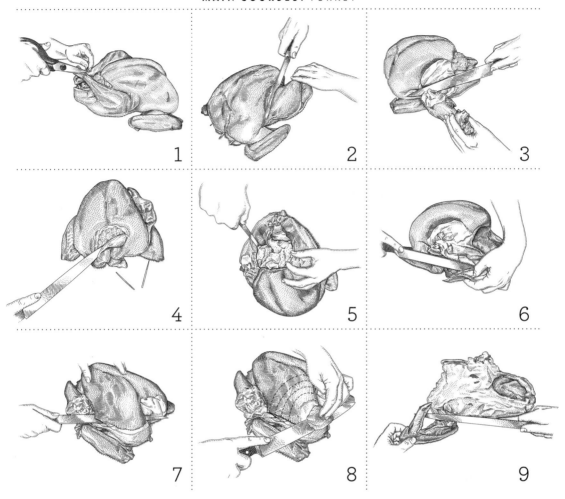

## HOW TO CARVE A TURKEY

*1.* With scissors, cut through trussing, taking care to remove all of the string.

*2.* Remove drumsticks: Place knife against thigh; cut down to expose the leg's second joint.

*3.* Apply pressure at joint with knife point, twist knife, and cut through to sever drumsticks.

*4.* Slice open neck cavity with an oval cut that allows you to remove stuffing with skin intact.

*5.* Use a long-handled spoon to scoop out stuffing from cavity; transfer to a serving bowl.

*6.* Slice thigh meat from bone of both thighs; the dark meat should be tender from resting in the juices.

*7.* Place knife horizontally at bottom curve of one side of bird's breast; slice in toward rib cage to create a "guide cut." Slice again down rib cage, from the center top to the guide cut.

*8.* Cut vertically through breast meat to create medallion slices, being careful to preserve some skin on each slice. Repeat steps 7 and 8 on other side of breast.

*9.* Place knife at first wing joint, insert knife point, and twist it to sever wing. Repeat with other wing.

## cranberry glaze

MAKES ABOUT 1 CUP

*This glaze may be made up to two days ahead and refrigerated in an airtight container. It is also delicious with roasted chicken, duck, or pork.*

1   tablespoon unsalted butter
½   shallot, finely chopped (about 2 teaspoons)
2   fresh sage leaves
1   teaspoon whole juniper berries
1½  cups fresh or thawed frozen cranberries
1   cup pure maple syrup
1   cup apple cider, plus more if needed
¾   cup red-currant jelly
¼   teaspoon coarse salt
    Pinch of freshly ground pepper

**1.** In a medium saucepan, melt butter over medium heat. Add shallot, and cook until translucent, stirring occasionally, about 2 minutes. Add sage leaves and juniper berries; cook, stirring, 1 minute. Add cranberries, maple syrup, apple cider, jelly, salt, and pepper. Raise heat to medium-high, and simmer until cranberries are soft and starting to burst, about 3 minutes.

**2.** Transfer cranberry mixture to a food processor, and purée until smooth. Pass purée through a fine sieve into a small saucepan.

**3.** Return glaze to stove, and simmer gently over medium heat until it has thickened slightly, about 10 minutes; you should have about 1 cup. If glaze seems too thick, thin it with a little apple cider. Keep warm until ready to use.

## oven-roasted turkey breast

SERVES 6 WITH LEFTOVERS

1   tablespoon olive oil
1   whole turkey breast (about 5 pounds), rinsed and patted dry
1   tablespoon coarse salt
½   teaspoon freshly ground pepper
1   tablespoon all-purpose flour

**1.** Preheat oven to 350°F. Place a roasting rack in a small, heavy roasting pan. Drizzle oil over turkey breast, and season with salt and pepper. Center turkey breast on rack. Transfer to oven, and roast until juices run clear and a meat thermometer inserted into thickest part (avoiding bone) registers 165°F, about 1 hour 20 minutes. Transfer to a platter, and let rest 10 minutes before carving.

**2.** Make the gravy: Remove the rack, and place roasting pan over high heat. Add flour to pan; whisk 2 minutes, scraping up pan drippings and incorporating pan juices. Add ½ cup water; continue whisking until mixture is smooth and thickened, about 2 minutes. Transfer to a gravy boat, and serve with turkey.

## roast turkey breast with pennsylvania dutch stuffing
SERVES 10 TO 12

*If you'd like, ask your butcher to bone the turkey breast for you. Potatoes are often used to make stuffings in Pennsylvania Dutch cooking.*

- 1 *whole turkey breast (about 5 pounds)*
  *Coarse salt and freshly ground pepper*
- 1½ *pounds red potatoes*
- 1 *tablespoon unsalted butter, plus more, room temperature, for rubbing*
- 1 *tablespoon olive oil*
- 3 *garlic cloves, finely chopped*
- 1 *bunch leeks, white and pale-green parts only, thinly sliced crosswise, washed well and dried*
- 1 *tablespoon fresh rosemary leaves, chopped, or 1 teaspoon dried*
- 2 *cups day-old bread cubes*
- 1 *large egg, lightly beaten*
  *Rosemary sprigs, plus more for garnish*

**1.** To bone turkey, place it on a clean work surface, meat side down. Cut off wings. Starting at top of breast, make a cut where meat begins, then run knife against one side of rib cage in long, smooth strokes, letting meat fall away. When breastbone is reached, repeat with other side. Carefully loosen meat from breastbone without cutting through skin. Remove the bones. Loosen membrane from underneath large fillet on each side of breast, and open like a book. Rinse and pat dry. Season with salt and pepper, and refrigerate, wrapped well in plastic, until ready to stuff.

**2.** Bring a pot of water to a boil. Add potatoes, and boil until almost tender, about 20 minutes. Drain; when cool enough to handle, break potatoes into large pieces. Set aside.

**3.** In a large sauté pan, melt butter over medium-low heat, and add oil. Add garlic, and cook 1 minute. Add leeks, and cook, stirring, until softened, about 2 minutes. Add rosemary, reserved potatoes, and bread cubes; mix well. Season with salt and pepper. Let cool slightly, then mix in egg. Let cool to room temperature.

**4.** Lay turkey breast, skin side down, on work surface. Place stuffing in center of breast. From a short end, roll up turkey breast snugly around stuffing.

**5.** Preheat oven to 400°F. Lay 4 lengths of kitchen twine a few inches apart on work surface; place rolled turkey on top. Lay rosemary sprigs on both sides; tie strings around turkey. Tie another string around breast lengthwise; rub turkey with butter. Place on a rack in a roasting pan.

**6.** Transfer to oven, and roast turkey 15 minutes. Reduce oven heat to 375°F, and continue cooking, basting periodically with pan juices, until a meat thermometer inserted into meat and stuffing registers at least 165°F, about 1½ hours total. Let rest at least 15 minutes. Serve garnished with the additional rosemary sprigs.

CHICKEN

## double-crust chicken-and-mushroom pie

SERVES 6

2½ cups plus 6 tablespoons all-purpose flour, plus more for work surface

1 teaspoon table salt

1 teaspoon granulated sugar

1 cup (2 sticks) plus 5 tablespoons chilled unsalted butter, cut into small pieces

¼ to ½ cup ice water

1 whole chicken (3 to 4 pounds)

4 cups chicken stock, preferably homemade (page 179), or low-sodium canned chicken broth

8 ounces pearl onions

10 ounces red potatoes, scrubbed and cut into ½-inch pieces

5 medium carrots, cut into ½-inch pieces

14 ounces shiitake, cremini, or button mushrooms, quartered if large

¾ cup milk

1 package (10 ounces) frozen peas, thawed

2 tablespoons fresh thyme leaves

2 tablespoons chopped fresh sage
Coarse salt and freshly ground pepper

1 large egg, beaten with 1 teaspoon water, for egg wash

**1.** Combine 2½ cups flour, the table salt, and sugar in a food processor. Add 1 cup butter; pulse until mixture resembles coarse meal, 8 to 10 times. Add ice water in a slow steady stream through the feed tube with the machine running, until dough holds together; do not process more than 30 seconds. Turn out dough onto a clean work surface; divide in half. Flatten into disks; wrap each in plastic, and refrigerate at least 1 hour or overnight.

**2.** Place chicken and stock in a medium stockpot. Add enough water just to cover chicken. Bring to a boil; reduce heat, and simmer gently until chicken is cooked through, about 45 minutes. Using tongs, transfer chicken to a plate; set aside until cool enough to handle. Strain 2 cups stock into a measuring cup, and set aside. (The remaining stock may be frozen for another use.)

**3.** Preheat oven to 375°F, with rack in center. Cook onions in a medium pan of simmering water, about 15 minutes. Drain, and rinse under cool water. Peel onions, and set aside. Remove skin and bones from chicken, and discard. Shred chicken into bite-size pieces, and set aside.

**4.** Melt remaining 5 tablespoons butter in a large high-sided skillet over medium heat. Add potatoes, carrots, and reserved onions, and cook, stirring occasionally, until potatoes begin to turn golden. Add mushrooms; cook 5 minutes more. Add remaining 6 tablespoons flour, and cook, stirring, 1 minute. Add reserved chicken stock and the milk; bring to a simmer. Cook until thick and bubbly, stirring constantly. Stir in peas, thyme, sage, and reserved chicken; season with salt and pepper. Remove from heat, and let cool slightly.

**5.** On a lightly floured surface, roll out one disk of dough into a 12-inch round. Fit dough into a 9½-inch glass pie plate with dough overlapping top of pan. Trim dough to about a 1-inch overhang. Carefully spoon filling into dough.

**6.** Roll out remaining dough into a 10-inch circle; place on top of filling. Fold overlapping edges of dough under to firmly seal. Pinch to make a decorative border. Use a knife to make four or five slits in center of pie. Brush top of dough with egg wash.

**7.** Place pie plate on a baking sheet; transfer to oven. Bake until crust is golden brown, rotating pie halfway through, 45 to 60 minutes. Remove from oven; let cool slightly before serving.

## coq au vin

SERVES 6

*Serve this stew over rice or barley.*

- 6 *large garlic cloves, smashed*
- 4 *whole black peppercorns*
- 2 *sprigs thyme, plus more for garnish*
- 1 *fresh bay leaf*
- 7 *sprigs flat-leaf parsley, stems and leaves separated*
- 2 *whole skinless and boneless chicken breasts*
- 2 *tablespoons olive oil*
- 8 *ounces pearl onions, peeled*
- 12 *ounces white button mushrooms, halved or quartered*
- 1 *tablespoon unsalted butter*
  *Coarse salt and freshly ground pepper*
- 3 *tablespoons Cognac*
- 1 *cup dry red wine*
- 3¼ *cups chicken stock, preferably homemade (page 179), or low-sodium canned chicken broth*
- 1 *tablespoon tomato paste*
- 1 *tablespoon cornstarch*

1. Make a bouquet garni: Using a small piece of cheesecloth, wrap 3 garlic cloves, the peppercorns, thyme, bay leaf, and parsley stems; tie in a bundle with kitchen twine. Set aside.

2. Cut chicken into strips about 2 inches long and ¾ inch wide; set aside. In a large, deep skillet or a Dutch oven, heat 1 tablespoon oil over medium-high heat. Add onions and remaining 3 garlic cloves; cook, stirring occasionally, until beginning to brown, about 4 minutes. Add mushrooms; cook until golden, about 4 minutes. Transfer to a dish.

3. Add butter and remaining tablespoon oil to skillet. Season chicken strips with salt and pepper. Working in two batches, cook chicken until browned, about 1 minute per side. Return chicken to skillet. Add Cognac and wine; deglaze pan, stirring with a wooden spoon to scrape up any browned bits from the bottom. Stir in chicken stock and tomato paste. Add bouquet garni. Bring to a boil; reduce heat to a simmer, and cook, covered, 15 minutes. Add reserved mushrooms, onions, and garlic; cook 5 minutes more.

4. Using a slotted spoon, transfer chicken and vegetables to a bowl. Discard bouquet garni. Over high heat, reduce stock by half, about 12 minutes. In a small bowl, dissolve cornstarch in 1 tablespoon water. Pour mixture into stock, and stir until incorporated. Cook 2 minutes. Return chicken and vegetables to pot, and cook over medium-low heat until warmed through. Chop parsley leaves, and stir into chicken mixture. Serve stew immediately, garnished with thyme.

### HOW TO DEGLAZE A PAN

*Deglazing a pan is a technique using a liquid such as wine or stock to loosen the browned, caramelized bits of food or fat that remain in the pan after cooking. Once a pan has been deglazed, the remaining liquid can be used as a sauce to accompany the food you have cooked. To deglaze a pan, add wine, such as Madeira, or homemade or low-sodium canned chicken stock, skimmed of any fat. Stir with a wooden spoon until the liquid reduces and is thick enough to coat the back of the spoon.*

## tamale casserole with chicken and roasted-tomatillo salsa

### SERVES 6

*Corn tamales, with a variety of fillings, are enjoyed throughout Mexico in the days leading up to Christmas. This party dish uses the same classic batter, but is easier to put together than individual tamales steamed in banana leaves.*

- 8  medium tomatillos (12 ounces), husked and rinsed
- Olive oil, for pie plate and brushing
- 2  large garlic cloves (unpeeled)
- 3  medium fresh serrano chiles or 1 large jalapeño chile
- ½  white onion, finely chopped
- 3  tablespoons chopped fresh cilantro
- ¾  teaspoon coarse salt, plus more for seasoning
- 1  whole skinless and boneless chicken breast, cut into ½-inch dice
- Classic Tamale Batter (recipe follows)

**1.** Heat broiler. Place tomatillos on a rimmed baking sheet. Broil tomatillos 4 inches below heat element until soft and blackened in spots, 8 to 9 minutes, turning once. Remove from broiler; set aside until cool.

**2.** Reduce oven temperature to 425°F, with rack in upper third. Lightly oil an 8-inch pie plate; set aside. Place garlic in a medium skillet set over medium heat. Cook 5 minutes, then add chiles. Cook, turning occasionally, until chiles and garlic are soft and blackened in spots, about 10 minutes more. Remove from heat; let cool. Peel garlic.

**3.** Transfer tomatillos and any accumulated juices to a food processor or blender; add chiles and garlic. Process until a coarse purée forms. Transfer to a medium bowl.

**4.** Place onion in a sieve; rinse under cold running water. Drain; add to tomatillo purée along with cilantro and the salt. Stir to combine.

**5.** Measure ¾ cup salsa into a medium sauté pan, and stir in chicken. Cook over medium heat, stirring, until chicken is tender, 8 to 10 minutes; season with salt. Remove from heat; set aside to cool.

**6.** Spread half the tamale batter evenly over bottom of prepared pie plate. Spread chicken filling over batter; spread remaining batter over chicken.

**7.** Transfer to oven; bake until the crust is golden, about 35 minutes. Reduce oven temperature to 300°F, and lightly brush top of pie with oil; cover loosely with foil. Continue baking until golden and center springs back when touched, about 35 minutes more. Remove from oven; let stand 5 minutes.

**8.** Cut casserole into wedges. Serve warm, drizzled with remaining tomatillo salsa; if salsa is too thick to drizzle, thin with 1 or 2 tablespoons water.

## classic tamale batter

### MAKES 3¾ CUPS

- 1¾  cups masa harina
- 5  ounces (⅔ cup) fresh pork lard, chilled, or solid vegetable shortening
- 1  teaspoon baking powder
- 1  scant teaspoon salt
- ⅔  cup chicken stock, preferably homemade (page 179), or low-sodium canned chicken broth

**1.** In a small bowl, whisk masa harina into 1 cup plus 2 tablespoons hot water until smooth; let cool to room temperature.

**2.** In the bowl of an electric mixer, combine lard, baking powder, and salt. Beat until light and fluffy. Add 1 cup masa-harina mixture and ⅓ cup stock; beat until thoroughly combined. Add the remaining masa-harina mixture and ⅓ cup stock; beat until light and fluffy, about 2 minutes. The batter should be soft but hold its shape in a spoon. Refrigerate at least 1 hour. Store batter in an airtight container, refrigerated, up to 2 days.

## *roast capon with wild-rice sourdough stuffing*
### SERVES 8

*Coarse salt*

1½ cups mixed uncooked wild and brown rice

 4 ounces pancetta or bacon, cubed

 2 onions, coarsely chopped

 5 to 6 carrots, coarsely chopped

 4 stalks celery, coarsely chopped
   *Freshly ground pepper*

1½ to 2½ cups chicken stock, preferably homemade (page 179), or low-sodium canned chicken broth

 ¼ cup thinly sliced fresh sage leaves

 1 to 2 tablespoons unsalted butter (optional), plus more, room temperature, for rubbing

 5 cups cubed day-old sourdough bread

 ¼ cup chopped fresh flat-leaf parsley

 1 capon, rinsed and patted dry (7 to 8 pounds)

**1.** In a medium saucepan over high heat, bring 2½ cups water to a boil; add salt. Add rice, and return to a boil. Reduce heat to low, cover tightly, and cook until tender, about 45 minutes. Spread the rice on a plate to cool.

**2.** Meanwhile, place pancetta in a large, deep skillet over medium-low heat. Cook until fat is rendered and pancetta is browned, 10 to 15 minutes. Add onions; cook until soft, 2 to 3 minutes. Raise heat to medium; add carrots and celery. Cook until soft, 5 to 10 minutes. Season with salt and pepper.

**3.** Stir 1½ cups stock into skillet, and bring to a simmer; add sage. Over medium-high heat, reduce liquid until thick and soupy, about 5 minutes. Add butter, if desired, and stir until melted. Add cooked rice to skillet, and stir until moistened.

**4.** Preheat oven to 425°F. Place bread cubes in a large bowl, and combine with rice mixture. Add up to 1 cup more stock as needed until stuffing is slightly moist but not soggy. Stir in parsley.

**5.** Season cavity of capon with salt and pepper. Stuff with rice mixture just before roasting. Rub capon with a little butter, and sprinkle with salt and pepper. Tie legs together with kitchen twine; place in a roasting pan.

**6.** Transfer pan to oven; reduce oven temperature to 375°F. Roast capon until juices run clear when thigh is pricked with a fork, about 25 minutes per pound. Let rest, 10 minutes before carving, covered loosely with foil.

## cornish game hens with whole-grain stuffing

SERVES 4

*Triticale is a combination of wheat and rye, though its flavor is closer to the nutlike qualities of wheat. It is used mostly in multigrain flours and in cereal mixes.*

½   cup triticale or wheat berries

½   cup oat berries

½   ounce dried porcini mushrooms

½   cup boiling water

1½  tablespoons olive oil

½   onion, cut into ¼-inch dice

½   small bulb fennel, trimmed and
     cut into ¼-inch dice

1   stalk celery, cut into ¼-inch dice

1   small garlic clove, minced

4   ounces small button mushrooms, quartered

2   tablespoons Madeira or Calvados

⅓   cup dried figs, quartered

⅓   cup dried apricots, quartered

¾   cup chicken stock, preferably
     homemade (page 179), or low-sodium
     canned chicken broth

2   teaspoons fresh thyme leaves,
     coarsely chopped

     Coarse salt and freshly ground pepper

¼   cup toasted hazelnuts, skinned and
     coarsely chopped

4   Cornish game hens (about 1 pound each),
     rinsed and patted dry

2   tablespoons unsalted butter,
     room temperature

**1.** Bring a medium pot of water to a boil; add triticale and oat berries. Simmer until grains are al dente, about 30 minutes. Drain; rinse under cold water, and set aside.

**2.** Place porcini in a small bowl; cover with the boiling water, and let soak 20 minutes. Remove porcini from soaking liquid, and finely chop. Strain and reserve soaking liquid.

**3.** Preheat oven to 425°F. Heat oil in a large skillet over medium-low heat. Add onion, fennel, celery, and garlic; cook, stirring occasionally, until onion is translucent, 10 to 12 minutes. Add porcini and button mushrooms; simmer, stirring, until they begin to brown and soften slightly, about 5 minutes. Add Madeira and reserved mushroom soaking liquid, and cook until almost all liquid has evaporated, 1½ to 2 minutes.

**4.** Add figs, apricots, ½ cup stock, thyme, and reserved grains to skillet; season with salt and pepper. Simmer until grains have absorbed almost all liquid, about 2 minutes. Stir in hazelnuts; remove skillet from heat.

**5.** Sprinkle cavities and outer skin of hens with salt and pepper; rub skin with butter. Stuff each hen with ⅓ cup grain mixture. Tie legs of hens with kitchen twine; place in a roasting pan. Place remaining stuffing and ¼ cup chicken stock into a baking dish; cover with foil.

**6.** Transfer roasting pan to oven; bake hens, basting occasionally with pan juices, until golden and juices run clear, 30 to 35 minutes. After 15 minutes of cooking, transfer stuffing to oven; cook until heated through, 15 to 20 minutes. Serve hens with extra stuffing.

## roasted cornish game hens with pomegranate-molasses glaze

*photograph on page 48*
SERVES 4

⅓ cup pomegranate molasses

⅓ cup extra-virgin olive oil

¼ teaspoon freshly ground pepper, plus more for seasoning

2 Cornish hens (each 1 to 1½ pounds), rinsed and patted dry

2 onions, 1 thinly sliced, 1 cut into 8 wedges

4 garlic cloves, smashed

1 lemon, cut into 8 wedges

2 tablespoons unsalted butter, melted

Coarse salt

Pomegranate Pilaf (page 296)

Vegetable-oil cooking spray, for roasting rack

1. In a small bowl, whisk together pomegranate molasses, oil, and pepper. Place each hen in a large resealable plastic bag. Divide marinade, sliced onion, and garlic evenly among bags. Seal bags; turn to coat. Refrigerate at least 4 hours or overnight, turning occasionally.

2. Preheat oven to 350°F, with rack in lower third. Fit a shallow roasting pan or rimmed baking sheet with a roasting rack, and coat rack evenly with cooking spray; set aside.

3. Remove hens from plastic bags, letting excess marinade drip off. Place hens on rack, breast side up, and tuck wing tips under body. Fill each cavity with 4 onion and 4 lemon wedges; tie legs with kitchen twine. Brush skin with butter, and season with salt and pepper.

4. Transfer to oven, and roast until hens are golden and cooked through, about 1½ hours, rotating pan every 30 minutes. If skin starts to get too brown, cover loosely with foil. Remove from oven; serve hens with pomegranate pilaf.

## duck roasted in salt

SERVES 4

*This roasting method also works well with a four-pound chicken; adjust the cooking time to about one-and-a-half hours.*

1 cup orange marmalade

2 sprigs thyme

1 tablespoon grated fresh ginger, plus a 1-inch piece, peeled and sliced into ¼-inch rounds

2 tablespoons whole pink peppercorns, lightly crushed

1 duck (about 5 pounds), rinsed and patted dry

Freshly ground black pepper

1 onion, coarsely chopped

1 carrot, coarsely chopped

1 stalk celery, coarsely chopped

4 sprigs thyme

1 fresh bay leaf

1 sprig rosemary

3 whole cinnamon sticks

5 pounds coarse salt

1. In a small saucepan, heat orange marmalade over medium heat until liquefied. Remove from heat, and pass liquid through a fine sieve set over a small bowl. Stir in thyme, grated ginger, and pink peppercorns; set glaze aside.

2. Preheat oven to 400°F. Season duck cavity with black pepper; stuff with vegetables, ginger rounds, thyme, bay leaf, rosemary, and 1 cinnamon stick. Use kitchen twine and a trussing needle to sew cavity closed; tie legs together with twine.

3. Pour one-third of the salt into a Dutch oven slightly larger than the duck. Place duck on the salt; brush duck generously with glaze. Place the remaining 2 cinnamon sticks on the salt, next to duck. Cover duck completely with remaining salt.

**4.** Transfer duck to oven; roast until a meat thermometer inserted into thickest part of thigh (avoiding bone) registers 165°F, about 2 hours 15 minutes.

**5.** Remove duck from oven; let cool 30 minutes. Carefully invert pot onto a large cutting board. Break off salt from duck, and discard; brush off any excess salt. Remove skin; carve, and serve.

✳

## roasted duck with sour-cherry glaze
### SERVES 4

*This recipe was prepared by chef and owner Rocco di Spirito of Union Pacific in New York City when he appeared on Martha's television show.*

- 1 *Peking duck (5 to 6 pounds)*
  *Coarse salt and freshly ground pepper*
- 2 *pounds rutabagas (about 2 medium), peeled and cut into ½-inch pieces*
- ¼ *cup white-wine vinegar*
- 4 *tablespoons unsalted butter, room temperature*
- 2 *tablespoons honey*
- 2 *sprigs mint, leaves picked and thinly sliced*
  *Zinfandel Sour-Cherry Glaze (recipe follows)*
  *Evergreens and crushed pinecones, for serving (optional)*
- 1½ *cups mixed spices, such as whole allspice, star anise, cumin seeds, juniper berries, anise seeds, and dried bay leaves (optional)*

**1.** Preheat oven to 225°F, with racks in upper and lower thirds. Bring a large pot of water to a boil.

**2.** Using a sharp knife, score the fat on the breast of duck, making crosswise slashes at ½-inch intervals, being careful not to puncture the meat. Using kitchen twine, truss the duck, leaving enough twine to form a handle.

**3.** Holding twine handle, lower duck into the boiling water 10 seconds. Remove duck, and drain any water that has accumulated in the cavity. Place duck, breast side up, on a wire rack in a large roasting pan. Add 1 inch of water to pan to prevent the fat from smoking as it drips during cooking. Season duck with salt and pepper.

**4.** Place rutabagas in a small ovenproof saucepan. Season with salt and pepper. Drizzle with vinegar, and toss to combine. Cover saucepan, and place on upper rack in oven, with the duck on the lower rack. Roast until duck is golden brown and most of the fat has rendered, 2½ to 3 hours.

**5.** Remove rutabagas from oven; set aside. Raise oven temperature to 500°F. Transfer duck to upper rack; continue roasting until skin is well browned and crisp, about 10 minutes more.

**6.** Meanwhile, pass rutabagas through a food mill fitted with a large disk into a medium saucepan. Add butter and honey; season with salt and pepper, stirring to combine. Stir in mint. Transfer to a serving dish; keep warm.

**7.** Remove duck from oven, and immediately brush with half the sour-cherry glaze. Transfer to a serving platter. If using, arrange evergreens and pinecones around the perimeter of a platter larger than the serving platter, and sprinkle with spices. Place duck platter on top. If desired, use a kitchen torch to sear the evergreens, pinecones, and spices until aromatic. Serve duck with rutabagas and remaining sour-cherry glaze.

## zinfandel sour-cherry glaze
### MAKES ABOUT 2 CUPS

*The glaze may be prepared in advance and stored in an airtight container in the refrigerator up to two days. The sauce will thicken upon standing; reheat gently before serving.*

- 1 cup dried sour cherries
- 1 cup red-wine vinegar
- 1 cup sugar
- 2 750-ml bottles zinfandel or other dry red wine
- 3 tablespoons hot mustard
  Coarse salt

**1.** In a small saucepan, combine cherries and vinegar. Place over medium heat just until steam rises from the pan. Remove from heat; set aside until cherries have rehydrated, about 20 minutes. Drain cherries, reserving vinegar, and chop; set aside.

**2.** Place sugar in a large skillet over medium heat; cook, stirring, until sugar dissolves and turns a light caramel color, about 10 minutes.

**3.** Remove caramel from heat. Add reserved vinegar carefully, as it may spatter. Stir until caramel melts. Add wine; simmer over medium-low heat until mixture has reduced by about two-thirds and is the consistency of a thin syrup. Stir in reserved cherries. Whisk in mustard, and season with salt. Serve glaze warm with roasted duck.

## roast goose
### photograph on page 46
### SERVES 6

*If using a frozen goose, thaw it overnight in the refrigerator; let stand at room temperature thirty minutes before proceeding.*

- 1 fresh or frozen goose, giblets reserved (about 12 pounds), rinsed and patted dry
  Coarse salt and freshly ground pepper
- 3 carrots, cut in half
- 3 stalks celery, cut in half
- 1 head garlic, cut in half crosswise
- 1 bunch fresh thyme
- 1 bunch fresh sage
- 1 onion, cut in half
- 8 sprigs flat-leaf parsley
- 1 fresh bay leaf
- 1 teaspoon whole black peppercorns
- ½ cup dry white wine
- 1 tablespoon unsalted butter

**1.** Preheat oven to 400°F. Trim as much excess fat as possible from the opening of the goose cavity. Remove first and second joints of wings; set aside for making goose stock.

**2.** With a sharp knife, prick entire surface of goose skin, being careful not to cut into the meat. Fold neck flap under body, and pin flap down with a toothpick. Generously sprinkle cavity with salt and pepper; insert two carrot halves, two celery-stalk halves, the garlic, thyme, and sage. Tie the legs together with kitchen twine. Generously sprinkle outside of goose with salt and pepper; place, breast side up, on a wire rack set in a large roasting pan.

**3.** Transfer goose to oven, and roast until golden brown, about 1 hour. Using a baster, remove as much fat as possible from pan every 30 minutes; reserve fat for another use. Reduce oven heat to 325°F, and continue roasting until goose is very well browned all over and a meat thermometer inserted into a breast (avoiding bone) registers 180°F, about 1 hour more.

**4.** Meanwhile, prepare goose stock for the gravy and dressing: Trim and discard any excess fat from wing tips, neck, and giblets, and place in a small stockpot. Add remaining four carrot and celery-stalk halves, both onion halves, parsley, bay leaf, peppercorns, and enough water to cover bones and vegetables by 1 inch (about 2½ quarts water).

**5.** Place stockpot over high heat; bring to a boil. Reduce heat to medium-low; simmer, skimming foam from surface as it forms, 2 hours. Strain the stock through a cheesecloth-lined sieve into a container. Remove and discard the fat floating on surface of stock; set stock aside.

**6.** Remove goose from oven; transfer to a cutting board with a drainage well. Let goose stand 15 to 20 minutes before carving.

**7.** Meanwhile, prepare gravy: Pour off all the fat from the roasting pan, and place pan over high heat. Pour in wine; deglaze pan, stirring up any browned bits from bottom with a wooden spoon, until liquid has reduced by three-quarters. Add 2 cups reserved goose stock; cook, stirring until liquid is again reduced by three-quarters. Season with salt and pepper. Stir in butter, and cook until gravy is slightly thickened. Pass gravy through a cheesecloth-lined sieve into a gravy boat, and serve hot with the roast goose.

# roasted pheasant with chestnut-fennel fricassée

SERVES 4

- 2 cups fresh chestnuts
- ¾ cup wild rice, rinsed well
- 1 teaspoon coarse salt, plus more for seasoning
- ¼ cup fresh rosemary, finely chopped, plus whole sprigs for garnish
- 1 garlic clove, minced
- 6 shallots, 2 minced and 4 slivered lengthwise
  Freshly ground pepper
- 1 pheasant (about 3 pounds), rinsed and patted dry
- 2 tablespoons plus 1 teaspoon unsalted butter
- 1 teaspoon olive oil
- 2 bulbs fennel (about 1 pound), sliced thinly crosswise
- 1 cup Brown Game Stock (recipe follows) or low-sodium canned chicken stock

**1.** Preheat oven to 400°F. Score each chestnut using a sharp paring knife or a chestnut knife: Make an X on one side of each chestnut or make one long slit crosswise around circumference. Place chestnuts in a single layer on a rimmed baking sheet, and roast until flesh is tender and golden, about 25 minutes. Using a clean kitchen towel, immediately rub to remove shells; set chestnuts aside.

**2.** In a medium saucepan, combine rice with 3 cups water. Bring to a boil; reduce heat, cover partially, and simmer 25 minutes. Remove from heat; stir in ½ teaspoon salt, and let stand 10 minutes. Drain rice, and set aside.

**3.** In a small bowl, combine rosemary, garlic, and minced shallots; season with salt and pepper. Rub pheasant cavity with mixture. Season outside of pheasant with salt and pepper.

**4.** Reduce oven heat to 350°F. Truss pheasant with kitchen twine. Melt 1 tablespoon butter in a roasting pan over medium heat. Place pheasant in pan; brown evenly on all sides, about 15 minutes total. Place pheasant breast side up; transfer pan to oven. Cook, basting often with pan juices, until legs are a little loose when you pull them, about 40 minutes. Remove from oven; let rest 15 to 20 minutes before carving.

**5.** Meanwhile, melt ½ teaspoon each butter and oil in a medium skillet. Add slivered shallots; cook, stirring, over medium heat until soft, 5 to 6 minutes. Transfer shallots to a bowl.

**6.** Melt another ½ teaspoon each butter and oil in skillet. Add fennel slices; cook until soft, about 5 minutes. Transfer fennel to bowl with shallots.

**7.** Melt remaining tablespoon butter in skillet. Add reserved chestnuts; cook 2 minutes. Add half the game stock and ½ teaspoon salt. Bring to a boil, and simmer until stock is reduced to a glaze, about 10 minutes. Add remaining ½ cup stock; simmer again until reduced to a glaze, about 5 minutes. Transfer chestnuts to a plate.

**8.** Add reserved rice, shallots, and fennel to skillet along with 1 cup water; cook 5 minutes over medium heat. Add chestnut mixture. Season with salt and pepper; stir to combine. Serve fricassée hot with sliced pheasant. Garnish with rosemary.

## brown game stock
### MAKES ABOUT 1 QUART

*For the clearest stock, simmer over very low heat without stirring. Refrigerate stock in airtight containers for up to three days or freeze for up to six months.*

- 2 pounds game-bird or poultry bones, rinsed and patted dry
- 3 carrots, coarsely chopped
- 3 stalks celery, coarsely chopped
- 1 onion, quartered (unpeeled)
- 1 tablespoon tomato paste
- 2 garlic cloves (unpeeled)
- 2 dried bay leaves
  Fresh flat-leaf parsley stems
- 1 sprig rosemary or a large pinch of dried rosemary
- 4 sprigs thyme or a pinch of dried thyme
- 1 scant tablespoon whole black peppercorns

**1.** Preheat oven to 400°F. Place bones in a roasting pan; roast in oven until they begin to brown, about 20 minutes.

**2.** Add carrots, celery, onion, and tomato paste to pan; stir to combine. Continue roasting, stirring occasionally, until brown and caramelized, about 30 minutes more. Using a slotted spoon, transfer bones and vegetables to a stockpot.

**3.** Skim off and discard fat from pan; add 1 cup water. Bring to a boil over medium heat, scraping up browned bits from bottom of pan with a wooden spoon; transfer liquid and bits to stockpot. Add 11 cups water along with the garlic, bay leaves, parsley, rosemary, thyme, and peppercorns.

**4.** Bring stock to a boil; reduce heat to lowest setting, and simmer about 5 hours, skimming foam from surface occasionally.

**5.** Remove pot from heat; let cool slightly. Strain stock carefully through a cheesecloth-lined sieve into storage containers. Let cool completely.

## roast guinea fowl
### SERVES 6

*Cornish game hens can be substituted for the guinea hens; reduce the roasting time to one hour, total.*

- 3 guinea hens (2½ pounds each), rinsed and patted dry
- 1 bunch fresh flat-leaf parsley, plus 12 leaves for tucking
- 4 cups Wild-Rice Stuffing (page 295)
- 4 tablespoons unsalted butter, melted
  Coarse salt and freshly ground pepper
- 1 bunch fresh chervil
- 8 garlic cloves, unpeeled
- 1 cup dry white wine

**1.** Preheat oven to 450°F. Gently loosen skin of each hen breast, and tuck 4 parsley leaves under each. Fill cavities of birds with stuffing, and truss with kitchen twine. Place in a foil-lined roasting pan. Brush some butter over birds; sprinkle with salt and pepper. Strew chervil and parsley sprigs over birds, and surround with garlic.

**2.** Transfer pan to oven; roast 15 minutes. Pour wine into pan, and brush birds again with melted butter. Reduce oven heat to 400°F; continue roasting 1 hour more. Cover with foil; roast until birds are cooked through, 15 to 30 minutes. Remove from oven; let rest 10 minutes before carving.

## quail with brussels sprouts and shallots
### SERVES 8

*Boning a quail may seem like finicky work, but the result is worth the effort. You can also use the bones to make stock.*

- 8 quail, rinsed and patted dry
- 2 cups Couscous Stuffing (page 293)
  Coarse salt
- 3 pounds brussels sprouts, trimmed
- 3 tablespoons olive oil, or more if needed
- 16 large shallots
- 4 sprigs thyme
- 1 cup dry white wine

**1.** Bone each quail by placing breast side down on a cutting board; cut along both sides of backbone with a sharp knife or kitchen scissors. Cut meat away from rib cage, and pull entire carcass from meat. Cut out thigh bones.

**2.** With quail skin side down, spoon about 3 tablespoons stuffing onto each one. Secure the back of each quail with a bamboo or steel skewer, and truss with kitchen twine. Place quail in one layer in a large roasting pan.

**3.** Preheat oven to 350°F. Bring a large pot of water to a boil; add salt. Blanch brussels sprouts in water 5 minutes; drain, and set aside. Heat olive oil in a large, heavy skillet; add shallots, and sauté 8 to 10 minutes, adding more oil if needed. Transfer shallots and brussels sprouts to pan around birds. Strew thyme over birds. Pour wine into pan.

**4.** Transfer pan to oven, and roast until birds are cooked through and browned, about 30 minutes. Serve quail with vegetables.

FISH AND SHELLFISH

## halibut à la barigoule
### SERVES 4

*This fish is braised in white wine and flavored with bacon and carrots, a preparation inspired by a method known as "à la barigoule," which is used in many Provençal dishes.*

- 3  ounces thick-cut bacon,
   cut into ½-inch pieces
- 3  shallots, sliced into ¼-inch rings
- 2  garlic cloves, coarsely chopped
- 5  carrots, sliced into ½-inch rounds
- 6  sprigs thyme
- 1  teaspoon coarse salt, plus more
   for seasoning
- ¼  teaspoon freshly ground pepper,
   plus more for seasoning
- 1½  cups dry white wine
- 4  halibut fillets (about 8 ounces each),
   cut into 4 equal pieces
- 2  tablespoons fresh flat-leaf parsley,
   coarsely chopped

**1.** In a large sauté pan, cook bacon over medium heat until crisp and brown, and fat is rendered, about 10 minutes. Transfer to paper towels to drain. Discard all but 2 tablespoons rendered fat.

**2.** Add shallots to pan; cook until caramelized, scraping up browned bits from bottom with a wooden spoon, about 6 minutes. Add garlic; cook until soft, about 4 minutes. Add carrots, thyme, salt, and pepper to pan; cook until carrots are just tender, about 9 minutes.

**3.** Raise heat to high. Slowly add wine and ¾ cup water, and bring to a boil, scraping up remaining browned bits from bottom of pan. Reduce heat to medium; add halibut. Cook, covered, until fish is opaque and cooked through, about 8 minutes.

**4.** Transfer fish to a serving plate; discard thyme. Raise heat to high. Stir in parsley, and season with salt and pepper; cook 2 to 3 minutes more. Spoon vegetables and sauce over fish; garnish with reserved bacon. Serve immediately.

## poached halibut
### SERVES 4

- 1  tablespoon Dijon mustard
- 1  cup Herb Vinaigrette (recipe follows)
- 1  small shallot, finely diced
- 3  cups Court Bouillon (page 233)
- 4  halibut steaks (about 8 ounces each)
   with skin
   Fine sea salt and freshly ground
   white pepper
- ½  teaspoon chopped fresh tarragon
- 1½  teaspoons chopped fresh flat-leaf parsley
- 2  tablespoons chopped fresh chives
- 2  tablespoons fresh chervil

**1.** Place mustard in a medium bowl, and slowly whisk in vinaigrette. Add shallot. Transfer to a small saucepan; set aside.

**2.** In a large saucepan over high heat, bring court bouillon to a boil. Season halibut with salt and pepper. Add halibut to pan; reduce heat to a simmer. Poach fish 5 to 6 minutes for rare. Transfer to a warm plate; set aside.

**3.** Add herbs to reserved vinaigrette; warm over low heat. Remove skin from halibut, and place one steak in the center of each plate. Spoon vinaigrette over the fish. Serve immediately.

### herb vinaigrette
MAKES 1⅓ CUPS

2  teaspoons Dijon mustard

1  teaspoon fine sea salt

2  pinches freshly ground white pepper

3  tablespoons red-wine vinegar

3  tablespoons sherry vinegar

½  cup plus 1 tablespoon olive oil

½  cup plus 1 tablespoon corn oil

In a small bowl, whisk together mustard, salt, pepper, and vinegars. Whisking constantly, slowly pour in olive oil, then corn oil, until mixture is emulsified. Store vinaigrette, tightly covered, in the refrigerator up to 1 week.

## horseradish-crusted halibut
SERVES 4

*We use halibut in this recipe, but any firm-flesh white fish, such as cod or flounder, would also be good.*

10  tablespoons freshly grated or drained
     prepared horseradish

½  cup plain breadcrumbs,
    preferably homemade

2  tablespoons unsalted butter

1  tablespoon fresh chervil leaves

1  tablespoon fresh tarragon leaves
    Freshly ground pepper

2  teaspoons egg white

4  skinless halibut fillets (6 to 8 ounces each)
    Coarse salt

1  teaspoon olive oil

2  bunches spinach, trimmed and washed well

2  tablespoons balsamic vinegar

**1.** Preheat oven to 400°F. In a food processor, combine horseradish, breadcrumbs, butter, herbs, and a pinch of pepper. Pulse until combined and herbs are coarsely chopped, 2 or 3 times. Add egg white, and pulse 2 or 3 times more.

**2.** Season both sides of fish fillets with salt and pepper. Pat 3 or 4 tablespoons horseradish mixture firmly onto one side of each fillet.

**3.** Heat a large nonstick ovenproof sauté pan over medium-low heat. Add oil and fish fillets, coated side down. Cook until crust is golden brown, 2 to 3 minutes. Carefully turn fillets, then transfer pan to oven; bake until fish is cooked through, 7 to 10 minutes.

**4.** While fish is baking, place spinach in a medium saucepan (the leaves should still have water clinging to them; if they don't, sprinkle with a few drops). Season with salt; cover, and cook over medium heat, stirring occasionally, until spinach is just wilted, 2 to 3 minutes. Pour vinegar into a small saucepan; cook over high heat until reduced by half, about 2 minutes.

**5.** Remove fish from oven. Serve each fillet with some of the wilted spinach and drizzle with the reduced vinegar.

## red snapper livornese style
SERVES 12

3½ pounds red snapper fillets
    (4 to 5 ounces each) with skin
¼ cup all-purpose flour
    Coarse salt and freshly ground pepper
½ cup olive oil
4 large garlic cloves, finely chopped
2 cans (28 ounces each) whole Italian peeled
    plum tomatoes, crushed
1 cup dry white wine
½ cup finely chopped fresh flat-leaf parsley

**1.** Dredge snapper fillets in the flour; tap off excess. Season with salt and pepper.

**2.** Heat 3 tablespoons oil in a large skillet over medium-high heat. Add half the fillets, flesh side down; cook until golden brown, about 2 minutes per side. Transfer to a platter. Add 3 tablespoons oil to skillet; repeat with remaining snapper.

**3.** Add remaining 2 tablespoons oil to skillet; reduce heat to medium. Add garlic; cook, stirring, until lightly browned, about 30 seconds. Stir in tomatoes and wine; season with salt and pepper. Pour half the mixture into another large skillet; simmer both over medium-low heat until sauce thickens, 20 to 30 minutes.

**4.** Divide parsley between skillets. Place half the fillets, skin side down, in each skillet, and simmer until fish is cooked through, 6 to 8 minutes. Remove from heat. Transfer fish to serving platters; spoon sauce over fish. Serve immediately.

## red snapper one, two, three
SERVES 4

½ cup packed fresh flat-leaf parsley leaves
½ cup packed fresh mint leaves
1 large garlic clove, finely chopped
⅓ cup extra-virgin olive oil
2 tablespoons freshly squeezed lemon juice
1 teaspoon red-wine vinegar
    Coarse salt
4 skinless red snapper fillets (5 ounces each),
    halved crosswise

**1.** Mound parsley, mint, and garlic together on a cutting board; chop finely. Transfer to a small bowl. Add oil, lemon juice, and vinegar, and whisk to combine. Set aside.

**2.** Heat a large nonstick skillet over high heat. Sprinkle skillet with salt to sparsely cover bottom. Place fish in skillet; cook until just opaque, 1 to 3 minutes per side. Carefully transfer to a serving platter. Spoon sauce over fish; serve immediately.

## poached salmon

SERVES 12

*If you don't have a fish poacher, you can use a large, deep roasting pan with a wire rack placed in the bottom.*

1 *whole salmon (about 8 pounds),
head and tail on*
*Court Bouillon (recipe follows)*
*Garnishes for salmon, such as herb sprigs or thinly sliced carrots, cucumbers, radishes, or citrus*
*Aspic (recipe follows)*

**1.** Rinse fish under cold running water, washing away any blood around gills, which would cloud the stock. Pat fish dry inside and out with paper towels; place on a clean work surface. Trim fins from back, belly, and near gills with a pair of kitchen scissors. If the fish is too long to fit in poacher, remove head and tail with a sharp knife; cut off tail right below tail fins.

**2.** Cut a double thickness of cheesecloth 17 inches wide and the length of the salmon plus 8 inches. Place cheesecloth on a clean work surface. Lay fish lengthwise on cloth; wrap cloth around fish. Tie ends of cheesecloth with kitchen twine.

**3.** Place the rack in the bottom of poacher, and fill with cooled court bouillon; add water if necessary to cover fish. Using ends of cloth as handles, lower salmon into poacher. Cover, and set poacher over two burners. Bring liquid to a boil; reduce heat to very low. Cook at a bare simmer 25 minutes.

**4.** Slide a wooden spoon through each handle of poaching rack; lift out rack, and prop spoons on edges of poacher so fish is elevated. Raise one of the spoons to lift the side of rack that supports the head end, and expose the widest part of the fish's back. Insert an instant-read thermometer near where the fin was. The fish is fully cooked when

the temperature registers 135°F. If it hasn't, return to liquid, and continue poaching, checking temperature every 5 minutes.

**5.** Using wooden spoons as described in step 4, remove rack from liquid, and prop it on top of poacher at an angle to drain, reserving court bouillon to make aspic. When salmon is cool enough to handle, transfer to a clean work surface; let cool completely, about 45 minutes.

**6.** Unwrap fish, leaving cheesecloth in place underneath. If head and tail are still attached and are in good shape, you may want to leave them on for presentation. If not, remove tail with kitchen scissors; the head will pull off easily. Turn fish over so that the side that was on the rack faces up. Peel skin using a paring knife and your fingers.

**7.** Using cheesecloth to support the fish, flip it onto a serving platter, skin side up. Remove remaining skin. Using the back of the paring knife, gently scrape off any brown fat.

**8.** Arrange garnishes on top of fish; secure with toothpicks. Prepare an ice bath. Pour aspic into a large bowl; set bowl in ice bath. Stir aspic until it begins to thicken, 5 to 10 minutes. Remove from ice bath, and ladle some over the salmon. Refrigerate salmon 15 minutes. Repeat glazing process, if desired. If aspic becomes too thick to ladle, warm over a pan of simmering water. Remove toothpicks. Refrigerate salmon, uncovered, up to 24 hours.

**9.** When ready to serve, cut with a fish server: Start at the wide end of the fish; slide the server under or between the garnishes, rather than cutting through them. Cut down to the bones, working the server gently between the flakes. Lift a section of fish with garnishes on top, and transfer to a dinner plate. Repeat with remaining portions.

## court bouillon

MAKES 6 QUARTS

*If you're preparing this easy bouillon the day you poach the salmon, make it right in the poacher. The bouillon can also be made up to three days ahead in a stockpot and refrigerated in an airtight container.*

- 1   *bunch fresh thyme*
- 1   *bunch fresh flat-leaf parsley*
- ½   *teaspoon whole black peppercorns*
- ½   *teaspoon fennel seeds*
- 1   *750-ml bottle dry white wine*
- 1   *leek, white and pale-green parts only, sliced into ¼-inch-thick rounds, and washed well*
- 2   *carrots, sliced into ¼-inch-thick rounds*
- 1   *lemon, sliced into ¼-inch-thick rounds*
- 3   *dried bay leaves*
- 2   *tablespoons coarse salt*

Fill a 10-quart stockpot with 7 quarts water (about three-quarters full). Using kitchen twine, tie thyme and parsley together in a tight bundle. Place bundle in pot, along with the remaining ingredients. Cover, and bring to a boil. Remove lid, and reduce heat; gently simmer 30 minutes. Remove and discard herb bundle. Let bouillon cool to room temperature, about 1 hour.

## aspic

- 6   *cups Court Bouillon, reserved from poaching salmon*
- 6   *large egg whites*
- 3   *envelopes unflavored gelatin (1 tablespoon each)*

**1.** Strain court bouillon through a fine sieve into a stockpot. In a separate bowl, whisk egg whites until frothy. Whisk egg whites into bouillon. Place over medium heat, whisking constantly, until mixture comes to a simmer. The egg whites will draw all the cloudy particles out of the stock and begin to coagulate on top. Simmer until all the foam has coagulated, about 10 minutes.

**2.** Using a slotted spoon, skim off foam, and discard. Soak a 12-inch square of cheesecloth in ice water. Squeeze out any excess water, and line sieve with cheesecloth. Strain broth through sieve into a saucepan. Repeat, using fresh cheesecloth each time, until all the foam has been removed.

**3.** Place ⅓ cup cold water in a small bowl, and sprinkle with gelatin. Let stand until softened, about 10 minutes. Add gelatin mixture to clarified stock, and bring to a simmer over medium heat, whisking constantly; do not boil. Remove from heat.

## seared salmon with creamy leek sauce

SERVES 4

3 tablespoons unsalted butter

3 leeks, white and pale-green parts only, sliced into ½-inch-thick rounds, washed well (about 1½ cups)

⅓ cup dry white wine

⅓ cup heavy cream

3 tablespoons finely chopped fresh chives
Coarse salt and freshly ground pepper

¼ cup low-sodium canned chicken broth or water

1 tablespoon olive oil

4 salmon fillets (about 6 ounces each) with skin
Arugula, washed well and dried, for garnish
Lemon wedges, for garnish

**1.** Melt butter in a medium skillet over medium-low heat. Add leeks; cook, stirring occasionally, until they begin to soften, about 5 minutes. Add wine, and simmer until leeks are very tender, about 4 minutes. Add cream and 2 tablespoons chives; return to a simmer. Season mixture with salt and pepper. Reserve half; transfer remaining mixture to a blender. Add chicken broth, and purée until leek sauce is smooth.

**2.** Heat oil in a large sauté pan over medium heat. Season salmon fillets with salt and pepper; place skin side down in pan. Cook until skin side is well browned, about 5 minutes. Turn fillets, and sauté just until fish is cooked through, 3 to 6 minutes more; it should still be slightly pink in the center. Transfer to a serving platter.

**3.** Serve salmon with puréed leek sauce. Garnish with reserved leek mixture, the remaining chives, and the arugula and lemon wedges.

## slow-roasted salmon with green sauce

SERVES 4

Save any remaining green sauce to use as a salad dressing or sandwich spread.

1 small white onion, chopped

2 garlic cloves, minced

1 cup packed fresh flat-leaf parsley

4 ounces watercress leaves, plus 2 bunches for serving

½ pound spinach, trimmed and washed well

½ cup buttermilk

½ cup sour cream
Juice of 1 lemon

2 teaspoons coarse salt

½ teaspoon freshly ground pepper
Extra-virgin olive oil, for baking dish and fish

4 skinless salmon fillets (about 5 ounces each)

**1.** Place onion, garlic, parsley, watercress, spinach, buttermilk, sour cream, lemon juice, 1 teaspoon salt, and ¼ teaspoon pepper in a food processor. Purée until smooth; transfer to the refrigerator.

**2.** Preheat oven to 300°F. Rub the bottom of a 9-by-13-inch glass baking dish with oil. Place salmon fillets in dish, and rub tops with oil. Sprinkle with remaining teaspoon salt and ¼ teaspoon pepper. Pour ¼ cup water in dish.

**3.** Transfer baking dish to oven; cook fish until just cooked through, 20 to 25 minutes. Serve immediately over watercress; drizzle with herb sauce. Extra sauce can be refrigerated up to 4 days.

## whole roasted salmon with pickled-beet salad

*photograph on page 51*

SERVES 12

4  leeks, white and pale-green parts only, sliced in half lengthwise, washed well

4  oranges

1  whole salmon (about 8 pounds), scaled and cleaned, head and tail on

1  teaspoon coarse salt

½  teaspoon freshly ground pepper

6  sprigs cilantro

1  red onion, sliced into ⅛-inch-thick rounds

1  tablespoon unsalted butter

1  cup dry white wine
   Pickled-Beet Salad (recipe follows)

**1.** Preheat oven to 400°F. Strew bottom of a 12-by-18-inch rimmed baking sheet with leeks; set aside. With a sharp knife, cut away peel, pith, and outer membranes from 2 oranges, following the curve of the fruit. Slice flesh into ¼-inch-thick rounds.

**2.** Rinse salmon under cold water, making sure cavity is completely clean. Pat fish dry with paper towels. Cut three shallow slits, about 3 inches apart, through the skin on each side of fish. Sprinkle cavity with salt and pepper.

**3.** Stuff cavity with the cilantro, reserved orange rounds, and onion rounds. Drape a large piece of cheesecloth over leeks in bottom of roasting pan. Place salmon on top of cheesecloth.

**4.** Squeeze juice from remaining 2 oranges into a small saucepan; bring to a boil. Add butter, and stir until melted; remove from heat.

**5.** Brush salmon with orange-juice mixture. Place roasting pan in oven, and roast salmon, basting every 10 minutes with orange-juice mixture, until skin is crisp and browned and meat is pink and firm to the touch, about 1 hour. If head or tail of fish become too dark, tent with aluminum foil.

**6.** Remove pan from oven; immediately pour wine into pan to help loosen salmon. Using cheesecloth to lift fish, carefully transfer fish and leeks to a serving platter. Gently remove cheesecloth; discard pan juices. Serve with beet salad.

## pickled-beet salad

SERVES 12

6  large beets, peeled and cut into matchsticks

1  red onion, sliced into ⅛-inch-thick rounds

3  oranges

1  cup red-wine vinegar

6  tablespoons sugar

1½  cups dried cranberries

1  pound watercress

**1.** Place beets and onion in a medium bowl, and toss to combine; set aside. Working over a bowl to catch the juices, cut away peel, pith, and outer membranes from oranges, following the curve of the fruit. Cut between membranes to remove whole segments; add to bowl with juice. Squeeze juice from membranes into bowl. Set aside.

**2.** In a small saucepan over medium heat, bring vinegar, sugar, and ½ cup water to a boil. Stir until sugar has dissolved, about 2 minutes. Pour liquid over reserved beet mixture; let cool to room temperature, about 30 minutes. Add reserved orange segments and juice, along with the dried cranberries; toss gently to combine.

**3.** Place watercress in a large serving bowl. With a slotted spoon, arrange pickled-beet mixture over watercress, and serve.

**235**

## whole roasted salmon with christmas glaze

### SERVES 8 TO 10

1    whole salmon (6 to 8 pounds), scaled
     and cleaned, head and tail on
     Coarse salt and freshly ground pepper

6    sprigs rosemary

3    tablespoons sugar

¼    cup plus 3 tablespoons rice vinegar

1    tablespoon grated fresh ginger

1¼   cups clam juice
     Pinch of ground allspice
     Pinch of ground cloves
     Pinch of ground nutmeg

1½   tablespoons arrowroot
     or 2 tablespoons cornstarch
     Sautéed Leeks and Potatoes (page 261)

10   lady apples, for garnish

**1.** Preheat oven to 450°F. Rinse salmon well. Using a sharp knife, trim 2 inches of flesh from each side of the fish belly; discard. Cut crisscross marks 2½ inches apart on both sides of the salmon, deep enough to go through the skin.

**2.** Season salmon liberally inside and out with salt and pepper, and fill cavity with rosemary sprigs. Transfer salmon to a 16½-by-12-inch roasting pan, standing it up on its belly and curving it to fit in the pan. Place pan in oven.

**3.** Heat sugar in a small saucepan over medium-low heat, stirring it several times, until melted and golden, about 5 minutes. Stir in vinegar and ginger; cook until reduced by half, 2 to 3 minutes. Add clam juice and spices, and bring to a boil. Reduce heat, and simmer a few minutes. Combine arrowroot or cornstarch with 1 tablespoon water in a small bowl; mix to dissolve. Stir into glaze. Cook, stirring constantly, until the glaze is thick and syrupy, about 1 minute.

**4.** When the salmon begins to brown (after 20 to 25 minutes), reduce oven temperature to 375°F. Brush salmon liberally on all sides with glaze. Continue brushing every 5 minutes until fish is cooked through; salmon should feel firm when touched at its thickest point. Total cooking time should be 35 to 45 minutes.

**5.** Remove salmon from oven; let rest 5 minutes. Arrange potatoes and leeks on a serving platter. Using 2 spatulas, place salmon on top of vegetables. Garnish platter with lady apples.

## striped sea bass with blood oranges and olives

*photograph on page 50*
### SERVES 4

6    blood or navel oranges

4    striped sea bass fillets
     (about 6 ounces each) with skin
     Coarse salt and freshly ground pepper

1    tablespoon canola oil

6    tablespoons chilled unsalted butter

2    shallots, cut into ¼-inch pieces

1    ounce small pitted green olives, quartered

**1.** Squeeze 3 to 4 oranges to make 1 cup juice; set aside. Using a sharp paring knife, remove the peel and pith from the remaining oranges, following the curve of the fruit. Cut between membranes to remove whole segments, and set segments aside in a small bowl.

**2.** Score skin side of fish, and season with salt and pepper. Heat oil in a medium skillet over medium-high heat. Add fish, skin side up; cook until golden brown, about 3 minutes. Turn fish; reduce heat to medium, and continue to cook until opaque and cooked through, about 3 minutes. Transfer to a serving platter; keep warm.

**3.** While fish is cooking, melt 1 tablespoon butter in a small saucepan over medium heat. Add shallots; cook, stirring frequently, until golden, about 5 minutes. Add reserved orange juice, and bring to a simmer. Cook until juice has reduced by half, about 5 minutes.

**4.** Remove pan from heat, and whisk in remaining 5 tablespoons butter, 1 tablespoon at a time. Stir in reserved orange segments and the olives. Pour sauce over fish, and serve immediately.

## sole florentine
SERVES 12

2½  cups milk
 7  tablespoons unsalted butter
 ¼  cup plus 1 tablespoon all-purpose flour
 ⅛  teaspoon ground nutmeg
    Coarse salt
 3  pounds (about 3 bunches) spinach, washed well, tough stems trimmed
    Freshly ground pepper
3⅓  cups dry white wine
12  fillets of sole (about 3 pounds)
 ¼  cup freshly grated Parmesan cheese (about 1 ounce)

**1.** Preheat oven to 450°F, with rack in upper third. Make béchamel sauce: Bring milk just to a simmer in a small saucepan over medium-high heat. Melt 5 tablespoons butter in a medium saucepan over medium-low heat. Add flour to butter; cook, whisking constantly, until mixture is smooth and bubbling, about 5 minutes.

**2.** Slowly whisk hot milk into flour mixture, a little at a time. Add nutmeg, and season with salt. Cook, stirring constantly with a wooden spoon, until sauce begins to boil and is thick enough to coat the back of the spoon, about 5 minutes. Remove from heat; cover loosely, and set aside.

**3.** Working in batches, steam spinach over 1 to 2 inches boiling water until it is tender and bright green, 1 to 2 minutes. Transfer to a colander; let drain 10 minutes. Pat dry with paper towels, removing as much moisture as possible. Arrange in an even layer on a large ovenproof serving platter or in a 4-quart shallow casserole. Season with salt and pepper; cover loosely, and set aside.

**4.** Place wine and remaining 2 tablespoons butter in a large, deep skillet; bring to a boil. Reduce heat to medium-low, and keep at a steady simmer. Season fish with salt and pepper; carefully add fillets to skillet, working in batches so as not to overcrowd the pan. Rest a large metal spatula on top of fillets to keep them submerged; cook until just beginning to turn opaque, 1 to 2 minutes. Transfer cooked fillets to a wire rack set in a rimmed baking sheet; let drain, about 2 minutes.

**5.** Arrange fish in a single layer over spinach, leaving a 1-inch border all around. Spoon béchamel sauce over fish, and sprinkle with cheese. Bake until béchamel is golden brown in spots and fish is heated through, 8 to 10 minutes. Remove from oven, and serve immediately.

## sole rolls with spinach and lemon slices

*photograph on page 50*

SERVES 4

1  teaspoon olive oil

1  shallot, minced

¾  pound spinach, trimmed and washed, water clinging to leaves

   Coarse salt and freshly ground pepper

1  large lemon

1  tablespoon finely chopped almonds

1  tablespoon finely chopped mixed fresh herbs, such as chervil, flat-leaf parsley, chives, and tarragon

4  fillets gray sole, lemon sole, or flounder (about 4 ounces each)

¼  cup dry white wine

**1.** Preheat oven to 375°F, with rack in center. In a large sauté pan, heat oil over low heat. Add shallot; cook, stirring frequently, until soft, about 2 minutes. Raise heat to medium. Add spinach; season with salt and pepper. Cook, tossing frequently, until wilted and bright green, about 2 minutes. Transfer mixture to a colander, pressing down to remove liquid. Chop finely; squeeze out remaining liquid. Divide mixture into four equal parts.

**2.** Halve lemon crosswise. Grate zest of half, and combine with almonds and herbs in a small bowl; set aside. Slice other lemon half into thin rounds.

**3.** Lay fillets flat on a work surface, smoothest side down; place one part spinach mixture at the narrow end of each fillet. Roll into cylinders, enclosing spinach. Place rolls in a gratin dish, seam sides down, with lemon rounds between each. Pour wine into dish. Sprinkle one-quarter of almond mixture on top of each roll; cover dish with parchment paper and then aluminum foil.

**4.** Transfer dish to oven, and bake until fish is opaque and cooked through, 15 to 20 minutes.

## crab cakes with chicory salad

SERVES 4

*These cakes are extra meaty because they are bound with a minimum of eggs and breadcrumbs.*

¼  cup finely chopped shallots (about 4)

½  cup olive oil

1  pound jumbo lump crabmeat, rinsed and picked over

2  large eggs, lightly beaten

   Grated zest of 2 lemons

2  tablespoons chopped fresh chives

   Coarse salt and freshly ground pepper

2  tablespoons plain breadcrumbs, plus more for dusting

1  tablespoon unsalted butter

1  head radicchio

1  head frisée or curly endive

2  heads red or white Belgian endive

2  tablespoons cider vinegar

   Mashed-Potato Tartar Sauce (recipe follows)

**1.** Preheat oven to 350°F. In a small sauté pan over low heat, cook shallots in 2 tablespoons olive oil until transparent, 2 to 3 minutes.

**2.** In a large bowl, combine crabmeat, shallots, eggs, lemon zest, and chives; season with salt and pepper. Add breadcrumbs, and stir to combine. Shape mixture into eight cakes, and dust lightly with additional breadcrumbs.

**3.** In a large ovenproof sauté pan over medium heat, melt butter with 2 tablespoons oil. Sauté crab cakes until golden brown on one side, 1 to 2 minutes. Turn cakes, and transfer pan to oven. Bake until cakes are cooked through, 5 to 8 minutes.

**4.** Combine greens. In a small bowl, whisk together remaining ¼ cup oil and the vinegar; season with salt and pepper. Toss with greens. Serve salad with crab cakes and tartar sauce.

## mashed-potato tartar sauce
MAKES 2 CUPS

1 large or 2 small russet potatoes
   (about 8 ounces), scrubbed
1 large yellow or red bell pepper
1 cup mayonnaise
2 tablespoons capers, rinsed and drained
1 tablespoon Dijon mustard
   Juice and grated zest of 2 lemons
2 tablespoons chopped fresh flat-leaf parsley
   Dash of hot-pepper sauce, such as Tabasco
   Coarse salt and freshly ground pepper

**1.** Preheat oven to 425°F. Pierce potato with a fork, and bake until soft, about 1 hour.

**2.** Meanwhile, roast pepper over a gas flame or under the broiler until skin is charred, turning as each side blackens. Place in a bowl, and cover with plastic wrap; let steam about 10 minutes. Peel and seed pepper, then cut into small pieces.

**3.** Scoop flesh of potato into a medium bowl; mash with a potato masher or fork. Stir in mayonnaise, then add pepper and remaining ingredients. Chill until ready to serve.

## lobster fricassée
SERVES 4

*Every part of the lobster is used in this fricassée. The shells are roasted with garlic and bay leaves, and then simmered with wine. The resulting sauce intensely flavors the lobster meat and accompanying vegetables.*

**for lobster sauce:**

5 cups dry white wine
3½ pounds lobster (about 2 large or 3 small)
1 onion, coarsely chopped
2 carrots, coarsely chopped
4 garlic cloves
4 dried bay leaves
3 cups chicken stock,
   preferably homemade (page 179),
   or low-sodium canned chicken broth
3 tablespoons tomato paste

**for fricassée:**

½ cup dried flageolets or great Northern
   beans, picked over and rinsed
1 dried bay leaf
1 teaspoon coarse salt
2 tablespoons olive oil
6 shallots, chopped
12 pearl onions, peeled
2 carrots, cut into 1½-inch pieces
2 Yukon gold potatoes, peeled and
   cut into 1½-inch pieces
8 pattypan squash or small zucchini,
   stems trimmed
2 cups chicken stock, preferably
   homemade (page 179), or low-sodium
   canned chicken broth
1 cup mixed wild fresh mushrooms, such
   as chanterelle, shiitake, and oyster
¼ cup heavy cream
   Fresh flat-leaf parsley, for garnish

**1.** Preheat oven to 400°F. Make sauce: Fill a 10-quart stockpot three-quarters full with water; add 1 cup wine, and bring to a boil Add 1 lobster, and cook 5 minutes; remove. Return cooking liquid to a boil; repeat with remaining lobsters. Let cool.

**2.** Remove tails and claws from lobsters. With a sharp knife, carefully cut underside of tails three-fourths of the way down. Remove meat, and cut into four pieces; set aside. Reserve tail fans for garnish; reserve all other shells for lobster stock. Crack claws; remove meat in one piece. Cut bodies in half, remove meat, and rinse shells well to clean out interior.

**3.** Place shells in an 11-by-14-inch roasting pan. Add onion, carrots, garlic, and bay leaves. Roast until shells are very brown but not burnt, about 40 minutes. Remove pan from oven. Add 1 cup wine; deglaze pan, scraping up browned bits from bottom with a wooden spoon. Transfer mixture to a stockpot; add remaining 3 cups wine, the stock, and tomato paste, and simmer until reduced by half, about 45 minutes. Strain sauce through a fine sieve into a bowl, pressing on solids. Set sauce aside.

**4.** Make fricassée: Place beans in a medium saucepan, and add water to cover by 2 inches. Bring to a boil; remove from heat, and drain. Return beans to saucepan, and add fresh water to cover. Add bay leaf, and bring to a boil; reduce heat, and simmer until beans are tender, about 35 minutes. Add boiling water, if necessary, to keep beans completely covered. Add salt, and continue simmering 10 minutes more. Let beans cool in liquid, then drain and rinse; set beans aside.

**5.** Heat oil in a large sauté pan over medium heat. Add shallots; cook, stirring, until transparent, about 5 minutes; do not brown. Add onions, car-

rots, potatoes, squash, and stock; cook, stirring occasionally, until vegetables are tender and liquid has evaporated, about 20 minutes. Add mushrooms; cook, stirring, until wilted, 3 to 4 minutes. Add reserved beans, lobster meat, and sauce; add cream, and bring to a boil. Divide fricassée among four serving bowls; garnish each serving with parsley leaves and reserved tail fans.

### *mussels in white wine and garlic*
SERVES 4

*Be sure to buy live mussels from a reliable source. Discard any open mussels that do not close when you press on their shells a few times.*

- 4 *pounds fresh mussels*
- 2 *cups dry white wine*
- 4 *large shallots, finely chopped*
- 4 *garlic cloves, finely chopped*
- ½ *teaspoon coarse salt*
- ⅓ *cup mixed fresh herbs, such as flat-leaf parsley, chervil, and basil, chopped*
- 6 *tablespoons unsalted butter, cut into pieces*

**1.** Rinse and scrub mussels under cold running water. Using your fingers or a paring knife, remove the stringy beards, and discard.

**2.** In a stockpot over medium heat, combine wine, shallots, garlic, and salt. Bring to a boil; reduce heat, and simmer 5 minutes.

**3.** Add mussels to pot. Cover, and raise heat to high. Cook until all mussels are open, about 5 minutes; discard any mussels that did not open. Remove from heat. Divide mussels among four bowls. Strain broth through a cheesecloth-lined sieve; place in a clean saucepan over medium heat. Stir in herbs and butter, and divide among bowls with mussels. Serve immediately.

## oyster pie

### SERVES 10 TO 12

*This oyster pie is a favorite recipe of Martha's friend Salli LaGrone from Tennessee.*

- 14 tablespoons (1¾ sticks) unsalted butter, plus more for dish
- 1½ quarts shucked oysters and their liquor
- 7 scallions, finely chopped
- 1 teaspoon Worcestershire sauce
- ¾ teaspoon hot-pepper sauce, such as Tabasco
- 1 cup chopped fresh flat-leaf parsley
- 1 teaspoon coarse salt
- ¼ teaspoon freshly ground pepper
- 3 cups saltine-cracker crumbs, crumbled by hand (about 46 crackers)
- 3 tablespoons half-and-half or milk

**1.** Preheat oven to 450°F, with rack in center. Butter a shallow 10-inch baking or pie dish. Reserving liquid, drain the oysters. Check oysters for shells, and discard. Set oysters aside.

**2.** Melt 3 tablespoons butter over medium heat in a medium skillet; add scallions, and cook, stirring, until soft, about 3 minutes. Stir in Worcestershire and hot-pepper sauce. Transfer mixture to a medium bowl, and let cool.

**3.** Stir oysters, ¼ cup parsley, the salt, and pepper into scallion mixture. In a medium bowl, combine cracker crumbs and remaining ¾ cup parsley. Melt remaining 11 tablespoons butter, and stir into crumb mixture. In a small bowl, combine ¼ cup of the reserved oyster liquor with the half-and-half.

**4.** Spread a thin layer of the crumb mixture evenly in bottom of prepared baking dish. Cover with one-third of the oyster mixture, followed by ½ cup crumb mixture; top with one-third of the oyster liquid. Continue layering until all ingredients are used, ending with crumb mixture. Bake until golden brown on top, 25 to 35 minutes. Serve hot.

## scallops in white wine

### photograph on page 50

### SERVES 4

*Serve with your favorite wild-rice blend.*

- 2 dozen sea scallops (about 1½ pounds), tough muscles removed
- 12 cherry tomatoes, halved
- 1 large red onion, halved and sliced into ¼-inch-thick half-moons
- ½ cup dry white wine
- 4 tablespoons unsalted butter
- 1 tablespoon chopped fresh thyme
  Coarse salt and freshly ground pepper

**1.** Preheat oven to 400°F. Fold four 18-inch lengths of parchment paper in half crosswise. Cut out one half-heart shape from folded side of each. Lay hearts flat on a work surface; place 6 scallops on one half of each parchment heart near the crease. Top each with one-quarter of the tomatoes and onion; drizzle with 2 tablespoons wine. Dot each with 1 tablespoon butter. Sprinkle with thyme; season with salt and pepper.

**2.** Fold other half of parchment over ingredients. Make small overlapping folds to seal the edges, starting at top of heart. Two inches from pointed end, twist paper twice, gently but firmly, to seal.

**3.** Place scallop packets on a large rimmed baking sheet or in a heavy ovenproof skillet (preferably cast iron); bake until fully puffed, about 20 minutes. Remove from oven; open packets carefully. Transfer scallops, tomatoes, and onion to plates; spoon some cooking liquid from the packets over top. Serve immediately.

## sea scallops with sherry and saffron couscous

SERVES 4

1 pound sea scallops, tough muscles removed
  Coarse salt and freshly ground pepper
2 to 3 tablespoons olive oil
¼ cup dry sherry
2½ cups chicken stock, preferably homemade (page 179), or low-sodium canned chicken broth
3 tablespoons unsalted butter, cut into small pieces
  Pinch of saffron
1 tablespoon fresh thyme
2 cups couscous

1. Season scallops with salt and pepper. Heat 2 tablespoons oil in a large sauté pan over medium-high heat. Add scallops, working in batches (add 1 tablespoon oil if necessary). Sear until golden brown and caramelized, about 1 minute per side. Transfer scallops to a plate, and cover with foil.

2. Pour off any fat remaining in pan; return pan to heat. Add sherry; deglaze pan, scraping up browned bits from bottom with a wooden spoon. Simmer until sherry is reduced by two-thirds. Add stock, butter, saffron, and thyme; season with salt. Bring to a boil; add couscous. Cover the pan; remove from heat. Let stand 5 minutes. Fluff couscous with a fork, and season with salt and pepper. Serve scallops with couscous.

## seared shrimp with lemon and garlic

SERVES 12

*This dish is equally delicious served piping hot or at room temperature.*

4 lemons
4 pounds large shrimp, peeled, deveined, and rinsed
3 garlic cloves, minced
½ cup extra-virgin olive oil
  Coarse salt and freshly ground pepper

1. Finely grate zest of 3 lemons. Juice all 4 lemons; set juice aside. Place shrimp in a large bowl; add lemon zest, garlic, and ¼ cup oil; toss to coat evenly. Season with salt and pepper.

2. Heat a large sauté pan over medium heat. Add 1 tablespoon oil, and heat until hot but not smoking. Arrange one-quarter of the shrimp in a single layer in pan. Cook until undersides are golden brown, 45 to 60 seconds. Turn shrimp, and continue cooking until other sides are golden brown and shrimp are opaque, about 1 minute more. Transfer to a large serving platter.

3. Add 1½ tablespoons reserved lemon juice to pan; deglaze pan, stirring up browned bits from bottom with a wooden spoon. Pour pan sauce over shrimp. Cover loosely with foil while repeating process with remaining shrimp, adding 1 tablespoon oil each time, then deglazing with lemon juice.

## PASTA

### rigatoni with pumpkin and bacon

SERVES 4 TO 6

*Pepitas, or pumpkin seeds, can be found in most health-food stores; look for hulled pepitas.*

- 8 slices bacon, cut into 1-inch pieces
- 1 onion, cut into ½-inch dice
  Coarse salt and freshly ground pepper
- 1 pumpkin (about 2 pounds), such as
  'Cheese' or 'Small Sugar Pie,' peeled
  and cut into ¾-inch cubes
- 1 tablespoon chopped fresh sage
- ¼ teaspoon ground allspice
- 1½ cups chicken stock,
  preferably homemade (page 179),
  or low-sodium canned chicken broth
- 3 tablespoons heavy cream
- 1 pound rigatoni
- 1 cup freshly grated Parmesan cheese
- 2 tablespoons hulled pepitas

**1.** Cook bacon in a large, deep skillet over medium heat until fat is rendered and bacon is almost crisp, about 5 minutes. Using a slotted spoon, transfer to paper towels; drain, and set aside.

**2.** Add onion to skillet, and season with salt and pepper. Cook, stirring occasionally, until onion is soft, about 5 minutes. Add pumpkin, sage, and allspice; cook, stirring frequently, until pumpkin is well coated, about 5 minutes.

**3.** Add chicken stock to skillet; bring to a boil. Reduce heat to medium-low. Stir in cream; gently simmer until pumpkin is soft and sauce has thickened slightly, about 20 minutes.

**4.** Meanwhile, bring a large pot of water to a boil. Add salt and rigatoni; cook until pasta is al dente according to package instructions, about 9 minutes. Drain, and transfer to skillet.

**5.** Return bacon to skillet; toss gently to combine. Divide pasta among serving bowls. Sprinkle each with grated Parmesan and pepitas.

### pasta puttanesca

SERVES 4 TO 6

- Coarse salt
- 1 pound spaghetti or linguine
- 3 tablespoons olive oil
- 6 medium garlic cloves, finely chopped
- ½ teaspoon crushed red-pepper flakes
- 10 anchovy fillets, crushed
- 1 can (28 ounces) Italian plum
  tomatoes, seeded, chopped, and
  strained, juice reserved
- 3 tablespoons capers, drained
- ½ cup Kalamata olives (3 ounces),
  pitted and coarsely chopped
- 2 tablespoons coarsely chopped
  fresh flat-leaf parsley

**1.** Bring a large pot of water to a boil; add salt. Add pasta; cook until al dente according to package instructions, about 9 minutes; drain.

**2.** Meanwhile, heat oil in a large skillet over medium heat. Add garlic, red-pepper flakes, and anchovies. Cook, stirring, until aromatic, 1 to 2 minutes. Add tomatoes and reserved juice, capers, and olives. Bring to a boil; reduce heat to a simmer, and cook, stirring frequently, until sauce has thickened slightly, about 5 minutes.

**3.** Stir pasta into sauce. Cook, stirring, until sauce clings to pasta, about 2 minutes. Stir in parsley. Serve immediately.

## fettuccine with brussels-sprout leaves, brown butter, and toasted walnuts

SERVES 4 TO 6

*To remove individual brussels-sprout leaves, cut the stem off of each sprout, and gently ease apart all the leaves.*

- 2 ounces walnuts
  Coarse salt
- 1 pound fettuccine
- ½ cup (1 stick) plus 3 tablespoons unsalted butter
- 1 red onion, halved and sliced into thin wedges
- 2 garlic cloves, minced
- 1 pound brussels sprouts, leaves separated
- ½ teaspoon finely chopped fresh sage
- ¼ teaspoon finely chopped fresh thyme
  Freshly ground pepper
  Freshly grated Parmesan cheese, for serving

**1.** Preheat oven to 350°F. Spread walnuts on a rimmed baking sheet; toast in oven until fragrant, about 10 minutes. When cool enough to handle, coarsely chop; set aside.

**2.** Bring a large pot of water to a boil; add salt. Add pasta, and cook until al dente according to package instructions, about 9 minutes. Drain; transfer to a medium bowl, and toss with 1 tablespoon butter. Cover, and keep warm.

**3.** While pasta is cooking, place ½ cup butter in a small saucepan over medium-high heat. Cook until butter begins to brown and is very fragrant, about 8 minutes. Strain into a glass measuring cup or a small bowl; let stand 10 minutes, then discard solids, and set brown butter aside.

**4.** Heat remaining 2 tablespoons butter in a large skillet over medium heat. Add onion and garlic, and cook until starting to soften, about 2 minutes. Add sprout leaves and herbs; season with salt and pepper. Continue cooking until leaves are bright green and tender, and onions are translucent, 3 to 5 minutes.

**5.** Add pasta to skillet, and drizzle with reserved brown butter. Toss to combine, and cook until heated through, seasoning with more salt and pepper, if desired. Transfer to a serving dish; garnish with toasted walnuts and grated Parmesan cheese. Serve immediately.

## orecchiette with caramelized shallots, pancetta, and herbs

SERVES 4 TO 6

*Orecchiette (Italian for "little ears") are perfectly shaped for catching the morsels in this sauce. You can instead use other short pasta shapes, such as penne, gemelli, or farfalle. The sauce can be prepared (up to the addition of the cream) several hours ahead and kept, covered, in the refrigerator; rewarm over low heat.*

- ¾ pound pancetta or bacon, cut into ¼-inch cubes
- 1 tablespoon unsalted butter
- 1 garlic clove, minced
- 1 pound shallots (12 to 15 large), thickly sliced
- ½ teaspoon sugar
  Coarse salt and freshly ground pepper
- 1½ cups chicken stock, preferably homemade (page 179), or low-sodium canned chicken broth
- ¼ cup heavy cream (optional)
- 1 cup tightly packed mixed fresh herbs, including rosemary, sage, thyme, marjoram, flat-leaf parsley, and basil
- 1 pound orecchiette
- ½ teaspoon olive oil
- 1½ cups grated Parmesan cheese, (3 ounces) preferably Parmigiano-Reggiano

**1.** Place pancetta in a large sauté pan, and cook over medium-low heat, stirring occasionally, until crisp, about 15 minutes. Using a slotted spoon, transfer to paper towels; drain, and set aside.

**2.** Pour off all but 1 tablespoon fat from pan, and add butter. Heat until melted, then add garlic, shallots, and sugar; season lightly with salt and pepper. Reduce heat to low, and cook, covered, until shallots are soft and translucent, about 15 minutes. Raise heat to medium-high; cook, stirring constantly, until shallots are golden brown, about 10 minutes. Do not burn.

**3.** Bring a large pot of water to a boil. Meanwhile, add stock to pan; simmer until reduced by one-third, stirring up browned bits from bottom of pan, about 7 minutes. Add cream, if using, to sauce; simmer over high heat until sauce thickens slightly, about 2 minutes. Remove from heat; keep warm. Coarsely chop all but a small handful of herbs.

**4.** Add salt and pasta to boiling water; cook until pasta is al dente according to package instructions, about 8 minutes. Drain, and return to pot. Add chopped herbs to sauce, and cook 1 minute. Season with salt and pepper. Add pasta to sauce, and toss to combine over low heat, 1 minute.

**5.** In a small skillet, fry remaining herbs in the oil until crisp, about 30 seconds; drain on paper towels. Stir pancetta and ½ cup grated cheese into pasta mixture, and divide pasta among serving bowls. Garnish with fried herbs. Serve remaining cup cheese on the side.

## penne with fennel, sardines, and pine nuts

### SERVES 4

- 1 teaspoon coarse salt, plus more for cooking water
- 1 pound penne, trenette, or other short pasta
- 2 tablespoons extra-virgin olive oil
- ¼ cup pine nuts
- 1 onion, finely chopped
- 2 fennel bulbs, trimmed and thinly sliced, plus ¼ cup green fronds
- 4 garlic cloves, finely chopped
  Freshly ground pepper
- 2 cans (3.75 ounces each) sardines packed in olive oil
  Grated zest and juice of 1 lemon, plus 1 lemon for serving

**1.** Bring a large pot of water to a boil. Add salt and pasta, and cook until al dente according to package instructions, about 8 minutes.

**2.** Meanwhile, combine the oil and pine nuts in a large sauté pan. Cook over medium heat, stirring occasionally, until nuts are lightly toasted, 3 to 4 minutes.

**3.** Add onion, sliced fennel, garlic, and salt to pan; season with pepper. Cook, stirring occasionally, until onion is soft and light golden, 9 to 10 minutes. Add sardines; stir in lemon zest and juice. Chop reserved fennel fronds; stir into mixture.

**4.** Drain pasta, reserving about ¼ cup cooking liquid. Add pasta to mixture in pan along with enough cooking water to coat; toss to combine. Divide among four serving plates; grate lemon zest over each. Serve immediately.

## perciatelli with roasted chestnuts, butternut squash, and goat cheese

*photograph on page 52*

SERVES 4 TO 6

*Perciatelli is a thick, hollow, spaghetti-shaped pasta. Bucatini or linguine can be used instead.*

- 10   *ounces fresh chestnuts*
- 2   *tablespoons unsalted butter*
- 2   *tablespoons extra-virgin olive oil*
- 5   *leeks, white and pale-green parts only, sliced crosswise ¼ inch thick, washed well, and drained*
- 2   *garlic cloves, thinly sliced*
- 1   *small butternut squash (about 1 pound), peeled, seeded, and cut into ¾-inch dice*
     *Coarse salt and freshly ground pepper*
- ¾   *cup dry vermouth or white wine*
- 1   *cup chicken stock, preferably homemade (page 179), or low-sodium canned chicken broth*
- 1   *pound perciatelli*
- 4   *ounces fresh goat cheese, crumbled into small pieces*
- ½   *cup packed small fresh basil leaves*

**1.** Preheat oven to 400°F. Score each chestnut using a sharp paring knife or a chestnut knife: Make an X on one side of each chestnut or make one long slit crosswise around circumference. Place chestnuts in a single layer on a rimmed baking sheet, and roast until flesh is tender and golden, about 25 minutes. Turn oven off. Using a clean kitchen towel, immediately rub to remove shells. Discard shells and inner skin. Break chestnuts into halves or quarters; set aside.

**2.** Bring a large pot of water to a boil. In a large, deep sauté pan, melt butter and oil over medium heat. Add leeks and garlic; cook, stirring occasionally, until softened, about 6 minutes. Add reserved chestnuts and the squash; season with salt and pepper. Cook until squash is tender, 15 to 20 minutes. Add vermouth and stock, and raise heat to medium-high. Cook until liquid is reduced by a little more than half, about 2 minutes.

**3.** Meanwhile, add salt and pasta to boiling water; cook until pasta is al dente according to package instructions, about 9 minutes. Drain pasta, and add to sauté pan along with half the goat cheese; toss to combine. Transfer pasta mixture to a serving dish, and garnish with the remaining goat cheese and the basil leaves.

## three-nut pasta

SERVES 4 TO 6

*Peeled and roasted chestnuts are available at your grocery store; they are usually sold in vacuum-sealed packages. Pappardelle are flat, long, wide noodles with frilly edges; fettucine would also work.*

- ¾   *cup blanched hazelnuts*
- ¼   *cup pine nuts*
- 2   *tablespoons extra-virgin olive oil*
- 1   *tablespoon unsalted butter*
- 4   *shallots, minced*
- 16   *fresh large chestnuts, roasted, peeled, and cut into quarters*
- ½   *cup dry white wine*
- 1½   *cups chicken stock, preferably homemade (page 179), or low-sodium canned chicken broth*
- ½   *cup heavy cream*
     *Coarse salt*
- 1   *pound pappardelle*
- 2   *tablespoons fresh thyme leaves*
- ¼   *cup packed fresh flat-leaf parsley, coarsely chopped*
     *Freshly ground pepper*

**1.** Preheat oven to 350°F, with racks in upper and lower thirds. Spread hazelnuts and pine nuts separately in a single layer on two rimmed baking sheets. Toast until golden and aromatic and hazelnut skins begin to split, about 10 minutes. Set pine nuts aside to cool. Rub warm hazelnuts with a clean kitchen towel to remove the skins. Let cool, then coarsely chop.

**2.** Bring a large pot of water to a boil. In a large skillet, heat the oil and butter over low heat. Add shallots and chestnuts; cook until shallots are soft and translucent, about 7 minutes. Add wine, stock, and cream; raise heat to high, and cook until liquid is reduced by one-third, about 4 minutes.

**3.** Add salt and pasta to boiling water; cook until pasta is al dente according to package instructions, about 10 minutes. Drain.

**4.** Reduce cream mixture to medium-low; stir in chopped hazelnuts, thyme, and 2 tablespoons parsley. Season with salt and pepper; cook 2 minutes more. Add pasta; toss to combine, and remove from heat. Divide pasta among serving plates; drizzle with sauce. Garnish with pine nuts and remaining parsley.

## crab-stuffed shells with peas and leeks

*photograph on page 53*

SERVES 8 TO 10

- 9 tablespoons unsalted butter
- 2 leeks, white and pale-green parts only, halved lengthwise, cut into ¼-inch half-moons, washed well, and drained
- 1 cup fresh or frozen peas
  Coarse salt and freshly ground pepper
- 8 ounces lump crabmeat, picked over and rinsed
- 6 tablespoons all-purpose flour
- 2 cups milk
- 1 cup heavy cream
  Juice of 1 lemon
- 1 pound jumbo pasta shells
- ½ cup breadcrumbs, preferably homemade
- 6 garlic cloves, minced
- ¼ cup fresh flat-leaf parsley leaves
- 1 tablespoon extra-virgin olive oil

**1.** Melt 3 tablespoons butter in a medium skillet over medium heat. Add leeks, and cook until soft, about 5 minutes. Add peas; cook until bright green, about 3 minutes more. Transfer mixture to a bowl, and season with salt and pepper. Stir in the crabmeat; cover with plastic wrap, and refrigerate until ready to assemble.

**2.** Melt remaining 6 tablespoons butter in a large saucepan over medium heat. When bubbling, add flour. Cook, whisking constantly, 1 minute. While whisking, slowly pour in milk. Continue cooking, whisking constantly, until mixture bubbles and thickens. Remove from heat; stir in cream and lemon juice, and season with salt and pepper.

**3.** Preheat oven to 375°F. Bring a large pot of water to a boil. Add salt and pasta shells; cook 2 to 3 minutes less than package instructions. Drain.

**4.** Meanwhile, in a small bowl, stir together bread-crumbs, garlic, parsley, and oil; set aside. Stir 1 cup cream sauce into reserved crab mixture. Pour another cup cream sauce into the bottom of a 9-by-13-inch baking dish.

**5.** Fill each pasta shell with a heaping tablespoon of crab mixture; arrange in baking dish. Spoon remaining cream sauce over shells, and sprinkle with breadcrumb mixture. Transfer to oven; bake until mixture is bubbling and top is golden brown, about 30 minutes. Let cool 5 minutes before serving.

## baked buckwheat pasta with savoy cabbage

SERVES 6 TO 8

*Buckwheat noodles called pizzoccheri, are a specialty of the Valtellina region of northern Italy. Whole-wheat fettuccine can be used instead.*

    1   *pound small white or fingerling potatoes*
        *Coarse salt*
    1½  *tablespoons unsalted butter,*
        *plus more for baking dish*
    2   *garlic cloves, minced*
    2   *leeks, white and pale-green parts only,*
        *thinly sliced, washed well, and drained*
    ½   *head savoy cabbage (about 1 pound),*
        *cored and shredded*
    ½   *cup chicken stock, preferably*
        *homemade (page 179), or low-sodium*
        *canned chicken broth*
        *Freshly ground pepper*
    1   *pound pizzoccheri*
    1½  *cups freshly grated Parmesan*
        *cheese (3 ounces)*
    12  *fresh sage leaves*
    8   *ounces Taleggio cheese,*
        *cut into ½-inch cubes*

**1.** Fill a large saucepan with 6 cups cold water. Add potatoes and salt. Bring to a boil; reduce heat to medium, and simmer until potatoes are almost tender, about 45 minutes, depending on size and type of potato. Remove from heat; drain. When cool enough to handle, peel potatoes. (It is not necessary to peel fingerling potatoes; slice in half lengthwise.) Cut potatoes crosswise into ¼-inch-thick slices. Set aside.

**2.** Melt 1½ tablespoons butter in a large skillet over low heat. Add garlic and leeks, and cook until leeks are soft, about 5 minutes. Add cabbage and stock, and season with salt and pepper; continue cooking, covered, until the cabbage is tender, about 20 minutes.

**3.** Meanwhile, bring a large pot of water to a boil. Add salt and pasta; cook 2 to 3 minutes less than package instructions. Drain.

**4.** Preheat oven to 400°F. Add ½ cup Parmesan to cabbage mixture, and toss to combine. Slice 8 sage leaves into thin slivers; add to cabbage mixture.

**5.** Butter a 9-by-13-inch baking dish or large gratin dish. Arrange one-third of the noodles in the bottom of the dish. Layer half the cabbage mixture, half the sliced potatoes, one-third of the taleggio, and ½ cup Parmesan on top of the noodles. Arrange another third of the noodles over the cheese; cover with the remaining cabbage and potatoes and another third of the taleggio. Top with remaining pasta, and sprinkle with remaining ½ cup Parmesan, taleggio, and sage leaves.

**6.** Transfer to oven; bake until top is golden brown and cheese is bubbly, about 20 minutes. Let cool 5 minutes before serving.

## butternut squash cannelloni with sage-walnut cream sauce

*photograph on page 55*

SERVES 8 TO 10

3 tablespoons unsalted butter

1 onion, diced

1 large butternut squash (2½ to 3 pounds), peeled, seeded, and chopped into about 1-inch pieces

1 tablespoon plus 2½ teaspoons coarse salt

1 teaspoon ground cinnamon

1 teaspoon ground cumin

¼ teaspoon ground nutmeg

¼ teaspoon cayenne pepper

½ teaspoon freshly ground black pepper

1 cup freshly grated Parmesan cheese (2 ounces)

1 cup ricotta cheese

1 pound spinach, Swiss chard, or other greens, trimmed, washed, and coarsely chopped

2 tablespoons extra-virgin olive oil

8 ounces dried pasta sheets (about twelve 5-by-7-inch rectangles)

Sage-Walnut Cream Sauce (recipe follows)

Fresh sage leaves, for garnish

**1.** Make filling: Heat 2 tablespoons butter in a large skillet over medium heat. Add onion; cook until it begins to soften, about 3 minutes. Add squash; cook, stirring occasionally, until it begins to soften, about 5 minutes. Add 1½ teaspoons salt, the cinnamon, cumin, nutmeg, cayenne, ¼ teaspoon black pepper, and 1 cup water. Reduce heat; cover, and cook, stirring occasionally, until squash is very tender, about 20 minutes.

**2.** Remove skillet from heat. Mash squash mixture with a potato masher or wooden spoon, and transfer to a medium bowl. When cool, stir in Parmesan and ricotta. Cover with plastic wrap; refrigerate until ready to assemble.

**3.** Heat remaining tablespoon butter in a large skillet over medium heat. Add spinach a little at a time, tossing and cooking until wilted before adding more. Stir in 1 teaspoon salt and ¼ teaspoon black pepper. Transfer to a bowl; cover, and refrigerate until ready to assemble.

**4.** Preheat oven to 375°F. Bring a large pot of water to a boil. Add oil and remaining tablespoon salt. One at a time, add pasta sheets to the boiling water; cook 2 to 3 minutes less than the package instructions. Carefully remove pasta sheets with tongs, and drain in a colander.

**5.** Assemble cannelloni: Lay pasta sheets on a clean work surface. Spoon about ½ cup squash filling down the center of one sheet, and top with a heaping tablespoon of spinach mixture. Brush one long side of pasta sheet with water; roll up, starting with other long side, and seal. Repeat with remaining pasta, filling, and spinach.

**6.** Spread half the cream sauce on the bottom of a 9-by-13-inch baking dish. Arrange cannelloni, seam side down, in bottom of dish, and cover with remaining sauce. Garnish with a few sage leaves. Bake until tops start to brown and filling is bubbling, about 30 minutes. Remove from oven; let cool 5 minutes before serving.

## sage-walnut cream sauce
MAKES ABOUT 3 CUPS

4 tablespoons unsalted butter

¼ cup all-purpose flour

2 cups milk

1 cup heavy cream

2 sprigs sage

¼ cup chopped walnuts

Pinch of ground nutmeg

Coarse salt and freshly ground pepper

**1.** Heat butter in a large saucepan over medium heat. When bubbling, add flour. Cook, whisking constantly, 1 minute. While whisking, slowly pour in milk. Continue cooking, whisking constantly, until mixture bubbles and thickens.

**2.** Remove pan from heat; stir in cream, sage, walnuts, and nutmeg. Season with salt and pepper. Cover; set sauce aside to infuse 30 minutes.

## baked rigatoni with sausage meatballs and broccoli rabe
photograph on page 54
SERVES 8 TO 10

2 tablespoons extra-virgin olive oil

1 onion, diced

¼ cup vodka

1 can (16 ounces) tomato sauce

1 can (28 ounces) plum tomatoes, cut into pieces, juice reserved

1½ cups heavy cream

4 sprigs oregano

4 sprigs thyme

2 pounds sweet Italian sausage, casings removed

Coarse salt

1 pound rigatoni

Unsalted butter, for baking dish

1 bunch broccoli rabe, tough ends trimmed, leaves and stems cut into 1-inch lengths

4 ounces fontina cheese, cut into ½-inch cubes

**1.** Make the sauce: Heat oil in a large saucepan over medium heat. Add onion, and cook until soft, about 5 minutes. Add vodka; cook until liquid has almost evaporated, about 3 minutes. Stir in tomato sauce, canned tomatoes and juice, cream, oregano, and thyme. Cook at a gentle simmer until sauce has thickened, about 30 minutes.

**2.** While sauce is cooking, make meatballs: Using hands, roll sausage into balls about 1 inch in diameter. Heat a medium skillet over medium-high heat, and sauté meatballs in batches until well browned and cooked through, about 6 minutes. Transfer cooked meatballs to tomato sauce.

**3.** Bring a large pot of water to a boil. Add salt and pasta; cook 2 to 3 minutes less than the package instructions, about 5 minutes. Drain, and stir noodles into sauce.

**4.** Preheat oven to 375°F. Butter a 3-quart casserole or baking dish; set aside. Bring a large saucepan of water to a boil; add salt. Blanch broccoli rabe until bright green and just tender, about 1 minute. Drain, and rinse under cold water to stop the cooking. Add to pasta mixture, and toss to combine.

**5.** Pour pasta mixture into prepared baking dish; top with cheese. Bake until mixture is bubbling and top is slightly browned, about 30 minutes. Let cool 5 minutes before serving.

## baked mushroom linguine
### SERVES 8 TO 10

2  sprigs rosemary

2  sprigs thyme, plus 2 teaspoons finely chopped leaves

4  ounces dried mushrooms, such as porcini or chanterelle

4  cups boiling water

7  tablespoons unsalted butter, plus more for baking dish

5  tablespoons all-purpose flour

1½  cups heavy cream

1  onion, diced

1  pound button mushrooms, trimmed, cleaned, and quartered

1  pound shiitake mushrooms, trimmed, cleaned, and sliced

   Coarse salt and freshly ground pepper

1  pound linguine

½  cup freshly grated pecorino Romano cheese (1 ounce)

**1.** Wrap rosemary and thyme sprigs in cheesecloth, and tie with kitchen string; set aside. Place dried mushrooms in a bowl, and pour the boiling water over them. Let soak 30 minutes. Using a slotted spoon, transfer mushrooms to another bowl. Press mushrooms to release as much liquid as possible, and pour liquid back into bowl with soaking

liquid; set mushrooms aside. Strain liquid through a fine sieve lined with a paper towel; set aside. (You should have about 4 cups.)

**2.** Melt 5 tablespoons butter in a large saucepan over medium heat. When bubbling, add flour. Cook, stirring, until mixture begins to brown, about 3 minutes. While whisking, slowly pour in reserved mushroom liquid. Continue cooking, whisking constantly, until the mixture bubbles and becomes thick. Stir in cream and reserved herb bundle. Reduce to a gentle simmer, and cook sauce 30 minutes, stirring occasionally, to allow flavors to infuse. Discard herb bundle.

**3.** Preheat oven to 375°F. Butter a 9-by-13-inch baking dish; set aside. Heat remaining 2 tablespoons butter in a large skillet over medium heat. Add onion, and cook until it begins to soften, about 3 minutes. Add button mushrooms; cook until they release their juices, and make room in the pan. Add shiitake and reserved rehydrated mushrooms, and cook until tender, about 5 minutes. Add mushroom liquid to skillet, and stir to combine. Season with salt and pepper, and set aside.

**4.** Bring a large pot of water to a boil. Add salt and pasta; cook 2 to 3 minutes less than package instructions. Drain, and stir noodles into mushroom mixture; toss to combine.

**5.** Transfer pasta mixture to the prepared baking dish. Sprinkle with the grated cheese, and bake until browned on top and mixture is bubbling, about 30 minutes. Let cool 5 minutes before serving.

## wild mushroom and spinach lasagna

*photograph on page 54*

SERVES 8 TO 10

*This is a great dish to serve to vegetarian guests. Frozen spinach can be substituted for fresh, and plain lasagna sheets can be substituted for the spinach sheets.*

- 1 cup (2 sticks) unsalted butter
- 3 garlic cloves, finely sliced
- 5 pounds fresh spinach, trimmed and washed well
- 1 pound ricotta cheese
- 2 tablespoons salt
- 1¾ teaspoons freshly ground pepper
- 3 pounds mixed wild mushrooms, such as chanterelle, oyster, and shiitake, trimmed, cleaned, and cut into 1-inch pieces
- ¾ cup Madeira or dry sherry
- ½ cup chopped fresh flat-leaf parsley
- 4½ cups milk
- ½ cup all-purpose flour
- ½ teaspoon ground nutmeg
- 1 cup freshly grated pecorino Romano cheese (2 ounces)
- 1 pound fresh spinach-lasagna sheets

**1.** Melt 1 tablespoon butter in a large sauté pan over medium heat. Add half the garlic; sauté until light golden, about 2 minutes. Add half the spinach leaves; cover, and cook, stirring occasionally, until wilted, 4 to 5 minutes. Drain mixture in a colander. Repeat with another tablespoon butter and remaining garlic and spinach.

**2.** When spinach mixture is cool enough to handle, squeeze out excess liquid. Roughly chop, and place in a medium bowl. Add ricotta, 2 teaspoons salt, and 1 teaspoon pepper; stir until combined. Set mixture aside.

**3.** Melt 2 tablespoons butter in a large skillet over medium heat. Add one-third of the mushrooms;

sprinkle with 1 teaspoon salt and ¼ teaspoon pepper. Sauté until mushrooms are softened and browned, about 10 minutes. Add ¼ cup Madeira; deglaze skillet, scraping up browned bits from bottom with a wooden spoon. Continue cooking until liquid has almost evaporated. Transfer mushrooms to a medium bowl.

**4.** Repeat with another 2 tablespoons butter, another third of the mushrooms, and ¼ cup Madeira. (Reserve the remaining mushrooms and Madeira for topping.) Add two-thirds chopped parsley to mushrooms; stir to combine.

**5.** Warm 4 cups milk in a medium saucepan over medium heat. Melt 8 tablespoons butter in another saucepan over medium heat; when bubbling, add flour. Cook, whisking constantly, 1 minute. Slowly add warmed milk; cook, whisking constantly, until mixture bubbles and thickens. Remove from heat. Stir in 2 teaspoons salt, ¼ teaspoon pepper, the nutmeg, and ½ cup grated cheese. Measure out ½ cup sauce; set aside.

**6.** Preheat oven to 350°F. Assemble lasagna: Spread ½ cup sauce in the bottom of a 9-by-13-inch baking dish. Place a layer of lasagna sheets in dish, trimming to fit. Spread 1 cup spinach mixture over sheets, followed by 1 cup mushroom mixture and ½ cup sauce. Repeat, making several layers. For last layer, place lasagna sheets on top; spread ½ cup sauce over lasagna sheets. Sprinkle with remaining ½ cup grated cheese.

**7.** Transfer to oven; bake lasagna until top is golden brown, 1 to 1¼ hours. Let stand 20 minutes before serving. Just before serving, melt remaining 2 tablespoons butter in the skillet over medium heat. Add remaining uncooked mushrooms; season with remaining 1 teaspoon salt and ¼ teaspoon pepper. Cook until mushrooms are golden and tender, about 10 minutes. Add remaining ¼ cup

Madeira; deglaze skillet, scraping up browned bits from bottom with a wooden spoon. Stir in remaining parsley.

**8.** In a small saucepan, combine reserved ½ cup sauce with remaining ½ cup milk. Over medium heat, whisk until warm and smooth. Spoon cooked mushrooms over each serving. Serve lasagna with warmed sauce.

## CLEANING MUSHROOMS

*Not every type of mushroom gets cleaned the same way. To clean cultivated mushrooms, such as white button, shiitake, oyster, cremini, and portobello, wipe them with a mushroom brush or a damp paper towel. (Never rinse cultivated mushrooms with water; mushrooms absorb water like a sponge.) Trim the stems with a paring knife.*

*Edible wild mushrooms such as chanterelles, black trumpets, and morels require water for cleaning. Place the mushrooms in a bowl of cool water, and swish them until the dirt is removed. Contact with the water should be brief; remove them as soon as they are clean.*

*For best results, wait until just before you use mushrooms to clean them. Store unwashed mushrooms in a paper bag, or wrap them loosely in paper towels to keep them from drying out. Mushrooms sealed in packages should remain in packages until ready to use. Do not store mushrooms in the crisper, as the moist environment can cause spoilage; store them instead on a refrigerator shelf.*

## *traditional lasagna bolognese*
### SERVES 8 TO 10

*This lasagna was designed for a deep-dish baking pan. If you use a standard nine-by-thirteen-inch baking pan, you will have excess sauce, which you can freeze, and use over pasta. The lasagna can be assembled in advance before baking; cover, and refrigerate up to one day, or freeze up to three weeks. Let thaw overnight in the refrigerator; bake as directed below.*

> Bolognese Sauce (recipe follows)
> 3 pounds ricotta cheese
> 3 large egg yolks
> 1 cup freshly grated Parmesan cheese (2 ounces)
> ¼ teaspoon ground nutmeg
> Pinch of ground cayenne pepper
> Coarse salt and freshly ground black pepper
> Unsalted butter, for dish
> 2 tablespoons extra-virgin olive oil
> 1 pound dried lasagna noodles
> 1 pound fresh mozzarella, sliced into ¼-inch-thick rounds

**1.** Bring meat sauce to room temperature, if necessary. In a large bowl, whisk together ricotta, egg yolks, Parmesan, nutmeg, and cayenne; season with salt and pepper. Cover with plastic wrap; chill until ready to assemble.

**2.** Preheat oven to 400°F. Butter an 11-by-14-by-3-inch baking dish. Bring a large pot of water to a boil. Add oil and salt. One at a time, add lasagna noodles; cook 2 to 3 minutes less than the package instructions. Carefully remove noodles with tongs, and drain in a colander.

**3.** Spread about 3 cups sauce on the bottom of the prepared baking dish. Arrange a single layer of lasagna noodles over sauce, overlapping them slightly. Spread about 2 cups sauce over noodles and half the ricotta mixture over sauce.

**4.** Top with another layer of lasagna noodles. Spread with more sauce and the remaining ricotta mixture. Top with a final layer of lasagna noodles. Spread sauce over noodles, and finish with a layer of mozzarella rounds.

**5.** Transfer to oven, and bake until sauce is bubbling and cheese has melted, at least 1 hour. Cover with aluminum foil if the cheese starts to turn too brown. Let cool 10 to 15 minutes before serving.

## bolognese sauce
### MAKES ABOUT 3 QUARTS

*Sauce can be stored in the freezer in airtight containers for up to one month.*

- 3 tablespoons unsalted butter
- 3 tablespoons extra-virgin olive oil
- 2 onions, cut into ¼-inch dice
- 3 stalks celery, cut into ¼-inch dice
- 3 carrots, cut into ¼-inch dice
- 2 pounds ground sirloin
- 2 pounds ground veal
- 1 quart whole milk
- 2 cups dry red wine
- 3½ cups beef stock, preferably homemade (page 183), or low-sodium canned beef broth
- 1 cup tomato paste
  Coarse salt and freshly ground pepper

**1.** Heat butter and olive oil in a large cast-iron or enamel pot over medium heat.

**2.** Add onions; cook until they begin to soften, about 5 minutes. Add celery and carrots; cook until vegetables are tender, 8 to 10 minutes. Add ground sirloin and veal; cook, stirring occasionally, until meat is no longer pink. Add milk; cook at a gentle simmer, occasionally skimming fat from surface, until liquid has reduced by half, about 50 minutes.

**3.** Add wine to pot; simmer until liquid has reduced again by half, about 40 minutes.

**4.** Add stock and tomato paste to pot; season with salt and pepper. Simmer gently until sauce thickens, 40 to 45 minutes. Cool slightly before using, or cool completely before storing.

# *side dishes*

POTATOES, VEGETABLES

STUFFINGS

RICE AND GRAINS

CHUTNEYS, PICKLES, AND PRESERVES

✳

## mashed potatoes

### SERVES 4 TO 6

*For stiffer mashed potatoes, reduce milk or cream to three-fourths cup; for richer potatoes, add another two tablespoons butter. The traditional russet makes mashed potatoes that are fluffy but grainy; long white and Yukon gold varieties produce a creamier texture.*

- 2 pounds russet, Yukon gold, or long white potatoes
- 1 cup milk or cream
- 4 tablespoons unsalted butter
- ¼ teaspoon freshly grated nutmeg
  Coarse salt and freshly ground pepper

**1.** Peel potatoes, and cut into 1½-inch-thick slices. Place slices in a medium saucepan; cover with cold water by 2 inches, and bring to a boil. Reduce heat, and simmer until tender when pierced with the tip of a paring knife, about 10 minutes. Drain potatoes in a colander; return to pot, and place over low heat until dry, about 1 minute.

**2.** Heat milk just until steaming in a small saucepan over medium heat. Place a heatproof bowl over a pan of simmering water. Press hot, drained potatoes through a potato ricer into bowl.

**3.** Stir potatoes with a wooden spoon until smooth, about 1 minute. Using a whisk, incorporate butter. Drizzle in hot milk, whisking constantly. Add nutmeg, and season with salt and pepper; whisk to combine. Serve immediately.

## variations

### saffron mashed potatoes

While heating the milk, add a pinch of saffron. Let steep 5 minutes before adding to potatoes.

### garlic mashed potatoes

Add 3 smashed garlic cloves to milk. Cover, and simmer until garlic is mild and soft, about 20 minutes; add mixture to potatoes.

### roasted-garlic mashed potatoes
*photograph on page 56*

Wrap 1 small head of garlic in aluminum foil, and roast in a 400°F oven for 45 minutes. When cool enough to handle, squeeze garlic cloves into bowl of potatoes, along with the milk.

### herbed mashed potatoes

Add chopped fresh herbs such as parsley, dill, chives, or basil to potatoes at the end. For bright-green potatoes, substitute an herb-infused olive oil for the butter. To make, purée herbs and olive oil in a food processor until herbs are finely minced and oil is bright green.

### mashed potatoes
### and root vegetables

Substitute ⅓ pound cooked carrots, sweet potatoes, turnips, or parsnips for ⅓ pound potatoes.

## *mashed potatoes with caramelized roasted parsnips*

SERVES 12 TO 14

 5  *pounds (about 10) russet potatoes*

1½  *cups whole milk*

 ¾  *cup (1½ sticks) unsalted butter,*
     *cut into pieces*

 ½  *cup sour cream*
     *Coarse salt and freshly ground*
     *white pepper*
     *Caramelized Roasted Parsnips,*
     *for garnish (recipe follows)*

 1  *tablespoon snipped fresh*
     *chives, for garnish*

**1.** Peel potatoes, and cut into ¼-inch-thick slices. Place slices in a large saucepan; cover with cold water, and bring to a boil. Reduce heat; simmer until tender when pierced with the tip of a paring knife, 25 to 30 minutes. Drain potatoes in a colander.

**2.** In a small saucepan, heat milk and butter until just boiling. Transfer potatoes to the bowl of an electric mixer; whisk on low speed until smooth. Add hot milk mixture and sour cream; season with salt and pepper. Mix, increasing speed to high, until potatoes are fluffy. Serve immediately, garnished with roasted parsnips and chives.

## *caramelized roasted parsnips*

SERVES 12 TO 14 AS A GARNISH

 ½  *cup (1 stick) unsalted butter, melted*

 2  *tablespoons granulated sugar*

 2  *teaspoons light-brown sugar*

 3  *pounds parsnips, peeled and*
     *cut into 3-by-¼-inch julienne*

 1  *teaspoon garlic powder*
     *Coarse salt and freshly ground pepper*

**1.** Preheat oven to 350°F. In a large roasting pan, whisk together butter and sugars. Add parsnips, and toss to coat. Add garlic powder, and season with salt and pepper; toss to combine.

**2.** Cover pan with foil; bake 20 minutes. Remove foil, and stir. Continue roasting parsnips, uncovered, until lightly browned, about 20 minutes more. Season with salt and pepper.

## mashed potatoes with golden onions and roquefort

SERVES 10 TO 12

*The potatoes can be made a day in advance; to reheat, place in a heatproof bowl, cover with foil, and set over a pan of simmering water.*

  3  pounds (about 6) russet potatoes, peeled and quartered
  ¾  cup milk
  ½  cup (1 stick) unsalted butter, cut into pieces
     Coarse salt and freshly ground pepper
  2  tablespoons olive oil
  1  large yellow onion, quartered
3½  ounces Roquefort cheese, crumbled (½ cup)

**1.** Place potatoes in a large saucepan; cover with cold water, and bring to a boil. Reduce heat, and simmer until potatoes are tender when pierced with the tip of a paring knife, about 20 minutes. Drain and return to pan.

**2.** Heat milk and butter in a small saucepan until just boiling; pour mixture into pan with potatoes. Season with salt and pepper. Mash with a potato masher or wooden spoon until liquid is incorporated. Transfer mixture to a heatproof bowl. Cover with foil; set bowl over a pan of simmering water to keep warm.

**3.** Heat oil in a large skillet over medium heat. Add onion; sauté, stirring frequently, until golden brown, 10 to 12 minutes. Season with salt and pepper.

**4.** Transfer potatoes to a serving dish. Spoon onion over potatoes, and crumble cheese over top; serve.

## mashed potatoes and celery root

SERVES 10 TO 12

*For a completely smooth texture, pass potatoes and celery root through a food mill or potato ricer after they have been cooked.*

  4  pounds (about 12) Yukon gold potatoes
  1  pound celery root
  1  cup heavy cream
  6  tablespoons unsalted butter
  1  tablespoon coarse salt
  ¼  teaspoon freshly ground pepper

**1.** Peel potatoes, and cut into 1-inch pieces. Using a paring knife, peel celery root, following the shape of the vegetable. Cut into ½-inch pieces. Place potatoes and celery root in a small stockpot with cold water to cover, and bring to a boil. Reduce heat, and simmer until tender when pierced with the tip of a paring knife, about 10 minutes. Drain vegetables in a colander; return to pot, and place over low heat until dry, about 1 minute.

**2.** Combine cream, butter, salt, and pepper in a small saucepan, and place over medium heat until butter is melted and mixture comes to a simmer. Pour over potato mixture; using a potato masher or wooden spoon, mix until fluffy and smooth.

## potato-chive soufflé

SERVES 10 TO 12

*Chilling the dish ahead of time will make the soufflé rise even higher.*

- 2 tablespoons breadcrumbs
- 3 pounds (about 9) Yukon gold potatoes, peeled and cut into eighths
- 2 garlic cloves, thinly sliced
- 2 dried bay leaves
- ½ teaspoon baking soda
- 1 cup nonfat buttermilk
- 1¼ cups skim milk
- 3 tablespoons snipped fresh chives
- 2 teaspoons sugar
- Coarse salt and freshly ground pepper
- 4 large egg whites
- Pinch cream of tartar
- Nonstick vegetable cooking spray

**1.** Preheat oven to 425°F. Coat a 2½-quart soufflé dish with cooking spray; sprinkle with breadcrumbs, and tap out excess. Place dish in freezer to chill while proceeding.

**2.** Place potatoes, garlic, and bay leaves in a small stockpot. Fill with cold water to cover; bring to a boil. Reduce heat; simmer until potatoes are very soft and starting to fall apart, 12 to 15 minutes. Drain potatoes thoroughly; discard bay leaves.

**3.** Pass potatoes and garlic through a potato ricer or food mill into a large bowl. In a small bowl, mix together baking soda and buttermilk; stir mixture into potatoes, along with the skim milk, chives, and sugar. Season with salt and pepper. Mixture should be thick and soupy, not stiff. Set aside.

**4.** Place egg whites and cream of tartar in the bowl of an electric mixer, and whisk on medium speed until soft peaks form. Fold egg-white mixture into potato mixture. Remove soufflé dish from freezer, and pour mixture into dish.

**5.** Transfer dish to oven, and bake until soufflé has risen above edge and top is browned, about 45 minutes. Remove from oven, and serve immediately.

## braised potatoes

SERVES 4

*We used a combination of fingerling and tiny new potatoes, but you can also use quartered or halved larger new potatoes.*

- 3 tablespoons extra-virgin olive oil
- 1 tablespoon unsalted butter
- 1 onion, thinly sliced
- 1½ pounds fingerling and very small new white potatoes
- 6 small shallots
- 2 or 3 sprigs rosemary, plus 1 tablespoon roughly chopped leaves for garnish
- Coarse salt and freshly ground pepper
- 1 cup chicken stock, preferably homemade (page 179), or low-sodium canned chicken broth

**1.** Preheat oven to 375°F. Heat oil and butter over medium-low heat in a large ovenproof skillet. Add onion; cook, stirring, until very soft, about 15 minutes. Stir in potatoes, shallots, and half the rosemary sprigs; season with salt and pepper. Raise heat to medium-high; cook, stirring, until potatoes begin to brown, about 10 minutes. Remove from heat; add remaining rosemary sprigs and stock.

**2.** Cover skillet, and transfer to oven; cook until potatoes are tender when pierced with a fork, about 10 minutes (timing will vary with size of potatoes). Remove lid; cook until liquid is thickened and reduced, about 20 minutes. Remove from oven; garnish with chopped rosemary. Serve.

## roasted fennel and potatoes

### SERVES 4

*Preheating the roasting pan helps give the vegetables a crisp, golden crust.*

 2  bulbs fennel (about 4 ounces
    each), trimmed
 1  pound (about 8) red new potatoes, halved
 1  tablespoon olive oil
    Coarse salt and freshly ground pepper

**1.** Preheat oven to 425°F. Heat a heavy roasting pan in oven 20 minutes.

**2.** Meanwhile, cut each fennel bulb lengthwise into six wedges. In a medium bowl, toss fennel and potatoes with oil; season with salt and pepper.

**3.** Remove roasting pan from oven; place fennel and potatoes, cut sides down, in pan. Roast vegetables, without turning, until tender and golden brown, about 30 minutes. Serve immediately.

## rösti potatoes

### SERVES 6

3½  pounds (10 or 11) Yukon gold potatoes,
     peeled and placed in cold water
     Coarse salt and freshly ground pepper
¼   cup Clarified Butter (recipe follows)

**1.** Preheat oven to 400°F. Shred potatoes on the large holes of a box grater; wrap in a clean kitchen towel, and squeeze out liquid. Place potatoes in a medium bowl; season with salt and pepper.

**2.** Heat half the butter in a 10-inch, ovenproof nonstick sauté pan over medium-low heat. Spread potatoes in pan evenly; press down with a spatula to flatten cake. Cook until bottom is golden and turning crisp, about 18 minutes.

**3.** Invert cake onto a plate; slide back into pan, and spoon remaining butter around edges. Cook until other side begins to get crisp, about 10 minutes, shaking pan several times to loosen cake.

**4.** Transfer pan to oven; cook until potatoes are cooked through and tender in center, about 12 minutes. Cut cake into wedges; serve immediately.

## clarified butter

### MAKES ⅔ CUP

*Because clarified butter has no milk solids, it can withstand higher cooking temperatures than regular butter without burning.*

 1  cup (2 sticks) unsalted butter

**1.** Melt butter in a small saucepan over low heat until foamy and milk solids have fallen to bottom, about 15 minutes. Remove from heat; let cool.

**2.** Carefully skim foam from top, and discard. Slowly pour liquid butter into a bowl or storage container, leaving solids behind. Use immediately, or keep covered in refrigerator up to 1 month.

## sautéed leeks and potatoes

SERVES 8

2   pounds (about 6) Yukon gold potatoes

3   tablespoons unsalted butter

8   leeks, white and pale-green parts only, sliced into ¼-inch rounds and washed well
    Coarse salt and freshly ground pepper

**1.** Place potatoes in a large saucepan; cover with cold water, and bring to a boil. Reduce heat, and simmer until just tender when pierced with a fork, 15 to 20 minutes. Drain, and set aside to cool.

**2.** Melt butter in a large sauté pan over low heat. Add leeks; cook, partially covered, until soft and translucent, about 20 minutes.

**3.** Slice potatoes into ⅓-inch rounds, and add to leeks. Season with salt and pepper; cook, covered, until potatoes are heated through, about 5 minutes. Serve immediately.

## gratin dauphinoise

photograph on page 59

SERVES 4 TO 6

2   tablespoons unsalted butter, room temperature, plus more for baking dish

3   pounds (about 9) Yukon gold potatoes

1   large garlic clove, minced

1¼  cups milk

1   cup heavy cream

1½  teaspoons coarse salt

¼   teaspoon freshly grated nutmeg

1   dried bay leaf
    Freshly ground pepper

4   ounces Gruyère cheese, finely grated (about 1 cup)

**1.** Preheat oven to 400°F, with rack in center. Generously butter a 12-by-9-inch glass baking dish. Peel potatoes, and slice into ⅛-inch-thick rounds. Place slices in a bowl of cold water while you work to prevent discoloration.

**2.** In a medium saucepan, combine garlic, milk, heavy cream, salt, nutmeg, and bay leaf. Bring just to a simmer over medium heat, and pour into prepared baking dish. Discard bay leaf.

**3.** Drain potatoes, and pat dry with paper towels. Transfer to baking dish. Using a large spoon, toss potatoes with milk mixture, pressing down gently to distribute slices evenly. Season with pepper. Dot with butter, distributing evenly over entire surface; sprinkle with cheese.

**4.** Bake until potatoes are tender when pierced with the tip of a paring knife and top is brown, 45 to 50 minutes. Serve immediately.

## three-potato gratin

SERVES 12 TO 14

*To prevent Yukon gold and russet potatoes from discoloring, drop the slices into a bowl of cold water while you work. Drain well, and pat dry with paper towels before proceeding.*

  *Unsalted butter, for dish*
2 *pounds (3 large) sweet potatoes, peeled and sliced ⅛ inch thick*
1 *pound (about 2) russet potatoes, peeled and sliced ⅛ inch thick*
2 *pounds (about 6) Yukon gold potatoes, peeled and sliced ⅛ inch thick*
1 *onion, thinly sliced*
4 *garlic cloves, minced*
4 *ounces white cheddar cheese, grated (about 1 cup)*
4 *ounces Gruyère cheese, grated (about 1 cup)*
1 *tablespoon fresh thyme leaves, plus 3 sprigs*
  *Coarse salt and freshly ground pepper*
1 *cup heavy cream*

**1.** Preheat oven to 375°F. Butter a 13-by-9-inch baking dish. In a large bowl, toss together potatoes, onion, garlic, half the cheddar and Gruyère, and 1 tablespoon thyme; season with salt and pepper.

**2.** Arrange potato mixture in prepared baking dish, distributing evenly. Pour cream over mixture. Scatter thyme sprigs over top. Cover tightly with foil; bake until potatoes are tender when pierced with the tip of a paring knife, about 1 hour.

**3.** Remove foil; sprinkle remaining cheddar and Gruyère cheese over potato mixture. Bake until top is golden brown and crusty, 20 to 25 minutes more. Serve immediately.

## potato gratin with onions and herring

SERVES 10 TO 12

*This dish is also delicious without fish, as a potato-onion gratin.*

2 *tablespoons unsalted butter, plus more for dish*
2 *yellow onions, thinly sliced*
  *Coarse salt and freshly ground pepper*
3½ *pounds (about 7) russet potatoes*
3 *ounces matjes herring fillet or Swedish anchovy fillets, cut crosswise into ¼-inch pieces*
2 *cups heavy cream*
2 *tablespoons dry breadcrumbs*

**1.** Preheat oven to 375°F. Butter a 12-by-6-inch ovenproof dish; set aside. Melt butter in a large skillet over low heat. Add onions, and season with salt and pepper. Cover, and cook, stirring occasionally, until onions are soft and translucent, about 20 minutes. Continue cooking, uncovered, 10 minutes more. Remove from heat.

**2.** Meanwhile, peel potatoes, and slice lengthwise ¼ inch thick. Cut each slice again lengthwise into very thin strips.

**3.** Arrange half the potatoes in prepared baking dish; season with salt and pepper. Cover with cooked onions; arrange herring or anchovies on top. Cover with remaining potatoes; season with salt and pepper. Pour cream over potatoes; sprinkle with breadcrumbs. Cover with foil, and bake 50 minutes. Remove foil; bake until top is browned, 40 to 50 minutes more. Serve immediately.

## twice-baked potatoes stuffed with spinach and parsnip soufflés

### SERVES 6

*Use leftover potato flesh for mashed potatoes.*

- 6  russet potatoes (about 3 pounds), scrubbed well
- 4  tablespoons unsalted butter
- 4  parsnips (1 pound), trimmed, peeled, and cut into 2-inch chunks
- 2  tablespoons fresh thyme leaves
   Coarse salt and freshly ground pepper
- 2  tablespoons pure maple syrup
- 1  bunch spinach, trimmed and washed well, with water clinging to leaves
- 1  cup heavy cream
   Freshly grated nutmeg
- 4  large egg whites, beaten to soft peaks

**1.** Preheat oven to 400°F. Bake potatoes on a baking sheet until tender when pierced with a fork, about 1 hour. Set aside to cool.

**2.** Melt 2 tablespoons butter in a large roasting pan in oven. Remove pan from oven; add parsnips and thyme, and season with salt and pepper; toss to coat. Roast until parsnips are tender when pierced with a fork, about 30 minutes.

**3.** Add maple syrup to pan, and toss to combine. Continue roasting parsnips until they start to caramelize, about 10 minutes. Remove from oven; let cool slightly. Pass parsnips through a food mill or potato ricer into a medium bowl; set aside.

**4.** Line a baking sheet with parchment paper; set aside. Using a serrated knife, carefully slice potatoes in half crosswise. Using a soup spoon, scoop out most of the flesh, leaving about a ¾-inch shell. Using the serrated knife, trim just enough off bottoms of potato shells so they sit flat. Transfer shells to sheet, cup sides up.

**5.** Reserve one-third potato flesh for another use. Pass the rest through a food mill or potato ricer into a bowl. Cover bowl with foil, and set aside.

**6.** Melt 1 tablespoon butter in a large skillet. Add spinach, and season with salt and pepper. Cook over medium heat until spinach has wilted. Transfer spinach to a food processor. Add ½ cup cream, and process until smooth. Transfer spinach mixture to a medium bowl.

**7.** Divide potato flesh in half. Add half to spinach mixture and half to parsnip mixture.

**8.** Combine remaining 1 tablespoon butter and ½ cup cream in a small skillet. Cook over medium-low heat until butter has melted. Pour cream mixture into parsnip mixture; season with salt and pepper. Add nutmeg to spinach mixture. Divide beaten egg whites in half; fold half into parsnips and half into spinach until combined.

**9.** Using a spoon, fill six potato shells with spinach mixture and six with parsnip mixture (enough so cups are just overflowing). Transfer shells to oven; bake until potatoes are heated through and filling is puffed and golden brown, about 30 minutes. Serve immediately.

## savory twice-baked sweet potatoes

*photograph on page 58*

SERVES 6

*For a less formal presentation, you can spoon, rather than pipe, the filling into the shells.*

- 3 medium sweet potatoes (about 2 pounds), scrubbed well
- 4 ounces smoked bacon (about 5 slices)
- 2 tablespoons dark-brown sugar
- 3 tablespoons unsalted butter, room temperature
- 2 small shallots, finely minced
- 1 teaspoon minced fresh rosemary, plus more for garnish
- 1 large egg
- 2 tablespoons heavy cream
- 2 ounces Gruyère cheese, finely grated (½ cup), plus more for garnish
  Coarse salt and freshly ground pepper

**1.** Preheat oven to 400°F. Place sweet potatoes on a parchment-lined baking sheet, and pierce each several times with a fork. Bake until tender when pierced with the tip of a paring knife, about 45 minutes. Remove from oven; set aside to cool.

**2.** Line a rimmed baking sheet with aluminum foil; fit with a wire rack. Arrange bacon strips on rack, and sprinkle with brown sugar. Cook until well glazed and crisp, 12 to 15 minutes. Remove from oven; let cool slightly, and roughly chop.

**3.** Melt 1 tablespoon butter in a small skillet over medium heat. Add shallots; cook until soft and fragrant, about 2 minutes. Add rosemary, and cook 1 minute more. Remove from heat.

**4.** Using a serrated knife, carefully slice sweet potatoes in half lengthwise. Using a soup spoon, scoop out flesh, leaving about a ¼-inch shell; set halves on a baking sheet. Place flesh in the bowl of an electric mixer fitted with the paddle attachment.

Add remaining 2 tablespoons butter, reserved shallot mixture, the egg, cream, and Gruyère. Mix well until combined. Season with salt and pepper.

**5.** Transfer mixture to a pastry bag fitted with a star tip. Pipe mixture into reserved sweet-potato shells. Bake until golden, about 20 minutes. Remove from oven; garnish with Gruyère, rosemary, and reserved bacon. Serve immediately.

## baked sweet potatoes and pecans

*photograph on page 56*

SERVES 8

- 7 tablespoons unsalted butter, room temperature, plus more for dish
- 5 pounds (about 8) sweet potatoes
- 7 tablespoons dark-brown sugar
- 1½ teaspoons ground cinnamon
  Pinch of cayenne pepper
  Coarse salt and freshly ground black pepper
- ⅔ cup pecan halves

**1.** Preheat oven to 400°F. Generously butter a 2-quart casserole dish, and set aside. Place sweet potatoes on a parchment-lined baking sheet, and pierce each several times with a fork. Bake until almost tender when pierced with the tip of a paring knife, 25 to 30 minutes. Remove potatoes from oven; set aside until cool enough to handle. Slip off skins. Slice potatoes into 1½-inch-thick rounds, and transfer to a large bowl.

**2.** Add 5 tablespoons each butter and brown sugar to potatoes along with the cinnamon and cayenne; season with salt and black pepper. Stir to combine.

**3.** Melt remaining 2 tablespoons butter in a medium sauté pan over medium-high heat. Add remaining 2 tablespoons brown sugar and the pecans. Cook, stirring occasionally, until pecans are caramelized, about 3 minutes. Transfer to bowl with potatoes; stir gently to combine.

**4.** Transfer mixture to prepared casserole dish; bake, stirring occasionally, until potatoes are caramelized and liquid is bubbling, 30 to 35 minutes. Serve immediately.

## balsamic-roasted sweet potatoes and butternut squash
### SERVES 10 TO 12

- 4 pounds (about 6) sweet potatoes, peeled and cut into 3-by-¾-inch wedges
- 2 pounds (2 medium) butternut squash, peeled, seeded, and cut into 3-by-¾-inch wedges
- ¼ cup olive oil, plus more for drizzling
- 3 tablespoons balsamic vinegar, plus more for drizzling
- 2 tablespoons unsalted butter, melted
- 1 tablespoon chopped fresh rosemary
  Coarse salt and freshly ground pepper
- 1 small bunch arugula, trimmed and washed well

**1.** Preheat oven to 400°F. In a large bowl, toss together potatoes, squash, oil, vinegar, butter, and rosemary; season with salt and pepper.

**2.** Arrange vegetable mixture in a single layer in two 13-by-9-inch baking pans. Roast until vegetables are tender and golden, 45 to 50 minutes, rotating pans halfway through.

**3.** Transfer vegetable mixture to a large bowl; let cool slightly. Toss in arugula; drizzle with oil and vinegar, and serve immediately.

## sweet-potato gratin
### SERVES 6

*Gratin can be made through step three several hours ahead, and finished just before serving.*

- 3 pounds (4 or 5) sweet potatoes
- 4 ounces pecans, coarsely chopped (1 cup)
- ½ cup packed dark-brown sugar
- 2 teaspoons ground ginger
- 1 teaspoon ground cinnamon
  Pinch of freshly grated nutmeg
- 4 tablespoons unsalted butter, plus more for baking dish
- 2 cups miniature marshmallows

**1.** Place potatoes in a large saucepan of cold water, and bring to a boil. Reduce heat, and simmer until potatoes are just tender when pierced with the tip of a paring knife, about 20 minutes; drain. Place potatoes in a bowl of cold water until skins begin to loosen. Peel potatoes; set aside.

**2.** In a small bowl, combine pecans, brown sugar, ginger, cinnamon, nutmeg, and butter. Slice the reserved potatoes ¼ inch thick.

**3.** Preheat oven to 450°F. Butter an 8-inch square baking dish. Arrange one-third of potatoes on bottom of dish in a single layer. Sprinkle one-third of nut mixture over top. Repeat, making two more layers of potatoes and nut mixture.

**4.** Cover dish with foil; bake until heated through, about 40 minutes. Remove dish from oven, and heat broiler. Arrange marshmallows evenly over top of gratin, and broil until just browned, 30 to 60 seconds. Serve hot.

## *artichoke gratin*
SERVES 6 TO 8

**for artichoke base:**

4 *lemons, halved*

6 *globe artichokes*

1 *tablespoon coarse salt*

1 *teaspoon whole black peppercorns*

1 *large sprig thyme*

2 *garlic cloves*

2 *tablespoons olive oil*

**for béchamel:**

2 *tablespoons unsalted butter*

1 *tablespoon diced shallot*

*Coarse salt and freshly ground black pepper*

*Pinch of cayenne pepper*

*Pinch of freshly grated nutmeg*

¼ *cup all-purpose flour*

2 *cups whole milk, heated*

1 *dried bay leaf*

3 *ounces Gruyère cheese, grated (¾ cup)*

**1.** Make artichoke base: Squeeze juice of 1 lemon into a large bowl of cold water; add juiced halves. Using a serrated knife, cut off artichoke leaves, starting about 1 inch from stem. Discard tough outer leaves. Scrape out purple chokes with a spoon. Generously rub hearts with lemon water. Using a paring knife, trim and peel stems; rub with more lemon water. Add stems to bowl of lemon water.

**2.** Bring a large saucepan of water to a boil. Add salt, peppercorns, thyme, garlic, and olive oil. Squeeze in juice of remaining 3 lemons. Add artichoke hearts; simmer until tender when pierced with the tip of a paring knife, about 15 minutes. Drain. Cut hearts into ½-inch-thick slices.

**3.** Make béchamel: Heat broiler. Melt butter in a large skillet over medium heat. Add shallot, and cook until translucent but not browned, 1 to 2 minutes. Season with salt, black pepper, cayenne, and nutmeg; stir to combine. Reduce heat to low. Add flour, 1 tablespoon at a time, whisking constantly until fully incorporated. Cook, without browning, until floury taste is gone, 3 to 5 minutes more.

**4.** Whisk hot milk into mixture, a third at a time, whisking constantly, until béchamel is thick and completely smooth. Add bay leaf, and cook, stirring occasionally, 8 minutes more. Strain through a sieve. Add ½ cup Gruyère to hot béchamel.

**5.** Arrange artichoke slices in an 8-inch ovenproof dish. Pour béchamel over artichokes, and sprinkle with remaining ¼ cup Gruyère. Just before serving, broil until top is golden brown, 1 to 2 minutes.

## chopped roasted beets with feta and pecans

SERVES 12 TO 14

*We used several types of beets—including golden globe and Chioggia—for a colorful side dish, but you may use any variety you like.*

2 ounces (½ cup) pecan halves

4 bunches small beets (16 to 20 beets), trimmed and scrubbed

3 tablespoons cider vinegar

3 tablespoons olive oil

4 ounces feta cheese, crumbled

2 tablespoons chopped fresh flat-leaf parsley, plus sprigs for garnish

Coarse salt and freshly ground pepper

**1.** Preheat oven to 350°F. Spread pecans in a single layer on a rimmed baking sheet; toast in oven until fragrant and browned, about 10 minutes. Transfer to a bowl to cool. Coarsely chop, and set aside. Raise oven temperature to 450°F.

**2.** Wrap beets loosely in several aluminum-foil packets, grouping them according to size. Roast on a baking sheet until tender when pierced with the tip of a paring knife, about 1 hour. Using paper towels, rub off skins. Cut into wedges, and place in a serving bowl. Drizzle vinegar and oil over beets; toss to coat (beets can be made up to this point several hours ahead and kept at room temperature, covered with plastic wrap).

**3.** Just before serving, add feta, parsley, and pecans; season with salt and pepper. Toss to combine. Garnish with parsley sprigs.

## roasted beets with orange and ginger

SERVES 4

*Roasting beets concentrates their sweet flavor and makes them easy to peel.*

1 ounce (¼ cup) pecan halves

4 beets (about 1½ pounds), trimmed and scrubbed

3 tablespoons olive oil

Coarse salt and freshly ground pepper

1 orange

1½ teaspoons sherry vinegar

¾ teaspoon grated fresh ginger

**1.** Preheat oven to 350°F. Spread pecans in a single layer on a rimmed baking sheet; toast in oven until fragrant and browned, about 10 minutes. Transfer to a bowl to cool. Break in half, and set aside. Raise oven temperature to 425°F.

**2.** Place beets on a large piece of aluminum foil; drizzle with 1 tablespoon oil, and season with salt and pepper. Wrap foil loosely around beets, and roast on a baking sheet until beets are tender when pierced with the tip of a paring knife, about 1 hour. Using paper towels, rub off skins from beets. Quarter beets, and place in a serving bowl.

**3.** Using a zester or vegetable peeler, remove one-quarter of the orange peel in long, thin strips; set aside. Cut away remaining peel and pith with a sharp paring knife, following the shape of the fruit. Remove segments from half the orange; cut in half crosswise, and set aside. Squeeze juice from remaining half; measure out 1 tablespoon juice, and place in a small bowl. Add vinegar and ginger, and whisk in remaining 2 tablespoons oil. Season with salt and pepper.

**4.** Drizzle vinaigrette over beets, and toss to coat. Add reserved orange segments, peel, and pecans. Serve immediately.

## beet and herring salad

SERVES 10 TO 12

5  large beets (about 2 pounds),
   trimmed and scrubbed

1½ cups white vinegar

1½ cups sugar

1½ teaspoons coarse salt

1  red onion, halved and thinly sliced

4  garlic cloves

1½ tablespoons whole allspice

2  dried bay leaves

4  Yukon gold potatoes (about 1⅓ pounds)

2  fillets pickled herring (about 6 ounces)

1  whole dill pickle

1  Granny Smith apple, peeled and cored
   Freshly ground pepper

2  hard-boiled eggs, peeled, for garnish

6  sprigs dill, for garnish

1  cup sour cream, for serving (optional)

**1.** Place beets in a large saucepan; add enough cold water to cover by 2 inches. Bring to a boil, then reduce heat, and simmer until tender when pierced with a fork, about 1¼ hours. Drain, and rinse under cold water.

**2.** Meanwhile, combine vinegar, sugar, salt, and 3 cups water in a saucepan; bring to a boil. Add onion, garlic, allspice, and bay leaves. Reduce heat, and simmer until fragrant, 10 to 15 minutes.

**3.** Peel beets, and place in a 2½-quart jar. Pour vinegar mixture over beets to cover. Let liquid cool completely; refrigerate, covered, 3 to 4 days.

**4.** Place potatoes in a large saucepan; add enough cold water to cover by 2 inches. Bring to a boil; reduce heat, and simmer until tender when pierced with a fork, about 25 minutes. Drain, and let stand until cool enough to handle. Peel potatoes; set aside to cool completely.

**5.** Remove beets from refrigerator. Drain beets, reserving ½ cup pickling liquid. Cut beets, herring, pickle, apple, and 3 potatoes into ¼-inch dice, and combine in a large nonreactive bowl. Strain reserved liquid into bowl, season with pepper, and toss to coat. Slice remaining potato and the hard-boiled eggs lengthwise, ¼ inch thick.

**6.** Transfer beet mixture to a serving bowl, and garnish with sliced potato, eggs, and dill sprigs; serve with sour cream on the side, if desired.

## christmas-bean salad

SERVES 10 TO 12

*Christmas beans are large, flat beans that are purplish in color. They have a meaty texture and a slightly sweet flavor when cooked.*

1  pound Christmas beans

2  garlic cloves, finely chopped

2  tablespoons red-wine vinegar

5  tablespoons freshly squeezed orange juice

½  cup olive oil
   Coarse salt and freshly ground pepper

1  head curly endive or frisée

1  bunch radishes, trimmed and washed

**1.** Place beans in a small pot; add enough cold water to cover by 2 inches. Bring to a boil; remove from heat, and drain. Return beans to pot; cover again with cold water, and bring to a steady simmer. Cook, uncovered, until beans are tender, about 45 minutes, adding boiling water, if necessary, to keep beans covered. Let beans cool in liquid, then drain and rinse. Set aside.

**2.** In a medium bowl, whisk together garlic, vinegar, and orange juice. Whisk in oil in a slow, steady stream until emulsified. Season with salt and pepper. Toss with beans, and let marinate in refrigerator, at least 1 hour.

**3.** Tear endive into bite-size pieces. Thinly slice radishes. In a serving bowl, toss endive and radishes with beans; season with salt and pepper. Serve.

## green beans with tasso ham

### SERVES 10 TO 12

*Tasso ham is a cured pork used primarily for seasoning. Salt pork can also be used.*

- 2 ounces tasso ham
- 3 pounds fresh green beans, trimmed
- 3 tablespoons unsalted butter
- 2 tablespoons olive oil
- 1 small onion, finely chopped
- 4 garlic cloves, minced
- 2 teaspoons cider vinegar
- 2 teaspoons sugar
  Coarse salt and freshly ground pepper

**1.** Place ham in freezer until almost frozen, 3 to 4 hours. Cut into fine strips; set aside.

**2.** Bring a large pot of water to a boil. Add beans; cook until just tender and bright green, 2 to 3 minutes. Drain, and rinse with cold water. Set aside.

**3.** Heat butter and oil in a large skillet over medium heat. Add onion and garlic; cook, stirring occasionally, until onion is translucent, about 5 minutes. Add green beans, and raise heat to high; cook, tossing, 2 minutes.

**4.** Add ham, vinegar, and sugar to skillet; season with salt and pepper. Cook, stirring, until heated through, about 3 minutes. Serve hot.

## green beans with pecans and pomegranate seeds

### SERVES 6 TO 8

*We used haricots verts, wax beans, and snap peas. Choose one or a mixture, to equal one-and-one-half pounds.*

- 2 ounces (½ cup) pecan halves
  Coarse salt
- 1 pound mixed haricots verts and yellow wax beans
- ½ pound sugar snap peas
- 1 large shallot, minced
- 1 teaspoon Dijon mustard
- 2 tablespoons champagne vinegar
  Freshly ground pepper
- 3 tablespoons walnut oil
  Seeds from 1 pomegranate

**1.** Preheat oven to 350°F. Spread pecan halves in a single layer on a rimmed baking sheet, and toast in oven until fragrant and browned, about 10 minutes. Set aside to cool.

**2.** Prepare a large ice bath; set aside. In a small pot, bring 3 quarts of water to a boil over high heat. Add salt, beans, and peas; cook until just tender, 3 to 4 minutes. Transfer to ice bath to stop cooking. Drain beans and peas; let dry on paper towels.

**3.** In a medium bowl, whisk together shallot, mustard, and vinegar; season with salt and pepper. Whisk in oil in a slow, steady stream until emulsified. Toss beans and peas with vinaigrette. Refrigerate, covered, until ready to serve. Just before serving, sprinkle salad with pomegranate seeds and toasted pecans.

## cranberry-bean salad with butternut squash and broccoli rabe

*photograph on page 61*

SERVES 10 TO 12

- 1 onion
- 1 dried bay leaf
- 4 to 5 whole black peppercorns
- 2½ pounds fresh cranberry beans (about 3 cups), shelled
- 5 tablespoons olive oil
  Coarse salt and freshly ground pepper
- 4 slices bacon (about 4 ounces)
- 1 small butternut squash (about 1¾ pounds), cut into ½-inch pieces
- 4 garlic cloves, minced
- 1 bunch (about 1 pound) broccoli rabe, washed and trimmed

**1.** Using a sharp knife, slice off stem end of onion and score shallow slits all over, making sure it stays intact. Place in a large saucepan with bay leaf and peppercorns; fill with enough water to just cover. Bring to a boil, then reduce heat, and simmer 20 minutes.

**2.** Add beans to pan; simmer until cooked through, about 15 minutes. Drain beans; reserve 1 tablespoon cooking liquid, and discard onion and spices. In a medium bowl, toss beans with 1 tablespoon oil and reserved cooking liquid; season with salt and pepper. Set aside.

**3.** Cook bacon in a large skillet over medium heat until crisp. Transfer to paper towels to drain. Pour off all but 2 tablespoons rendered bacon fat, and return skillet to medium heat. Working in batches if necessary, cook squash until soft and golden, about 10 minutes. Season with salt and pepper, and transfer to a bowl; set aside.

**4.** Heat 3 tablespoons oil in same skillet over medium heat. Add garlic, and cook until just golden,

1 to 2 minutes. Add broccoli rabe, and cook until wilted and heated through, about 5 minutes. Season with salt and pepper.

**5.** Add beans and squash to skillet, and cook just until heated through. Drizzle with remaining tablespoon oil, and season with salt and pepper. Transfer mixture to a serving bowl, and crumble reserved bacon on top; serve.

## marinated green-bean and lima-bean salad

SERVES 10

- Coarse salt
- 2 pounds fresh green beans, trimmed
- 1¼ pounds fresh or frozen lima beans
- ¼ cup white-wine vinegar
- 3 tablespoons Dijon mustard
- 1 shallot, minced
  Freshly ground pepper
- ¾ cup extra-virgin olive oil
- 2 tablespoons chopped fresh tarragon, plus more for garnish
- 2 tablespoons chopped fresh flat-leaf parsley, plus more for garnish

**1.** Prepare a large ice bath; set aside. Bring a medium saucepan of water to a boil over high heat. Add salt and the green beans; cook until just tender and bright green, about 5 minutes. Using a slotted spoon, transfer beans to ice bath to stop the cooking. Drain beans in a colander.

**2.** Cook lima beans in the boiling water, until just tender, about 2 minutes (5 minutes if frozen). Drain in a colander; place under cold, running water to stop the cooking. Set aside.

**3.** In a medium bowl, combine vinegar, mustard, and shallot; season with salt and pepper. Whisk in oil in a slow, steady stream until emulsified. Whisk in tarragon and parsley.

**4.** In a large bowl, toss green beans with enough vinaigrette to coat. In a large bowl or on a platter, arrange green beans in an even layer. Sprinkle reserved lima beans over top. Drizzle more vinaigrette over beans. Garnish with tarragon and parsley, and serve.

## green-beans vinaigrette
### SERVES 6

Coarse salt
1½ pounds green beans, trimmed
 2 medium shallots, thinly sliced
 1 teaspoon Dijon mustard
 1 tablespoon freshly squeezed
  lemon juice
 3 tablespoons olive oil

**1.** Prepare an ice bath; set aside. Bring a medium saucepan of water to a boil over high heat. Add salt and the beans; cook until beans are just tender and bright green, about 5 minutes. Transfer beans to ice bath to stop cooking. Drain in a colander; pat dry with paper towels. Combine beans and shallots in a large bowl.

**2.** In a small bowl, whisk together mustard and lemon juice, and season with salt. Whisk in oil in a slow, steady stream until emulsified. Drizzle over beans, and toss to coat evenly. Serve.

## white beans
### SERVES 4

 1 cup dried cannellini beans, picked over
 3 tablespoons olive oil
 1 large onion, diced
 4 garlic cloves, minced
 1 to 1½ cups chicken stock, preferably
  homemade (page 179), or low-sodium
  canned chicken broth
 6 fresh sage leaves, sliced into thin strips
  Coarse salt and freshly ground pepper

**1.** Place beans in a bowl; cover with cold water. Let soak overnight at room temperature; drain.

**2.** Place beans in a medium saucepan, and cover with cold water. Simmer, covered, over medium-low heat, until tender but not mushy, 45 to 60 minutes. Drain beans in a colander, reserving 1 cup cooking liquid.

**3.** Heat oil in a medium sauté pan over medium heat. Add onion, and cook until translucent, stirring occasionally, about 7 minutes. Add garlic, and cook until fragrant but not brown, 1 to 2 minutes more. Add beans, reserved cooking liquid, and 1 cup chicken stock. Simmer, covered, until beans are very tender, about 25 minutes.

**4.** Stir in sage, and season with salt and pepper. If mixture is dry, add up to ½ cup of the remaining chicken stock. Serve hot.

## brussels sprouts with pearl onions

SERVES 6 TO 8

4  slices bacon (about 4 ounces)

12  ounces pearl onions, trimmed

2  pounds brussels sprouts, trimmed and halved

⅔  cup chicken stock, preferably homemade (page 179), or low-sodium canned chicken broth

2  teaspoons chopped fresh oregano or rosemary
    Coarse salt and freshly ground pepper

**1.** Cook bacon in a large skillet over medium heat until crisp and fat is rendered. Using a slotted spatula, transfer bacon to paper towels to drain.

**2.** Add the pearl onions to rendered fat in skillet; cook over medium heat, tossing occasionally, until lightly caramelized, about 5 minutes. Add brussels sprouts, cut sides down; cook until undersides are golden brown, about 5 minutes. Turn sprouts, and add chicken stock. Reduce heat to medium-low; cook, covered, 5 minutes. Remove lid, and continue cooking until the liquid has reduced to a few tablespoons and the vegetables are tender, about 8 minutes more.

**3.** Transfer mixture to a serving bowl. Crumble bacon over the top, and sprinkle with oregano. Season with salt and pepper. Serve hot.

## caramelized chestnuts and brussels sprouts

SERVES 8

¾  pound fresh chestnuts

2  tablespoons unsalted butter

1  tablespoon olive oil

2  pounds brussels sprouts, trimmed and halved
    Coarse salt and freshly ground pepper

½  cup cider vinegar

¼  cup sugar

¼  cup Homemade Turkey Stock (recipe follows), or low-sodium canned chicken broth

**1.** Preheat oven to 400°F. Score each chestnut using a sharp paring knife or a chestnut knife: Make an X on one side of each chestnut or make one long slit crosswise around the circumference. Place chestnuts in a single layer on a rimmed baking sheet, and roast until flesh is tender and golden, about 25 minutes. Remove from oven. Using a clean kitchen towel, immediately rub to remove shells. Set chestnuts aside.

**2.** Melt butter and oil in a large sauté pan over medium-high heat. Add brussels sprouts; season with salt and pepper. Cook, stirring occasionally, until golden, 16 to 18 minutes.

**3.** Add roasted chestnuts to pan. Cook, gently stirring occasionally, until brussels sprouts are tender and deep brown in spots, 20 to 25 minutes.

**4.** Add vinegar, sugar, and stock to pan. Cook, stirring occasionally, until liquid is reduced to a syrup, 4 to 5 minutes. Transfer to a platter, and serve.

## homemade turkey stock

MAKES 1¼ QUARTS

*Stock can be made ahead and stored in an airtight container; refrigerate for up to three days or freeze for up to six months.*

> Turkey neck and giblets (heart, gizzard, and liver), reserved from turkey
> 1 onion, cut into large chunks
> 2 stalks celery, cut into large chunks
> 2 carrots, cut into large chunks
> 6 sprigs flat-leaf parsley
> 1 dried bay leaf
> 1 teaspoon whole black peppercorns

**1.** Rinse neck and giblets well. Combine all ingredients and 7 cups water in a medium stockpot. Bring to a boil; reduce heat, and simmer 1½ hours, skimming foam from surface as needed.

**2.** Pass stock through a cheesecloth-lined sieve into an airtight container; discard solids. Let stock cool completely, then cover, and store.

## roasted brussels sprouts with apples and red onions

SERVES 6 TO 8

*You may substitute Granny Smith apples for the lady apples; core and cut each apple into six wedges before cooking.*

> 2 tablespoons unsalted butter
> 2 tablespoons olive oil
> 1 pound brussels sprouts, trimmed and halved
> 5 lady apples, halved crosswise, seeds removed
> 1 red onion, cut into ¼-inch-thick wedges
> Juice of ½ lemon
> Coarse salt and freshly ground pepper
> 6 sprigs thyme
> 1 cup apple cider

**1.** Preheat oven to 425°F. In a roasting pan, melt butter with olive oil. Add brussels sprouts, apples, onion, and lemon juice; season with salt and pepper. Toss to coat. Turn apples, cut sides down, and scatter thyme sprigs over top. Roast until tender and golden brown, about 30 minutes.

**2.** Transfer mixture to a serving dish. Place roasting pan over medium-high heat. Add cider; deglaze pan, scraping up browned bits on bottom of pan with a wooden spoon. Continue cooking until cider has reduced slightly, 3 to 4 minutes. Pour sauce over brussels sprouts; serve.

## sautéed brussels sprouts with raisins

SERVES 4

1   tablespoon extra-virgin olive oil

10  ounces brussels sprouts, trimmed
    and thinly sliced

2   carrots, cut into ¼-inch pieces

¼   cup golden raisins

1   cup chicken stock, preferably
    homemade (page 179), or low-sodium
    canned chicken broth
    Coarse salt and freshly ground pepper

Heat oil in a large skillet over medium heat. Add
brussels sprouts and carrots; cook until sprouts
start to turn golden brown, about 3 minutes. Add
raisins and chicken stock; cook, stirring occasionally, until sprouts are tender when pierced
with the tip of a paring knife, about 12 minutes. (If
skillet becomes too dry before sprouts are tender,
add up to 3 tablespoons water.) Remove from heat,
and season with salt and pepper. Serve hot.

## sweet-and-sour red cabbage

MAKES 5 CUPS

*This side dish can be made in advance and
warmed over low heat just before serving.*

1   small head red cabbage (about 2 pounds)

2   tablespoons vegetable oil

7   tablespoons red-wine vinegar

3   tablespoons honey

1   teaspoon ground cinnamon
    Pinch of ground allspice
    Coarse salt and freshly ground pepper

1   Granny Smith apple

1. Halve cabbage lengthwise; remove core, and
slice leaves as thinly as possible.

2. Heat oil in a large saucepan over medium-low
heat. Add cabbage, and cook, stirring frequently,
until wilted, about 10 minutes. Add vinegar, honey,
cinnamon, and allspice. Season with salt and pepper. Add 3 tablespoons water, and continue cooking cabbage until almost soft, about 1½ hours.
(Add more water as needed if pan looks dry.)

3. Halve apple lengthwise, remove core, and slice
apple into very thin wedges. Add to cabbage, and
continue cooking until cabbage is soft and almost
dry, about 20 minutes more. Serve warm.

## buttered carrots
SERVES 6

- 3 tablespoons unsalted butter
- 1 tablespoon sugar
- 8 large carrots, halved crosswise
  and cut into thin matchsticks
  Coarse salt and freshly ground pepper

Melt butter over medium heat in a large skillet. Sprinkle in sugar, and cook until melted. Add carrots, and toss until they are coated. Cover partially, and cook until carrots are just tender, about 3 minutes. Season with salt and pepper, and toss to coat. Serve immediately.

## glazed carrots and ginger
SERVES 4

*For a less spicy dish, omit the chile.*

- 20 baby carrots (about ½ pound),
  with 1-inch green top left on
- 1 tablespoon unsalted butter
- 1 tablespoon honey
- 1 3-inch-long piece fresh ginger, peeled
  and cut into ¼-inch-thick matchsticks
- ½ teaspoon thinly sliced red chile

**1.** Bring a large saucepan of water to a boil. Add carrots; cook until just tender, 3 to 4 minutes. Drain carrots, and pat dry with paper towels.

**2.** Melt butter in a large skillet over medium-low heat. Add carrots, honey, and ginger; cook, turning carrots frequently, until browned, about 8 minutes. Add chile, and cook until soft, about 1 minute more. Remove from heat; serve.

## kale-rutabaga purée
SERVES 8

*For a slightly sharper flavor, substitute two pounds of turnips for the rutabaga. If using turnips, you may need less milk—add it gradually, stopping when the mixture is fairly smooth.*

- 1 rutabaga (2 pounds), peeled
  and cut into 1-inch chunks
- 2 tablespoons olive oil
- 1 yellow onion, coarsely chopped
- 2 tablespoons minced garlic
- 2 pounds kale, trimmed, washed,
  and roughly chopped
  Coarse salt and freshly ground pepper
- ¾ cup milk

**1.** Place rutabaga in a medium saucepan; add enough water to cover, and bring to a boil over medium-high heat. Reduce to a simmer, and cook until tender, about 25 minutes. Drain; set aside.

**2.** Heat oil in a large sauté pan over medium-high heat. Add onion and garlic, and cook, stirring occasionally, until translucent, about 3 minutes. Add kale in batches, allowing each batch to wilt before adding the next. Season with salt and pepper.

**3.** Transfer mixture to a food processor. Purée until smooth; add reserved rutabaga. With machine running, gradually add milk through the feed tube; process until mixture is smooth. Serve.

## cauliflower with hazelnut brown butter

SERVES 12 TO 14

- 1 cup hazelnuts
- 3 small or 2 large heads cauliflower (about 3½ pounds)
  Coarse salt
- 10 tablespoons (1¼ sticks) unsalted butter
- 2 tablespoons freshly squeezed lemon juice
- 2 tablespoons finely chopped fresh chives

**1.** Preheat oven to 350°F. Spread hazelnuts on a rimmed baking sheet; toast in oven until fragrant and skins are beginning to split, about 10 minutes. Using a clean kitchen towel, vigorously rub off papery skins. Coarsely chop nuts; set aside.

**2.** Trim stems of cauliflower heads so they sit flat, keeping heads intact. Bring several inches of water to a boil in a large steamer or in a pot fitted with a rack; add salt. Steam cauliflower until just tender, about 10 minutes. Transfer to a platter.

**3.** Combine butter and reserved hazelnuts in a small saucepan. Cook over medium heat until butter turns brown, 3 to 4 minutes. Remove from heat, and add lemon juice and chives. Season with salt, and whisk to combine. Pour butter sauce over cauliflower, and serve immediately.

## butternut squash with brown butter

SERVES 4

*The easiest way to peel butternut squash is with a vegetable peeler. The harp-shape variety works particularly well.*

- 2 tablespoons unsalted butter
- 1 butternut squash (about 1¾ pounds), peeled, seeded, and cut into ¾-inch chunks
- ½ cup chicken stock, preferably homemade (page 179), or low-sodium canned chicken broth
- 1 tablespoon dark-brown sugar
  Coarse salt and freshly ground pepper

**1.** Melt butter in a large skillet over medium-high heat until golden brown. Add squash; cook, stirring occasionally, until golden brown and tender when pierced with a fork, about 16 minutes.

**2.** Add stock, ¼ cup water, and the brown sugar; cook until liquid has evaporated and squash is caramelized, about 6 minutes. Remove from heat; season with salt and pepper. Serve immediately.

## roasted fennel

SERVES 8 TO 12

- 6 large bulbs fennel, trimmed
- ¼ cup olive oil
  Coarse salt and freshly ground pepper
- 1 cup grated Parmesan cheese

**1.** Preheat oven to 400°F. Bring a large pot of water to a boil. Blanch fennel bulbs in water, 10 minutes; drain. Halve bulbs lengthwise, and arrange in a roasting pan, cut sides down. Drizzle with oil, and season with salt and pepper.

**2.** Transfer pan to oven, and roast 20 minutes. Sprinkle with cheese, and continue roasting until golden on top, 10 to 15 minutes more. Serve hot.

## braised leeks, parsnips, and fennel

### SERVES 12

8   parsnips (about 2½ pounds), peeled, quartered, and cut into 3-inch lengths

4   bulbs fennel (about 3 pounds), trimmed and cut into 1-inch wedges, fronds reserved

3   large leeks (about 2¼ pounds), white and pale-green parts only, quartered lengthwise and washed well

3   garlic cloves, halved lengthwise
    Coarse salt and freshly ground pepper

1½  teaspoons roughly chopped fresh thyme leaves

3   tablespoons chilled unsalted butter, cut into small pieces

¾   cup chicken stock, preferably homemade (page 179), or low-sodium canned chicken broth

¾   cup dry white wine

**1.** Preheat oven to 350°F. In a 4-quart ovenproof casserole, combine parsnips, fennel, leeks, and garlic; season with salt and pepper. Sprinkle thyme over the top, and dot with butter. Pour in stock and wine. Cover with aluminum foil, and bake 1 hour.

**2.** Remove foil, and continue baking until vegetables are tender, 20 to 30 minutes more. Remove from oven; let cool slightly, about 10 minutes. Garnish with snipped fennel fronds, and serve.

## braised endive with orange

### SERVES 6

1   orange

2   cups chicken stock, preferably homemade (page 179), or low-sodium canned chicken broth

3   whole star anise

6   heads (about 2 pounds) Belgian endive, cut in half lengthwise
    Coarse salt and freshly ground pepper

**1.** Slice off both ends of the orange. Using a sharp paring knife, cut away the peel and white pith, following the curve of the fruit. Slice between membranes to remove segments. Cut segments crosswise into thirds. Set aside.

**2.** Combine stock and star anise in a large, shallow, nonreactive saucepan; bring to a boil. Add endive halves, and season with salt and pepper. Reduce heat to medium-low. Cover endive with cheesecloth or a round of parchment paper to keep it moist. Cover pan, and simmer until endive is tender when pierced with the tip of a paring knife, about 10 minutes per side. Using a slotted spoon, transfer endive to a plate, and cover with cheesecloth to keep moist. Discard star anise.

**3.** Raise heat to high, and cook remaining liquid until reduced by half, about 5 minutes. Pour hot liquid over endive. Arrange reserved orange segments on top, and serve immediately.

## braised escarole with currants

SERVES 6

1 tablespoon extra-virgin olive oil
½ teaspoon crushed red-pepper flakes
4 garlic cloves, thinly sliced
1 ounce slivered almonds (about ⅓ cup)
4 anchovy fillets, rinsed (optional)
¼ cup dry sherry
½ cup chicken stock, preferably homemade (page 179), or low-sodium canned chicken broth
1 tablespoon dark-brown sugar
2 bunches (about 2½ pounds) escarole, cleaned, drained, and torn into 2-inch pieces
¼ cup currants

1. Heat oil in a large, deep skillet over medium-low heat. Add pepper flakes; stir until fragrant, about 1 minute. Add garlic and almonds; cook, stirring, until light golden, about 3 minutes. Add anchovies, if desired; stir until mashed and combined. Add sherry; cook until almost evaporated. Add stock and sugar; stir until sugar has dissolved.

2. Add escarole to skillet in batches, tossing until each batch starts to wilt before adding the next. Cover, and cook over low heat, stirring occasionally, until completely wilted, about 5 minutes.

3. Add currants to skillet; cook until escarole is tender, about 10 minutes more. Serve.

## mushroom-potato pie

photograph on page 60

SERVES 10 TO 12

2 tablespoons unsalted butter, plus more for baking dish
1 onion, cut into ½-inch dice
2 pounds assorted wild mushrooms, such as chanterelle, oyster, and black trumpet, trimmed, cleaned, and coarsely chopped
¼ cup dry white wine
  Coarse salt and freshly ground pepper
1 cup freshly grated Gruyère cheese (4 ounces)
1 cup freshly grated Parmesan cheese (about 3½ ounces)
1½ pounds (4 to 5) Yukon gold potatoes, peeled
1 tablespoon chopped fresh thyme
¾ cup milk
½ cup heavy cream

1. Preheat oven to 350°F. Butter a 13-by-9-inch casserole or baking dish; set aside. Melt butter in a large skillet over medium heat. Add onion; cook, stirring occasionally, until soft, about 5 minutes. Add mushrooms in two batches; cook, stirring occasionally, until they have released their juices and most of the liquid has evaporated, about 5 minutes. Add white wine; cook, stirring occasionally, until evaporated, 3 to 5 minutes more. Remove from heat; season with salt and pepper.

2. Combine Gruyère and Parmesan in a small bowl, and set aside. Cut potatoes into ⅛-inch-thick slices. Arrange a layer of potato slices, slightly overlapping, in bottom of casserole dish. Sprinkle with half the thyme; season with salt and pepper. Sprinkle one-third of the cheese over the top, followed by half the mushroom mixture. Arrange another layer of potatoes over the top. Sprinkle with remaining thyme; season with salt and pepper. Sprinkle all but 2 tablespoons cheese over the top, followed by the remaining mushroom mixture. Arrange the remaining potato slices around edge of casserole.

**3.** Combine milk and cream; pour over top of casserole. Cover loosely with foil, and bake until liquid is bubbling, about 1 hour. Remove foil, and sprinkle with remaining 2 tablespoons cheese; continue baking until top is golden, about 20 to 30 minutes more. Let stand about 10 minutes before cutting into squares. Serve warm.

## scalloped mushrooms
SERVES 8 TO 10

*We used frozen pearl onions, but fresh can be used instead. To peel, place them in boiling water for one minute, then let them cool slightly before slipping off their papery skins.*

- 9 tablespoons unsalted butter
- 1 pound frozen pearl onions, thawed and drained
- 3 pounds assorted mushrooms, such as button, cremini, and shiitake, trimmed, cleaned, and halved (large ones should be quartered)
- ¾ cup heavy cream
- 1 cup freshly grated Parmesan cheese (4 ounces)
  Coarse salt and freshly ground pepper
- 1 cup plain coarse breadcrumbs, preferably homemade

**1.** Preheat oven to 350°F. Heat 1 tablespoon butter in a large cast-iron or other ovenproof skillet over medium-high heat. Add onions; cook, stirring occasionally, until soft and just starting to brown, about 5 minutes. Transfer to a large bowl.

**2.** Melt 2 tablespoons butter in skillet; add one-quarter of the mushrooms, tossing to coat. Cook until mushrooms have released their juices and most of the liquid has evaporated, about 5 minutes. Transfer to bowl with onions. Repeat with remaining mushrooms and butter.

**3.** Add cream and ½ cup Parmesan to bowl, and season with salt and pepper. Stir to combine.

Return mixture to skillet or a baking dish. Sprinkle breadcrumbs and remaining ½ cup Parmesan over top, and bake until bubbling and golden, about 25 minutes. Serve hot.

## wild-mushroom ragout
SERVES 4

- 1½ pounds wild mushrooms, such as chanterelle or shiitake, trimmed and cleaned
- 2 tablespoons unsalted butter
- 1 tablespoon extra-virgin olive oil
- 2 garlic cloves, minced
- ¼ cup dry white wine
  Coarse salt and freshly ground pepper
  Juice of ½ lemon
- 3 tablespoons coarsely chopped fresh flat-leaf parsley

**1.** Cut mushrooms into ½-inch-thick strips, and set aside. Melt butter with oil in a large skillet over high heat. Add garlic, and cook until fragrant but not brown, about 30 seconds.

**2.** Add mushrooms to skillet, and toss quickly in butter mixture to coat. Add wine; continue cooking until most of the liquid has evaporated and mushrooms turn golden, about 8 minutes. Season generously with salt and pepper. Add lemon juice and parsley; toss to combine. Serve immediately.

## madeira-glazed baked quinces and wild mushroom
### SERVES 8

1   lemon, halved
4   quinces
1½  cups Madeira
    Coarse salt and freshly ground pepper
1   ounce dried porcini mushrooms
1   cup boiling water
3   tablespoons unsalted butter
1   onion, finely chopped
2   teaspoons minced fresh thyme leaves,
    plus sprigs for garnish
½   pound wild mushrooms, such as
    shiitake or oyster, trimmed, cleaned,
    and cut into 1-inch pieces

1. Preheat oven to 350°F. Juice lemon; place the juice and both halves in a large bowl of water. Peel quinces one at a time; halve and core, transferring each half to the lemon water as you work to prevent discoloration.

2. Arrange quince halves, cut sides up, in a roasting pan. Drizzle with 1 cup Madeira; season with salt and pepper. Pour 2 cups water into pan. Cover tightly with foil. Cook until quinces are tender and translucent, about 1½ hours. Remove from oven, and reduce heat to 325°F.

3. Meanwhile, place dried porcini in a bowl, and cover with the boiling water; let stand until soft, about 30 minutes. Remove from water, reserving liquid; finely chop mushrooms.

4. Heat butter in a large sauté pan over medium heat. Add onion; cook, stirring occasionally, until translucent, about 5 minutes. Add porcini, thyme, and wild mushrooms; cook over medium heat, stirring until mushrooms have released their juices, about 5 minutes. Reduce heat to medium-low; add reserved porcini liquid and remaining ½ cup Madeira, and season with salt and pepper.

Continue cooking until liquid is reduced to a glaze and mushrooms are tender, 8 to 10 minutes.

5. Generously spoon mushroom mixture over each quince. Cover dish with foil. Return to oven; cook until quinces are heated through, about 30 minutes. Remove foil; continue baking until golden, 10 to 15 minutes. Serve garnished with thyme sprigs.

## wild-mushroom and leek beggar's purses
### MAKES 8

*Any combination of wild mushrooms can be used; try chanterelles and shiitakes. If using a variety, cook each type separately. When working with each sheet of phyllo, keep others covered with a clean damp kitchen towel.*

4   leeks, washed well
4   tablespoons olive oil
1½  pounds wild mushrooms,
    cleaned and sliced
1   to 2 tablespoons fresh thyme leaves
¼   cup Madeira or beef stock
    Coarse salt and freshly ground pepper
6   sheets frozen phyllo dough, thawed
    Unsalted butter, melted

1. Split leeks in half lengthwise, leaving the root attached. Remove some of the inner layers to use for tying purses; blanch them 30 seconds in boiling water. Plunge in cool water; drain, and set aside.

2. Slice off green tops, and thinly slice leeks. Heat 1 tablespoon oil in a sauté pan over medium heat. Add leeks; cook, stirring, until soft but not browned, about 5 minutes. Transfer to a large bowl.

3. Add 1 tablespoon oil to pan, and raise heat to medium-high. Add one-third of the mushrooms in a single layer. Cook, stirring frequently, until just softened, about 3 minutes. Add to bowl with leeks. Repeat with remaining oil and mushrooms.

4. Return mushrooms and leeks to pan. Add thyme and Madeira, and season with salt and pepper. Cook over high heat, stirring, until liquid is reduced to a syrup consistency. Set aside to cool.

5. Lay 1 phyllo sheet flat on a clean work surface; brush sparingly with melted butter. Lay another sheet on top; brush with butter. Repeat to make another layer. Cut stack into 4 rectangles. Place ⅓ cup filling in center of each, and gather into a cinched-purse shape. Repeat process with remaining phyllo and filling. Place purses on a baking sheet, and chill until firm.

6. Preheat oven to 400°F. Bake purses until evenly golden brown, about 15 minutes. Tie each purse with a leek ribbon, and serve immediately.

## braised onions
### SERVES 12 TO 14

3 pounds red and white onions
   (about 15 small onions)
3 tablespoons unsalted butter
3 tablespoons sugar
   Coarse salt and freshly ground pepper

1. Trim roots from onions, leaving enough to keep onion intact. Cut them lengthwise in halves or quarters, depending on their size.

2. Place onions in a large skillet; add butter and sugar. Season with salt and pepper. Add enough water to reach halfway up sides of onions. Bring to a boil over medium-high heat; reduce heat to medium-low, and cook, covered, until onions are tender, about 20 minutes. Raise heat to medium, and cook, uncovered, stirring occasionally, until caramelized, 30 to 40 minutes. Serve hot.

## apricot-and-thyme-glazed onions
### SERVES 10 TO 12

*This dish can be prepared ahead up to the point when you bake the onions. The rest of the recipe can be completed thirty minutes before serving. You can also prepare it in a thirteen-by-nine-inch glass baking dish: Bake, covered with aluminum foil, about forty-five minutes, basting once after twenty minutes.*

1 jar (10 ounces) apricot all-fruit preserves
¼ cup dry white wine
½ bunch thyme
3 large Spanish onions, sliced
   crosswise ½ inch thick
3 large red onions, sliced
   crosswise ½ inch thick
   Coarse salt

1. Immerse an extra-large clay baker in cold water; let soak 10 to 15 minutes. Combine apricot preserves and 1 tablespoon water in a small saucepan; cook over medium-high heat until liquefied, 1 to 2 minutes. Remove from heat; set aside.

2. Preheat oven to 450°F. Remove baker from water, and invert to drain off excess. Pour wine into baker, and arrange all but 8 sprigs of thyme over bottom. Arrange onion slices over thyme, layering them three across and alternating Spanish and red onions. Brush onions with half the melted apricot preserves; season with salt.

3. Bake, covered, until onions begin to soften and are translucent, about 1 hour 20 minutes, basting with pan juices after 45 minutes. Brush onions with remaining preserves. If preserves have thickened, stir in several drops of water. Continue baking, uncovered, until onions are tender and slightly caramelized, about 30 minutes. To serve, drizzle each serving with pan juices, and garnish with remaining thyme sprigs.

## creamed pearl onions

SERVES 8

*To roast garlic, wrap the head in foil and place in a 400-degree oven for forty-five minutes.*

2¾ cups chicken stock, preferably homemade (page 179), or low-sodium canned chicken broth

¾ cup dry white wine

1½ pounds pearl onions

5 tablespoons all-purpose flour

2½ teaspoons fresh thyme leaves

¼ teaspoon freshly ground pepper

1 head roasted garlic

2 tablespoons grated Parmesan cheese

**1.** Preheat oven to 350°F. Place stock and wine in a medium saucepan over high heat, and cook until reduced by half.

**2.** Meanwhile, bring a medium saucepan of water to a boil. Add onions; cook 10 minutes. Drain; let cool. Using a paring knife, remove skins. Set aside.

**3.** Place flour and reduced liquid in a food processor, and pulse until combined. Transfer mixture to a small saucepan; whisk constantly over medium heat until thickened, about 10 minutes. Remove from heat. Stir in 1½ teaspoons thyme and the pepper. Slice off top of garlic head, and squeeze cloves into sauce; stir to combine.

**4.** Place onions and sauce in a 10-inch round baking dish. Sprinkle with Parmesan and remaining teaspoon thyme. Bake until golden on top, about 1 hour 15 minutes. Serve hot.

## spicy parsnips with sautéed red swiss chard and garlic

SERVES 10 TO 12

Coarse salt

8 parsnips (2½ to 3 pounds), peeled and sliced ¼ inch thick

6½ tablespoons unsalted butter

4½ tablespoons olive oil

3 dried ancho chiles

1 tablespoon coriander seeds, lightly crushed

1 tablespoon pink peppercorns, lightly crushed

1 tablespoon green peppercorns, lightly crushed

1 tablespoon cardamom pods

6 fresh curry leaves

3 small garlic cloves, sliced ⅛ inch thick

4 bunches red Swiss chard (2 pounds), stems trimmed, leaves torn from center vein

Freshly ground black pepper

**1.** Preheat oven to 300°F. Bring a large pot of water to a boil over high heat. Add salt and parsnips. Cook parsnips until just tender when pierced with the tip of a paring knife, about 7 minutes. Drain in a colander; rinse with cold water, and pat dry.

**2.** Heat 1½ tablespoons each butter and oil in a large skillet over medium-high heat. Add 1 dried chile and one-third each of the coriander seeds, pink peppercorns, green peppercorns, cardamom pods, and curry leaves; cook, stirring, until fragrant, 1 to 2 minutes.

**3.** Add one-third of the parsnips to skillet, and reduce heat to medium. Season with salt; cook, tossing often, until golden brown, 8 to 9 minutes. Transfer parsnips to a roasting pan; place in oven to keep warm. Repeat steps 2 and 3 twice.

**4.** Meanwhile, heat remaining 2 tablespoons butter in a large, deep skillet over medium heat. Add garlic; cook, stirring frequently, until golden, 2 to 3 minutes. Working in batches, add chard to pan, tossing each batch until wilted before adding the next. Cook until chard is very tender, about 8 minutes. Season with salt and pepper. Transfer mixture to a warm serving platter, and top with parsnip mixture. Serve hot.

## savory roasted apples, onions, and shallots

### SERVES 10 TO 12

*Select the smallest onions possible—the same size as the shallots—so they will cook evenly.*

- 5 tablespoons rendered bacon fat or olive oil
- 4 shallots
- 4 small yellow onions
- 4 small red onions
  Coarse salt and freshly ground pepper
- 2 dried bay leaves
- 1 tablespoon juniper berries, lightly crushed
- 1 tablespoon mustard seeds
- ½ cup spiced rum or brandy
- ¼ cup molasses
- 1 cup chicken stock, preferably homemade (page 179), or low-sodium canned chicken broth
- 3 cups apple cider
- 4 small firm-fleshed apples, such as Empire, Northern Spy, or Granny Smith

**1.** Preheat oven to 400°F, with racks in lower third and center. In a 12-inch ovenproof skillet, heat 3 tablespoons bacon fat over medium-high heat. Make a deep cut along the length of each shallot and onion. Add shallots and onions to skillet; season with salt and pepper. Add one bay leaf, half the juniper berries, and half the mustard seeds. Cook, shaking pan frequently, until shallots and onions begin to turn golden brown, 6 to 7 minutes.

**2.** In a small measuring cup, combine ¼ cup rum and 2 tablespoons molasses; stir to combine. Pour mixture into skillet, and stir to combine. Reduce heat to medium; cook until onions and shallots begin to caramelize and liquid has almost evaporated, about 1 minute. Pour ½ cup stock and 1½ cups cider into skillet, and stir to combine. Raise heat to medium-high; bring to a boil.

**3.** Transfer onion mixture to a large roasting pan; roast on lower rack 1 hour 30 minutes.

**4.** Meanwhile, heat remaining 2 tablespoons bacon fat in skillet over medium-high heat. With a sharp knife, cut apples in half lengthwise; remove seeds and stems. Season cut sides of apples with salt and pepper. Place halves, cut sides down, in skillet; sear until golden brown, 3 to 4 minutes. Add remaining bay leaf, juniper berries, and mustard seeds.

**5.** In a small measuring cup, combine remaining ¼ cup rum and 2 tablespoons molasses; stir to combine. Pour into skillet; cook until apples begin to caramelize and liquid has almost evaporated, about 3 minutes. With tongs, turn apple halves. Pour remaining ½ cup stock and 1½ cups cider into skillet, and stir to combine. Bring liquid to a boil; remove skillet from heat.

**6.** When onion mixture has cooked 1 hour, transfer skillet to center rack of oven, and roast until apples are very tender, about 30 minutes. With a slotted spoon, transfer apples and onion mixture to a hot platter. Place skillet over high heat. Cook liquid from apples until reduced to about ½ cup, about 5 minutes. Drizzle liquid over apples and onions, and serve immediately.

## green pea purée

SERVES 8 TO 10

*The purée may be made up to one hour ahead and kept warm, covered with foil, in a heatproof bowl set over a pan of simmering water.*

Coarse salt
3  pounds shelled fresh or thawed frozen peas (9 cups)
2  tablespoons unsalted butter
   Pinch of freshly grated nutmeg
   Freshly ground pepper

**1.** Prepare a large ice bath; set aside. Bring a large pot of water to a boil; add salt. Working in two batches, cook peas in boiling water until bright green, about 1 minute. Using a slotted spoon, immediately transfer peas to ice bath to stop the cooking. Drain peas in a large colander.

**2.** Using a food mill fitted with the finest disk, pass peas into a medium bowl. Transfer purée to a medium saucepan placed over medium heat. Add butter and nutmeg; season with salt and pepper. Cook, stirring, until just warmed through. Serve.

## peas and prosciutto

SERVES 6 TO 8

¼  cup extra-virgin olive oil
2  teaspoons unsalted butter
1  onion, finely chopped
2  pounds shelled fresh or thawed frozen peas (6 cups)
½  to ¾ cup chicken stock, preferably homemade (page 179), or low-sodium canned chicken broth
4  ounces prosciutto, finely chopped
   Coarse salt and freshly ground pepper

**1.** In a large skillet, heat oil and butter over medium-high heat until butter is melted and foamy. Add onion, and cook, stirring occasionally, until it begins to soften, about 2 minutes.

**2.** Add peas and ½ cup stock to skillet. Lower heat to medium, and cook, stirring occasionally, until peas are tender, 5 to 10 minutes. If mixture becomes too dry, add up to ¼ cup more stock; the dish should be moist but not soupy. Add prosciutto, and stir to combine. Season with salt and pepper. Serve hot or at room temperature.

## creamed spinach

SERVES 4

2½  pounds fresh spinach, trimmed and washed well, with water clinging to leaves
3  tablespoons unsalted butter
¼  cup all-purpose flour
1  cup milk
1  teaspoon sugar
   Coarse salt and freshly ground pepper
   Freshly grated nutmeg
   Sour cream, for serving (optional)

**1.** Place spinach in a large saucepan over high heat. Cover, and cook, tossing occasionally, until wilted, 2 to 4 minutes. Drain in a colander set over a bowl; squeeze out excess liquid, and reserve. Roughly chop spinach, and set aside.

**2.** In a medium skillet, melt butter over medium heat. Add flour, and cook, stirring, 1 to 2 minutes. Slowly whisk in milk; add sugar, and season with salt and pepper. Thin mixture with reserved spinach liquid, as desired. Stir in spinach. Sprinkle with nutmeg, and top with a dollop of sour cream, if desired. Serve immediately.

## galette of root vegetables

SERVES 8

*A variation on the traditional French potato galette, this pancake can be made with almost any combination of root vegetables.*

- 2 carrots
- 2 white turnips, peeled
- 1 parsnip, peeled
- 3 large russet potatoes (about 2½ pounds), peeled
- ½ cup Clarified Butter (page 260)
  Coarse salt and freshly ground pepper

**1.** Coarsely grate vegetables, using a mandoline if possible. Dry grated potatoes by rubbing them between paper towels.

**2.** Heat clarified butter in a 12-inch nonstick skillet until it sizzles. Mix together grated vegetables; place in skillet in a flat, even layer. Season with salt and pepper. Cook over medium-high heat, shaking pan gently to prevent sticking, until underside is golden brown, about 10 minutes.

**3.** Invert galette onto a plate, then slide it back into skillet; reduce heat to low, and cook until other side is golden brown, 20 to 30 minutes, shaking pan occasionally. Serve warm, cut into wedges.

## roasted winter vegetables

SERVES 8 TO 10

- 2 to 3 pounds assorted winter vegetables, such as carrots, turnips, rutabagas, parsnips, pearl onions, and potatoes
- 4 tablespoons unsalted butter
- ¼ to ½ cup chicken stock, preferably homemade (page 179), or low-sodium canned chicken broth
  Coarse salt and freshly ground pepper
  Handful of chopped fresh herbs, such as thyme, parsley, or oregano

**1.** Preheat oven to 375°F. Scrub vegetables, and peel as desired. Cut into 1-to-2-inch pieces (they should all be of similar size).

**2.** Place butter in a roasting pan, and heat in oven until melted. Add vegetables and ¼ cup stock to pan; season with salt and pepper. Stir well to coat.

**3.** Roast until vegetables are tender and golden brown, 1 to 1½ hours, stirring occasionally and adding up to ¼ cup more stock as needed to keep vegetables slightly moist. Stir in herbs, and serve.

## root vegetables anna

SERVES 8 TO 10

*We added rutabagas to pommes Anna, a French dish traditionally made with potatoes.*

- 1 head garlic
- ¼ teaspoon olive oil
- 1½ pounds (4 to 5) Yukon Gold potatoes
- 2 pounds large rutabagas
- 6 tablespoons unsalted butter
- 1 teaspoon roughly chopped fresh thyme leaves, plus ½ teaspoon for garnish
  Coarse salt and freshly ground pepper

**1.** Preheat oven to 450°F. Place garlic head in an ovenproof dish, and drizzle with oil. Roast until flesh is very soft, about 20 minutes. Remove from oven; let cool. Squeeze out cloves, and cut into slivers; set aside. Reduce oven heat to 425°F.

**2.** Meanwhile, peel potatoes, then thinly slice with a mandoline or sharp knife. Place slices in a bowl, and cover with a damp paper towel to prevent discoloration. Peel rutabagas, then halve and thinly slice. Place in a separate bowl, and cover with a damp paper towel.

**3.** In a 10-inch, nonstick ovenproof skillet, melt 2 tablespoons butter, swirling pan to coat evenly. Remove from heat. Starting at the outside edge, arrange half the rutabaga in overlapping concentric circles to cover bottom of pan; press down on top to compress. Sprinkle with ½ teaspoon thyme and one-third of the roasted garlic; season with salt and pepper, and dot with 1 tablespoon butter. Repeat two more times, using potatoes for the second layer and remaining rutabagas for the last (omit thyme from last layer).

**4.** Spread remaining tablespoon butter over a large piece of aluminum foil; cover skillet tightly with foil, buttered side down. Weight foil with

another ovenproof skillet, and transfer to oven. Bake until vegetables are tender when pierced with the tip of a paring knife, 50 to 60 minutes.

**5.** Transfer skillet to a wire rack; remove weight, and let cool 15 minutes. Remove foil, and carefully invert cake onto a serving dish. Serve warm, garnished with remaining ½ teaspoon thyme.

## winter vegetable cobbler

SERVES 10 TO 12

- 1 rutabaga, peeled and cut into 1-inch pieces
- 1 turnip, peeled and cut into 1-inch pieces
- 1 small butternut squash, peeled, seeded, and cut into 1-inch cubes
- 8 ounces pearl onions, peeled
- 2 parsnips, peeled and cut into 2-inch lengths
- 2 carrots, cut into 2-inch lengths
- 2 cups white and/or shiitake mushrooms, cleaned and sliced ¼ inch thick
- ½ bunch fresh thyme, plus more for garnish
  Wild Mushroom Sauce (recipe follows)
  Coarse salt and freshly ground pepper
  Herb Pastry (recipe follows)
- 1 large egg yolk beaten with 1 tablespoon heavy cream, for egg wash

**1.** Preheat oven to 375°F. Combine vegetables, thyme, and mushroom sauce in a large bowl. Season with salt and pepper. Transfer mixture to a 10-inch round baking dish.

**2.** Roll out pastry dough to a 10-inch round, about ⅛ inch thick. Place dough over vegetables, crimping edge against inside edge of dish to seal. Cut a few slits in top of pastry to allow steam to escape; brush pastry with egg wash.

**3.** Bake cobbler until crust is golden brown and juices are bubbling, about 40 minutes. Garnish with several sprigs of thyme. Serve hot.

## wild mushroom sauce
MAKES 1½ CUPS

*1 cup (about 2 ounces) dried*
*porcini mushrooms*

*2 tablespoons unsalted butter*

*1 tablespoon olive oil*

*1 large onion, finely chopped*

*3 garlic cloves, minced*

*3 tablespoons all-purpose flour*

*1 cup dry white wine*

*Bouquet garni, made with bay leaves,*
*thyme, peppercorns, parsley, and*
*celery tied in cheesecloth*

*Coarse salt and freshly ground pepper*

**1.** In a glass measuring cup, soak mushrooms in 1½ cups hot water until soft, about 15 minutes. With a slotted spoon, remove mushrooms, and squeeze over cup, reserving the soaking liquid. Coarsely chop mushrooms, and set aside.

**2.** Heat butter and oil in a medium saucepan over medium heat. Add onion and garlic; cook, stirring occasionally, until softened, 3 to 4 minutes. Stir in flour until smooth. Add wine, and bring to a boil. Pour in mushroom liquid, leaving behind any sediment at bottom of measuring cup.

**3.** Add reserved mushrooms and bouquet garni to pan; reduce heat, and simmer, stirring occasionally, until sauce is the consistency of gravy, about 35 minutes. Remove bouquet garni. Season with salt and pepper; let cool before using. Sauce can be refrigerated in an airtight container up to 2 days; warm over low heat before using.

## herb pastry
MAKES 1 TEN-INCH CRUST

*1¼ cups all-purpose flour*

*½ teaspoon salt*

*4 tablespoons chilled unsalted*
*butter, cut into small pieces*

*¼ cup solid vegetable shortening, chilled*

*3 tablespoons fresh thyme leaves*

*¼ cup ice water*

**1.** In a food processor, combine flour and salt; pulse to combine. Add butter and shortening; process until mixture resembles coarse meal, about 10 seconds. Add thyme; pulse 1 or 2 times.

**2.** With machine running, add ice water a little at a time through the feed tube; process until dough just holds together (no more than 30 seconds). Form dough into a disk, wrap in plastic, and chill until firm, at least 30 minutes.

## winter greens and bacon

SERVES 4

*Any combination of kale, chard, and mustard or collard greens works well in this recipe.*

- 4 slices thick-cut bacon, cut crosswise into ½-inch pieces
- 1 pound kale, trimmed and torn into 2-inch pieces
- 1 bunch Swiss chard, trimmed and torn into 2-inch pieces
- 2 teaspoons cider vinegar
  Coarse salt and freshly ground pepper

**1.** In a large skillet over medium heat, cook bacon until browned, about 5 minutes. Using a slotted spoon, transfer to a paper-towel–lined plate; set aside. Pour off all but 2 tablespoons rendered fat.

**2.** Add greens and ¾ cup water to skillet; bring to a boil. Cover skillet; reduce heat, and simmer, tossing occasionally, until greens are wilted and almost all water has evaporated, about 8 minutes.

**3.** Remove from heat. Stir in vinegar, and season with salt and pepper. Toss in bacon. Serve warm.

## winter vegetable purée

SERVES 8 TO 12

*The pears add a slight sweetness to this purée.*

- 4 tablespoons unsalted butter
- 1 butternut squash (1 pound), peeled, seeded, and coarsely chopped
- 4 parsnips, peeled and coarsely chopped
- 2 onions, coarsely chopped
- 6 carrots, coarsely chopped
- 2 ripe but firm pears, peeled, cored, and coarsely chopped
- ¼ teaspoon freshly grated nutmeg
  Coarse salt and freshly ground pepper

**1.** Melt butter in a large skillet over medium heat. Add vegetables and pears, and cook until tender, stirring occasionally, 20 to 25 minutes. Add a little water if necessary to prevent sticking.

**2.** Transfer mixture to a food processor, and purée until smooth. Stir in nutmeg, and season with salt and pepper. Serve warm.

## *apple-chestnut stuffing*
### SERVES 8 TO 10, WITH LEFTOVERS

*To save time, you can complete the first three steps and chop the onions and celery the day before. If using shelled chestnuts, chop them, then proceed with step two.*

- 2 cups chestnuts (12 ounces)
- 1 loaf (about 1 pound) rustic Italian or French bread
- 2 cups prunes, coarsely chopped (12 ounces)
- 1 cup apple cider
- 3 tablespoons unsalted butter
- 1 large red onion, finely chopped
- 2 stalks celery, cut into ¼-inch dice
- 2 green apples, cored and cut into ¼-inch dice
- 2 large eggs, lightly beaten
- ½ cup heavy cream
- 3 tablespoons chopped fresh sage
  Coarse salt and freshly ground pepper

**1.** Preheat oven to 400°F. Score each chestnut using a sharp paring knife or a chestnut knife: Make an X on one side of nut or make one long slit crosswise around circumference of chestnut. Place chestnuts in a single layer on a rimmed baking sheet, and roast until flesh is tender and golden, about 25 minutes. Remove from oven. Using a kitchen towel, immediately rub to remove shells. Coarsely chop chestnuts, and set aside.

**2.** Reduce oven heat to 350°F. Remove crust from bread; reserve crust. Slice bread 1 inch thick; cut slices into 1-inch cubes. Place in a single layer on two baking sheets; toast in oven until dry, tossing occasionally, 5 to 7 minutes. Set aside to cool. Place reserved crust in a food processor, and pulse until coarse crumbs form. Set aside.

**3.** Place prunes and apple cider in a small saucepan, and bring to a boil over medium-high heat. Reduce to a simmer, and cook until prunes have absorbed liquid, 20 to 25 minutes. Set aside.

**4.** Melt butter in a large skillet over medium heat, and add chestnuts, onion, half the celery, and half the apples. Cook, stirring occasionally, until onion is translucent, about 7 minutes. Let cool.

**5.** In a large bowl, combine the bread cubes and crumbs, prune and chestnut mixtures, remaining celery and apples, eggs, heavy cream, and sage. Stir to combine. Season with salt and pepper. Cook stuffing in a turkey or baking dish as directed in Cooking Stuffing (below).

### COOKING STUFFING

*If cooking stuffing in a turkey, let it cool completely after preparing, and stuff turkey just before it goes into the oven, to prevent bacteria from forming. Fill large cavity and neck cavity of turkey loosely with as much stuffing as they hold comfortably. Don't pack the stuffing too tightly, or it will not cook evenly. Cook until a meat thermometer inserted into stuffing registers at least 165°F (turkey should register 180°F).*

*If cooking on its own, place stuffing in a buttered baking dish. Cover with foil, and bake in a 375-degree oven thirty-five minutes. Remove foil, and continue baking until stuffing is golden brown on top, about ten minutes more.*

## classic stuffing

SERVES 10 TO 12, WITH LEFTOVERS

¾ cup (1½ sticks) unsalted butter

4 onions (2 pounds), cut into ¼-inch dice

16 stalks celery, cut into ¼-inch dice

10 large fresh sage leaves, chopped,
or 2 teaspoons crushed dried sage

1½ quarts chicken stock, preferably
homemade (page 179), or low-sodium
canned chicken broth

2 loaves day-old white bread (about 36
slices), crusts on, cut into 1-inch cubes

2 teaspoons coarse salt

4 teaspoons freshly ground pepper

3 cups coarsely chopped fresh flat-leaf
parsley (about 2 bunches)

8 ounces (2 cups) pecans, toasted
and chopped (optional)

2 cups dried cherries (optional)

**1.** Melt butter in a large skillet. Add onions and celery; cook, stirring occasionally, over medium heat until onions are translucent, about 10 minutes. Add sage; stir to combine, and cook 3 to 4 minutes. Stir in ½ cup stock. Cook until liquid has reduced by half, about 5 minutes.

**2.** Transfer onion mixture to a large bowl. Add remaining ingredients, including remaining stock; mix to combine. Cook stuffing in a turkey or baking dish as directed in Cooking Stuffing (page 289).

## cornbread stuffing with sage, sun-dried tomatoes, and sausage

SERVES 8 TO 10, WITH LEFTOVERS

*To toast pine nuts, place them in a dry skillet over medium-high heat until golden and fragrant, about five minutes, tossing frequently.*

Cornbread (recipe follows)

½ pound sweet Italian sausage,
casings removed

½ pound hot Italian sausage,
casings removed

2 small onions, finely chopped
(about 1½ cups)

6 stalks celery, finely chopped
(about 2½ cups)

2 garlic cloves, minced

½ cup pine nuts, toasted

⅓ cup sun-dried tomatoes (oil-packed),
coarsely chopped

2 tablespoons chopped fresh sage leaves,
or 1 tablespoon dried sage

1 cup chicken stock, preferably
homemade (page 179), or low-sodium
canned chicken broth

4 tablespoons unsalted butter, melted
Coarse salt and freshly ground pepper

**1.** Preheat oven to 350°F. Cut cornbread into ¾-inch pieces, and spread evenly on a rimmed baking sheet. Toast bread, tossing occasionally, until golden brown, about 20 minutes.

**2.** Heat a large skillet over medium-high heat, and add sausage. Cook, stirring frequently, until there is no trace of pink, 6 to 8 minutes. Using a slotted spoon, transfer sausage to a bowl, and set aside. Pour off all but 1 teaspoon of fat from skillet.

**3.** Add onions to skillet; cook over medium heat, stirring occasionally, until translucent, about 5 minutes. Add celery and garlic; cook, stirring, until celery is soft, 6 to 8 minutes.

**4.** Combine cornbread, sausage, onion mixture, pine nuts, tomatoes, and sage in a large bowl; mix well. Add chicken stock and melted butter, and toss to combine. Season with salt and pepper. Cook stuffing in a turkey or baking dish as directed in Cooking Stuffing (page 289).

### cornbread

MAKES 1 EIGHT-INCH SQUARE

*Bake the cornbread at least one day before you assemble the stuffing.*

- 4  tablespoons unsalted butter, melted and cooled, plus more for pan
- 1  cup yellow cornmeal
- 1  cup all-purpose flour
- ¼  cup sugar
- 1  tablespoon baking powder
- ½  teaspoon coarse salt
- 1  cup milk
- 1  large egg

**1.** Preheat oven to 425°F. Generously butter an 8-by-2-inch square baking pan, and set aside.

**2.** In a medium bowl, combine cornmeal, flour, sugar, baking powder, and salt. In a small bowl, whisk together milk and egg. Add milk mixture to flour mixture; stir to combine. Add melted butter, and whisk until just combined.

**3.** Pour mixture into prepared pan; bake until golden brown and firm to the touch, 18 to 20 minutes. Transfer pan to a wire rack to cool completely. Let stand overnight, uncovered.

### classic cornbread-sourdough stuffing

SERVES 8 TO 10, WITH LEFTOVERS

- 6  tablespoons unsalted butter
- 1  onion, cut into ¼-inch dice
- 2  garlic cloves, minced
- 2  carrots, cut into ¼-inch dice
- ½  bulb fennel, trimmed and cut into ¼-inch dice
    Cornbread (recipe above), cut into ½-inch cubes
- 1  day-old, 10-ounce sourdough ficelle, cut into ½-inch cubes
- 3  tablespoons finely chopped assorted fresh herbs, such as rosemary, sage, thyme, parsley, and marjoram
- 1  cup pitted prunes, cut into ½-inch dice
- 5  dried pears, cut into ½-inch dice
    Coarse salt and freshly ground pepper
- ½  cup Homemade Turkey Stock (page 273), or low-sodium canned chicken broth

**1.** Preheat oven to 350°F. Melt 2 tablespoons butter in a large skillet over medium-low heat. Add onion, garlic, carrots, and fennel; cook, stirring occasionally, until vegetables are tender, about 10 minutes. Remove from heat.

**2.** In a large bowl, combine cornbread and sourdough. Add vegetables, herbs, prunes, and pears; season with salt and pepper.

**3.** Melt remaining 4 tablespoons butter in a small saucepan. Add melted butter and turkey stock to stuffing mixture. Toss to combine. Cook stuffing in a turkey or baking dish as directed in Cooking Stuffing (page 289).

## cranberry-cornbread stuffing

SERVES 8 TO 10, WITH LEFTOVERS

8 ounces (2 cups) pecans

¾ cup (1½ sticks) unsalted butter

3 large onions, cut into ¼-inch dice

6 stalks celery, cut into ¼-inch dice

¼ cup fresh oregano leaves, chopped

1½ quarts chicken stock, preferably homemade (page 179), or low-sodium canned chicken broth

Skillet Cornbread (recipe follows), crumbled

1 loaf day-old white bread, crust on, cut into 1-inch cubes (10 heaping cups)

3 large eggs, lightly beaten

2 cups dried cranberries

1 cup coarsely chopped fresh flat-leaf parsley (1 large bunch)

1 tablespoon coarse salt

1 tablespoon freshly ground black pepper

½ teaspoon cayenne pepper

**1.** Preheat oven to 350°F. Spread pecans in a single layer on a rimmed baking sheet; toast in oven until golden and fragrant, 8 to 12 minutes, tossing occasionally. Let cool, then roughly chop; set aside.

**2.** Melt butter in a large skillet. Add onions and celery; cook over medium heat, stirring occasionally, until onions are translucent, about 8 minutes. Add oregano; stir to combine, and cook 2 minutes. Stir in ½ cup stock. Cook until liquid has reduced by half, about 5 minutes.

**3.** Transfer onion mixture to a large bowl. Add pecans, cornbread, bread cubes, eggs, cranberries, parsley, salt, black pepper, cayenne, and remaining cup stock; mix to combine. Cook stuffing in a turkey or baking dish as directed in Cooking Stuffing (page 289).

## skillet cornbread

MAKES 1 NINE-TO-TEN-INCH ROUND

*The cornbread should be made at least a day before the stuffing.*

¼ cup solid vegetable shortening

2 cups all-purpose flour

2 cups yellow cornmeal

2 tablespoons sugar

1 tablespoon plus 1 teaspoon baking powder

1½ teaspoons salt

2 cups milk

4 large eggs

**1.** Preheat oven to 425°F, with rack in center. Place shortening in a 9-to-10-inch cast-iron or other ovenproof skillet. Heat in oven.

**2.** In a medium bowl, whisk together flour, cornmeal, sugar, baking powder, and salt; set aside. In another bowl, whisk together milk and eggs. Pour milk mixture into flour mixture; stir just until combined. Do not overmix; batter should be lumpy.

**3.** Carefully slide out oven rack. Pour batter into hot skillet. Cook until cornbread is golden brown and firm to the touch, about 25 minutes. Let stand overnight, uncovered.

## couscous dressing

SERVES 4

1½ cups chicken stock, preferably homemade (page 179), or low-sodium canned chicken broth
1 tablespoon olive oil
6 scallions, chopped
1 garlic clove, minced
1 cup uncooked couscous
1 tablespoon curry powder
¼ teaspoon ground turmeric
¼ teaspoon cayenne pepper
1 teaspoon coarse salt

In a medium saucepan, bring chicken stock just to a boil; remove from heat, and keep covered. Heat oil in a large skillet. Add scallions and garlic; cook, stirring occasionally, until soft, about 3 minutes. Add couscous, and stir to combine. Stir in spices and salt; cook 1 to 2 minutes more. Add hot chicken stock; remove from heat, and let stand until couscous is tender and has absorbed all liquid, 10 to 15 minutes. Serve hot.

## oyster brioche stuffing

photograph on page 59

SERVES 6 TO 8

12 slices (¾ inch thick) brioche, crusts removed
4 tablespoons unsalted butter
1 onion, cut into ½-inch dice
2 stalks celery, cut into ¼-inch dice
1 garlic clove, minced
1 teaspoon coarse salt
½ teaspoon freshly ground black pepper
⅛ teaspoon freshly grated nutmeg
⅛ teaspoon cayenne pepper
2 dozen shucked oysters, ⅓ cup of liquor reserved
2 tablespoons Cognac (optional)
½ cup heavy cream
1½ cups fresh flat-leaf parsley, chopped

**1.** Preheat oven to 350°F. Cut brioche into ¾-inch cubes. Spread on a rimmed baking sheet, and toast until dry and golden, about 10 minutes. Let cool.

**2.** Melt butter in a medium skillet over medium heat. Add onion, celery, garlic, salt, and black pepper. Cook, stirring occasionally, until onion is soft, about 3 minutes. Add nutmeg, cayenne, oyster liquor, and Cognac, if using; cook until liquid has evaporated, about 1 minute. Add oysters and cream; cook 30 seconds more. Remove from heat.

**3.** In a large bowl, toss together brioche, oyster mixture, and parsley. Cook stuffing in a turkey or baking dish as directed in Cooking Stuffing (page 289).

## sausage stuffing

SERVES 12 TO 14, WITH LEFTOVERS

½  cup (1 stick) unsalted butter

10  garlic cloves, minced

4  large onions, coarsely chopped

8  stalks celery, coarsely chopped

4  tart apples, cored and cut
   into ½-inch chunks
   Coarse salt and freshly ground pepper
   Poultry seasoning, such as Bell's

2  loaves sourdough bread,
   cut into ¾-inch cubes

1  pound Italian sausage, casings removed

4  large eggs, lightly beaten

**1.** Melt butter in a Dutch oven or stockpot over low heat. Add garlic and onions; cook, stirring occasionally, until slightly softened, about 5 minutes. Add celery, and cook until soft, stirring frequently, 10 to 15 minutes. Add apples, and cook until soft, about 5 minutes more. Season with salt, pepper, and poultry seasoning. Add bread, and toss well to coat. Set aside.

**2.** Form sausage into 1-inch balls. In a medium sauté pan over medium heat, brown sausage balls until no trace of pink remains. Remove with a slotted spoon, and add to stuffing. Mix well, and let cool slightly. Thoroughly mix in eggs; let cool completely. Cook stuffing in a turkey or baking dish as directed in Cooking Stuffing (page 289).

## wild-rice and sausage dressing

SERVES 10 TO 12

¼  cup slivered almonds
   Unsalted butter, for casserole

3  tablespoons olive oil

1  onion, finely chopped

2  stalks celery, cut into ½-inch dice

3  large garlic cloves, minced

1  tablespoon finely chopped fresh rosemary

1  tablespoon finely chopped fresh sage
   Coarse salt and freshly ground pepper

2  tablespoons finely chopped
   fresh flat-leaf parsley

4  ounces sweet Italian sausage,
   casings removed

1  Granny Smith apple, peeled, cored,
   and cut into ½-inch dice

¼  cup Calvados or dry white wine

3  cups cooked wild rice

2  cups cooked white rice

10  dried apricots, quartered

6  dried pitted prunes, halved

**1.** Preheat oven to 375°F. Spread almonds on a rimmed baking sheet, and toast in oven until golden, 5 to 7 minutes. Set aside to cool.

**2.** Raise oven heat to 425°F. Generously butter a 2½-quart casserole or baking dish. Heat 2 tablespoons oil in a large sauté pan over medium heat. Add onion, celery, and garlic; cook, stirring occasionally, until onion is soft, about 7 minutes.

**3.** Raise heat to high, and add rosemary and sage; season with salt and pepper. Continue cooking until onion is golden, 2 to 3 minutes. Remove pan from heat; stir in parsley. Transfer mixture to a large bowl; return pan to heat.

**4.** Crumble sausage, separating meat. Add ½ tablespoon oil to pan. Add sausage, and cook, stirring and breaking up meat, until well browned, about

3 minutes. Transfer sausage to bowl with reserved vegetables. Return pan to heat.

**5.** Add remaining ½ tablespoon oil to pan. Add apple; cook, stirring occasionally, until browned, 2 to 3 minutes. Add Calvados; deglaze pan, scraping up any browned bits on bottom with a wooden spoon. Continue cooking until most of the liquid has evaporated, about 1 minute more.

**6.** Transfer apple mixture to bowl with sausage and vegetables. Add rice, apricots, prunes, and toasted almonds; season with salt and pepper.

**7.** Transfer dressing to prepared casserole; cover with aluminum foil. Bake until heated through, about 20 minutes. Serve hot.

## wild-rice stuffing
### SERVES 6 TO 8

4   *tablespoons unsalted butter*

1   *onion, finely chopped*

2   *garlic cloves, minced*

2   *oranges, peeled and coarsely chopped*

½   *cup coarsely chopped dried apricots*

½   *cup coarsely chopped dried apples*

½   *cup dried currants*

1   *tablespoon finely chopped fresh sage*

1   *tablespoon finely chopped fresh chervil*

3   *cups cooked wild rice*
    *Coarse salt and freshly ground pepper*

Melt butter in a large skillet. Add onion and garlic; cook, stirring occasionally, until soft, about 5 minutes. Add oranges, dried fruit, and herbs; cook until heated through. Add cooked rice, and season with salt and pepper. Serve hot.

## lemon-saffron millet pilaf
### SERVES 8 TO 10

*We served this pilaf with grilled shrimp, but it would be good with any roasted or grilled fish.*

2   *teaspoons olive oil*

2   *shallots, minced*

2   *garlic cloves, minced*

3   *carrots, finely chopped*

2   *stalks celery, finely chopped*
    *Coarse salt and freshly ground pepper*

¼   *teaspoon saffron threads, crumbled*

1½  *cups millet*

3   *tablespoons freshly squeezed lemon juice (about 1 lemon)*

1   *tablespoon finely chopped lemon zest, plus more for garnish*

¾   *cup finely chopped fresh flat-leaf parsley*

**1.** Heat oil in a medium saucepan over medium heat. Add shallots, garlic, carrots, and celery; season with salt and pepper. Cook, stirring occasionally, until vegetables are beginning to brown, about 5 minutes. Add saffron and millet, and cook, stirring, 1 minute more.

**2.** Add 3 cups water, lemon juice, and lemon zest to saucepan. Bring to a boil; cover, reduce heat to low, and cook until millet has absorbed all the liquid, about 25 minutes. Turn off heat. Let stand, covered, until millet is tender, about 10 minutes.

**3.** Stir in parsley with a fork, and fluff pilaf. Serve hot, garnished with lemon zest.

## pomegranate pilaf

*photograph on page 48*

SERVES 4 TO 6

- 2 tablespoons unsalted butter
- 1 small red onion, cut into ¼-inch dice
- 1 cup basmati or jasmine rice
- 1½ cups chicken stock, preferably homemade (page 179), or low-sodium canned chicken broth
- ½ cup chopped dried apricots
- ½ cup chopped unsalted pistachios or almonds
- ½ cup pomegranate seeds (about ½ pomegranate)
- 1 tablespoon chopped fresh thyme leaves
  Coarse salt and freshly ground pepper

**1.** Melt butter in a medium saucepan over medium-low heat. Add onion; cook, stirring occasionally, until softened, about 4 minutes. Add rice; cook, stirring to coat, 1 minute. Add chicken stock; bring to a boil. Cover, and reduce heat to low. Cook until rice has absorbed all liquid, 15 to 20 minutes.

**2.** Remove pan from heat, and fluff with a fork. Stir in apricots, nuts, pomegranate seeds, and thyme. Season with salt and pepper; serve hot.

## spiced pilaf

SERVES 6

- 2 teaspoons canola oil
- 1 small red onion, cut into ¼-inch dice
- 2 small carrots, cut into ¼-inch dice
- 1 stalk celery, cut into ¼-inch slices
- ¼ cup dry white wine
- 1½ cups brown rice
- ½ teaspoon paprika
- ¼ teaspoon ground turmeric
- ½ teaspoon ground cumin
  Coarse salt and freshly ground pepper

**1.** Heat oil in a medium skillet over medium heat. Add onion, carrots, and celery; cook, stirring occasionally, until soft, 3 to 4 minutes. Add wine, and cook until most of the liquid has evaporated, about 2 minutes. Transfer vegetables to a medium bowl, and set aside to cool.

**2.** Bring a medium saucepan of water to a boil. Stir in rice; cook, uncovered, stirring frequently, until tender, 25 to 30 minutes. Drain, and add to bowl of vegetables. Stir in paprika, turmeric, and cumin; season with salt and pepper. Serve hot.

## quick polenta with bacon and sage

### SERVES 4

*Water or stock can be substituted for part or all of the milk. The more milk you use, the creamier the polenta will be.*

- 2 ounces thickly sliced bacon, cut crosswise into ½-inch-thick pieces
- 1 teaspoon finely chopped fresh sage leaves, plus more whole leaves for garnish
- 4 cups milk
- ¾ cup plus 2 tablespoons quick-cooking polenta
- 3 tablespoons unsalted butter
  Coarse salt and freshly ground pepper
- 2 tablespoons extra-virgin olive oil

**1.** Heat a medium saucepan over low heat. Add bacon; cook, stirring frequently, until crisp and golden, about 8 minutes. Using a slotted spoon, transfer bacon to a paper-towel–lined plate. Set aside. Add chopped sage to saucepan; cook, stirring constantly, until fragrant, about 30 seconds. Add milk; bring to a boil.

**2.** Whisking constantly, add polenta in a slow, steady stream. Reduce heat to medium-low; cook, stirring constantly with a wooden spoon, until polenta has thickened, about 6 minutes. Whisk in butter, and season with salt and pepper. Transfer mixture to a serving bowl, and crumble reserved bacon on top. Heat oil in a small sauté pan over medium heat. Add whole sage leaves, and fry until crisp, about 30 seconds. Scatter leaves over polenta, and serve immediately.

## polenta wedges

*photograph on page 60*

### SERVES 6

- 3 cups skim milk
- 3 tablespoons finely chopped fresh chives
- 2 garlic cloves, minced
  Coarse salt
- ¼ teaspoon paprika
- ¾ cup quick-cooking polenta
- 2 ounces Parmesan cheese, finely grated
- 1 tablespoon unsalted butter, melted, plus more for brushing

**1.** Combine milk, chives, garlic, salt, and paprika in a medium saucepan, and bring to a boil over high heat. Whisking constantly, add polenta in a slow, steady stream. Reduce heat to medium-low; cook, stirring occasionally with a wooden spoon, until polenta has thickened, about 6 minutes. Add Parmesan and butter; stir until combined.

**2.** Pour polenta into an 8½-inch springform pan; let stand at room temperature until completely set, about 45 minutes.

**3.** Heat broiler. Remove outer ring from springform pan. Cut polenta into six wedges. Brush top with melted butter. Broil wedges until golden on top and heated through, about 8 minutes. Serve.

## soft polenta

SERVES 4

*We served the polenta with Braised Lamb Shanks with Tomato and Fennel (page 197), but it is equally delicious with chicken, veal, or pork.*

- 1 teaspoon coarse salt
- 1 cup polenta (not quick-cooking)
- 2 tablespoons unsalted butter

Bring 4 cups water to a boil in a medium saucepan; add salt. Stirring constantly with a wooden spoon, slowly add polenta, letting grains pass through your fingers in a steady stream. Reduce heat; simmer, stirring constantly, until polenta is tender but not mushy, 30 to 35 minutes. Remove from heat; stir in butter. Serve immediately.

## spoon bread with chorizo

SERVES 8

*Our version of the traditional cornmeal pudding includes onion and sausage, but the creamy texture of this side dish recalls its Southern roots. To reheat, cover with foil and place in a 350-degree oven until heated through, fifteen to twenty minutes.*

- 3 tablespoons unsalted butter, plus more for baking dish
- 1 onion, cut into ½-inch dice
- 5 ounces chorizo, cut into ½-inch dice
- 1 cup white cornmeal
- 1½ cups fresh or frozen corn
- 1½ teaspoons coarse salt
- 5 large eggs
- 1½ cups heavy cream

**1.** Preheat oven to 350°F. Melt 2 tablespoons butter in a medium skillet over medium heat. Add onion; cook, stirring occasionally, until softened, about 4 minutes. Add chorizo; cook, stirring, until lightly browned, about 4 minutes more. Using a slotted spoon, transfer mixture to a medium bowl. Set aside to cool.

**2.** Bring 2 cups water to a boil in a small saucepan. Stirring constantly, add cornmeal in a slow, steady stream. Reduce heat to medium-low; cook until mixture has thickened, about 2 minutes. Transfer to bowl with sausage mixture. Stir in corn, salt, and remaining tablespoon butter.

**3.** In a separate bowl, whisk together eggs and cream; stir mixture into sausage mixture until well incorporated. Pour into a buttered 2-quart soufflé dish or deep-dish pie plate. Bake spoon bread until set and top is golden brown, about 1 hour. Serve hot or at room temperature.

## risotto with farro

SERVES 4

*Cooked farro retains a slightly chewy texture that makes this an especially hearty risotto.*

- 6 cups chicken stock, preferably homemade (page 179), or low-sodium canned chicken broth
- 2 tablespoons olive oil
- 2 large shallots, finely chopped
- 2¼ cups farro
- ⅔ cup dry white wine
- 4 ounces fontina cheese, finely grated
  Coarse salt and freshly ground pepper
- ½ head escarole (about 5 ounces), sliced ½ inch thick
- 2 ounces (½ cup) toasted walnuts, coarsely chopped

**1.** Place chicken stock and 4 cups water in a medium saucepan, and bring to a gentle simmer.

**2.** In a large saucepan, heat oil over medium heat. Add shallots; cook, stirring, until translucent, about 5 minutes. Add farro, and cook, stirring, until coated with oil and beginning to darken, about 5 minutes. Add wine, and cook until almost completely evaporated.

**3.** Add enough chicken-stock mixture to just cover farro mixture; stir constantly until liquid is almost absorbed. Continue adding simmering stock, ½ cup at a time, stirring constantly until it is absorbed before adding more, about 1 hour. Farro should be tender but slightly firm in center and suspended in liquid the consistency of heavy cream.

**4.** Stir cheese into farro mixture; season with salt and pepper. Add escarole, and cook until just wilted, about 1 minute. Serve immediately, sprinkled with walnuts.

## french lentil and swiss chard risotto
### SERVES 6

1   *dried bay leaf*
6   *sprigs thyme, plus 2 teaspoons leaves*
⅓   *cup French green lentils,
     picked over and rinsed*
1   *large bunch Swiss chard
     (about 1¼ pounds), washed well*
4   *cups chicken stock, preferably
     homemade (page 179), or low-sodium
     canned chicken broth*
1   *tablespoon olive oil*
2   *large leeks (about ¾ pound), white and
     pale-green parts only, halved lengthwise,
     thinly sliced crosswise, and washed well*
1   *small onion, finely chopped*
2   *garlic cloves, minced*
1¼  *cups Arborio rice*
½   *cup dry white wine
     Coarse salt and freshly ground pepper*
¼   *cup freshly grated Parmesan cheese*
⅓   *cup finely shredded radicchio, for garnish*

**1.** In a medium saucepan, combine 6 cups water, bay leaf, and thyme sprigs; bring to a boil. Simmer 5 minutes. Add lentils, reduce heat to low, and simmer until tender, 15 to 20 minutes. Drain lentils; set aside. Discard bay leaf and thyme sprigs.

**2.** Meanwhile, separate Swiss chard leaves from stalks. Slice leaves into very thin 2-inch-long strips, and cut smaller stems into ¼-inch pieces. Discard larger stems. Cook Swiss chard in a dry wok or large skillet over high heat, tossing constantly until just wilted, about 3 minutes. Set chard aside in a colander.

**3.** In a medium saucepan, bring stock to a boil; reduce heat, and keep at a gentle simmer.

**4.** Heat oil in a heavy 4-quart saucepan over medium heat; add leeks, onion, and garlic; cook, stirring frequently, until vegetables are soft but not browned, about 6 minutes. Add rice and thyme leaves; cook, stirring constantly, until edges of rice are translucent, about 3 minutes. Add wine, and cook, stirring constantly, until almost all wine is absorbed, about 30 seconds.

**5.** Raise heat to medium-high, and season with salt and pepper. Add ½ cup simmering stock; cook, stirring constantly, until nearly all stock is absorbed. Continue adding simmering stock ½ cup at a time, stirring constantly until it is absorbed before adding more, 15 to 20 minutes. Rice should be tender but still firm in the center and suspended in liquid the consistency of heavy cream.

**6.** Remove pan from heat, and stir in lentils, Swiss chard, and Parmesan. Season with salt and pepper. Divide risotto among six shallow bowls; garnish with shredded radicchio. Serve immediately.

## *risotto with three mushrooms*

photograph on page 57

SERVES 4

*Any wild mushroom or combination of mushrooms will give this risotto a rich, intense flavor.*

- 4 ounces each chanterelle, shiitake, and black trumpet mushrooms
- ½ cup (1 stick) unsalted butter
  Coarse salt and freshly ground pepper
- 6 to 8 cups chicken stock, preferably homemade (page 179), or low-sodium canned chicken broth
- 3 tablespoons olive oil
- 2 shallots, finely chopped
- 1 cup Arborio rice
- ½ cup dry white wine
- 1 cup freshly grated Parmesan cheese, plus more for garnish
  Fresh chervil, for garnish

**1.** Gently clean mushrooms with a mushroom brush or paper towel. Trim tough stems, and discard. Cut mushrooms into ½-inch pieces.

**2.** Melt 2 tablespoons butter in a large skillet over medium-high heat. Add chanterelles, and season with salt and pepper. Cook, stirring occasionally, until softened, about 3 minutes. Transfer to a bowl. In the same skillet, melt another 2 tablespoons butter. Add remaining mushrooms, and season with salt and pepper. Cook, stirring occasionally, until softened, about 2 minutes. Transfer mushrooms to bowl with chanterelles.

**3.** In a medium saucepan, bring stock to a boil; reduce heat, and keep at a gentle simmer.

**4.** Heat oil in a large, heavy-bottom saucepan over medium heat. Add shallots, and cook, stirring occasionally, until translucent, about 3 minutes. Add rice, and cook, stirring constantly, until edges are translucent, about 3 minutes. Add wine, and cook, stirring constantly, until almost all wine is absorbed, about 30 seconds.

**5.** Raise heat to medium-high, and season with salt and pepper. Add ½ cup simmering stock; cook, stirring constantly, until nearly all stock is absorbed. Continue adding simmering stock, ½ cup at a time, stirring constantly until it is absorbed before adding more, 15 to 20 minutes. Rice should be tender but still firm in the center and suspended in liquid that is the consistency of heavy cream.

**6.** Remove pan from heat. Stir in remaining 4 tablespoons butter, the reserved mushrooms, and 1 cup Parmesan. Season with salt and pepper. Divide risotto among four shallow bowls. Grate or shave additional Parmesan over risotto, and sprinkle with chervil. Serve immediately.

## *beetroot risotto*

SERVES 6

*If you cannot find beets with tops, use red or green Swiss chard in place of beet greens.*

- 3 small beets
- 2 small onions, halved (unpeeled)
- 4 garlic cloves (unpeeled)
- 3 sprigs thyme
- 4½ cups chicken stock, preferably homemade (page 179), or low-sodium canned chicken broth
- 1 tablespoon olive oil
- 2 large leeks (about ¾ pound), white and pale-green parts only, halved lengthwise, thinly sliced crosswise, and washed well
- 1¼ cups Arborio rice
- ½ cup dry red wine
  Coarse salt and freshly ground pepper
- ¼ cup freshly grated Parmesan cheese
- 1 teaspoon minced fresh tarragon
- ½ teaspoon balsamic vinegar

**1.** Preheat oven to 375°F. Remove greens from beets, leaving 1 inch of stem intact. Set greens aside. Wrap beets, onions, garlic, and thyme in a double layer of aluminum foil, sealing edges tightly. Roast on a baking sheet 1½ hours. Remove packet from oven, and open to let contents cool.

**2.** Meanwhile, trim tough stems from beet greens, and discard. Wash leaves, and slice them into very thin 2-inch-long strips. Cook beet greens in a dry wok or large skillet over high heat, tossing constantly until just wilted, 1 to 2 minutes. Set greens aside in a colander.

**3.** Using a paper towel, remove skins from beets; cut into ¼-inch dice. (You will have about 1 cup diced beets.) Set aside. Discard onion peels, and finely chop onions. Squeeze garlic cloves from skins; discard skins and thyme sprigs. Set onions and garlic aside.

**4.** In a medium saucepan, bring stock to a boil; reduce heat, and keep at a gentle simmer.

**5.** Heat oil in a heavy 4-quart saucepan over medium heat. Add leeks; cook, stirring frequently, until soft but not browned, about 6 minutes. Stir in reserved onions and garlic. Add rice; cook, stirring constantly, until edges are translucent, about 3 minutes. Add wine; cook, stirring, until almost all wine is absorbed, about 30 seconds.

**6.** Raise heat to medium-high; season with salt and pepper. Add ½ cup simmering stock; cook, stirring constantly, until nearly all stock is absorbed. Continue adding simmering stock, ½ cup at a time, stirring constantly until it is absorbed before adding more, 15 to 20 minutes. With the last addition of stock, stir in diced beets. Rice should be tender but still firm in the center and suspended in liquid that is the consistency of heavy cream.

**7.** Remove pan from heat, and stir in reserved beet greens, Parmesan, tarragon, and vinegar; season with salt and pepper. Divide risotto among six shallow bowls. Serve immediately.

## *wheat berries with vegetables*
### SERVES 8 TO 10

1  cup wheat berries
1  small head broccoli (about 15 ounces), trimmed and cut into florets
2  teaspoons olive oil
1  yellow onion, coarsely chopped
2  garlic cloves, minced
1  can (28 ounces) tomatoes, drained and chopped
1  large yellow squash, quartered lengthwise and cut into ¼-inch slices
½  small eggplant, cut into ½-inch pieces
¼  cup chopped fresh oregano
   Coarse salt and freshly ground pepper

**1.** Place wheat berries in a small stockpot; add 1 quart water. Cover, and bring to a boil; reduce heat, and simmer until tender, at least 40 minutes. Drain in a colander, and set aside.

**2.** Prepare a large ice bath; set aside. Bring a medium pot of water to a boil. Add broccoli, and blanch until bright green, 1 to 2 minutes. Transfer to ice bath to stop cooking. Drain, and set aside.

**3.** Heat oil in a large skillet over medium-low heat. Add onion and garlic; cook, stirring frequently, until translucent, about 10 minutes. Raise heat to medium; add tomatoes, yellow squash, eggplant, and oregano. Season with salt and pepper. Cook, stirring occasionally, until vegetables are softened, about 15 minutes. Add reserved broccoli and wheat berries; continue cooking until heated through, about 3 minutes more. Serve.

## wild-rice and fruit salad

*photograph on page 59*

SERVES 8

*This rice dish can be made a day ahead and refrigerated, covered with plastic wrap. Before serving, let it come to room temperature, and garnish with almonds.*

- 2 cups wild rice
- 1 tablespoon unsalted butter
- 1 red apple, cored and cut into ¼-inch dice
  Pinch of ground cloves
- 3 tablespoons extra-virgin olive oil
- 1 small red onion, cut into ¼-inch dice
- 1 stalk celery, cut into ¼-inch dice
- 1 small carrot, cut into ¼-inch dice
- 2 garlic cloves, minced
- ¼ cup dried currants
  Coarse salt and freshly ground pepper
- 3 tablespoons balsamic vinegar
- 2 tablespoons cider vinegar
- 1 tablespoon freshly squeezed lemon juice
- 2 ounces (½ cup) slivered almonds, toasted

**1.** Bring a medium saucepan of water to a boil over high heat. Stir in rice, and reduce heat to medium-low. Cook, stirring frequently, until rice is tender and most of the kernels have burst, about 55 minutes. Drain rice; rinse under cold water, and set aside in a large bowl.

**2.** Melt butter in a medium skillet. Add apple and cloves; cook, stirring occasionally, until apples are golden, about 3 minutes. Transfer to bowl with rice. In same skillet, heat 1 tablespoon oil over medium heat. Add onion, celery, carrot, and garlic; cook until onion is just beginning to brown, about 6 minutes. Transfer to bowl with rice mixture; add currants. Season with salt and pepper.

**3.** Return skillet to heat; add vinegars, lemon juice, and 2 tablespoons water. Cook, whisking constantly, until mixture has reduced by half, about

2 minutes. Whisk in remaining 2 tablespoons oil. Drizzle dressing over salad, and toss to combine. Serve warm or at room temperature, garnished with toasted almonds.

## wild-rice cakes

SERVES 8

- 8 thin slices white bread, trimmed of crusts
- 1 cup wild rice
  Coarse salt
- 4 tablespoons canola oil
- 2 garlic cloves, minced
- 1 carrot, cut into ¼-inch dice (about ⅓ cup)
- 1 stalk celery, cut into ¼-inch dice (about ⅓ cup)
- ½ yellow bell pepper, ribs and seeds removed, cut into ¼-inch dice (about ⅓ cup)
- 2 large eggs, lightly beaten
  Freshly ground pepper

**1.** Preheat oven to 250°F. Place bread on a baking sheet. Toast in oven until dry, about 15 minutes. Transfer to a wire rack to cool. Chop bread very finely (you should have about 1¼ cups); set aside.

**2.** Rinse rice under cold water until water runs clear. In a medium saucepan, bring 4 cups water to a boil over high heat; add salt. Stir in rice, and reduce heat to medium-low. Cook, stirring frequently, until most of the kernels have burst, about 55 minutes. Drain; rinse under cold water, and set aside in a large bowl.

**3.** Heat 2 tablespoons oil in a nonstick sauté pan over medium heat. Add garlic; cook, stirring, until fragrant, about 1 minute. Add carrot, celery, and pepper; cook, stirring, until softened, about 5 minutes. Transfer to bowl with rice. Add eggs; stir to combine. Gently fold in breadcrumbs. Season with salt and pepper. Cover; refrigerate until breadcrumbs have absorbed all liquid, about 1 hour.

**4.** Line a baking sheet with a Silpat baking mat or parchment paper. Using a 2-ounce ice-cream scoop, pack rice mixture into a ball; place on baking sheet. Gently press down with your damp palm to form a cake. Repeat with remaining rice.

**5.** Heat remaining 2 tablespoons canola oil in a medium nonstick sauté pan over medium heat. Using a spatula, transfer 4 rice cakes to pan. Cook until lightly browned and set around edges, about 5 minutes. Gently flip cakes; cook 5 minutes more. Repeat with remaining cakes. Serve hot.

---

CHUTNEYS, PICKLES, AND PRESERVES

---

## cranberry chutney

### MAKES 6 HALF-PINT JARS

⅔  cup packed light-brown sugar

½  cup cider vinegar

1  teaspoon coarse salt

½  teaspoon ground cardamom

1  cup candied orange peel,
     cut into ¼-inch dice

2  stalks celery, finely diced

1  red onion, finely diced

2  apples, peeled, cored, and cut
     into ¼-inch dice

5  cups fresh or frozen cranberries

**1.** Combine sugar, vinegar, salt, cardamom, orange peel, celery, onion, apples, and 2 cups water in a shallow 6-quart saucepan. Bring to a boil. Reduce heat to a simmer; cook until apples are tender and most liquid has been absorbed, 30 to 40 minutes.

**2.** Stir cranberries into mixture; cook until they begin to pop, 10 to 15 minutes. Remove from heat. Immediately transfer chutney to jars as directed in Canning Tips (right). Alternatively, let cool completely; store in an airtight container in the refrigerator, up to 1 month.

## CANNING TIPS

*Follow these instructions for safe canning:*

*1. Discard any jars that have chips or cracks. Wash jars, lids, and screw bands in hot, soapy water; rinse well. Place jars upright on a wire rack set in a large pot, leaving at least one inch between jars. Fill pot with hot water until jars are submerged, and bring to a boil. Continue boiling fifteen minutes. Turn off heat, leaving jars in water. Sterilize lids according to manufacturer's instructions; never reuse lids.*

*2. Using a jar lifter and stainless-steel tongs, lift jars from pot, emptying water back into pot; place jars on clean kitchen towels. Place a stainless-steel canning funnel in mouth of a jar; fill with hot chutney or preserves to a quarter inch from rim. Remove funnel; run a small rubber spatula around edge to release excess air bubbles. Clean rim and threads of jar with a towel dipped in hot water. Repeat with other jars. Lift prepared lids with tongs; place on rims of jars. Screw on bands until secure but not too tight, or air in jars will not be able to escape and jars will not properly seal.*

*3. After each jar is filled, place it back into pot of water. When all jars have been returned to pot, cover and bring to a full boil. Process jars in steadily but gently boiling water twenty to forty-five minutes (longer times will be needed at altitudes higher than one thousand feet).*

*4. Remove jars from water bath with jar lifter, and place them on a rack to cool twenty-four hours. As chutneys and preserves cool, a vacuum will form inside jars, sealing them. Check seals by pressing center of lids with your finger. They should not spring back; if a lid springs up when your finger is released, the jar is not sealed. Unsealed jars should be refrigerated up to one month. Store sealed jars in a cool, dry, dark place up to one year.*

## cranberry-pear chutney

MAKES 6 HALF-PINT JARS

3 ripe but firm pears, peeled, cored, and cut into ½-inch dice

1 tablespoon grated lemon zest plus 1 tablespoon freshly squeezed lemon juice

3 cups fresh or frozen cranberries

1 cup sugar

½ cup freshly squeezed orange juice

¼ cup golden raisins

5 dried pitted dates, coarsely chopped (¼ cup)

**1.** Place pears in a medium bowl. Toss with lemon zest and juice. Set aside.

**2.** Combine cranberries and sugar in a large saucepan; cook over medium-low heat until berries pop and release juices, about 8 minutes. Add orange juice, raisins, and dates. Raise heat to medium-high. Cook, stirring occasionally, until mixture begins to bubble. Add pears; cook, stirring, until mixture thickens and pears turn red and are cooked through, about 10 minutes. Remove from heat.

**3.** Immediately transfer chutney to jars as directed in Canning Tips (page 303). Alternatively, let cool completely; store in an airtight container in the refrigerator, up to 1 month.

## dried-cherry, pearl-onion, and pear chutney

MAKES 6 HALF-PINT JARS

4 Bartlett pears, peeled, cored, and cut into ¼-inch dice

Juice of 2 lemons

2½ cups dried cherries

1 pound pearl onions, trimmed, peeled, and halved lengthwise

1½ cups red-wine vinegar

1 cup sugar

1 teaspoon coarse salt

¼ teaspoon ground cloves

**1.** In a large bowl, toss pears with lemon juice. Place cherries, onions, half the pears, the vinegar, sugar, salt, cloves, and 2 cups water in a shallow, 6-quart saucepan. Bring to a boil over high heat. Reduce heat to medium-low, and simmer until fruit is tender, about 45 minutes.

**2.** Raise heat to high; cook until liquid has been absorbed, about 10 minutes. Stir in remaining pears; reduce heat to low. Cook until pears are heated through, about 5 minutes. Remove from heat.

**3.** Immediately transfer chutney to jars as directed in Canning Tips (page 303). Alternatively, let cool completely; store in an airtight container in the refrigerator, up to 1 month.

## peppery fig chutney
MAKES 6 HALF-PINT JARS

*We used Calimyrna figs for this chutney, but the Black Mission variety can also be used.*

- 1 pound dried figs, trimmed and cut into eighths
- 2 cups coarsely chopped shallots
- 2 cups dry red wine
- 1 cup red-wine vinegar
- ¾ cup sugar
- 6 sprigs thyme, tied in a bundle with kitchen twine
- 2 teaspoons whole black peppercorns, crushed
- 1 teaspoon coarse salt
- 2 pounds very ripe fresh figs, trimmed and cut into ½-inch chunks

**1.** Place dried figs, shallots, wine, red-wine vinegar, sugar, thyme, crushed peppercorns, and salt in a medium saucepan. Bring to a boil over medium-high heat. Reduce heat to medium-low; simmer, stirring occasionally, until figs are soft and liquid has thickened, about 45 minutes.

**2.** Remove and discard thyme bundle. Stir in fresh figs. Cook, stirring frequently, until figs break down, 10 to 15 minutes. Remove from heat.

**3.** Immediately transfer chutney to jars as directed in Canning Tips (page 303). Alternatively, let cool completely; store in an airtight container in the refrigerator, up to 1 month.

## prune and apple chutney
MAKES 6 HALF-PINT JARS

- 1 large or 2 small Spanish onions (about 1 pound), cut into ¼-inch-thick wedges
- ½ cup raisins
- 12 pitted prunes, cut lengthwise into strips
- 1½ tablespoons minced fresh ginger
- 1 cup white vinegar
- ⅓ cup sugar
- ¾ teaspoon ground cumin
- ¾ teaspoon coarse salt
- 6 tart apples (2½ pounds), peeled, cored, and cut into 1-inch cubes

**1.** Place onion, raisins, prunes, ginger, vinegar, sugar, cumin, salt, and 2 cups water in a shallow, 6-quart saucepan. Bring to a boil over medium-high heat. Reduce heat to medium-low; simmer, stirring occasionally, until most of the liquid has been absorbed, about 40 minutes.

**2.** Add apples and 1½ cups water to saucepan. Cook, stirring frequently, until apples are soft and translucent and all liquid has been absorbed, about 50 minutes. Remove from heat.

**3.** Immediately transfer chutney to jars as directed in Canning Tips (page 303). Alternatively, let cool completely; store in an airtight container in the refrigerator, up to 1 month.

## spicy mango chutney
MAKES 6 HALF-PINT JARS

*Slightly underripe mangoes work best.*

15 whole cloves

15 whole pink peppercorns

⅔ cup white vinegar

1 large red onion, finely diced (2 cups)

2 cups sugar

1½ teaspoons coarse salt

1 teaspoon crushed red-pepper flakes

3 tablespoons freshly grated lime zest,
plus ⅔ cup freshly squeezed lime juice
(about 4 limes)

2 tablespoons grated fresh ginger

7 mangoes (7½ pounds), peeled,
pitted, and cut into ½-inch chunks

1. Place cloves and peppercorns in the center of a 4-inch square of cheesecloth; secure with kitchen twine to form a bundle. Place bundle in a shallow, 6-quart saucepan. Add vinegar, onion, sugar, salt, and crushed red pepper. Bring to a boil over medium-high heat. Reduce heat to medium-low, and simmer 15 minutes.

2. Add lime zest and juice, ginger, and mangoes; cook, stirring frequently, until mangoes begin to soften and liquid has thickened, about 40 minutes. Remove from heat.

3. Immediately transfer chutney to jars as directed in Canning Tips (page 303). Alternatively, let cool completely; store in an airtight container in the refrigerator, up to 1 month.

## pear chutney
MAKES 1¾ CUPS

*This chutney makes a nice accompaniment to roasted pork or turkey.*

1½ tablespoons unsalted butter

2 large shallots, peeled and thinly sliced

2 teaspoons sugar

2 ripe but firm Bartlett pears (about 1 pound),
peeled and cut into ¼-inch dice

1 teaspoon five-spice powder
Coarse salt and freshly ground pepper

1½ tablespoons balsamic vinegar

1. Melt butter in a large skillet over medium heat. Add shallots; cook, stirring occasionally, until golden, about 8 minutes. Sprinkle with sugar; cook, stirring frequently, until sugar has caramelized slightly, about 3 minutes.

2. Add pears and five-spice powder to shallot mixture; season with salt and pepper. Raise heat to medium-high; cook until pears have softened, about 5 minutes. Add vinegar; cook, tossing until absorbed, about 4 minutes. Serve warm.

## spiced oranges
MAKES 2 QUARTS

9  *Valencia or blood oranges, scrubbed and sliced ¼ inch thick*
4  *cups sugar*
2  *cups white-wine vinegar*
2  *whole cinnamon sticks*
15  *whole black peppercorns*
10  *whole cloves*

**1.** Place orange slices in a large, nonreactive saucepan; cover with cold water. Simmer until skins are tender, about 1¼ hours. Using a slotted spoon, transfer to a colander; discard water.

**2.** Combine sugar and vinegar in saucepan over low heat. Bring to a boil, stirring until sugar is dissolved. Reduce heat to a simmer. Add spices, and cook 10 minutes. Add oranges; simmer, covered, until skins are translucent, about 40 minutes. Let cool completely in liquid.

**3.** Immediately layer oranges in sterilized jars (see Canning Tips, page 303). Cover with cooking liquid, and seal. The oranges can be used right away, but the flavor will be improved after 4 to 6 weeks.

## basic pickling recipe
MAKES 3½ QUARTS

*This recipe is sufficient to pickle three cantaloupes, two medium pumpkins, or two pounds of pearl onions. Before pickling, peel the items, and cut into slightly larger than one-inch chunks; pearl onions can be left whole. To peel pearl onions, drop them in boiling water for one minute, and then drain in a colander. When cool enough to handle, slip off the papery skins.*

3  *cups sugar*
2  *cups cider vinegar*
2  *teaspoons whole cloves*
2  *teaspoons whole allspice*
1  *whole cinnamon stick*
1  *half-inch piece fresh ginger, peeled*
1  *lemon, thinly sliced*
   *Fruit or vegetables to be pickled*

**1.** Heat sugar and vinegar in a nonreactive stockpot over medium-high heat, stirring until sugar has dissolved. Add remaining ingredients (including items to be pickled), and bring to a boil. Reduce heat; cover, and simmer 30 minutes. Remove from heat; let stand overnight at room temperature.

**2.** Transfer mixture to jars or airtight containers; store, covered, in the refrigerator up to 2 weeks.

## bread-and-butter pickles
### MAKES 3 QUARTS

*These are the familiar pickles that are a staple at delis. For best results, use only kirby cucumbers to make pickles; they are firmer and have fewer seeds than other types.*

- 3 pounds kirby cucumbers, washed well
- 1½ pounds white onions, thinly sliced
- ½ cup coarse salt
- 3 cups cider vinegar
- 2 cups sugar
- 2½ teaspoons mustard seed
- 1½ teaspoons ground turmeric
- 1 teaspoon ground celery seed

**1.** Cut away any bruises or blemishes from cucumbers; cut cucumbers into ¼-inch slices. Place in a large bowl, and add onions and salt; toss well to combine, and add enough cold water to cover by about 1 inch. Let stand, covered, at room temperature at least 2 hours.

**2.** Transfer mixture to a colander to drain, discarding liquid; rinse cucumbers and onions with cold running water, and drain again. Set aside.

**3.** Combine vinegar, sugar, mustard seed, turmeric, and celery seed in a large saucepan; bring to a boil over high heat. Add cucumbers and onions, and return to a boil. Cook 1 minute.

**4.** Transfer mixture to jars or airtight containers, and store, covered, in the refrigerator up to 2 weeks.

## pickled fennel
### MAKES 3 PINTS

- 3 pounds fennel (about 9 bulbs)
- 1 orange
- 2 cups white vinegar
- 5 tablespoons coarse salt
- 2 tablespoons sugar
- 6 whole star anise

**1.** Wash fennel, and cut away any bruises or bad spots. Trim tops and remove core; slice bulbs into very thin rings. Cut three 1-inch-long strips of peel from the orange; remove any white pith.

**2.** Combine vinegar, salt, sugar, and 1½ cups water in a large pot; bring to a boil.

**3.** Meanwhile, fill three pint jars halfway with fennel rings, dividing evenly. Place one strip of orange peel and 2 star anise on top of fennel. Fill jars with remaining fennel, using the back of a clean spoon to pack it down. Leave ¾ inch of space beneath the rim.

**4.** Pour hot liquid over fennel, covering it by ¼ inch and leaving ½ inch of space beneath the rims. Place lids on jars, and let cool completely. Store in refrigerator up to 5 days.

## pickled green beans
MAKES 2 QUARTS

2   pounds green beans, trimmed
2   cups white-wine vinegar
3   tablespoons coarse salt
1   teaspoon whole black peppercorns
¾   teaspoon cayenne pepper
2   garlic cloves
¼   cup fresh dill

**1.** Bring a large pot of water to a boil over high heat. Add beans, and cook until crisp-tender and bright green, about 5 minutes. Drain beans in a colander. Transfer to a heatproof bowl or storage container; set aside.

**2.** Combine vinegar, salt, peppercorns, cayenne, and 2¼ cups water in a medium saucepan. Bring mixture to a boil over high heat. Add garlic and dill; remove from heat. While still hot, pour vinegar mixture over green beans; let cool completely. Cover tightly; store in refrigerator up to 2 weeks.

## cranberry-fig relish
MAKES ABOUT 2 CUPS

*Frozen orange-juice concentrate can be substituted for the apple for a stronger orange flavor.*

1   orange, cut into eighths (unpeeled)
12  large dried figs (about 8 ounces),
     cut into quarters
12  ounces fresh cranberries
½   cup frozen apple-juice concentrate

**1.** Place orange pieces in a food processor, and process until finely diced, about 30 seconds. Add figs, cranberries, and concentrate; pulse until fruit is coarsely chopped, 5 to 6 times.

**2.** Transfer mixture to a bowl; cover, and chill in refrigerator overnight. Before serving, let stand at room temperature about 2 hours.

## cranberry relish two ways
MAKES 1 QUART

*This recipe is courtesy of Sara Foster, owner of Foster's Market in Durham, North Carolina. She likes to serve two versions of relish during the holidays, one traditional, the other more spicy. Be sure to remove all the white pith from the orange segments, as it is quite bitter.*

1   pound fresh cranberries
1   cup sugar
½   cup freshly squeezed orange juice
     Grated zest of 1 orange
4   oranges, peeled and segmented
1   cup seven-pepper jelly
1   tablespoon chopped fresh herbs,
     such as rosemary and thyme

**1.** In a medium saucepan, bring 1 cup water to a simmer over medium heat. Add cranberries, sugar, and orange juice and zest. Cook, stirring frequently, until all the sugar is dissolved and cranberries begin to pop, about 15 minutes.

**2.** Divide cranberry mixture evenly between two small bowls. Add orange segments to one bowl and jelly and herbs to the other; stir both to combine. Serve, or store in separate airtight containers in the refrigerator up to 1 week.

## chunky apple-cranberry sauce

*photograph on page 56*

MAKES ABOUT 3 CUPS

- 1 onion, cut into ½-inch-thick wedges
- ⅔ cup granulated sugar, or more as desired
- ½ cup dry red wine
- 12 ounces fresh cranberries
- ¼ cup cider vinegar
- 1 Granny Smith apple, peeled, cored, and cut into ½-inch dice
- 2 teaspoons grated fresh ginger
- ¼ teaspoon ground mace
- ¼ teaspoon curry powder
  Grated zest and juice of 1 orange
- ⅓ cup dried currants

**1.** In a medium saucepan, combine onion, sugar, and wine. Bring to a boil over medium-high heat. Reduce heat to medium, and simmer, covered, about 4 minutes.

**2.** Add remaining ingredients except currants; cook until cranberries have popped, about 8 minutes. Add more sugar, if desired. Remove from heat; stir in currants. Transfer to a bowl to cool. Serve at room temperature.

## cranberry sauce with dried cherries

MAKES 3 CUPS

*You can substitute dried cranberries or raisins for the dried cherries in this recipe.*

- 12 ounces fresh cranberries
- ¾ cup dried cherries
- ½ cup finely chopped shallots
- 2 tablespoons red-wine vinegar
  Zest and juice of 1 orange (about ½ cup)
- 2 teaspoons grated fresh ginger
- ¾ cup packed light-brown sugar

Combine all ingredients in a medium saucepan; cook over medium heat until cranberries begin to pop. Reduce heat to low; cook, stirring occasionally, until cranberries release their juices, about 15 minutes. If sauce becomes too thick, add water until desired consistency is reached. Transfer to a bowl to cool. Serve at room temperature.

## mrs. gubler's pomegranate jelly

*photograph on page 73*

MAKES 3 PINTS

*This recipe was provided by Julie Gubler, the mother of Angela Gubler, senior art director for Martha Stewart Living. To obtain pomegranate juice, purée seeds in a food processor until smooth, then strain in a sieve, discarding pulp.*

- 1 package pectin (1¾ ounces)
- 5 cups sugar
- 5 cups fresh pomegranate juice
  (from about 10 pomegranates)

**1.** In a small bowl, mix pectin with ¼ cup sugar. Place juice in a large saucepan, and stir in pectin mixture. Bring to a boil, and add remaining 4¾ cups sugar. Return to a boil, stirring to dissolve sugar; cook 2 minutes more. Remove from heat.

**2.** Immediately transfer jelly to jars as directed in Canning Tips (page 303). Alternatively, let cool completely; store in an airtight container in the refrigerator, up to 1 month.

# desserts

FRUIT DESSERTS

CUSTARDS AND PUDDINGS

CHARLOTTES AND TRIFLES

PASTRIES

FROZEN DESSERTS

FESTIVE CAKES

FRUITCAKES

GINGERBREADS

PIES AND TARTS

✳

## caramel-coated seckel pears

SERVES 8

*The pears must be poached at least a day ahead of serving, so plan accordingly.*

1   750-ml bottle dry white wine
3   cups sugar
1   lemon, halved
1   whole cinnamon stick
    Several whole cloves
    Several whole black peppercorns
16   ripe Seckel pears
    Canola oil, for baking sheet

**1.** Combine wine, 1 cup sugar, 1 lemon half, and spices in a medium saucepan. Bring to a boil; reduce heat, and simmer 10 minutes.

**2.** Peel pears carefully, leaving stems intact. Sprinkle with juice from remaining lemon half. Add pears to poaching liquid; bring to a bare simmer.

**3.** Cover pears with a lid slightly smaller than the pan to keep them submerged. Cook until tender, 10 to 30 minutes, depending on size and ripeness of pears; rearrange pears once or twice to ensure even cooking. Let cool completely in poaching liquid; refrigerate pears and liquid overnight.

**4.** Remove pears from liquid, and drain on paper towels; discard poaching liquid. Dry pears as much as possible, and set aside.

**5.** Set a large pan of cold water near stove. Combine remaining 2 cups sugar with ½ cup water in a heavy, medium saucepan over low heat. Stir occasionally, until sugar dissolves. Cover pan, and bring to a boil over medium-high heat; leave covered 1 minute to let condensation wash down insides of pan. Continue boiling syrup, uncovered, without stirring, until it becomes a deep amber.

Carefully plunge bottom of saucepan into pan of cold water to stop cooking.

**6.** Holding each pear by the stem, carefully dip in hot caramel, and set on a lightly oiled baking sheet. When all pears have been dipped, drizzle remaining caramel over tops. Serve within 30 minutes.

## pears and figs poached in red wine

SERVES 4

*Left in its cooking liquid and tightly covered, poached fruit will keep in the refrigerator for up to three days. Serve with cookies, whipped cream, or a sweet dessert cheese, such as Gorgonzola dolce.*

1   750-ml bottle dry red wine
¾   cup sugar
1   whole cinnamon stick
20   whole black peppercorns
¼   cup honey
1   vanilla bean, split lengthwise
1   lemon, halved
4   firm but ripe Bosc pears
4   fresh or dried figs, halved

**1.** Combine 2 cups water, wine, sugar, cinnamon, peppercorns, honey, and vanilla bean in a large saucepan. Squeeze in lemon juice, using a sieve to catch seeds, and toss in one of the halves. Bring to a boil; lower heat, and simmer 10 minutes.

**2.** Meanwhile, peel pears carefully, leaving stems intact. Place pears in the simmering poaching liquid, and cover with a lid slightly smaller than pan to keep pears submerged.

**3.** Reduce heat to a bare simmer; poach pears, rotating occasionally, until tender, 20 to 30 minutes, depending on ripeness of fruit. Let cool slightly in liquid. Transfer pears to a bowl. Simmer poaching liquid until reduced by half.

**4.** Add figs to liquid, cut side down. Simmer 2 to 3 minutes. (If using dried figs, poach until tender, 15 to 20 minutes.)

**5.** Carefully transfer figs, cut side down, to bowl with pears; pour reduced poaching liquid over fruit. Let cool; chill at least 4 hours, or overnight.

**6.** With a slotted spoon, remove fruit from liquid, and place 1 pear and 2 fig halves on each serving plate. Reduce remaining poaching liquid over medium heat until thick enough to coat the back of a spoon. Serve hot or cold with the fruit.

## *vacherin*
*photograph on page 63*
SERVES 10

6  large egg whites, room temperature

2½  cups granulated sugar

2  teaspoons pure vanilla extract

4  cups fresh or frozen cranberries
   (about 14 ounces)

½  cup plus 1 tablespoon freshly
   squeezed orange juice

2  cups fresh raspberries (about 8 ounces)

1½  cups heavy cream

2  tablespoons confectioners' sugar,
   plus more for dusting

   Mint sprigs, for garnish (optional)

**1.** Preheat oven to 200°F, with racks in upper and lower thirds. Using an inverted round cake pan as a guide, trace a 9-inch circle on each of two pieces of parchment paper. Place each sheet, marked side down, on a baking sheet. Set aside.

**2.** In the bowl of an electric mixer, whisk egg whites on high speed until soft peaks form, about 2 minutes. With mixer on medium speed, gradually add ¼ cup granulated sugar; whip to combine. Add 1¼ cups granulated sugar, 1 tablespoon at a time, and whip until whites are very stiff and glossy. Add 1 teaspoon vanilla; beat just until combined. Divide batter between traced circles, and spread evenly to edges.

**3.** Transfer baking sheets to separate racks in the oven; bake, rotating sheets every 30 minutes, until meringues are dried and crisp on the outside but soft inside, about 3½ hours; lower oven heat if meringues start to brown. Remove from oven; let cool completely on baking sheets.

**4.** In a large saucepan over medium heat, combine cranberries, ½ cup orange juice, and remaining 1 cup granulated sugar. Cook, stirring frequently, until cranberries begin to break down and syrup has thickened slightly, about 8 minutes.

**5.** Remove pan from heat; transfer syrup to a medium bowl. Fold in raspberries and remaining tablespoon orange juice. Let cool; refrigerate, covered, until ready to assemble. (If you are assembling the dessert right away, you can chill the berry mixture over an ice bath, stirring frequently until cool.)

**6.** Combine cream, remaining teaspoon vanilla, and confectioners' sugar in a chilled metal mixing bowl; whip until mixture is stiff but not grainy. Cover with plastic wrap, and place in the refrigerator until ready to use.

**7.** To assemble vacherin, place one meringue disk on a serving plate, and spread half the whipped cream on top. Drizzle with half the berry mixture, and place second meringue disk on top. Spoon remaining cream onto center of meringue, and heap remaining berry mixture on top. Dust vacherin with confectioners' sugar, and garnish plate with mint sprigs, if desired. Slice vacherin with a serrated knife, and serve immediately.

## pear pavlova

SERVES 6

### for pears:

- 1 750-ml bottle dry red wine, such as cabernet or zinfandel
- 1 cup sugar
- 1 teaspoon whole black peppercorns
- 3 dried bay leaves
- 2 whole cinnamon sticks
- 6 medium firm but ripe Bosc pears

### for meringue base:

- 4 large egg whites
  Pinch of salt
- ¾ cup packed light-brown sugar
- ¼ cup superfine sugar
- 1 teaspoon distilled white vinegar
- 1 teaspoon pure vanilla extract

### for topping:

- 1 cup heavy cream
- 2 tablespoons superfine sugar

**1.** Poach pears: Combine 3 cups water, wine, sugar, peppercorns, bay leaves, and cinnamon sticks in a large saucepan. Bring to a boil, and stir until sugar has dissolved. Reduce heat to a gentle simmer.

**2.** Carefully peel pears, leaving stems intact. Place in simmering poaching liquid; cover with a lid slightly smaller than pan to keep pears submerged. Cook, rotating pears occasionally, until bases are tender, 20 to 25 minutes, depending on ripeness of fruit. Meanwhile, prepare an ice bath.

**3.** Using a large slotted spoon, carefully transfer pears to a large metal bowl set in the ice bath. Pour poaching liquid through a fine sieve into bowl with pears; let cool completely. Cover bowl with plastic wrap; refrigerate overnight.

**4.** Preheat oven to 300°F, with rack in center. Line a baking sheet with parchment paper. Using an inverted cake pan or bowl as a guide, trace an 8-inch circle on parchment; turn parchment over, marked side down.

**5.** Make meringue base: Place egg whites, salt, and light-brown sugar in the bowl of an electric mixer. Whisk on low speed until no lumps of sugar remain. Increase speed to medium; beat until soft peaks form, about 9 minutes. With mixer running, gradually add superfine sugar. Continue beating until peaks are stiff and glossy, about 2 minutes more. Beat in vinegar and vanilla.

### FORMING A PAVLOVA

*1. Line a baking sheet with parchment paper. Using an inverted 8-inch cake pan or bowl as a guide, trace a circle on the parchment; turn parchment over, marked side down. Using a rubber spatula, spread the meringue onto the traced circle.*

*2. Form peaks around the edge of the circle and a well in the center before baking.*

**6.** Using a rubber spatula, spread the meringue onto traced circle on prepared baking sheet; form peaks around the edge and a well in the center.

**7.** Bake meringue until crisp around the edge and just set in the center, about 1¼ hours. Transfer baking sheet to a wire rack; when meringue is cool enough to handle, carefully peel off parchment. Let meringue cool completely on rack.

**8.** Make topping: In a mixing bowl, whip heavy cream and sugar until stiff peaks form. Cover with plastic wrap; refrigerate until ready to use.

**9.** Slice pears in half lengthwise; remove seeds and stems with a spoon or melon baller, and discard. Cut pears into ¾-inch pieces, and place in a bowl; cover with plastic wrap, and set aside.

**10.** Bring 3 cups poaching liquid to a boil in a medium saucepan; reduce heat, and simmer until syrupy and reduced to about 1 cup, 20 to 25 minutes. Meanwhile, prepare another ice bath. Pour syrup into a clean bowl set in the ice bath; stir frequently until cool and thickened.

**11.** To assemble pavlova, carefully place meringue on a serving platter. Spoon whipped cream on top, and then add pears. Serve, sliced into wedges and drizzled with syrup.

## winter fruit crisp
*photograph on page 73*
SERVES 8 TO 10

*The cooking time for the figs will vary depending on how moist they are. The first step can be done up to six hours ahead.*

- 3½ cups dried Calimyrna figs (about 20 ounces)
- ¼ cup honey
- ¼ cup sugar
- 1 heaping teaspoon whole black peppercorns, wrapped in cheesecloth
- 2 whole cinnamon sticks
- 2 cups dry red wine
- ¾ cup dried cherries
- 4 Granny Smith apples (about 2 pounds)
- 4 ripe but firm Bartlett pears (about 1¾ pounds)
- 2 tablespoons freshly squeezed lemon juice
- 4 cups Crisp Topping (recipe follows)
  Crème fraîche, whipped cream, or ice cream, for serving (optional)

**1.** Cut tips of stems off figs; discard. Cut figs in half lengthwise if small or in quarters if large. Place in a small saucepan along with honey, sugar, wrapped peppercorns, cinnamon sticks, and wine. Stir well, and bring to a boil. Reduce heat to low; simmer, stirring gently occasionally, until figs are soft and liquid is reduced to about ¼ inch, about 30 minutes. Discard cinnamon and peppercorns. Stir in the cherries.

**2.** Preheat oven to 375°F. Peel and core apples, and cut each into 16 wedges. Peel and core pears, and cut into 1-inch chunks. Place fruit in a 3½-quart oval gratin dish; sprinkle with lemon juice.

**3.** Transfer fig mixture to gratin dish; mix well. Sprinkle topping evenly over the top. Transfer to oven; bake 30 minutes.

**4.** Reduce oven temperature to 350°F, and continue baking until topping is brown and juices are bubbling, about 15 minutes more. If the top begins to get too brown, cover it loosely with aluminum foil. Remove from oven. Serve warm with crème fraîche, whipped cream, or ice cream, as desired.

—

## crisp topping
### MAKES 8 CUPS

*This makes enough for two large crisps—freeze extra in an airtight container up to one month.*

- ½   cup whole blanched almonds (about 2½ ounces)
- 2¼  cups all-purpose flour
- ¾   cup packed light-brown sugar
- ⅓   cup granulated sugar
- ½   teaspoon ground cinnamon
- ½   teaspoon salt
- 1   cup (2 sticks) very cold unsalted butter, cut into small pieces

**1.** Preheat oven to 350°F. Spread almonds in a single layer on a rimmed baking sheet; toast in oven until golden and fragrant, about 10 minutes, shaking sheet frequently. Remove from oven; let cool.

**2.** Finely grind almonds in a food processor; transfer to the bowl of an electric mixer. Add flour, sugars, cinnamon, and salt; mix until just combined. Add butter, and mix on low until clumps form, 4 to 5 minutes. Refrigerate until ready to use.

## eggnog panna cotta
### MAKES 12 THREE-OUNCE SERVINGS

- 3½  cups milk
- 5   large egg yolks
- ¾   cup sugar
- 1   cup cold heavy cream
- 2   tablespoons light rum
-     Freshly grated nutmeg
- 1   tablespoon powdered gelatin (1½ envelopes)

**1.** Prepare a large ice bath; set aside. Place 2 cups milk in a small saucepan, and bring to a boil over medium-high heat. Combine egg yolks and sugar in a medium bowl, and whisk until pale yellow. Pour half the hot milk into egg-yolk mixture, whisking constantly. Return mixture to pan; cook over low heat, stirring constantly with a wooden spoon, until thick enough to coat back of spoon.

**2.** Remove pan from heat, and immediately stir in remaining 1½ cups milk and the cream. Pour through a fine sieve into a bowl set over the ice bath. Add rum and nutmeg. Let stand, stirring frequently, until chilled.

**3.** Measure out ½ cup eggnog; sprinkle with gelatin. Let stand until softened, about 5 minutes. Pour remaining eggnog into a medium saucepan, and place over medium heat. Cook until just barely steaming. Add gelatin mixture, and stir to dissolve. Strain through a fine sieve. Pour into 3-ounce ramekins or teacups, and refrigerate until set, 2½ to 3 hours. Serve chilled.

## apricot-lemon steamed pudding with kumquat marmalade

### SERVES 8

*This recipe can be made using any steamed-pudding mold. If kumquats are not available, substitute one-third cup orange marmalade for the kumquat marmalade made in step one.*

- 1 pound fresh kumquats (3½ cups), plus more, sliced, for garnish
- 1½ cups granulated sugar
- 1 cup dried apricots
- ¼ cup brandy
- 1 one-inch piece fresh ginger, peeled and halved

  Grated zest of 2 lemons
- ½ cup (1 stick) unsalted butter, plus more, room temperature, for mold and parchment
- 1¾ cups all-purpose flour
- 2½ teaspoons baking powder
- ⅛ teaspoon salt
- 1 cup packed dark-brown sugar
- 3 large eggs
- ½ teaspoon pure vanilla extract
- 1 cup milk
- 1 cup crème fraîche or double cream

**1.** Cut kumquats into ¼-inch-thick pieces; remove seeds. Combine kumquats and sugar in a medium saucepan. Cook slowly over low heat, stirring frequently with a wooden spoon, until kumquats are soft and released liquid has thickened slightly, 25 to 35 minutes. Transfer to a small bowl, and set marmalade aside.

**2.** Combine apricots, brandy, ½ cup water, ginger, and zest of 1 lemon in a medium saucepan. Cover, and bring to a boil over medium-high heat. Reduce heat to a simmer, and cook until almost all liquid has evaporated, 15 to 20 minutes. Discard ginger. Transfer apricot mixture to a food processor. Purée until smooth; set aside.

**3.** Butter an 8- to 10-cup pudding mold. Cut out a round of parchment paper that is 4 inches larger than the mold; butter parchment. Into a medium bowl, sift together flour, baking powder, and salt.

**4.** In the bowl of an electric mixer fitted with the paddle attachment, cream butter and brown sugar on medium speed until lightened, 1 to 2 minutes. Add eggs, one at a time, beating until incorporated after each. Add vanilla and remaining zest. Slowly beat in apricot purée. Add flour mixture in two additions, alternating with the milk.

**5.** Spoon about ¾ cup kumquat marmalade into prepared mold, arranging kumquats around sides of mold to follow pattern if there is one; reserve remaining marmalade. Pour batter into mold. Tap mold sharply against counter to distribute batter evenly. Cover with parchment, buttered side down, and secure with a rubber band; cover with foil. Secure mold lid over foil.

**6.** Place a wire rack in a stockpot, and set mold, lid side up, on rack. Pour in enough boiling water to reach halfway up side of mold. Cover pot, and bring to a boil over high heat. Reduce heat to medium-low; steam 2 hours 20 minutes.

**7.** Remove mold from pot; let stand 15 minutes. Remove lid, foil, and parchment; invert mold onto a serving plate, and garnish with sliced kumquats. Serve pudding warm or at room temperature, with a dollop of crème fraîche or double cream and reserved kumquat marmalade on the side.

## *chocolate-soufflé crêpes*

MAKES 1 DOZEN

*Crêpes can be refrigerated in a resealable plastic bag for up to three days or frozen for up to one month. Refrigerate sauce in an air-tight container for up to one week. Bring both to room temperature before assembling dessert.*

### for crêpes and assembling dessert:

- ½ cup unsweetened cocoa powder, sifted, plus more for dusting
- ¼ cup confectioners' sugar, sifted
- 3 tablespoons all-purpose flour
- 3 large eggs
- 3 tablespoons unsalted butter, melted, plus more for pan
- 5 tablespoons heavy cream
- ½ cup milk
- 2 pints fresh raspberries

### for espresso sauce:

- 1 cup heavy cream
- 1 tablespoon instant espresso powder
- 8 ounces bittersweet chocolate, finely chopped

### for chocolate soufflé:

- Pastry Cream (recipe follows)
- ¼ cup unsweetened cocoa powder
- 6 large egg whites, room temperature
- 1 teaspoon freshly squeezed lemon juice
- ½ cup superfine sugar

**1.** Make crêpes: In a medium bowl, combine cocoa powder, confectioners' sugar, flour, eggs, butter, and cream. Whisk together until combined; do not overmix. Add milk, whisking constantly, until batter is smooth. Cover with plastic wrap; let rest at room temperature 30 minutes.

**2.** Heat a 7-inch nonstick sauté pan over medium-high heat. When pan is hot, lightly coat bottom with melted butter. Pour 2 tablespoons batter into pan; swirl pan immediately, covering entire surface. Cook crêpe until center is set, 45 to 55 seconds. Using a thin spatula, carefully flip crêpe; cook 1 minute more. Transfer to a plate.

**3.** Repeat cooking process with remaining batter, brushing pan with butter each time. Stack crêpes between layers of wax or parchment paper. Let cool completely; cover with plastic wrap, and keep at room temperature until ready to use.

**4.** Make espresso sauce: In a small saucepan, bring cream to a boil over medium-high heat. Add espresso powder, and whisk to dissolve.

**5.** Place chopped chocolate in a medium bowl; pour hot cream mixture over it. Let stand 5 minutes, then stir until smooth; let cool completely.

**6.** Make chocolate soufflé: Place pastry cream in a heatproof bowl. Set bowl over a pan of simmering water until cream is warm to the touch, about 2½ minutes. Remove from heat; sift cocoa powder over cream, and whisk to combine. Set mixture aside in a warm place.

**7.** In the bowl of an electric mixer, whisk egg whites and lemon juice on medium speed until whites are frothy, about 3 minutes. Increase speed to medium-high; gradually add sugar, whisking until meringue forms stiff, but not dry, peaks.

**8.** Whisk one-third of meringue into chocolate pastry cream. Using a rubber spatula, gently fold in remaining meringue just until combined.

**9.** Preheat oven to 400°F; heat two baking sheets. Assemble dessert: Lay six crêpes on each hot sheet. Place ⅓ cup chocolate soufflé in center of each crêpe; fold crêpes in half without pressing.

**10.** Bake until soufflé has set, about 5 minutes. Remove crêpes from oven; dust with cocoa powder. Transfer to serving plates with a spatula. Serve immediately with espresso sauce and raspberries.

## pastry cream

MAKES ABOUT 1 CUP

- 3 large egg yolks
- ¼ cup sugar
- 2 tablespoons all-purpose flour
- 1 cup milk
- 1 vanilla bean, split lengthwise

**1.** Prepare an ice bath; set aside. In a medium bowl, whisk egg yolks with 2 tablespoons sugar and flour until light and pale; set aside.

**2.** Place milk and remaining 2 tablespoons sugar in a medium saucepan. Scrape in vanilla seeds; add pod. Bring mixture just to a boil. Pour approximately half the milk mixture over reserved egg mixture; whisk to combine. Pour mixture back into the saucepan. Return to a boil, whisking constantly; cook until thick enough to coat the back of a spoon, 2 to 3 minutes.

**3.** Pour pastry cream into a medium bowl; discard vanilla pod. Set bowl in ice bath until cream is chilled, stirring frequently.

**4.** Lay plastic wrap directly on surface of pastry cream to prevent a skin from forming. Refrigerate until ready to use, up to 1 day.

## montebianco

SERVES 12

*This dessert is mounded into the shape of a mountain and covered with whipped cream. Twenty ounces of frozen chestnuts can be substituted for two pounds of fresh ones.*

- 2 pounds fresh chestnuts, in shells
- ½ teaspoon coarse salt
- 3½ cups milk
- 1 cup confectioners' sugar
- 2 tablespoons unsalted butter
- 1 vanilla bean, split lengthwise and scraped
- 3 tablespoons light rum
- 1 quart heavy cream
- ¼ cup unsweetened cocoa powder, for dusting

**1.** Using a small paring knife, cut an X into one side of each chestnut. Fill a large saucepan with water; add chestnuts and salt. Bring to a boil; reduce heat to medium, and cook until tender, about 20 minutes. Remove 2 or 3 at a time from water; peel outer shells and scrape off inner skins.

**2.** Combine chestnuts, milk, ¾ cup sugar, butter, and vanilla pod and scrapings in saucepan; bring to a simmer over medium heat. Cook until chestnuts are falling apart, 30 to 35 minutes. Drain, reserving cooking liquid. Discard vanilla pod; set chestnuts aside to cool.

**3.** Pass chestnuts through a food mill into a medium bowl. Stir in rum and 5 to 6 tablespoons of the reserved cooking liquid until combined. Working in batches, place chestnut mixture in a potato ricer fitted with large-hole blade. Press strands of mixture into serving bowls. It should look like a small mound of spaghetti.

**4.** Whip cream with remaining ¼ cup sugar. Using a pastry bag fitted with a large star tip, pipe the whipped cream over chestnut mixture, covering the entire exposed surface. Dust with cocoa; serve.

**319**

## date-nut puddings

*photograph on page 65*

MAKES 8 SIX-OUNCE SERVINGS

*Choose only plump dates with dark, shiny skins.*

- 4   tablespoons unsalted butter, cut into small pieces, plus more for cups
- 1½   cups all-purpose flour
- 1   teaspoon baking soda
- ½   teaspoon baking powder
- ½   teaspoon salt
- ¼   teaspoon ground cardamom
- 1½   cups pitted dates (about 10 ounces), coarsely chopped
- 2   cups boiling water
- 1   cup packed light-brown sugar, plus about ⅓ cup for sprinkling
- 1   large egg, lightly beaten
- 1   teaspoon pure vanilla extract
- 1   cup coarsely chopped walnuts (about 4 ounces), plus 8 halves for garnish
- 1   cup crème fraîche
- 3   tablespoons confectioners' sugar
- 1   tablespoon Cognac or brandy

**1.** Preheat oven to 325°F. Butter eight 6-ounce ramekins or custard cups, and place on a rimmed baking sheet. Set aside. In a medium bowl, whisk together flour, baking soda, baking powder, salt, and cardamom; set aside.

**2.** In a large bowl, combine dates, 1½ cups boiling water, and the butter. Stir until butter is melted and dates are soft, 2 to 3 minutes. Stir in brown sugar, egg, and vanilla. Add flour mixture, and stir until combined. Stir in walnuts.

**3.** Sprinkle 2 teaspoons brown sugar into bottom of each prepared ramekin. Divide batter evenly (about ¾ cup each) among ramekins; sprinkle each with 2 teaspoons brown sugar. Pour 1 tablespoon boiling water over batter in each ramekin.

**4.** Transfer baking sheet to oven; bake until a cake tester inserted in centers comes out clean, 35 to 40 minutes. Remove from oven.

**5.** In a small bowl, whisk together crème fraîche, confectioners' sugar, and Cognac. To unmold, invert puddings onto serving plates. Serve warm, with a dollop of crème fraîche mixture; garnish each plate with a walnut half.

## festive figgy pudding

SERVES 10 TO 12

- 1½   cups dried Calimyrna figs (8½ ounces)
- ¼   cup brandy
- ½   cup dried apricots
- ½   cup (1 stick) unsalted butter, plus more for mold and parchment
- 1   cup packed dark-brown sugar
- 2   large eggs
- ½   teaspoon pure vanilla extract
- 1½   cups all-purpose flour
- 1½   teaspoons baking powder
     Pinch of salt
- 1   cup milk
- 2   tablespoons apricot jam

**1.** In a large saucepan over medium-low heat, combine 1 cup figs, ½ cup water, and brandy; cook 15 minutes. Transfer mixture to a food processor; process until smooth, and set aside.

**2.** Place remaining ½ cup figs and the apricots in a small bowl. Cover with hot water; let soak until fruit is plump. Drain thoroughly; slice figs in half.

**3.** Butter a 5-cup pudding mold. Cut out a round of parchment paper several inches larger than the mold; butter parchment, and set aside.

**4.** In the bowl of an electric mixer fitted with the paddle attachment, cream butter and sugar on medium speed until light and fluffy. Add eggs and vanilla, and beat until combined. Add puréed fig mixture; beat until smooth and combined. Into a bowl, sift together flour, baking powder, and salt; add to fig mixture in three batches, alternating with milk and starting and ending with flour.

**5.** Spoon jam into bottom of prepared pudding mold. Arrange reserved fruit on bottom and sides of mold with cut ends of figs facing down. Pour in batter. Cover mold with prepared parchment, buttered side down; secure with a rubber band, and cover tightly with aluminum foil.

**6.** Place a wire rack in the bottom of a 10-quart stockpot; set pudding mold on top of rack. Pour enough boiling water into pot to reach halfway up sides of mold. Cover pot; steam pudding over medium-low heat until a cake tester inserted into center comes out clean, about 2 hours 20 minutes. Carefully remove mold from pot; remove foil and parchment. Let pudding stand, uncovered, 15 minutes before turning out onto a serving plate.

### MEASURING BROWN SUGAR

*When a recipe calls for "packed" brown sugar (don't use "brownulated"), it should look compact. Compress the sugar tightly with your fingers so that the sugar is level with the top of the measuring cup and firmly enough to make sure that there are no air pockets.*

## kumquat toffee puddings
### MAKES 8 SIX-OUNCE SERVINGS

*Members of the citrus family, kumquats resemble tiny oranges. They have an edible, sweet rind and a tart flesh, and are available throughout the holiday season. Choose firm fruit without any bruises. For an elegant garnish, reserve some of the poaching liquid, and gently simmer eight whole kumquats for fifteen to twenty minutes; serve one on each plate.*

- 4 *tablespoons unsalted butter, room temperature, plus more for ramekins*
- 1 *cup plus 8 teaspoons granulated sugar*
- 8 *teaspoons light corn syrup*
- 8 *ounces kumquats, sliced ¼ inch thick, seeds removed*
- 8 *ounces pitted dates, finely chopped*
- 1 *teaspoon baking soda*
- 1 *cup boiling water*
- 1 *cup all-purpose flour*
- 1 *teaspoon baking powder*
- ¼ *teaspoon salt*
- ¾ *cup firmly packed light-brown sugar*
- 2 *large eggs*
- 4 *ounces walnuts, toasted and roughly chopped*
  *Toffee Sauce (recipe follows)*

**1.** Butter eight 6-ounce ramekins. Sprinkle 1 teaspoon sugar in bottom of each, and drizzle with 1 teaspoon corn syrup; set aside.

**2.** Combine kumquats, remaining cup sugar, and ½ cup water in a saucepan over medium heat. Bring to a boil; reduce heat to low. Simmer until kumquats are soft, 15 to 20 minutes. Remove from heat. Let cool slightly. Arrange slices in the bottom of each ramekin, and set aside.

**3.** Preheat oven to 350°F. Combine dates and baking soda in a small bowl; cover with the boiling water. Stir to combine. Into a separate bowl, sift together flour, baking powder, and salt; set aside.

**4.** In the bowl of an electric mixer fitted with the paddle attachment, cream butter and brown sugar until fluffy. Add eggs one at a time, beating until combined after each addition. Add the flour mixture; beat until combined. Add the date mixture and walnuts, and beat until combined. Pour the batter into ramekins.

**5.** Bake until a cake tester inserted in centers comes out clean, about 30 minutes. Remove from oven. To unmold, run a knife around edges, and invert onto serving plates. Serve puddings warm, drizzled with toffee sauce.

### toffee sauce
MAKES 2⅔ CUPS

1½ cups firmly packed light-brown sugar
2 tablespoons unsalted butter
2 cups heavy cream
1 teaspoon pure vanilla extract

In a medium saucepan over medium heat, bring all ingredients to a boil. Simmer, stirring occasionally, until just slightly thickened, about 5 minutes. Remove from heat; serve warm.

## orange rice pudding
SERVES 10

*This dish is best when prepared a few hours ahead and served at room temperature.*

6 oranges
2 cups Arborio rice
¾ cup sugar
1 whole cinnamon stick
1 vanilla bean, split lengthwise and scraped, or 1 teaspoon pure vanilla extract
2 cups heavy cream
⅓ cup whole blanched almonds

**1.** Grate the zest from 1 orange. Slice this and one other orange in half; squeeze juice into a saucepan; add zest and rice, sugar, 5 cups water, cinnamon stick, and vanilla bean and scrapings. Bring mixture to a boil over high heat, stirring constantly. Reduce heat; cover, and simmer until almost all liquid is absorbed, about 20 minutes.

**2.** Remove pan from heat. Stir several times, cover, and let stand about 15 minutes; discard vanilla bean and cinnamon stick. Transfer to a large bowl; cover with a clean kitchen towel, and let cool.

**3.** Using a sharp paring knife, remove peel and pith from remaining oranges, following the curve of the fruit. Carefully cut between membranes to remove whole segments; discard seeds. Set aside.

**4.** Just before serving, whip the cream in a mixing bowl until stiff. Fold cream, almonds, and all but 10 orange segments into rice mixture. Transfer pudding to a large bowl; garnish with remaining orange segments.

## semolina puddings

MAKES 8 FOUR-OUNCE PUDDINGS
OR 1 SEVEN-CUP PUDDING

*Couscous is a tiny pasta made from semolina.*

Unsalted butter, for ramekins
4 cups milk
1 vanilla bean, split lengthwise and scraped
Grated zest of 1 orange
½ cup sugar
1 cup couscous
3 large egg yolks
1 teaspoon baking soda
1 cup dried cranberries
Candied orange zest, for garnish (optional)
Cranberry Coulis (recipe follows)

**1.** Butter eight 4-ounce ramekins or a 7-cup pudding mold or bowl; set aside.

**2.** In a medium saucepan over medium heat, bring milk to a boil. Add vanilla bean and scrapings, orange zest, and sugar. Remove from heat; cover, and let stand 30 minutes. Discard vanilla bean.

**3.** Return pan to medium heat. Bring mixture to a boil, and stir in couscous. Bring to a simmer, and cook 10 minutes. Remove pan from heat; cover, and let stand until couscous has absorbed all liquid, about 15 minutes.

**4.** Preheat oven to 350°F. Stir egg yolks, baking soda, and cranberries into couscous. Pour mixture into ramekins, and place in a roasting pan. Pour enough boiling water into pan to reach halfway up sides of ramekins.

**5.** Transfer pan to oven; bake 35 to 40 minutes, or until puddings are set. Add boiling water as necessary to maintain water level. Garnish with candied orange zest, if desired, and serve with coulis.

## cranberry coulis

MAKES 1 CUP

1½ cups fresh cranberries
⅓ cup sugar
Zest of 1 orange

Combine cranberries, ¾ cup water, sugar, and zest in a small saucepan over medium heat. Bring to a boil; reduce heat, and simmer until cranberries have burst, about 12 minutes. Pass through a sieve into a small bowl, and discard solids. Serve chilled.

## persimmon pudding

SERVES 8 TO 10

*Persimmons are similar to tomatoes in shape and color. When fully ripe, they are soft and sweet.*

3 tablespoons unsalted butter, room temperature, plus more for mold
¼ cup brandy
¼ cup golden raisins
¼ cup currants
1 cup sugar
2 large eggs, separated
1 teaspoon pure vanilla extract
2 teaspoons freshly squeezed lemon juice
2 to 3 very ripe persimmons
¾ cup half-and-half
1 teaspoon baking soda
1¼ cups all-purpose flour
1½ teaspoons ground cinnamon
½ teaspoon ground nutmeg
¼ teaspoon salt
¾ cup pecans, toasted and coarsely chopped

**1.** Butter an 8-cup lidded pudding mold, and set aside. In a small saucepan over low heat, combine brandy, raisins, and currants, and bring to a simmer. Remove from heat, and let stand 15 minutes; drain, discarding liquid.

**2.** Meanwhile, in the bowl of an electric mixer fitted with the paddle attachment, cream together butter and sugar until light and fluffy. Beat in egg yolks, vanilla, and lemon juice until combined.

**3.** Cut tops off persimmons. Scoop out pulp, and pass through a sieve into bowl with egg mixture, discarding seeds and skins. Add half-and-half. Dissolve baking soda in 1 tablespoon hot water, and add to egg mixture.

**4.** Sift together flour, spices, and salt into a medium bowl, and add to egg mixture. Beat just until combined. Stir in pecans. In a clean bowl, beat egg whites until stiff peaks form; fold into batter. Scatter raisins and currants in bottom of prepared mold. Pour batter into mold, and clamp on lid.

**5.** Choose a pot large enough to hold the mold, with a 2-inch clearance on all sides. Place a wire rack or folded dish towel in bottom of pot, and fill with enough water to reach halfway up sides of mold. Remove mold, cover pot, and bring to a boil; reduce heat to a simmer. Return mold to pot. Cover, and steam pudding 2 hours 20 minutes. Add boiling water as necessary to maintain water level. Remove mold from pot; let cool, uncovered, 15 minutes before serving.

## sabayon with roasted chestnuts
### SERVES 12

5 large egg yolks
  Pinch of salt
¼ cup plus 2 tablespoons sugar
1 cup Muscat de Beaumes-de-Venise
  or other sweet dessert wine
¾ cup heavy cream
2 teaspoons freshly squeezed lemon juice
1 jar (7.4 ounces) roasted whole chestnuts
  Chocolate Straws (recipe follows)
  Cocoa powder, for sprinkling

**1.** Prepare a large ice bath, and set aside. In a large nonreactive bowl, whisk together egg yolks, salt, and sugar until mixture is very pale. Add Muscat, and whisk to combine.

**2.** Place bowl over a pan of simmering water; whisk until mixture has thickened and tripled in volume, 8 to 10 minutes. Immediately transfer to ice bath, and whisk until chilled.

**3.** In a large bowl, whip cream until soft peaks form. Add lemon juice, and fold whipped cream into chilled egg mixture. Divide among twelve serving dishes; top each with 2 roasted chestnuts and 1 chocolate straw; sprinkle with cocoa. Serve.

## chocolate straws

MAKES 1 DOZEN

*If your first attempt is unsuccessful, you can remelt the chocolate and start over.*

6 ounces bittersweet chocolate, finely chopped

**1.** Melt chocolate in a heatproof bowl set over a pan of simmering water. Pour chocolate onto an inverted 11-by-17-inch baking sheet. Using an off-set spatula, spread into a thin even rectangle, covering sheet entirely. Transfer to refrigerator; chill until chocolate sets slightly, about 15 minutes.

**2.** Remove chocolate from refrigerator. Holding sheet vertically, score chocolate in a line down the middle with a metal bench scraper. Starting on the left side, approximately 2½ inches from the top, and holding scraper at a 45-degree angle, gently push away from you, forming a tight curl or straw. Repeat making straws down left side of sheet and then right side, moving bench scraper 2½ inches down sheet each time, for a total of twelve straws. If chocolate becomes too soft, chill 5 minutes. Store straws between layers of parchment paper in an airtight container; refrigerate until ready to use.

## tangerine parfaits

MAKES 6

2 envelopes unflavored gelatin (about 4½ teaspoons)

3 cups freshly squeezed tangerine juice (8 to 12 tangerines)

1 cup buttermilk

½ cup heavy cream

¼ cup sugar

Blood-orange segments, for garnish (about 2 blood oranges)

Mint sprigs, for garnish

**1.** Prepare an ice bath, and set aside. Measure out 1 teaspoon gelatin; set aside. Sprinkle remaining gelatin over ½ cup tangerine juice, and let soften 5 minutes. Meanwhile, heat the remaining 2½ cups tangerine juice in a small saucepan over medium heat. Add softened gelatin; cook, stirring, over medium-low heat until gelatin has dissolved, about 2 minutes. Set pan in ice bath; stir until cool. Divide mixture evenly among six 10-ounce glasses. Refrigerate until set, about 1½ hours.

**2.** Prepare another ice bath. Sprinkle reserved teaspoon gelatin over ½ cup buttermilk; let soften 5 minutes. In a small saucepan, heat heavy cream and sugar until sugar has dissolved. Add softened gelatin; cook, stirring, over medium-low heat until gelatin has dissolved, about 2 minutes. Stir in remaining ½ cup buttermilk. Set pan in ice bath; stir until cool. Carefully pour buttermilk mixture over chilled tangerine layers, dividing evenly. Return to refrigerator until set, about 1 hour.

**3.** Serve parfaits garnished with blood-orange segments and mint.

# pistachio charlotte

*photograph on page 66*

SERVES 8 TO 10

*Store-bought ladyfingers can be used for forming charlotte and cake layers.*

¼ cup sugar

1 tablespoon kirsch

Ladyfingers and Cake Rounds (recipe follows), bottoms trimmed flat

Pistachio Praline and Pistachio Bavarian Cream (recipe follows)

**1.** Combine sugar and ½ cup water in a small saucepan; bring to a simmer over low heat, stirring occasionally, until sugar has dissolved, 1 to 2 minutes. Remove from heat, and let cool. Add kirsch, and stir to combine.

## FORMING A CHARLOTTE

*Brush baked ladyfingers and cake rounds with syrup. Stand ladyfingers upright around edge of springform pan; arrange a cake layer on bottom.*

**2.** Brush ladyfingers and cake rounds with the syrup. Arrange ladyfingers upright around edge of an 8½-inch springform pan. Lay a cake round in the bottom, trimming to fit if needed.

**3.** Spoon in one-third Bavarian cream; smooth top, and sprinkle with one-third praline. Repeat with remaining cake rounds, Bavarian cream, and praline to form two more layers. Refrigerate until set, at least 4 hours or overnight. Serve chilled.

## ladyfingers and cake rounds

MAKES ABOUT 22 LADYFINGERS PLUS THREE 8½-INCH CAKE ROUNDS

6 large eggs, separated

¾ cup sugar

1¼ cups all-purpose flour

Confectioners' sugar

**1.** Using an inverted cake pan or bowl, draw three 8½-inch circles on two pieces of parchment paper and four rows 3½ inches wide on two more pieces of parchment paper; place paper, marking side down, on baking sheets; set aside.

**2.** Preheat oven to 350°F. In the bowl of an electric mixer, whisk yolks and ½ cup plus 3 tablespoons sugar on high speed until mixture is thick and pale, 1 to 2 minutes. Add flour, and fold in gently.

**3.** In a clean mixing bowl, whisk egg whites until frothy. Gradually whisk in remaining tablespoon sugar; beat until stiff, 1 to 2 minutes. Fold one-third whites into reserved yolk mixture, then gently fold in remaining whites until just incorporated.

**4.** Using an offset spatula, spread batter evenly inside traced circles, making rounds ¼ inch thick. Transfer to oven; bake, rotating sheets halfway through, until rounds are light golden, about 15 minutes. Transfer to wire racks to cool.

**5.** Meanwhile, fill a large pastry bag fitted with ½-inch plain tip with remaining batter; pipe ladyfingers, ½ inch thick, between traced lines. Sprinkle ladyfingers generously with confectioners' sugar; let sugar soak in, about 3 minutes.

**6.** Place baking sheets in oven; bake, rotating sheets halfway through, until ladyfingers are light golden, 15 to 18 minutes. Transfer to wire racks to cool. Once cake rounds and ladyfingers are cool, remove from parchment paper.

### pistachio praline and pistachio bavarian cream
MAKES 2 CUPS PRALINE
AND ABOUT 4½ CUPS CREAM

*The toasted pistachios are used to make both the praline and the Bavarian cream. Whole blanched almonds may be substituted for shelled pistachio nuts; if so, skip step one.*

5½  cups shelled pistachio nuts
 3  cups milk
1¾  cups sugar
 6  large egg yolks
 2  envelopes unflavored gelatin (4½ teaspoons), softened in 6 tablespoons water
1½  tablespoons kirsch
1¼  cups heavy cream

**1.** Preheat oven to 325°F. Bring a medium pot of water to a boil over high heat. Add pistachio nuts, and blanch 30 seconds; drain. When nuts are cool enough to handle, remove skins.

**2.** Spread nuts on a rimmed baking sheet, and place in oven until nuts are dry but still green, 15 to 20 minutes. Remove from oven; let cool. Set aside 1¼ cups nuts.

**3.** Transfer remaining nuts to a food processor, and pulse until coarsely ground. Combine ground nuts and milk in a medium saucepan; bring to a boil over medium heat. Transfer mixture to a bowl; chill in refrigerator 3 hours.

**4.** Make praline: Line a baking sheet with a Silpat baking mat; set aside. Combine ¾ cup sugar and ¼ cup water in a small saucepan over medium heat. Cook, stirring occasionally and brushing down sides of pan with water to prevent crystals from forming, until sugar is golden, about 10 minutes. Add reserved 1¼ cups nuts, and stir to combine. Pour mixture onto prepared baking sheet, spreading evenly, and let cool. Break into pieces, and pulse in a food processor until coarsely chopped; set aside until ready to assemble charlotte.

**5.** Make Bavarian cream: Prepare an ice bath, and set aside. Remove milk-nut mixture from refrigerator, and strain through a cheesecloth-lined sieve into a medium saucepan, squeezing all milk from nuts (you should have 2 cups). Discard nuts.

**6.** Bring strained milk to a simmer over medium-low heat. Whisk egg yolks with remaining cup sugar in a medium bowl until pale. Pour hot milk slowly into egg mixture, whisking constantly. Return mixture to saucepan; cook, stirring constantly, until thick enough to coat back of spoon, 3 to 5 minutes. Do not allow mixture to boil.

**7.** Remove pan from heat, and stir in softened gelatin until dissolved. Strain mixture through a fine sieve into a clean bowl set in the ice bath; stir occasionally until chilled. Add kirsch; stir to combine.

**8.** In the bowl of an electric mixer fitted with the paddle attachment, whip heavy cream to soft peaks. Fold whipped cream into egg mixture until just combined. Use immediately to assemble charlotte.

## gingerbread trifle with cognac custard and pears

SERVES 8

*The gingerbread may be made up to two days ahead, or kept frozen up to one month.*

- ¾ cup (1½ sticks) unsalted butter, room temperature, plus more for pan
- 2⅓ cups sifted all-purpose flour
- 1½ teaspoons baking soda
- ¼ teaspoon salt
- 1½ teaspoons ground ginger
- 1½ teaspoons ground cinnamon
- 1½ cups sugar
- 2 large eggs, room temperature
- ¾ cup unsulfured molasses
- ¾ cup nonfat buttermilk
- 1 lemon
- 10 ripe pears, such as Bosc or Anjou
  Cognac Pastry Cream (recipe follows)

**1.** Preheat oven to 350°F. Butter a 9-by-2-inch round cake pan; line bottom with parchment. Sift together flour, baking soda, salt, and 1 teaspoon each ginger and cinnamon into a large bowl.

**2.** In the bowl of an electric mixer fitted with the paddle attachment, cream ½ cup butter on medium-high speed until lightened, 3 to 4 minutes. Scrape down sides of bowl. Add ½ cup sugar in two batches, scraping down sides after each addition. Beat until fluffy, 3 to 4 minutes more. Add eggs, one at a time, beating 1 minute after each addition. With mixer on medium speed, slowly add molasses, beating about 10 seconds. Slowly pour in buttermilk; beat until combined.

**3.** On low speed, slowly add reserved flour mixture in three batches, beating to combine after each addition. Transfer to prepared pan. Bake until a cake tester inserted into center comes out clean, 35 to 45 minutes. Let cool on a wire rack.

**4.** Juice the lemon; place juice and both halves in a large bowl of cold water. Peel pears one at a time, then quarter, core, and cut into 1- to 1½-inch chunks; place each in lemon water to prevent discoloration as you work.

**5.** Drain pears; transfer half to a 12-inch skillet. Add ½ cup sugar, 2 tablespoons butter, and ¼ teaspoon each cinnamon and ginger. Sauté over high heat, stirring, until sugar and butter melt to form caramel, 4 to 5 minutes. Reduce heat to medium-high; cover, and continue cooking 10 minutes more, stirring occasionally.

**6.** Transfer pears and liquid to a large bowl to cool; repeat with remaining pears, sugar, butter, ginger, and cinnamon. Let cool completely.

**7.** Slice gingerbread into three rounds of equal thickness. Cut each round into eight triangles. Line the bottom of a trifle bowl with eight triangles; trim to fit if needed. Spoon 1 cup pastry cream over gingerbread, followed by 2 cups pear mixture. Repeat process two times, layering with remaining gingerbread, cream, and pears. Refrigerate until ready to serve, up to 1 day.

## cognac pastry cream
MAKES 3⅓ CUPS

9 large egg yolks
¾ cup sugar
4½ tablespoons all-purpose flour
3 cups milk
¾ teaspoon pure vanilla extract
3 tablespoons Cognac

**1.** In the bowl of an electric mixer fitted with the paddle attachment, combine yolks and sugar. Beat on medium-high until mixture is pale yellow and thick, 2 to 3 minutes. Reduce speed to medium-low. Add flour; beat to combine.

**2.** Bring milk to a boil in a medium saucepan. Slowly pour half the milk into the egg mixture; beat until smooth. Pour mixture back into saucepan. Whisk over medium heat until mixture comes to a boil, 6 to 8 minutes.

**3.** Transfer mixture to a large bowl. Stir in vanilla and Cognac. Let cool completely. Cover with plastic wrap, and refrigerate until needed, up to 3 days.

### BAKING WITH EGGS

*Use fresh white or brown eggs at room temperature, graded large. To bring eggs to room temperature quickly, place them in a bowl of warm water for ten to fifteen minutes. Use cold eggs when separating; the yolks will be less likely to break. After you separate the eggs, bring them to room temperature. Refrigerate extra whites in an airtight container for up to five days, or freeze for up to two months.*

## poached pear and almond holiday trifle
*photograph on page 73*
SERVES 10 TO 12

1 cup (2 sticks) unsalted butter,
   plus more for pans
3¼ cups all-purpose flour, sifted,
   plus more for pans
1 cup sliced almonds
¼ cup cornstarch
4½ teaspoons baking powder
1 teaspoon salt
2 cups sugar
1⅓ cups milk
2½ teaspoons pure vanilla extract
6 large egg whites
½ teaspoon cream of tartar
   Muscat-Poached Pears (recipe follows)
   Custard Sauce (recipe follows)
1 cup heavy cream

**1.** Preheat oven to 350°F. Butter three 8-inch round cake pans. Line bottoms with parchment paper; butter paper, and dust with flour. Spread almonds on a rimmed baking sheet. Toast in oven until fragrant, shaking occasionally, about 10 minutes. Let cool on a plate. Sift together flour, cornstarch, baking powder, and salt into a medium bowl.

**2.** Place butter in the bowl of an electric mixer fitted with the paddle attachment, and cream on medium speed until lightened. Gradually add sugar; beat until light and fluffy, about 4 minutes. Reduce speed to low. Add flour mixture in three batches, alternating with the milk, and starting and ending with the flour. Stir in vanilla. Transfer mixture to a large bowl.

**3.** In a clean mixing bowl, whisk egg whites and cream of tartar on medium-high speed until peaks are stiff but not dry, 2 to 3 minutes. Fold mixture into batter.

**4.** Divide batter among prepared pans. Bake until a cake tester inserted into centers comes out clean, 25 to 30 minutes. Transfer pans to wire racks to cool 10 minutes. Invert cakes onto racks; reinvert, and let cool completely.

**5.** Reserve the prettiest 4 pear halves to decorate top of trifle. Cut remaining halves into quarters. Place poaching liquid over high heat, and reduce until syrupy and thick enough to coat the back of a spoon; let cool completely.

**6.** Trim tops of cakes with a serrated knife to make level. Cut cakes into 1- to 2-inch cubes. Arrange one-third of cake cubes in bottom of a trifle dish with white (cut) sides facing out. Press together pieces to create a tight layer. Brush top of layer with ⅓ cup reduced poaching liquid. Arrange half the pear quarters on top. Pour half the custard sauce over pears; sprinkle with half the almonds. Repeat process with one-third cake, ⅓ cup poaching liquid, and the remaining pear quarters, custard sauce, and almonds.

**7.** Arrange remaining cake in a layer on top; press down to eliminate any air bubbles and create a level surface. Brush with ⅓ cup syrup. Thinly slice reserved pear halves, and fan over top of cake. The trifle may be made 1 day ahead to this point and refrigerated until ready to serve.

**8.** When ready to serve, remove trifle from refrigerator; whip heavy cream to soft peaks, and spoon onto center of trifle.

### muscat-poached pears
MAKES 8

2  375-ml bottles Muscat wine
½  cup sugar
8  ripe but firm pears, such as Anjou or
   Bartlett, peeled and halved

**1.** Combine Muscat, sugar, and 3 cups water in a wide 6-quart saucepan; bring to a boil over high heat. Stir until sugar has dissolved. Add pear halves; reduce heat to a low simmer. Cut out round of parchment paper to fit just inside pan; cover pears. Cook until pears are just barely tender, about 20 minutes. Remove from heat; remove parchment paper, and let pears cool in liquid.

**2.** Remove pears from liquid, and use a melon baller or paring knife to remove core. If preparing pears in advance, store in poaching liquid, and refrigerate in an airtight container up to 2 days.

### custard sauce
MAKES 2⅓ CUPS

1¼  cups milk
¾  cup heavy cream
6  large egg yolks
½  cup sugar

**1.** Prepare a large ice bath; set aside. Combine milk and cream in a medium saucepan; bring to a boil over medium-high heat.

**2.** Combine egg yolks and sugar in a medium bowl; whisk until pale yellow. Pour half the hot mixture into egg-yolk mixture, whisking constantly. Return to pan with remaining milk mixture; cook over low heat, stirring constantly with a wooden spoon, until thick enough to coat spoon.

**3.** Remove pan from heat; pour mixture through a fine sieve into a bowl set over the ice bath. Let cool, stirring occasionally. Store in an airtight container in the refrigerator up to 2 days.

PASTRIES

## apple strudel

MAKES 2

2¾  cups all-purpose flour, plus more
     for pan and plastic wrap

1¼  cups (2½ sticks) unsalted butter, plus
     more, melted, for pan and brushing

 3   large whole eggs

 ½   teaspoon salt

 1   cup sugar

 3   to 4 slices white bread

 ⅔   cup pine nuts (4 ounces)

3½  pounds assorted apples, such as
     Macoun, Granny Smith, or Cortland,
     peeled, cored, and sliced ½ inch thick

     Zest of 1 lemon

1½  cups raisins

 1   large egg yolk, lightly beaten
     Confectioners' sugar, for dusting

**1.** Place flour, 8 tablespoons butter, eggs, salt, 1 teaspoon sugar, and 1 tablespoon water in a food processor, and pulse until dough comes together. Divide dough in half; flatten into two disks, and wrap each in plastic wrap. Refrigerate at least 2 hours or overnight.

**2.** Preheat oven to 375°F. Generously butter a large baking pan. Sprinkle with flour, and tap out excess; set aside. Pulse bread in a food processor to form coarse crumbs (you should have about 1½ cups crumbs). Melt 10 tablespoons butter in a large skillet over medium-low heat. Add pine nuts and breadcrumbs; cook, stirring frequently, until fragrant and golden brown, 8 to 10 minutes; set aside.

**3.** Melt 2 tablespoons butter in a large Dutch oven over medium-high heat. Add apples and remaining sugar; cook, stirring frequently, until apples have softened, 10 to 12 minutes. Transfer to a large bowl. Stir in pine-nut mixture, lemon zest, and raisins; let cool about 15 minutes.

**4.** Spread a 24-inch square of plastic wrap on a clean work surface, and dust with flour. Remove one piece of dough from refrigerator, and place in center of plastic. Roll out into a 20-inch-diameter paper-thin round. Brush top with butter. Spread half the reserved apple mixture on dough. Lift closest edge of plastic, and fold dough over onto itself. Pull plastic back, and use it to fold the dough in half again. Gently lift top fold, and brush with egg yolk; gently press to seal. Brush ends of dough with egg; fold up, and seal. Repeat process with second piece of dough and remaining apple mixture. Transfer to prepared baking pan. Brush entire surface of dough with egg yolk. Using a wooden skewer, pierce strudels all over.

**5.** Transfer pan to oven; bake, rotating halfway through, until golden brown, 30 to 35 minutes. Transfer pan to a wire rack to cool, about 45 minutes. Sprinkle with confectioners' sugar; serve.

### PREPARING PANS FOR BAKING

*When coating a baking pan with softened butter, a pastry brush works best. It not only ensures that the entire surface is evenly coated but also helps cover hard-to-reach nooks. If adding flour, lightly dust buttered surface and gently tap out excess.*

## pecan croquembouche ring
*photograph on page 68*
SERVES 8 TO 10

*Croquembouche, which means "crisp in the mouth" in French, is made with cream-filled pastry puffs that are coated in caramel. Instead of the traditional pyramid shape, our rendition resembles a holiday wreath crowned with a halo of spun sugar. Although there are several components to the recipe, each can be made in advance and then assembled just before serving. You may need to make several batches of caramel, because it hardens quickly.*

½ recipe Pâte à Choux Puffs
  (about 48; recipe follows)
  Pecan Pastry Cream (recipe follows)
1½ cups sugar
  Pinch cream of tartar
18 pecan halves (about 1 ounce)

**1.** Prepare an ice bath; set aside. Using an inverted 9-inch cake pan, trace a 9-inch circle on a piece of parchment paper; place paper, marked side down, on a baking sheet. Line another baking sheet with parchment; set sheets aside.

**2.** Spread choux puffs on a piece of parchment paper on a work surface. Using a pastry bag fitted with a ¼-inch round tip, pipe pastry cream into puffs, inserting tip into bottom of each. Set aside.

**3.** In a small saucepan, bring 1 cup sugar, cream of tartar, and 3 tablespoons water to a boil over medium heat. Continue cooking without stirring until sugar has dissolved, 5 to 6 minutes, washing down sides of pan with a wet pastry brush to prevent crystals from forming. Raise heat to high; cook until syrup is amber, about 5 minutes, swirling pan to color evenly. Remove from heat; dip bottom of pan in ice bath 3 seconds to stop cooking.

**4.** Using long-handled tweezers or small tongs, dip one of the pecan halves into caramel, letting the excess drip back into the pan; place on prepared (unmarked) baking sheet. Repeat with the remaining pecans. Let cool.

**5.** Dip bottom half of each filled puff into caramel, letting excess drip back into pan. Place puffs, dipped side down, on prepared (marked) baking sheet in a ring, using traced circle as a guide. Make sure the puffs are touching and adhere to one another. Once ring is complete, make another one inside the first. Once second ring is complete, begin making a third on top, centering puffs between the two bottom rings and placing them dipped side down. If at any point caramel begins to harden in pan, reheat briefly over low heat.

**6.** Dip bottom (flat side) of candied pecans again in caramel, and arrange them in a ring around outside edge of top row of puffs, centering them between the puffs.

**7.** For the spun sugar, make a second batch of caramel with the remaining ½ cup sugar and 3 tablespoons water. Let cool slightly. Test by dipping a fork into caramel and holding it over pan; the caramel should fall back into pan in long golden threads. Dip a balloon whisk with top cut off or two forks into caramel, and spin caramel threads over a large piece of parchment paper to form a nest. Transfer assembled ring to a serving plate, and place spun-sugar nest in center.

## pâte-à-choux puffs

MAKES ABOUT 8 DOZEN

*Puffs can be made up to one day ahead and stored in airtight containers at room temperature. Any extras can be frozen up to one month.*

½ cup (1 stick) unsalted butter

1 teaspoon sugar

½ teaspoon salt

1 cup all-purpose flour

4 to 5 large eggs, plus 1 egg, lightly beaten with 1 tablespoon water, for egg wash

**1.** Preheat oven to 425°F. Line two baking sheets with parchment paper or Silpat baking mats. Combine 1 cup water, butter, sugar, and salt in a medium saucepan; bring to a boil over medium-high heat. Remove from heat; using a wooden spoon, stir in flour until thoroughly combined. Return pan to medium heat; cook, stirring constantly, until mixture pulls away from sides and a film forms on bottom of pan, about 4 minutes.

**2.** Transfer mixture to the bowl of an electric mixer fitted with the paddle attachment, and beat on low speed until slightly cooled, about 2 minutes. With mixer on medium speed, add 4 eggs, one at a time, beating until incorporated after each addition. Dough should be shiny and form a string when touched and lifted with your finger. If no string forms, lightly beat another egg; add it a little at a time. If a string still doesn't form, add water 1 teaspoon at a time.

**3.** Using a pastry bag fitted with a ½-inch round tip, pipe 1-inch rounds 1 inch apart onto prepared baking sheets. Brush egg wash over tops of rounds.

**4.** Bake until rounds are puffed and lightly golden, about 10 minutes. Reduce oven temperature to 350°F; continue baking until puffs are golden, 20 to 25 minutes more. Turn off oven; prop open oven door with a wooden spoon to release steam. Let puffs dry in oven about 15 minutes, then transfer to a wire rack to cool completely.

### ASSEMBLING THE CROQUEMBOUCHE

*1. To form ring, dip cream-filled pâte-à-choux puffs in caramel, and place in a circle on a baking sheet. Create a second circle inside the first, and a third circle on top.*

*2. To create a nest for center of ring, cut tip from a balloon whisk, dip it into caramel, and spin threads over a large piece of parchment paper.*

## pecan pastry cream

MAKES 1¾ CUPS

*Pastry cream can be made up to four days ahead and stored in the refrigerator.*

- 2 ounces pecans (½ cup)
- 2 cups milk
- ½ vanilla bean, split lengthwise and scraped
- 1 large whole egg
- 1 large egg yolk
- 2 tablespoons cornstarch
- 2 tablespoons all-purpose flour
- ¼ teaspoon salt
- ½ cup sugar
- 1 tablespoon chilled unsalted butter, cut into ½-inch pieces
- 2 teaspoons walnut or hazelnut liqueur (optional)

**1.** Preheat oven to 350°F. Spread pecans in a single layer on a rimmed baking sheet; toast until fragrant, 7 to 9 minutes, turning once. Remove from oven; let cool. Pulse in a food processor until finely ground; you should have about ½ cup.

**2.** Combine milk, vanilla bean and scrapings, and ground pecans in a small saucepan, and bring to a boil. Cover, and remove from heat. Let steep 15 minutes. Discard vanilla bean.

**3.** Meanwhile, in a medium bowl, whisk together egg, egg yolk, cornstarch, flour, and salt until mixture is smooth. Strain mixture through a fine sieve into a medium saucepan, pressing down with a rubber spatula or wooden spoon to extract as much liquid as possible; discard solids.

**4.** Prepare an ice bath; set aside. Add sugar to milk mixture, and stir to combine. Bring to a boil; remove from heat, and slowly whisk into strained egg mixture in saucepan. Return mixture to medium heat; cook, whisking constantly, until thick and bubbling, 1 to 2 minutes.

**5.** Transfer mixture to a large bowl, and whisk in butter and liqueur, if using. Set bowl in ice bath until mixture is completely cool, stirring occasionally. Cover with plastic wrap, pressing it directly onto surface to prevent a skin from forming. Refrigerate until ready to use.

## GENERAL TIPS FOR SUCCESSFUL BAKING

- *Read the entire recipe carefully, noting how long each step should take and how far in advance the recipe needs to be started. Also look over the ingredients beforehand, checking you have everything you will need before starting.*

- *Remember to preheat the oven. It should be turned on twenty to thirty minutes before use.*

- *To ensure even baking, place pans in the center of the oven. If you have to use two racks, rotate pans between them halfway through suggested baking time.*

- *Watch carefully for doneness. Oven temperatures can vary widely, so use an oven thermometer. Baking times are good guidelines, but you should always pay attention to visual cues (such as change of color or texture).*

## epiphany cake

*photograph on page 67*

SERVES 10 TO 12

*Epiphany cake, also known as kings' cake, is traditionally served on the twelfth night of Christmas, in honor of the three kings who came bearing gifts. A clean coin, dried bean, or small figure is traditionally placed in the almond mixture; whoever finds the prize is crowned king or queen for the day.*

- ⅔ *cup whole blanched almonds (about 4 ounces)*
- ½ *cup granulated sugar*
- 1 *large egg yolk, plus 1 yolk lightly beaten with 1 tablespoon heavy cream, for egg wash*
- 3 *tablespoons unsalted butter*
- 2 *tablespoons dark rum*
  *All-purpose flour, for work surface*
- 2 *packages (17.3 ounces each) frozen puff pastry, thawed*
- ¼ *cup seedless red-raspberry jam*
- 1 *tablespoon sanding sugar*

**1.** Line two baking sheets with parchment paper; set aside. Combine almonds and granulated sugar in a food processor, and pulse until nuts are finely ground. Add 1 egg yolk, butter, and rum; process until mixture is combined. Add prize, if using.

**2.** Carefully unfold dough from one package onto a lightly floured work surface; place one sheet of dough on top of the other, squaring corners. Roll out dough to an 11-inch square. Transfer to one of the prepared baking sheets. Repeat with the second package of pastry.

**3.** Invert and gently press a 10-inch round cake pan into center of one dough square to mark a circle to use as a guide. Working quickly, lightly brush water over dough circle, leaving a ½-inch border. Place half the almond mixture in the center of the circle; using an offset spatula, spread mixture evenly, leaving a ½-inch border. Spread jam on top of the almond mixture, followed by the remaining almond mixture.

**4.** Carefully place reserved pastry square on top, squaring corners. Gently lift edges to allow air to escape; smooth out any remaining air bubbles with your hands. Press edges firmly to seal. Invert and place the 10-inch round cake pan on top of dough again, centering it over filling. Using a pastry wheel or sharp knife, cut out a 10-inch circle around inverted pan. Discard scraps; place filled round in freezer about 10 minutes.

**5.** Remove sheet from freezer. Using the tip of a sharp knife, lightly score a decorative three-pointed crown in center of round. Using a ¼-inch pastry tip or a straw, cut out three circles above points of crown. Make ¾-inch-long shallow cuts 1 inch apart all around edge of pastry. Very lightly brush top of pastry with egg wash, being careful not to let any drip over the edges, as it will inhibit rising. Sprinkle crown with sanding sugar. Recut edges of pastry with ¾-inch-long slits, wiping knife clean after each cut. (This will prevent cuts from sealing back up.) Place in freezer at least 1 hour.

**6.** Preheat oven to 400°F, with rack in center. Transfer sheet to oven, and bake 30 minutes. Reduce oven heat to 375°F; cover outer edge of pastry with foil to prevent it from burning. Continue baking until center is browned, about 30 minutes more. Remove from oven; slide cake onto a wire rack to cool. Serve at room temperature.

## hazelnut-brittle caramel ice cream

### MAKES 1 QUART

*To avoid overcooking, have the milk and cream measured before you begin.*

- 1 cup sugar
- 2¼ cups milk
- ¾ cup heavy cream
- 6 large egg yolks
- ¼ teaspoon salt
- ¾ cup Hazelnut Brittle (recipe follows), finely chopped
  Caramel Bowls, for serving (recipe follows; optional)

**1.** Prepare a large ice bath; set aside. Place ⅔ cup sugar in a large saucepan; cook over medium heat until dark amber, about 6 minutes. Slowly add milk and cream, whisking to dissolve the caramelized sugar. Raise heat to high, and bring the mixture to a boil.

**2.** In a medium bowl, whisk together egg yolks, remaining ⅓ cup sugar, and salt until pale. Whisking constantly, add hot cream mixture to yolks. Return mixture to saucepan over medium heat; cook, stirring constantly with a wooden spoon, until cream is thick enough to coat the back of the spoon, 4 to 6 minutes.

**3.** Remove pan from heat; pour mixture through a fine sieve into a heatproof bowl. Place bowl in ice bath; stir occasionally until chilled. Freeze in an ice-cream maker according to manufacturer's instructions. Transfer to an airtight container, and fold in the hazelnut brittle; place in freezer until set, at least 4 hours or preferably overnight.

**4.** When ready to serve, remove ice cream from freezer, and scoop into caramel bowls, if desired.

## hazelnut brittle

### MAKES ONE 11-BY-17-INCH SHEET

*You can also make this brittle with other nuts, such as pistachios or slivered almonds.*

- Vegetable oil, for pan and knife
- 4 cups sugar
- ¼ teaspoon cider vinegar
- 5½ cups hazelnuts

**1.** Oil an 11-by-17-inch rimmed baking sheet; set aside. Combine sugar, vinegar, and 1 cup water in a medium saucepan over medium heat. Cook until amber, 20 to 22 minutes, washing down sides with a wet pastry brush to prevent crystals from forming. Stir in nuts.

**2.** Pour hot mixture onto prepared sheet. Let stand until firm but still soft enough to cut. Invert onto a cutting board. Working quickly, use a sharp, oiled knife to cut sheet into six equal rectangles. Store brittle in an airtight container up to 1 week.

## caramel bowls

MAKES 2 DOZEN

*Make sure the caramel coating has cooled enough so that it forms a line when dripped from a spoon. With your first attempts, be patient and allow plenty of time.*

Vegetable oil, for ladle
Caramel Coating (recipe follows)

**1.** Lightly oil the outside of an eight-ounce ladle. Working over a piece of parchment or baking sheet, drizzle caramel from a tablespoon onto oiled side of inverted ladle, making thin intersecting lines until almost entire surface is covered. Turn ladle right side up, and place 2 ice cubes inside ladle. Swirl to cool coating, being careful not to spill ice or any drops of water on caramel. Let caramel set completely.

**2.** Gently cup ladle with your hand, and ease hardened caramel off ladle. Immediately transfer bowl to an airtight container. Discard ice, dry ladle, and repeat with remaining coating, oiling ladle each time. If caramel hardens at any point, reheat over low heat. Bowls can be stored in airtight containers up to 2 days at room temperature.

## caramel coating

MAKES 1⅓ CUPS

4½ cups sugar
½ cup distilled or bottled water
⅓ cup light corn syrup

**1.** Fill a large bowl with cold tap water, and set aside. Place sugar and distilled water in a medium saucepan over low heat; stir, dissolving sugar. Raise heat to medium-high, and bring to a boil. Skim surface foam as needed. Add corn syrup, and return to a boil.

**2.** Continue cooking syrup mixture until light golden brown and a candy thermometer registers 340°F, about 18 minutes, washing down sides of pan with a wet pastry brush to prevent crystals from forming. Place pan in cold water 5 seconds to stop cooking. Remove pan from water; let caramel thicken slightly, about 5 minutes, before using. If caramel starts to harden while working, set over low heat for a few minutes.

### MEASURING LIQUID SUGAR

*Before measuring a liquid sweetener, such as honey or corn syrup, lightly coat your measuring cup with nonstick cooking spray or a small amount of vegetable oil—the liquid will slide out more easily.*

## coconut snowmen

*photograph on page 62*

MAKES 4

*You will need three ice-cream scoops in varied sizes. Shoestring licorice cut into pieces can also be used for the buttons, eyes, and mouth.*

2½  pints best-quality vanilla ice cream

  2  packages sweetened shredded
     coconut (7 ounces each)
     Orange food coloring

  1  tablespoon marzipan (¼ ounce)

 40  Sen Sen licorice candies

  4  marshmallows

  4  chocolate wafers
     Sifted confectioners' sugar

**1.** Line a baking pan that fits in your freezer with parchment paper. Scoop vanilla ice cream, rounding scoops as much as possible, until you have 4 of each size; place in prepared baking pan. Transfer to freezer to harden 15 minutes.

**2.** Spread coconut onto a plate. Remove ice cream from freezer; roll scoops in coconut. Return to pan, then return pan to freezer. Add food coloring to marzipan until carrot color. Shape marzipan into small carrot shapes, using a paring knife to make ridges. Remove one small scoop of ice cream at a time from freezer, and make faces using Sen Sen for eyes and mouth and marzipan carrots for nose. Return to freezer.

**3.** Remove middle-size scoops from freezer one at a time; place Sen Sen in a row down front for the buttons. Remove remaining scoops from freezer, and stack to create snowmen, pressing slightly to adhere. Return snowmen to freezer.

**4.** Make top hats by roasting marshmallows on skewers over a gas burner or on a baking sheet under the broiler until browned, rotating every few seconds. Place toasted marshmallows on chocolate wafers, and dust with confectioners' sugar. Place hats on snowmen just before serving.

## champagne granita

MAKES 2 QUARTS

*The time it takes to freeze the granita will vary depending on the temperature of your freezer. If there is enough space in the freezer to do so, dividing the mixture between two pans will speed up the process.*

2½  cups sugar

  1  750-ml bottle dry Champagne

**1.** Prepare a large ice bath; set aside. Combine sugar and 2½ cups water in a medium saucepan; bring to a boil. Cook over medium-high heat until sugar has dissolved completely. Transfer to a large bowl set in ice bath; let cool, stirring occasionally.

**2.** Add Champagne to syrup; stir to combine. Pour into a 9-by-13-inch metal pan, and place in freezer, uncovered, 30 minutes. Stir with the tines of a fork, scraping up icy parts. Return to freezer, and stir every 20 minutes until consistency of mixture is similar to that of shaved ice. Cover with plastic wrap until ready to serve.

## chestnut-espresso caramel-swirl ice cream

MAKES ABOUT 1½ QUARTS

*Let ice cream stand at room temperature for ten to fifteen minutes to soften slightly before serving. Store extra caramel sauce, covered, in the refrigerator up to one month.*

12  ounces fresh chestnuts

3½  cups heavy cream

2  cups whole milk

1½  cups sugar

1  vanilla bean, split lengthwise and scraped

8  large egg yolks

¼  cup freshly brewed espresso or very strong freshly brewed coffee

½  tablespoon unsalted butter

**1.** Preheat oven to 400°F. Score each chestnut using a sharp paring knife or a chestnut knife: Make an X on one side of nut or make one long slit crosswise around circumference of chestnut. Place chestnuts in a single layer on a rimmed baking sheet, and roast until flesh is tender and golden, about 25 minutes. Remove from oven. Using a kitchen towel, immediately rub to remove shells.

**2.** Make custard mixture: Combine 2 cups cream, milk, ½ cup sugar, vanilla bean and scrapings, and chestnuts in a medium saucepan. Cook over medium-low heat, stirring occasionally, until chestnuts are falling apart, 20 to 25 minutes.

**3.** Prepare a large ice bath; set aside. In a large bowl, whisk together egg yolks and ½ cup sugar until pale, about 2 minutes. Pour 1 cup hot cream mixture into egg yolks, and whisk to combine. Pour egg mixture back into remaining cream mixture, and whisk to combine.

**4.** Return saucepan to medium heat; stir constantly with a wooden spoon until mixture thickens and holds a line when a finger is drawn across back of spoon, 3 to 5 minutes. Remove from heat, and immediately stir in 1 cup cream.

**5.** Working in batches if necessary, transfer mixture to a food processor or blender, filling no more than halfway; purée until smooth. Pass mixture through a fine sieve into a large bowl, pressing down on chestnuts to extract as much liquid as possible; discard solids. Chill in refrigerator.

**6.** Make caramel sauce: Stir together espresso and remaining ½ cup cream; set aside. Combine remaining ½ cup sugar and 2 tablespoons water in a small saucepan; cook over medium-high heat, washing down sides of pan with a wet pastry brush to prevent crystals from forming, until mixture turns dark golden, 13 to 15 minutes.

**7.** Carefully add espresso mixture to pan (it will spatter); do not stir. When bubbling has subsided, about 1 minute, add butter. Stir with a wooden spoon until combined. Transfer pan to ice bath to cool, stirring frequently.

**8.** Transfer chilled custard mixture to an ice-cream maker, and freeze according to manufacturer's instructions. Quickly transfer half the ice cream to a 1½-quart storage container. Drizzle 4 or 5 tablespoons caramel over ice cream. Cover with remaining ice cream, and drizzle with 4 or 5 tablespoons more caramel. Drag a knife through caramel and ice cream to create swirls. Cover; place in freezer about 6 hours or overnight.

## spice ice cream

MAKES ABOUT 1½ QUARTS

1 vanilla bean, split lengthwise and scraped
4 whole cinnamon sticks
2 cups milk
1 whole star anise (optional)
6 large egg yolks
¾ cup plus 2 tablespoons sugar
2 cups heavy cream, chilled

**1.** Place vanilla bean and seeds, cinnamon sticks, milk, and star anise, if using, in a saucepan over medium-high heat. Bring mixture to a simmer; cover, and remove from heat. Let steep 30 minutes, then strain into a saucepan, discarding solids.

**2.** Combine egg yolks and sugar in a mixing bowl, and whisk until pale and thick, about 3 minutes.

**3.** Prepare a large ice bath; set aside. Place strained milk mixture over medium-low heat, and bring just to a simmer. Slowly pour milk mixture into yolk mixture, whisking constantly. Return mixture to saucepan; cook over low heat, stirring constantly, until mixture is thick enough to coat back of a spoon, about 5 minutes. The custard should retain a line drawn across back of spoon with your finger.

**4.** Remove pan from heat, and immediately stir in chilled cream. Pass through a fine-mesh sieve into a bowl set in ice bath. Stir occasionally until cool. Cover bowl, and place in refrigerator until well chilled, preferably overnight.

**5.** Transfer custard to an ice-cream maker, and freeze according to manufacturer's instructions. Transfer ice cream to an airtight container, and freeze at least 4 hours or up to 1 week.

## pear and cranberry sorbet

SERVES 6

¾ cup plus 2 tablespoons sugar
9 Comice or other green-skinned pears
½ cup freshly squeezed lemon juice
½ cup fresh or frozen cranberries

**1.** Prepare an ice bath; set aside. Combine sugar with 1¾ cups water in a medium saucepan. Cook over medium-high heat, stirring until sugar has dissolved, 5 to 8 minutes. Transfer syrup to a metal bowl; set bowl over ice bath to chill, stirring occasionally, about 30 minutes.

**2.** Meanwhile, peel and core 3 pears. Cut into ¼-inch dice, and toss with 2 tablespoons lemon juice. Transfer to a medium saucepan; add cranberries. Cover, and cook over medium heat until cranberries burst and release their juices, 6 to 8 minutes. Reduce heat to medium-low; cook, covered, until pears are very soft, 12 to 18 minutes more. Transfer mixture to a food processor, and process until smooth. If desired, pass the purée through a fine sieve for a smoother texture. Transfer purée to another metal bowl; chill over ice bath or in refrigerator, about 30 minutes.

**3.** Combine chilled syrup and purée with ¼ cup lemon juice. Transfer mixture to an ice-cream maker, and freeze according to manufacturer's instructions. (Alternatively, place mixture in a metal pan, and freeze 1 hour. Stir with a fork, then continue to freeze, stirring every 30 minutes, until sorbet is granular and frozen, about 4 hours.)

**4.** Meanwhile, make the serving shells. Cut the top inch from remaining 6 pears, and reserve tops. Using a melon baller, scoop out as much flesh from pears as possible, leaving skin intact. Brush insides of pears with remaining 2 tablespoons lemon juice. Place pears and their tops in a large plastic container, and cover; transfer to freezer at least 2 hours. The shells may be prepared 2 to 3 days ahead. To serve, fill frozen shells with sorbet, and garnish with pear tops. Serve immediately.

## peppermint semifreddo
*photograph on page 63*
SERVES 6

½  cup peppermint candies (about 4 ounces)
1½  cups heavy cream
3  large eggs, separated
9  tablespoons sugar
6  tablespoons peppermint liqueur
   Chocolate Sauce, for serving
   (recipe follows)
   Peppermint sticks, for serving

**1.** Using a rolling pin, finely crush 5 tablespoons candies between sheets of parchment paper. Place cream in a medium bowl; whisk in crushed candy, and whip until stiff peaks form. Chill until ready to use. Roughly crush remaining 3 tablespoons candy, and set aside.

**2.** Prepare an ice bath; set aside. In a large heatproof bowl set over a pan of simmering water, whisk egg yolks and 3 tablespoons sugar until pale. Add liqueur, and whisk vigorously until mixture is thick, 3 to 4 minutes. Transfer to ice bath, and whisk until cool.

**3.** In the heatproof bowl of an electric mixer set over a pan of simmering water, whisk egg whites and remaining 6 tablespoons sugar until sugar dissolves and mixture is warm to the touch, about 2 minutes. Remove from heat, and whisk until stiff and glossy peaks form.

**4.** Fold egg-white mixture into egg-yolk mixture in three additions. Fold in whipped-cream mixture. Spoon mixture into six individual serving dishes, layering it with reserved crushed candies. Freeze until firm, about 1½ hours. Serve semifreddo with chocolate sauce and peppermint sticks.

## chocolate sauce
MAKES 2 CUPS

8  ounces bittersweet chocolate,
   finely chopped
1¼  cups heavy cream

Place chocolate in a heatproof bowl. Bring cream to a boil; pour over chocolate. Let stand 15 minutes; stir until smooth and combined. Store in an airtight container in the refrigerator up to 1 week. Before using, reheat gently in a heatproof bowl set over a pan of simmering water.

## chestnut chocolate layer cake

MAKES 1 NINE-INCH LAYER CAKE

*This cake is best served the day it is made. You can bake it in the morning and finish it later in the day. It can stand in a cool place for about three hours before serving. Marrons glacés, whole candied chestnuts, are available at specialty food stores.*

 Unsalted butter, for pans

14 ounces fresh chestnuts

 1 cup sugar

 4 large eggs, room temperature, separated

½ teaspoon cream of tartar

 1 cup sifted cake flour (not self-rising)

⅔ cup sifted chestnut flour

 2 teaspoons baking powder

½ teaspoon ground cinnamon

¼ teaspoon salt

½ cup vegetable oil

 1 teaspoon pure vanilla extract

 6 ounces very finely ground semisweet chocolate

 Pastry-Cream Filling (recipe follows)

 Chocolate Ganache Icing (recipe follows)

 8 marrons glacés (optional)

**1.** Preheat oven to 400°F. Butter two 9-by-2-inch round baking pans, and line bottoms with parchment. Butter parchment, and set aside. Score each chestnut using a sharp paring knife or a chestnut knife: Make an X on one side of nut or make one long slit crosswise around circumference of chestnut. Place chestnuts in a single layer on a rimmed baking sheet, and roast until flesh is tender and golden, about 25 minutes. Remove from oven. Using a clean kitchen towel, immediately rub to remove shells. Let chestnuts cool completely. Transfer chestnuts to a food processor. Add 2 tablespoons sugar, and pulse until very finely ground; set aside.

**2.** Reduce oven heat to 325°F. In the bowl of an electric mixer, whisk egg whites and cream of tartar on medium-low speed until foamy, 5 to 6 minutes. With mixer running, slowly add ½ cup sugar. Raise speed to medium-high; beat until stiff peaks form, 6 to 7 minutes. Transfer mixture to a bowl.

**3.** Into clean mixing bowl, sift together cake flour, chestnut flour, baking powder, cinnamon, salt, and remaining 6 tablespoons sugar. Add egg yolks, oil, vanilla, and ½ cup water; beat on medium speed until smooth and combined, about 1 minute.

**4.** Using a rubber spatula, gently fold flour mixture in four or five additions into egg-white mixture until combined. Gently fold in reserved ground chestnuts and the chocolate. Evenly divide batter between prepared pans; bake on one shelf, rotating pans halfway through, until golden and a cake tester inserted in centers comes out clean, about 65 minutes. Transfer to a wire rack; let cool completely in pans. Invert cakes onto racks; remove parchment paper.

**5.** Place one layer on a cake round or serving platter. Using an offset spatula, evenly spread pastry cream on top, leaving a ½-inch border. Place other layer on top.

**6.** Pour ganache on top, and carefully spread, leaving a ¼-inch border. Ganache will overflow slightly and gently brim over edges. If desired, arrange marrons glacés around top edge of cake, spacing evenly. Set cake aside in a cool place to allow ganache to set.

## pastry-cream filling

MAKES ENOUGH FOR 1 NINE-INCH
LAYER CAKE

1½  cups milk
1½  tablespoons cornstarch
1½  tablespoons all-purpose flour
⅓  cup sugar
    Pinch of salt
 1  large whole egg
 1  large egg yolk
 1  tablespoon unsalted butter
 1  teaspoon pure vanilla extract

**1.** In a medium saucepan, bring milk to a boil. Prepare a large ice bath; set aside.

**2.** Meanwhile, in a medium bowl, combine cornstarch, flour, sugar, salt, egg, and egg yolk; whisk until combined. Pour one-quarter of boiling milk into egg mixture, whisking until combined. Whisk mixture back into remaining milk; place over medium-low heat. Whisk until mixture begins to bubble and has thickened, 4 to 5 minutes.

**3.** Remove from heat; whisk in butter and vanilla until butter is melted. Transfer mixture to a medium bowl; set bowl in ice bath. Let stand until cold, stirring occasionally, about 10 minutes. Place plastic wrap directly on surface to prevent a skin from forming, and store in the refrigerator until ready to use, up to 3 days.

## chocolate ganache icing

MAKES ENOUGH FOR 1 NINE-INCH
LAYER CAKE

*This recipe can easily be doubled or tripled.*

 6  ounces semisweet or bittersweet chocolate, finely chopped
 6  ounces heavy cream

Place chocolate in a small heatproof bowl. Bring cream to a boil in a small saucepan over medium-high heat; pour cream over chocolate. Let stand 5 minutes, then stir until chocolate has melted and mixture is smooth. Set ganache aside in a cool place; let stand until thickened to the consistency of thick cake batter, 10 to 15 minutes.

### TIPS FOR MAKING LAYER CAKES

• *Always use ingredients that are at room temperature when baking layer cakes, to ensure that the texture, crumb, and density of the finished cake will be just right.*

• *Cake layers can be baked ahead of time, then wrapped in plastic and frozen for up to one month. Be sure to let the layers thaw completely before covering them with frosting.*

## chocolate cake with golden leaves

*photograph on page 68*

MAKES 1 TEN-INCH BUNDT CAKE

- 1  cup (2 sticks) unsalted butter, plus more, room temperature, for pan
   Unsweetened cocoa powder, for pan
- 22  ounces semisweet chocolate (about 3⅔ cups), finely chopped
- 2  cups all-purpose flour
- 1  teaspoon baking powder
- ½  teaspoon salt
- 4  large eggs
- 2  cups sugar
- 1  tablespoon pure vanilla extract
- 1½  cups milk
- 1  cup heavy cream
   Gold petal dust, for garnish (optional)
   Chocolate leaves, for garnish (optional)

**1.** Preheat oven to 350°F. Butter a 10-inch Bundt pan; dust with cocoa, tapping out excess. Set aside. Combine 14 ounces chocolate and the butter in a heatproof bowl set over a pan of simmering water; heat, stirring occasionally, until chocolate has melted and mixture is smooth. Remove from heat.

**2.** Into a medium bowl, sift together flour, baking powder, and salt. In the bowl of an electric mixer fitted with the paddle attachment, beat eggs and sugar until pale, about 4 minutes. Beat in vanilla. With mixer on low speed, beat in chocolate mixture until smooth. Add flour mixture in three batches, alternating with the milk and beginning and ending with flour; beat until mixture is smooth after each addition.

**3.** Pour batter into prepared pan. Bake until a cake tester inserted in center comes out clean, about 1 hour 5 minutes. Transfer to a wire rack; let cool completely in pan, at least 1 hour 15 minutes.

**4.** Bring cream to a boil in a small saucepan; remove from heat. Add remaining 8 ounces chocolate, swirling pan so cream covers chocolate; let stand 5 minutes. Whisk until combined. Set aside until mixture is cool to the touch. Strain through a fine sieve into a small bowl.

**5.** Invert cake onto a wire rack set in a rimmed baking sheet. Pour chocolate glaze over cake, using an offset spatula if necessary, to completely cover cake. Pour off excess glaze from baking sheet, straining it again into a bowl. If glaze has started to set, reheat over a pan of simmering water. Repeat to make a second coating. Set cake aside in a cool place to let glaze set, at least 20 minutes.

**6.** Garnish cake: If desired, sift gold petal dust over cake; decorate tops of chocolate leaves with gold petal dust, and attach to cake.

### BUYING GOOD-QUALITY CHOCOLATE

*Use the best chocolate available when baking. Indications of quality include:*

• *Purity. Look on the label for the chocolate's cocoa content, or the percentage of chocolate liquor it contains. The higher the cocoa content, the more intense the chocolate flavor. Semisweet chocolate by definition has at least 35 percent chocolate liquor.*

• *Aroma. When choosing chocolate, make sure its scent is simply chocolatey, free of any dusty or chemical odor, and not overly sweet.*

• *Appearance. Chocolate comes in a range of deep, rich colors. A whitish-gray blemish called bloom may appear on chocolate that was exposed to fluctuations in temperature or humidity—but this will not affect the chocolate's taste or quality if used for baking.*

# chocolate-applesauce cake
*photograph on page 71*
MAKES ONE 9½-INCH CAKE

*This moist cake is better when made one day before serving. A kugelhopf mold is a tube pan with swirled sides. You can also use a Bundt pan.*

- 1 cup (2 sticks) unsalted butter, room temperature, plus more for pan
- 2¼ cups superfine sugar
- 2 large eggs
- 2½ cups unsweetened applesauce, preferably homemade
- 1¾ cups all-purpose flour
- 1 cup unsweetened cocoa powder
- 2 teaspoons baking powder
- 1 teaspoon ground cinnamon
- 1 teaspoon ground ginger
- ½ teaspoon ground nutmeg
- Pinch of salt
- 6 ounces bittersweet chocolate, cut into ½-inch pieces
- 2 tablespoons Calvados or brandy
- 1 teaspoon pure vanilla extract
- 1 tablespoon confectioners' sugar
- Cider Glaze, Apple Chips, and Crystallized Ginger (recipe follows)
- 2 cups whipped cream, for serving (optional)

**1.** Preheat oven to 325°F. Butter a 9½-inch kugelhopf mold. Coat with ¼ cup superfine sugar; tap out excess sugar, and set mold aside.

**2.** In the bowl of an electric mixer fitted with the paddle attachment, beat butter and remaining 2 cups superfine sugar on medium speed, scraping down sides as needed, until mixture is light and fluffy, about 5 minutes. Add eggs, and beat 2 to 3 minutes more. Fold in applesauce, being careful not to overmix.

**3.** Into a large bowl, sift together flour, cocoa powder, baking powder, cinnamon, ginger, nutmeg, and salt. Fold mixture into applesauce mixture. Add chocolate pieces, Calvados, and vanilla; mix until just combined. Pour batter into prepared pan; smooth top with a rubber spatula.

**4.** Bake until cake pulls away from sides of pan and is springy to the touch, and a cake tester inserted in center comes out clean, about 2 hours. Transfer to a wire rack to cool slightly before inverting cake onto rack. Reinvert; let cool completely.

**5.** Sift confectioners' sugar over cake. Pour cider glaze over top of cake, allowing it to drip down sides. Garnish with apple chips and crystallized ginger. Serve cake with whipped cream, if desired.

## THE BEST VANILLA EXTRACT

*Check that the label reads "pure vanilla extract" when making a recipe that calls for vanilla—imitation varieties do not taste as complex. We prefer varieties made from Bourbon-Madagascar beans.*

## cider glaze, apple chips, and crystallized ginger

MAKES ENOUGH TO GARNISH
ONE 9½-INCH CAKE

2   cups apple cider, plus more as needed

4   cups confectioners' sugar, sifted

2   lemons

2   Cortland or other firm red apples

1   two-inch piece fresh ginger, peeled

**1.** Combine cider and 1 cup sugar in a small saucepan; bring to a boil over medium heat. Skim surface, removing any cider sediment that rises to top. Reduce heat; simmer until liquid begins to thicken into a glaze, about 30 minutes.

**2.** Preheat oven to 200°F. Squeeze juice from lemons into a small bowl filled with cold water. Using a very sharp knife, slice apples into rounds as thinly as possible. Place rounds in the lemon water. Line a baking sheet with a Silpat baking mat; set sheet aside.

**3.** Remove cider glaze from heat; let stand until cool enough to touch. Carefully dip each apple round into glaze, and place on baking sheet.

**4.** Bake apple rounds until golden and edges have curled, about 2 hours. Transfer apples to a wire rack; let cool until crisp. Brush with cider glaze.

**5.** Return cider glaze to low heat. Slice ginger into ⅛-inch-thick slices crosswise, and add to glaze. Cook over low heat until ginger is soft and translucent, about 30 minutes. Using a slotted spoon, transfer ginger to a wire rack to cool. The glaze should have reduced to just less than ¾ cup.

**6.** Whisk remaining 3 cups confectioners' sugar into glaze. Remove from heat. If glaze is too thin, let it cool slightly. If it is too thick, add a little more cider. Use immediately.

## chocolate mousse cake

MAKES 1 TEN-INCH LAYERED LOAF

Chocolate Sponge Cake (recipe follows)

8   ounces bittersweet chocolate, finely chopped

3   large egg yolks

¼   cup sugar

2   tablespoons all-purpose flour

1   tablespoon cornstarch

1½  cups milk

1½  cups heavy cream

2   recipes Chocolate Ganache Icing (page 343)

    Edible roses and rose petals, for garnish (optional)

    Cinnamon Crème Anglaise, for serving (recipe follows)

**1.** Line a 10-by-4½-by-3-inch loaf pan with plastic wrap; let excess hang over sides. Line pan with chocolate sponge cake: Cut a 10½-by-5-inch rectangle to fit the top; set aside. Cut one 9-by-4-inch rectangle to fit bottom and two 9-by-3-inch rectangles to fit sides. Cut four 4½-by-2¼-inch pieces; use two to fit each end of the pan.

**2.** Place chocolate in a large heatproof bowl set over a pan of barely simmering water; stir until melted. Set aside.

**3.** Combine yolks and sugar in a medium bowl; whisk until pale. Add flour and cornstarch; whisk to combine. Place milk in a small saucepan; bring to a boil. Gradually pour milk into yolk mixture, whisking constantly. Return mixture to pan; set over medium-low heat. Cook, whisking constantly, until mixture just comes to a boil.

**4.** Remove pan from heat; immediately pass mixture through a fine sieve into the melted chocolate. Stir with a rubber spatula until combined; let cool. Whip heavy cream to soft peaks, and fold into chocolate mixture.

**5.** Spoon chocolate mixture into prepared loaf pan, and top with reserved sponge cake. Wrap excess plastic over loaf, and place in freezer overnight.

**6.** Invert cake onto a wire rack set in a rimmed baking sheet. Pour ganache over cake, using an offset spatula if necessary, to completely cover cake. Scrape excess ganache from baking sheet back into bowl. If ganache has started to set, reheat over a pan of simmering water. Repeat to make a second coating. Allow ganache to set, about 10 minutes.

**7.** Transfer cake to a serving platter; refrigerate 1 hour or until ready to serve. If desired, garnish with edible roses and rose petals just before serving. Thinly slice with a serrated knife. Serve with cinnamon crème anglaise.

### chocolate sponge cake
MAKES 1 TWELVE-BY-SEVENTEEN-INCH CAKE

*This sponge cake is best the day it is made.*

> Unsalted butter, room temperature, for baking sheet
¼ cup plus 1 tablespoon all-purpose flour
¼ cup plus 1 tablespoon unsweetened cocoa powder
6 large eggs, separated
¾ cup sugar

**1.** Preheat oven to 400°F. Butter a 12-by-17-inch rimmed baking sheet; line with parchment paper, and butter the paper. Combine 1 tablespoon flour and 1 tablespoon cocoa; sprinkle over baking sheet, and tap out excess. Set sheet aside.

**2.** In the bowl of an electric mixer, whisk egg yolks on high speed until pale, about 5 minutes. Transfer to a medium bowl, and set aside.

**3.** Place egg whites in clean mixing bowl; whisk on medium speed until soft peaks form, about 3 minutes. Increase speed to medium-high; gradually

add sugar, beating until stiff, glossy peaks form, about 3 minutes. Transfer mixture to a large bowl.

**4.** Using a rubber spatula, fold egg yolks into egg-white mixture. Sift remaining ¼ cup each flour and cocoa over mixture; gently fold to combine. Gently pour batter into prepared baking sheet; smooth top with an offset spatula.

**5.** Bake until cake springs back to the touch, 10 to 12 minutes. Remove from oven; immediately invert cake onto a wire rack lined with parchment paper. Peel parchment from cake; let cake cool completely.

### cinnamon crème anglaise
MAKES 2 CUPS

1 cup milk
¾ cup heavy cream
2 whole cinnamon sticks
4 large egg yolks
¼ cup sugar

**1.** Combine milk, cream, and cinnamon sticks in a small saucepan; bring to a boil over medium-high heat. Remove from heat; let steep 30 minutes.

**2.** Prepare a large ice bath; set aside. In a medium bowl, whisk egg yolks and sugar until pale, about 2 minutes. Return milk mixture to medium heat, and bring to a simmer; reduce heat to low. Whisk about ½ cup milk mixture into egg-yolk mixture. Return mixture to saucepan; cook, stirring, until thick enough to coat the back of a wooden spoon.

**3.** Strain crème anglaise through a fine sieve into a bowl set in ice bath; discard cinnamon. Store in an airtight container in refrigerator up to 3 days.

## freedom hall chocolate-beet cake

MAKES 1 TEN-INCH TUBE CAKE

*This recipe comes from Litchfield Carpenter, who named the cake after his great-aunt's house. We garnished the side of the cake with Gingerbread Angels (page 432).*

### for cake:

- 3 pounds beets
- 3½ cups all-purpose flour
- 4 teaspoons baking soda
- ½ teaspoon salt
- ¼ teaspoon ground cloves
- ¼ teaspoon ground cinnamon
- 5 ounces unsweetened chocolate, chopped
- 6 large eggs
- 2½ cups granulated sugar
- ¼ cup packed dark-brown sugar
- 1½ cups vegetable oil
- 1½ teaspoons pure vanilla extract

### for glaze:

- 6 ounces semisweet or good-quality bittersweet chocolate, chopped
- 1 tablespoon unsalted butter
- 1 tablespoon light corn syrup
- ¾ cup heavy cream
- ½ teaspoon pure vanilla extract
- ¼ teaspoon ground cinnamon
  Pinch of salt

**1.** Make cake: Wash beets; trim stems to 1 inch. Place beets in a large saucepan of cold water, and bring to a boil over high heat. Reduce heat to a simmer; cook beets until very tender when pierced with a paring knife, about 1 hour. Drain, and let rest until cool enough to handle. Using paper towels, rub off skin. Cut beets into large pieces, and transfer to a food processor. Process until smooth, about 5 minutes. Measure out 4 cups beet purée; set aside.

**2.** In a large bowl, whisk together flour, baking soda, salt, cloves, and cinnamon; set aside. In a heatproof bowl set over a pan of simmering water, heat chocolate, stirring, until melted. Let cool.

**3.** Preheat oven to 350°F, with rack in lower third. In the bowl of an electric mixer, whisk eggs and granulated sugar on medium-low speed until combined. Beat in brown sugar, and then vegetable oil. On low speed, gradually beat in reserved beet purée. Add flour mixture in three batches, alternating with melted chocolate and beginning and ending with flour.

**4.** Add vanilla; beat until combined. Pour batter into a 12-cup tube pan. Bake until a cake tester inserted in middle comes out clean, about 1 hour 35 minutes. Transfer to a wire rack to cool in pan; invert cake onto rack. If desired, trim top so cake will sit level on the plate. Cake can be stored at room temperature, wrapped in plastic, 2 to 3 days.

**5.** When ready to serve, make the glaze: Melt chocolate in a heatproof bowl set over a pan of simmering water. Add butter, corn syrup, and cream; stir until smooth. Stir in vanilla, cinnamon, and salt. Pour glaze over cake; use an offset spatula, if necessary, to spread glaze over sides of cake. Serve at room temperature.

## lemon chiffon cake with citrus compote

*photograph on page 72*

MAKES 1 NINE-INCH TUBE CAKE

*A tube pan is also known as an angel-food-cake pan. We prefer pans with removable bottoms.*

- 1½ cups cake flour (not self-rising)
- ½ teaspoon baking soda
- ½ teaspoon salt
- 1½ cups plus 2 tablespoons granulated sugar
- 6 large eggs, separated
- ½ cup vegetable oil
- 2 tablespoons freshly squeezed lemon juice, plus ¼ cup grated lemon zest (about 4 lemons)
- 1 teaspoon pure vanilla extract
- ½ teaspoon cream of tartar
  Citrus Compote (recipe follows)
  Blood-Orange Chips (recipe follows; optional)
  Confectioners' sugar, for dusting

**1.** Preheat oven to 325°F, with rack in center. In a medium bowl, sift together flour, baking soda, salt, and 1½ cups granulated sugar; set aside.

**2.** In a large bowl, whisk together egg yolks, vegetable oil, ⅔ cup water, lemon juice and zest, and vanilla. Add reserved flour mixture, and stir until smooth. Set aside.

**3.** In the bowl of an electric mixer, whisk egg whites on medium speed until foamy. Add cream of tartar; beat on high speed until soft peaks form, about 1 minute. Gradually add remaining 2 tablespoons granulated sugar; beat on high speed until stiff peaks form, about 3 minutes more.

**4.** Fold one-third of egg-white mixture into egg-yolk mixture, then gently fold in remaining two-thirds. Pour batter into a 9-inch tube pan. Using an offset spatula, smooth the top. Bake until a cake

tester inserted in middle comes out clean and cake is just golden, about 50 minutes.

**5.** Remove cake from oven; invert pan over the neck of a wine bottle 2 hours to cool. Turn cake right side up. Run a knife around edge to loosen cake; invert cake onto a serving platter. Fill center of cake with citrus compote. Drain some of the citrus sections, and arrange on top of cake. Top with blood-orange chips, if using. Dust cake with confectioners' sugar just before serving. Serve with remaining citrus compote on the side.

### citrus compote

MAKES ENOUGH FOR 1 NINE-INCH TUBE CAKE

- 3 blood oranges
- 3 oranges
- 3 ruby-red or pink grapefruit
- 2 cups sugar

**1.** Slice off both ends of each orange and grapefruit. Place fruit on a work surface, cut side down. Using a sharp paring knife, remove peel and pith in a single curved motion, following the shape of the fruit. Working over a bowl to catch the juices, slice carefully between sections to remove whole segments. Squeeze membranes over the bowl to release any remaining juice before discarding. Measure out 1 cup juice; set aside. Place segments in bowl with remaining juice.

**2.** Combine sugar and reserved cup juice in a small saucepan. Bring to a boil over medium heat. Reduce heat to a simmer, and cook until liquid has reduced by half, about 10 minutes. Let cool to room temperature. Drain orange and grapefruit segments; combine with syrup in a serving bowl. Keep refrigerated until ready to serve.

### blood-orange chips
MAKES ABOUT 1 DOZEN

1 blood orange
  Confectioners' sugar

**1.** Preheat oven to 225°F. Cut unpeeled orange into very thin slices. Line a baking sheet with parchment paper, and arrange slices on top. Place sugar in a sieve, and generously dust slices. Flip slices, and dust other sides with sugar.

**2.** Bake slices until they begin to dry out, about 30 minutes; turn each slice over. Continue baking until slices are dry but still colorful and not too browned, about 3 minutes more. Let cool. The chips may be stored in an airtight container at room temperature up to 1 month.

### citrus cake
MAKES 1 NINE-INCH CAKE

*You may choose to cut the cake and then garnish each slice with the candied peel, or decorate the whole cake with the peel before slicing.*

½  cup unsalted butter (1 stick), plus more for pan and parchment
1½  cups cake flour (not self-rising), plus more for pan
¾  teaspoon baking powder
¾  teaspoon salt
¼  teaspoon baking soda
1  cup granulated sugar
2  large eggs
  Zest of 2 lemons
½  cup buttermilk
1  cup confectioners' sugar
2½  tablespoons freshly squeezed lemon juice
1½  cups Candied Citrus Peel, cut into ¼-inch strips (page 438)

**1.** Preheat oven to 350°F. Butter a 9-inch round cake pan; line bottom with parchment paper. Butter parchment, and dust pan with flour, tapping out excess; set aside. Sift together flour, baking powder, salt, and baking soda into a bowl; set aside.

**2.** In the bowl of an electric mixer fitted with the paddle attachment, cream butter until pale. Gradually add granulated sugar; beat until light and fluffy, 1 to 2 minutes more. Add eggs one at a time, beating until incorporated after each addition. Add lemon zest; beat to combine.

**3.** Add the flour mixture to the egg mixture in three batches, alternating with the buttermilk and beginning and ending with the flour.

**4.** Spread batter evenly in pan. Bake until golden brown and a cake tester inserted in center comes out clean, about 30 minutes. Transfer to a wire rack to cool completely. Invert cake onto a serving dish.

**5.** Whisk together confectioners' sugar and lemon juice until smooth and opaque. Spread over top of cake with an offset spatula, allowing glaze to drip over side. Garnish with candied citrus peel.

## orange cake with candied citrus slices

MAKES 1 TEN-INCH CAKE

*When using slices of citrus as garnish, choose fruits with thin skins and not too much pith.*

- 2 lemons
- 2 small oranges
- 4 kumquats (optional)
- 4 cups sugar
- 1 cup (2 sticks) unsalted butter, room temperature, plus more for pan
- 4 large eggs
- 3 cups all-purpose flour, sifted
- 2 teaspoons baking powder
- ½ teaspoon salt
- ¼ cup freshly squeezed orange juice (about 1 orange)
- 1 cup sour cream
- 2 tablespoons freshly grated orange zest (about 2 oranges)
- ½ cup orange marmalade

**1.** Wash fruit, and cut into ⅛-inch-thick slices (do not peel). Remove seeds. In a small saucepan over medium heat, combine 2 cups each sugar and water. Bring to a boil, and simmer until clear, about 5 minutes. Add enough lemon slices to make one layer; simmer until transparent, 20 to 40 minutes.

**2.** Using a slotted spoon, transfer slices to a bowl; continue with remaining lemons, followed by oranges and then kumquats, if desired. When all fruit has been candied, pour remaining syrup over fruit; let cool. Refrigerate until ready to use.

**3.** Preheat oven to 350°F. Butter a 10-by-3-inch professional round cake pan, and set aside. In the bowl of an electric mixer fitted with the paddle attachment, cream butter and remaining 2 cups sugar until light and fluffy. Beat in eggs one at a time.

**4.** Sift together flour, baking powder, and salt. Mix together juice and sour cream. Add flour mixture to butter mixture in three batches, alternating with the juice mixture and beginning and ending with the flour. Beat in zest.

**5.** Pour batter into prepared pan, and smooth top with an offset spatula. Bake until a cake tester inserted in center comes out clean, about 1½ hours. Let cake cool 10 minutes in pan, then invert onto a wire rack. Reinvert; let cool completely.

**6.** Heat marmalade and a few drops of water in a small saucepan over low heat until melted. To decorate, brush whole cake with marmalade; arrange drained candied citrus slices on top.

### ROOM-TEMPERATURE BUTTER

*When a recipe calls for butter at room temperature, test its firmness by pressing your forefinger into the top. When the indentation from your finger remains but the butter still holds its shape, it is ready. To soften butter quickly, microwave in five-second intervals, rotating often; or slice ¼-inch-thick pieces and lay them flat on a stainless-steel surface for about ten minutes.*

## fig holiday roll

MAKES 1 SIXTEEN-INCH ROLL

*Frozen grapes can be substituted for the currants, and cream cheese (mixed with two more table-spoons sugar and a half teaspoon vanilla extract) can be used instead of the mascarpone.*

### for cake:

½  cup (1 stick) unsalted butter, melted and cooled, plus more for sheet and foil

1  pound soft dried figs, trimmed and quartered

¼  cup dried currants

1½  cups milk

1½  cups all-purpose flour

¾  cup packed light-brown sugar

2½  teaspoons baking powder

1  teaspoon ground cinnamon

½  teaspoon salt

½  teaspoon freshly grated nutmeg

¼  teaspoon ground ginger

¼  teaspoon ground cloves

3  slices white sandwich bread

4  large eggs

2  tablespoons chopped Candied Lemons and Kumquats (page 398; optional)

2  tablespoons crystallized ginger (optional)

### for filling and garnish:

2  pounds mascarpone cheese

½  cup heavy cream

½  cup confectioners' sugar

   Red currants, for garnish

   Candied Lemons and Kumquats, for garnish (page 398; optional)

   Raspberry Coulis, for garnish (recipe follows)

**1.** Preheat oven to 350°F, with rack in center. Make cake: Butter a 17-by-11-inch rimmed baking sheet. Line with parchment paper, and butter parchment. Place figs, dried currants, and milk in a medium saucepan; bring to a simmer over medium heat.

Cook until liquid is absorbed, 8 to 10 minutes. Remove from heat; place mixture in a food processor, and process until a thick paste forms (it should not be completely smooth). Set aside.

**2.** Sift together flour, brown sugar, baking powder, cinnamon, salt, nutmeg, ground ginger, and cloves into a medium bowl; set aside. Tear bread into small pieces; place in a food processor. Pulse until fine crumbs form, about 10 times; you should have about 1½ cups breadcrumbs.

**3.** Place eggs in the bowl of an electric mixer; beat on high speed until frothy. Add reserved fig mixture, along with the breadcrumbs, melted butter, candied fruit, and crystallized ginger, if using. Beat until combined. With mixer on low speed, add reserved flour mixture; beat until just combined.

**4.** Using an offset spatula, spread batter evenly on prepared baking sheet. Cover loosely with buttered foil, and place in oven. Place a baking pan filled with boiling water on rack beneath cake.

**5.** Bake until cake is golden and springy to the touch, about 40 minutes, rotating once halfway through. Remove from oven, and let cool on a wire rack 10 minutes.

**6.** Meanwhile, make filling: Combine mascarpone, cream, and sugar in a large bowl; fold until smooth. Refrigerate, covered, until ready to use; cake will be easier to roll if mixture is cold.

**7.** Lay a clean kitchen towel over cake, and invert onto a baking sheet. Let cool 10 minutes. Starting with a long end, roll gently into a log, incorporating the towel; curl the cake without applying too much pressure, to prevent excessive cracking. Keep roll wrapped in towel 10 minutes. Unroll, and let cool to room temperature. Don't worry if there are breaks in the cake; once filled, it can be rolled with cracked pieces on bottom.

1. Preheat oven to 350°F. Butter a 17-by-11-inch rimmed baking sheet; line with parchment paper. Butter parchment, and sprinkle with flour, tapping out excess. Place a clean kitchen towel on a work surface; sift confectioners' sugar evenly over towel. In a medium bowl, whisk together flour, ginger, cinnamon, cloves, and nutmeg; set aside.

2. In the heatproof bowl of an electric mixer set over a pan of simmering water, combine brown sugar and eggs; whisk until a candy thermometer registers 110°F (warm to the touch), about 2 minutes. Remove bowl from heat. Beat on high speed, using paddle attachment, until thick and pale, 6 to 8 minutes. Transfer mixture to a large bowl.

3. In a small bowl, combine butter and molasses. Add flour mixture to egg mixture in thirds, folding until combined after each batch; add molasses mixture in a steady stream while folding in last batch. Pour mixture onto prepared sheet; smooth top with an offset spatula.

4. Bake until cake is springy to the touch and golden brown, about 14 minutes. Transfer sheet to a wire rack to cool 5 minutes. Carefully invert cake onto sugared towel. With short end closest to you, pick up edge of towel, and begin rolling cake. As you roll, incorporate towel; continue rolling into a log. Clip with clothespins to help hold shape. Transfer to a wire rack to cool.

### calvados soaking syrup
MAKES 1½ CUPS

- 1 cup sugar
- 5 tablespoons Calvados or brandy

In a saucepan over medium-high heat, combine sugar and 1 cup water. Cook, stirring occasionally, until sugar has dissolved, 4 to 5 minutes. Remove from heat; let cool. Stir in Calvados. Cover with plastic wrap until ready to use.

### semifreddo mixture
MAKES ENOUGH FOR
1 SEVENTEEN-INCH ROLL

- 6 large egg yolks
- ⅓ cup sugar
- ⅓ cup Calvados or brandy
- 2 cups heavy cream

1. In the bowl of an electric mixer fitted with the paddle attachment, beat yolks on medium speed until pale and thick. Gradually add sugar; beat until fluffy. Slowly add Calvados, and combine.

2. Set bowl over a pan of simmering water. Whisk until mixture is shiny and thick, about 8 minutes. Return to mixer; beat on medium speed until cool, about 10 minutes.

3. In another bowl, whip cream until soft peaks form. Add one-fourth of whipped cream to egg mixture, and whisk to combine. Fold in remaining whipped cream. Transfer to a 13-by-9-inch metal pan. Cover with plastic wrap, and freeze at least 3 hours or overnight.

### spiced cranberry coulis
MAKES 1⅔ CUPS

- 8 ounces fresh cranberries
- 6 tablespoons sugar
- 2 strips orange peel (about 1 inch wide and 3 inches long)
- 1 whole cinnamon stick

1. In a small saucepan, combine all ingredients with 1½ cups water, and bring to a boil. Reduce heat to medium-low, and cook until cranberries have burst, 8 to 10 minutes. Discard orange peel and cinnamon stick.

2. Pass mixture through a food mill, then through a fine sieve to remove solids; let cool.

### sugared cranberries and rosemary

MAKES ½ CUP

¾ cup Calvados Soaking Syrup (page 355)
½ teaspoon sugar
½ cup fresh cranberries
12 sprigs rosemary

Pour soaking syrup into a medium bowl; place sugar in another bowl. Insert a toothpick into a cranberry. Dip cranberry into syrup; let excess drip off, then roll in sugar, tapping off excess. Set aside on parchment paper. Repeat with remaining cranberries. Dip a rosemary sprig in syrup; let excess drip off, then dip into sugar; tap off excess. Set aside on parchment paper. Repeat with remaining rosemary sprigs.

✻

### bûche de noël

photograph on page 74

SERVES 10 TO 12

*This fanciful "Yule log" is a classic French holiday dessert. When making génoise for this recipe, let cool ten minutes, then invert onto a clean kitchen towel. Starting with a long end, roll gently into a log, incorporating the towel. Keep roll wrapped in towel ten minutes. Unroll, and let cool to room temperature.*

Chocolate Génoise (page 377)
Chocolate Mousse (recipe follows)
Chocolate Ganache (recipe follows)
4 ounces bittersweet chocolate, melted
Meringue Mushrooms (recipe follows)
Confectioners' sugar, for dusting

**1.** To assemble cake, place génoise, still on towel, on a baking sheet. Spread chocolate mousse evenly over cake, leaving a 2-inch border on one long end. Reroll cake, starting from other long end, using towel to help roll. Cover with plastic wrap; chill until firm, about 1 hour.

**2.** Place cake, seam side down, on a serving platter; tuck strips of parchment under edge to keep platter clean while decorating.

**3.** Whip ganache at medium speed until it is the consistency of soft butter. Cut a wedge off each end of cake at a 45-degree angle for branches; set aside. Ice log with a thin layer of ganache. Attach one branch, cut side up, to top of cake and one to its side. Spread ganache all over log, using a small spatula to form barklike ridges. Chill.

**4.** Line a baking sheet with parchment. Spread melted chocolate ⅛ inch thick over parchment. Refrigerate until cold, 10 to 15 minutes. Roll paper back and forth until chocolate splinters; sprinkle evenly over cake. Chill cake until ready to serve.

**5.** When ready to serve, arrange meringue mushrooms around and on top of cake, and dust lightly with confectioners' sugar.

### chocolate mousse

MAKES ENOUGH FOR 1 BUCHE DE NOEL

4 ounces semisweet chocolate
4 tablespoons unsalted butter
4 large eggs, separated
  Pinch cream of tartar
½ cup heavy cream

**1.** In a heatproof bowl over a pan of simmering water, melt chocolate and butter, stirring occasionally until smooth. Remove from heat, and transfer to a large bowl. Whisk in egg yolks, stirring well. Let cool to room temperature.

**2.** Beat egg whites with cream of tartar until stiff. Whisk a third of the whites into chocolate mixture; gently fold in remainder.

**3.** Whip cream until soft peaks form, and fold in. Chill until set, about 1 hour.

## chocolate ganache
### MAKES 1½ CUPS

6  ounces bittersweet or semisweet chocolate
1  cup heavy cream

Chop chocolate into small pieces, and place in a medium bowl. In a small saucepan, heat cream until scalding; pour over chocolate. Let stand 5 minutes, then stir until smooth. Refrigerate until cold but not solid, stirring occasionally.

## meringue mushrooms
### MAKES ABOUT 30

When using these with Bûche de Noël, omit white chocolate from this recipe and skip step four. In step five, use remaining bittersweet chocolate to attach stems to caps.

   Swiss Meringue (recipe follows)
2  ounces bittersweet chocolate, chopped
3  ounces white chocolate, chopped

**1.** Preheat oven to 200°F. Line two baking sheets with parchment paper. Using an 18-inch pastry bag fitted with a large round tip, pipe meringue onto parchment, forming domes 1 to 2 inches in diameter. Pipe a stem shape for each cap separately.

**2.** Bake 1 hour, then reduce oven heat to 175°F. Continue baking until meringues are completely dry to the touch but are still white, 45 to 60 minutes. Remove from oven.

**3.** Place bittersweet chocolate in a heatproof bowl, and set over a pan of simmering water; stir occasionally, until completely melted. Using an offset spatula, spread bottoms of caps with chocolate; let set at room temperature.

**4.** Melt white chocolate in another heatproof bowl set over simmering water; let cool slightly. Spread white chocolate over dark chocolate, and use a toothpick to create lines from center of cap to edges. Let set in a cool, dry place.

**5.** Using a paring knife, poke a small hole in center of each coated mushroom cap. Dip pointed end of each mushroom stem in melted white chocolate (reheat over simmering water, if necessary); insert stem into hole in center of cap. Allow to set. Mushrooms should be kept in an airtight container in a cool, dry place until ready to use, up to 2 days.

## swiss meringue
### MAKES 4 CUPS

When making meringue mushrooms for Bûche de Noël, fold one tablespoon cocoa powder into Swiss Meringue after vanilla has been added; sprinkle piped mushrooms with more cocoa powder before baking.

4   large egg whites
1   cup sugar
    Pinch cream of tartar
½   teaspoon pure vanilla extract

**1.** Combine egg whites, sugar, and cream of tartar in the bowl of an electric mixer; place bowl over a pan of simmering water. Whisk constantly until sugar has dissolved and whites are warm to the touch, about 3 minutes. Rub mixture between your fingers to test; it should be smooth.

**2.** Remove bowl from heat. Whisk, starting on low speed and gradually increasing to high, until meringue is cool and stiff and glossy peaks form, about 10 minutes. Add vanilla; mix until combined. Use immediately.

## *birch de noël*

MAKES 1 TEN-BY-FIVE-INCH LOG

*We created this version of the classic French Yule log as part of an all-white dessert display when we ran a story about a white Christmas in* Martha Stewart Living. *It has since become a holiday classic in its own right. To make sugared rosemary sprigs, wash sprigs, then make a glaze by thinning one egg white with one tablespoon water; brush glaze over sprigs, then coat in superfine sugar.*

 1  *whole fresh coconut*
 6  *large eggs, separated*
 ¾  *cup sugar*
 ¼  *cup unsweetened cocoa powder*
 ¼  *cup all-purpose flour*
 2  *tablespoons rum*
     *White Chocolate Mousse (page 360)*
     *Seven-Minute Frosting (page 360)*
     *Meringue Mushrooms (page 357)*
     *Snowy Chocolate Truffles (page 361)*
     *Sugared rosemary sprigs,
     for garnish (optional)*

**1.** Preheat oven to 350°F. Wrap coconut in a clean kitchen towel, and place in oven 20 minutes. Remove from oven, and place on a work surface. Reduce oven heat to 250°F. Tap coconut with a hammer until it cracks in several places; break it into pieces. The white flesh should be pulling away slightly from the hard shell. Separate flesh, keeping pieces of coconut as large as possible.

**2.** Using a vegetable peeler, shave the largest pieces of coconut into long curls, and place on a baking sheet. Bake 15 to 20 minutes, just until dry. Grate smaller pieces on the small holes of a box grater. You will need ½ cup grated coconut for the cake filling. Set aside shavings and grated coconut.

**3.** Raise oven heat to 400°F. Line a 17-by-12-inch rimmed baking sheet with parchment paper, and

set aside. Place egg yolks in the bowl of an electric mixer, and whisk on high speed until pale, 4 to 5 minutes. Transfer to a large bowl; set aside.

**4.** Place egg whites in clean mixing bowl; whisk on medium speed until soft peaks form, 1 to 2 minutes. Increase speed to medium-high; gradually add sugar, whipping until stiff peaks form.

**5.** Using a rubber spatula, fold one-third of egg-white mixture into egg-yolk mixture to lighten; fold in the rest until just combined. Sift cocoa powder and flour over top of mixture, and gently fold in. Pour batter onto prepared sheet, and smooth top with an offset spatula.

**6.** Bake until cake is golden and springy to the touch, 9 to 10 minutes. Remove from oven, and immediately invert cake onto a wire rack lined with parchment paper. Peel parchment paper from bottom of cake, and let cake cool completely.

**7.** Lay a clean kitchen towel flat on a work surface. Transfer cake on parchment paper to towel. Using a pastry brush, coat cake with rum. Using an offset spatula, spread chocolate mousse evenly over cake. Sprinkle with reserved grated coconut.

**8.** With a short end of the cake facing you, roll carefully into a log. Wrap in towel, and secure with clothespins or binder clips to help hold the shape. Place on a baking sheet; refrigerate until firm, at least 2 hours or overnight.

**9.** When ready to serve, remove cake from refrigerator. Using a serrated knife, trim ends of roll, cutting on the bias. Choose the prettier end, and place it, cut side up, on the log, forming a branch.

**10.** Transfer log to a serving platter, and coat with frosting using an offset spatula. Decorate with meringue mushrooms, truffles, coconut shavings, and rosemary sprigs, if desired.

## HOW TO MAKE A YULE LOG AND MERINGUE MUSHROOMS

*1.* To form a yule log, place sheet cake, still on kitchen towel, on work surface. With a short end of the cake facing you, roll carefully into a log, using towel to help guide the shape.

*2.* Wrap log in towel, and secure with clothespins or binder clips to help hold the shape. Place wrapped log on a baking sheet; refrigerate until firm.

*3.* Using a serrated knife, trim ends of roll, cutting on the bias. Choose the prettier end for a branch, and place it, cut side up, on top of log. If desired, place other branch on side of log. Frost log and branches.

*4.* For Meringue Mushrooms, pipe meringue onto a parchment-paper-lined baking sheet, forming domes one to two inches in diameter for caps. Pipe a stem shape for each cap separately; bake until dry.

*5.* Spread the bottoms of the cooked caps with melted bittersweet chocolate. Let them set, then spread white chocolate over dark, if using.

*6.* Run a toothpick from center of cap to edges to create ribs. Attach stems with more melted chocolate.

## white chocolate mousse
MAKES 5½ CUPS

1½ teaspoons unflavored gelatin
12 ounces best-quality white chocolate, roughly chopped
2½ cups heavy cream

**1.** Sprinkle gelatin over ¼ cup cold water, and let soften 5 minutes. Place chocolate in a food processor, and pulse until very finely chopped.

**2.** Place ¾ cup cream in a small saucepan, and bring just to a boil over medium-high heat. Add gelatin mixture, and stir 30 seconds to dissolve completely. With motor running, pour mixture into food processor; process until smooth.

**3.** Transfer mixture to a medium bowl; cover with plastic wrap. Chill until thick enough to hold ribbons on the surface when mixture is lifted with a spoon, about 20 minutes.

**4.** Whip remaining 1¾ cups cream to stiff peaks. Gently fold into chocolate mixture until just combined. If not using immediately, refrigerate in an airtight container.

## seven-minute frosting
MAKES 4½ CUPS

*For best results, start whisking the egg whites once the syrup has reached a boil. This recipe can easily be doubled.*

¾ cup plus 1 tablespoon sugar
1 tablespoon light corn syrup
3 large egg whites
¾ teaspoon pure vanilla extract

**1.** In a small, heavy saucepan over medium heat, combine ¾ cup sugar, ⅓ cup water, and corn syrup, stirring until sugar dissolves. Raise heat to medium-high; bring to a boil. Wash down sides of pan with a wet pastry brush to prevent sugar crystals from forming. Cook without stirring until a candy thermometer registers 235°F (soft-ball stage).

**2.** Meanwhile, in the bowl of an electric mixer, whisk egg whites on medium speed until soft peaks form, about 2½ minutes. Gradually add remaining tablespoon sugar, and reduce speed to medium-low. Remove syrup from heat, and carefully pour it in a steady stream down side of bowl.

**3.** Increase speed to medium-high, and beat until frosting is completely cool, about 7 minutes. Add vanilla, and beat until fully incorporated. Frosting should be shiny and smooth and hold stiff peaks. Use frosting immediately.

### candied lemon slices
MAKES ABOUT 1½ DOZEN

*Store slices in syrup in an airtight container in the refrigerator, up to one week.*

1 lemon (unpeeled)
2 cups sugar

**1.** Using a mandoline or sharp knife, slice lemon as thinly as possible.

**2.** In a medium saucepan, combine sugar and 2 cups water. Bring to a boil over medium-high heat. Add lemon slices; return just to a boil, and immediately remove from heat. Let cool completely.

### poppy-seed layer cake
MAKES 1 EIGHT-INCH LAYER CAKE

*Cake can be assembled the day before serving.*

1 cup (2 sticks) unsalted butter, room temperature, plus more for pans
2½ cups sifted all-purpose flour, plus more for pans
1 tablespoon baking powder
Pinch of salt
2 lemons
1 cup milk
½ cup poppy seeds, plus more for garnish
1 tablespoon vanilla extract
1½ cups sugar
4 large eggs, room temperature
2 cups Lemon Curd (recipe follows)
1 cup (½ pint) heavy cream

**1.** Preheat oven to 350°F. Butter two 8-inch round cake pans. Line bottoms with parchment paper; butter and flour paper and sides of pans, tapping out excess flour. Sift together flour, baking powder, and salt two times into a bowl; set aside.

**2.** Zest 1 lemon into long strips; set aside for garnish. Grate zest of second lemon; place in a small saucepan along with the milk and poppy seeds. Heat over high heat until steaming; let cool to room temperature. Add vanilla.

**3.** In the bowl of an electric mixer fitted with the paddle attachment, cream butter until soft. Gradually add sugar; beat on medium speed until very fluffy, about 5 minutes, scraping down sides of bowl several times. Add eggs one at a time, beating well after each addition; continue beating on medium-high speed until smooth, about 1 minute.

**4.** Add flour mixture in three additions, alternating with milk mixture and beginning and ending with flour. Beat on low speed until just combined.

**5.** Divide batter evenly between prepared pans; smooth with an offset spatula. Bake until a cake tester inserted in center of cakes comes out clean, 25 to 30 minutes. Let cakes cool in pans 5 minutes, then invert onto wire racks. Peel off paper; let cakes cool completely.

**6.** To assemble the cake, place one layer, top side down, on a serving plate. Spread about 1 cup chilled lemon curd on top, leaving a ¾-inch border. Place second layer, top side up, on filling; press gently. Chill 30 minutes.

**7.** Prepare an ice bath; set aside. In a bowl, whip cream until soft peaks form. Fold into remaining cup lemon curd. Place bowl in ice bath. Quickly spread top and sides of cake with a thick layer of cream mixture. Chill cake 15 to 30 minutes.

**8.** Remove cake from refrigerator; coat with another layer of cream mixture, covering entirely. Chill until set, about 15 minutes. Tipping cake slightly, sprinkle sides with poppy seeds. Decorate top with lemon-zest strips. Chill until ready to serve.

### lemon curd

MAKES ABOUT 3 CUPS

1  cup sugar

6  large egg yolks, lightly beaten and strained

½  cup freshly squeezed lemon juice

½  cup (1 stick) unsalted butter,
   cut into small pieces
   Grated zest of 1 lemon

**1.** Place sugar, egg yolks, and lemon juice in a medium saucepan over low heat; whisk to combine. Cook, stirring constantly with a wooden spoon, until thick enough to coat the back of the spoon. Continue cooking a few minutes more, but do not let boil.

**2.** Remove pan from heat. Stir in butter a few pieces at a time until melted; stir in zest. Let cool; chill, covered, until ready to use, up to 1 day.

### red-velvet cake

MAKES 1 NINE-INCH CAKE

*To get this cake's distinctive red color, we used Spectrum Super Red food coloring by Ateco.*

   Unsalted butter, room
   temperature, for pans

2½  cups cake flour (not self-rising),
    plus more for pans

1  teaspoon salt

¼  cup unsweetened cocoa powder

1½  cups sugar

1½  cups canola oil

2  large eggs

¼  cup red food coloring

1  teaspoon pure vanilla extract

1  cup buttermilk

1½  teaspoons baking soda

2  teaspoons white vinegar
   Seven-Minute Frosting (page 360)

**1.** Preheat oven to 350°F. Generously butter two 9-inch round cake pans. Dust with flour, and tap out excess; set aside. In a medium bowl, whisk together flour, salt, and cocoa; set aside.

**2.** In the bowl of an electric mixer, whisk sugar and oil on medium speed until well combined. Add eggs one at a time, beating well after each addition. Add food coloring and vanilla, and beat until combined. Add the flour mixture and buttermilk in two alternating batches, starting with the flour; scrape down sides of bowl as needed.

**3.** In a small bowl, whisk together baking soda and vinegar. Add to batter, and beat 10 seconds. Divide batter evenly between prepared pans. Bake until a cake tester inserted in centers comes out clean, 30 to 35 minutes.

**4.** Transfer pans to a wire rack to cool 5 minutes. Invert cakes onto rack; reinvert so they are top side up, and let cool completely.

**5.** Place one cake layer on a serving platter. Using an offset spatula, spread about 1½ cups frosting on top of layer. Place second layer on top, and spread a thick layer of frosting on entire cake, swirling to create peaks, as desired. The cake can be refrigerated, covered, up to 6 hours. Before serving, bring to room temperature.

## almond tortes

MAKES 2 EIGHT-INCH TORTES

10 tablespoons (1¼ sticks) unsalted butter, melted and cooled, plus more, room temperature, for pans

1½ cups whole almonds (unblanched)

1 cup plus 2 tablespoons granulated sugar

¼ cup cornstarch

¼ cup all-purpose flour

1 teaspoon baking powder

¼ teaspoon salt

6 large eggs

¼ cup orange-flavored liqueur

1 cup seedless raspberry jam

⅓ cup confectioners' sugar, for dusting
Marzipan holly leaf and berries, for decorating (optional)
Vegetable-oil cooking spray

**1.** Preheat oven to 375°F. Butter two 8-inch round cake pans. Line bottoms with parchment paper; butter parchment, and set aside. In a food processor, process almonds and sugar to a powder. Into a medium bowl, sift together cornstarch, flour, baking powder, and salt; set aside.

**2.** In the bowl of an electric mixer fitted with the paddle attachment, beat 2 eggs with the ground almond mixture on low speed until blended, about 1 minute. Add remaining 4 eggs one at a time, beating on high speed 3 to 4 minutes and scraping down sides of bowl after each addition. Add liqueur, and beat until combined.

**3.** Sprinkle cornstarch mixture over egg mixture; fold in until just combined. Fold in melted butter. Divide batter evenly between prepared pans. Bake until a cake tester inserted in centers comes out clean, about 30 minutes, rotating pans halfway through. Line 2 wire racks with parchment paper; coat parchment with cooking spray. Invert cakes onto parchment; let cool, about 45 minutes.

**4.** In a small saucepan, warm jam over low heat until melted, stirring occasionally. Spread warm jam on top of one cake layer; place second layer on top, and dust with confectioners' sugar. Decorate with marzipan, if desired.

## linzertorte with lingonberry jam

MAKES 1 EIGHT-INCH TART

*This rich torte, a recipe from Carolina Bunce, is best served chilled with whipped cream.*

3 ounces best-quality bittersweet chocolate, chilled

¾ cup sugar

5 ounces whole almonds (unblanched)

1½ cups all-purpose flour, plus more for work surface

½ teaspoon ground cinnamon
Pinch of salt

9 tablespoons chilled unsalted butter, cut into small pieces

1 large egg

1½ tablespoons freshly squeezed lemon juice

1 cup lingonberry or raspberry jam
Confectioners' sugar, for dusting

**1.** Preheat oven to 350°F. Break the chocolate into pieces. In a food processor, combine chocolate, sugar, and almonds; pulse until finely ground, about 45 seconds.

**2.** Add flour, cinnamon, and salt; pulse 3 to 4 times to combine. Add butter; pulse until mixture resembles coarse meal. Transfer to a medium bowl.

**3.** In a small bowl, whisk together egg and lemon juice. Add to flour mixture, stirring with a fork until mixture comes together.

**4.** Place an 8-inch springform pan or bottomless tart ring on a parchment-lined baking sheet. Press about two-thirds of dough into pan, forming a

½-inch-thick crust; crust should be thicker on the sides (about 1 inch). Using a rubber spatula, spread jam evenly over bottom of crust.

**5.** Divide remaining dough into quarters. On a lightly floured work surface, roll dough into long thin ropes about ⅓ inch in diameter. Arrange ropes along top of tart, pressing to flatten.

**6.** Bake tart until slightly golden brown around the edges, about 50 minutes. Let cool to room temperature. Chill, and dust lightly with confectioners' sugar before serving.

## hazelnut chocolate torte
### MAKES 1 EIGHT-INCH SQUARE TORTE

2¾  cups hazelnuts
¾  cup (1½ sticks) unsalted butter, melted, plus more for pan
¾  cup Dutch-process cocoa powder, plus more for pan and dusting
⅓  cup all-purpose flour
6  large eggs, separated
½  cup packed light-brown sugar
   Pinch of salt
½  cup superfine sugar
3  recipes Chocolate Ganache Icing (page 343)

**1.** Preheat oven to 350°F. Spread hazelnuts in a single layer on a rimmed baking sheet. Toast until fragrant and skins begin to split, about 10 minutes. Remove from oven. While still warm, rub nuts vigorously in a clean kitchen towel to remove loose skins. Let cool, and roughly chop 1 cup nuts; set aside. In a food processor, pulse remaining nuts until finely ground.

**2.** Butter an 8-inch square cake pan, and dust with cocoa powder, tapping out excess; set aside. In a small bowl, whisk together cocoa powder, ground hazelnuts, and flour; set aside.

**3.** In the bowl of an electric mixer, whisk egg yolks and brown sugar on medium-high speed until mixture holds a ribbon-like trail on the surface for 3 seconds when whisk is lifted, about 45 seconds. Transfer mixture to a large bowl.

**4.** In a clean mixing bowl, whisk egg whites and salt on medium-high speed until soft peaks form, about 1 minute. With mixer running, slowly add superfine sugar; beat until peaks are stiff and glossy. Fold egg-white mixture into egg-yolk mixture in three additions. Sift reserved cocoa mixture over egg mixture; gently fold in with a rubber spatula until just combined. Fold in melted butter.

**5.** Transfer batter to prepared pan; smooth top with an offset spatula. Bake until a cake tester inserted in center comes out clean, 35 to 40 minutes. Transfer to a wire rack to cool completely, about 1½ hours.

**6.** Invert cake onto wire rack; reinvert, and trim top with a serrated knife to level, if desired. Brush away any loose crumbs. Set rack over a rimmed baking sheet lined with plastic wrap. Pour icing over top of cake, completely covering top and sides. Set cake and rack over another rimmed baking sheet; refrigerate 5 minutes.

**7.** Meanwhile, lift up plastic from baking sheet; pour ganache through a fine sieve into a bowl, pressing down with a rubber spatula. Remove cake from refrigerator, and pour strained ganache over top to give it a second coat. Refrigerate 5 minutes.

**8.** Transfer torte to a serving platter. Dust top with cocoa powder; press chopped hazelnuts onto sides, and serve.

## three-nut torte

*photograph on page 69*

MAKES 1 EIGHT-INCH TORTE

*Whisk one teaspoon corn syrup into Chocolate Ganache Icing recipe before setting aside to cool.*

> Unsalted butter, room temperature, for pans
>
> All-purpose flour, for pans

6 large eggs, separated

¼ cup plus 3 tablespoons sugar

¾ cup finely ground toasted walnuts

½ cup finely ground toasted hazelnuts

½ cup finely ground toasted blanched almonds

3 ounces bittersweet chocolate, finely chopped or grated

1 tablespoon finely grated orange zest

½ teaspoon baking powder

¼ teaspoon salt

> Praline Buttercream (recipe follows)
>
> Chocolate Ganache Icing (page 343)

**1.** Preheat oven to 300°F. Butter three 8-inch round cake pans. Line bottoms with parchment paper; butter parchment, and dust with flour, tapping out excess. Set aside.

**2.** In the bowl of an electric mixer, whisk egg yolks and ¼ cup sugar on medium-high speed until thick and pale, about 3 minutes. Transfer to a large bowl. In a separate bowl, toss together nuts, chocolate, zest, baking powder, and salt. Sprinkle over yolk mixture; do not mix in.

**3.** Whisk egg whites in clean bowl of an electric mixer set over a pan of simmering water until whites are warm to the touch. Remove bowl from heat; with clean whisk attachment, beat on high until soft peaks form. Beat in remaining 3 tablespoons sugar until stiff and glossy peaks form.

**4.** Fold egg-white mixture into egg-yolk mixture, one-third at a time. Divide batter evenly among prepared pans; smooth with an offset spatula.

**5.** Bake cakes until springy to the touch, about 20 minutes. Transfer pans to wire racks to cool, about 10 minutes. Run a knife around edge of each cake to loosen, and invert cakes onto wire racks; peel off parchment paper. Let cool completely.

**6.** Place one cake layer on a turntable or flat work surface. Spread 1¼ cups buttercream evenly over top. Place second cake layer on buttercream, and spread 1¼ cups buttercream over top. Place final cake layer on top, and spread remaining ½ cup buttercream on top. Refrigerate at least 30 minutes while you make the ganache.

**7.** Transfer cake to a wire rack set over a rimmed baking sheet. Pour ganache over top of cake; use an offset spatula to smooth top and sides. Place cake in refrigerator, and let ganache set, at least 30 minutes, before serving.

### TORTES

*The classic torte is a series of sponge-cake layers alternated with a cream or jam filling, but torte can refer to any number of Central European cakes. Although tortes are rich, most are not very sweet, so the flavors of the ingredients shine through.*

## praline buttercream

MAKES 3 CUPS

1 cup (2 sticks) unsalted butter, room temperature, cut into small pieces, plus more for baking sheet

1½ cups sugar

¾ cup chopped toasted blanched almonds

4 large egg whites

**1.** Make the praline: Butter a baking sheet; set aside. In a small, heavy saucepan, bring 1 cup sugar and ¼ cup water to a boil over medium heat, stirring until sugar dissolves; wash down sides of pan with a wet pastry brush to prevent crystals from forming. Continue cooking, without stirring, until dark amber, swirling pan to color evenly. Remove from heat; stir in nuts, distributing evenly. Immediately pour mixture onto prepared baking sheet. Let sit until hardened and completely cool.

**2.** Break praline into pieces, and place in a food processor; pulse to a fine powder. Measure out 1½ cups praline powder, and set aside. Reserve remaining powder for another use.

**3.** Make the buttercream: In the heatproof bowl of an electric mixer set over a pan of simmering water, whisk together egg whites and remaining ½ cup sugar until mixture is warm to the touch and sugar has dissolved.

**4.** Remove bowl from heat; whisk on high speed until mixture is cool and stiff, about 5 minutes. Add butter, several pieces at a time, and beat until mixture has a smooth, spreadable consistency. If the buttercream appears curdled, keep beating until smooth again.

**5.** Add praline powder to buttercream; beat to combine. If using the same day, set aside, covered with plastic wrap, at room temperature. Or refrigerate in an airtight container up to 3 days. Before using, bring to room temperature; beat with paddle attachment until smooth.

## cranberry upside-down cake

MAKES 1 EIGHT-INCH CAKE

*This almond-flavored cake is baked on top of cranberries that have been simmered in maple syrup. When the cake is turned out of its pan, the cranberries make a dramatic topping. Serve it plain for breakfast or with a scoop of vanilla ice cream for dessert.*

¾ cup (1½ sticks) unsalted butter, room temperature, plus more for pan

¾ cup all-purpose flour, plus more for pan

2¾ cups fresh or thawed frozen cranberries

½ cup plus 1 tablespoon pure maple syrup

½ teaspoon ground cinnamon

1 teaspoon baking powder

¼ teaspoon salt

¼ cup plus 2 tablespoons yellow cornmeal, preferably coarse

¼ cup almond paste

¾ cup plus 2 tablespoons sugar

3 large eggs, separated

¼ teaspoon pure vanilla extract

¼ teaspoon pure almond extract

½ cup milk

**1.** Butter and flour an 8-by-2-inch round cake pan; set aside. In a large skillet, heat 6 tablespoons butter over medium heat until sizzling. Add cranberries, and cook until shiny, 2 to 3 minutes.

**2.** Add maple syrup and cinnamon to skillet. Cook, stirring frequently, until cranberries soften but still hold their shape, about 5 minutes. Using a slotted spoon, transfer cranberries to a baking sheet; let cool slightly. Set aside skillet containing syrup.

**3.** Arrange cranberries in the prepared cake pan. Return skillet with syrup to medium heat, and boil 3 to 4 minutes. Immediately pour syrup over cranberries; let cool 10 minutes.

**4.** Preheat oven to 350°F, with rack in center. Into a large bowl, sift together flour, baking powder, and salt. Whisk in cornmeal. Set aside.

**5.** Place remaining 6 tablespoons butter in the bowl of an electric mixer fitted with the paddle attachment. Crumble in almond paste, and beat on medium speed until smooth and combined, about 30 seconds.

**6.** With mixer running, gradually add ¾ cup sugar to butter mixture, and beat until creamy. Add egg yolks; beat until combined. Beat in vanilla and almond extracts. Add flour mixture in two batches, alternating with milk. Set batter aside.

**7.** In a clean mixing bowl, whisk egg whites until foamy. Gradually add remaining 2 tablespoons sugar, and beat until soft peaks form. Whisk one-third of the egg whites into batter, then fold in the remaining whites.

**8.** Spread batter over cranberries in pan, smoothing with an offset spatula, and bake until a cake tester inserted in center comes out clean, about 45 minutes. Transfer to a wire rack to cool completely, about 2 hours. Invert cake onto a serving plate, and serve at room temperature.

## gingerbread-pear upside-down cake
*photograph on page 70*
MAKES 1 NINE-INCH SQUARE CAKE

- 10 *tablespoons butter (1¼ sticks), room temperature, plus more for pan*
- 5 *ripe but firm Bartlett pears, peeled, cored, and quartered*
- 2 *tablespoons freshly squeezed lemon juice*
- 4 *tablespoons granulated sugar*
- 6 *tablespoons brandy*
- 1 *cup all-purpose flour*
- 1 *tablespoon ground ginger*
- 1 *teaspoon ground cinnamon*
- ¼ *teaspoon ground cloves*
- ¼ *teaspoon ground nutmeg*
- ¼ *teaspoon salt*
- ¼ *cup packed dark-brown sugar*
- 3 *large eggs*
- ½ *cup unsulfured molasses*
- 1 *tablespoon freshly grated ginger*
- 1 *teaspoon baking soda*
- 2 *tablespoons boiling water*

**1.** Preheat oven to 350°F. Butter a 9-inch square cake pan; set aside. In a large bowl, toss pears with lemon juice. In a large skillet over medium-high heat, melt 2 tablespoons butter; sprinkle with 2 tablespoons granulated sugar.

**2.** Arrange half the pears, cut sides down, in a single layer in skillet; cook until brown, 2 to 3 minutes. Turn pears over; cook other sides until brown, 2 to 3 minutes. Using a slotted spoon, transfer pears to a plate. Add remaining pears to skillet, and cook until brown; transfer to plate.

**3.** Carefully pour brandy into skillet, and sprinkle with remaining 2 tablespoons granulated sugar. Cook, stirring, until reduced to a syrup, about 1 minute. Pour into prepared cake pan; swirl to cover evenly. Starting in one corner of pan, fan out pears, cut sides down, in a single layer; arrange so the tapered sides lie in the same direction. Set aside.

**4.** In a medium bowl, whisk together flour, ground ginger, cinnamon, cloves, nutmeg, and salt; set aside. In the bowl of an electric mixer fitted with the paddle attachment, cream the remaining 8 tablespoons butter until light. Add brown sugar; beat on medium-high speed until fluffy, about 3 minutes. Add eggs, and beat to combine. Beat in molasses and grated ginger.

**5.** Add half the flour mixture; beat to combine on low speed. In a small bowl, combine baking soda and boiling water; beat into batter. Add remaining flour mixture, and beat until combined.

**6.** Pour batter into pan over pears; smooth with an offset spatula. Bake 25 minutes. Reduce oven heat to 325°F; continue baking until springy to the touch, 15 to 20 minutes. Transfer to a wire rack to cool 1 hour. Run a knife around cake to loosen. Invert cake onto a serving plate, tapping bottom to help release pears. Serve at room temperature.

## *pear and raisin upside-down cake*

*photograph on page 68*

MAKES 1 TEN-INCH CAKE

*To keep pears from turning brown, submerge them in cold water mixed with a bit of lemon juice; pat dry with paper towels before using.*

- 14 *tablespoons (1¾ sticks) unsalted butter, room temperature, plus more for pan*
- 1¾ *cups packed light-brown sugar*
- 2 *cups all-purpose flour*
- 2 *teaspoons baking powder*
- ½ *teaspoon salt*
- ½ *teaspoon ground cinnamon*
- ⅛ *teaspoon ground cloves*
- 3 *large eggs, room temperature*
- 1 *teaspoon pure vanilla extract*
- ¾ *cup milk*
- 4 *ripe but firm Bosc pears (about 2 pounds)*
- 1 *cup golden raisins*

**1.** Preheat oven to 350°F. Butter a 10-by-2-inch round cake pan. Line the bottom with parchment paper, and butter parchment. Set aside.

**2.** In a small saucepan over medium heat, melt 6 tablespoons butter with ¾ cup brown sugar; cook, stirring occasionally, until mixture is combined and bubbling, 6 to 7 minutes. Pour into prepared pan; swirl to cover bottom evenly. Let cool completely, 15 to 20 minutes.

**3.** Meanwhile, make batter: Into a medium bowl, sift together flour, baking powder, salt, cinnamon, and cloves. In the bowl of an electric mixer fitted with the paddle attachment, cream remaining 8 tablespoons butter and 1 cup brown sugar until smooth. Add eggs one at a time, beating until combined after each addition. Beat in vanilla. Add flour mixture in three batches, alternating with the milk and beginning and ending with the flour. Set aside.

**4.** Peel, core, and slice pears lengthwise into ¼-inch-thick slices. Arrange slices in a circle around the outside edge of the pan, overlapping slightly. Sprinkle raisins over top, making sure to fill center. Carefully pour batter on top; smooth with an offset spatula.

**5.** Bake until a cake tester inserted into center comes out clean, about 1 hour. Transfer to a wire rack; let cool in pan 20 minutes before inverting onto a serving plate. Serve at room temperature.

## brownie cupcakes
### MAKES 1 DOZEN

  6  *tablespoons unsalted butter*
 11  *ounces best-quality semisweet chocolate, coarsely chopped*
  3  *large eggs*
  1  *cup sugar*
  ¾  *cup all-purpose flour*
  ¼  *cup unsweetened cocoa powder*
  ⅛  *teaspoon baking soda*
  1  *cup coarsely chopped walnuts (optional)*
     *Mrs. Milman's Chocolate Frosting (recipe follows)*
     *Nonstick cooking spray*

**1.** Preheat oven to 350°F. Line a 12-cup muffin tin with paper liners. Coat generously with cooking spray, and set aside.

**2.** In a small saucepan over low heat, melt butter and 8 ounces chocolate; stir until smooth. Remove from heat, and set aside.

**3.** In a large bowl, whisk together eggs and sugar. Add flour, cocoa, and baking soda. Stir in melted chocolate mixture until combined. Stir in remaining 3 ounces chocolate and the nuts, if desired.

**4.** Using an ice-cream scoop, fill prepared muffin cups three-quarters full with batter. Bake until a firm crust forms on cupcakes, about 20 minutes. Transfer tin to a wire rack to cool, about 10 minutes. Remove cupcakes from tin; cool completely on wire rack. Ice cupcakes generously with frosting.

## mrs. milman's chocolate frosting
### MAKES ABOUT 3 CUPS, ENOUGH FOR 1 DOZEN CUPCAKES

 12  *ounces best-quality semisweet chocolate, finely chopped*
  2  *cups heavy cream*
  ½  *teaspoon light corn syrup*

**1.** Combine chocolate and cream in a medium saucepan. Cook over low heat, stirring constantly, until mixture has thickened, 20 to 30 minutes. Raise heat to medium-low, and cook, stirring constantly, 3 minutes more. Remove from heat, and stir in corn syrup.

**2.** Transfer mixture to a large bowl. Chill, covered, until thick enough to spread, about 2 hours, stirring every 15 to 20 minutes.

## christmas cupcakes

*photograph on page 73*

MAKES 3 DOZEN

### for cupcakes:

1½ cups cake flour (not self-rising), sifted

½ teaspoon baking powder

¼ teaspoon salt

¾ cup (1½ sticks) unsalted butter, room temperature

1 cup sugar

2 large eggs

1 teaspoon pure vanilla extract

½ teaspoon pure almond extract

½ cup nonfat buttermilk

### for butter glaze and decorating:

2 cups sifted confectioners' sugar

½ cup (1 stick) unsalted butter

8 teaspoons milk

Royal Icing (page 428)

**1.** Preheat oven to 350°F. Make cupcakes: Line three 12-cup mini-muffin tins with paper liners, and set aside. In a medium bowl, sift together flour, baking powder, and salt; set aside.

**2.** In the bowl of an electric mixer fitted with the paddle attachment, cream butter and sugar on medium speed until light and fluffy, about 3 minutes. Add eggs one at a time, beating until incorporated after each addition; beat in vanilla and almond extracts.

**3.** Add flour mixture in three batches, alternating with the buttermilk and beginning and ending with the flour.

**4.** Using a pastry bag fitted with a plastic coupler, fill prepared muffin cups three-quarters full. Use an offset spatula to carefully smooth tops. Bake until a cake tester inserted in centers comes out clean, about 18 minutes. Transfer tins to wire racks to cool. Remove cupcakes from tins.

**5.** Make one batch of glaze: Place 1 cup confectioners' sugar in a medium bowl. In a small saucepan, melt 4 tablespoons butter over medium heat. Remove from heat; immediately pour butter into bowl with sugar. Add 4 teaspoons milk; whisk until smooth. Working quickly, dip tops of half the cupcakes into glaze, and place cupcakes right side up on wire rack. Repeat to make a second batch of glaze, and use to coat remaining cupcakes.

**6.** Allow glaze to set, about 20 minutes. Fill a pastry bag fitted with a plain writing tip with royal icing, and decorate as desired.

## gingerbread cupcakes

MAKES 10

*Use large cupcake papers and two jumbo-muffin tins to bake these cupcakes. Coat them with either a butter or chocolate glaze, and then decorate with meringue buttercream.*

1 cup boiling water

2 teaspoons baking soda

2½ cups all-purpose flour

2 teaspoons baking powder

2 teaspoons ground ginger

1½ teaspoons ground cinnamon

½ teaspoon ground cloves

½ teaspoon ground nutmeg

½ teaspoon salt

½ cup (1 stick) unsalted butter, room temperature

⅔ cup packed dark-brown sugar

1 cup unsulfured molasses

2 large eggs, room temperature, lightly beaten

Butter Glaze or Shiny Chocolate Glaze (recipes follow)

Meringue Buttercream (recipe follows)

**1.** Preheat oven to 350°F. Line ten cups of two jumbo-muffin tins with paper liners, and set aside. In a bowl, combine the boiling water and baking soda; set aside. In a large bowl, sift together flour, baking powder, ground spices, and salt; set aside.

**2.** In the bowl of an electric mixer fitted with the paddle attachment, cream butter until light. Beat in brown sugar until fluffy, 1 to 2 minutes. Beat in molasses, baking-soda mixture, and flour mixture, then beat in eggs.

**3.** Fill each prepared muffin cup three-quarters full, dividing batter evenly. Bake cupcakes until a cake tester inserted in centers comes out clean, about 30 minutes. Transfer tins to a wire rack to cool a few minutes, then remove cupcakes from tins, and let cool completely on rack.

**4.** Working quickly, dip tops of cupcakes into butter or chocolate glaze, and place cupcakes right side up on a wire rack. Let glaze set, about 20 minutes, before decorating with piped buttercream.

### butter glaze

MAKES 1½ CUPS

*To tint glaze, add food coloring a drop at a time, stirring well before adding more.*

2½ cups sifted confectioners' sugar
½ cup (1 stick) unsalted butter
2 tablespoons plus 2 teaspoons milk

Place confectioners' sugar in a medium bowl. In a small saucepan, melt butter over medium heat; immediately pour melted butter into bowl with sugar. Add milk; whisk until mixture is smooth. Use immediately.

### shiny chocolate glaze

MAKES 2⅓ CUPS

10 ounces semisweet chocolate, finely chopped
1¼ cups heavy cream
4 teaspoons unsalted butter

In a heatproof bowl set over a pan of simmering water, combine chocolate, heavy cream, and butter. Let mixture melt slowly, stirring occasionally. Use immediately, or cover, and keep warm over simmering water until ready to use.

## meringue buttercream

MAKES 5 CUPS

*Meringue buttercream is an excellent icing to use for piping. To tint, add food coloring a drop at a time, stirring well before adding more. Since this recipe makes a large amount of buttercream, it can easily be divided among small bowls and each bowl tinted a different color.*

- 1¼ cups sugar
- 5 large egg whites
  Pinch cream of tartar
- 2 cups (4 sticks) chilled unsalted butter, cut into small pieces
- 1 teaspoon pure vanilla extract

**1.** In a small saucepan over medium heat, bring sugar and ⅓ cup water to a boil; continue boiling, washing down sides of pan with a wet pastry brush to prevent crystals from forming, until a candy thermometer registers 238°F (soft-ball stage).

**2.** In the bowl of an electric mixer, whisk egg whites on low speed until foamy. Add cream of tartar, and beat on medium-high speed until stiff but not dry peaks form.

**3.** With mixer running, carefully pour sugar syrup into egg-white mixture in a steady stream down side of bowl; beat on high speed until steam is no longer visible, about 3 minutes. Add butter, piece by piece, with mixer on medium speed, beating until incorporated after each addition.

**4.** Add vanilla; continue beating until frosting is smooth and spreadable, 3 to 5 minutes. If frosting looks curdled at any point, keep beating until it is smooth. If frosting becomes too soft for piping, stir it over a large bowl of ice water until stiff.

**Note:** Raw eggs should not be used in food prepared for pregnant women, babies, young children, the elderly, or anyone whose health is compromised.

## ginger baba au rhum

MAKES ABOUT 20 MINI BABA

*These miniature versions of baba au rhum are baked in mini-brioche molds. You will need about twenty molds.*

- 1 cup all-purpose flour, plus more for dough and work surface
  Pinch of salt
- ¼ cup warm milk (about 110°F)
- 1 cup plus 4 teaspoons granulated sugar
- 1 envelope active dry yeast (1 scant tablespoon)
- 1 large egg, lightly beaten
- 3 tablespoons unsalted butter, melted, plus more for molds
- 6 tablespoons rum
- 1 one-inch piece fresh ginger, peeled and cut into four pieces
- 1 large egg, lightly beaten with 1 tablespoon water, for egg wash
- 4 teaspoons sanding sugar

**1.** Sift flour and salt into a large bowl. In a small bowl, combine warm milk, 4 teaspoons granulated sugar, and yeast. Stir to dissolve; let stand until foamy, about 5 minutes. Add yeast mixture to flour mixture; stir with a wooden spoon. Add beaten egg and butter; stir 5 minutes (dough will still be sticky). Cover with plastic wrap; let rise in a warm place until doubled in bulk, about 45 minutes.

**2.** Preheat oven to 425°F. Beat the dough with a wooden spoon to remove air bubbles, adding 1 to 2 tablespoons flour if needed. Turn out dough onto a floured work surface. Form into 1-inch balls with floured hands. Place dough in well-buttered 2-by-1-inch molds. Cover; let proof 10 minutes.

**3.** Meanwhile, combine remaining 1 cup granulated sugar, ¾ cup water, the rum, and ginger in a small saucepan. Stir over medium heat until sugar dissolves, about 3 minutes, then cook 5 minutes more. Set aside to steep.

4. Brush the tops of dough with egg wash, and sprinkle with sanding sugar. Bake until golden, about 10 minutes. Remove from oven. Strain syrup into a large bowl. Turn baba out of pan; place in syrup, turning to coat, and let soak up to 4 hours. Serve baba in syrup at room temperature.

✳

## mini angel-food cakes
*photograph on page 67*
MAKES 6

⅔  cup superfine sugar
½  cup cake flour (not self-rising)
6  large egg whites
½  teaspoon cream of tartar
¼  teaspoon salt
½  teaspoon pure vanilla extract
   Clementine Mousse (recipe follows)

1. Preheat oven to 350°F. Into a medium bowl, sift together ¼ cup sugar and the cake flour three times. In the bowl of an electric mixer, whisk egg whites, cream of tartar, salt, and vanilla on low speed until mixture is frothy. Add remaining sugar; raise speed to medium-high, and beat until stiff peaks form. Sift flour mixture over top, and gently fold in until well combined.

2. Rinse 6 mini angel-food-cake pans, and shake out water so only a few drops remain. Distribute batter evenly among pans. Tap pans gently against countertop to remove any air pockets. Transfer to oven, and bake until cakes are golden and springy to the touch, 18 to 20 minutes.

3. Remove pans from oven; invert and rest each pan on the neck of a bottle or on two glasses. Let stand until completely cool. Run a knife around edges; tap pan on counter to loosen, then invert cakes onto serving plates. Top each with a dollop of clementine mousse.

## clementine mousse
*photograph on page 67*
MAKES ENOUGH FOR 6 MINI
ANGEL-FOOD CAKES

*You can use almost any other citrus fruit— tangerines, oranges, or lemons—instead of the clementines in this recipe.*

1½  cups freshly squeezed clementine juice
    Finely grated zest of 1 clementine
¼   cup sugar
1   teaspoon unflavored gelatin
1   cup heavy cream

1. Prepare an ice bath; set aside. Place 2 tablespoons clementine juice in a small heatproof bowl; cover with plastic wrap, and chill in refrigerator. Place remaining juice in a medium saucepan; add zest and sugar, and bring to a boil. Reduce heat to a simmer; cook until liquid has reduced to ½ cup, about 20 minutes. Transfer syrup to a bowl set over ice bath; stir frequently until syrup is cool.

2. Remove reserved juice from refrigerator, and sprinkle gelatin over top. Let stand until softened, about 5 minutes. Set bowl over a pan of simmering water until gelatin has dissolved. Stir mixture into clementine syrup. Refrigerate 5 minutes.

3. In a mixing bowl, whip cream until stiff peaks form. Fold in clementine mixture until well combined. Cover with plastic wrap; refrigerate until mixture is set, about 1 to 2 hours.

## individual no-bake cheesecakes

*photograph on page 73*

MAKES 6

3  tablespoons granulated sugar

7  ounces graham crackers (about 13)

½  cup (1 stick) unsalted butter, melted

10  ounces cream cheese, room temperature

6  ounces crème fraîche

⅔  cup sifted confectioners' sugar

1  cup heavy cream

1  cup Mrs. Gubler's Pomegranate Jelly, for serving (page 310)

Pomegranate seeds, for garnish

**1.** Line six cups of a jumbo-muffin tin with plastic wrap; set aside. Combine sugar and crackers in a food processor; pulse until very finely chopped. Transfer to a small bowl, and stir in melted butter. Press mixture into prepared muffin cups. Transfer to freezer while preparing filling.

**2.** In the bowl of an electric mixer fitted with the paddle attachment, beat cream cheese, crème fraîche, and confectioners' sugar until combined. In another bowl, beat heavy cream until stiff peaks form; fold into cream-cheese mixture. Spoon filling into crusts; freeze until firm, about 30 minutes.

**3.** Meanwhile, heat pomegranate jelly in a small saucepan over low heat, stirring until melted and smooth. Remove from heat; let stand until jelly is cool but still pourable.

**4.** To serve, remove muffin tin from freezer. Lift out cheesecakes by gently pulling up on plastic wrap. Carefully remove plastic; set cakes on serving plates. Drizzle each with jelly, and sprinkle with pomegranate seeds.

## shiny chocolate petits fours

MAKES 4 DOZEN

*These bite-size cakes can be stored, uncovered, for up to two days in the refrigerator.*

⅔  cup brewed strong coffee

½  cup sugar

Chocolate Génoise (recipe follows)

3  recipes Shiny Chocolate Glaze, warm (page 373)

192  gold dragées (optional)

**1.** Place coffee and sugar in a small saucepan. Bring to a boil over medium heat, stirring constantly until sugar has dissolved. Remove from heat, and let cool.

**2.** Turn génoise out onto a cutting board, and peel off parchment paper. Trim ½ inch from each long edge and 1 inch from each short edge with a serrated knife. Cut génoise in half, making two 10-by-7½-inch pieces. Brush tops generously with cooled coffee syrup.

**3.** Prepare an ice bath. Transfer ¾ cup chocolate glaze to a medium bowl; place over ice bath. Whisk glaze until fluffy, lightened, and thick. Using an offset spatula, evenly spread whipped glaze over one piece of génoise. Place second piece of génoise squarely on top of first.

**4.** Using a ruler and a serrated knife, cut stacked cake into 48 1¼-inch squares. Fit two rimmed baking sheets with wire racks. Arrange cake squares on racks, spacing them 1½ inches apart.

**5.** Generously ladle warm glaze over squares, covering tops and sides. Refrigerate 10 minutes.

**6.** Remove sheets from refrigerator; place four dragées, if desired, in the center of each petit four. Using a small offset spatula, transfer petits fours to a cake stand or serving platter.

## chocolate génoise

MAKES 1 SEVENTEEN-BY-ELEVEN-INCH CAKE

*Génoise is best when made the day before you plan to use it.*

- 5 tablespoons unsalted butter, melted, plus more for pan
- ⅓ cup sifted cocoa powder, plus more for pan
- ⅔ cup sifted cake flour (not self-rising)
  Pinch of baking soda
- 7 large eggs
- ¾ cup sugar
- 2 teaspoons pure vanilla extract

**1.** Preheat oven to 350°F. Butter a 17-by-11-inch baking pan. Line with parchment paper; butter paper, and dust with cocoa. Set aside. Into a medium bowl, sift together flour, cocoa, and baking soda; set mixture aside.

**2.** In the bowl of an electric mixer, whisk together eggs, sugar, and vanilla. Set bowl over a pan of simmering water; whisk until mixture is warm and sugar has dissolved. Remove from heat. Whisk on high speed until mixture is thick, pale, and tripled in bulk, about 6 minutes.

**3.** In three batches, sift reserved flour mixture over egg mixture, folding in after each addition. While folding in last addition, pour in melted butter; fold in thoroughly.

**4.** Transfer batter to prepared pan; smooth with an offset spatula. Tap pan against counter to remove air bubbles. Bake until cake springs back when touched in center, 15 to 20 minutes. Transfer pan to a wire rack. Let cake cool completely. Cover pan with plastic wrap until ready to use.

## backhouse family fruitcake

MAKES 1 EIGHT-INCH CAKE

*This recipe comes from the mother of Sara Backhouse, former associate food editor at Martha Stewart Living.*

- ¾ cup (1½ sticks) unsalted butter, room temperature, plus more for pan
- 4 ounces glacéed or dried pineapple, chopped into ½-inch pieces (½ cup)
- 4 ounces glacéed or dried apricots, chopped into ½-inch pieces (½ cup)
- 8 ounces dates, pitted and chopped (1½ cups)
- 4 ounces dried cherries (½ cup)
- 4 ounces whole blanched almonds (¾ cup)
- 8 ounces Brazil nuts (1½ cups)
- ⅔ cup all-purpose flour
- ½ cup cake flour (not self-rising)
- ½ teaspoon baking powder
  Pinch of salt
- 1 cup packed light-brown sugar
- 3 large eggs
- 2 tablespoons rum, plus more for dousing
- 1 teaspoon pure vanilla extract

**1.** Preheat oven to 300°F. Brush an 8-inch springform pan with butter. Line bottom with parchment paper; butter parchment. Set aside.

**2.** Combine fruit and nuts in a bowl; set aside. Sift together the flours, baking powder, and salt into a medium bowl. In the bowl of an electric mixer fitted with the paddle attachment, cream butter and sugar until fluffy, about 3 minutes. Reduce speed; add eggs one at a time, mixing well after each addition. Beat in rum and vanilla.

**3.** In two additions, add flour mixture to butter mixture. Scrape down bowl between additions. Fold in fruit and nuts. Pour batter into prepared pan. Bake until golden and set, about 2½ hours. If cake begins to brown too quickly, tent with foil.

**4.** Transfer pan to a wire rack, and let cool completely. Remove cake from pan; peel off parchment. Wrap cake in cheesecloth or muslin. Douse with ¼ cup rum. Store in a cool, dry place, dousing cake with ¼ cup rum once a week for at least 1 month before serving.

## chocolate panforte

MAKES 1 NINE-INCH CAKE

*Unlike most fruitcakes, this one, a specialty of Siena, Italy, is ready to eat as soon as it cools.*

4   ounces whole hazelnuts (¾ cup)
    Unsalted butter, room temperature, for pan
3   ounces dried cherries (½ cup)
2   tablespoons brandy
3   ounces best-quality unsweetened chocolate, finely chopped (¾ cup)
1¼  ounces best-quality bittersweet chocolate, finely chopped (¼ cup)
1   cup plus ½ tablespoon all-purpose flour
1½  teaspoons ground cinnamon
⅔   cup honey
⅔   cup packed light-brown sugar
½   teaspoon Dutch-process cocoa powder

**1.** Preheat oven to 350°F. Spread hazelnuts on a rimmed baking sheet. Toast in oven until fragrant and skins are beginning to split, about 10 minutes. Rub warm nuts in a clean kitchen towel to remove skins. Set nuts aside.

**2.** Reduce oven heat to 300°F. Butter a 9-inch springform pan. Line bottom with parchment paper; butter parchment, and set aside.

**3.** Combine cherries, nuts, brandy, and chocolates in a medium bowl; set aside. Sift 1 cup flour and ½ teaspoon cinnamon into a small bowl.

**4.** Combine honey and sugar in a small saucepan. Bring to a boil, stirring constantly. Reduce heat to a simmer, and cook 2 minutes. Combine with dried-fruit mixture. Fold in flour mixture. Pour batter into prepared pan.

**5.** With wet hands or a small metal spatula, press mixture to form a level layer. In a small bowl, combine remaining ½ tablespoon flour, 1 teaspoon cinnamon, and the cocoa. Sift over cake batter.

**6.** Bake until set, about 30 minutes. Remove from oven, and let cool completely. Gently brush off flour coating before serving. Keep in an airtight container up to 1 week at room temperature.

## dowager duchess fruitcakes

MAKES 5 SMALL LOAVES

*This cake is best served thinly sliced.*

2   cups (4 sticks) unsalted butter, room temperature, plus more for pan
2½  cups sugar
5   large eggs
3   tablespoons dry sherry, plus more for dousing
    Grated zest of 1 lemon
    Grated zest of 1 orange
4   cups all-purpose flour, sifted
2   pounds 4 ounces candied citrus peel, such as grapefruit, orange, or lemon, cut into ½-inch pieces (6 cups)
15  ounces whole blanched almonds (2½ cups)

**1.** Preheat oven to 300°F. Line bottoms of five 5¾-by-3-inch loaf pans with parchment paper; butter parchment, and set aside.

**2.** In the bowl of an electric mixer fitted with the paddle attachment, cream butter and sugar until light and fluffy, about 3 minutes. Add eggs one at a time, beating well after each addition and scraping down sides of bowl at least twice. Stir in sherry and citrus zest.

**3.** Reduce speed to low. Add flour 1 cup at a time, beating until just combined after each addition. Fold in candied peel and almonds.

**4.** Pour batter into prepared pans. Bake until golden and a cake tester inserted in centers comes out clean, about 1 hour 15 minutes.

**5.** Remove cakes from oven, and douse each with 3 tablespoons sherry. Cool cakes completely in pans on a wire rack. Remove cakes from loaf pans, and peel off parchment. Wrap cakes in muslin or cheesecloth. Store in a cool, dry place, dousing cakes with several tablespoons of sherry once a week for at least 1 month before serving.

## figgy christmas fruit rolls
### MAKES 4 TWELVE-INCH ROLLS

12 ounces walnuts (3¼ cups)

4½ pounds dried figs (about 10 cups), stems removed

4 ounces dates, pitted and roughly chopped (¾ cup)

6 ounces candied citrus peel, such as orange or lemon, roughly chopped (1 cup)

7 ounces bittersweet chocolate, chopped into ¼-inch pieces

5 ounces shelled pistachios (1 cup)

6 tablespoons brandy, plus more for dousing

2 tablespoons anisette

1 teaspoon ground cinnamon

¼ teaspoon freshly grated nutmeg

1 teaspoon pure vanilla extract

Pinch of salt

Confectioners' sugar, for work surface

**1.** Preheat oven to 350°F. Spread walnuts in a single layer on a rimmed baking sheet. Toast in oven until fragrant, about 10 minutes. Let cool completely, and roughly chop.

**2.** Working in two batches, process figs in a food processor until finely minced. Transfer figs to a large bowl; add walnuts, dates, citrus peel, chocolate, pistachios, 2 tablespoons brandy, anisette, cinnamon, nutmeg, vanilla, and salt; mix well, using your hands for best results.

**3.** Divide mixture into four equal parts. Dust a clean work surface with confectioners' sugar. Gently roll each part into a log about 2 inches in diameter and 12 inches long. Gently brush off excess sugar with a pastry brush. Roll each log in rice paper. Brush each log with 1 tablespoon brandy. Do not worry if rice paper tears.

**4.** Wrap logs in parchment paper, and secure with kitchen string. Store in a cool, dry place, unwrapping parchment and dousing rice paper with brandy once a week for at least 1 month before serving. (Rewrap in parchment each time.) To serve, slice rolls into thin rounds.

## fruit and stout cake

MAKES 1 NINE-INCH LOAF

1 cup (2 sticks) unsalted butter, room
   temperature, plus more for pan

12 ounces prunes, pitted and chopped
   into ½-inch pieces (2 cups)

8 ounces golden raisins (1½ cups)

8 ounces dried currants (1½ cups)

1¼ cups stout, such as Guinness,
   plus more for dousing

2⅔ cups all-purpose flour

½ teaspoon baking powder

¼ teaspoon freshly grated nutmeg

¼ teaspoon ground cinnamon

1¼ cups packed light-brown sugar

2 large eggs

**1.** Preheat oven to 300°F. Brush a 9-by-4½-inch loaf
pan with butter. Line bottom of pan with parchment paper; butter paper, and set aside.

**2.** Combine the prunes, raisins, and currants in
a medium bowl. Add ½ cup stout, and set aside.
Into a medium bowl, sift together flour, baking
powder, nutmeg, and cinnamon.

**3.** In the bowl of an electric mixer fitted with the
paddle attachment, cream butter and sugar until
fluffy, about 3 minutes. Add eggs one at a time,
mixing well after each, and scraping down sides
of bowl twice. Add flour mixture in two batches,
beating just until combined after each addition.
Fold in reserved fruit mixture.

**4.** Pour batter into prepared pan. Transfer to oven;
bake until dark brown and a cake tester inserted
in center comes out clean, about 3½ hours. (Cracks
will appear on top of cake.)

**5.** Remove cake from oven; sprinkle with ½ cup
stout. Let cool on a wire rack 30 minutes. Remove
from pan; peel off parchment. Let cool completely.
Wrap cake in cheesecloth or muslin. Douse fruitcake with remaining ¼ cup stout. Store in a cool,
dry place, dousing with ¼ cup stout once a week
for at least 1 month before serving.

## lardy cakes

MAKES 2 SEVENTEEN-BY-ELEVEN-INCH CAKES

*Martha was inspired to develop this recipe after
sampling a huge lardy cake at the Flour Bag
Bakery in Gloucestershire, England. In the north
of England, it is traditional to serve lardy cakes
on holidays and special occasions.*

All-purpose flour, for work surface
Sour Lardy-Cake Dough (recipe follows)

2 tablespoons ground ginger

2 tablespoons ground cinnamon

2 teaspoons ground coriander

½ teaspoon ground nutmeg

½ teaspoon ground mace

6 cups mixed dried fruit, such as currants,
   cranberries, and golden raisins

8 ounces (1¼ cups) solid vegetable shortening

1½ cups turbinado or packed light-brown sugar

½ cup apricot jam

4 tablespoons Cognac or brandy

**1.** On a lightly floured work surface, roll out half
the dough into a 16-inch square. Cover remaining
half with plastic; set aside. In a small bowl, combine spices. In a large bowl, combine dried fruit.

**2.** Spread 2 ounces shortening over top of dough,
leaving a ½-inch border around perimeter. Sprinkle 6 tablespoons brown sugar over shortening.
Sprinkle one-fourth of combined spices over sugar.
Sprinkle one-fourth of dried fruit over spices. Using
your palms, gently press toppings into dough.

**3.** Fold four corners of square into center to create
a smaller square, enclosing filling completely.
Gently press down on dough with rolling pin.
Spread 2 ounces shortening over dough, again

leaving a ½-inch border. Sprinkle with 6 table-spoons sugar and another one-fourth each spices and fruit. Gently press topping into dough; fold dough into thirds like a business letter.

**4.** Transfer dough to a piece of parchment paper; roll out into a 17-by-11-inch rectangle. Lifting parchment carefully, transfer to a baking sheet. Let rest about 20 minutes.

**5.** Repeat steps 1 through 4 with remaining dough, shortening, brown sugar, spices, and fruit.

**6.** Preheat oven to 350°F. Combine jam and Cognac in a small saucepan; cook over low heat until liquefied. Pour mixture through a fine sieve into a small bowl; discard solids. Brush surface of dough rectangles with strained glaze.

**7.** Bake cakes until golden and puffed, 35 to 45 minutes. Let cool slightly before serving. Lardy cakes will keep at room temperature up to 1 day, wrapped in foil; reheat in a 300°F oven, about 10 minutes, before serving.

### sour lardy-cake dough

MAKES ENOUGH FOR 2
SEVENTEEN-BY-ELEVEN-INCH CAKES

*To make this dough, substitute all-purpose flour for the bread flour in the Sponge recipe.*

1½  cups warm water (about 110°F)

 5  teaspoons (about 1⅔ envelopes)
     active dry yeast

 3  cups Sponge (page 103), pulled
     into small pieces

 4  cups bread flour

 1  tablespoon salt
     All-purpose flour, for work surface
     Vegetable oil, for bowl and plastic wrap

**1.** In the bowl of an electric mixer, combine 1 cup warm water and yeast. Let stand until foamy, about 10 minutes. Add remaining ½ cup warm water

and the sponge. Using the paddle attachment, mix on low speed until combined, about 2 minutes.

**2.** In a medium bowl, combine flour and salt. Add to sponge mixture, and mix on low speed 1 minute. Switch to the dough-hook attachment, and mix on medium-low speed until dough is smooth, about 8 minutes. Dough will still be sticky.

**3.** Turn out dough onto a lightly floured work surface, and knead 4 or 5 times to form a ball. Place dough, smooth side up, in a lightly oiled bowl, and cover with oiled plastic wrap. Let rise in a warm place until dough has doubled in bulk and is slightly blistered and satiny, about 1 hour.

**4.** Punch down dough, and fold over 4 or 5 times. Place folded side down in bowl. Cover, and let rise again in a warm place until doubled in bulk and satiny, about 50 minutes. Divide dough in half, and wrap each half in plastic until ready to use.

## mr. and mrs. maus's fruitcakes

*photograph on page 67*

MAKES 2 NINE-INCH CAKES

- 2 cups (4 sticks) unsalted butter, room temperature, plus more for pans
- 2½ cups all-purpose flour, plus more for pans
- 2 cups sugar
- 12 large eggs
- 6 pounds mixed candied fruits and fresh nuts, such as citron, lemon, and orange peel, and cherries, apricots, walnuts, and pecans
- ½ cup unsulfured molasses
- 2 tablespoons ground allspice
- 1 cup apricot jam
- ⅓ cup brandy
  - Whole dried apricots, for garnish
  - Pecan halves, for garnish

**1.** Preheat oven to 275°F. Butter two 9-inch round cake pans. Line bottoms of pans with wax paper; butter paper, and dust with flour. Tap out excess, and set aside.

**2.** In the bowl of an electric mixer fitted with the paddle attachment, cream butter and sugar until pale. Add eggs one at a time, beating until incorporated after each addition and scraping down sides of bowl at least twice. Batter should be fluffy. Stir in fruits, nuts, and molasses until blended.

**3.** Sift flour and allspice into a medium bowl; stir mixture, 1 cup at a time, into batter.

**4.** Spoon batter into prepared pans. Set pans in a larger baking pan filled with 1½ to 2 inches of hot water. Bake until a cake tester inserted in centers comes out clean, 3 to 3½ hours. Cool cakes in pans on a wire rack.

**5.** Remove cakes from pans; peel off paper. Place apricot jam in a small saucepan. Add brandy; heat over low heat until mixture is warm and syrupy.

Strain mixture through a fine sieve. Brush fruitcakes with glaze. Garnish cakes with dried apricots and pecan halves, and glaze again. Let glaze harden before wrapping fruitcakes in parchment paper. Store, wrapped again in plastic in a cool, dry place for several weeks.

GINGERBREADS

## gingerbread

MAKES 1 EIGHT-INCH SQUARE
OR 16 INDIVIDUAL CAKES

*We like to pair this gingerbread with Caramel-Coated Seckel Pears (page 312).*

- ½ cup (1 stick) unsalted butter, plus more for pan
- 1 cup boiling water
- 2 teaspoons baking soda
- 2½ cups all-purpose flour
- 2 teaspoons ground ginger
- 1½ teaspoons ground cinnamon
- ½ teaspoon ground cloves
- 2 teaspoons baking powder
- ¾ cup packed dark-brown sugar
- 1 cup unsulfured molasses
- 2 large eggs, lightly beaten
  - Confectioners' sugar, for dusting
  - Whipped cream, for serving
  - Crystallized ginger, thinly sliced, for garnish

**1.** Preheat oven to 350°F. Butter an 8-inch square cake pan or sixteen 3-inch oval molds, and set aside. Combine boiling water and baking soda in a small bowl. Into a large bowl, sift together flour, spices, and baking powder. Set both aside.

**2.** In the bowl of an electric mixer fitted with the paddle attachment, cream butter until pale. Add brown sugar, and beat until fluffy. Beat in molasses and baking-soda mixture. Gradually add flour mixture, beating until combined, and scraping down sides of bowl as necessary. Add eggs, and beat until incorporated.

**3.** Pour batter into prepared pan, and bake until a cake tester inserted in center comes out clean, 35 to 40 minutes (if baking in molds, reduce baking time to 25 to 30 minutes). Let cool on a wire rack. To serve, dust gingerbread with confectioners' sugar, and top with whipped cream; garnish with crystallized ginger.

## gingerbread cake with chocolate ganache
### MAKES 1 NINE-INCH CAKE

- 4 tablespoons unsalted butter, room temperature, plus more for mold
- 1¼ cups all-purpose flour, plus more for mold
- ½ cup boiling water
- 1 teaspoon baking soda
- 1 teaspoon baking powder
- 1 teaspoon ground ginger
- ¾ teaspoon ground cinnamon
- ¼ teaspoon ground cloves
- ¼ teaspoon ground nutmeg
- ¼ teaspoon salt
- ⅓ cup packed dark-brown sugar
- ½ cup unsulfured molasses
- 1½ teaspoons grated fresh ginger
- 1 large egg, room temperature, lightly beaten
- 2 recipes Chocolate Ganache Icing (page 343)
- ⅓ cup crystallized ginger, very thinly sliced

**1.** Preheat oven to 350°F. Butter and flour a 9-inch savarin mold, tapping out excess flour; set aside. In a small bowl, combine the boiling water and baking soda. Into a large bowl, sift together flour, baking powder, ground ginger, cinnamon, cloves, nutmeg, and salt. Set both aside.

**2.** In the bowl of an electric mixer fitted with the paddle attachment, cream butter and brown sugar on medium speed until fluffy, 2 to 3 minutes. Add molasses, grated ginger, and baking-soda and flour mixtures; beat until smooth and well combined, scraping down sides of bowl as necessary. Add egg, and beat until combined.

**3.** Pour batter into prepared mold; place on a baking sheet. Bake until a cake tester inserted in center comes out clean, about 25 minutes. Transfer to a wire rack to cool completely.

**4.** Unmold cake onto a wire rack set over a rimmed baking sheet lined with plastic wrap. Pour icing over cake to cover completely, making sure top and sides are completely covered. Set cake on rack over another rimmed baking sheet; chill 5 minutes.

**5.** Meanwhile, lift up plastic wrap from baking sheet; pour pooled ganache through a fine sieve into a bowl, pressing with a rubber spatula. Remove cake from refrigerator, and coat with another layer of ganache; chill another 5 minutes.

**6.** Transfer cake to a serving platter. Arrange crystallized ginger over top of cake, and serve.

## gingerbread petits fours

MAKES 2 DOZEN

1½  cups (3 sticks) unsalted butter, room
    temperature, plus more for baking sheet

1½  cups all-purpose flour, plus more
    for baking sheet

2  tablespoons ground ginger

2  teaspoons ground cinnamon

¼  teaspoon ground nutmeg

¼  teaspoon ground cloves

1½  cups sugar

3  tablespoons unsulfured molasses

6  large eggs, room temperature

1  teaspoon pure vanilla extract

   Ginger Simple Syrup (recipe follows)

   Swiss Meringue Buttercream
   (recipe follows)

   Poured Fondant (recipe follows)

   Gel-paste food coloring

**1.** Preheat oven to 350°F. Butter a 10½-by-15½-inch
rimmed baking sheet; line with parchment paper.
Butter parchment, and sprinkle with flour; tap out
excess, and set aside. Sift flour, ginger, cinnamon,
nutmeg, and cloves into a medium bowl; set aside.

**2.** In the bowl of an electric mixer fitted with the
paddle attachment, cream butter and sugar on
medium-high speed until pale and fluffy. Add
molasses, and beat until combined.

**3.** Add eggs one at a time, beating until incorporated and scraping down sides of bowl after each
addition. Add vanilla; reduce speed to low. Gradually add flour mixture. Pour batter onto prepared
baking sheet; use an offset spatula to smooth into
an even layer. Bake until a cake tester inserted in
center comes out clean, about 20 minutes.

**4.** Cool cake on sheet on a wire rack 10 minutes.
Invert cake onto rack, and let cool completely. Cut
cake in half crosswise, forming two 10½-by-7¾-
inch rectangles. Using a pastry brush, coat one

rectangle with some ginger syrup. Spread 1 cup
buttercream over syrup-coated cake. Using a 1½-
inch cookie cutter, cut a round out of unfrosted
rectangle. Leaving first round in cutter, cut a second round from frosted layer, so layers are neatly
stacked. Transfer petit four to a wire rack. Repeat
until 2 dozen petits fours are cut.

**5.** Divide fondant equally among three separate
heatproof bowls; tint each a pastel shade with food
coloring. Working with one color at a time, warm
fondant over a pan of barely simmering water just
until pourable. Remove bowl from heat.

**6.** Place one petit four on a chocolate dipping fork
or a large dinner fork; hold it over pan of fondant.
Use a small ladle to pour fondant over the petit
four until well coated. Allow fondant to drip for a
few seconds before setting petit four on wire rack.

**7.** Repeat with remaining petits fours and remaining colored fondant. If needed, rewarm fondant
over simmering water periodically. Let fondant set
at least 10 minutes before decorating cakes with
remaining buttercream, as desired.

## ginger simple syrup

MAKES 1¼ CUPS

1  cup sugar

1  two-inch piece fresh ginger, thinly sliced

Combine sugar and 1 cup water in a small saucepan over medium-high heat; bring to a boil. Add
ginger; reduce heat to a simmer, and cook 5 minutes. Set aside to cool, about 1½ hours. Strain
before using. Store, refrigerated in an airtight
container, up to 1 month.

## swiss meringue buttercream
MAKES 1¼ CUPS

*If buttercream appears curdled after adding butter, continue beating until it becomes smooth.*

½  cup sugar

2  large egg whites

10  tablespoons (1¼ sticks) unsalted butter, room temperature, cut into tablespoons

½  teaspoon pure vanilla extract

**1.** Combine sugar and egg whites in the bowl of an electric mixer. Place bowl over a pan of simmering water. Whisk constantly until sugar is dissolved and mixture is warm to the touch. Test by rubbing the mixture between your fingers; it should feel smooth.

**2.** Remove bowl from heat. Using whisk attachment, beat egg-white mixture on medium speed until shiny and cooled, about 10 minutes. Increase speed to high, and whisk until stiff and glossy peaks form. Reduce speed to medium-low, and add butter 1 tablespoon at a time, beating well after each addition. Beat in vanilla.

**3.** Switch to paddle attachment; beat on lowest speed to remove all air pockets, 3 to 5 minutes. If using the same day, cover with plastic wrap, and leave at room temperature. If not, store in an airtight container in the refrigerator up to 3 days. Before using buttercream, bring to room temperature, and beat until smooth with the paddle attachment, 5 to 10 minutes.

## poured fondant
MAKES ABOUT 2 CUPS

*Fondant should be liquid enough to pour. It will thicken as it sits over heat. If it is too thick, add Ginger Simple Syrup as needed, one tablespoon at a time.*

24  ounces powdered fondant

¼  cup hot water

Pinch of salt

2  teaspoons corn syrup

2  tablespoons unsalted butter

1  teaspoon pure vanilla extract

Break up any lumps in powdered fondant, and combine half with the hot water, salt, corn syrup, and butter in a large heatproof bowl. Place bowl over a pan of simmering water. Using a rubber spatula, stir until smooth, about 3 minutes. Add remaining powdered fondant and vanilla; stir until well combined and smooth. Work quickly; fondant will lose its sheen if heated too long.

## gingerbread with poached pears

SERVES 6

*Bake the gingerbread and poach the pears a day ahead; whip the cream and slice the pears when you're ready to assemble the cake.*

### for gingerbread cake:

- 1 cup (2 sticks) unsalted butter, room temperature, plus more for pan
- ½ cup packed dark-brown sugar
- ½ cup granulated sugar
- 4 large eggs
- 1 teaspoon pure vanilla extract
- 1¼ cups all-purpose flour
- 1 teaspoon salt
- 1 teaspoon ground cinnamon
- ¾ teaspoon ground ginger
- ¾ teaspoon ground nutmeg
- ½ teaspoon baking soda
- ½ teaspoon baking powder
- ¼ teaspoon ground cloves
  Confectioners' sugar, for dusting

### for poached pears:

- 3 ripe but firm pears, such as Anjou, Bartlett, or Bosc
- 1 750-ml bottle dry red wine, such as cabernet sauvignon, cabernet franc, or merlot
- ½ cup sugar
- 1 vanilla bean, split lengthwise
- 1 whole cinnamon stick
  Zest of 1 orange
  Zest of 1 lemon
- 2 whole cloves
- 1 whole star anise
- 1 dried bay leaf

### for cinnamon cream:

- 1 cup heavy cream
- 2 tablespoons confectioners' sugar
- ¼ teaspoon ground cinnamon

**1.** Preheat oven to 350°F. Make gingerbread cake: Butter a 9-by-5-inch loaf pan; set aside. In the bowl of an electric mixer fitted with the paddle attachment, cream butter and both sugars on medium speed until light and fluffy. Add eggs one at a time, mixing well after each addition. Beat in vanilla.

**2.** In a large bowl, sift together flour, salt, cinnamon, ginger, nutmeg, baking soda, baking powder, and cloves. Gradually add flour mixture to butter mixture, mixing on low speed until just combined. Pour batter into prepared pan, and smooth top with an offset spatula.

**3.** Bake until a cake tester inserted in center comes out clean, 50 to 55 minutes. Transfer to a wire rack to cool completely. Run a knife around cake to loosen, and invert onto a serving platter.

**4.** Using a paring knife, make a trough in top of cake: With knife about ¾ inch from edge, insert knife halfway down into cake; cut a rectangle, leaving a ¾-inch border all around. Insert a serrated knife through one long side of cake, intersecting cut made by paring knife through top. Cut bottom of trough, being careful not to cut through shorter sides or all the way through cake. Lift out trough, and reserve for another use. Cover cake with plastic wrap until ready to assemble.

**5.** Make poached pears: Peel pears, leaving stems intact; place in a medium saucepan. Add remaining ingredients and just enough water to cover.

**6.** Bring to a boil over high heat. Reduce heat to medium-low. Cook, stirring gently, until a paring knife easily pierces pears, about 15 minutes. Remove from heat; let pears cool in liquid.

**7.** Using a slotted spoon, transfer pears to a plate. Pour poaching liquid through a fine sieve set over a bowl; discard solids, and return liquid to saucepan. Cook over medium-high heat until liquid has reduced and is thick enough to coat the back of a wooden spoon, about 45 minutes. Let cool completely. If making ahead, store pears in the same container as the syrup.

**8.** Make cinnamon cream: Place all ingredients in a mixing bowl. Whip until soft peaks form. Cover with plastic wrap; refrigerate until ready to use.

**9.** To assemble dessert, slice poached pears in half, and remove cores with a melon baller. Dust cake with confectioners' sugar. Stand halved pears upright in trough of cake. Drizzle 2 tablespoons red-wine syrup over tops. Serve slices with more syrup; top each with a dollop of cinnamon cream.

## three-ginger gingerbread
MAKES 1 NINE-INCH SQUARE

*This gingerbread has a pudding-like texture.*

2½  cups all-purpose flour, plus more for pan
  1  cup packed dark-brown sugar
  1  teaspoon baking powder
  1  teaspoon baking soda
  1  teaspoon instant espresso powder
  1  teaspoon ground cinnamon
  ¼  teaspoon ground ginger
  ¼  teaspoon cayenne (or less to taste)
  ¼  teaspoon salt
  ⅛  teaspoon ground coriander seeds
  ⅛  teaspoon ground cloves
  1  cup unsulfured molasses
  8  ounces plain nonfat yogurt
  ½  cup unsweetened applesauce
  ⅓  cup canola oil
  2  tablespoons minced crystallized ginger
  1  tablespoon balsamic vinegar
1½  teaspoons grated lemon zest
  1  teaspoon grated fresh ginger
     Nonstick cooking spray

**1.** Preheat oven to 325°F. Line bottom of a 9-inch square baking pan with parchment paper; coat with cooking spray, and sprinkle with flour. Tap out excess; set aside.

**2.** In a large bowl, whisk together flour, brown sugar, baking powder, baking soda, espresso powder, cinnamon, ground ginger, cayenne, salt, coriander, and cloves.

**3.** In a medium bowl, whisk together remaining ingredients until smooth. Add to flour mixture; stir with a wooden spoon until blended.

**4.** Pour batter into prepared pan, and bake until a cake tester inserted in center comes out clean, 60 to 70 minutes. Transfer to a wire rack; let cool in pan. To serve, cut into 12 squares.

## *apple pie*

photograph on page 75

MAKES 1 NINE-INCH PIE

*For the flakiest and most evenly browned crust, use a glass pie dish. Freezing the top layer of dough before cutting out the leaves will help produce very smooth edges.*

3 tablespoons all-purpose flour, plus more for work surface

1½ recipes Pâte Brisée (recipe follows)

3 pounds (about 9) assorted apples, such as Macoun, Granny Smith, Cortland, Jonagold, or Empire, peeled, cored, and cut into ¼-inch-thick slices

2 tablespoons freshly squeezed lemon juice

¼ cup granulated sugar

1 teaspoon ground cinnamon

¼ teaspoon ground nutmeg

⅛ teaspoon salt

1 tablespoon unsalted butter, cut into small pieces

1 large egg yolk, whisked with 1 tablespoon heavy cream, for egg wash

Sanding sugar, for sprinkling

**1.** On a lightly floured work surface, roll out one pâte brisée disk into a 13-inch round about ⅛ inch thick. Fit dough into a 9-inch pie plate. With a sharp paring knife, trim dough flush with rim. Cover plate with plastic wrap; freeze until firm, at least 30 minutes.

**2.** Roll out remaining two disks of pâte brisée about ⅛ inch thick. Place on a parchment-lined baking sheet; cover, and freeze until firm, at least 30 minutes. Remove sheet from freezer; using a 2¼-inch leaf-shape cutter, cut out about 65 leaves. Place leaves in a single layer on baking sheet. Cover; refrigerate until firm, at least 30 minutes.

**3.** Preheat oven to 400°F. In a large bowl, toss apples with lemon juice, granulated sugar, flour, cinnamon, nutmeg, and salt. Remove pie shell from freezer; fill with apple mixture. Dot with butter.

**4.** Remove leaves from refrigerator, and score with a paring knife to make veins. Lightly brush edge of pie shell with water. Brush bottom of each leaf with water; beginning with outside edge, arrange leaves in a slightly overlapping ring. Repeat to form another ring slightly overlapping the first. Continue until only a small circle of filling is left uncovered in the center.

**5.** Carefully brush tops of leaves and pie edge with egg wash, and sprinkle generously with sanding sugar. Refrigerate until firm, at least 30 minutes.

**6.** Place pie plate on a baking sheet, and bake until crust just begins to brown, about 20 minutes. Reduce oven temperature to 350°F, and continue baking until crust is golden brown and juices are bubbling, 35 to 45 minutes. If crust begins to brown too quickly, drape a piece of foil over the top. Transfer to a wire rack to cool before serving.

## pâte brisée

MAKES ENOUGH FOR 2 SINGLE-CRUST
NINE-INCH PIES, 1 TWELVE-INCH PIE, AND
TWENTY-FOUR 2¼-INCH TARTLETS

*The dough can be stored, wrapped in plastic, for up to one week in the refrigerator or up to one month in the freezer. Before using frozen dough, thaw at room temperature. For best results, make sure all ingredients are thoroughly chilled before you begin. To make using a food processor, see how-to on page 391.*

2½ cups all-purpose flour
1 teaspoon salt
1 teaspoon sugar
1 cup (2 sticks) chilled unsalted butter, cut into small pieces
4 to 6 tablespoons ice water

**1.** Place flour, salt, and sugar in a medium bowl, and stir to combine. With a pastry blender or two knives, cut butter into flour mixture by pressing down quickly, using as few strokes as possible. Mixture should resemble coarse meal, with only a few pea-size pieces remaining.

**2.** Add 4 tablespoons ice water. Using your hands, gather dough, and gently press into a ball. It should come together loosely; if not, add up to 2 tablespoons more water, 1 tablespoon at a time. Divide dough in half; place each on plastic wrap. Flatten into disks. Wrap tightly; refrigerate at least 1 hour before using.

## autumn harvest pie

MAKES 1 TWELVE-INCH PIE

*When making pâte brisée for this recipe, do not divide dough in half before flattening and wrapping in plastic.*

7 baking apples (about 2 pounds), such as Rome, Granny Smith, or Cortland, peeled, cored, and sliced ½ inch thick
7 ripe but firm Bosc pears (about 2 pounds), peeled, cored, and sliced ½ inch thick
4 tablespoons all-purpose flour, plus more for work surface
1⅓ cups sugar, plus more for sprinkling
½ teaspoon grated fresh nutmeg
  Juice and zest of 1 lemon
3 cups fresh cranberries (about 12 ounces)
  Pâte Brisée (recipe above)
4 tablespoons unsalted butter, cut into small pieces
2 tablespoons heavy cream

**1.** Preheat oven to 400°F. In a large bowl, combine apples and pears with flour, sugar, nutmeg, and lemon juice and zest. Add cranberries; toss gently to combine. Set aside.

**2.** On a lightly floured work surface, roll out pâte brisée to an 18-inch round about ⅛ inch thick. Fit dough into a 12-inch pie plate.

**3.** Fill pie shell with fruit mixture; dot with butter. Fold edge of dough over fruit. Brush dough with cream. Sprinkle sugar lightly and evenly over the filling. Place the pie plate on a parchment-paper-lined baking sheet.

**4.** Bake 20 minutes. Reduce oven heat to 350°F; continue baking until crust is golden brown and juices are bubbling, about 1½ hours more. If crust begins to brown too quickly, drape aluminum foil over the top. Transfer to a wire rack to cool completely before serving.

## pear and sour-cherry pie
MAKES 1 NINE-INCH PIE

1½ cups dried sour cherries

4 pounds ripe but firm pears (about 7)

¼ cup freshly squeezed lemon juice (2 lemons)

1 cup sugar

½ cup all-purpose flour, plus more for work surface

1½ teaspoons ground cinnamon

½ teaspoon ground nutmeg

¼ teaspoon ground cloves

Pâte Brisée (page 389)

1 tablespoon unsalted butter, cut into small pieces

1 large egg yolk, whisked with 1 tablespoon heavy cream, for egg wash

1. In a small bowl, soak cherries in hot water just to cover until soft, about 20 minutes. Peel, core, and thinly slice pears; toss in a bowl with lemon juice. Drain cherries, and add to pears; discard liquid. Add sugar, flour, and spices; toss to combine.

2. Preheat oven to 400°F. On a lightly floured work surface, roll out one pâte brisée disk into a 13-inch round about ⅛ inch thick. Fit dough into a 9-inch pie plate. Fill with pear mixture; dot with butter.

3. Roll out remaining dough to about ⅛ inch thick. Using a 2-inch star-shape cutter, cut out a star from center. Brush edge of pie shell with water; place rolled dough on top. Using a sharp paring knife, trim edge, leaving a 1-inch overhang. Tuck dough under edge; crimp to seal. Brush dough with egg wash.

4. Place pie plate on a baking sheet. Bake 20 minutes; reduce oven heat to 350°F. Continue baking until crust is golden brown and juices are bubbling, 40 to 50 minutes more. If crust begins to brown too quickly, drape aluminum foil over top. Transfer to a wire rack to cool before serving.

## pecan pie
MAKES 1 NINE-INCH PIE

All-purpose flour, for work surface

Pâte Brisée (page 389)

1 cup sugar

4 tablespoons unsalted butter, melted

4 large whole eggs

1 cup plus 2 tablespoons dark corn syrup

½ cup pure maple syrup

2 tablespoons bourbon or dark rum

1 teaspoon pure vanilla extract

1½ cups pecan halves (about 5¼ ounces)

1 large egg yolk, whisked with 1 tablespoon heavy cream, for egg wash

Whipped cream, for serving (optional)

1. On a lightly floured work surface, roll out one pâte brisée disk into a 13-inch round about ⅛ inch thick. Fit dough into a 9-inch pie plate. With a sharp knife, trim dough flush with rim. Refrigerate until firm, at least 30 minutes.

2. Roll out remaining dough to about ⅛ inch thick. Using a small leaf-shape cutter, cut out leaves. Remove pie plate from refrigerator. Lightly brush edge of dough with water. Lightly brush bottom of leaves with water, and arrange on top edge of pie dough so that leaves are slightly overlapping. Refrigerate until firm, about 30 minutes.

3. Preheat oven to 375°F. In a medium bowl, whisk together sugar, butter, eggs, corn syrup, maple syrup, bourbon, and vanilla. Fold in pecans. Pour filling into prepared pie shell. Carefully brush egg wash on top of leaves.

4. Bake 15 minutes; reduce oven heat to 350°F. Bake until the tip of a paring knife inserted in the center comes out clean, about 1 hour 15 minutes. Transfer to a wire rack. Serve pie warm or at room temperature with whipped cream, if desired.

## MAKING PATE BRISEE WITH A FOOD PROCESSOR

*1. In the bowl of a food processor fitted with the metal blade, process to combine flour, salt, and sugar.*

*2. Add butter; process until mixture resembles coarse meal, 8 to 10 seconds. Add 4 tablespoons ice water; pulse just until dough holds together without becoming wet or sticky, no longer than 30 seconds.*

*3. Pinch off a piece of dough, and feel its texture: If it is crumbly, add ice water, 1 tablespoon at a time. Divide dough in half; flatten into two even disks, and wrap in plastic. Chill at least 1 hour or overnight.*

## PATE BRISEE BY HAND

*1. With a pastry blender or two knives, cut cold butter into flour mixture by pressing down quickly; use as few strokes as possible. You may leave a few pea-size pieces.*

*2. Add 4 tablespoons ice water. Gather dough with your hands, and gently press it into a ball. It should come together loosely; if not, add more water a tablespoon at a time.*

### ROLLING OUT DOUGH

*1. On a lightly floured surface, press rolling pin gently all over chilled dough to flatten it slightly. Working from the center, roll out dough into a round about 3 inches larger than the pie plate.*

*2. Wrap dough around rolling pin; lift and center it over pie plate. Gently unroll dough over pie plate, leaving an even amount of overhang.*

### FINISHING TOUCHES

*1. For a two-crust pie, dip a star-shape cutter in flour, then cut a star in center of second dough disk. Wrap dough around rolling pin; lift, and center over pie plate.*

*2. Using the knuckle of your forefinger on one hand and the thumb and forefinger on the other, pinch together both layers of the dough around the entire perimeter to seal.*

## quince apple pie

SERVES 8

*You will need three-quarters of the pâte brisée dough; instead of dividing the dough in half, as instructed, pinch off one-quarter of the dough, and save for another use (dough can be stored in the freezer for up to one month). Pat the rest of the dough into a disk, wrap in plastic, and refrigerate until ready to use. You may substitute four additional Granny Smith apples for the poached quinces; for added apple flavor, soak the raisins in one-third cup warmed Calvados instead of the poaching liquid.*

- 4   quinces, peeled and halved, peels reserved
- 1   375-ml bottle sweet dessert wine, such as Muscat
- 1   vanilla bean, split lengthwise and scraped
- 1   cup sugar, plus more for sprinkling
- ½   cup mixed golden and dark raisins
- 4   Granny Smith apples
     Juice of 1 lemon
- ¼   cup all-purpose flour, plus more for work surface
- 1   teaspoon ground cinnamon
     Pâte Brisée (page 389)
- 1   to 2 tablespoons unsalted butter

**1.** In a medium saucepan, combine quinces and their peels with the wine, vanilla bean and scrapings, ¼ cup sugar, and enough water to cover. Place cheesecloth over fruit to keep it submerged; bring to a boil over medium-high heat. Reduce heat, and simmer until quinces are tender when pierced with the tip of a paring knife, 25 to 35 minutes. Using a slotted spoon, transfer fruit to a plate; set aside. Continue cooking liquid until syrupy and reduced by two-thirds, about 30 minutes.

**2.** Preheat oven to 375°F. Place raisins in a medium bowl, and cover with reduced poaching liquid. Let cool completely.

**3.** Peel and core apples, and cut into ¾-inch-thick wedges. Transfer to a large bowl; add lemon juice, and toss to coat. Add remaining ¾ cup sugar, the flour, and cinnamon; toss to combine. Drain raisins, and add to apple mixture; reserve poaching liquid. Using a melon baller, remove core from poached quinces; cut fruit into ¾-inch-thick wedges, and add to apple mixture.

**4.** On a lightly floured work surface, roll out pâte brisée to ⅛ inch thick. Fit dough into a 9-inch ceramic pie plate, allowing excess pastry to hang over the edges. Fill with apple mixture and dot with butter; fold edges of dough over fruit, overlapping as needed and leaving center open. Brush dough with water; sprinkle with sugar.

**5.** Bake until crust is deep golden brown and juices are bubbling, about 1 hour 25 minutes. If fruit in center appears dry, brush with poaching liquid. If fruit or crust begins to brown too quickly, drape with aluminum foil. Transfer to a wire rack to cool.

### HOW TO MAKE THE BEST PATE BRISEE

- *All the ingredients should be ice cold. Even the flour should be chilled.*

- *Keep tools handy. Have a dry brush, bench scraper, and bowl of flour out when rolling.*

- *Preshape dough before chilling. Form dough into a disk; cover with plastic. Chill at least one hour or overnight.*

- *Roll quickly. Using only a minimal amount of flour to prevent sticking, evenly roll out a round without overworking the dough.*

- *Keep the dough as cold as possible. If at any point the dough sticks to the work surface, refrigerate for about fifteen minutes.*

## black-bottom tart

*photograph on page 70*

MAKES 1 NINE-INCH TART

*All-purpose flour, for work surface*

½ *recipe Pâte Brisée (page 389)*

4 *ounces semisweet chocolate, coarsely chopped*

1¼ *teaspoons unflavored gelatin*

2 *tablespoons cold water*

4 *large egg yolks*

¾ *cup sugar*

2 *tablespoons cornstarch*

2 *cups milk*

2 *teaspoons pure vanilla extract*

2 *large egg whites*

*Pinch of salt*

*Pinch cream of tartar*

1 *cup heavy cream*

¼ *cup chocolate shavings, for decorating (optional)*

**1.** Preheat oven to 400°F. On a lightly floured work surface, roll out pâte brisée disk into a 13-inch round about ⅛ inch thick. Fit dough into a 9-inch bottomless tart ring set on a baking sheet. Using a sharp paring knife, trim dough flush with rim. Prick bottom of dough all over with a fork. Chill until firm, about 30 minutes.

**2.** Remove baking sheet from refrigerator. Line tart ring with parchment paper, leaving about 3 inches overhang. Fill with pie weights or dried beans. Bake 20 minutes. Remove weights and parchment; continue baking until crust is deep golden, 10 to 15 minutes. Transfer to a wire rack to cool completely.

**3.** In a microwave or a medium heatproof bowl set over a pan of simmering water, melt chocolate. In a small bowl, sprinkle gelatin over cold water; let stand until softened, about 5 minutes.

**4.** In a medium bowl, whisk together egg yolks, ¼ cup sugar, and cornstarch; set aside. In a medium saucepan, combine milk and ¼ cup sugar; cook over medium heat until mixture begins to bubble around the edge, about 3 minutes. Whisking constantly, gradually add hot milk mixture to egg-yolk mixture. Return mixture to pan; cook, stirring constantly over medium heat until custard is thick and just starting to boil, 5 to 7 minutes.

**5.** Prepare an ice bath. Measure out ½ cup custard, and place in a medium bowl; immediately whisk in gelatin mixture until smooth. Place bowl in the ice bath several seconds to set mixture. Press a piece of plastic wrap directly onto surface to prevent a skin from forming. Set aside.

**6.** Stir remaining custard into melted chocolate, and add vanilla. Set bowl in ice bath. Let cool completely, stirring occasionally. Spread the mixture evenly in the bottom of prepared tart shell. Refrigerate until set, at least 5 minutes.

**7.** In the bowl of an electric mixer, whisk egg whites with salt and cream of tartar on medium speed until soft peaks form, about 2 minutes. With mixer running, gradually add remaining ¼ cup sugar; beat until peaks are stiff and glossy, 1 to 3 minutes. Whisk one-third meringue into reserved custard mixture until completely smooth. (You may need to beat the custard again at this point until smooth.) Gently but thoroughly fold remaining meringue into custard mixture. Spread over chocolate layer in tart shell. Cover with plastic wrap; refrigerate at least 3 hours or overnight.

**8.** In a small bowl, whip heavy cream until stiff peaks form. Transfer to a pastry bag fitted with a star tip (Ateco #825), and pipe decoratively over custard (alternatively, spread with an offset spatula). Sprinkle chocolate shavings on top, if desired. Refrigerate until ready to serve.

## caramel-nut tarts

MAKES 2 NINE-INCH TARTS

*Tarts can be stored in an airtight container at room temperature for up to two days.*

- 1 cup (2 sticks) unsalted butter
- 1 cup packed light-brown sugar
- ¼ cup granulated sugar
- ¾ cup honey
- ¼ cup heavy cream
- ½ teaspoon salt
- 1 pound assorted mixed nuts, such as hazelnuts, pistachios, almonds, pecans, or cashews
- 1 teaspoon pure vanilla extract
  Pâte Sucrée Tart Shells (recipe follows), still in tart pans

**1.** Preheat oven to 325°F, with rack in center. Place butter, both sugars, honey, heavy cream, and salt in a large saucepan. Bring to a boil over high heat, stirring constantly; continue boiling 5 minutes. Stir in nuts and vanilla; remove from heat. Pour filling into tart shells.

**2.** Bake tarts until filling is bubbling, 15 to 20 minutes. Transfer to a wire rack to cool before serving.

## pâte sucrée tart shells

MAKES 2 NINE-INCH TART SHELLS

*You can freeze the unbaked tart shells for up to three weeks; cover tightly with plastic wrap. The tart shells can be baked a day in advance and kept uncovered at room temperature before being filled.*

- 2½ cups all-purpose flour, plus more for work surface
- 3 tablespoons sugar
- 1 teaspoon salt
- 1 cup (2 sticks) chilled unsalted butter, cut into small pieces
- 2 large egg yolks, plus 1 lightly beaten
- ¼ cup ice water

**1.** In a food processor, combine flour, sugar, and salt; pulse to combine. Add butter, and process until mixture resembles coarse meal, about 20 seconds. Beat 2 egg yolks and the ice water in a small bowl. Add to flour mixture; pulse until dough just comes together, 10 to 15 seconds. Divide dough in half, and flatten into two disks. Wrap well with plastic, and refrigerate at least 1 hour or overnight.

**2.** Preheat oven to 400°F. Remove one disk from the refrigerator; place on a lightly floured work surface. Roll out dough into a 10½-inch round, about ⅛ inch thick. Carefully lift and place over a 9-inch tart pan, preferably with a removable bottom; fit dough into sides and bottom. Trim excess dough flush with edge with a paring knife. Prick bottom of shell all over with a fork. Freeze until firm, about 15 minutes. Repeat with second disk.

**3.** Remove pans from freezer; line with parchment paper extending over sides by 1 inch. Fill with pie weights or dried beans, and place on a baking sheet. Bake 20 minutes. Remove parchment and weights; immediately brush with beaten yolk. Bake until golden brown, 10 to 12 minutes. Transfer to a wire rack to cool before filling.

## grapefruit tart

MAKES 1 NINE-INCH TART

3 large ruby red or pink grapefruits

⅔ cup sugar

3 large whole eggs

2 large egg yolks

¾ cup heavy cream

1 Pâte Sucrée Tart Shell (page 395),
   still in tart pan

   Confectioners' sugar, for dusting

**1.** Preheat oven to 300°F. Squeeze juice from 1 grapefruit into a large measuring cup, and set aside; you should have ¾ cup. Cut off both ends of remaining 2 grapefruits; using a sharp paring knife, remove peel, pith, and outer membranes, following curve of fruit. Working over a bowl to catch juices, carefully slice between sections to remove whole segments. Set segments aside. Squeeze membranes to extract as much juice as possible. Cover bowl with plastic wrap; set aside.

**2.** In a large bowl, whisk together sugar, eggs, and yolks. Slowly whisk in cream and reserved grapefruit juice until combined and smooth. Pour through a fine sieve into a medium bowl; discard solids. Skim off surface foam with a spoon.

**3.** Pour custard mixture into tart shell. Place in oven, and bake until center is set when gently touched with your finger, about 40 minutes. Transfer to a wire rack to cool completely. The tart can be refrigerated at this point up to 1 day.

**4.** To serve, hold a plate or bottom of tart pan over filling (do not touch); dust edges of crust with confectioners' sugar. Slice into wedges; serve with reserved grapefruit segments.

## holiday fruit tart

MAKES ONE 13½-BY-4-INCH TART

*This dessert is so sweet, a thin slice at the end of the meal will do. When following the pâte brisée recipe, omit the sugar; instead of dividing in half, as instructed, pinch off one-quarter of the dough, and wrap separately. Pat the rest of the dough into a disk, and cover with plastic wrap until ready to use.*

1 cup all-purpose flour, plus
   more for work surface

   Pâte Brisée (page 389)

1 teaspoon ground ginger

½ teaspoon ground allspice

½ teaspoon freshly grated nutmeg

½ teaspoon ground cinnamon

¼ teaspoon salt

½ cup plus 2 tablespoons packed
   dark-brown sugar

¼ cup dried currants

¼ cup golden raisins

¼ cup dried cranberries

¼ cup candied citron

¼ cup candied orange peel, chopped
   into ¼-inch pieces

1 cup (4 ounces) finely chopped
   blanched almonds, toasted

   Finely grated zest of 1 lemon, plus 2
   tablespoons freshly squeezed lemon juice

3 tablespoons brandy

¼ cup unsulfured molasses

1 large egg, plus 1, lightly beaten with
   1 tablespoon water, for egg wash

**1.** On a lightly floured work surface, roll out dough to fit a rectangular 13¼-by-4-inch tart pan, about ⅛ inch thick. Carefully place pastry in pan; gently press into sides and corners. Trim dough flush with edge of pan. Cover with plastic; refrigerate while making filling.

**2.** Sift flour, spices, and salt into a large bowl. Add brown sugar, dried fruit, citron, orange peel, almonds, and lemon zest and juice. Stir in brandy, molasses, and 1 egg. Pack mixture into tart shell.

**3.** On a lightly floured work surface, roll out the remaining dough into a rectangle approximately the same size as the pan, about ⅛ inch thick. Moisten edges of tart shell with water; place rolled dough on top. Press edges to seal well, and trim excess dough. Chill tart 1 hour.

**4.** Preheat oven to 325°F. Remove tart from refrigerator; make three slits in top of dough with a sharp knife to let steam escape. Brush dough with egg wash, and bake until golden brown and flaky, about 1 hour 40 minutes. Let tart cool on a wire rack before serving.

✳

## pear tart
### MAKES 1 TEN-INCH TART

*This rustic pear tart is made in a ten-inch round cake pan that is two inches deep. The base of a ten-inch tart pan is used to shape and chill the dough for the top of the tart.*

1½  *cups sugar*

2  *whole cinnamon sticks*

½  *teaspoon ground cinnamon*

2  *whole cloves*

10  *ripe but firm Anjou pears (about 5½ pounds), peeled and cut into 1-inch pieces*

¼  *cup finely chopped crystallized ginger*

1  *cup (2 sticks) unsalted butter, room temperature, plus more for pan*

1½  *tablespoons pure vanilla extract*

4  *whole egg yolks, plus 1 whole egg, lightly beaten*

2¾  *cups all-purpose flour, plus more for pans*

⅛  *teaspoon salt*

**1.** Combine ½ cup sugar, cinnamon sticks, ground cinnamon, cloves, and 3 cups water in a large saucepan; bring to a simmer over medium heat. Allow to simmer until sugar has dissolved, about 5 minutes. Add pears; cover, and simmer, stirring occasionally, until pears are very tender and falling apart, about 25 minutes.

**2.** Remove lid; continue simmering, stirring frequently, until all liquid has evaporated, 30 to 40 minutes. Remove from heat, and transfer mixture to a medium bowl; stir in crystallized ginger. Let cool completely; discard cinnamon sticks.

**3.** Preheat oven to 350°F. Butter the bottom of a 10-by-2-inch round cake pan. Cut parchment to fit bottom of pan; place in pan. Set aside. In the bowl of an electric mixer fitted with the paddle attachment, cream butter and remaining cup sugar until light and fluffy. Add vanilla and egg yolks, one at a time, beating well after each addition. Add flour and salt; beat until just combined. Divide dough in half. Wrap one half in plastic; chill.

**4.** With fingers, spread remaining dough evenly over bottom and about 1½ inches up sides of prepared pan, sprinkling lightly with flour if dough becomes too sticky. Spread pear mixture evenly over dough. Refrigerate 15 minutes.

**5.** For top crust, lightly flour the bottom of a 10-inch tart pan. Remove dough from refrigerator; press evenly on pan bottom to make a thick, even disk; chill 15 minutes. Using a spatula, slide disk of dough over filling. Press disk into place, and smooth with an offset spatula.

**6.** Brush beaten egg over top of tart. With a fork, score the top in a lattice pattern, and brush again with egg. Bake until crust is golden brown, about 50 minutes. Let tart cool in pan on a wire rack, until just warm. Invert to remove from pan; turn right side up to serve.

## lemon tart with candied lemons and kumquats

*photograph on page 68*

MAKES 1 NINE-INCH TART

6  *large egg yolks*

3  *large whole eggs*

1  *cup plus 2 tablespoons sugar*

   *Finely grated zest of 2 lemons*

¾  *cup freshly squeezed lemon juice
(about 6 lemons)*

6  *tablespoons unsalted butter,
cut into small pieces*

1  *Pâte Sucrée Tart Shell (page 395),
still in tart pan*

   *Candied Lemons and Kumquats
(recipe follows)*

**1.** Prepare an ice bath; set aside. Make lemon curd: In a large heatproof bowl set over a pan of simmering water, whisk egg yolks with the eggs, sugar, and lemon zest and juice. Cook, stirring constantly, until mixture thickens, 5 to 6 minutes. Remove from heat, and stir in butter until melted. Pour through a fine sieve into a large bowl set in the ice bath; let cool completely.

**2.** Remove tart shell from tart pan. Fill with chilled lemon curd. Decorate with candied lemons and kumquats. Serve immediately.

## candied lemons and kumquats

MAKES ENOUGH TO DECORATE
1 NINE-INCH TART

*Candied citrus can be made several days in advance and stored in the cooking syrup. Before assembling tart, drain slices on a wire rack about five minutes or gently scrape them with an offset spatula to remove excess liquid.*

3  *cups sugar*

2  *lemons, thinly sliced into rounds*

6  *kumquats, thinly sliced into rounds*

In a 12-inch sauté pan, bring sugar and 3 cups water to a boil, stirring constantly until sugar dissolves. Reduce heat to a gentle simmer. Add fruit slices in a single layer, arranging them so they do not overlap. Cook until white pith is translucent, 30 to 40 minutes, turning slices two or three times during cooking. Using a slotted spatula, carefully transfer slices to a wire rack to cool completely before using or storing.

## rice pudding tartlets with blood oranges

MAKES 6 FOUR-INCH TARTLETS

*Rice pudding will continue to thicken as it cools, so be careful not to overcook.*

   *All-purpose flour, for work surface*

   *Pâte Sucrée (recipe follows)*

4  *blood oranges*

1  *cup Arborio rice*

4  *cups milk*

½  *vanilla bean, split lengthwise and scraped*

½  *cup sugar*

   *Pinch of salt*

1  *cup heavy cream*

2  *large egg yolks*

**1.** Preheat oven to 400°F. Place six 4-inch tart rings on a baking sheet lined with a Silpat baking mat or parchment paper. Set aside.

**2.** On a lightly floured work surface, roll out pâte sucrée to ⅛ inch thick. Using an inverted 6-inch bowl as a guide, cut out six 6-inch rounds of dough with a sharp paring knife. Press dough into tart rings; trim excess with knife. Prick bottom of tart shells all over with a fork. Transfer to freezer until firm, about 15 minutes.

**3.** Cut out six 6-inch parchment-paper rounds, and line rings; fill with pie weights or dried beans. Bake until edges begin to brown, about 20 minutes. Remove from oven, and carefully remove parchment and weights. Return to oven; continue baking until golden brown all over, about 10 minutes more. Transfer to a wire rack to cool completely. Carefully remove tart shells from tart rings, and set aside.

**4.** Grate zest of 1 orange, and set aside. Cut ends off all four oranges, and remove peel and pith with a paring knife, following the curve of the fruit. Working over a bowl to catch the juices, slice between sections to remove whole segments. Set segments aside. Squeeze membranes to extract as much juice as possible; reserve ¼ cup juice.

**5.** Fill a medium saucepan with water; bring to a boil. Add rice, and blanch 2 minutes. Drain well, and return to saucepan. Add milk, reserved orange zest, vanilla bean and scrapings, sugar, and salt; cook at a gentle simmer over medium heat, stirring occasionally, until rice is tender and has absorbed most of the liquid, 30 to 35 minutes. Remove from heat; discard vanilla bean.

**6.** In a large bowl, whisk together heavy cream, egg yolks, and reserved orange juice. Gradually whisk in rice mixture, and return to saucepan. Place pan over medium-low heat; cook, stirring constantly, until mixture boils and thickens, about 10 minutes. Remove from heat; let stand 5 minutes. Pour filling into baked tart shells. Arrange orange segments in an overlapping floral pattern (to resemble rose petals) over rice pudding, and serve warm or at room temperature.

### *pâte sucrée*
MAKES 6 FOUR-INCH ROUND TARTLET SHELLS

2½  cups all-purpose flour
3  tablespoons sugar
1  cup (2 sticks) chilled unsalted butter, cut into small pieces
2  large egg yolks
¼  cup ice water

**1.** Place flour and sugar in a food processor; pulse a few seconds to combine. Add butter; process until mixture resembles coarse meal, about 20 seconds. In a small bowl, lightly beat egg yolks and ice water until combined. With the machine running, pour egg mixture through the feed tube in a slow, steady stream. Process until dough just holds together, no more than 30 seconds.

**2.** Turn out dough onto a clean work surface, and divide into two equal pieces. Place each on plastic wrap. Flatten into disks; wrap, and refrigerate at least 1 hour or overnight.

## persimmon tartlets with caramel cream and ginger crust

MAKES 12 FOUR-INCH TARTLETS

*For best results, we recommend using fluted tartlet tins with removable bottoms.*

- 2 cans sweetened condensed milk (14 ounces each)
- 1 box (1 pound) graham crackers
- ¼ cup ground ginger
- ½ teaspoon ground cinnamon
- ¼ teaspoon freshly ground pepper
- 1 cup plus 3 tablespoons unsalted butter, melted
- 4 large egg yolks
- 24 ounces crème fraîche
- 3 ripe persimmons, sliced ¼ inch thick

**1.** In the top of a double boiler, cook condensed milk over low heat, covered, until thick and a light caramel color, about 3 hours. While cooking, stir milk occasionally, and add water to pan as needed to maintain water level.

**2.** Meanwhile, preheat oven to 350°F. Process graham crackers in a food processor until fine crumbs form, about 2 minutes; transfer to a medium bowl. Add ginger, cinnamon, and pepper; whisk to combine. Stir in melted butter. Press 4 to 5 loosely packed tablespoons graham-cracker mixture on bottom and sides of each of twelve 4-inch tart pans. Place pans on a baking sheet; bake crusts until set, about 10 minutes. Let cool on a wire rack.

**3.** Prepare an ice bath; set aside. In a medium bowl, lightly whisk egg yolks. Place caramelized milk and crème fraîche in a medium saucepan over medium-low heat; cook, stirring often, until small bubbles appear around edge, about 10 minutes.

**4.** Whisking constantly, pour half the hot crème-fraîche mixture into egg yolks in a slow, steady stream. When well combined, return mixture to saucepan. Bring to a boil over medium heat, stirring constantly; continue boiling, stirring, until mixture has thickened, about 3 minutes. Remove from heat; strain mixture through a fine sieve into a medium bowl set over the ice bath. Let stand until cool but not set.

**5.** Fill cooled crusts with strained crème-fraîche mixture. Transfer to the refrigerator, and chill until set, 15 to 20 minutes. Arrange persimmon slices decoratively on top. Serve chilled.

## tangerine-curd tartlets

MAKES 2 DOZEN

*The curd (steps one through three) and tartlet shells (steps four and five) can be made up to three days before you assemble the dessert. If you don't have forty-eight 2¼-inch fluted tartlet pans, bake tartlets in batches.*

- 3 large whole eggs
- 3 large egg yolks
- ½ cup sugar
  Juice of 1 lemon
- ½ cup freshly squeezed tangerine juice, plus grated zest of 3 tangerines, plus 48 tangerine sections (about 9 tangerines total)
- 6 tablespoons chilled unsalted butter, cut into small pieces
  All-purpose flour, for work surface
  Pâte Brisée (page 389)

**1.** Prepare an ice bath; set aside. In a medium heat-proof bowl, whisk together eggs, yolks, and ¼ cup sugar; set mixture aside. Place lemon juice, tangerine juice, two-thirds of zest, and remaining ¼ cup sugar in a small, heavy-bottom, nonreactive saucepan. Bring to a boil.

**2.** Pour the boiling liquid into egg mixture, whisking constantly. Return mixture to saucepan, and bring to a boil again, whisking constantly. As soon as curd starts to boil, remove from heat.

**3.** Pour curd through a fine sieve set over a medium bowl, pressing with the back of a wooden spoon or ladle to extract as much liquid as possible; discard solids. Gradually whisk in butter until incorporated. Set the bowl over the ice bath, stirring occasionally until completely cool. Lay plastic wrap directly on surface of curd to prevent a skin from forming. Chill until firm, about 3 hours.

**4.** Preheat oven to 375°F. On a lightly floured work surface, roll out each disk of dough to about ⅛ inch thick. Using a 3-inch cookie cutter, cut out 12 rounds from each piece. Press rounds into pans, and place a second pan on top; gently press two pans together. Chill until firm, about 30 minutes.

**5.** Bake shells until edges begin to brown, about 12 minutes. Remove top pans, and continue baking until crust dries completely and becomes golden brown, 12 to 14 minutes more. Transfer shells to a wire rack to cool completely.

**6.** To serve, place about 1 tablespoon curd in each shell. Top each with 2 tangerine sections, and sprinkle with the remaining zest.

## tiny tartes tatin
*photograph on page 70*
MAKES 1 DOZEN

- 1 cup sugar
- 4 tablespoons unsalted butter
- ¼ cup chopped fresh cranberries
- ¼ cup chopped walnut halves
- 3 medium apples, peeled, cored, and cut into ½-inch cubes
  All-purpose flour, for work surface
- 1 package frozen puff pastry (17.3 ounces), thawed

**1.** Preheat oven to 375°F. In a small saucepan, combine sugar and ¼ cup water over medium heat, stirring until sugar dissolves. Without stirring, cook until mixture is dark amber, 10 to 12 minutes, washing down sides of pan with a wet pastry brush to prevent crystals from forming.

**2.** Immediately pour 1 tablespoon caramel mixture into each cup of a standard 10½-by-13½-inch muffin tin. Add 1 teaspoon butter to each cup. Combine cranberries, walnuts, and apples in a medium bowl. Divide filling evenly among cups.

**3.** On a lightly floured work surface, roll out 1 sheet of puff pastry into a 12-inch square. (Reserve remaining sheet for another use; wrap well in plastic, and store in the freezer.) Using a 2½-inch cookie cutter, cut out 12 rounds. Lay pastry rounds over apple mixture in muffin cups.

**4.** Bake until pastry is golden brown and puffed, 30 to 35 minutes. Transfer to a wire rack to cool 3 minutes before inverting tarts onto a baking sheet lined with parchment paper. Replace any dislodged pieces of apple; serve immediately.

## winter fruit tart

MAKES 1 TEN-INCH TART

*This tart can also be baked in a ten-inch spring-form pan or a tart ring on a baking sheet.*

12 ounces dried figs (about 18 figs),
    cut in half

6 ounces dried apricots (about ¾ cup),
    cut in half

4 ounces golden raisins (about ¾ cup)

2 cups dry white wine

1 vanilla bean, split lengthwise and scraped

1¼ cups sugar

1 cup fresh cranberries

¾ cup pitted dates (6 ounces), chopped

1 cup (2 sticks) unsalted butter,
    plus more for pan

1½ tablespoons pure vanilla extract

4 large egg yolks, plus 1 whole egg,
    lightly beaten, for glaze

2¾ cups all-purpose flour, plus more for pans

⅛ teaspoon salt

**1.** Place figs, apricots, raisins, wine, vanilla bean and scrapings, and ¼ cup sugar in a large sauce-pan over medium-low heat; simmer, stirring often, until fruit is very soft, about 10 minutes. Remove from heat; discard vanilla pod. Stir in cranberries and dates. Set aside to cool.

**2.** In the bowl of an electric mixer fitted with the paddle attachment, cream butter and remaining cup sugar until light and fluffy. Add vanilla extract and then egg yolks, one at a time, beating well after each. Add flour and salt; beat until combined.

**3.** Preheat oven to 350°F. Butter bottom of a 10-by-2-inch round cake pan. Cut parchment to fit bottom of pan; place in pan. Divide dough in half. Wrap one half in plastic; chill.

**4.** With fingers, spread remaining dough evenly over bottom and about 1½ inches up sides of pre-pared pan; sprinkle lightly with flour if it becomes too sticky. Spread fruit filling evenly over dough. Refrigerate 15 minutes.

**5.** For top crust, flour the bottom of a 10-inch tart pan. Remove dough from refrigerator; press evenly on pan bottom to make a thick, even disk; chill 15 minutes. Using a spatula, slide disk of dough over filling; press into place, and smooth with an offset spatula.

**6.** Brush egg glaze over top of tart. With a fork, score top in a lattice pattern; brush again with egg. Bake until golden brown, 50 to 60 minutes. Let tart cool slightly in pan on a wire rack. Invert to remove from pan; turn right side up to serve.

# *cookies and confections*

BAR COOKIES, DROP COOKIES

FILLED AND SANDWICH COOKIES

ICEBOX COOKIES

HAND-SHAPED AND ROLLED COOKIES

CONFECTIONS

✳

## apricot windows

*photograph on page 77*

MAKES 4 DOZEN 1½-BY-3-INCH BARS
OR 2 DOZEN 3-INCH SQUARES

3½  cups all-purpose flour

1⅓  cups yellow cornmeal

½  teaspoon salt

2¼  cups (4½ sticks) unsalted butter,
    room temperature

1½  cups sugar

3  large eggs, room temperature

2¼  cups apricot jam, room temperature

**1.** Preheat oven to 375°F. In a medium bowl, whisk together flour, cornmeal, and salt. In the bowl of an electric mixer fitted with the paddle attachment, cream butter and sugar on medium speed until light and fluffy. Add eggs one at a time, beating to incorporate after each addition. Reduce speed to low, and gradually add flour mixture; combine thoroughly.

**2.** Line a 17-by-11-inch rimmed baking sheet with parchment paper. Press half the dough evenly onto sheet. Place another piece of parchment over dough; rub the back of a spoon over parchment to smooth dough. Remove parchment. Using an offset spatula, spread jam evenly over dough.

**3.** Fit a pastry bag with a plain tip; fill bag with remaining dough. Pipe parallel lines of dough ½ inch apart over jam. Pipe perpendicular lines ½ inch apart across first lines. Bake until golden, about 30 minutes. Transfer sheet to a wire rack to cool. Cut into bars or squares. Store in an airtight container at room temperature up to 2 days.

## chocolate chip cookie bars

*photograph on page 77*

MAKES 32

1  cup (2 sticks) unsalted butter, room
    temperature, plus more for pans

1½  cups all-purpose flour, plus more for pans

1½  cups packed light-brown sugar

2  large eggs

1  teaspoon pure vanilla extract

2  cups quick-cooking oats

½  teaspoon salt

½  teaspoon baking soda

1  package (12 ounces) semisweet
    chocolate chips

**1.** Preheat oven to 350°F. Brush two 8-inch square cake pans with butter, and dust with flour, tapping out excess; set aside.

**2.** In the bowl of an electric mixer fitted with the paddle attachment, cream butter and brown sugar on medium speed until light and fluffy. Add eggs and vanilla, and mix until combined. Add flour, oats, salt, and baking soda, and mix until combined. Stir in chocolate chips.

**3.** Divide dough evenly between prepared pans. Using a large rubber spatula, flatten dough to fill pan bottoms, pressing it into edges of pans.

**4.** Bake until golden brown and set in center, about 35 minutes, rotating pans halfway through. Transfer to wire racks to cool completely before removing from pans. Cut each square in half to form two 8-by-4-inch rectangles, then cut each half into eight 4-by-1-inch bars. Store in an airtight container at room temperature up to 4 days.

## brownies

*photograph on page 77*

MAKES ABOUT 8

*Brownies are traditionally cut into bars, but we baked ours in a shallow muffin tin so that each one is surrounded by a delicious crust. To make bars, bake batter in a buttered thirteen-by-nine-inch baking pan.*

- ¾ cup (1½ sticks) unsalted butter, cut into small pieces
- 8 ounces bittersweet or semisweet chocolate, roughly chopped
- 4 large eggs
- 1½ cups granulated sugar
- ½ cup packed dark-brown sugar
- 1 tablespoon pure vanilla extract
- 1⅓ cups sifted all-purpose flour
- ½ teaspoon salt

**1.** Preheat oven to 350°F. Line eight cups of shallow muffin tins with paper liners; set aside. In a heatproof bowl set over a pan of simmering water, melt butter and chocolate, stirring frequently. Remove from heat; let cool completely.

**2.** In a large mixing bowl, whisk together eggs, sugars, and vanilla until combined. In a separate bowl, combine sifted flour and salt. Add chocolate mixture to egg mixture; stir with a wooden spoon until combined. Gradually add flour mixture, stirring until thoroughly combined. Pour a scant ⅔ cup batter into each prepared muffin cup.

**3.** Bake until brownies are firm around edges but still soft in centers, about 30 minutes. Do not overbake, or brownies will be dry. Transfer tin to a wire rack to cool completely, then turn out brownies onto rack. Brownies can be stored in an airtight container at room temperature up to 4 days.

## congo bars

*photograph on page 77*

MAKES ABOUT 16 DOZEN

*Cashews, hazelnuts, almonds, or pecans can be substituted for the macadamia nuts.*

- 6 cups (about 2 pounds) macadamia nuts, halved
- 1 package (16 ounces) graham crackers
- ½ cup (1 stick) unsalted butter, melted
- 10 ounces bittersweet chocolate, finely chopped
- 1½ cups packed sweetened shredded coconut
  Caramel for Cookies (recipe follows)

**1.** Preheat oven to 350°F. Spread macadamia nuts in a single layer on a rimmed baking sheet, and toast in oven until golden, about 10 minutes. Set nuts aside to cool.

**2.** Line a 17-by-11-inch rimmed baking sheet with parchment paper. In a food processor, pulse graham crackers until fine crumbs form. Place crumbs in a medium bowl; stir in melted butter. Press mixture onto prepared sheet. Sprinkle chocolate evenly over graham-cracker crust, followed by coconut and then the reserved nuts.

**3.** In a heatproof bowl set over a pan of simmering water, heat the caramel until liquefied; drizzle over top of mixture on sheet. Bake until golden, about 20 minutes. Transfer to a wire rack to cool. Cut into bars, about 1¼ by ¾ inches. Store in an airtight container at room temperature up to 4 days.

## caramel for cookies

MAKES 3¾ CUPS

*This recipe can easily be halved or multiplied.*

- 4 cups sugar
- ½ teaspoon cream of tartar
- ¼ teaspoon salt
- ½ cup heavy cream

**1.** Combine sugar, cream of tartar, salt, and ⅔ cup water in a wide, heavy-bottom saucepan. Place over high heat. Cook, without stirring, until sugar begins to melt and turn golden, 2 to 5 minutes; wash down sides of pan with a wet pastry brush to prevent crystals from forming.

**2.** Reduce heat to medium, and continue cooking, stirring occasionally, until sugar has melted, mixture is deep golden, and a candy thermometer registers 300°F (hard-crack stage).

**3.** Stirring constantly, carefully pour cream slowly down side of pan. After cream is incorporated, remove from heat. Transfer to a heatproof bowl; keep at room temperature until ready to use.

## golden popcorn bars

MAKES ABOUT 3 DOZEN

*For a quicker version of these squares, substitute air-popped popcorn.*

- 2 tablespoons vegetable oil, plus more for pans
- ¾ cup popping corn (enough to make 12 cups popcorn)
- 2 cups salted peanuts
- 1½ recipes Caramel for Cookies (recipe above)

**1.** Preheat oven to 350°F. Oil two 13-by-9-inch baking pans; line bottom of pans with parchment paper, and oil parchment. Set aside.

**2.** Heat oil in a heavy-bottom stockpot over medium heat. Add popping corn. Cover, and cook until corn starts to pop. Continue cooking, shaking pot frequently, until popping noises subside; remove from heat. Transfer popped corn to a large bowl, and add peanuts.

**3.** In a heatproof bowl set over a pan of simmering water, heat caramel until liquefied. Drizzle caramel over popcorn mixture; toss to coat thoroughly. Transfer mixture to one of the prepared pans; using the back of a wooden spoon, pack mixture as tightly as possible.

**4.** Bake until caramel darkens, about 20 minutes. Transfer to a wire rack to cool 5 minutes. Invert other prepared pan; place on top. Using hot pads, flip pans, letting popcorn mixture fall into second pan. Let cool on a wire rack. When completely cool and hard, cut into bars, about 2 by 1½ inches.

## pecan caramel shortbread

*photograph on page 77 and 80*

MAKES ABOUT 11 DOZEN

3½  cups pecans
1½  cups (3 sticks) unsalted butter
¾  cup packed light-brown sugar
2¼  cups all-purpose flour
    Caramel for Cookies (page 406)

**1.** Preheat oven to 350°F. Spread pecans in a single layer on a rimmed baking sheet. Toast in oven until golden and fragrant, 10 to 15 minutes. Let cool on a wire rack. Roughly chop, and set aside.

**2.** In the bowl of an electric mixer fitted with the paddle attachment, cream butter and sugar on medium speed until light and fluffy. With mixer on low, gradually add flour; mix until combined.

**3.** Line a 17-by-11-inch rimmed baking sheet with parchment paper. Press dough evenly onto bottom of sheet. Bake until golden, about 20 minutes.

**4.** In a heatproof bowl set over a pan of simmering water, heat caramel until liquefied. Using a wooden spoon, stir in reserved pecans, and spread mixture evenly over dough. Return to oven, and bake until caramel is slightly darkened, about 10 minutes. Transfer sheet to a wire rack to cool. Cut into bars, about 2¾ by ½ inches. Store in an airtight container at room temperature up to 3 days.

## shaker lemon bars

MAKES ABOUT 6 DOZEN

*Make the recipe through step one the day before you plan to bake these lemony treats.*

2  lemons, washed and dried
2¾  cups sugar
1  cup plus 2 tablespoons (2¼ sticks) chilled unsalted butter, cut into small pieces
3  cups all-purpose flour
½  teaspoon salt
4  large eggs, lightly beaten
    Confectioners' sugar, for dusting

**1.** With a sharp knife, slice lemons as thinly as possible; remove seeds. Toss slices with 2 cups sugar; transfer mixture to a shallow airtight container. Place in the refrigerator overnight.

**2.** Place butter, remaining ¾ cup sugar, flour, and salt in a food processor. Pulse until crumbs form and mixture starts to hold together.

**3.** Preheat oven to 400°F. Line a 17-by-11-inch rimmed baking sheet with parchment paper. Press dough evenly onto bottom and up sides of sheet, making sure there are no holes. Bake until golden brown, about 20 minutes. Transfer sheet to a wire rack to cool completely, about 15 minutes.

**4.** Place lemon mixture and eggs in a food processor. Process until lemon rinds are in ¼-to-½-inch pieces, 30 to 40 seconds. Pour mixture over cookie crust, and bake until set, 15 to 20 minutes. Let cool on a wire rack. Trim ½ inch from edges. Cut remaining sheet into bars, about 2 by 1¼ inches. Dust with confectioners' sugar. Store in an airtight container at room temperature up to 3 days.

## rocky road brownies

MAKES 1 DOZEN

**for brownies:**

 4 ounces walnuts, coarsely chopped (1 cup)

 1 cup (2 sticks) unsalted butter,
   plus more, room temperature, for pan

 8 ounces best-quality unsweetened
   chocolate

 5 large eggs

3½ cups sugar

 2 teaspoons instant espresso powder

 1 tablespoon pure vanilla extract

1⅔ cups all-purpose flour

 ½ teaspoon salt

 3 ounces best-quality semisweet chocolate,
   coarsely chopped (½ cup)

**for topping:**

 4 ounces walnuts, coarsely chopped (1 cup)

 6 ounces best-quality semisweet chocolate,
   coarsely chopped (1 cup)

 2 cups miniature marshmallows

**1.** Make brownies: Preheat oven to 350°F. Spread walnuts in a single layer on a rimmed baking sheet; toast in oven until golden and fragrant, 5 to 10 minutes. Set aside to cool.

**2.** Raise oven temperature to 400°F. Butter a 13-by-9-inch baking pan; line bottom with parchment paper, and butter parchment; set aside.

**3.** Melt unsweetened chocolate and butter in a heatproof bowl set over a pan of simmering water, stirring frequently. Remove from heat; set aside.

**4.** In the bowl of an electric mixer fitted with the paddle attachment, beat eggs, sugar, and espresso powder on high speed until light and fluffy, about 5 minutes. Reduce speed to low, and add chocolate mixture and vanilla; beat until combined. Gradually add flour and salt; beat until just incorporated. Fold in semisweet chocolate and reserved toasted walnuts.

**5.** Pour batter into prepared pan; spread evenly with a rubber spatula. Bake until edges are set but center is still soft, about 35 minutes.

**6.** Make topping: In a medium bowl, combine walnuts, chocolate, and marshmallows. Sprinkle topping evenly over brownies.

**7.** Return to oven; bake until chocolate is partially melted and marshmallows are soft and lightly browned, about 5 minutes. Transfer to a wire rack; let cool 20 minutes. Using a serrated knife, cut into squares, about 3¼ by 3 inches; serve warm or at room temperature. Store in an airtight container at room temperature up to 2 days.

## rugelach fingers

*photograph on page 77*
MAKES ABOUT 5 DOZEN

*These cookies use the ingredients of the traditional crescent-shaped rugelach but are instead cut into bars.*

 4 ounces walnuts (1 cup)

 ¾ cup (1½ sticks) chilled unsalted butter,
   cut into small pieces, plus 3 tablespoons,
   melted, for filling

 8 ounces cream cheese

 2 cups all-purpose flour

 ½ teaspoon salt

 6 ounces bittersweet chocolate,
   coarsely chopped (1 cup)

 ½ cup granulated sugar

 1 tablespoon ground cinnamon

 ¾ cup dried currants
   Grated zest of 1 orange

 3 tablespoons light corn syrup

 1 large egg yolk, beaten with 1 tablespoon
   water, for egg wash

 3 tablespoons fine sanding sugar
   or granulated sugar

**1.** Preheat oven to 350°F. Spread walnuts in a single layer on a rimmed baking sheet; toast in oven until golden and fragrant, 10 to 15 minutes. Let cool, then finely chop. Set aside. Turn off oven.

**2.** In the bowl of an electric mixer fitted with the paddle attachment, beat ¾ cup butter and the cream cheese on low speed until mixture is soft, with pieces of butter still visible. With mixer running, gradually add flour and salt; beat until crumbly and just beginning to hold together, about 20 seconds (there should still be some small pieces of butter). Divide dough in half. Flatten each half into a disk, and wrap in plastic. Transfer to refrigerator; chill at least 5 hours.

**3.** Preheat oven to 350°F. Place chocolate in a food processor; pulse until very finely chopped, about 7 times. Transfer to a large bowl. Add sugar, cinnamon, currants, orange zest, corn syrup, melted butter, and reserved walnuts; stir until combined.

**4.** Line a 13-by-9-inch baking pan with parchment paper. Place one disk of dough between two pieces of wax paper; roll dough into a rectangle the size of prepared baking pan; fit dough into pan. Spread chocolate mixture evenly over dough. Roll out remaining disk of dough into another 13-by-9-inch rectangle; place on top of mixture in pan.

**5.** Brush top of dough with egg wash, and sprinkle with sanding sugar. Bake until golden, about 35 minutes. Let cool on a wire rack. Cut into bars, about 2½ by ¾ inches. Store in an airtight container at room temperature up to 3 days.

## buttery pecan rounds
### MAKES ABOUT 3 DOZEN

*This is a wonderfully simple drop cookie.*

- 1   cup (2 sticks) unsalted butter
- ¾   cup packed dark-brown sugar
- 1   large egg yolk
- 1   cup sifted all-purpose flour
- ½   teaspoon salt
- ⅔   cup chopped pecans
- 36   pecan halves, for decorating

**1.** Preheat oven to 325°F. In the bowl of an electric mixer fitted with the paddle attachment, cream butter and sugar on medium speed until light and fluffy. Add egg yolk; beat until combined. Into a medium bowl, sift together flour and salt; add to butter mixture, and beat until incorporated. Stir in chopped pecans.

**2.** Drop batter by the teaspoon onto a baking sheet. Press one pecan half into center of each cookie. Bake until light brown, 12 to 15 minutes; let cool on wire racks. Store in an airtight container at room temperature up to 3 days.

## mudslide cookies

MAKES ABOUT 4 DOZEN

*These cookies are made with three types of chocolate for a rich, deep flavor.*

⅔ cup all-purpose flour

2 teaspoons baking powder

1 teaspoon salt

6 tablespoons unsalted butter

6 ounces unsweetened chocolate, coarsely chopped (1 cup)

16 ounces semisweet chocolate, coarsely chopped (2⅔ cups)

5 large eggs

1¾ cups sugar

1½ teaspoons pure vanilla extract

16 ounces milk chocolate, coarsely chopped (2⅔ cups)

**1.** Preheat oven to 400°F. Line baking sheets with Silpat baking mats or parchment paper; set aside. Into a small bowl, sift together flour, baking powder, and salt; set aside.

**2.** In a heatproof bowl set over a pan of simmering water, melt butter and both dark chocolates, stirring to combine; set aside to cool.

**3.** In the bowl of an electric mixer, whisk eggs, sugar, and vanilla on medium speed until light and fluffy, about 3 minutes. Add cooled chocolate mixture, and combine on low speed. Add flour mixture, and continue to beat on low speed until almost combined, about 1 minute. Stir in milk chocolate until combined.

**4.** Using a spoon, drop dough onto prepared baking sheets, about 3 inches apart. Bake until cookies are set, 12 to 15 minutes. Transfer to wire racks; let cookies cool completely on baking sheets before serving. Store in an airtight container at room temperature up to 4 days.

## oatmeal cookies

*photograph on page 76*

MAKES 1 DOZEN LARGE
OR 3 DOZEN SMALL

1 cup packed light-brown sugar

1 cup granulated sugar

1 cup (2 sticks) unsalted butter, room temperature

2 large eggs, room temperature

1 teaspoon pure vanilla extract

3 cups rolled oats

1 cup plus 2 tablespoons all-purpose flour

½ cup wheat germ

1 teaspoon baking soda

1 teaspoon baking powder

12 ounces semisweet chocolate, chopped into chunks, 1½ cups golden raisins, or 10 ounces toffee pieces

**1.** Preheat oven to 350°F. In the bowl of an electric mixer fitted with the paddle attachment, cream brown sugar, granulated sugar, and butter, starting on low speed and increasing to medium, until mixture is light and fluffy, about 5 minutes. Add eggs and vanilla; scrape down sides of bowl with a rubber spatula, and beat to combine.

**2.** Place oats, flour, wheat germ, baking soda, and baking powder in a large bowl; stir to combine. Add flour mixture to butter mixture; mix on low speed until just combined, 10 to 15 seconds. Stir in chocolate, raisins, or toffee pieces, as desired.

**3.** Line two large baking sheets with parchment paper. Use a large (2½-ounce) or small (1¼-ounce) ice-cream scoop to form balls of dough. Place balls about 4 inches apart (2 inches for small) on baking sheets. Bake until cookies are golden and just set, about 18 minutes for large and 14 minutes for small. Let cookies cool on sheets 5 minutes before transferring to a wire rack. Store in an airtight container at room temperature up to 4 days.

## chocolate thumbprints

*photograph on page 80*

MAKES 2 DOZEN

¾ cup (1½ sticks) unsalted butter,
room temperature

½ cup confectioners' sugar

¼ teaspoon salt

1 teaspoon pure vanilla extract

1¼ cups all-purpose flour

4 ounces semisweet chocolate, coarsely
chopped (about ⅔ cup)

1½ teaspoons light corn syrup

**1.** Preheat oven to 350°F. In the bowl of an electric mixer fitted with the paddle attachment, cream ½ cup butter with the sugar, salt, and vanilla on medium speed until smooth, about 2 minutes. Gradually beat in flour, beginning on low speed and increasing to medium-high.

**2.** Roll dough by the teaspoon into balls; place 1 inch apart on a baking sheet. Bake 10 minutes; remove from oven, and make an indentation in top of each cookie with thumb. Return to oven; bake until light brown around edges, 7 to 9 minutes more. Transfer cookies to a wire rack to cool.

**3.** In a heatproof bowl set over a pan of simmering water, combine chocolate, remaining ¼ cup butter, and the corn syrup; stir occasionally until melted and smooth. Let cool slightly. When cookies are cool, fill thumbprints with chocolate mixture. Store cookies in airtight containers at room temperature up to 3 days.

## jam thumbprints

*photograph on page 77*

MAKES ABOUT 3 DOZEN

½ cup (1 stick) unsalted butter,
room temperature

½ cup plus 2 tablespoons granulated sugar

1 large egg yolk

1 teaspoon pure vanilla extract

1¼ cups all-purpose flour

⅛ teaspoon salt

5 ounces (½ cup) whole blanched almonds,
finely ground

1 large egg white, lightly beaten

½ cup jam or preserves

**1.** Preheat oven to 325°F. Line two baking sheets with parchment paper; set aside. In the bowl of an electric mixer fitted with the paddle attachment, cream butter and ½ cup sugar on medium speed until light and fluffy, about 3 minutes. Add egg yolk and vanilla, and beat until combined. In a medium bowl, whisk together flour and salt; gradually add flour mixture to butter mixture, beating on low speed until combined.

**2.** On a plate, combine ground almonds with the remaining 2 tablespoons sugar. Form dough into 1-inch balls; dip in egg white, then in almond mixture, coating completely. Transfer to prepared baking sheets. Make a deep indentation in the center of each ball with your finger or the bottom of a thick wooden spoon.

**3.** Bake 10 minutes; remove from oven, and press down centers again. Rotate sheets, and bake until golden brown, 8 to 10 minutes more. Remove from oven; let cool slightly on a wire rack before filling thumbprints with jam. Store in airtight containers at room temperature up to 3 days.

## cream-filled chocolate cookies

MAKES ABOUT 30

*The dough for these cookies can be made ahead and stored, wrapped well in plastic, in the refrigerator for up to one week or in the freezer for up to one month; thaw completely in the refrigerator before proceeding with recipe. After assembling the cookies, you can roll the sides in crushed candy canes.*

1¼ cups all-purpose flour
¾ cup Dutch-process cocoa powder
1 teaspoon baking soda
¼ teaspoon baking powder
¼ teaspoon salt
10 tablespoons (1¼ sticks) unsalted butter, room temperature
1½ cups sugar, plus more for glass
1 large egg, room temperature
Vanilla Cream Filling (recipe follows)

**1.** Preheat oven to 375°F. Line two baking sheets with parchment paper; set aside. Into a medium bowl, sift together flour, cocoa powder, baking soda, baking powder, and salt; set aside.

**2.** In the bowl of an electric mixer fitted with the paddle attachment, cream butter and sugar until light and fluffy, about 2 minutes. Add the egg, and beat to combine. With mixer on low speed, gradually add the flour mixture; continue beating until dough just comes together.

**3.** Using a spoon, drop balls of dough about 2 inches apart on prepared baking sheets. Dip the bottom of a glass in sugar; press to flatten balls to about ⅛ inch thick. (If necessary, remove dough from glass with a thin spatula.)

**4.** Bake until cookies are firm, 10 to 12 minutes, rotating sheets halfway through. Transfer to wire racks to cool completely. Turn half the cookies over.

**5.** Using a pastry bag fitted with a plastic coupler, pipe about 1 tablespoon filling onto inverted cookies. Place remaining cookies on top; gently press on each to squeeze filling to edges. Filled cookies can be stored in airtight containers at room temperature up to 2 days.

## vanilla cream filling

MAKES ABOUT 1 CUP

½ cup (1 stick) unsalted butter, room temperature
½ cup solid vegetable shortening
3½ cups confectioners' sugar
1 tablespoon pure vanilla extract

In the bowl of an electric mixer fitted with the paddle attachment, cream butter and shortening until smooth and combined. With the mixer on low speed, gradually add confectioners' sugar, and continue beating until light and fluffy, about 2 minutes. Beat in vanilla. Set filling aside at room temperature until ready to use.

# linzer sandwiches

*photograph on page 80*
MAKES ABOUT 14

*If the dough begins to soften while rolling or cutting, return it to the refrigerator or freezer until firm, about fifteen minutes.*

- 5   ounces (1 cup) unblanched hazelnuts
- 1   cup (2 sticks) unsalted butter, room temperature
- ½   cup granulated sugar
- 1   large egg
- 1   teaspoon pure vanilla extract
- 2   cups plus 2 tablespoons all-purpose flour, plus more for work surface
- 1   teaspoon baking powder
- 1   teaspoon ground cinnamon
- ¼   teaspoon ground nutmeg
- ¼   teaspoon salt
     Confectioners' sugar, for dusting
- ⅔   cup raspberry or cherry jam

**1.** Preheat oven to 375°F. Spread hazelnuts in a single layer on a rimmed baking sheet; toast in oven until skins begin to split, about 10 minutes. Remove from oven; vigorously rub nuts in a clean kitchen towel to remove as much skin as possible. Let cool completely. Transfer to a food processor; pulse until finely ground. Set aside. Turn off oven.

**2.** In the bowl of an electric mixer fitted with the paddle attachment, cream butter and sugar on medium speed until light and fluffy, about 2 minutes. Add egg; beat to combine. Beat in vanilla.

**3.** In a medium bowl, whisk reserved ground hazelnuts with the flour, baking powder, cinnamon, nutmeg, and salt. With the mixer on low speed, gradually add flour mixture to butter mixture; beat on low speed until combined, about 2 minutes. Divide dough in half, and flatten each into a disk. Wrap disks in plastic, and refrigerate until firm, at least 1 hour or overnight.

**4.** Preheat oven to 350°F. Line two baking sheets with parchment paper; set aside. Place a piece of parchment on a work surface, and generously dust with flour. Roll out one disk of dough to ¼ inch thick. Transfer dough on parchment to freezer; chill until firm, about 20 minutes. Repeat rolling and freezing with the other disk of dough.

**5.** Remove one sheet of dough from freezer. Using a 3-inch fluted cutter, cut out rounds. With a spatula, transfer rounds to prepared baking sheets. Using a ½-inch star cutter, cut centers from half the cookies. Repeat with other dough sheet. Return cookies to freezer; chill until firm, about 15 minutes.

**6.** Bake cookies until edges are golden, 14 to 16 minutes, rotating sheets halfway through. Transfer cookies to wire racks to cool completely.

**7.** Lightly dust star-cut cookies with confectioners' sugar. Invert remaining uncut cookies, and spread about 1 tablespoon jam over each. Place cut cookies on top, and press gently to adhere. Filled cookies can be stored in an airtight container at room temperature up to 2 days.

## lime sablés
MAKES 2 DOZEN

1⅓  cups all-purpose flour,
     plus more for rolling
1½  tablespoons granulated sugar
⅓   cup confectioners' sugar,
     plus more for dusting
¼   teaspoon salt
¾   cup (1½ sticks) chilled unsalted
     butter, cut into small pieces
1½  teaspoons pure lime extract
     Lime Curd (recipe follows)

**1.** Place flour, granulated sugar, confectioners' sugar, and salt in a food processor. Pulse until combined. Add butter; pulse until coarse crumbs form. Add lime extract, and pulse to combine.

**2.** Turn out dough onto plastic wrap, and flatten into a disk. Wrap in plastic, and refrigerate until very firm, at least 2 hours.

**3.** Preheat oven to 325°F. Line two baking sheets with Silpat baking mats or parchment paper; set aside. On a lightly floured work surface, roll out dough to ⅛ inch thick. Using a 1¾-inch cookie cutter, cut the dough into squares. Using a 1-inch fluted cutter, cut windows from center of half the squares. Place all squares on prepared baking sheets, about 1 inch apart.

**4.** Bake cookies until just golden, 15 to 17 minutes, rotating sheets halfway through. Transfer cookies to a wire rack to cool completely.

**5.** Lightly dust cut cookies with confectioners' sugar. Invert uncut cookies, and spread with about 1 teaspoon lime curd. Place cut cookies on top, and press gently to adhere. Refrigerate until firm, about 20 minutes. Store filled cookies in airtight containers in the refrigerator up to 2 days.

## lime curd
MAKES ¾ CUP

½   cup sugar
2   large eggs, lightly beaten
¼   cup freshly squeezed lime juice (6 limes)
2   teaspoons grated lime zest (2 limes)
4   tablespoons unsalted butter,
     cut into small pieces

**1.** Combine sugar, eggs, lime juice, and zest in a medium saucepan. Cook over medium-low heat, whisking constantly, until mixture thickens and holds mark of whisk, about 20 minutes.

**2.** Remove pan from heat; whisk in butter, one piece at a time, until combined. Strain through a fine sieve into a nonreactive bowl. Lay plastic wrap directly on surface to prevent a skin from forming. Chill at least 3 hours and up to 1 day.

ICEBOX COOKIES

## cornmeal-pecan biscuits
photograph on page 76
MAKES 2½ DOZEN

2   ounces (½ cup) whole pecans
½   cup (1 stick) unsalted butter,
     room temperature
1   cup sugar
1   large egg
1   teaspoon pure vanilla extract
1¼  cups all-purpose flour
½   cup yellow cornmeal
1   teaspoon baking powder
¼   teaspoon salt
2   tablespoons dark-brown sugar
1   teaspoon ground cinnamon
1   large egg white, lightly beaten with
     1 tablespoon water, for egg wash

**1.** Preheat oven to 400°F. Spread pecans in a single layer on a rimmed baking sheet. Toast in oven until golden and fragrant, 8 to 10 minutes. Set pecans aside to cool.

**2.** In the bowl of an electric mixer fitted with the paddle attachment, cream butter and sugar on medium speed until light and fluffy, 2 to 4 minutes. Add egg and vanilla; beat to combine.

**3.** In a medium bowl, whisk together flour, cornmeal, baking powder, and salt. With mixer on low speed, gradually add flour mixture to butter mixture. Beat until combined, about 30 seconds.

**4.** Transfer dough to a clean work surface, and divide into four equal pieces. Place each piece between two 12-inch square pieces of parchment. Roll out pieces of dough into 9-by-3½-inch rectangles. Transfer dough, still between parchment, to baking sheets; chill at least 10 minutes.

**5.** In a food processor, process reserved pecans, the brown sugar, and cinnamon until nuts are finely chopped, 12 to 15 seconds. Transfer mixture to a medium bowl.

**6.** Remove dough from refrigerator; remove parchment from tops. Brush one rectangle lightly with egg wash; sprinkle with ¼ cup pecan mixture. Brush second rectangle lightly with egg wash; invert over first, and remove parchment. Repeat layering process with remaining two rectangles, leaving top rectangle uncoated. Trim to an 8½-by-3¼-inch brick. Wrap in plastic; chill overnight.

**7.** Preheat oven to 350°F. Line two baking sheets with parchment paper. Cut brick crosswise into ¼-inch-thick slices; place slices on prepared baking sheets, about 2½ inches apart.

**8.** Bake biscuits until light golden, 12 to 15 minutes. Transfer to a wire rack to cool. Store in airtight containers at room temperature up to 2 weeks.

## orange poppy-seed spirals

*photograph on page 76*
MAKES ABOUT 3 DOZEN

*Orange Sablé Dough (page 416)*
⅓ cup poppy seeds

**1.** Remove dough from refrigerator; let it come to room temperature. Roll out dough between two 14-by-12-inch pieces of parchment into a 14-by-12-inch rectangle. Transfer dough, still between parchment, to a baking sheet; chill 30 minutes.

**2.** Transfer dough to a clean work surface, with a short side facing you. Remove parchment from top; sprinkle with poppy seeds. Using bottom parchment to support dough, fold over bottom of dough to the center. Fold over dough in the same direction two more times, forming a 3½-inch-wide rectangle about 1½ inches tall. Wrap in parchment; chill at least 2 hours.

**3.** Preheat oven to 350°F. Line two baking sheets with parchment paper. Remove dough from refrigerator; remove parchment. Cut dough into ¼-inch-thick slices. Place slices on prepared baking sheets, about 2½ inches apart.

**4.** Bake cookies until edges are light golden, about 15 minutes. Transfer cookies to a wire rack to cool. Store cookies in airtight containers at room temperature up to 2 weeks.

## orange sablé cookies

*photograph on page 76*

MAKES ABOUT 5 DOZEN

*Orange Sablé Dough (recipe follows)*

*1 cup sanding or granulated sugar, for rolling*

**1.** Remove dough from refrigerator; divide in half. Form each half into a rough log. Place each log on a 16-by-12-inch piece of parchment paper. Fold parchment over dough; roll and press dough into 1½-inch-diameter logs. Wrap in parchment. Refrigerate at least 3 hours.

**2.** Preheat oven to 350°F. Line two baking sheets with parchment paper. Spread sanding sugar in a shallow dish. Remove logs from refrigerator; remove parchment. Roll logs in sugar to coat. Slice logs into ¼-inch-thick rounds; place rounds on prepared baking sheets, about 2 inches apart.

**3.** Bake until edges are golden, about 15 minutes, rotating sheets halfway through. Transfer cookies to a wire rack to cool. Store cookies in an airtight container at room temperature up to 2 weeks.

**Variation:** To make Orange-Ginger Cookies, substitute 6 ounces finely chopped crystallized ginger for the sanding sugar.

## orange sablé dough

MAKES ABOUT 1½ POUNDS

*6 ounces (1¼ cups) whole blanched almonds*

*1 cup confectioners' sugar*

*¾ cup (1½ sticks) unsalted butter, room temperature*

*3 tablespoons finely grated orange zest (2 to 3 oranges)*

*1 large egg*

*1 tablespoon freshly squeezed orange juice*

*1½ cups all-purpose flour*

**1.** Process almonds and sugar in a food processor until mixture resembles coarse meal; set aside.

**2.** In the bowl of an electric mixer fitted with the paddle attachment, cream butter and zest on medium speed until light and fluffy, 2 to 3 minutes. On low speed, gradually add almond mixture; beat until combined, 10 to 15 seconds. Add egg and orange juice; beat until combined. Add flour all at once and beat until combined. Wrap dough in plastic; refrigerate until ready to use, up to 1 week, or freeze up to 6 weeks.

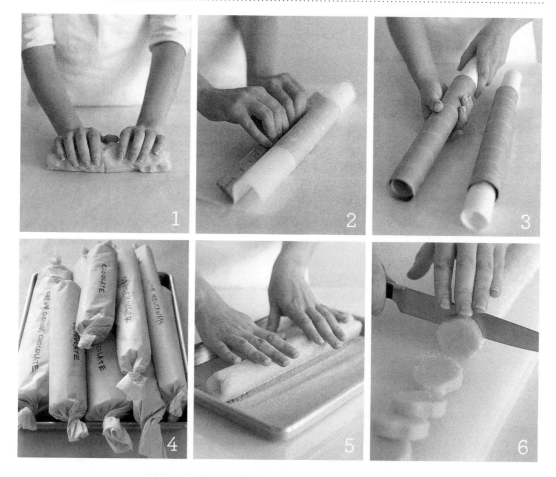

## HOW TO FORM PERFECT LOGS OF DOUGH

**1.** *When making classic icebox cookies such as Orange Sablé Cookies, form the dough into a rough log shape on a sheet of parchment paper. Place the dough slightly off center, toward one end of the parchment. Fold parchment paper over the dough.*

**2.** *Push with a ruler to mold the wrapped dough into a narrow cylinder just smaller than the diameter of a paper-towel tube (about 1½ inches). Press hard to remove air pockets and to keep the dough even.*

**3.** *Slip the parchment-wrapped dough into an empty paper-towel tube to maintain its shape as it chills. Refrigerate until very firm, at least 3 hours. Remove paper-towel tube.*

**4.** *If desired, wrap logs of dough in parchment paper, and label. You can store logs in the refrigerator up to 10 days, or in the freezer up to 3 months (let frozen logs thaw slightly before slicing).*

**5.** *When ready to bake, roll the chilled dough back and forth in a rimmed baking sheet sprinkled with sanding sugar or another coating, such as cocoa, chopped nuts, candied fruit, or crystallized ginger.*

**6.** *Slice the refrigerated or frozen logs into ¼-to-½-inch-thick rounds, depending on recipe, and bake.*

## wheatmeal peanut-butter fingers

*photograph on page 76*

MAKES ABOUT 3 DOZEN

1 cup (2 sticks) unsalted butter, room temperature

¾ cup confectioners' sugar

1 large egg

1¼ cups toasted wheat germ

1¼ cups whole-grain pastry flour

¼ teaspoon salt

¼ cup cornstarch

¼ cup smooth peanut butter

¼ cup granulated sugar

1. In the bowl of an electric mixer fitted with the paddle attachment, cream butter and confectioners' sugar on medium speed until light and fluffy, 2 to 3 minutes. Add egg; beat until incorporated.

2. In a medium bowl, whisk together wheat germ, pastry flour, salt, and cornstarch. Add mixture to butter mixture all at once, and beat on low speed until combined, about 1 minute.

3. Divide dough into two equal pieces; place each piece between 12-inch squares of parchment paper. Roll out each piece into a 10-by-7-inch rectangle, about ¼ inch thick.

4. Remove top pieces of parchment from dough rectangles; spread peanut butter over one rectangle. Invert second rectangle on top of first. Fold over any overhanging parchment to wrap dough. Transfer to a baking sheet; chill at least 1 hour.

5. Preheat oven to 350°F. Line two baking sheets with parchment paper. Remove dough from refrigerator; remove parchment. Generously sprinkle top and bottom of dough with sugar. Trim ⅛ inch from all edges, creating a clean rectangle. Cut into slices, about 3½ by ½ inches; place slices on prepared sheets, about 1½ inches apart.

6. Bake cookies until barely golden, about 22 minutes. Transfer to a wire rack to cool. Store in airtight containers up to 2 weeks.

## striped cookies

*photograph on page 76*

MAKES ABOUT 6½ DOZEN

*Black and White Dough (recipe follows), room temperature*

1. Divide black dough into four equal pieces. Place each piece between two 12-by-14-inch pieces of parchment paper. Roll out dough into 3½-by-12-inch rectangles. Transfer dough, still between parchment, to baking sheets; chill at least 30 minutes. Repeat process with white dough.

2. Remove dough from refrigerator; remove parchment from tops. Invert one white rectangle onto a black one; remove parchment. Repeat stacking with another white and black rectangle, for a total of four layers. Trim ⅛ inch from all edges. Wrap stacked brick in plastic. Make a second brick with remaining four rectangles. Chill at least 1 hour.

3. Preheat oven to 375°F. Line two baking sheets with parchment paper. Cut bricks crosswise into ¼-inch-thick slices; place slices on prepared sheets, about 2½ inches apart.

4. Bake cookies until barely golden, 10 to 12 minutes; transfer to wire racks to cool. Store in airtight containers at room temperature up to 2 weeks.

## black and white dough

MAKES ABOUT 4¾ POUNDS

- 4 cups (8 sticks) unsalted butter, room temperature
- 7½ cups bread flour
- 3 cups confectioners' sugar
- 1 teaspoon pure vanilla extract
- ⅓ cup Dutch-process cocoa powder

**1.** In the bowl of an electric mixer fitted with the paddle attachment, cream butter, flour, sugar, and vanilla on medium speed until combined.

**2.** Turn out dough onto a work surface; divide in half. Return one half to the mixing bowl, and beat in cocoa powder until combined.

**3.** Wrap both dough halves in plastic; refrigerate until ready to use, up to 1 day.

## bull's-eye cookies

photograph on page 76
MAKES ABOUT 7½ DOZEN

Black and White Dough (recipe above), room temperature

**1.** Divide black dough in half. Between two 12-by-14-inch pieces of parchment paper, roll out one half to a 7-by-12-inch rectangle, about ⅓ inch thick. Repeat with white dough. Chill both rectangles at least 30 minutes.

**2.** Take two-thirds of remaining black dough, and roll between two 12-by-14-inch pieces of parchment paper into a 4¾-by-12-inch rectangle. Repeat with white dough. Chill at least 15 minutes.

**3.** Roll out remaining black dough on a clean work surface into a 12-inch log, about ¾ inch in diameter. Repeat with white dough. Wrap in parchment paper. Chill at least 15 minutes.

**4.** Remove smaller black rectangle from refrigerator; remove parchment from top. Remove white log from refrigerator, and place lengthwise on black rectangle. Using bottom piece of parchment for support, wrap black dough around white log, pressing with fingers to seal seam. Roll log back and forth to smooth seam.

**5.** Repeat step 4 with smaller white rectangle and black log. Remove larger white rectangle from refrigerator; remove top piece of parchment. Place white log wrapped in black dough lengthwise on white rectangle. Using bottom piece of parchment for support, wrap white dough around log, pressing with fingers to seal seam. Roll log back and forth to smooth seam.

**6.** Repeat step six with larger black rectangle and black log wrapped in white dough. Wrap both logs in parchment paper. Chill 1 hour.

**7.** Preheat oven to 375°F. Line two baking sheets with parchment paper. Remove logs from refrigerator, and remove parchment. Slice each into ¼-inch-thick rounds; place on prepared baking sheets, about 2 inches apart.

**8.** Bake cookies until barely golden, about 15 minutes. Transfer cookies to a wire rack to cool. Store in airtight containers up to 2 weeks.

## chewy coconut-chocolate pinwheels

*photograph on page 76 and 80*

MAKES ABOUT 3 DOZEN

9 tablespoons unsalted butter,
  room temperature
1 cup sugar
1 large egg
1 teaspoon pure vanilla extract
2 cups cake flour (not self-rising)
½ teaspoon baking soda
¼ teaspoon salt
1½ cups shredded unsweetened coconut
6 ounces bittersweet chocolate,
  coarsely chopped (1 cup)
⅓ cup sweetened condensed milk

1. In the bowl of an electric mixer fitted with the paddle attachment, cream 8 tablespoons butter and the sugar until light and fluffy. Add egg and vanilla, and beat until combined.

2. In a medium bowl, whisk together flour, baking soda, and salt. With mixer on low speed, gradually add flour mixture to butter mixture until combined. Add coconut, and beat until combined.

3. Roll out dough between two 12-by-17-inch pieces of parchment into a 10-by-15-inch rectangle, about ⅛ inch thick. Transfer dough, still between parchment, to a baking sheet; chill at least 1 hour.

4. Place chocolate and remaining tablespoon butter in a heatproof bowl set over a pan of simmering water. Melt completely, stirring occasionally; remove from heat. Stir in condensed milk. Let stand until thickened slightly, about 5 minutes.

5. Remove dough from refrigerator; remove parchment from top. Using an offset spatula, spread melted chocolate mixture over dough. Using bottom piece of parchment for support, roll dough into a log. Wrap in parchment; chill overnight.

6. Preheat oven to 350°F. Line two baking sheets with parchment paper. Remove log from refrigerator; remove parchment. Slice log into ¼-inch-thick rounds. Place rounds, about 1½ inches apart, on prepared baking sheets. Bake until edges are lightly golden, 8 to 10 minutes, rotating sheets halfway through. Transfer cookies to a wire rack to cool. Store in airtight containers at room temperature up to 2 weeks.

### ROLLING PINWHEELS

*After spreading evenly with melted chocolate mixture, roll dough into a log using parchment paper for support. For the best presentation, and for uniformity, try to keep the log perfectly round.*

## cranberry noëls

*photograph on page 75*
MAKES ABOUT 3 DOZEN

*The dough can be stored, wrapped well in plastic, in the freezer for up to one month. Before slicing, thaw slightly at room temperature. For a festive variation, roll the edges in colored sanding sugar before baking.*

- 1 cup (2 sticks) unsalted butter, room temperature
- ¾ cup sugar
- 2 tablespoons milk
- 1 teaspoon pure vanilla extract
- 2½ cups all-purpose flour
- ½ teaspoon salt
- ¾ cup dried cranberries
- ½ cup chopped pecans

**1.** In the bowl of an electric mixer fitted with the paddle attachment, cream butter and sugar on medium speed until light and fluffy, about 2 minutes. Add milk and vanilla. Beat until just combined. With mixer on low speed, gradually add flour and salt; beat until fully combined. Beat in cranberries and pecans.

**2.** Turn out dough onto a clean work surface, and divide in half. Shape each half into an 8-inch log, about 2 inches in diameter. Wrap logs in plastic, and refrigerate until firm, about 2 hours.

**3.** Line baking sheets with parchment paper, and set aside. Preheat oven to 375°F. Remove logs from refrigerator. Using a sharp knife, slice logs into ¼-inch-thick rounds. Place rounds, about 1½ inches apart, on prepared baking sheets. Bake until edges are golden, 14 to 16 minutes, rotating sheets halfway through. Transfer cookies to a wire rack to cool completely. Store cookies in airtight containers at room temperature up to 2 weeks.

## lacy nut cookies

*photograph on page 76*
MAKES ABOUT 3 DOZEN

- 1 cup (2 sticks) plus 5 tablespoons unsalted butter, room temperature
- 2¼ cups confectioners' sugar
- ¼ cup corn syrup
- 1¼ cups bread flour
- 1¼ cups chopped nuts, such as almonds, blanched hazelnuts, or pecans

**1.** Preheat oven to 350°F. In the bowl of an electric mixer fitted with the paddle attachment, cream butter and sugar on medium speed until light and fluffy. With mixer running, add corn syrup. Reduce speed to low; gradually add flour, and beat to combine. Beat in nuts.

**2.** Place a 12-by-16-inch piece of parchment paper on a clean work surface. Spoon dough lengthwise down center of parchment. Fold parchment over dough; press and roll dough into a 1½-inch-diameter log. Chill log at least 30 minutes.

**3.** Line two baking sheets with parchment paper. Remove log from refrigerator; remove parchment. Slice into ½-inch-thick rounds. Place rounds, about 3½ inches apart, on prepared baking sheets.

**4.** Bake cookies until golden brown, 15 to 20 minutes, rotating sheets halfway through. Transfer cookies to a wire rack to cool. Store in an airtight container at room temperature up to 2 weeks.

HAND-SHAPED
AND ROLLED COOKIES

## apricot shortbread trees

photograph on page 75
MAKES ABOUT 2½ DOZEN

*We like to cut this buttery shortbread into tree shapes, and then decorate some with glittery dragées. Lightly brush the edges of the cookies with beaten egg white, and then spoon dragées over top, pressing gently to adhere.*

 1  cup (2 sticks) unsalted butter,
    room temperature
 ¾  cup sifted confectioners' sugar
 1  teaspoon pure vanilla extract
 2  cups sifted all-purpose flour, plus more
    for rolling dough
 ½  teaspoon salt
 ½  cup finely chopped dried apricots

**1.** Line a baking sheet with parchment paper; set aside. In a large bowl, stir together the butter, sugar, vanilla, flour, and salt with a wooden spoon until mixture is just combined. Stir in dried apricots. Turn out dough onto a piece of plastic wrap, and flatten into a disk. Wrap in plastic, and chill until firm, about 1 hour.

**2.** Preheat oven to 325°F, with rack in center. Transfer dough to a lightly floured sheet of parchment paper; roll out to ¼ inch thick. If dough starts to get too soft, place in the freezer or refrigerator for a few minutes. Using a tree-shape cookie cutter, cut out trees, and place, about 1 inch apart, on prepared baking sheet.

**3.** Bake cookies until golden, 12 to 15 minutes, rotating sheet halfway through. Transfer cookies to a wire rack to cool. Store cookies in airtight containers at room temperature up to 5 days.

## chocolate charms

MAKES 40

*Dust these cookies with cocoa just before serving. If you're giving the cookies as a gift, enclose instructions for dusting along with about three tablespoons of cocoa powder.*

 2  cups all-purpose flour
 ¼  cup unsweetened cocoa powder,
    plus more for dusting
 ¼  teaspoon salt
 1  cup (2 sticks) unsalted butter,
    room temperature
 ¾  cup sugar
 1  teaspoon pure vanilla extract

**1.** Line two baking sheets with parchment paper; set aside. Sift together flour, cocoa, and salt into a small bowl; set aside. In the bowl of an electric mixer fitted with the paddle attachment, cream butter on medium speed until pale and smooth, about 5 minutes. Add sugar, and beat until very light and fluffy, about 2 minutes more, scraping down sides of bowl as needed. Beat in vanilla.

**2.** With the mixer on low speed, gradually add flour mixture to butter mixture; beat until just combined and dough sticks together when squeezed. Cover bowl with plastic wrap, and refrigerate until firm, about 1 hour.

**3.** Preheat oven to 325°F. Using a spoon, form dough into 1-inch balls; place about 1 inch apart on prepared baking sheets. Bake until firm, 20 to 25 minutes, rotating sheets halfway through. Let cool on wire racks. Just before serving, dust with cocoa powder. Store cookies in airtight containers at room temperature up to 1 week.

## chocolate orange cookies

MAKES ABOUT 3 DOZEN 2-INCH COOKIES

1 ¾ cups sifted all-purpose flour
1 teaspoon baking powder
Pinch of salt
½ cup (1 stick) unsalted butter, room temperature
⅔ cup sugar
1 large egg
Zest of 1 orange
1 tablespoon orange-flavored liqueur
½ cup grated semisweet chocolate

**1.** Into a bowl, sift together flour, baking powder, and salt; set aside. In the bowl of an electric mixer fitted with the paddle attachment, cream butter and sugar on medium speed until light and fluffy. Beat in egg, orange zest, and liqueur until smooth.

**2.** With mixer on low speed, gradually add flour mixture to butter mixture, beating until just combined. Beat in chocolate. Turn out dough onto plastic wrap; flatten into a disk. Wrap; chill 3 hours.

**3.** Preheat oven to 350°F. Remove dough from the refrigerator, and roll out to ¼ inch thick. Cut into shapes, as desired. Place shapes on baking sheets, and bake cookies until golden, about 15 minutes. Transfer to wire racks to cool. Store in airtight containers at room temperature up to 3 days.

## coconut almond cookies

MAKES ABOUT 3 DOZEN 2-INCH COOKIES

1 cup finely shredded coconut
1 cup (2 sticks) unsalted butter, room temperature
¼ teaspoon salt
½ cup sifted confectioners' sugar
1 teaspoon pure almond extract
2¼ cups sifted cake flour (not self-rising)
4 ounces (¾ cup) blanched almonds, finely ground

**1.** Preheat oven to 325°F. Spread shredded coconut in a single layer on a rimmed baking sheet, and toast in oven, stirring occasionally, until lightly golden, about 20 minutes.

**2.** In the bowl of an electric mixer fitted with the paddle attachment, cream butter and salt on medium speed until smooth. Gradually add sugar, beating until light and fluffy. Beat in almond extract and toasted coconut. With mixture on low speed, gradually add flour, beating until combined. Stir in almonds. Turn out dough onto plastic wrap; flatten into a disk. Wrap, and chill 3 hours.

**3.** Preheat oven to 325°F. Remove dough from refrigerator, and roll out to ¼ inch thick. Cut into shapes, as desired. Place shapes on baking sheets, and bake cookies until golden, 18 to 20 minutes. Transfer cookies to wire racks to cool. Store in airtight containers at room temperature up to 3 days.

## coconut pyramids

*photograph on page 80*

MAKES 45

*The dough can be made up to one week in advance and refrigerated until ready to use.*

5¼  cups unsweetened shredded
      desiccated coconut

1¾  cups sugar

  7  large egg whites, lightly beaten
      Pinch of salt

  2  tablespoons unsalted butter,
      melted and cooled

  1  teaspoon pure almond extract

  1  teaspoon pure vanilla extract

  4  ounces semisweet chocolate,
      finely chopped

  ½  teaspoon solid vegetable shortening

**1.** Preheat oven to 350°F. Line baking sheets with parchment paper; set aside. In a large bowl, using your hands, mix together coconut, sugar, egg whites, and salt. Add butter and extracts, and combine. Cover bowl with plastic; chill at least 1 hour.

**2.** Remove dough from refrigerator. Moisten palms with cold water. Roll 1 tablespoon of dough in palms, squeezing tightly to form a compact ball. Place ball on a clean work surface; using a bench scraper, flatten each side to form a pyramid. Repeat process with remaining dough.

**3.** Place pyramids about 1 inch apart on prepared baking sheets; bake until edges are golden brown, about 15 minutes, rotating sheets halfway through. Transfer sheets to a wire rack to cool completely.

**4.** Place chocolate and shortening in a heatproof bowl set over a pan of simmering water; stir occasionally, until melted. Dip top ½ inch of pyramids into melted chocolate; return to baking sheets. Let chocolate cool and harden. Store in airtight containers at room temperature up to 2 days.

## honey lebkuchen

MAKES ABOUT 12 DOZEN

*An old German recipe, lebkuchen are often decorated with icing, but our version is rich enough to serve undecorated.*

1½  cups sugar

  ⅔  cup honey

  ½  cup (1 stick) unsalted butter

  6  cups sifted all-purpose flour

  ½  teaspoon salt

1½  teaspoons baking soda

  ¼  teaspoon ground ginger

  1  teaspoon ground cinnamon
      Grated zest of 1 lemon

  3  ounces (½ cup) blanched almonds,
      finely chopped

  2  small eggs, lightly beaten

**FORMING COCONUT PYRAMIDS**

*Place a ball of coconut dough on a work surface. Using a bench scraper, flatten dough on each side to form a three-sided pyramid.*

**1.** In a large saucepan, warm sugar, honey, and butter over low heat, stirring until sugar has dissolved and mixture is smooth. Remove from heat. Sift together flour, salt, baking soda, and spices into a medium bowl; add to honey mixture, and stir until blended. Stir in lemon zest, almonds, and eggs. Let cool; turn out dough onto a piece of plastic wrap; flatten into a disk. Chill at least 3 hours.

**2.** Preheat oven to 350°F. Remove dough from refrigerator, and roll out to ¼ inch thick. Cut into shapes, as desired. Place shapes on baking sheets, and bake cookies until golden brown, 10 to 12 minutes, rotating sheets halfway through. Transfer cookies to wire racks to cool. Store cookies in airtight containers at room temperature up to 2 days.

## lime-glazed cornmeal cookies
*photograph on page 72*
MAKES ABOUT 5 DOZEN

*These not-too-sweet cookies are a nice alternative for the holiday season.*

- 1   cup (2 sticks) unsalted butter, room temperature
- 1   cup sugar
- 1   large egg
- 2   tablespoons freshly squeezed lime juice (about 1 lime)
- 1   tablespoon plus 1 teaspoon grated lime zest (about 6 limes)
- 2   teaspoons grated orange zest (about ½ orange)
- ½   teaspoon pure almond extract
- 1½ cups all-purpose flour
- 1   cup yellow cornmeal, plus more for glass
     Lime Glaze (recipe follows)
     Sugared Lime Zest (optional; recipe follows)

**1.** In the bowl of an electric mixer fitted with the paddle attachment, cream butter and sugar on medium speed until light and fluffy, about 4 minutes. Add egg, and beat until combined. Add lime juice and zest, orange zest, and almond extract. Beat to combine.

**2.** With mixer on low speed, add flour and cornmeal to butter mixture. Beat until well combined. Turn out dough onto a piece of plastic wrap; flatten into a disk, and chill until firm, about 1 hour.

**3.** Preheat oven to 350°F. Line two baking sheets with parchment paper. Remove dough from the refrigerator. Using a 1¼-inch ice-cream scoop, form dough into uniform balls. (Alternatively, drop rounded heaps from a tablespoon.) Place balls about 3 inches apart on prepared baking sheets. Spread some cornmeal on a plate; dip the bottom of a glass in cornmeal, and use it to flatten each ball until it is ¼ inch thick.

**4.** Bake until edges are crisp and lightly golden, about 15 minutes, rotating sheets halfway through. Let cookies cool completely on a wire rack.

**5.** Place rack with cookies on a sheet of wax paper. Dip a fork into glaze, and drizzle glaze over each cookie. Let it dry. Store cookies in airtight containers at room temperature up to 1 week. Before serving, garnish with sugared lime zest, if desired.

**Variation:** To make Lemon-Glazed Cornmeal Cookies, substitute lemons for the limes.

### lime glaze
MAKES ENOUGH FOR 5 DOZEN COOKIES

*If you're making Lemon-Glazed Cornmeal Cookies, substitute freshly squeezed lemon juice for the lime juice in this recipe.*

1½  cups confectioners' sugar, sifted
¼  cup freshly squeezed lime juice

In a medium bowl, whisk together confectioners' sugar and lime juice until very smooth. Continue whisking vigorously until glaze is thick and shiny, about 3 minutes. The glaze may be stored in an airtight container at room temperature up to 3 hours; whisk again just before drizzling.

### sugared lime zest
MAKES ENOUGH FOR 5 DOZEN COOKIES

*Reserve the poaching syrup to use in making dessert glazes, limeade, and cocktails.*

1  cup granulated sugar
2  limes
½  cup superfine sugar

1. Combine granulated sugar and 1 cup water in a small saucepan. Bring to a boil over medium-high heat, and cook, stirring occasionally, until sugar has dissolved, about 3 minutes. Set aside.

2. Use a citrus zester to remove long strips of zest from each lime. Add lime zest to sugar syrup, and simmer over low heat until zest is slightly transparent and very soft, about 30 minutes.

3. Place superfine sugar in a small bowl. Using a slotted spoon, transfer several zest strips to bowl; turn to coat evenly. Using your fingers or tweezers, transfer strips to a piece of wax paper to dry. Repeat until all zest is coated. Store in an airtight container at room temperature up to 4 days.

### mocha almond cookies
MAKES ABOUT 2 DOZEN

4  ounces unsweetened chocolate, finely chopped
½  cup (1 stick) unsalted butter
6  tablespoons coffee-flavored liqueur
2  large eggs
¾  cup sugar, plus more for rolling
1⅓  cups sifted all-purpose flour
¾  teaspoon baking powder
4  ounces (1 cup) blanched almonds, finely ground
   *Sifted confectioners' sugar, for rolling*

1. In a small saucepan, melt chocolate and butter over low heat, stirring occasionally. Stir in coffee liqueur; remove saucepan from heat, and cover to keep warm. In the bowl of an electric mixer fitted with the paddle attachment, beat eggs and sugar on medium speed until fluffy. Beat chocolate mixture into egg mixture.

2. Sift together flour and baking powder into a small bowl; add to chocolate mixture, and beat well. Stir in ground almonds. Cover bowl with plastic wrap, and chill until firm, about 1 hour.

3. Remove dough from refrigerator. Form dough into 1-inch balls; place on a baking sheet, and chill 10 minutes more.

4. Preheat oven to 325°F. Place granulated and confectioners' sugars in two separate bowls. Remove sheet from refrigerator; roll balls first in granulated sugar, then in confectioners' sugar, coating evenly. Return balls to baking sheet, spaced 2 inches apart, and bake until firm and crackly, about 15 minutes, rotating sheet halfway through. Let cool on wire racks. Store in airtight containers at room temperature up to 3 days.

## *palmiers*

photograph on page 80

MAKES ABOUT 4 DOZEN

1  package (17.3 ounces) frozen
   puff pastry, thawed
1  cup granulated sugar

**1.** Unfold pastry sheets, and stack; trim edges to make a 10-inch square. Place one sheet flat on a work surface; cover other sheet with plastic wrap. Sprinkle top of one square with ¼ cup sugar. Gently press sugar into dough. Roll up one side of dough to middle, making sure pastry is even. Roll up the opposite side to the middle, meeting first side. Repeat process with the second pastry sheet and ¼ cup sugar. Wrap rolls separately in plastic; chill until very firm, about 1 hour.

**2.** Preheat oven to 475°F. Lightly spritz two baking sheets evenly with water. Remove logs from refrigerator; remove plastic, and cut crosswise into ¼-inch-thick slices. Place slices 2 inches apart on prepared baking sheets. Freeze 15 minutes.

**3.** Remove baking sheets from freezer; sprinkle each pastry shape with ½ teaspoon sugar. Bake cookies until bottoms begin to caramelize, 5 to 6 minutes, rotating sheets halfway through. Remove sheets from oven, and quickly flip cookies. Continue baking cookies until evenly caramelized but not burned, 1 to 2 minutes more.

**4.** Transfer baking sheets to wire racks, and let cool 1 to 2 minutes. Using a thin spatula, transfer palmiers to wire racks to cool completely. Store in airtight containers at room temperature up to 3 days.

**MAKING PALMIERS**

*1. Roll up one side of sugar-covered pastry dough to the middle, making sure pastry is even. Roll up the opposite side to the middle, meeting the first side.*

*2. Once chilled, use a sharp knife to cut logs crosswise into ¼-inch-thick slices.*

## gingerbread cookies

MAKES ABOUT 16 LARGE COOKIES

  6  cups sifted all-purpose flour,
     plus more for work surface
  1  teaspoon baking soda
  ½  teaspoon baking powder
  1  cup (2 sticks) unsalted butter,
     room temperature
  1  cup packed dark-brown sugar
  4  teaspoons ground ginger
  4  teaspoons ground cinnamon
1½  teaspoons ground cloves
  1  teaspoon freshly ground pepper
1½  teaspoons salt
  2  large eggs
  1  cup unsulfured molasses
     Royal Icing (recipe follows)

**1.** Into a large bowl, sift together flour, baking soda, and baking powder. Set aside.

**2.** In the bowl of an electric mixer fitted with the paddle attachment, cream butter and sugar on medium speed until fluffy. Beat in spices and salt, then beat in eggs and molasses until combined. Reduce speed to low. Gradually add flour mixture; beat until combined. Divide dough in half; flatten into disks. Wrap in plastic; chill at least 1 hour.

**3.** Preheat oven to 350°F. Remove dough from the refrigerator, and let stand at room temperature to temper slightly. (This prevents dough from cracking.) Place a large piece of parchment paper on a clean work surface, and dust generously with flour.

**4.** Roll out dough to a ¼-inch thickness, running an offset spatula under dough and dusting with flour as needed to prevent sticking. Transfer dough on parchment paper to freezer to chill until very firm, about 15 minutes.

**5.** Remove dough from freezer; working quickly, cut into desired shapes. If dough begins to soften, return to freezer a few minutes. Using a spatula, transfer shapes to baking sheets; freeze until firm, about 15 minutes.

**6.** Transfer baking sheets to oven; bake until cookies are crisp but not darkened, 8 to 10 minutes, rotating sheets halfway through. Transfer cookies to wire racks to cool, then ice as desired.

## royal icing

MAKES ABOUT 2½ CUPS

*If you use egg whites, omit the water from step one, and refrigerate icing until ready to use.*

  1  pound confectioners' sugar
  5  tablespoons meringue powder or 2 large
     egg whites
     Liquid gel or gel-paste food coloring
     (optional)

**1.** In the bowl of an electric mixer fitted with the paddle attachment, combine sugar, meringue powder, and a scant ½ cup water on low speed. Mix until fluffy yet dense, 7 to 8 minutes. Use icing immediately, or transfer to an airtight container (icing hardens quickly when exposed to air). Beat well with a rubber spatula before using.

**2.** To thin icing for flooding (filling in areas with a thin layer of icing), stir in additional water 1 teaspoon at a time. Test consistency by lifting spoon and letting icing drip back into bowl; a ribbon of icing on surface should remain 5 to 7 seconds.

**3.** To tint icing, dip a toothpick into food coloring, and gradually mix into icing with toothpick until desired shade is reached.

**Note:** Raw eggs should not be used in food prepared for pregnant women, babies, young children, the elderly, or anyone whose health is compromised.

### DECORATING COOKIES WITH ROYAL ICING

**1.** *Outline cookie using a small plain tip (Ateco #2). Let icing set 5 to 10 minutes. Using a plain tip (Ateco #5), draw several zigzags across the entire surface of the cookie (this is called flooding).*

**2.** *Spread icing over cookie with an offset spatula. Let dry overnight. When ready to decorate, pipe a design with the small plain tip.*

**3.** *To create a leafy vine motif, pipe wavy horizontal "stems" on each cookie, starting at the top. Next, add leaves: Apply pressure to pastry bag to make a leaf's base, letting up on pressure as you move toward the tip. Stagger leaves along the stem. If desired, apply silver dragées or other decorations before icing hardens.*

**4.** *Place sanding sugar in a bowl. While icing is wet, hold cookie over a clean paper towel; sprinkle liberally with sanding sugar (this is called flocking). Let sit for 5 minutes before shaking off excess sugar. Let icing dry completely, for several hours, before gently removing stray crystals with a soft pastry brush.*

## sugar cookies

MAKES ABOUT 16 LARGE COOKIES

- 4 cups sifted all-purpose flour, plus more for work surface
- 1 teaspoon baking powder
- ½ teaspoon salt
- 1 cup (2 sticks) unsalted butter, room temperature
- 2 cups sugar
- 2 large eggs
- 2 teaspoons pure vanilla extract
  Royal Icing (page 428), for decorating (optional)
  Sanding sugar, for decorating (optional)

**1.** Into a large bowl, sift together flour, baking powder, and salt; set aside. In the bowl of an electric mixer fitted with the paddle attachment, cream butter and sugar on medium speed until light and fluffy. Beat in eggs and vanilla until combined.

**2.** With mixer on low speed, gradually add flour mixture, and beat until thoroughly combined. Divide dough in half, and wrap each in plastic. Flatten with a rolling pin so dough is even. Refrigerate until firm, at least 1 hour.

**3.** Preheat oven to 325°F. Line two baking sheets with parchment paper. Remove dough from refrigerator; let stand at room temperature to temper slightly. (This prevents dough from cracking.) Place a large piece of parchment on a clean work surface; dust generously with flour.

**4.** Roll out dough to a ¼-inch thickness, running an offset spatula under dough and dusting with flour as needed to prevent dough from sticking. Transfer dough on parchment to freezer to chill until very firm, about 15 minutes.

**5.** Remove dough from freezer; working quickly, cut into desired shapes. If dough begins to soften, return to freezer for a few minutes. Using a spatula, transfer shapes to prepared baking sheets; freeze cookies until firm, about 15 minutes.

**6.** Transfer baking sheets to oven; bake until edges of cookies just begin to brown, 15 to 18 minutes, rotating sheets halfway through. Transfer cookies to wire racks to cool completely, then decorate as desired with icing and sanding sugar.

### CHILLING COOKIE SHAPES

Soft cookie dough (below right) loses its shape when moved; to retain crisp cut edges, refrigerate dough until firm (below left) before baking.

## TIPS FOR ROLLED COOKIES

• *Line baking sheets with parchment paper or a Silpat baking mat before you begin so you can transfer shapes as soon as they are cut.*

• *Avoid pressing hard when rolling over dough edges, as this will thin them.*

• *Use only the amount of flour you need to reduce sticking, since the dough will incorporate the flour; too much added flour can toughen cookies.*

• *For easy release, dip cookie cutters in flour before cutting. When moving shapes, pull scraps away so you can maneuver the spatula without damaging edges of shapes.*

• *Chill dough before cutting to make it easier to transfer shapes to baking sheets. Chilling the dough again after it is cut into shapes helps cookies hold their shape while baking.*

• *Reroll scraps of dough only once or your cookies could be tough. Bake leftover scraps from the second batch for snacking.*

## *spritz cookies*

*photograph on page 75*
MAKES 2 TO 3 DOZEN

1½  cups (3 sticks) unsalted butter, room temperature
1  cup sugar
2  large egg yolks
1  tablespoon pure vanilla extract
3¾  cups sifted all-purpose flour
¼  teaspoon salt
   Silver or gold dragées, for decorating (optional)

**1.** Preheat oven to 350°F. In the bowl of an electric mixer fitted with the paddle attachment, cream butter and sugar until light and fluffy. Add egg yolks and vanilla; beat until combined. With mixer on low speed, gradually add flour and then salt; beat until combined.

**2.** Working in batches, transfer dough to a cookie press; press out desired shapes, 2 inches apart, onto baking sheets. Decorate with dragées, if desired.

**3.** Bake until cookies are golden around edges, 7 to 10 minutes, rotating sheets halfway through. Transfer cookies to a wire rack to cool completely. Repeat until all dough is used. (If using the same baking sheets, cool them under cold running water and then dry thoroughly before pressing out more shapes.) Store cookies in an airtight container at room temperature up to 3 days.

## gingerbread angels

MAKES 10 DOZEN

*This recipe is a favorite of Martha's friend Salli LaGrone. The dough freezes well. You can bake half the batch if you like; freeze remaining dough, wrapped in plastic, up to one month.*

3½ cups all-purpose flour, plus more for work surface

 2 teaspoons baking soda

 1 teaspoon ground cinnamon

 1 teaspoon ground ginger

 1 teaspoon ground cloves

 1 teaspoon allspice

 ¼ teaspoon salt

 1 cup (2 sticks) unsalted butter, room temperature

 ¾ cup granulated sugar

 ¾ cup packed dark-brown sugar

 1 large egg

 2 tablespoons light corn syrup
   Grated zest of 1 orange
   Grated zest of 1 lemon
   Royal Icing (optional; page 428)

**1.** In a medium bowl, whisk together flour, baking soda, cinnamon, ginger, cloves, allspice, and salt. In the bowl of an electric mixer fitted with the paddle attachment, cream butter and sugars on medium speed until fluffy. Add egg and corn syrup; beat until combined.

**2.** Add half the flour mixture to the butter mixture; beat on low speed until well combined. Add remaining flour mixture and the orange and lemon zests; beat until combined. Cover bowl with plastic wrap; chill dough, until firm, at least 1 hour.

**3.** Preheat oven to 350°F. On a floured work surface, roll out dough ¼ inch thick. Using a large angel-shape cookie cutter, cut out shapes; place ¾ inch apart on a baking sheet. Bake until firm, 6 to 8 minutes, rotating halfway through; cool on a wire rack.

**4.** Meanwhile, gather scraps into a ball; wrap in plastic, and chill 30 minutes. Roll out again; cut out more angels, and bake 6 to 8 minutes. If desired, pipe icing with a pastry bag fitted with a small round tip. Store cookies in airtight containers at room temperature up to 3 days.

## viennese almond crescents

*photograph on page 80*

MAKES ABOUT 3½ DOZEN

2¼ cups all-purpose flour

 ⅛ teaspoon salt

3½ ounces blanched almonds (⅔ cup)

 ⅔ cup superfine sugar

 12 tablespoons (1½ sticks) cold unsalted butter, cut into very small pieces

 3 large egg yolks

 1 teaspoon pure vanilla extract

 ¾ cup confectioners' sugar, for dusting

**1.** Sift together flour and salt into a small bowl. In a food processor, pulse almonds until finely ground. Add superfine sugar and flour mixture to the almonds; pulse to combine. With machine running, gradually add butter through the feed tube. Add yolks and vanilla; process 20 seconds. Wrap dough in plastic; chill at least 1 hour.

**2.** Line two baking sheets with parchment paper. Remove dough from refrigerator. Roll 1 tablespoon of dough into a 3-inch log; taper ends, and shape into a crescent. Repeat with the remaining dough. Place crescents about 1 inch apart on prepared baking sheets. Chill 30 minutes.

**3.** Preheat oven to 350°F. Transfer baking sheets to oven; bake until cookies are firm but not brown, about 18 minutes, rotating sheets halfway through. Transfer cookies on parchment to a wire rack, and let cool 5 minutes. Dust with confectioners' sugar before serving.

## pistachio-cranberry biscotti
### MAKES ABOUT 2 DOZEN

*Biscotti make good gifts because they keep well and travel without crumbling.*

- 1½ cups shelled green pistachios
- 1 cup dried cranberries
- Grated zest of 1 lemon
- 2½ cups all-purpose flour, plus more for work surface
- 1¼ cups sugar
- 1 teaspoon baking powder
- ⅛ teaspoon salt
- 3 large whole eggs
- 2 large egg yolks
- 1 teaspoon pure vanilla extract

**1.** Preheat oven to 350°F. Spread pistachios in a single layer on a rimmed baking sheet; toast in oven until fragrant, about 8 minutes. Let cool, then finely chop half of them.

**2.** Line a rimmed baking sheet with parchment paper, and set aside. In a small bowl, combine chopped and whole pistachios, the cranberries, and lemon zest; set aside.

**3.** In the bowl of an electric mixer, combine flour, sugar, baking powder, and salt. In a medium bowl, whisk together eggs, yolks, and vanilla. Add egg mixture to flour mixture; using the paddle attachment, beat on medium-low speed until a sticky dough forms. Stir in nut mixture.

**4.** Turn out dough onto a well-floured work surface; knead slightly. Shape into two 9-by-3½-inch logs. Transfer to prepared baking sheet. Bake until golden brown, 25 to 30 minutes. Remove from oven. Reduce oven heat to 275°F. Let logs stand until cool enough to handle, about 10 minutes.

**5.** On a cutting board, cut logs diagonally into ½-inch-thick slices. Return slices, cut side down, to baking sheet. Bake until lightly toasted, about 20 minutes. Turn over; bake 20 minutes more, or until slightly dry. Cool on a wire rack. Store in an airtight container at room temperature up to 2 weeks.

## classic shortbread wedges
### MAKES 8 TO 12

*The baking times for each variety of shortbread will vary depending on the kind of baking pan and size of cutters used. If rolling out dough to cut into shapes, form into a flat disk, and wrap in plastic. Chill until firm, at least 1 hour.*

- 1 cup (2 sticks) unsalted butter, room temperature, plus more for pan
- 2 cups all-purpose flour
- ¾ teaspoon salt
- ½ cup confectioners' or granulated sugar
- 1 teaspoon pure vanilla extract

**1.** Butter an 8½-inch round cake or springform pan; set aside. Sift together flour and salt into a small bowl; set aside. In the bowl of an electric mixer fitted with the paddle attachment, cream butter on medium speed until smooth, 3 to 5 minutes. Add sugar, and continue beating until very light and fluffy, about 2 minutes more, scraping down sides of bowl as needed. Beat in vanilla.

**2.** With mixer on low speed, gradually add flour mixture to butter mixture; beat until just combined and dough sticks together when squeezed.

**3.** Pat dough into prepared pan; score into wedges with a paring knife, and chill 30 minutes.

**4.** Bake until firm and just starting to brown, about 50 minutes. Let cool completely on a wire rack before storing. Store at room temperature up to 1 month in an airtight container.

**Variation:** To make Chocolate Wedges, sift ½ cup unsweetened cocoa powder with the flour and salt.

## black-and-white triangles

MAKES 2 DOZEN

*Ingredients for Classic Shortbread Wedges
(page 433)*
*Ingredients for Chocolate Wedges (page 433)*
*All-purpose flour, for work surface*

Follow recipe for shortbread wedges and chocolate wedges variation through step 2. On a lightly
floured work surface, roll out both doughs ¼ inch
thick; chill 30 minutes. Place classic dough on top
of chocolate dough; cut into 3-by-1½-inch triangles; place on baking sheets. Bake until firm and
just starting to color, 20 to 25 minutes, rotating
sheets halfway through. Let cool on a wire rack.

## ginger shortbread

MAKES 1 DOZEN

*Ingredients for Classic Shortbread Wedges
(page 433), replacing confectioners' sugar
with ½ cup packed dark-brown sugar*
1 *teaspoon ground ginger*
1 *teaspoon ground cinnamon*
  *Pinch of ground cloves*
  *Pinch of freshly ground pepper*
  *All-purpose flour, for work surface*
  *Crystal sugar*

Follow recipe for shortbread wedges through step
2, sifting ginger, cinnamon, cloves, and pepper
with flour and salt in step 1. On a lightly floured
work surface, roll out dough ½ inch thick. Cut out
gingerbread with a 3-inch cookie cutter, and sprinkle with crystal sugar; place shapes on baking
sheets, and chill 30 minutes, rotating sheets halfway through. Bake until firm, about 30 minutes.
Let cool completely on a wire rack.

## christmas-tree sandwiches

MAKES 1 DOZEN

*Ingredients for Classic Shortbread Wedges
(page 433)*
*All-purpose flour, for work surface*
*Raspberry or strawberry jam*

Follow recipe for shortbread wedges through step
2. On a lightly floured work surface, roll out dough
¼ inch thick. Cut into 24 tree shapes with a 3-inch
cookie cutter. Cut decorative holes (for ornaments)
in half the trees with a ¼-inch round pastry tip or
straw; place shapes on baking sheets, and chill 30
minutes. Bake until firm and just starting to brown,
10 to 15 minutes, rotating sheets halfway through.
Let cool completely on a wire rack. Spread uncut
trees with jam, and top with cut trees.

## almond shortbread stars

MAKES ABOUT 2 DOZEN

*Ingredients for Classic Shortbread Wedges
(page 433)*
2 *ounces (½ cup) blanched almonds,
finely ground*
1 *teaspoon pure almond extract*
  *All-purpose flour, for work surface*
  *Confectioners' sugar*

Follow recipe for shortbread wedges through step
2, adding ground almonds and extract to creamed
butter mixture at the end of step 1. On a lightly
floured surface, roll out dough ¼ inch thick. Cut
into star shapes with a 1½-inch cookie cutter; place
shapes on a baking sheet, and chill 30 minutes.
Bake until firm and just starting to brown, 15 to 20
minutes, rotating sheet halfway through. Let cool
completely on wire racks. Toss shortbread in confectioners' sugar before serving.

## chocolate-glazed nut balls

### MAKES ABOUT 3 DOZEN

*Ingredients for Classic Shortbread Wedges
(page 433)*
*Chocolate Glaze (recipe follows)*
½  *cup finely chopped pistachios or pecans*

Follow recipe for shortbread wedges through step
2. Roll dough into 1-inch balls with your hands;
place on baking sheets, and chill 30 minutes. Bake
until firm and just starting to brown, 20 to 25 minutes, rotating sheets halfway through. Let cool
completely on wire racks. Dip shortbread balls into
chocolate glaze, letting excess drip off; then dip
into chopped nuts. Set balls aside on wax paper
until the glaze has set.

## chocolate glaze

### MAKES ABOUT 1 CUP

9  *ounces semisweet chocolate,
   finely chopped*
2  *tablespoons sugar*
1  *tablespoon light corn syrup*
½  *teaspoon pure vanilla extract*

**1.** Place half the chocolate in a heatproof bowl set
over a pan of simmering water; stir until melted.
Gradually add remaining chocolate, stirring until
smooth. Remove from heat.

**2.** Combine sugar, corn syrup, and ¼ cup water
in a small saucepan. Bring mixture to a boil, stirring until sugar has dissolved. Remove from heat.

**3.** Whisk sugar syrup into melted chocolate until
smooth. Stir in vanilla. If using immediately, keep
glaze warm by setting it over a bowl of simmering
water. Store glaze up to 2 days in the refrigerator;
rewarm in a hot-water bath before using.

## citrus coins

### MAKES ABOUT 2 DOZEN

*Ingredients for Classic Shortbread Wedges
(page 433)*
¼  *cup grated lemon or orange zest
   (about 5 lemons or 3 oranges)*
1  *tablespoon freshly squeezed lemon or
   orange juice*
   *All-purpose flour, for work surface*
   *Sanding sugar*

Follow recipe for shortbread wedges through step
2, adding zest and juice to creamed butter mixture
at the end of step 1. Combine well before adding
flour mixture. On a lightly floured surface, roll out
dough ¼ inch thick. Cut out coins with a 2-inch
round cookie cutter. Roll edges in sanding sugar;
place on baking sheets, and chill 30 minutes. Bake
until firm and just starting to brown, about 20 minutes, rotating sheets halfway through. Let cool
completely on wire racks.

## espresso shortbread

### MAKES ABOUT 2 DOZEN

2  *tablespoons instant espresso powder*
   *Ingredients for Classic Shortbread Wedges
   (page 433)*
   *All-purpose flour, for work surface*

Dissolve espresso powder in 1 teaspoon hot water.
Follow recipe for shortbread wedges through step
2, adding espresso mixture to creamed butter mixture at the end of step 1. On a lightly floured work
surface, roll out dough ¼ inch thick. Cut out ovals
with a 2-inch cookie cutter. Score a line down center of ovals with the back of a butter knife. Place
on baking sheets; chill 30 minutes. Bake until firm,
about 20 minutes, rotating sheets halfway through.
Let cool on wire racks.

## hazelnut shortbread balls

MAKES ABOUT 3 DOZEN

*Ingredients for Classic Shortbread Wedges
(page 433)*
½  *cup finely chopped hazelnuts (or pecans)*

Follow recipe for shortbread wedges through step
2, adding nuts to creamed butter mixture at the
end of step 1. Roll dough into 1-inch balls with your
hands; place on baking sheets, and chill 30 minutes. Bake until firm and just starting to brown, 20
to 25 minutes, rotating sheets halfway through.
Let cool completely on wire racks.

## chocolate-glazed fingers

MAKES ABOUT 1½ DOZEN

*Ingredients for Classic Shortbread Wedges
(page 433)*
*All-purpose flour, for work surface*
*Chocolate Glaze (page 435)*

Follow recipe for shortbread wedges. On a lightly
floured work surface, roll out dough ½ inch thick.
Cut into 3-by-1-inch rectangles. Place on baking
sheets; chill 30 minutes. Bake until firm and just
starting to brown, 20 to 25 minutes, rotating sheets
halfway through. Let cool on a wire rack before
drizzling with glaze.

## lemon-poppy balls

MAKES ABOUT 3 DOZEN

*Ingredients for Classic Shortbread Wedges
(page 433)*
*Lemon Poppy-Seed Glaze (recipe follows)*

Follow recipe for shortbread wedges through step
2. Roll dough into 1-inch balls with your hands;
place on baking sheets, and chill 30 minutes. Bake
until firm and just starting to brown, 20 to 25 min-

utes, rotating sheets halfway through. Let cool
completely on a wire rack. Dip balls into glaze,
letting excess to drip off. Set aside on wax paper
until glaze has set.

## lemon poppy-seed glaze

MAKES ABOUT ¾ CUP

1  *cup confectioners' sugar*
¼  *cup heavy cream*
1  *tablespoon freshly squeezed lemon juice*
1  *teaspoon poppy seeds*

In a small bowl, whisk together sugar, cream, and
lemon juice until combined and smooth. Stir in
poppy seeds; use immediately, or refrigerate in an
airtight container up to 2 days.

CONFECTIONS

## almond croquant

MAKES ONE 13-BY-9-INCH PAN

*This almond brittle is enjoyed in the south of
France as part of "Treize Desserts," a Christmas
Eve tradition of serving thirteen sweets, repre-
senting Jesus and the twelve apostles.*

*Unsalted butter, room temperature,
for baking sheet*
1½  *cups sugar*
½  *cup light corn syrup*
2  *cups finely chopped blanched almonds
(about 9 ounces)*
*Vegetable oil*

**1.** Butter a 13-by-9-inch rimmed baking sheet; set
aside. Combine sugar and corn syrup in a small
saucepan. Bring to a boil, stirring until sugar has
dissolved. Cook, without stirring, until a candy thermometer registers 238°F (soft-ball stage), washing
down sides of pan with a wet pastry brush to pre-

vent crystals from forming. Stir in almonds; cook, stirring occasionally, until mixture is light amber.

**2.** Pour mixture onto prepared baking sheet; spread quickly into a ¼-inch-thick layer with an oiled metal spatula. Let stand 2 minutes before cutting with a sharp, oiled knife (or let cool completely before breaking into pieces). Set aside until completely cool. Store in an airtight container at room temperature up to 1 month.

**Variation:** To make Sesame Seed Crunch, substitute 1½ cups toasted sesame seeds for the blanched almonds. Stir in 2 teaspoons freshly squeezed lemon juice before pouring mixture onto prepared baking sheet.

## bourbon pralines
*photograph on page 79*
MAKES ABOUT 18

- *2   cups sugar*
- *1   cup nonfat buttermilk*
- *1   teaspoon baking soda*
- *5   tablespoons unsalted butter*
- *1   tablespoon bourbon*
- *1   cup pecan halves*

**1.** Line two baking sheets with parchment paper. In a 4-quart saucepan, combine sugar, buttermilk, and baking soda. Bring to a rolling boil over medium-high heat, stirring constantly. Cook, stirring constantly, until a candy thermometer registers 240°F (soft-ball stage), about 15 minutes, washing down sides of pan with a wet pastry brush to prevent crystals from forming. Remove from heat.

**2.** Add butter and bourbon to syrup mixture; stir with a wooden spoon until butter melts. Stir in pecans; beat with wooden spoon 30 seconds.

**3.** Spoon 1 tablespoon mixture onto a prepared sheet, forming a 2-inch disk. Repeat with remaining mixture. (If mixture begins to harden, return to heat 1 minute, stirring and scraping down sides.) Let disks stand until set, about 1 hour. Refrigerate in an airtight container up to 2 weeks.

## chocolate-nut patties
*photograph on page 79*
MAKES 30

- *1   pound semisweet chocolate*
- *¾   cup assorted roasted and raw nuts, such as cashews, macadamias, pecans, walnuts, and hazelnuts, roughly chopped*

**1.** Line two baking sheets with parchment paper, and set aside. Using a serrated knife, chop chocolate into bean-size pieces; place two-thirds in a dry heatproof bowl. Set remaining chocolate aside.

**2.** Fill a saucepan with 2 inches of water, and bring to a simmer; turn off heat. Set bowl with chocolate over pan, and stir gently with a rubber spatula until chocolate has melted and an instant-read thermometer registers 118°F.

**3.** Remove bowl from pan. Add reserved chopped chocolate. Stir constantly, bringing chocolate up sides and back down into bowl, until temperature cools to about 86°F. To determine if chocolate is tempered, drizzle a thin line onto a cool stainless-steel surface. The chocolate should dry to a matte finish in about 5 minutes.

**4.** Return bowl to saucepan; stir occasionally to maintain temperature between 86°F and 89°F, returning to heat, if necessary.

**5.** Working quickly, pour 2 tablespoons tempered chocolate onto a prepared baking sheet to form a 2-inch patty. Continue forming patties, spacing them 2 inches apart. Let chocolate stand until it just begins to set. Sprinkle 1 teaspoon nuts in center of each; set aside in a cool place to harden. Once completely set, store in an airtight container at room temperature up to 1 month.

## chocolate-covered turtles
### photograph on page 79
### MAKES 55 TO 60

1½ pounds (about 7½ cups) pecan halves

½ cup (1 stick) unsalted butter, cut into small pieces, plus more for baking sheets

2 cups light corn syrup

½ cup whole milk

2 cups sugar

Pinch of baking soda

1 can (12 ounces) evaporated milk

1 pound semisweet chocolate

**1.** Preheat oven to 350°F. Spread pecans in a single layer on a rimmed baking sheet; toast in oven until fragrant. Let cool. Generously butter baking sheets. Arrange 5 pecan halves in a snowflake-shaped cluster, overlapping nuts in center, on one of the prepared sheets. Repeat with remaining nuts, spacing clusters 2 inches apart.

**2.** In a heavy saucepan, combine corn syrup, milk, and sugar. Place over medium-high heat; cook, stirring occasionally, until mixture comes to a boil, about 6 minutes. Stir in baking soda.

**3.** Clip a candy thermometer to pan; add butter, stirring constantly until melted and keeping mixture at a full boil. Slowly pour in evaporated milk; cook at a boil, stirring constantly, until temperature registers 240°F (soft-ball stage), about 45 minutes. If pan starts to overflow, reduce heat for a few minutes, then return to a boil.

**4.** Remove caramel from heat; transfer to a medium heatproof bowl. Let cool to 200°F; caramel should have the consistency of thick honey.

**5.** Using a spoon, gently drizzle 1 tablespoon of the caramel on top of each nut cluster. If caramel becomes too stiff, place bowl over low heat; stir constantly for several minutes until returned to proper consistency. Let caramel clusters set.

**6.** Temper chocolate, following steps 1 through 3 in Chocolate-Nut Patties (recipe above).

**7.** Drizzle 1 tablespoon tempered chocolate over each cluster; set aside in a cool place to harden. Store turtles in an airtight container at room temperature up to 1 month.

## candied citrus peel
### MAKES 1½ CUPS

8 oranges, 10 lemons, or 6 grapefruits

6 cups sugar

**1.** Using a sharp knife, cut ends off each piece of fruit; cut fruit in half lengthwise. Insert tip of knife between fruit and white pith of peel, and run about halfway down fruit. Turn fruit on other end; repeat, following curve of fruit and keeping peel in one piece. Using your fingers, gently pull flesh away from peel. Reserve flesh for another use.

**2.** Place citrus peel in a 6-quart pot, and fill with enough cold water to cover (about 3 quarts). Bring to a boil over medium heat. Reduce heat; simmer 20 minutes. Drain peel; soak in cold water until cool enough to handle, about 5 minutes.

**3.** Using a melon baller, scrape soft white pith from peel, being careful not to tear or cut into skin. If making candied grapefruit peel, after scraping pith, simmer peel 20 minutes more; drain, cool, and scrape again to remove remaining pith.

**4.** Slice each piece of peel lengthwise into thin strips, about ¼ inch wide if garnishing a cake, or ⅜ inch wide if rolling in sugar.

5. In a saucepan, combine sugar with 3 cups water. Bring to a boil over medium heat, stirring occasionally until sugar has dissolved, about 8 minutes. Add peel strips to boiling syrup; reduce heat to medium-low. Wash down sides of pan with a wet pastry brush to prevent crystals from forming. Simmer strips until translucent and syrup thickens, about 40 minutes. Remove from heat; let strips cool in syrup at least 3 hours or overnight. Once cool, strips can be stored in syrup in an airtight container up to 3 weeks in the refrigerator.

**Variation:** To make sugared candied peel, remove cooled strips from syrup with a slotted spoon, wiping off excess syrup with your fingers. Roll strips in granulated sugar, and place on racks to dry.

## chewy nut toffees
### MAKES ABOUT 75

*Toffees should be individually wrapped in cellophane or wax paper to maintain their shape. This recipe can easily be doubled; for plain toffees, omit the nuts.*

- 2 *cups heavy cream*
- ½ *cup sweetened condensed milk*
- 2 *cups light corn syrup*
- 2 *cups sugar*
- ½ *teaspoon salt*
- ½ *cup (1 stick) unsalted butter, cut into tablespoons*
- 1 *tablespoon bourbon or pure vanilla extract*
- 1 *cup chopped nuts, such as pecans or peanuts (optional)*
  *Vegetable-oil cooking spray*

1. Coat a 13-by-9-inch baking pan that is at least 1½ inches deep with cooking spray. Set aside. In a 2-quart saucepan, combine cream and condensed milk; set aside.

2. In a heavy 3- to 4-quart saucepan, combine corn syrup, ½ cup water, sugar, and salt. Cook over high heat, stirring with a wooden spoon, until sugar has dissolved, about 5 minutes.

3. Reduce heat to medium. Bring to a boil. Cook, without stirring, until a candy thermometer registers 260°F (hard-ball stage), about 20 minutes, washing down sides of pan with a wet pastry brush to prevent crystals from forming. Meanwhile, cook cream mixture over low heat until just warm; do not let boil.

4. When sugar syrup reaches 260°F, gradually stir in butter and warmed cream mixture, keeping mixture at a boil. Stirring constantly, cook over medium heat until mixture reaches 248°F (firm-ball stage), about 15 minutes. Stir in bourbon and nuts, if desired. Immediately pour into prepared pan; do not scrape saucepan. Let stand uncovered at room temperature 24 hours.

5. Coat a large cutting board generously with cooking spray. Invert toffee onto board. Cut into pieces, and wrap each in cellophane or wax paper. Store in an airtight container at room temperature up to 1 month.

## chocolate-covered almonds

*photograph on page 79*

MAKES ABOUT 2 POUNDS

- 13 ounces (2½ cups) unblanched whole almonds
- 1¼ cups granulated sugar
- 1 teaspoon ground cinnamon
- 1 pound semisweet chocolate, finely chopped
- ½ cup Dutch-process cocoa powder
- ½ cup confectioners' sugar

**1.** Preheat oven to 350°F. Spread almonds in a single layer on a rimmed baking sheet; toast in oven until fragrant and golden, about 15 minutes. Line two rimmed baking sheets with parchment paper.

**2.** In a medium saucepan, combine granulated sugar, ¼ cup water, the toasted almonds, and cinnamon. Cook, stirring constantly, until sugar is golden and granular and almonds are completely coated and separated. Pour mixture onto a prepared sheet. Freeze, about 15 minutes.

**3.** Meanwhile, melt chocolate in a heatproof bowl set over a pan of simmering water, stirring occasionally, until melted. Transfer half the coated almonds to a large bowl, and pour half the melted chocolate over nuts; stir until thoroughly coated. Transfer nuts to second prepared baking sheet. Using two forks, separate nuts so they are not sticking together. Refrigerate until chocolate has set, about 20 minutes. Place remaining almonds in a bowl; coat with remaining chocolate. Return nuts to baking sheet, and refrigerate until set.

**4.** Place cocoa powder and confectioners' sugar in two separate bowls. Toss half the nuts in cocoa; toss the other half in sugar, and gently tap off any excess. Store separately in airtight containers in the refrigerator up to 1 month.

## classic truffles

*photograph on page 78*

MAKES ABOUT 4 DOZEN

*When working with chocolate, be sure to do so in a cool room. Since chocolate is the primary ingredient in truffles, use the best-quality chocolate you can find. We like to use Valrhona, Callebaut, or Scharffen Berger. Butter melts at a lower temperature than chocolate and helps to give truffles their rich flavor. If you like, roll the coated truffles in finely chopped pistachios instead of cocoa powder; you will need about two cups for this recipe.*

- 1 cup heavy cream
- 4 tablespoons unsalted butter
- 2 teaspoons light corn syrup
- 1 pound semisweet chocolate, finely chopped, plus 12 ounces for dipping
- 1 cup Dutch-process cocoa powder, sifted

**1.** Make ganache: In a small saucepan, bring cream, butter, and corn syrup to a full boil. Turn off heat. Add 1 pound chopped chocolate; do not stir. Gently swirl pan to cover chocolate completely with cream. Let stand 5 minutes; slowly whisk until chocolate is melted and combined.

**2.** Transfer mixture to a large bowl; place in refrigerator, stirring every 15 minutes. After 45 minutes, mixture will begin to thicken very quickly, so begin stirring every 3 to 5 minutes until thick enough to scoop with a spoon, 10 to 20 minutes more; consistency should be similar to pudding.

**3.** Using two spoons or a 1¼-inch ice-cream scoop, form ganache into 1-inch balls, and transfer to a parchment-lined baking sheet. Refrigerate until firm but not hard, about 10 minutes. Remove sheet from refrigerator; squeeze pieces with your fingers to soften slightly, then quickly reshape into roughly shaped balls. Return to refrigerator until ready to dip. The truffle balls can be refrigerated, covered, up to 1 week before finishing.

**4.** Fill a medium saucepan one-quarter full with water; bring to a boil. Reduce heat to a gentle simmer. Place remaining 12 ounces chocolate in a medium heatproof bowl set over a pan of simmering water; stir occasionally until chocolate is melted. Remove from heat; let cool slightly.

**5.** Line another baking sheet with parchment paper. Place cocoa powder in a small bowl. Remove truffle balls from refrigerator. Using one hand, dip a ball into melted chocolate, and roll in your hand to evenly coat. Let excess drip back into bowl. Drop coated ball into cocoa powder and turn to coat using your other hand. Let set in bowl, about 20 seconds, then pick up the ball and roll in your hand to evenly coat.

**6.** Set coated truffle on prepared baking sheet. Repeat process with remaining truffles. If the kitchen is not cool enough for truffles to set immediately, refrigerate 5 minutes. Store up to 1 week in an airtight container in the refrigerator.

✳

## champagne truffles
MAKES 5½ DOZEN

*These truffles do not contain any Champagne. Instead, the name refers to "Fine Champagne," which is a grade of Cognac.*

*Ingredients for Classic Truffles (page 440), increasing chocolate for ganache to 1 pound 2 ounces and omitting cocoa powder*

6  *tablespoons Cognac*

1  *cup sifted confectioners' sugar*

Follow recipe for Classic Truffles. Once cream mixture and chocolate have been fully combined at the end of step 1, stir in Cognac. Proceed with recipe. Finish dipped truffles by rolling in confectioners' sugar.

## candy cane truffles
*photograph on page 78*
MAKES 5½ DOZEN

18  *candy canes or 8 ounces round peppermint candy*

*Ingredients for Classic Truffles (recipe above), omitting cocoa powder*

1  *tablespoon pure peppermint extract*

**1.** Working in two batches, place candy in a food processor; pulse until finely chopped. (Alternatively, place on a large cutting board, cover with plastic wrap, and crush with a rolling pin.) Using a sieve, sift out and discard powdery residue. Measure out 1 cup chopped candy; reserve the rest for rolling.

**2.** Follow recipe for Classic Truffles. Once cream mixture and chocolate have been fully combined at the end of step 1, stir in peppermint extract. When ganache has been chilled to a pudding consistency at the end of step 2, stir in chopped candy. Proceed with recipe. Finish dipped truffles by rolling in reserved chopped candy.

## hazelnut truffles
*photograph on page 78*
MAKES 5½ DOZEN

*Ingredients for Classic Truffles (page 440), increasing chocolate for ganache to 1 pound 2 ounces and omitting cocoa powder*

¼  *cup Nutella (chocolate-hazelnut spread)*

2½  *cups (about 11 ounces) toasted hazelnuts, finely chopped*

Follow recipe for Classic Truffles. Once cream mixture and chocolate have been fully combined at the end of step 1, stir in Nutella. Proceed with recipe. Finish dipped truffles by rolling in hazelnuts.

## coconut truffles

*photograph on page 78*

MAKES ABOUT 5 DOZEN

- 4 cups (11 ounces) sweetened shredded coconut
  Ingredients for Classic Truffles (page 440), omitting cocoa powder
- 4 teaspoons coconut oil

**1.** Preheat oven to 300°F. Spread coconut in a thin layer on a rimmed baking sheet, and transfer to oven. Cook, stirring occasionally, until coconut is dry, but without any color, about 15 minutes. Let cool completely, then very finely chop. Set aside.

**2.** Follow recipe for Classic Truffles. Once cream mixture and chocolate have been fully combined at the end of step 1, stir in coconut oil. Proceed with recipe. Finish dipped truffles by rolling in toasted coconut.

## orange truffles

*photograph on page 78*

MAKES 5 DOZEN

Ingredients for Classic Truffles (page 440), increasing the chocolate for ganache to 1 pound 2 ounces and omitting cocoa powder

- 6 tablespoons Grand Marnier or other orange-flavored liqueur
- 12 ounces semisweet chocolate, very finely chopped, and sifted to remove powdery residue

Follow recipe for Classic Truffles. Once cream mixture and chocolate have been fully combined at the end of step 1, stir in liqueur. Proceed with recipe. Finish dipped truffles by rolling in chopped semisweet chocolate.

## mocha truffles

MAKES 4 DOZEN

- 2 cups heavy cream
- 2 tablespoons best-quality ground coffee
  Ingredients for Classic Truffles (page 440), omitting cream

In a small saucepan, bring heavy cream and ground coffee to a boil. Turn off heat, cover, and let steep 20 minutes. Strain mixture through a fine sieve into a clean bowl, discarding solids. Measure out 1 cup liquid, and use in place of cream in step 1 of Classic Truffles recipe; proceed with recipe.

## ginger truffles

MAKES 4½ DOZEN

Ingredients for Classic Truffles (page 440), omitting cocoa powder

- 4 teaspoons finely grated orange zest (about 3 oranges)
- 1 cup confectioners' sugar
- 1 tablespoon ground ginger

Follow recipe for Classic Truffles. Once cream mixture and chocolate have been fully combined at the end of step 1, stir in grated orange zest. Proceed with recipe. Sift together confectioners' sugar and ginger into a small bowl. Finish dipped truffles by rolling in sugar mixture.

## pistachio truffles

*photograph on page 78*

MAKES 4 DOZEN

Ingredients for Classic Truffles (page 440), omitting cocoa powder

- 2 cups (11 ounces) shelled pistachios, finely chopped

Follow recipe for Classic Truffles. Finish dipped truffles by rolling in pistachios.

## praline truffles

MAKES 5 DOZEN

  5  cups (about 1 pound) sliced almonds
2½  cups sugar
     Ingredients for Classic Truffles (page 440), omitting cocoa powder

**1.** Preheat oven to 400°F. To make praline, spread almonds on a rimmed baking sheet; toast in oven, stirring occasionally, until lightly browned, about 10 minutes. Set aside. Line a baking sheet with parchment paper or a Silpat baking mat.

**2.** In a medium saucepan, bring sugar and ½ cup water to a boil over medium heat, stirring until sugar has dissolved. Increase heat to medium-high; continue cooking, without stirring, until syrup is light amber, washing down sides of pan with a wet pastry brush to prevent crystals from forming. Remove from heat. Stir in almonds with a wooden spoon.

**3.** Working quickly, pour mixture onto prepared baking sheet, and spread evenly with the back of a large spoon. Let cool completely. Break into pieces, and finely chop. Using a sieve, sift out and discard powdery residue. Set praline aside.

**4.** Follow recipe for Classic Truffles. Once ganache has been chilled to a pudding consistency at the end of step 2, stir in 1½ cups chopped praline. Proceed with recipe. Pulse remaining praline pieces in a food processor until coarsely ground; do not let praline become powdery. Finish dipped truffles by rolling in ground praline.

## sambuca truffles

MAKES 5 DOZEN

1½  cups heavy cream
  1  tablespoon anise seed
     Ingredients for Classic Truffles (page 440), increasing chocolate for ganache to 1 pound 2 ounces and omitting cream and cocoa powder
  6  tablespoons sambuca
  1  cup sifted confectioners' sugar

**1.** In a small saucepan, bring cream and anise seed to a boil. Turn off heat. Cover; steep 20 minutes. Strain through a fine sieve into a clean bowl; discard solids. Measure out 1 cup liquid; use in place of cream in step 1 of Classic Truffles recipe.

**2.** Proceed with recipe. Once cream mixture and chocolate have been fully combined at the end of step 1, stir in sambuca. Proceed with recipe. Finish dipped truffles by rolling in confectioners' sugar.

## peppermint bark

*photograph on page 78*

MAKES 1 SEVENTEEN-BY-ELEVEN-INCH SHEET

  2  pounds white chocolate, chopped into ½-inch pieces
12  large candy canes
 ½  teaspoon peppermint oil

Line a 17-by-11-inch rimmed baking sheet with parchment paper. Place chocolate in a heatproof bowl set over a pan of simmering water until melted, stirring constantly. Place candy on a cutting board; cover with plastic, and crush with a rolling pin. Stir candy and peppermint oil into melted chocolate. Remove from heat, and pour mixture onto prepared baking sheet; spread evenly. Chill until firm, 25 to 30 minutes. Break into pieces. Store in an airtight container, refrigerated, up to 1 week.

**443**

## nut brittle

MAKES 1 THIRTEEN-BY-NINE-INCH PAN

*Although peanut brittle may be the most common variety of this candy, you can also use other whole nuts, such as cashews, hazelnuts, almonds, or pecans, as well as toasted pumpkin seeds. For a Caribbean twist, add one cup shredded coconut along with the cashews.*

Unsalted butter, room temperature, for baking pan
1½  cups sugar
½  cup light corn syrup
Pinch of salt
2½  cups unsalted dry-roasted peanuts
1  teaspoon pure vanilla extract
1  teaspoon baking soda
Vegetable oil, for spatula

**1.** Butter a 13-by-9-inch baking pan, and set aside. Combine sugar, corn syrup, ¾ cup water, and salt in a medium saucepan. Bring to a boil over medium-high heat, stirring until sugar has dissolved. Cook, without stirring, until a candy thermometer registers 238°F (soft-ball stage), washing down sides of pan with a wet pastry brush to prevent crystals from forming. Stir in nuts; continue to cook, stirring often so nuts do not burn, until mixture is golden amber.

**2.** Carefully stir in vanilla and baking soda; the mixture will foam up in pan. Pour mixture into prepared pan, and quickly spread into a ½-inch-thick layer with an oiled metal spatula. Let brittle cool completely.

**3.** Break brittle into pieces; store in an airtight container at room temperature up to 1 month.

## toffee

MAKES ABOUT 70 PIECES

*The pans recommended below are the ideal fit for the toffee; if you use other size pans, pour the toffee to a thickness of an eighth of an inch.*

2  cups (4 sticks) unsalted butter, cut into tablespoons
¼  cup light corn syrup
2½  cups sugar
1  pound bittersweet chocolate, chopped into small pieces
3  cups pecans, chopped very fine, sifted to remove powdery residue
Vegetable-oil cooking spray

**1.** Coat a 15-by-10-inch baking pan, a 16½-by-11½-inch baking pan, and an 8-inch square baking pan with cooking spray. In a heavy 3-quart saucepan, combine butter, ½ cup water, corn syrup, and sugar. Bring to a boil, stirring until sugar dissolves and mixture thickens, about 2 minutes. Reduce heat to low; cook without stirring until mixture reaches a boil, washing down sides of pan with a wet pastry brush to prevent crystals from forming.

**2.** Keep at a boil, without stirring, until a candy thermometer registers 280°F (soft-crack stage), 35 minutes to just over 1 hour. Remove from heat. Without scraping pot, pour evenly into prepared pans. If needed, use an oiled spatula to smooth. Let cool at room temperature 45 minutes.

**3.** Melt chocolate in a heatproof bowl set over a pan of simmering water, stirring with a rubber spatula. Pour evenly over toffee; spread with a spatula if necessary. Let cool about 15 minutes; sprinkle with nuts, pressing them into chocolate.

**4.** Using a large knife, lightly score into 1¾-by-2¾-inch rectangles. Let stand at room temperature 24 hours. Cut or break toffee along scored lines. Store in an airtight container up to 4 weeks.

# food sources

✳

*Addresses and telephone numbers of sources may change prior to or following publication, as may availability of listed items.*

**ACTIVE DRY YEAST**
The Baker's Catalogue at King Arthur Flour

**AMBER SUGAR, BURNT**
The Baker's Catalogue at King Arthur Flour

**APRICOTS, DRIED**
A.L. Bazzini Company

**ARBORIO RICE**
Salumeria Italiana

**AVOCADO LEAVES, DRIED**
Kitchen/Market

**BARLEY MALT**
Whole Foods Market

**BLACK SESAME SEEDS**
Pacific Rim Gourmet

**BREAD FLOUR**
The Baker's Catalogue at King Arthur Flour

**BROWN FIGS, DRIED**
A.L. Bazzini Company

**BUCKWHEAT KASHA**
Quality Natural Foods

**BULGHUR WHEAT**
Whole Foods Market

**CAULIFLOWER MUSHROOMS**
Marché Aux Délices, Da Rosario Truffles & Caviar

**CHANTERELLE MUSHROOMS**
Marché Aux Délices, Da Rosario Truffles & Caviar, Gourmet Mushrooms

**CHESTNUT FLOUR**
Fante's Kitchen Wares Shop

**CHESTNUTS, FRESH**
Grace's Marketplace

**CHIPOTLE CHILES, CANNED IN ADOBO**
Kitchen/Market

**CHIPOTLE CHILES, DRIED**
Kitchen/Market

**CHOCOLATE (FOR CHOCOLATE LEAVES)**
Dorothy McNett's Place

**COOKIE DECORATING KIT**
Martha Stewart: The Catalog for Living

**CORN HUSKS, DRIED**
Kitchen/Market

**CRACKED WHEAT**
Whole Foods Market

**CREME FRAICHE**
Vermont Butter & Cheese Company

**CRYSTALLIZED GINGER**
The Ginger People

**CURRANTS, DRIED**
A.L. Bazzini Company

**DESICCATED COCONUT**
Foods of India, Kalustyan's

**EDIBLE CRYSTALLIZED ROSE PIECES**
Sweet Celebrations

**FIGS, DRIED**
A.L. Bazzini Company

**FINE SANDING SUGAR**
Beryl's Cake Decorating & Pastry Supplies, Martha Stewart: The Catalog for Living, Sweet Celebrations

**FLAX SEED**
Whole Foods Market

**FLEUR DE SEL (FLAKY SEA SALT)**
Zingerman's

**GEL-PASTE FOOD COLOR**
Sweet Celebrations

**GOLD PETAL DUST**
Sweet Celebrations

**GOOSE FAT**
Dean & DeLuca

**GOOSE, FRESH**
D'Artagnan, Polarica

**GRAVLAX**
Zabar's

**JUNIPER BERRIES, DRIED**
Dandelion Botanical Company

**LINGONBERRY PRESERVES**
Dean & DeLuca

**MACADAMIA NUTS**
A.L. Bazzini Company

**MARRONS GLACES**
Earthy Delights, Grace's Marketplace

**MASA HARINA, DRIED**
Kitchen/Market

**MASCARPONE CHEESE**
Dean & DeLuca

**MEATS AND SAUSAGES**
Schaller & Weber

**MERINGUE POWDER**
Martha Stewart: The Catalog for Living

**OAT BERRIES**
Various health food stores

**ORANGE-FLOWER WATER**
Caswell-Massey

**OYSTERS, SHUCKED**
Citarella

**PARMIGIANO REGGIANO**
Murray's Cheese

**PECORINO ROMANO CHEESE**
Murray's Cheese

**PEKING DUCK**
D'Artagnan, Polarica

**PEPPER JELLY**
Foster's Market

**PERSIMMONS**
Indian Rock Produce

**PHEASANT**
Polarica

**POLENTA, INSTANT**
Salumeria Italiana

**POMEGRANATE MOLASSES**
Pars International Foods, Sultan's Delight

**POMEGRANATES**
Indian Rock Produce

**PORCINI MUSHROOMS, FRESH**
Da Rosario Truffles & Caviar

**RICE-PAPER WRAPPERS, EDIBLE**
Pacific Rim Gourmet

**RICOTTA SALATA**
Murray's Cheese

**ROLLED OATS**
Whole Foods Market

**ROQUEFORT CHEESE**
Murray's Cheese, Zingerman's

**RUTABAGAS**
Indian Rock Produce

**RYE MEAL**
Various health food stores

**SCALLOP SHELLS**
Citarella

**SEA SCALLOPS, SMOKED**
Sullivan Harbor Farm

**SMOKED SABLE**
Russ & Daughters

**SOUR CHERRIES, DRIED**
A.L. Bazzini Company

**SOY NUGGETS (FLAKES)**
Various health food stores

**STAR ANISE**
Kitchen/Market

**STEEL-CUT OATS**
Whole Foods Market

**SUN-DRIED-TOMATO PASTE**
Zabar's

**SUPERFINE SUGAR**
The Baker's Catalogue at King Arthur Flour

**TOASTED WHEAT GERM**
Whole Foods Market, Various health food stores

**TRITICALE**
Whole Foods Market, Various health food stores

**TRUFFLES (WHITE AND BLACK)**
Zabar's

**VANILLA BEANS**
Penzeys Spices

**WHEAT BERRIES**
Whole Foods Market

**WHOLE BLACK PEPPERCORNS**
Penzeys Spices

**WHOLE CANDIED CHESTNUTS**
Specialty food stores

**WHOLE PEPPERCORNS**
Zabar's

**WHOLE-WHEAT FLOUR**
The Baker's Catalogue at King Arthur Flour

**WILD MUSHROOMS**
Da Rosario Truffles & Caviar, Gourmet Mushrooms

# *equipment sources*

**BAKING DISHES (GLASS AND PORCELAIN)**
Bridge Kitchenware, Broadway Panhandler, Cooking.com

**BAKING SHEETS, RIMMED**
Broadway Panhandler,
Kitchen Etc.

**BROTFORM**
The Baker's Catalogue at
King Arthur Flour

**CANDY THERMOMETER WITH CLIP**
Broadway Panhandler

**CHESTNUT ROASTING PAN**
Bridge Kitchenware

**CITRUS ZESTER**
Bridge Kitchenware

**COOKIE CUTTERS**
Martha Stewart: The Catalog
for Living

**CREPE OR BLINI PANS**
Bridge Kitchenware

**DUTCH OVEN (LE CREUSET)**
Sur La Table, Williams-Sonoma

**EGG CODDLERS**
Sur La Table

**FLUTED TARTLET MOLD/TIN WITH REMOVABLE BOTTOM**
Bridge Kitchenware

**INSTANT-READ THERMOMETER**
Bridge Kitchenware

**KITCHEN TWINE**
Broadway Panhandler

**KUGELHOPF PAN**
Bridge Kitchenware

**MANDOLINE**
Katagiri & Co.

**MINI LOAF PANS**
Broadway Panhandler

**MOLDS (CHOCOLATE LEAVES)**
Dorothy McNett's Place

**MUFFIN TINS**
Bridge Kitchenware

**NONSTICK TUBE PAN (12-CUP)**
Bridge Kitchenware

**OFFSET SPATULA**
Broadway Panhandler

**PANDORO MOLD (9-CUP)**
Bridge Kitchenware

**PASTRY BAG**
Martha Stewart: The Catalog
for Living

**PIPING TIPS**
Bridge Kitchenware,
Broadway Panhandler

**POPOVER TIN**
Bridge Kitchenware

**POTATO RICER**
Bridge Kitchenware,
Broadway Panhandler

**REHRUCKEN PANS**
Bridge Kitchenware

**ROUND CAKE PAN**
Broadway Panhandler

**RUBBER SPATULA, HEATPROOF**
Bridge Kitchenware

**SAVARIN MOLD**
Bridge Kitchenware

**SILPAT BAKING MAT**
Martha Stewart: The Catalog
for Living

**STEAMED PUDDING MOLDS**
Bridge Kitchenware

**STRAIGHTEDGE RAZOR (JAPANESE RED KAI RAZOR)**
Katagiri & Co.

**TART PANS**
Bridge Kitchenware

**TERRINES**
Bridge Kitchenware

**TRUSSING NEEDLE**
Broadway Panhandler

# directory

✳

**A.L. BAZZINI COMPANY**
212-334-1280

**THE BAKER'S CATALOGUE
AT KING ARTHUR FLOUR**
800-827-6836
www.kingarthurflour.com

**BERYL'S CAKE DECORATING
& PASTRY SUPPLIES**
P.O. Box 1584
North Springfield, VA 22151
800-488-2749
www.beryls.com

**BRIDGE KITCHENWARE**
214 East 52nd Street
New York, NY 10022
212-838-6746
800-274-3435 (outside NY only)
www.bridgekitchenware.com

**BROADWAY PANHANDLER**
477 Broome Street
New York, NY 10013
212-966-3434
866-266-5927

**CASWELL-MASSEY**
518 Lexington Avenue
New York, NY 10017
212-755-2254

**CITARELLA**
2135 Broadway
New York, NY 10023
212-874-0383

**COOKING.COM**
800-663-8810
www.cooking.com

**DA ROSARIO TRUFFLES
& CAVIAR**
800-281-2330

**DANDELION BOTANICAL
COMPANY**
708 North 34th Street
Seattle, WA 98103
206-545-8892
877-778-4869

**D'ARTAGNAN**
280 Wilson Avenue
Newark, NJ 07105
800-327-8246
www.dartagnan.com

**DEAN & DELUCA**
800-999-0306
www.deandeluca.com

**DOROTHY MCNETT'S PLACE**
831-637-6444
www.happycookers.com

**EARTHY DELIGHTS**
800-367-4709

**FANTE'S KITCHEN WARES SHOP**
800-443-2683
www.fantes.com

**FOODS OF INDIA**
212-683-4419

**FOSTER'S MARKET**
2694 Durham Chapel Hill Blvd.
Durham, NC 27707
877-455-3944
www.fostersmarket.com

**THE GINGER PEOPLE**
800-551-5284
www.gingerpeople.com

**GOURMET MUSHROOMS**
P.O. Box 391
Sebastopol, CA 95473
707-823-1743
www.mycopia.com

**GRACE'S MARKETPLACE**
1237 Third Avenue
New York, NY 10021
212-737-0600

**INDIAN ROCK PRODUCE**
800-882-0512
www.indianrockproduce.com

**KALUSTYAN'S**
212-685-3451
800-352-3451
www.kalustyans.com

**KATAGIRI & CO.**
224 East 59th Street
New York, NY 10022
212-755-3566

**KITCHEN ETC.**
800-232-4070
www.kitchenetc.com

**KITCHEN/MARKET**
888-468-4433
www.kitchenmarket.com

**MARCHE AUX DELICES**
888-547-5471
www.auxdelices.com

**MARTHA STEWART:
THE CATALOG FOR LIVING**
800-950-7130
www.marthastewart.com

**MURRAY'S CHEESE**
888-692-4339

**PACIFIC RIM GOURMET**
4905 Morena Blvd.
Suite 1313
San Diego, CA 92117
800-910-9657
www.pacificrim-gourmet.com

**PARS INTERNATIONAL FOODS**
212-760-7277

**PENZEYS SPICES**
P.O. Box 924
Brookfield, WI 53008
800-741-7787
www.penzeys.com

**POLARICA**
800-426-3872

**QUALITY NATURAL FOODS**
888-392-9237
www.qualitynaturalfoods.com

**RUSS & DAUGHTERS**
212-475-4880
800-787-7229 (outside
NY area only)
www.russanddaughters.com

**SALUMERIA ITALIANA**
800-400-5916
www.salumeriaitaliana.com

**SCHALLER & WEBER**
1654 Second Avenue
New York, NY 10028
212-879-3047

**SULLIVAN HARBOR FARM**
P.O. Box 96
Sullivan Harbor, ME 04664
800-422-4014
www.sullivanharborfarm.com

**SULTAN'S DELIGHT**
800-852-5046
www.sultansdelight.com
($20 minimum for mail orders)

**SUR LA TABLE**
1765 6th Avenue South
Seattle, WA 98134
800-243-0852
www.surlatable.com

**SWEET CELEBRATIONS**
7009 Washington Avenue South
Edina, MN 55439
612-943-1661
800-328-6722
www.sweetc.com

**VERMONT BUTTER & CHEESE
COMPANY**
800-884-6287

**WHOLE FOODS MARKET**
2421 Broadway
New York, NY 10024
212-874-4000
www.wholefoodsmarket.com

**WILLIAMS-SONOMA**
877-812-6235
www.williams-sonoma.com

**ZABAR'S**
212-787-2000
800-697-6301 (outside NY only)
www.zabars.com

**ZINGERMAN'S**
888-636-8162
www.zingermans.com

# index

# photography credits

✳